JAMES JOYCE

POEMS *and* EXILES

EDITED WITH AN INTRODUCTION AND
NOTES BY J. C. C. MAYS

PENGUIN BOOKS

PENGUIN BOOKS

Published by the Penguin Group
Penguin Books Ltd, 27 Wrights Lane, London w8 5tz, England
Penguin Books USA Inc., 375 Hudson Street, New York, New York 10014, USA
Penguin Books Australia Ltd, Ringwood, Victoria, Australia
Penguin Books Canada Ltd, 10 Alcorn Avenue, Toronto, Ontario, Canada m4v 3b2
Penguin Books (NZ) Ltd, 182–190 Wairau Road, Auckland 10, New Zealand

Penguin Books Ltd, Registered Offices: Harmondsworth, Middlesex, England

First published 1992

This edition copyright © J. C. C. Mays, 1992
The acknowledgements on p. 378 constitute an extension of this copyright page
All rights reserved

The moral right of the editor has been asserted

Printed in England by Clays Ltd, St Ives plc
Set in 10/12 pt Monophoto Sabon

CONTENTS*

* Joyce's own titles are given in italic; editorial titles are in roman.

* Joyce's notes and the draft scenes are given in the Notes, pp. 342–54
and pp. 360–70.

CONTENTS

FOREWORD

The present volume has changed its character as it has moved towards publication. It was conceived and prepared as a volume that brought together Joyce's poems with his play, *Exiles*. The 1936 *Collected Poems* contained the sequences *Chamber Music* and *Pomes Penyeach*, to which was added Joyce's poem on the birth of his grandson, *Ecce Puer*. The enlarged *Collected Poems* published after his death also gathered in two satirical broadsides, *The Holy Office* and *Gas from a Burner*. A few other poems had meanwhile been published in periodicals and elsewhere, and others included in Herbert Gorman's biography. The remainder, which had been for the most part sent or given to friends, remained in manuscript.

A large number of Joyce's occasional poems, previously published or unpublished, were included in Richard Ellmann's biography, and the full extent of the material was made publicly available in the first volume of *The James Joyce Archive*. Ellmann's texts were not, however, always reliable (of *Dooleysprudence* and *Post Ulixem Scriptum*, for example) and, though the *Archive* included drafts and proofs of the two sequences as well, it was still not complete. Again, the notes for *Exiles* were published in the 1951 edition of the play, and these were reproduced along with draft scenes and the fair-copy manuscript of the text itself in Volume XI of the *Archive*. The elaborate analysis by John Mac-Nicholas (NY, 1979) had meanwhile demonstrated the inadequacy of the versions in print, and the need to make a corrected version available.

Such was the position when I began. The bringing together of all Joyce's poems had been previously attempted only in Italian and French editions. The first of these, *Poesie*, translated by Alfredo Giuliani and others (Milan, 1961), has English and Italian texts *en face*, but was incomplete and contained patent errors in the printing of the English originals. The French edition (Paris,

1982) formed part of Volume I of the Bibliothèque de la Pléiade Joyce, edited by Jacques Aubert. It is far more comprehensive and sophisticated, but has the disadvantage for English readers of being wholly in French. The time was obviously ripe to bring forward Joyce's occasional poems, now that fashion had brought the high modernist mode to heel and such poems could be read without apology.

I prepared a collection of Joyce's poems that owed something to the arrangement of the Italian edition and much to the example and annotation of the French. They were presented alongside a freshly edited text of *Exiles*, and the whole was ready to go to press at the end of 1989. The permission of the Joyce Estate was sought for the poems still affected by copyright, but, because another edition was in hand, they declined to grant it. This other edition, edited by Richard Ellmann, A. Walton Litz and John Whittier-Ferguson, appeared from Faber/Viking in 1991. It presents a full collection of Joyce's poems alongside a number of early prose writings, namely *Epiphanies*, *Giacomo Joyce* and the 1904 essay *A Portrait of the Artist*.

This new *Poems and Shorter Writings* represents an improvement on previous collections. It makes widely available texts that had previously appeared only in the *Archive* or elsewhere, or had not been published at all. Its versions of already published poems are more accurate; later Ellmann silently supersedes his earlier self. That said, however, its editorial decisions are not inevitable, and their execution is not perfect. Though the Joyce Estate has prevented the present collection from being as complete as it aimed to be, there is room for another edition representing a different perspective on Joyce.

The new Faber collection reflects different editorial decisions. Its version of Joyce's two published collections rests on different base texts from mine; and my reading of the manuscripts often differs, so the texts of several unpublished and uncollected poems are also not the same. Thus, the Faber editors follow the 1907 edition of *Chamber Music*, which can be challenged on literary grounds (see my note on Poem XXVII, line 4); but they do not follow 1907 exactly, with unfortunate results (see note on Poem

XXXIII, line 14). Similarly for *Pomes Penyeach*; and attentive readers will notice texts like *New Tipperary; or, the C.G. is Not Literary*, 'Quatrain for Richard Wallace' and 'A Come-all-ye, by a Thanksgiving Turkey' are also different. Some differences can be attributed to Joyce's or his transcriber's difficult handwriting; others – as in these three last-named instances – I cannot explain.

In addition the Faber collection brings Joyce's poems into conjunction with a selection of his prose-poetry instead of with his only play, as here. The different make-up of each collection changes the understanding of the shared material each contains. The conjunction of material in the Faber suggests a perspective on Joyce that is perhaps the usual one: that his poems were early prentice work, like his beginnings in prose, and that their interest is introductory or supplementary. The perspective provided by bringing Joyce's poems together with his play, as here, is different and critical. Verse and drama constitute a single area outside the prose fiction in which Joyce most famously performed, and they constitute an area in which he explored singular effects.

My Introduction and Notes supplement one another, and provide a third point of contrast with *Poems and Shorter Writings*. It seems to me that readers of Joyce's published collections of verse require guidance if the point is not to be missed; his play might appear a sport unless its background in the way he understood drama is borne in mind. In particular, the uncollected occasional verses can begin to exist only when the network of allusions they depend on is made evident. When this is done, his other writings – which appear more independent of circumstances but which are equally sceptical of their own claim to independence – are also better understood. His poems have different public and private status, but this is not a difference between poems that are worth reading and poems of interest only to Joyceans.

The annotation in the Faber collection is light throughout, and it is particularly spare with respect to the poems. Readers might try to make what they can of *Pour la rîme seulement* as presented there before turning to the Notes below. I cannot help them with all the poems that the Estate would not license, but I include the notes on Joyce's Father Delan(e)y limerick as a memorial to what has been excluded. There is meanwhile enough in the present collection to show what, in relation to his play, Joyce's poems have to offer. (I might add, in case readers assume the Faber collection is itself complete, that it does not include two of the pieces below, and that it omits a further four poems that had a place below before they were disallowed.)

I owe much to the work of previous editors – Jacques Aubert, John MacNicholas and William York Tindall, especially – as will be evident in the Notes. A number of friends and colleagues at University College Dublin helped me on points of detail, for which I am again very grateful. I have named them in relation to the help they supplied, though of course they should not be held responsible for the use to which their information has been put. I should name here my wife, who helped revise the Introduction. I have most reason to be thankful to my former pupils at the School of Irish Studies in Dublin, who encouraged me to learn what I know about Joyce and taught me more besides; and also to the two Deans of the School, the late Michael Scott and Seán White, whose arrangements made for one of the most rewarding educational experiences I have known. If this book carried a dedication, it would be to my grandson born in Paris at the time I submitted the original manuscript: *Pour Jack, Ecce Puer*.

J. C. C. Mays
York, 25 June 1991

ABBREVIATIONS

Aubert   James Joyce, Œuvres, Vol. I, ed. Jacques Aubert (Biblio-
thèque de la Pléiade, Paris, 1982)

Archive   The James Joyce Archive, eds. Michael Groden, Hans
Walter Gabler, David Hayman, A. Walton Litz and Danis
Rose with John O'Hanlon (NY, 1977–9)

Bauerle   The James Joyce Song Book, ed. Ruth Bauerle (NY,
1982)

Budgen   Frank Budgen, James Joyce and the Making of
'Ulysses' and Other Writings, introd. Clive Hart (London,
1972)

CDD   The Complete Dublin Diary of Stanislaus Joyce, ed.
George H. Healy (Ithaca, NY, 1971)

CH   James Joyce: The Critical Heritage, ed. Robert H. Deming
(London, 1970)

Colum   Mary and Padraic Colum, Our Friend James Joyce
(NY, 1958)

Curran   C. P. Curran, James Joyce Remembered (London,
1968)

CW   The Critical Writings of James Joyce, ed. Ellsworth Mason
and Richard Ellmann (London, 1959)

Gorman   Herbert Gorman, James Joyce: A Definitive Life
(London, 1941)

D   James Joyce, Dubliners: Text, Criticism, and Notes, eds.
Robert Scholes and A. Walton Litz (NY, 1969)

Doyle   Paul A. Doyle, 'Joyce's Miscellaneous Verse', James
Joyce Quarterly II (Winter 1965) 90–96; 'Joyce's Miscellane-
ous Verse, Part II', James Joyce Quarterly V (Fall 1967)
71. The Joyce items are listed in a continuous series
through the two articles

FW   James Joyce, Finnegans Wake (London, 1939). References
are to page and line numbers, which are the same in all
editions

GJ   James Joyce, *Giacomo Joyce*, ed. Richard Ellmann (London, 1968)

JJ   Richard Ellmann, *James Joyce* (revised edition, Oxford, 1982)

JJQ   *James Joyce Quarterly* (Tulsa, Okla., 1963–   )

L   *Letters of James Joyce*, Vol. I, ed. Stuart Gilbert (London, 1957); Vols. II and III, ed. Richard Ellmann (London, 1966). Vol. I was reissued with corrections in NY (only) in 1966

Lund   Steven Lund, *James Joyce: Letters, Manuscripts, and Photographs at Southern Illinois University* (Troy, NY, 1983)

MacNicholas   John MacNicholas, *James Joyce's 'Exiles': A Textual Companion* (NY, 1979)

MBK   Stanislaus Joyce, *My Brother's Keeper*, ed. Richard Ellmann (London, 1958)

O'Connor   *The Joyce We Knew*, ed. Ulick O'Connor (Cork, 1967)

OED   James A. H. Murray, *et al.*, *The Oxford English Dictionary* (Oxford, 1888–1928)

P   James Joyce, *A Portrait of the Artist as a Young Man: Text, Criticism, and Notes*, ed. Chester B. Anderson (NY, 1968)

P/J   *Pound/Joyce: The Letters of Ezra Pound to James Joyce, with Pound's Essays on Joyce*, ed. Forrest Read (London, 1968)

Potts   *Portraits of the Artist in Exile: Recollections of James Joyce by Europeans*, ed. Willard Potts (Seattle, Wash., 1979)

P&SW   *Poems and Shorter Writings*, eds. Richard Ellmann, A. Walton Litz and John Whittier-Ferguson (London, 1991)

SB   *James Joyce's Letters to Sylvia Beach 1921–1940*, eds. Melissa Banta and Oscar A. Silverman (Bloomington, Ill., 1987)

Scholes   Robert E. Scholes, *The Cornell Joyce Collection: A Catalogue* (Ithaca, NY, 1961)

SH   James Joyce, *Stephen Hero*, ed. Theodore Spencer (revised edition, London, 1956)

Skeat   Walter W. Skeat, *An Etymological Dictionary of the English Language* (Oxford, 1882)

Slocum   John J. Slocum and Herbert Cahoon, *A Bibliography of James Joyce* (London, 1953)

Spielberg   Peter Spielberg, *James Joyce's Manuscripts and Letters at the University of Buffalo: A Catalogue* (Buffalo, NY, 1962)

Tindall   James Joyce, *Chamber Music*, ed. William York Tindall (NY, 1954)

U   James Joyce, *Ulysses: The Corrected Text*, ed. Hans Walter Gabler, with Wolfhard Steppe and Claus Melchior (London, 1986)

INTRODUCTION

I

When an author has written fiction of the order of the accessible *Dubliners* and *A Portrait of the Artist as a Young Man*, the masterpiece *Ulysses* and the unreadable *Finnegans Wake*, there is a perhaps inevitable impression that anything else he wrote in other forms must be of a lesser order: interesting, perhaps, to the Joycean specialist, but not to the general reader. Analogies may be drawn with William Faulkner (who began as a poet), Dr Johnson (who wrote a play called *Irene*) and Shelley (who wrote some novels). The implication is that great writers do sometimes stray into areas where they have no competence, and the results are best left to the attentions of specialists who are prepared to tease out motives and parallels.

If I shared these apologetic attitudes I would not be writing about Joyce's poems and play. 'A man of genius makes no mistakes. His errors are volitional and are the portals of discovery' (*U* 156). Joyce's poems are very varied. *Chamber Music* is fascinating in that it is neither good nor bad, nor these two mixed: it possesses a capacity to turn contradictory responses back on to themselves and remain simultaneously a demonstration of the mastery of a style and a critique of the same. *Pomes Penyeach* appears to offer something different and more available, that is, a sensitive register of some specific, personal occasions; in fact, as the sequence comes into focus, the promise of confession is displaced by contrivance, poetry is used to manipulate biography. Then, again, in a wide range of occasional poems, Joyce shows himself master of a third way of writing poetry. The occasional poems together should be measured against any current Poetry Book Society Choice: they contain parody, word-games, political poems, verses to friends that celebrate a wide range of ordinary social values. Specimens of any one genre would be enough to launch a reputation; that so many genres are represented is a *tour de force.* When one recalls that these occasional poems were written by the author of two different kinds of conventional verse, the idea that Joyce's poems are ancillary reading appears absurd.

Exiles is of interest because it is completely successful in a highly original way, and also because, as the only play of Joyce's to survive, it bears a complicated relation to his other writings. The relation with *Pomes Penyeach* is particularly interesting since both were written during a period in Joyce's career that was a sort of crossroads: he had finished *Dubliners* and was completing the *Portrait*; *Ulysses* was gestating from the idea of a story he had decided not to include in *Dubliners*. *Pomes Penyeach* and the play explore experiences he needed to be more sure about before approaching them in fiction; verse and drama promised more direct access to what he wanted to write and, in their different ways, more control over it. In the process, however, Joyce somehow estranged himself from the means he had employed. He wrote only one other poem of the same kind thereafter – when his grandson was born – and never attempted another play.

This Introduction concentrates on disentangling these sometimes complicated interrelationships, and information on the background and composition of Joyce's poems and *Exiles* is held over to the Notes. Readers who want to learn about or be reminded of dates and facts might prefer to turn straightaway to the Notes. The discussion of implications and connections here in the Introduction takes particular background information largely for granted.

II

Chamber Music was the first book of any kind by Joyce to be published. It was praised by Yeats and Arthur Symons as one of the best collections of its time,[1] and their understanding of the tradition in which he was writing requires their judgement to be taken seriously: the collection is an extraordinary début in the way it displays a complete mastery of a tradition and at the same time turns that tradition inside out. It inscribes Joyce in one kind of poetry then in fashion in advanced circles – announces his arrival; and it simultaneously supersedes that same kind of poetry – announces that he has left it behind and reckons it rubbish. For all the fluency that Yeats and Symons responded to, and that in *Dubliners* Joyce chose to work against, it contains a parodic dimension that *Dubliners* also builds upon.

Pomes Penyeach is less ambitious in this respect, and works more comfortably within the limits of what it pretends to be. The displacement of Joyce's formal ambitions on to fiction in the interim years led to a different transaction with poetic conventions. But though it is less ambitious in a formal sense, the turning-aside from fiction to verse at this point in his career suggests that he thought of verse as a medium to explore and clarify concerns in ways fiction could not. The later sequence engages the reader more directly, in that the supposed biographical thread exerts a more immediate pressure. But the biography is a fictive process, in which events are rearranged, and the lyric voice is constructed at a distance from the author's own. Even if the form is not actually turned inside out, as in *Chamber Music*, Joyce's attitude to form is still askew.

The kind of writing represented by Joyce's two collections of poetry reflects interests that are not duplicated by his fiction. One collection contributes to the style in which Joyce discovered himself as a writer, and extends the accomplishment of this style to a point where it constitutes a radical critique of what it is. The later collection continues in an apparently less ambitious mode, with another intent and other results. Because it aims to be less perfect, it can be less obviously disabling. It is closer to the ordinary methods of verse, and the space in which it works is thereby more intimate, but it is, at the same time, no less original for this. Biographical fact is distorted in such a way as to be displaced, with the result that form levers life into a position where biographical facts are differently understood.

Joyce provides some justification for discounting *Chamber Music* and *Pomes Penyeach*, by growing tired of the one and being diffident about the other,[2] but it is less often recalled that he also disparaged the *Portrait* and judged *Ulysses* to be fundamentally flawed. His writing always gained inspiration from dissatisfaction, and always moved forward by demolishing the foundation each previous work rested upon. I have noted that the picture of paralysis in *Dubliners* complements the verse exercise in *fin de siècle* aestheticism in the *Portrait*; but then Stephen Dedalus emerges as hero from the picture of paralysis, and Stephen is in turn complemented by Bloom in *Ulysses*. The complete record of one day in the city is finally destabilized by the book of night, *Finnegans Wake*. Similarly *Exiles* has something in common with *Chamber Music*, in that it constitutes a radical exploration of the form in which it is written; it overlaps thematically with *Pomes Penyeach* and the contemporary fiction, and in other ways it complements them.

The bringing together of Joyce's poems and his play in the present volume is illuminating, therefore, because they make up the common ground of his writings outside fiction. *Chamber Music* is not a false start, but in a profound sense the starting-point of everything he subsequently wrote. It represents the beginning he returned to with each fresh venture, rather than a position abandoned. Each novel discovers a different compromise in the face of such an impasse. Again, the fact that Joyce's main attention shifted on to fiction when he came to write *Pomes Penyeach* and *Exiles* is what, literally, enables them. They display qualities that his more conscious and continuing concerns left no space for. The poems and the play are utterly finished pieces of writing that come from a position in Joyce's mind that is less off-centre than his main fictional *œuvre*. Comparisons with Beckett and Yeats will explain what might seem a paradox.

Beckett was also drawn to writing by the possibilities that verse seemed to offer, but he found the openness of the possibilities numbing. At the moment he made his appearance in verse, in poems like *Whoroscope*, self-consciousness prompted him to hide; a carapace of allusion accumulated to prevent forward movement and self-reflexive cleverness clogged the rhythms. Only by saying less could he say anything at all, and narcissism displays itself through echo's bones in his first and only published collection.[3] Technical obligations clearly offered no distraction, as they do to some. The invitation to lyric proved to be frost in the veins. It is perhaps why the avatar first abandoned by the Unnamable is called Basil - a basilisk.

Beckett's release came through fiction, which establishes an enabling distance between author and language. Saying through somebody else, you can say more fully and more fluently than by attempting to speak yourself. The same considerations apply to *Chamber Music*. The several kinds of poem Joyce wrote previously, and poems like *Cabra*, later named *Tilly*, which were not included in the sequence, provide a measure of the narrow constraints he encountered as a lyric poet. It was inevitable that he should turn to fiction, though, like Beckett, he always understood fiction in the terms that prompted him to take it up, as an outsider, as opposed to an 'insider' storyteller, like Proust; as an enabling form whose limits were a source of inspiration equal to anything they might encompass.

Like Beckett between *Malone Dies* and *The Unnamable*, Joyce also wrote a play at a turning-point in his career. *Exiles* and *Godot* both remove their authors from the fiction with which they had become embroiled, to a position where they could assess the next step more clearly. Joyce was in the process of completing the *Portrait* and beginning *Ulysses*; he had written several parts of *Pomes Penyeach*, but not completed the sequence or determined its order. The play makes up a form of statement that is further removed from his real-life order of experience than verse, but not complicated by narrative as fiction is. The play converts story into situation and frames it for meditative analysis in scrupulously detached terms. The detachment has been understood, for the most part, but the neutrality has been lost in a fog of disbelief or misunderstanding. If one respects the processes of the play, they open into a rich piece of theatre.

Exiles is none the less a use of theatre in the way Joyce's novels are uses of fiction. The connection with the poems is that here too the form – that of the lyric – is used manipulatively. *Pomes Penyeach* is closer to the undisguised source of all Joyce's writings but none the less literary for that. At this point one might compare the occasional poems that are included in this edition. They are of many kinds, but what most have in common is that they move to a pre-set tune; the words are carried by the rhythms of popular or music-hall songs, or nursery rhymes, or convention. What does this say to Coleridge's claim, that he who has not music in his soul will never be a genuine poet? Joyce's music was constantly somebody else's, and his misplaced words have an edge of pastiche. Most of the uncollected poems are slight, and of a quite different order from those discussed so far, but they too have this essential feature in common.

Chamber Music moves to Elizabethan rhythms, and is not unaffected by Joyce's reading of Yeats, Verlaine and others. *Pomes Penyeach* contains rhythms connected more obviously with personality and more centred or rooted in a sense of self. But at the same time several poems are frankly dependent on other kinds of inspiration than a simply personal one – an opera or a folk-tune or Browning – and the difference of rhythm from poem to poem makes the point that the author is not reaching for a single, lyric voice. The dimensions of self-consciousness left Joyce exposed as a lyric poet, and the way in which he makes himself as a writer has parallels in Yeats as well as Beckett. Joyce as Giacomo Joyce, or something near it in these poems, is as much a created mask as any one of Yeats's created selves. Perhaps the fact of writing out of and in spite of a small community necessitates some kind of distancing, whether it be through the cultivation of masks, or physical exile, or removal to the margins of literary form. It is a form of protection, which appears like obliquity, until the energies on the margin accumulate and displace those of the centre.

Ecce Puer is Joyce's most conventionally successful poem, the one most widely accepted as worthy of the author of *Ulysses*. The reasons for its acceptance are probably its evident sincerity, the way it brings into alignment the effects of Joyce's father's death and his grandson's birth, compressing them into a form that does not betray its origins. The source of its attraction is undoubtedly some such sense of centred experience, but it should be noted that it works largely by allusion and quotation. It contrives a structure of language in which meaning appears to resound firmly but which in fact oscillates between irreconcilables. The title announces death and suffering as well as birth; opposite implications converge on lines of the text throughout; the only thing that is stable is indeed the text. It makes up a more complicated reality than its admirers usually assume.

III

The background of Joyce's early poems is clear enough, though it is not always appreciated. It might be described as a fusion of Irish Revival and English nineties, with other elements thrown in with the purpose, or at least the effect, of keeping the fusion volatile. Joyce was not working towards a compromise: any one element destabilizes the authority any other element might impose. For this reason it is probably more useful to begin with the English background, since it is the one Joyce consciously reached towards to counteract the position he found himself in. That background was made up of writers like Lionel Johnson, Arthur Symons, Ernest Dowson, John Gray and Victor Plarr, the core of the Rhymers' Club. Derek Stanford's Everyman anthology, *Writing of the 'Nineties: From Wilde to Beerbohm* (London, 1971), provides a selection.

Joyce's early title of lost prose sketches, *Silhouettes*, is borrowed from the 1892 collection by Symons; his first, lost collection of verse was called *Moods*, which is straight out of Whistler; and another lost verse collection, *Light and Dark*, would seem to echo Symons's *Days and Nights* (1889). Stephen's villanelle in the *Portrait* is a form that in itself advertises allegiance to the new fashion, as does Joyce's interest in the Elizabethans. Writers like Jonson and Herrick were the toast of the Rhymers' Club;[4] Verlaine and Mallarmé were enthusiasms shared with Symons and Dowson; John Davidson was also a follower of Nietzsche. The English nineties looked back to Rossetti and Swinburne rather than Tennyson and Browning, and to Pater rather than to Matthew Arnold. Their interest was in art for art's sake rather than for the sake of earnestly instilling moral values; they carefully distinguished Newman the prose stylist from Newman the sage.

Some aspects of nineties writing were obviously not congenial to Joyce. For instance, he did not share Lionel Johnson's and Aubrey Beardsley's interest in the ritualistic aspect of Catholicism, and his very different interest in scholastic theology might be understood less as a prophylactic than a protest against their indulgence. He was not interested in drugs or the Beardsley-decadent side of nineties writing, though his analysis of his relations with J. F. Byrne and Oliver St John Gogarty reveal an interest in the homosexual dimensions of masculine friendship. One might note that allusions to Oscar Wilde tend to cluster round Mulligan in *Ulysses* (and even to be hinted at in Robert Hand, in *Exiles*), both of whom are dismissed in the end for similarly betraying their talent.

In particular, Joyce did not share the conscious interest the English group took in Celticism, as a form of cultural resistance to the idea of Empire.[5] Ernest Rhys rediscovered his Welshness, John Davidson his Scottishness, the Bedford Park Yeats his Irishness. It was as fashionable to be Irish in London in 1890 as in the same circles a hundred years later, and for not dissimilar reasons. Joyce could have made much of his claim to Irishness, especially in the light of some of the other contemporary claimants, but the grounds were obvious to the point where such a claim would be wholly banal. The fact that he laughed about it, where others were solemn, underlines the point. He saw through the 'nationalism above party' of O'Leary's and Yeats's Fenianism as a twilit delusion, and was more interested in forging connections with Europe beyond Ireland, over the head of England: with Hauptmann and Ibsen, Flaubert and Dante, instead of with Queen Maeve.

One could go on accumulating parallels and differences. Joyce's dandy dressing – his tennis shoes and walking stick, for instance – sartorially signal the same message as the bow ties of the more successful Yeats. He retained to the end of his days a taste for swank cafés and restaurants of the order of magnitude of the old Café Royal. He was part of that wave of reaction against Victorian England that was more than a literary fashion when it became mixed with Irish nationalism, and Joyce was no less nationalist than the speech-making Yeats. Also, the anti-Romantic stance he took in Ireland was not without parallel, though he was not anxious to make such parallels evident. George Moore, for one, was also sceptical of Yeats's Celtic interests and used French Realist models to forge a counter-statement. Other minor poets, like James Starkey ('Seumas O'Sullivan') and later Oliver St John Gogarty, developed the nineties connection in their lyric poetry.

Joyce's early manner is distinguished not so much by the style in which he wrote, which is largely that of his place and time, as by his understanding of what he was doing. Yeats said the poems 'might have been the work of a young man who had lived in an Oxford literary set' (*JJ* 104), and Joyce's poems are better than Starkey's and Gogarty's because of their sophistication. There is a good essay by Myra Russel on the Elizabethan element of *Chamber Music*,[6] in which she points out how Joyce employs various stylistic features in a very fluent way. The musical background affects the cadence and the rhymes, in particular, as well as determining the artificial-seeming quality of the content and images.

At other times Elizabethan rhythms are crossed with other kinds. I have recorded some of these buried echoes in my notes, but they are elusive and difficult to prove. An example I did not include is in Poem XXXI. The conjunction of the phrases 'did walk together' and 'Was the kiss she gave to me' might recall to some readers' ears the close of Coleridge's *Ancient Mariner*: ''Tis sweeter far to me, / To walk together . . . ' The echo remains only a possibility, which comes and goes even to those who hear it. It coexists with similar echoes elsewhere of Wyatt and nameless Elizabethans. In the end it situates Joyce's poems in a limbo rather than firmly in an intertextual nexus. The quotations are not in quotation marks, and are therefore in several senses buried. Archaisms – what Stephen calls 'feudal terminology' (*SH* 179) – are instead used to manipulate levels of meaning, but in an anonymous way, without tangling meaning with specific sources.

Pound praised Joyce's poems 'for the sake of the clean-cut ivory finish, and for the interest of the rhythms, the cross run of the beat and the word, as of a stiff wind cutting the ripple-tops of bright water' (*P/J* 137). Stanislaus Joyce reports that the collection

that preceded *Chamber Music*, of which only fragments now
remain, would have included the villanelle that is given to Stephen
in the *Portrait* (*MBK* 100, 158). If this is the case, and taken
alongside the other evidence, it seems that *Chamber Music* repre-
sents a significant step forward in Joyce's control of rhythm. He
was interested enough to make handwritten copies of sixteenth-
century poems by Ben Jonson and Henry VIII (Scholes Nos. 19,
20), among others, and he planned to sing 'old English songs' to
the lute as a summer holiday job (*L* I 54).[7] At the same time he
excluded something as obviously, even if suavely, fashionable as
his villanelle.

The poems of *Chamber Music* are in the end distinguished
from the fashion in which they participate by the way they turn
negative energy, the instigation to be different, into positive pas-
tiche. This is most important of all, and is not always understood.
Joyce mastered the manner for which Yeats and Pound praised
him to the extent that his use becomes a critique. He writes so
completely within the style that the style is literally written out of
– in the sense of on to the outside, wholly away from – his
personality. It is utter to an extreme by means of which it is made
outer; the mimicry is intense to the point where it liberates the
mimic. Joyce is thereby able to detach himself from what he
wrote, and his judgement on its application and merits is independ-
ently open to change, even reversal. The record of his comments
on the poems, which traces a change from commitment to disgust,
is not as surprising as it has seemed to some commentators. The
poems are no more good or bad than Stephen Dedalus in the
Portrait is a hero or a fool, his theories true or hollow, his
villanelle evidence of achievement or pretension.

The early poems included in the present collection make it
evident that *Chamber Music* is a deliberately contrived selection.
It rests on choices that excluded poems like 'Come out to where
the youth is met' because they did not fit. The sequence is largely
determined by a structural idea, which became a proto-narrative.
It tells the same story as other early prose narratives, of love and
betrayal. Since the pattern preceded or at best accompanied the
events in Joyce's life that match it – the climactic meeting with

Nora, the 'betrayal' by Gogarty – it is likely that it has a literary source. George Meredith's *Modern Love* is a possible contender, if only because of Joyce's known admiration for it and because the influence of Elizabethan sonnet sequences is less obvious than that of songs.

The other determinant of what went into the collection was their suitability for singing, and this quality is undoubtedly more important than the narrative connection. Horace Gregory remarked in general that 'Joyce's gift was nine tenths auditory'. In the present instance, musicality is connected with the special surface Joyce was trying to achieve, and he was always eager to encourage settings and accompaniments.[8] The poems are, however, different from the models they follow, and this is the result of his peculiar concentration, even fixation, upon some words. It distinguishes *Chamber Music* from the poems Joyce wrote earlier, from the fragments which remain, as far as one can tell, and from comparable poems he did not include. These others share the same rhythms, but do not contain the same verbal constituent.

Joyce is known to have taken an interest in R. C. Trench's *On the Study of Words* (1858), as well as Walter Skeat's *Etymological Dictionary*,[9] but his interest was not historical. It is described in *Stephen Hero*: 'It was not only in Skeat that he found words for his treasure-house, he found them also at haphazard in the shops, on advertisements, in the mouths of the plodding public. He kept repeating them to himself till they lost all instantaneous meaning for him and became wonderful vocables' (*SH* 36). Some words in *Chamber Music*, like 'plenilune' and 'enaisled', draw attention to themselves by being manifestly unusual. Others, ordinary words like 'swoon' and 'brown', are used in special senses, as my notes explain. Others again, like 'snood', derive from what appears to be a misunderstanding and became in effect a private, privatizing usage. Any one poem in a sequence that has been put together from such radioactive particles at once exerts a different field of force on the others in the sequence from either an Elizabethan or a nineties counterpart.

The effect of using words in this idiosyncratic way might be compared with the quotations and literary allusions that the poems include. These come from a variety of sources, but the point is what is made of them, not where they come from. Identification of a source does not necessarily add to the meaning of what has been borrowed in its new context. Individual words are likewise handled like pebbles gathered from a beach, polished and treasured, and placed on a mantelpiece or table for contemplation. Removed from their original context, they have a different intrinsic meaning. They are freed from history and become vortexes of intense concentration, in a process described by Joyce as epiphany, or again by Stephen in his lucubrations on the wholeness, harmony and radiance of beauty (*P* 212–13). They work towards an instant of 'luminous silent stasis' that creates a pleasure that is an 'enchantment of the heart'.

The only way to demonstrate the process is to retrace it, the effect repeating the cause. The notes on *Chamber Music* indicate the materials, which indeed extend beyond words to rhymes and rhythmical effects. The process can be misunderstood: William York Tindall and other first-generation Joyce scholars were often criticized for atomizing Joyce's texts, picking on words and details and connecting them with others in an obsessive way. The result need not be trivializing if one bears in mind that the way of reading derives from the demands of the texts themselves. The method Joyce discovered for himself is exposed and relatively uncomplicated by other features in the early writing, but it is continuous with the later obsessive habits that resulted in Swahili in *Finnegans Wake* and composition with coloured pencils. It is sustained here by the Elizabethan rhythms. The form, which maintains delicate forward momentum with the assistance of an air of pastiche, contains particles that have been prepared by intense, still brooding.

Together, the several intertextual relationships situate the poem not at the intersection of those relationships but outside them, nowhere. It is a curious consequence of Joyce's essay in a mode that in literary history devoured its most faithful adherents. All the artists who appear in Stanford's nineties anthology – with the extraordinary exception of Yeats – failed to develop. Dowson is representative. As Symons said of him: 'he had already said, in his first book of verse, all that he had to say. Had he lived, had he gone on writing, he could only have echoed himself; and probably it would have been the less essential part of himself.'[10] Joyce contrived to master the factitious; he wrote a collection that is outstanding in the genre precisely because it is as well judged as it is skilled.

IV

The method of *Chamber Music* leaves the author and the reader paring their fingernails. We pass through the creation as if it were clear glass, emerging to stand at a distance in dispassionate contemplation. *Pomes Penyeach* has us more involved, though not wholly or directly. Joyce turned to verse to get close to feelings he could not explore satisfactorily in the kind of prose represented by *Dubliners* and the *Portrait*. Though an adjacent area of emotional experience was framed in *Giacomo Joyce*, it was not worked through and it was not published during his lifetime. It is clear that prose narrative removed Joyce to a border situation where he could write beyond himself and more flexibly about himself, but also that it easily led him astray. Verse encouraged him to remain closer to his feelings. It is more deeply personal just because it left less room for manoeuvre.

Pomes Penyeach were variously, inspirationally composed. Apart from the first poem, which is carried forward from the earlier time, and the last, which was added six years after the rest, the poems were written independently of each other between 1913 and 1916. They are arranged to form a narrative, centred on jealousy, emotional indulgence, and a sense of changing responsibilities and of ageing. The feelings go back to Joyce's thoughts about Nora in 1909 and before, and his sentimentally indulged crush on his Triestine pupil, Amalia Popper. They are extended with poems about his children and about his removal by age and illness from scenes of romantic passion.

Ezra Pound noted that the narrative motif in the *Chamber Music* poems was so slight that separately they hardly exist until one thinks of them as set to music (*P/J* 137); the workmanship is delicate to a point where the poems appear to elude anything as crass as an identifiable subject. The sense of autobiographical content and narrative arrangement in *Pomes Penyeach* is stronger. It should be emphasized that this is factitious, a contrived aspect of a more open-textured kind of poetry that engages the reader in a different way. The poems have titles, for instance, not simply numbers, and several of the titles are deliberately circumstantial or cumbrous. The appended places and dates are also part of their method. The details are poetic means, not autobiographical facts: Joyce altered them as he thought fit to revise the order of the sequence. The composition is deliberately fragmented in its narrative and its separate components, and the surface deliberately less finished.

Pound also noted that the last two poems in the *Chamber Music* sequence differed in quality from the others; they were less musical – in Pound's expressive word, more 'fibrous' (*P/J* 139). The rhythms of the *Penyeach* poems likewise. *Tilly*, when Joyce wrote it under the title *Cabra*, would never have fitted into *Chamber Music*, for exactly this reason. It has a rhythmic and metaphoric texture that unsuits it for song. It draws attention to its separate parts in a way that would only interrupt the smooth unfolding of the earlier lyric style.

All the later poems are filled with an accentuated sense of personality, and ask to be read as dramatic monologues, but the sense of personality is removed from directly personal expression. Joyce speaks in a voice which to all intents and purposes is his own in *Watching the Needleboats* and *A Flower given to my Daughter*, but *She weeps over Rahoon* is spoken as if by Nora. *A Memory of the Players in a Mirror at Midnight* is written in the language of Browning's play, *In a Balcony*, and *Flood* as a deliberate exercise in style. The sense of a single confessional voice is de-stabilized by these shifts, with the result that the reader becomes wary of taking a poem as apparently autobiographical as *Bahnhofstrasse* simply as it appears. Joyce invokes experience in a complicated way, to manipulate what the experience can express.

The peculiar focus on words (as in *Chamber Music*) undergoes a change here. The word 'needleboats' is an almost solitary example to set beside 'plenilune', 'snood' and the others, and its effect is subtly different. It brings Nora's Galway experiences into the suggested field of reference in a consciously controlled way, neither as a cherished possession, nor a private joke. The phrase 'swoon of shame', which crops up in *Alone*, is justified as an allusion to a known, published work; similarly, the allusions to opera and folk-song, or Odysseus and Syrinx, work more directly. The word 'Voidward' in *Nightpiece* is one of the few coinages in the later sequence, and it is characteristic in being a compound of elements that are not separately unusual: instead of 'plenilune', 'enaisled', 'innumerous' and the like, words such as 'Loveward', 'Rosefrail', 'Slimesilvered' and 'moondew' work in a more subdued way. The compounding is reinforcement, drawing attention to oddly joined elements, but the meanings are released more or less at once, without requiring separate acts of attention. Whereas Yeats pruned double epithets when he revised his earlier style, Joyce applied the principle of torque, which makes meanings work harder and acquire interest in themselves.

> Goldbrown upon the sated flood
> The rockvine clusters lift and sway;

Separately simple meanings flow together in a double strand in these lines from *Flood*, instead of delivering one at a terminus labelled Newman or Swinburne or whoever.

Chamber Music and *Pomes Penyeach* are Joyce's only two extant and published collections, though he included *Ecce Puer* in his 1936 *Collected Poems* and earlier published separately his two broadsides, *The Holy Office* and *Gas from a Burner*. *Ecce Puer* is significant, as I have already suggested, partly because Joyce turned to verse at such a crucial, personal moment; partly because, even then, he expressed himself in a way that appears transparent yet contains deep contradictions. *The Holy Office* can be read alongside the uncollected epigrams and other earlier satirical verse: the gap between *Chamber Music* and Joyce's realism and invective appears less extraordinary if one recalls, say, John Davidson among nineties poets. Again, *Gas from a Burner* might be related to *Pomes Penyeach*, since both of them have a more variable *persona* than *Chamber Music* and *The Holy Office*.

The occasional poems differ so much from one another that it is difficult to generalize about them as a group: what there is to be said is perhaps better left to the separate notes. They are, for the most part, doggerel, moving to the air of some popular tune or nursery rhyme. Even the limericks can be assimilated to this pattern, in that the form is prior to the words to a noticeably marked extent. The elements that Joyce drops into the pattern are sometimes verbally complicated, like his rhymes to advertise *Work in Progress* or the French poem to Valery Larbaud; sometimes they are wholly spontaneous and ephemeral, as in letters to Giorgio Joyce; at other times, as in the parody of Eliot's *Waste Land*, they make up memorable, telling satire.[11]

Readers who have come across these poems have usually assumed they were of anecdotal interest only. Joyce appears to have felt the same, since there was never any question of him collecting them. But take the limericks, which I have grouped separately together. Mostly they follow the traditional formula, 'There once was a — called — ' and maintain the traditional rhyming scheme, trimeter and dimeter lines and anapaestic rhythms. But Joyce diverges from the dominant tradition established by Edward Lear, in which the final line is a repetition, or varied repetition, of the first: his last lines characteristically deliver not a reversal, or a simple addition-repetition, but syntactical completion. On their way to it, his rhymes meet with a less cruel crack than Gogarty's; they do not flourish indecent discovery. Nor does he go in for trick rhyme, surprise non-rhyme and other such devices that construct elegant bridges of sound over an abyss of sense, like Ogden Nash and Morris Bishop. His rhymes establish real connections, and the poems centre on subjects both more varied and closer to the centre than the usual cast list of wild geographers and misendowed clerics. Their real-life subjects are not dismembered by the limerick form, which none the less contrives to place them in a distinctive light. The poem on Ezra Pound at Sirmione (*P&SW* 124) is as successful as *Ecce Puer*: it has not been recognized as such only because readers have no place for it and feel more at home with solemnity.

What is also interesting about Joyce's occasional poems is their relation to the poems he published as part of his fiction. His early uncollected poems either precede or accompany the composition of *Chamber Music*. They are written in the same manner, and remained unpublished either because they were judged not mature enough or simply because they did not fit. For instance, Stephen's villanelle in the *Portrait* survives from an earlier collection; it is a 'real' poem. The later, occasional poems are, by contrast, of a different kind from those in *Pomes Penyeach* and *Ecce Puer*. The poems that appear in Joyce's subsequent fiction – and there are a good many – are all in the manner of the ballad on Parnell in *Ivy Day in the Committee Room* (D 134–35). Why? Why are so many poems in this doggerel mode included in *Ulysses* and *Finnegans Wake*? What does it say about Joyce as a poet?

The materials are gathered together by Selwyn Jackson in his study *The Poems of James Joyce and the Use of Poems in His Novels* (Frankfurt/Main, 1978). Jackson's first two chapters are given over to a survey of the verse Joyce published separately, the remaining four to the verse in his novels. Whereas the pieces of verse quoted by Stephen in *Ulysses* are not dissimilar to Joyce's own early style, Bloom's efforts, such as his advertising rhyme for Plumtree's Potted Meat and his verses for Molly, are 'kinetic':

> *Poets oft have sung in rhyme*
> *Of music sweet their praise divine.*
> *Let them hymn it nine times nine.*
> *Dearer far than song or wine.*
> *You are mine. The world is mine.*

(U 555)

Ulysses also differs from Joyce's earlier fiction to the extent that it is filled with fragments of popular verse and songs that weave together in leitmotif.

Finnegans Wake is different again in that, besides multiplying the references to popular song, Joyce included five full-length poems written specially for the fiction: Hosty's ballad (*FW* 44–47), the poem in the Shem episode, 'In Nowhere has yet the Whole World' (*FW* 175), the song of the seaswans (*FW* 383), Tristan's song (*FW* 398–9), and the Gracehoper's poem (*FW* 418–

19). They can be read separately, but they also form nodes in a pattern of interrelationship, concentring major themes and routing them differently through the surrounding prose. In other words, they are important to the structure as well as the texture.

Jackson's argument is the conventional one: that Joyce made a false start as a writer of verse, and that as verse shifted from the centre of his attention it reappeared on the periphery, making another contribution. The aim of his study is to demonstrate how the poems in Joyce's novels show him assimilating poetry to prose, becoming a poetic novelist, as D. H. Lawrence also did, for example. I think the evidence he brings forward is open to a different interpretation. *Chamber Music* is demonstrably not a false start, and *Pomes Penyeach* is proof that Joyce felt verse was a form where the most personal themes might be – should be – explored. His later verse may be evidence that he had transferred his serious interest to fiction, but the fact that he continued to write verse proves a use for it that prose did not encompass. While from one point of view it is indeed doggerel, from another it is more interesting and more valuable.

Doggerel is used in *Finnegans Wake* with serious intent in a way that might alert one to serious consequences in a comic poem like *Dooleysprudence*. Joyce fell naturally into rhyme and rhythmical expression, and later poems that move to popular tunes are no more pastiche than *Chamber Music*, which moves to Elizabethan airs; the field of reference that binds the poems in *Finnegans Wake* to their context is merely a specified way of reading them. The same web of filiation extends from separately existing poems to a context that is less literary, less prepared: the 'A Come-all-ye, by a Thanksgiving Turkey', for instance, extends into expatriate life in Paris in the 1930s; *A Portrait of the Artist as an Ancient Mariner* is as lyric in expression as any *Pome Penyeach* – it is simply less 'romantic'.

What I have said about Joyce's limericks could be extended to all his parodies and imitations, which are variously kinetic. They are never static in the way described as an ideal by Stephen in the *Portrait*, passing 'from ecstasy to languor' (P 223), but this does not make them any the less interesting as poetry. The usual view is expressed by Stanislaus Joyce, when he says that 'not all Jim's personality nor even the most distinctive part of it found expression in verse, but only the emotive side, which in one respect was fictitious' (*MBK* 150). Stanislaus's attitude is reflected in the Faber editors' decision to include Stephen's villanelle (*P&SW* 72) and to omit the less 'poetical' verses that elsewhere play a part in Joyce's fiction. This takes a constrained, solemn view of what verse can encompass, and a view of Joyce's achievement that is too narrow.

V

Joyce's translation of Hauptmann's *Before Sunrise* is extant, and he is known to have sent a five-act play, *A Brilliant Career*, to William Archer.[12] *Exiles* is his only play to have survived, however, and it shares a similar background to the poems. The literary revival of the 1890s in Dublin also saw a new kind of theatre, which became properly established with the founding of the Abbey in 1904. Yeats was again its central organizing figure, accompanied this time by Edward Martyn and Lady Gregory in place of George Russell, and with Synge making a more striking contribution than Starkey was able to make in verse. The standards again came to be defined by Yeats and were nationalistic – that is, romantically rooted in place and community. Joyce was again attracted to the counter-tradition, and was again silent concerning his dependence on it.

Shaw had championed Ibsen, but so also had Martyn and George Moore. So even had Yeats, but Yeats was more committed to generalities, such as Ibsen's struggle to win an audience, than to Ibsen's dramaturgy and values; his real enthusiasm was for the symbolist drama of Villiers de l'Isle-Adam and Maeterlinck.[13] Martyn and Moore were committed to Ibsen in a closer way; they valued his realism for the same reason Moore valued Zola's fiction. Against this background Joyce's pose of the champion of an author without honour in Dublin is somewhat misleading. He took sides in a dispute that divided and ultimately split the Irish Dramatic Movement, though he did so without reference to the dispute. Characteristically remaining aloof from Martyn and

Moore, Joyce's championship of Ibsen is as much a counter-statement against mysticism, mumming and Yeats as genuine predilection for his author. He was friends enough with Synge in Paris, before Synge returned and was lost to view (from Joyce) in the Abbey design. It has even been suggested that his own *Brilliant Career* owed something to Martyn–Moore's *Bending of the Bough* (*JJ* 88, 454).

Critical discussion of *Exiles* has centred in part on Joyce's debt to Ibsen. The debt is evident in the way the play is made up of a debate over right and wrong, eschewing monologue. It has been compared to *Hedda Gabler* in the way it opens with the return home of the main character; the double set of partners has been taken to bear a strong resemblance to *When We Dead Awaken*; the theme of freedom for the wife has been said to derive from *The Lady from the Sea*; and so on. The discussion has often become an assessment of *Exiles* simply as an Ibsen play, and, measured in these terms, it has inevitably been found lacking, though this is not the point.

It is also evident that the relation I have sketched of Joyce's debt to his antecedents should not be interpreted rigidly. *Exiles* shows the influence of Wagner as well as Ibsen, which appears contradictory in terms of nineteenth-century literary politics until Joyce's allusions are seen as partly ironic. Discussion has also centred on the biographical dimension of the characters, connecting Richard Rowan with Joyce himself, Bertha with Nora, Robert Hand with Gogarty and several other 'betrayers', Beatrice with figures in Joyce's life extending from Mary Sheehy to Amalia Popper. I have supplied details of some of these connections in the Notes.

Exiles treats the same area of Joyce's experience as *Pomes Penyeach*, in terms of a different medium. It deals with the crisis he underwent – or manufactured – when he returned alone to Dublin in 1909 and became obsessed with the thought that Nora might have been unfaithful to him.[14] It was an experience connected with the fear of betrayal he expressed as early as Poems XVII, XVIII, XIX and XXI of *Chamber Music*, and which he explored from another direction in his own 'affair' with his

Triestine student. The play and the poems work the same materials through to kinds of resolution that are appropriate to their different mediums. The poems, though they are dramatic lyrics, remain close to Joyce's first feelings, and an outcome is arrived at by arrangement, almost adventitiously. The play displaces the same action into an impersonal space over which more control is exercised; the form organizes the experience Joyce would measure his distance from, frames it, holds it at a remove.

This is why Joyce insisted the play was not about adultery but exile.[15] While the possibility of adultery provides the ostensible plot, the impossibility of showing such an act onstage becomes for Joyce the opportunity to leave us in the dark. Like several crucial scenes in the action of *Ulysses*, it is simply omitted and we do not know if it took place. 'I can never know, never in this world,' Richard exclaims. Joyce is concerned to pursue consequences that are more pressing when the deed is in doubt; or rather absent, since we should not be sidetracked into thinking this is a problem play. It is also why we should not be distracted by the notes he made as he was writing. I have not included them as a separate appendix in order to keep them where they belong, subordinate to the level of the rest of the Notes. They establish and strengthen connections between the play and his life in a way that can distort what the play actually achieves, which is a peculiar kind of distance that complements the enterprise of *Pomes Penyeach*. As the one adjusts a lyric voice close, but in varying ways adjacent, to the experiences it describes, the other puts limits on a story, converts event into situation, for the assessment to be measured.

The success of the enterprise is not generally agreed upon because there is no agreement over Joyce's purpose. That is, the play has been found wooden and theatrical by turns, according to whether or not Joyce has been credited with control of the effects he creates. The most successful stage realization has been by Harold Pinter, which works on the premise that Joyce was aware of what might happen in the silences between his words, that Joyce worked self-consciously with humour instead of a myopic capacity for bathos.[16] Audiences have believed almost unanimously that Pinter's interpretation works and makes Joyce's play exciting, but Joyceans have asked if it is not more Pinter than Joyce. Though Joyce said a good deal about drama, it has not proved easy to reach a consensus on the basis of what he said, and the evidence can be argued either way.

The idea of drama that Stephen advances in the *Portrait* enlarges on what Joyce had worked out in 1903. Drama, according to Stephen, is the highest literary form because it is the most objective: whereas lyric records a self-conscious 'instant of emotion', and epic prolongs this instant, 'dramatic form is life purified in and reprojected from the human imagination. The mystery of esthetic like that of material creation is accomplished. The artist, like the god of the creation, remains within or behind or beyond or above his handiwork, invisible, refined out of existence, indifferent' (*P* 214–15; compare *CW* 145). This is the ideal Joyce found in Ibsen, when he wrote about him in 1900 in the *Fortnightly Review*. He distinguishes between the clever purveying of character, which he does not commend, and Ibsen's drama, which is 'wholly independent of his characters' (*CW* 65).

The play Joyce wrote as he completed the *Portrait* attempts to realize this same ideal of objectivity. It attempts to transpose a situation that had multiple implications into a form that was removed from personal accident and over which he had control. Unlike lyric, in which experience flows into and has no existence apart from words, words on a stage exist with spaces round them. They exist in relation with physical presence and gesture, nonverbal events. Thus ventilated, they can even afford laughter. The question is always whether the laughter is under the artist's control, since, if it is uncontrolled, it can also be at the artist's expense. Richard Rowan would play God paring his fingernails in his relation to the action he sets in motion: the argument is over whether he, and Joyce, should be allowed to maintain this equilibrium.

If the play can evidently be produced either way, Joyce appears to have incorporated his own revised reflections on drama in *Ulysses*. The theory of art that Stephen promulgates in the library chapter recalls Stephen's theory in the *Portrait*, with significant modifications. Shakespeare's plays are described as transpositions of his own experience, and this is stressed. Then later, the longest chapter in *Ulysses*, set in Nighttown, is cast in dramatic form, but it is made up of a series of illusions. The characters write themselves into plots of their own devising – Bloom into Mayor of Dublin, Stephen into a climactic confrontation with his mother – but overwrite would be more accurate. The plots are melodramatic rather than convincing: they imply that the relation art bears to reality here is a hallucination; that drama is not an objective form, it acts out dreams. The chapter contains more events we are aware do not happen, even while we see them happening, than any other.

The implications for drama contained in *Ulysses*, when set alongside the *Portrait*, appear to be that drama cannot escape its origins in life any more than a son can escape his father. As Stephen points out in his telegram (*U* 164), the belief that art can escape from life is a sentimental impossibility. At the same time drama can create a counter-reality in which real issues, in different, distorted form, can be manipulated. The paradox allows the illusion of freedom in art, even if art is doomed to be overtaken by life. Joyce put drama into a fictional context in his later writing, in the same way that he did his poems. He qualified its independent status, with the result that the operatic, stagy effects of *Circe* are comparable to doggerel in verse. There are also 'plays' in *Finnegans Wake* just as there are 'poems' – the Butt and Taff rehearsal of 'The abnihilisation of the etym' or the Mime of Mick and the Maggies – and their status is the same as the poems.

Pomes Penyeach and *Exiles* confront issues more directly than Joyce could in fiction, and in this respect are closer to the sources of his energy as a writer. Eventually, though, the access they gave was less useful than forms that enabled him to range more easily and widely on the margins of his personality. Put another way, verse and drama gave Joyce the most direct access to his feelings: one appeared like the shortest route, the other promised the most stable mode of appraisal; the feelings at the centre were meanwhile profoundly 'ordinary', as Joyce knew and often insisted,[17] and the excitement grew only with the attempt to harness them. If Joyce's

sense of what was central had been less secure, or if his ordinari-
ness had been less thoroughgoing, he would have suffered the fate
of Huysmans's Des Esseintes or Flann O'Brien's De Selby and
condemned himself to limbo.

VI

I have been describing how Joyce's poems and his play relate to
one another and to the rest of his writings. What bearings do they
have on his status as a writer? How do they situate him in relation
to Irish writing of his time and to modern writing as a whole? I
have suggested some of the qualities that distinguish them, but
what is the meaning of these qualities? Though the tendency of
Joyce's manner is to convert life into terms of art in order to come
to terms with life, is it possible to convert this general, generalizing
position into anything more obviously connected with here and
now? A good deal of the preceding discussion has been conducted
in terms that alternate between the metaphoric and the abstract –
centres and peripheries, for example – and some conclusions
couched in simpler terms might be welcome.

Joyce's early poems and his interest in drama both have particu-
lar origins in the literary Dublin of the 1890s; together they
encompass a set of interests, attitudes and responses that existed
in no other place at no other time. While in one light the milieu
was determined by fashions that were commonplace in France,
and constituted a special version of the English nineties, the
conditions that pertained in Ireland invested cultural fashions
with so much more explicit political meaning that it was trans-
formed utterly. The transformation of values is very obvious in
the case of Yeats, but the alternative Joyce pursued is not simply
an apolitical alternative; it is equally, though differently, political.

Irish writers had their own pressing reasons to be among the
first to react against Victorianism and the genteel tradition, to
turn from specifically English traditions to European models that
appeared to promise a critique and an alternative. A situation
evolved in which Ireland anticipated the Modern Movement
among English-speaking nations, one consequence of which was

that Modernism was a thing of the past in Ireland before it can be said to have begun in America or England.

This is not the place to write about the course of Irish literary history, which has delivered itself into its odd state at present, but it might be noted that the word 'Irish' in the present context is in effect equivalent to Dublin. The Revival was very much the product of the particular character of one city, not of other regions, though the rural west was reappraised by the cultural values of the capital and reinscribed. Dublin is a city with a minimal industrial base – in contrast to Belfast – and this was in decline.[18] It is also the centre of administration and the port of entry for ninety per cent of people and goods. Such economic and social conditions determine culture to the extent that fashions, when they arrive, tend quickly to be exclusive and as quickly to be exhausted. The architecture of Georgian Dublin is a striking example: it arrived late and spread over unusually large areas of the city; when the fashion eventually died, it did not feed into any continuing tradition but was superseded.

Chamber Music is a product of the same forces. It absorbs an incoming fashion in a way that is the more complete because it is not bothered with its background. Joyce sees a manner from the outside, and mimicks it perfectly because he is able to see it purely as style. In the process it becomes a new thing that surpasses its origins and bears a different kind of relation to reality. Joyce's method of concentration on isolated words is again peculiar, and requires distance from other distractions to be able to develop. It is a method of writing 'on the outside' or 'at a distance' that had a profound influence on Pound, and *Chamber Music* anticipates *Mauberley*. Indeed, it is natural that exactly the same problems of interpretation have faced writers on the two sequences.[19]

Yeats was lamenting the end of his version of the Revival even before the riots over Synge's *Playboy*, and *Chamber Music* deconstructed Modernism *avant la lettre* ('Romantic Ireland's dead and gone'). Modernism not only came early to Ireland, it also burnt out early; so that Yeats's Crazy Jane poems are already Post-Modern at a time when Auden was imitating Eliot, and Joyce was undoing the achievement of *Ulysses* while Wallace

Stevens was filling his fountain pen. If Joyce's occasional poems are considered in this light, their open texture, humour, kind of reference and sense of improvisation are no longer matters for Modernist regret. If a comparison is to be made between *Chamber Music* and *Mauberley*, the epigrams on Dr Rosenbach and on Samuel Roth (*P&SW* 130 and 135, as well as below) should be compared with the contents of James Fenton's *Manilla Envelope; To Budgen, Raughty Tinker* set alongside Gavin Ewart; the various occasional poems to Richard Wallace and to Giorgio Joyce (*P&SW* 147) are like rhyming Frank O'Hara.

The comparisons are worth making because they situate Joyce's poems alongside those that have similar pretensions, and make evident what his poems have to offer. Joyce's wit, the variability of his rhythms, his ability to adjust to different audiences, are striking. All his occasional poems are personal, yet those that attack do not founder on vituperation and those that are friendly are so varied as to suggest that they are not merely mechanical. The different versions of the same familiar style that Joyce produces for Sylvia Beach and Maria Jolas, or Richard Wallace and Stuart Gilbert (*P&SW* 148), make the poems he wrote for them occasional in the most complimentary sense. They demonstrate ways of writing when it would be easy to overwrite; each delicately adjusts to person and event.

It is fitting that Joyce left these poems for others to collect. There is something contradictory and discomfiting about authors' collections of occasional poems and trivia, 'more little ones', but not at all in the job being done for them. If Joyce had written his occasional poems for publication, or allowed publication in his lifetime outside the few that appeared as part of Gorman's biography, the way they relate to readers would necessarily change. They need to feed into and off the material that supports them in the notes, freely and casually. The transaction alters when the author supplies the surrounding material himself.

Exiles is similarly a study in contradiction, being made up of pure 'Ibsen' and pure 'Pinter'. It deals seriously with moral and social issues, such as women's role in marriage, and it is also a play in which actions are consistently hollow and at which we are invited to laugh. Like *Chamber Music*, it is a self-cancelling balancing act; like Beckett's plays, it operates on an evacuative premise, making what it achieves not repeatable; it is, as Francis Ferguson said long ago, 'a "drama to end dramas"' (*CH* I 157). Ellmann's biography records Joyce asking Arthur Laubenstein: '"Which would you say was the greater power in holding people together, complete faith or doubt?"' Laubenstein plumped for faith but Joyce was firm: '"No, doubt is the thing. Life is suspended in doubt like the world in the void. You might find this in some sense treated in *Exiles*"' (*JJ* 557).

The stage directions in the present edition follow Joyce's fair-copy manuscript. The difference between them and those in previously published texts is significant. Joyce was evidently careful about the way his text should be performed, preserving a fine adjustment between words and action. This might seem odd when the characteristic manner of the play is to set speech against speech. Though the immediate background is specific enough, with details in it as if for the close-up camera, it is isolated from the larger background. Joyce's Merrion is a nowhere-place and his Ranelagh another, and they might in many respects be suburbs of Trieste or Peking. The characters stand forward and declaim their lines at one another, in a time and space made devoid of echoes.

Carla de Petris observes that actors in *Exiles* 'have few actions to perform while speaking, often they are left on stage in utter silence and embarrassment'.[20] That is, when the actors speak, they do little else; when they are not speaking, their waiting surrounds words in silence, which puts action on the verge of melodrama. Stage directions most often indicate a pause or a form of dumb-show that indicates a thematic shift. Whereas in the case of a less sophisticated and experienced author one might suppose these features to be mistakes, in this instance one has to reckon they are used deliberately to isolate the drama. Their effect is numbing, and sometimes results in laughter, sometimes compels attention, should properly do both.

Joyce had earlier described drama as 'the least dependent of all arts on its material' (*CW* 43): it would seem he is after this kind of independence here. 'Drama has to do with the underlying laws first, in all their nakedness and divine severity, and only secondarily with the motley agents who bear them out' (CW 40). Whatever form it takes must not be superimposed or conventional. 'In literature we allow conventions, for literature is a comparatively low form of art. Literature is kept alive by tonics, it flourishes through conventions in all human relations, in all actuality. Drama will be for the future at war with convention, if it is to realize itself fully' (CW 41).

These quotations are from an essay written while Joyce was a student, but it applies to *Exiles*: the play assimilates Ibsenite possibilities and annihilates them with equal assurance. Joyce did not write a Post-Modern play thereafter, but there is enough theatre in *Ulysses* and *Finnegans Wake* to make evident what his idea of drama became. *Exiles* has found no place in the theatrical tradition because it refuses a place, like *Chamber Music* in verse. The carefully enunciated phrases of Pinter's plays allow comic dimensions to hover at the edge of serious predicaments; Bertha does not escape them, though she is none the less sympathetically portrayed; the anomalies are Irish and Joycean.

Transcendence in literature has been questioned in our time, and written off as Romantic ideology; materialist critics have argued that art cannot escape into a timeless world that is cut off from political and other responsibilities. Joyce was well aware of the impossibility of art, and his poems and his play demonstrate this and build on it. He told Harriet Weaver, in the course of *Work in Progress*, 'I know it is no more than a game but it is a game that I have learned to play in my own way. Children may just as well play as not. The ogre will come in any case' (L III 144). The point of the writing, however, is the game. It is rather different from Romantic *Spieltrieb*, but it is also rather different from what some commentary would reduce it to.

Irish literary politics are another matter again. Joyce has been situated in an argument between Irish-Irish and Anglo-Irish Ireland by polemicists as various as D. P. Moran, Thomas Kinsella and Seamus Deane. That is, his writing has been taken to represent a tradition more Catholic than Protestant, more Gaelic than Celtic, more urban-realist than rural-romantic.[21] The uses to which his writing might be put are none the less as various as the needs of his readers, in their different times and places; and his own consistently high regard for Yeats, as distinguished from the causes Yeats espoused, is to be borne in mind. He described his own position when he told Ernst Robert Curtius that he would rather be considered a rednosed comedian than a bluejawed tragedian (*JJ* 696). The position is anarchistically aslant, poised to soar above and let the liquid siftings fall upon those who would catch him in their nets.

NOTES

1. See also the press notices Joyce collected to insert in *Dubliners* (*L* II 332–3n).
2. References to Joyce's changing attitude towards *Chamber Music* and his uncertain attitude towards *Pomes Penyeach* can be traced most easily through the indexes to *L* III and *JJ*.
3. Beckett published *Echo's Bones and Other Precipitates* in 1935. I take the later collections in which it was included to be omnium gatherum collections in a different sense.
4. See Rhys's poem of this name in Stanford's *Writing of the 'Nineties* 128–9. References to Joyce's early lost collections may be traced through *JJ*.
5. The classic study is by John Kelleher, 'Matthew Arnold and the Celtic Revival' in *Perspectives of Criticism*, ed. Harry Levin (Cambridge, Mass., 1950) 197–221 – to which Seamus Deane has given a contemporary twist in *Civilians and Barbarians* (Derry, 1983) and, further, in *Celtic Revivals: Essays in Modern Irish Literature 1880–1980* (London, 1985).
6. Myra Russel, 'The Elizabethan Connection: The Missing Score of James Joyce's *Chamber Music*', *JJQ* XVIII (Winter 1981) 133–45.
7. Compare also Budgen 349 on Joyce's continuing admiration for the idiom of Elizabethan songs.
8. The Gregory quote is from *The Dying Gladiators* (NY, 1961) 163. A convenient place to begin to locate musical settings is Part F of Slocum 163–9, which can be supplemented by the annual listings in *JJQ*.
9. R. C. Trench, Church of Ireland Archbishop of Dublin, was grandfather of the Trench who stayed with Gogarty and Joyce at the Sandycove Tower and who appears as Haines in *Ulysses*. Aubert 1804 cites an

essay by Hugh Kenner, 'Joyce and the Nineteenth-century Linguistic Explosion' in *Atti del Third International James Joyce Symposium* (Trieste, 1974), on these early enthusiasms and connections.

10. Stanford's *Writing of the 'Nineties* 40.

11. Joyce's *Waste Land* parody can now be found in *P&SW*, as can most of the other occasional poems excluded from the present edition.

12. The Hauptmann has been published in an edition by Jill Perkins (San Marino, Calif. 1978); for *A Brilliant Career*, see the references in my note on 'Fragments from Shine and Dark' No. VI.

13. These matters are discussed by James W. Flannery, *W. B. Yeats and the Idea of a Theatre* (reprinted New Haven, Conn., 1989) 138, 155–7, etc., with further references for the material provided in the surrounding paragraphs.

14. The record preserved in *Selected Letters*, ed. Richard Ellmann (London, 1975) and *JJ* should be consulted, rather than the censored record contained in *L* and the first, 1959 edition of *JJ*.

15. See *L* I 138, in which he glossed the title for his Italian translator; also Padraic Colum's comments in his Introduction to *Exiles* (NY, 1951 edition) 7–8.

16. Descriptions of Pinter's 1970–71 production, and others, are offered by Katharine J. Worth 'Joyce via Pinter', *Revolutions in Modern English Drama* (London, 1972) 46–54, and John MacNicholas, 'The Stage History of *Exiles*', *JJQ* XIX (Fall 1981) 9–26.

17. In other words, I take Joyce's values, as family man and citizen, to approximate to Leopold Bloom's. Arthur Power used often to reflect on the discrepancy between Joyce's bourgeois habits of living and his commitment to experiment in art.

Some English readers at first responded to this 'ordinary' aspect of Joyce in class terms, Virginia Woolf finding him 'underbred' (*JJ* 528) and Wyndham Lewis 'shabby-genteel' (*CH* I 364). Its relation to his art has been understood better in the years since. For instance, Michael Begnal explicates the process by which history in a chapter of *Finnegans Wake* is 'reduced to a story which might be told over the bar in a pub, perhaps reduced to a tale told by four idiots which signifies, in itself, nothing' as a comment on history itself, 'remembore' ('Love that Dares to Speak its Name' in *A Conceptual Guide to 'Finnegans Wake'* ed. Michael H. Begnal and Fritz Senn, University Park, Pa., 1974, 145).

18. See the studies by Joseph V. O'Brien, *'Dear Dirty Dublin': A City in Distress 1899–1916* (Berkeley, Calif. 1982) and Mary E. Daly, *Dublin,*

the Deposed Capital: A Social and Economic History 1860–1914 (Cork, 1984).

19. As have bothered Donald Davie, for example, in a succession of well-known, contradictory discussions.

20. Carla de Petris, 'Exiles or the Necessity of Theatre' in Myriadminded Man: Jottings on Joyce ed. Rosa Maria Bosinelli, Paola Pugliatti and Romana Zacchi (Bologna, 1986) 70.

21. A summary and further references are provided by Terence Brown, 'Yeats, Joyce and the Irish Critical Debate', Ireland's Literature: Selected Essays (Mullingar, 1989) 77–90.

FURTHER READING

This list does not include all the titles that appear in the list of abbreviations, or all the books and articles cited in the Introduction and Notes. It concentrates on discussion rather than further annotation and is deliberately selective, omitting collateral reading as obvious as *CH* and *JJ*. Access to a very full list of material is conveniently to hand in Robert H. Deming, *A Bibliography of James Joyce Studies* (revised edition, Boston, Mass. 1977) and Thomas Jackson Rice, *James Joyce: A Guide to Research* (NY 1982).

VERSE

Chester G. Anderson, 'Joyce's Verses' in *A Companion to Joyce Studies* ed. Zack Bowen and James F. Carens (Westport, Conn., 1984) 129–55

Padraic Colum, 'James Joyce as Poet' in *The Joyce Book*, ed. Herbert Hughes (London, 1932) 13–15

A Concordance to the 'Collected Poems' of James Joyce ed. Paul A. Doyle (NY, 1966)

Francesco Gozzi, *La Poesia di James Joyce* (Bari, 1974)

Herbert Howarth, '*Chamber Music* and Its Place in the Joyce Canon' in *James Joyce Today: Essays on the Major Works*, ed. Thomas F. Staley (Bloomington, Ill. 1966) 11–27

Selwyn Jackson, *The Poems of James Joyce and the Use of Poems in His Novels* (Frankfurt/Main, 1978)

Myra Russel, 'The Elizabethan Connection: The Missing Score of James Joyce's *Chamber Music*', *JJQ* XVIII (Winter 1981) 133–45

Bonnie Kime Scott, *Joyce and Feminism* (Bloomington, Ill. 1984)

William York Tindall (ed.), *Chamber Music* (NY, 1954)

Max Wildi, 'The Lyrical Poems of James Joyce' in *Language and Society: Essays Presented to Arthur M. Jensen* (Copenhagen, 1961) 169–86

Morton D. Zabel, 'The Lyrics of James Joyce', *Poetry* (Chicago) XXXVI (July 1930) 206–13

EXILES

Ruth Bauerle, *A Word List to James Joyce's 'Exiles'* (NY, 1981)
— 'Bertha's Role in *Exiles*' in *Women in Joyce*, ed. Suzette Henke and Elaine Unkeless (Urbana, Ill. 1982) 108–31
Bernard Benstock, '*Exiles*' in *A Companion to Joyce Studies*, ed. Zack Bowen and James F. Carens (Westport, Conn., 1984) 361–86
— 'A Drama in Exile', *James Joyce* (Literature and Life Series, formerly Modern Literature and World Dramatists, NY 1985) 73–93
Hugh Kenner, '*Exiles*', *Dublin's Joyce* (London, 1955) 69–94
John MacNicholas, 'Joyce's *Exiles*: The Argument for Doubt', *JJQ* XI (Fall 1973) 33–40
— 'The Stage History of *Exiles*', *JJQ* XIX (Fall 1981) 9–26
Carla de Petris, '*Exiles* or the Necessity of Theatre' in *Myriad-minded Man: Jottings on Joyce* ed. Rosa Maria Bosinelli, Paola Pugliatti and Romana Zacchi (Bologna, 1986) 65–75
B. J. Tysdahl, *Joyce and Ibsen: A Study in Literary Influence* (Oslo/NY, 1968)
Raymond Williams in *Drama from Ibsen to Brecht* (London, 1968) 141–46; which is supplemented by *James Joyce: New Perspectives*, ed. Colin MacCabe (Brighton, 1982) 105–10
Katharine J. Worth, 'Joyce via Pinter', *Revolutions in Modern English Drama* (London, 1972) 46–54

A NOTE ON THE TEXTS

This edition does not attempt to collate variant readings. I have worked from original manuscripts in a few instances, but for the most part have been dependent on reproductions in the *Archive* and on photocopies. A proper analysis of the texts must wait for someone who can examine all the originals in person. Meanwhile, a partial collation of the manuscript and printed texts of *Chamber Music* is available in the edition by William York Tindall (NY, 1954). I have also taken advantage of the analysis of the text of *Exiles* by John MacNicholas (NY, 1979) to correct the previously available versions, though I have not accepted every one of his recommendations.

Because of the variousness of the texts, considerations apply that are best described in the notes on each poem separately and again on *Exiles*. In general, I have supplied improved texts of published material – that is, incorporating changes Joyce made in editions of the poems after the first edition, and revising the text of *Exiles* according to MacNicholas's prescription to bring it closer to what Joyce wanted to see in print – and I have gone back to manuscripts and typescripts for poems Joyce did not publish himself. This leads to some unevenness of texture and styling, but greater disadvantages would follow from imposing consistency. I have added only minimal punctuation to Joyce's manuscript versions, in the wake of his own practice.

Doyle attempts a comprehensive listing of Joyce's miscellaneous verse. His articles contain mistakes and omissions that are obvious enough in hindsight, but they also list poems I have excluded. My reasons are given at the beginning of the notes on Poems of Early Youth and on uncollected Occasional Poems. Some poems Doyle lists can be proved not to have been written by Joyce; others might be better described as loose or creative quotations; others again are drafts or variants of poems that are part of *Finnegans Wake*. Some of those I exclude are included in Aubert, but, while

1

the limits of occasional verse are by definition smudged, there is every reason in the present case not to smudge them further. Others again are excluded perforce, by reason of the decision of the Joyce Estate described above in my Foreword. They can now most conveniently be found in *P&SW*.

Other matters described in the Foreword are relevant here. In particular, texts that overlap with *P&SW* often differ because they rest on different editorial decisions. Such differences are sometimes noted, but not always.

PUBLISHED COLLECTIONS

Chamber Music

(published 1907)

I

Strings in the earth and air
   Make music sweet;
Strings by the river where
   The willows meet.

There's music along the river
   For Love wanders there,
Pale flowers on his mantle
   Dark leaves on his hair.

All softly playing,
   With head to the music bent,
And fingers straying
   Upon an instrument.

II

The twilight turns from amethyst
    To deep and deeper blue,
The lamp fills with a pale green glow
    The trees of the avenue.

The old piano plays an air,
    Sedate and slow and gay;
She bends upon the yellow keys,
    Her head inclines this way.

Shy thoughts and grave wide eyes and hands
    That wander as they list –
The twilight turns to darker blue
    With lights of amethyst.

III

At that hour when all things have repose,
  O lonely watcher of the skies,
  Do you hear the night wind and the sighs
Of harps playing unto Love to unclose
  The pale gates of sunrise?

When all things repose do you alone
  Awake to hear the sweet harps play
  To Love before him on his way,
And the night wind answering in antiphon
  Till night is overgone?

Play on, invisible harps, unto Love
  Whose way in heaven is aglow
  At that hour when soft lights come and go,
Soft sweet music in the air above
  And in the earth below.

IV

When the shy star goes forth in heaven
    All maidenly, disconsolate,
Hear you amid the drowsy even
    One who is singing by your gate.
His song is softer than the dew
    And he is come to visit you.

O bend no more in revery
    When he at eventide is calling
Nor muse: Who may this singer be
    Whose song about my heart is falling?
Know you by this, the lover's chant,
    'Tis I that am your visitant.

V

Lean out of the window,
    Goldenhair,
I heard you singing
    A merry air.

My book is closed;
    I read no more,
Watching the fire dance
    On the floor.

I have left my book:
    I have left my room:
For I heard you singing
    Through the gloom,

Singing and singing
    A merry air.
Lean out of the window,
    Goldenhair.

VI

I would in that sweet bosom be
    (O sweet it is and fair it is!)
Where no rude wind might visit me.
    Because of sad austerities
I would in that sweet bosom be.

I would be ever in that heart
    (O soft I knock and soft entreat her!)
Where only peace might be my part.
    Austerities were all the sweeter
So I were ever in that heart.

VII

My love is in a light attire
    Among the appletrees
Where the gay winds do most desire
    To run in companies.

There, where the gay winds stay to woo
    The young leaves as they pass,
My love goes slowly, bending to
    Her shadow on the grass;

And where the sky's a pale blue cup
    Over the laughing land,
My love goes lightly, holding up
    Her dress with dainty hand.

VIII

Who goes amid the green wood
　　With springtide all adorning her?
Who goes amid the merry green wood
　　To make it merrier?

Who passes in the sunlight
　　By ways that know the light footfall?
Who passes in the sweet sunlight
　　With mien so virginal?

The ways of all the woodland
　　Gleam with a soft and golden fire –
For whom does all the sunny woodland
　　Carry so brave attire?

O, it is for my true love
　　The woods their rich apparel wear –
O, it is for my own true love,
　　That is so young and fair.

IX

Winds of May, that dance on the sea,
　　Dancing a ringaround in glee
From furrow to furrow, while overhead
The foam flies up to be garlanded
In silvery arches spanning the air,
Saw you my true love anywhere?
　　　　Welladay! Welladay!
　　　　For the winds of May!
　　　Love is unhappy when love is away!

X

Bright cap and streamers,
    He sings in the hollow:
    Come follow, come follow,
        All you that love.
Leave dreams to the dreamers
    That will not after,
    That song and laughter
        Do nothing move.

With ribbons streaming
    He sings the bolder;
    In troop at his shoulder
        The wild bees hum.
And the time of dreaming
    Dreams is over –
    As lover to lover,
        Sweetheart, I come.

XI

Bid adieu, adieu, adieu,
   Bid adieu to girlish days.
Happy Love is come to woo
   Thee and woo thy girlish ways –
The zone that doth become thee fair,
The snood upon thy yellow hair,

When thou hast heard his name upon
   The bugles of the cherubim
Begin thou softly to unzone
Thy girlish bosom unto him
And softly to undo the snood
That is the sign of maidenhood.

XII

What counsel has the hooded moon
    Put in thy heart, my shyly sweet,
Of Love in ancient plenilune,
    Glory and stars beneath his feet –
A sage that is but kith and kin
With the comedian capuchin?

Believe me rather that am wise
    In disregard of the divine.
A glory kindles in those eyes,
    Trembles to starlight. Mine, O mine!
No more be tears in moon or mist
For thee, sweet sentimentalist.

XIII

Go seek her out all courteously
    And say I come,
Wind of spices whose song is ever
    Epithalamium.
O, hurry over the dark lands
    And run upon the sea
For seas and lands shall not divide us,
    My love and me.

Now, wind, of your good courtesy
    I pray you go
And come into her little garden
    And sing at her window;
Singing: The bridal wind is blowing
    For Love is at his noon;
And soon will your true love be with you,
    Soon, O soon.

XIV

My dove, my beautiful one,
   Arise, arise!
   The nightdew lies
Upon my lips and eyes.

The odorous winds are weaving
   A music of sighs:
   Arise, arise,
My dove, my beautiful one!

I wait by the cedar tree,
   My sister, my love.
   White breast of the dove,
My breast shall be your bed.

The pale dew lies
   Like a veil on my head.
   My fair one, my fair dove,
Arise, arise!

XV

From dewy dreams, my soul, arise,
   From love's deep slumber and from death,
For lo! the trees are full of sighs
   Whose leaves the morn admonisheth.

Eastward the gradual dawn prevails
   Where softly burning fires appear,
Making to tremble all those veils
   Of grey and golden gossamer.

While sweetly, gently, secretly,
   The flowery bells of morn are stirred
And the wise choirs of faery
   Begin (innumerous!) to be heard.

XVI

O cool is the valley now
   And there, love, will we go
For many a choir is singing now
   Where Love did sometime go.
And hear you not the thrushes calling,
   Calling us away?
O cool and pleasant is the valley
   And there, love, will we stay.

XVII

Because your voice was at my side
    I gave him pain,
Because within my hand I had
    Your hand again.

There is no word nor any sign
    Can make amend –
He is a stanger to me now
    Who was my friend.

XVIII

O sweetheart, hear you
   Your lover's tale;
A man shall have sorrow
   When friends him fail.

For he shall know then
   Friends be untrue
And a little ashes
   Their words come to.

But one unto him
   Will softly move
And softly woo him
   In ways of love.

His hand is under
   Her smooth round breast;
So he who has sorrow
   Shall have rest.

XIX

Be not sad because all men
   Prefer a lying clamour before you:
Sweetheart, be at peace again –
   Can they dishonour you?

They are sadder than all tears;
   Their lives ascend as a continual sigh.
Proudly answer to their tears:
   As they deny, deny.

XX

In the dark pinewood
 I would we lay,
In deep cool shadow
 At noon of day.

How sweet to lie there,
 Sweet to kiss,
Where the great pine forest
 Enaisled is!

Thy kiss descending
 Sweeter were
With a soft tumult
 Of thy hair.

O, unto the pinewood
 At noon of day
Come with me now,
 Sweet love, away.

XXI

He who hath glory lost nor hath
   Found any soul to fellow his,
Among his foes in scorn and wrath
   Holding to ancient nobleness,
That high unconsortable one –
His love is his companion.

XXII

Of that so sweet imprisonment
   My soul, dearest, is fain –
Soft arms that woo me to relent
   And woo me to detain.
Ah, could they ever hold me there,
Gladly were I a prisoner!

Dearest, through interwoven arms
   By love made tremulous,
That night allures me where alarms
   Nowise may trouble us
But sleep to dreamier sleep be wed
Where soul with soul lies prisoned.

XXIII

This heart that flutters near my heart
　　My hope and all my riches is,
Unhappy when we draw apart
　　And happy between kiss and kiss;
My hope and all my riches – yes! –
And all my happiness.

For there, as in some mossy nest
　　The wrens will divers treasures keep,
I laid those treasures I possessed
　　Ere that mine eyes had learned to weep.
Shall we not be as wise as they
Though love live but a day?

XXIV

Silently she's combing,
　　Combing her long hair,
Silently and graciously,
　　With many a pretty air.

The sun is in the willow leaves
　　And on the dappled grass
And still she's combing her long hair
　　Before the lookingglass.

I pray you, cease to comb out,
　　Comb out your long hair,
For I have heard of witchery
　　Under a pretty air,

That makes as one thing to the lover
　　Staying and going hence,
All fair, with many a pretty air
　　And many a negligence.

XXV

Lightly come or lightly go
    Though thy heart presage thee woe,
Vales and many a wasted sun,
    Oread let thy laughter run
Till the irreverent mountain air
Ripple all thy flying hair.

Lightly, lightly – ever so:
    Clouds that wrap the vales below
At the hour of evenstar
    Lowliest attendants are:
Love and laughter songconfessed
When the heart is heaviest.

XXVI

Thou leanest to the shell of night,
　　Dear lady, a divining ear.
In that soft choiring of delight
　　What sound hath made thy heart to fear?
Seemed it of rivers rushing forth
From the grey deserts of the north?

That mood of thine, O timorous,
　　Is his, if thou but scan it well,
Who a mad tale bequeaths to us
　　At ghosting hour conjurable –
And all for some strange name he read
In Purchas or in Holinshed.

XXVII

Though I thy Mithridates were
   Framed to defy the poisondart,
Yet must thou fold me unaware
   To know the rapture of thy heart
And I but render and confess
The malice of thy tenderness.

For elegant and antique phrase,
   Dearest, my lips wax all too wise;
Nor have I known a love whose praise
   Our piping poets solemnise,
Neither a love where may not be
Ever so little falsity.

XXVIII

Gentle lady, do not sing
   Sad songs about the end of love;
Lay aside sadness and sing
   How love that passes is enough.

Sing about the long deep sleep
   Of lovers that are dead and how
In the grave all love shall sleep.
   Love is aweary now.

XXIX

Dear heart, why will you use me so?
　Dear eyes that gently me upbraid
Still are you beautiful – but O,
　How is your beauty raimented!

Through the clear mirror of your eyes,
　Through the soft sigh of kiss to kiss,
Desolate winds assail with cries
　The shadowy garden where love is.

And soon shall love dissolved be
　When over us the wild winds blow –
But you, dear love, too dear to me,
　Alas! why will you use me so?

XXX

Love came to us in time gone by
   When one at twilight shyly played
And one in fear was standing nigh –
   For Love at first is all afraid.

We were grave lovers. Love is past
   That had his sweet hours many a one.
Welcome to us now at the last
   The ways that we shall go upon.

XXXI

O, it was out by Donnycarney
   When the bat flew from tree to tree
My love and I did walk together
   And sweet were the words she said to me.

Along with us the summer wind
   Went murmuring – O, happily! –
But softer than the breath of summer
   Was the kiss she gave to me.

XXXII

Rain has fallen all the day
    O come among the laden trees.
The leaves lie thick upon the way
    Of memories.

Staying a little by the way
    Of memories shall we depart.
Come, my beloved, where I may
    Speak to your heart.

XXXIII

Now, O now, in this brown land
    Where Love did so sweet music make
We two shall wander, hand in hand,
    Forbearing for old friendship' sake
Nor grieve because our love was gay
Which now is ended in this way.

A rogue in red and yellow dress
    Is knocking, knocking at the tree
And all around our loneliness
    The wind is whistling merrily.
The leaves – they do not sigh at all
When the year takes them in the fall.

Now, O now, we hear no more
    The vilanelle and roundelay!
Yet will we kiss, sweetheart, before
    We take sad leave at close of day.
Grieve not, sweetheart, for anything –
The year, the year is gathering.

XXXIV

Sleep now, O sleep now,
  O you unquiet heart!
A voice crying 'Sleep now'
  Is heard in my heart.

The voice of the winter
  Is heard at the door.
O sleep for the winter
  Is crying 'Sleep no more!'

My kiss will give peace now
  And quiet to your heart –
Sleep on in peace now,
  O you unquiet heart!

XXXV

All day I hear the noise of waters
    Making moan
Sad as the seabird is when going
    Forth alone
He hears the winds cry to the waters'
    Monotone.

The grey winds, the cold winds are blowing
    Where I go.
I hear the noise of many waters
    Far below.
All day, all night, I hear them flowing
    To and fro.

XXXVI

I hear an army charging upon the land
  And the thunder of horses plunging, foam about their knees.
Arrogant, in black armour, behind them stand,
  Disdaining the reins, with fluttering whips, the charioteers.

They cry unto the night their battlename:
  I moan in sleep when I hear afar their whirling laughter.
They cleave the gloom of dreams, a blinding flame,
  Clanging, clanging upon the heart as upon an anvil.

They come shaking in triumph their long green hair:
  They come out of the sea and run shouting by the shore.
My heart, have you no wisdom thus to despair?
  My love, my love, my love, why have you left me alone?

Pomes Penyeach

(*published 1927*)

Tilly

He travels after a winter sun,
Urging the cattle along a cold red road,
Calling to them, a voice they know,
He drives his beasts above Cabra.

The voice tells them home is warm.
They moo and make brute music with their hoofs.
He drives them with a flowering branch before him,
Smoke pluming their foreheads.

Boor, bond of the herd,
Tonight stretch full by the fire!
I bleed by the black stream
For my torn bough!

Dublin, 1904

Watching the Needleboats
at San Sabba

I heard their young hearts crying
Loveward above the glancing oar
And heard the prairie grasses sighing:
No more, return no more!

O hearts, O sighing grasses,
Vainly your loveblown bannerets mourn!
No more will the wild wind that passes
Return, no more return.

Trieste, 1912

A *Flower given to my Daughter*

Frail the white rose and frail are
Her hands that gave
Whose soul is sere and paler
Than time's wan wave.

Rosefrail and fair – yet frailest
A wonder wild
In gentle eyes thou veilest,
My blueveined child.

Trieste, 1913

She weeps over Rahoon

Rain on Rahoon falls softly, softly falling,
Where my dark lover lies.
Sad is his voice that calls me, sadly calling,
At grey moonrise.

Love, hear thou
How soft, how sad his voice is ever calling,
Ever unanswered, and the dark rain falling,
Then as now.

Dark too our hearts, O love, shall lie and cold
As his sad heart has lain
Under the moongrey nettles, the black mould
And muttering rain.

Trieste, 1913

Tutto è Sciolto

A birdless heaven, seadusk, one lone star
Piercing the west,
As thou, fond heart, love's time, so faint, so far,
Rememberest.

The clear young eyes' soft look, the candid brow,
The fragrant hair,
Falling as through the silence falleth now
Dusk of the air.

Why then, remembering those shy
Sweet lures, repine
When the dear love she yielded with a sigh
Was all but thine?

Trieste, 1914

On the Beach at Fontana

Wind whines and whines the shingle,
The crazy pierstakes groan;
A senile sea numbers each single
Slimesilvered stone.

From whining wind and colder
Grey sea I wrap him warm
And touch his trembling fineboned shoulder
And boyish arm.

Around us fear, descending
Darkness of fear above
And in my heart how deep unending
Ache of love!

Trieste, 1914

Simples

O bella bionda,
Sei come l'onda!

Of cool sweet dew and radiance mild
The moon a web of silence weaves
In the still garden where a child
Gathers the simple salad leaves.

A moondew stars her hanging hair
And moonlight kisses her young brow
And, gathering, she sings an air:
Fair as the wave is, fair, art thou!

Be mine, I pray, a waxen ear
To shield me from her childish croon
And mine a shielded heart for her
Who gathers simples of the moon.

Trieste, 1915

Flood

Goldbrown upon the sated flood
The rockvine clusters lift and sway;
Vast wings above the lambent waters brood
Of sullen day.

A waste of waters ruthlessly
Sways and uplifts its weedy mane
Where brooding day stares down upon the sea
In dull disdain.

Uplift and sway, O golden vine,
Your clustered fruits to love's full flood,
Lambent and vast and ruthless as is thine
Incertitude!

Trieste, 1915

Nightpiece

Gaunt in gloom,
The pale stars their torches,
Enshrouded, wave.
Ghostfires from heaven's far verges faint illume,
Arches on soaring arches,
Night's sindark nave.

Seraphim,
The lost hosts awaken
To service till
In moonless gloom each lapses muted, dim,
Raised when she has and shaken
Her thurible.

And long and loud,
To night's nave upsoaring,
A starknell tolls
As the bleak incense surges, cloud on cloud,
Voidward from the adoring
Waste of souls.

Trieste, 1915

Alone

The moon's greygolden meshes make
All night a veil,
The shorelamps in the sleeping lake
Laburnum tendrils trail.

The sly reeds whisper to the night
A name – her name –
And all my soul is a delight,
A swoon of shame.

Zurich, 1916

A Memory of the Players in
a Mirror at Midnight

They mouth love's language. Gnash
The thirteen teeth
Your lean jaws grin with. Lash
Your itch and quailing, nude greed of the flesh.
Love's breath in you is stale, worded or sung,
As sour as cat's breath,
Harsh of tongue.

This grey that stares
Lies not, stark skin and bone.
Leave greasy lips their kissing. None
Will choose her what you see to mouth upon.
Dire hunger holds his hour.
Pluck forth your heart, saltblood, a fruit of tears.
Pluck and devour!

Zurich, 1917

Bahnhofstrasse

The eyes that mock me sign the way
Whereto I pass at eve of day,

Grey way whose violet signals are
The trysting and the twining star.

Ah star of evil! star of pain!
Highhearted youth comes not again

Nor old heart's wisdom yet to know
The signs that mock me as I go.

Zurich, 1918

A Prayer

Again!
Come, give, yield all your strength to me!
From far a low word breathes on the breaking brain
Its cruel calm, submission's misery,
Gentling her awe as to a soul predestined.
Cease, silent love! My doom!

Blind me with your dark nearness, O have mercy,
    beloved enemy of my will!
I dare not withstand the cold touch that I dread.
Draw from me still
My slow life! Bend deeper on me, threatening head,
Proud by my downfall, remembering, pitying
Him who is, him who was!

Again!
Together, folded by the night, they lay on earth. I hear
From far her low word breathe on my breaking brain.
Come! I yield. Bend deeper upon me! I am here.
Subduer, do not leave me! Only joy, only anguish,
Take me, save me, soothe me, O spare me!

Paris, 1924

POEMS OF EARLY YOUTH

Satire on George O'Donnell

(in the style of Goldsmith)

Poor little Georgie, the son of a lackey,
Famous for 'murphies,' spirits, and 'baccy,
Renowned all around for a feathery head
Which had a tendency to become red.
His genius was such that all men used to stare,
His appearance was that of a bull at a fair.
The pride of Kilmainham, the joy of the class,
A moony, a loony, an idiot, an ass.
Drumcondra's production, and by the same rule,
The prince of all pot-boys, a regular fool.
All hail to the beauteous, the lovely, all hail
And hail to his residence in Portland gaol.

(1896–97)

Translation of Horace's 'O fons Bandusiae'

Brighter than glass Bandusian spring
   For mellow wine and flowers meet,
The morrow thee a kid shall bring
   Boding of rivalry and sweet
Love in his swelling forms. In vain
He, wanton offspring, deep shall stain
Thy clear cold streams with crimson rain.

The raging dog star's season thou,
   Still safe from in the heat of day,

When oxen weary of the plough
   Yieldst thankful cool for herds that stray.
Be of the noble founts! I sing
The oak tree o'er thine echoing
Crags, thy waters murmuring.

(1898)

Fragments from Shine and Dark
(perhaps also from the earlier collection Moods *and
other sources)*

[I]

I only ask you to give me your fair hands
Ah, dearest, this one grace, it will be the last
How fast are they fled, halcyon days, how fast
Nor you nor I can arrest time's running sands.
Enough that we have known the pleasure of love
Albeit pleasure, fraught with an heartfelt grief
Though our love season hath been marvellous
Yet we have loved and told our passion – [. . .]
Then fade the uncertain day and come the night

[II]

La scintelle de l'allumette
Qui se cachait entre vos mains
A ensorcelé ma cigarette –
Ah, l'étoile de l'allumette!

Il me plait bien d'obs [. . .]

[III]

Like viol strings
       Through the wane
Of the pale year
Lulleth me here
       With its strain.
My soul is faint
At the bell's plaint,
       Ringing deep;
I think upon

[IV]

Scalding tears shall not avail,
Love shall be to us for aye
       An heart-breaking tale.

Ah, how fast your warm heart beats
Fluttering upon my breast.
Lay aside your deep unrest;
We have eaten all the sweets,
The golden fruit falls from the tree

[V]

Yea, for this love of mine
I have given all I had;
For she was passing fair,
And I was passing mad.

All flesh, it is said,
Shall wither as the grass;

The fuel for the oven
Shall be consumed, alas!

[VI]

We will leave the village behind,
Merrily, you and I,
Tramp it smart and sing to the wind,
With the Rommany Rye.

(*Mullingar*, July, 1900)
(*A gypsy's song, in the third act of*
A Brilliant Career)

[VII]

Gladly above,
The lover listens
In deepest love.

(29 June 1900)

[VIII]

After the tribulation of dark strife,
And all the ills of the earth, crying for my release.

Why is the truth so hidden and the land of dreams so far,
That the feet of the climber fail on the upward way;
Although in the purple distance burns a red-gold star,
There are briers on the mountain and the weary feet have bled,
        The homesteads and the fireglow bid him stay:
And the burden of his body is like a burden of lead.

[IX]

Told sublimely in the language
Which the shining angels knew.
Tearless choirs of joyful servants,
Sounding cymbals, brazen shawms,
Distant hymns of myriad planets,
Heavenly maze of full-voiced psalms.
Only, when the heart is peaceful,
When the soul is moved to love,
May we hearken to those voices
Starry singing from above.

[X]

Love that I can give you, lady
Ah, that they haven't, lady
        Lady witchin', lady mine.

O, you say that I torment you
        With my verses, lady mine
Faith! the best I had I sent you,
        Don't be laughin', lady mine.
I am foolish to be hopin'
That you left your window open,

[XI]

. . . Wind thine arms round me, woman of sorcery,
While the lascivious music murmurs afar:
I will close mine eyes, and dream as I dance with thee,
And pass away from the world where my sorrows are.

Faster and faster! strike the harps in the hall!
Woman, I fear that this dance is the dance of death!
Faster! – ah, I am faint . . . and, ah, I fall.
The distant music mournfully murmureth.

[XII]

Where none murmureth,
Let all grieving cease
And fade as a breath,
And come the final peace
Which men call death.

Joy and sorrow
Pass away and be fled,
Welcome the morrow

[XIII]

Lord, thou knowest my misery,
See the gifts which I have brought,
Sunshine on a dying face
Stricken flowers, seldom sought.

See the pale moon, the sunless dawn
Of my fainting feebleness;
But only shed thy dew on me
And I shall teem in fruitfulness.

[XIV]

[?The]reg[?imental] rain
Thunders and sweeps along
The roadway. The rain is strong
And the tide of it lays all pain.

I am in no idle passion
That my threadbare coat is torn,
    And quaint of fashion.
My humour is devil-may-care,
As the labourer's song upborne
    On the quiet air.

[XV]

Though there is no resurrection from the past,
It matters not, for one pure thing I see,
On which no stain, no shadow has been cast.

I see the image of my love unclouded,
Like a white maiden in some hidden place,
In a bright cloak, woven of my hopes, enshrouded,
And looking at me with a smiling face.

I do not care for an honourable mention,

[XVI]

And I have sat amid the turbulent crowd,
And have assisted at their boisterous play;
I have unbent myself and shouted loud,
And been as blatant and as coarse as they.

I have consorted with vulgarity
And am indelibly marked with its fell kiss,
Meanly I lived upon casual charity
Eagerly drinking of the dregs of bliss.

[XVII]

[? Beautiful, ? undutiful.]
– Gorse-flower makes but sorry dining,
Mulberries make no winecups full,
Grass-threads lacing and entwining
Weave no linen by the waters –
Said the mother to her daughters.
The sisters viewed themselves reclining,
Heeding not, undutiful.
The first girl wished for spinning,
And she asked a spindle of gold;
The second sister wished to weave,

[XVIII]

That I am feeble, that my feet
Are weak as young twigs in the wind;

That this poor heart, which was of old
So reckless, passionate and proud,
Shivers at trifles and wanes cold
Whene'er thy fair face shows a cloud.

A golden bird in azure skies,
Late radiant with sunbright wings,
Is fallen down to earth, and sighs

[XIX]

The grieving soul. But no grief is thine
Who driftest the creeks and shallows among,
Shaking thy hair of the clinging brine.
Why is thy garment closer drawn?
Thine eyes are sad, my sorrowful one,
Thy tresses are strewn with the woe of dawn,
The pearly dawn weeping the sun.
Hast thou no word – to raise – to ease
Our souls? Well, go, for the faint far cry
Of the seabirds calls thee over the seas.

[XX]

Let us fling to the winds all moping and madness.
Play us a jig in the spirit of gladness
On the creaky, old squeaky strings of the fiddle.

The why of the world is an answerless riddle
Puzzlesome, tiresome, hard to unriddle
To the seventeen devils with sapient sadness:

       Tra la, tra la.

[XXI]

 Hands that soothe my burning eyes
 In the silence of moonrise
 At the midmost hour of night,
     Trouble me not.

 Fingers soft as rain alight,
 Like flowers borne upon the night
 From the pure deeps of sapphire skies

[XXII]

Now a whisper . . . now a gale
List, ah list, how drear it calls!

There is in it that appalls
As it wanders round the walls,
Like a forlorn woman, pale.
                    List the wind!

[XXIII]

O, queen, do on thy cloak
Of scarlet, passion hue,
And lift, attending folk,
A mournful ululù,
For flame-spun is the cloak.

* * * * * * *

Fling out thy voice, O lyre,
Forth of thy seven strings.

[XXIV]

'Requiem eternam dona ei, Domine';
Silently, sorrowfully I bent down my head,
For I had hated him – a poor creature of clay:
And all my envious, bitter, cruel thoughts that came
Out of the past and stood by the bier whereon he lay
Pointed their long, lean fingers through the
        gloom . . . O Name,
Ineffable, proud Name to whom the cries ascend
From lost, angelical orders, seraph flame to flame,
For this end have I hated him – for this poor end?

[XXV]

Of thy dark life, without a love, without a friend,
　　Here is, indeed, an end.

There are no lips to kiss this foul remains of thee,
　　O, dead Unchastity!
The curse of loneliness broods silent on thee still,
　　Doing its utmost will,
And men shall cast thee justly to thy narrow tomb,
　　A sad and bitter doom.

[XXVI]

I intone the high anthem,
Partaking in their festival.
Swing out, swing in, the night is dark,
Magical hair, alive with glee,
Winnowing spark after spark,
Star after star, rapturously.
Toss and toss, amazing arms;
Witches, weave upon the floor
Your subtle-woven web of charms

[XXVII]

Some are comely and some are sour,
Some are dark as wintry mould,
Some are fair as a golden shower.
To music liquid as a stream
They move with dazzling symmetry;

Their flashing limbs blend in a gleam
Of luminous-swift harmony
They wear gold crescents on their heads,
Hornèd and brilliant as the moon;

[XXVIII]

Flower to flower knits
Of willing lips and leaves:
Thy springtide of bliss
Maketh the breezes sing,
And blossoms yield their kiss
Unto amorous thieves.

But the arrow that flies
Must fall spent at last;

[XXIX]

In the soft nightfall
Hear thy lover call,
Hearken the guitar!
Lady, lady fair
Snatch a cloak in haste,
Let thy lover taste
The sweetness of thy hair.

(*This lyric and the following one are from
an unfinished play, 'Dream Stuff*')

[XXX]

[? Of] a [? mud- ? made] flower [? chain]
Discarded, broken in two.

Sing to mine ear, O rain,
Thine ultimate melody;
That the dearest loss is gain
In a holier treasury;

That a passionate cry in the night
For a woman, hidden and pale,

[XXXI]

And orient banners they outfling
Before the ripple-bearded king.

(1900?)

Translation of Verlaine's 'Chanson d'automne'

A voice that sings
Like viol strings
Through the wane
Of the pale year
Lulleth me here
With its strain.

My soul is faint
At the bell's plaint
  Ringing deep;
I think upon
A day bygone
  And I weep.

Away! Away!
I must obey
  This drear wind,
Like a dead leaf
In aimless grief
  Drifting blind.

(1900–1902)

'Alas, how sad the lover's lot'

Alas, how sad the lover's lot
Whose love to him can do offence!
Alas, that beauty should have not
Stability nor reverence!

My heart is taken in a net
Misled ill-used made captive too
By promises and shows – but yet
Happy with vows that are untrue.

Poor heart, alas, that such offence
Love all too reverent may not chide,
That winds that have no reverence
Abide where love doth still abide!

(1902)

'She is at peace where she is sleeping,'

She is at peace where she is sleeping,
Her pale hands folded on her shroud,
And I am wandering in the world
Alone and sorrowful and proud.
She heard, as standing on the shore,
A bell above the waters toll,
She heard the call of 'Come away'
Which is the calling of the soul.

They covered her with linen white
And laid her on a snow-white bed
And loosened out her glorious hair
And set white candles at her head.
I remember her moving of old
Amid grave days as one apart
O, little joy and great sorrow
Is all the music of my heart.

The fiddle has a mournful sound
That's playing in the street below –
I would I lay with her I love:
And who is there to say me no?
I would I lay in the dark earth
For sorrow bids me now depart
And the remembering of love
Makes a sad music in my heart.

(1902)

'I said: I will go down to where'

I said: I will go down to where
She waits amid the silences,
And look upon her face and smile;
And she will cover me with her hair
I shall forget what sorrow is
And rest with her a little while

I put aside sorrow and care
For these may not be where she is
For these are enemies. I came
And sought the glimmer of her hair
Amid the desolate silences
And cried upon the gloom her name.

(1902?)

'Though we are leaving youth behind'

Though we are leaving youth behind
And ways of pleasure would reprove
Thou hast engraven in the mind
Thy name, O many-weathered love

And should the grace, the presence – all
That was thy magic – cease to be.
Here in the bosom ever shall
Endure thy dear charactery.

(1902?)

'Come out to where the youth is met'

Come out to where the youth is met
Under the moon, beside the sea,
And leave your weapon and your net,
Your loom and your embroidery.

Bring back the pleasantness of days
And crystal moonlight on the shore.
Your feet have woven many a maze
In old times on the ivory floor.

The weapons and the looms are mute
And feet are hurrying by the sea.
I hear the viol and the flute,
The sackbut and the psaltery.

(1903–4?)

Latin Poem of Questionable Authorship

[*1*]

Seduxit miles virginem, receptus in hibernis,
Praecipitem quam[?] longius[?] se transtulit Avernis –
Impransius ille restitit – sed acrius potabat
Et conscius facinoris per vina clamitabat:
 'Mīsēram Baliam, infortunatam Baliam
 Proditem et traditam miserrimam Baliam.'

73

(2)

Ardente demum sanguine dum repsit ad cubile,
'O belle próditorcule, patrasti factum vile'
Nocturnae candent lampades – et ecce, imago dira,
Ante ora stabat militis, dixit, fumans ira –
  'Adspice Baliam, unfortunatam Baliam
  Proditam et traditam miserrimam Baliam.'

(3)

'Abito – cur me corporis pallore examinasti!'
'Perfidius munusculum, cui vis, administrasti
Pererro ripas Stygias – recusat justa Pontifex –
Suicidam quaestor nuncupat – sed tua culpa, carnifex!'
  'Tua culpa, carnifex, qui violasti Baliam,
  Proditam et traditam miserrimam Baliam.'

(4)

'Sunt mi bis deni solidi – quam nitidi, quam pulchri
Hos accipe et honores comparabere sepulcri –'
Tum lemuris non facis, ut antea, iracundos
Argentum ridens numerat – it ipsa vox jucundius[?]
  'Vale, vale corculum, lusisti fatu Baliam
  Vale, vale corculum, Nunc lude, si vis, aliam.'

(1900–1904?)

UNCOLLECTED OCCASIONAL POEMS

Satire on John Eglinton:
A Collaboration with Oliver St John Gogarty
(in the style of Burns)

John Eglinton, my Jo, John,
When last had you a   ?
I fear ye canna go, John,
Although ye are na spent.
O   begin to fel', John,
Ye canna mak' it flow,
And even if it swell, John
The lassies wadna know.

John Eglinton, my Jo, John,
I dinna like to say
Of course ye must have sinned, John
When ye were young and gay
It canna be remorse, John,
That keeps ye fra a ride
Your virtue is a farce, John,
Ye cardna if ye tried

(1903–4)

Satire on the Brothers Fay

O, there are two brothers, the Fays,
Who are excellent players of plays,
And, needless to mention, all
Most unconventional,
Filling the world with amaze.

But I angered these brothers, the Fays,
Whose ways are conventional ways,
   For I lay in my urine
    While ladies so pure in
White petticoats ravished my gaze.

(June 1904)

'The flower I gave rejected lies.'

The flower I gave rejected lies.
Sad is my lot for all to see.
Humiliation burns my eyes.
The Grace of God abandons me.

As Alberic sweet love forswore
The power of cursed gold to wield
So you, who lusts for metal ore,
Forswear me for a copperfield.

Rejoice not yet in false bravado
The pimpernel you flung away
Shall torchlike burn your El Dorado.
Vengeance is mine. I will repay.

(1902–4?)

On Rudolf Goldschmidt

(to the tune of the 'Amorous Goldfish')

A Goldschmidt swam in a Kriegsverein
As wise little Goldschmidts do,
And he loved every scion of the Habsburg line,
Each Archduke proud, the whole jimbang crowd,
And he felt that they loved him, too.
Herr Rosenbaum and Rosenfeld
And every other Feld except Schlachtfeld
All worked like niggers, totting rows of crazy figures,
To save Kaiser Karl and Goldschmidt, too.

Chorus:
For he said it is bet – bet – better
To stick stamps on some God-damned letter
Than be shot in a trench
Amid shells and stench,
Jesus Gott, Donnerwet – wet – wetter.

(November 1917?)

Dooleysprudence

(Air: 'Mr Dooley')

Who is the man when all the gallant nations run to war
Goes home to have his dinner by the very first cablecar
And as he eats his cantaloups contorts himself in mirth
To read the blatant bulletins of the rulers of the earth?

79

It's Mr Dooley,
Mr Dooley,
The coolest chap our country ever knew
'They are out to collar
The dime and dollar'
Says Mr Dooley-ooley-ooley-oo.

Who is the funny fellow who declines to go to church
Since pope and priest and parson left the poor man in the lurch
And taught their flocks the only way to save all human souls
Was piercing human bodies through with dumdum
    bulletholes?

It's Mr Dooley,
Mr Dooley,
The mildest man our country ever knew
'Who will release us
From Jingo Jesus?'
Prays Mr Dooley-ooley-ooley-oo.

Who is the meek philosopher who doesn't care a damn
About the yellow peril or problem of Siam
And disbelieves that British Tar is water from life's fount
And will not gulp the gospel of the German on the Mount?

It's Mr Dooley,
Mr Dooley,
The broadest brain our country ever knew
'The curse of Moses
On both your houses'
Cries Mr Dooley-ooley-ooley-oo.

Who is the cheerful imbecile who lights his long chibouk
With pages of the pandect, penal code and Doomsday Book
And wonders why bald justices are bound by law to wear
A toga and a wig made out of someone else's hair?

It's Mr Dooley,
Mr Dooley,
The finest fool our country ever knew
'They took that toilette
From Pontius Pilate'
Thinks Mr Dooley-ooley-ooley-oo.

Who is the man who says he'll go the whole and perfect hog
Before he pays an income tax or licence for a dog
And when he licks a postagestamp regards with smiling scorn
The face of king or emperor or snout of unicorn?
It's Mr Dooley,
Mr Dooley,
The wildest wag our country ever knew
'O my poor tummy
His backside gummy!'
Moans Mr Dooley-ooley-ooley-oo.

Who is the tranquil gentleman who won't salute the State
Or serve Nabuchodonosor or proletariat
But thinks that every son of man has quite enough to do
To paddle down the stream of life his personal canoe?
It's Mr Dooley,
Mr Dooley,
The wisest lad our country ever knew
'Poor Europe ambles
Like sheep to shambles!'
Sighs Mr Dooley-ooley-ooley-oo.

Who is the sunny sceptic who fights shy of Noah's arks
When they are made in Germany by Engels and by Marx
But when the social deluge comes and rain begins to pour
Takes off his coat and trousers and prepares to swim ashore?

It's Mr Dooley,
Mr Dooley,
The bravest boy our country ever knew
With arms akimbo
'I'll find that rainbow!'
Shouts Mr Dooley-ooley-ooley-oo.

(1916–18)

Lament for the Yeomen
(*from the German of Felix Beran*)

And now is come the war, the war:
And now is come the war, the war:
And now is come the war, the war.
War! War!

For soldiers are they gone now:
For soldiers all.
Soldiers and soldiers!
All! All!

Soldiers must die, must die.
Soldiers all must die.
Soldiers and soldiers and soldiers
Must die.

What man is there to kiss now,
To kiss, to kiss,
O white soft body, this
Thy soft sweet whiteness?

(1918)

To Budgen, Raughty Tinker

Oh! Budgen, boozer, bard, and canvas dauber
If to thine eyes these lines should sometime come
Bethink thee that the fleshpots of old Egypt
Nothing avail if beauty's heart would beat.
Wherefore forswear butter besmeared Ravioli
Which do the mainsprings of thy talent clog
On Roggenbrot, in Joghurt, and cold water,
Paint and be damned. We wait. Begin, and end.

James Joyce
Ethel Turner
Nora Joyce
W. H. Kerridge

(1918)

New Tipperary;
or, The C. G. is Not Literary

Up to rheumy Zurich came an Irishman one day
As the town was rather dull he thought he'd give a play
So that German propagandists might be rightly riled
But the bully British philistine once more made Oscar wild.

For the C.G. is not literairy
And his handymen are rogues
Our C.G.'s about as literary
As an Irish kish of brogues.

We paid all expenses,
As the good Swiss public knows,
But we'll be damn well damned before we pay for
Private Carr's swank hose.

When the play was over Carr with rage began to dance,
Howling 'I wants twenty quid for them there dandy pants:
Fork us out the tin or comrade Bennett here and me,
We're going to wring your bloddy necks. We're out for
    liberty.'

    Chorus (as above)

They found a Norse solicitor to prove that white was black,
That one can boss in Switzerland beneath the Union Jack,
They marched to the Gerichtshof but came down like Jack
    and Jill,
While the pants came tumbling after . . . and the judge is
    laughing still.

    No, the C.G. is not literairy
    And his handymen are rogues,
    Our C.G.'s about as literairy
    As an Irish kish of brogues.
    Goodbye, brother Bennett!
    Goodbye, chummy Carr!
    If you put a beggar upon horseback,
    Why 'e dunno where 'e are!

(October 1918)

The Right Man in the Wrong Place
(*Air:* 'My heart's in my highlands')

The pig's in the barley,
The fat's in the fire:
Old Europe can hardly
Find twopence to buy her.
Jack Spratt's in his office,
Puffed, powdered and curled:
Rumbold's in Warsaw –
All's right with the world.

(August 1920)

The Right Heart in the Wrong Place

Of spinach and gammon
Bull's full to his crupper:
White lice and black famine
Are the mayor of Cork's supper.
But the pride of old Ireland
Must be damnably humbled
If a Joyce is found cleaning
The boots of a Rumbold.

(August 1920)

Quatrain for Richard Wallace

And I shall have no peace there for Joyce comes more and
     more,
Dropping from a tram or a taxi to where the white wine swills.
Then midnight's all a shimmy and Bloom a bloody bore
And morning full — — — of bills! bills! bills!

(c. 1921)

To Sylvia Beach
(*following the publication of* Ulysses)

Who is Sylvia, what is she
That all our scribes commend her?
Yankee, young and brave is she
The west this grace did lend her,
That all books might published be.

Is she rich as she is brave
For wealth oft daring misses?
Throngs about her rant and rave
To subscribe for *Ulysses*
But, having signed, they ponder grave.

Then to Sylvia let us sing
Her daring lies in selling.

She can sell each mortal thing
That's boring beyond telling.
To her let us buyers bring.

J. J.
after
W. S.

(February 1922)

Fréderic's Duck
(Air: 'Dougherty's Duck')

Cantus Plenus
Now Wallace he heard that Fréderic's was the dearest place to
    dine
So he took the Joyces there to have combustible duck and wine.
The toothpicks cost a pound apiece, the salt a guinea a grain:
When Wallace saw the bill he felt an epigastric pain.

Chorus Coenatorum
Fréderic, Fréderic, Fréderic, O! My word, you pile it on!
A tour of the world is cheaper than a meal in the *Tour
    d'Argent.*
I'd rather eat hot dog in the street or dine for half a buck
Than sweat in full dress in your poultry-press and be bled like
    Fréderic's duck

(June 1923)

On a Fountain Pen Given Him by Richard Wallace

I never thought a fountain pen
Exemption gave as well as solace.
If critics blame my style again
I'll say 'twas given me by Wallace.

                    Shem the Penman
(February 1924)

On Kellog's Bran Poultice

Bran! Bran! The baker's ban!
Gobble it quick and die if you can.
Forgive us this day our deadly bread
But give us old Kellog's bran poultice instead.

(April 1925)

Fragment on Miss Moschos

Little Miss Moschos
Soft as a mouse goes

(1920s?)

Schevingen, 1927

Sáy, ain't thís succéss fool aúthor
Jést a dándy páradóx,
With that sílvier béach behínd him,
Hówling: Hélp! I'm ón the rócks!

(July 1927)

Hue's Hue? or Dalton's Dilemma

What colour's Jew Joyce when he's rude and grim both,
Varied virid from groening and rufous with rage
And if this allrotter's allred as a roth
Can he still blush unirish yet green as a gage?

(c. 1928)

Epigram on the Ladyfriends of St James

As I was going to Joyce Saint James'
I met with seven extravagant dames;
Every dame had a bee in her bonnet,
With bats from the belfry roosting upon it.
And Ah, I said, poor Joyce Saint James,
What can he do with these terrible dames?
Poor Saint James Joyce.

(January 1931)

Father O'Ford
(*Air: 'Father O'Flynn'*)

Oh Father O'Ford you've a masterful way with you.
Maid, wife and widow are wild to make hay with you.
Blonde and brunette turn about, run away with you.
You've such a way with you, Father O'Ford.

That instant they see the sun shine from your eye,
Their hearts flitterflutter, they sink and they sigh,
We kiss ground before thee, we madly adore thee
And crave and implore thee to take us Oh Lord.

(February 1931)

Rhyme to Advertise Extract from Work in Progress

Humptydump Dublin squeaks through his norse,
Humptydump Dublin hath a horriple vorse,
    And, with all his Kinks english
    Plus his irishmanx brogues,
Humptydump Dublin's grandada of all rogues.

(May 1931?)

To Mrs Herbert Gorman Who Complained That Her Visitors Kept Late Hours

Go ca'canny with the cognac
And of the Wine fight shy,
Keep your eye upon the hourglass
That leaves the beaker dry.

Guestfriendliness to callers
Is your surest thief of time,
They're so much at holmes when with you
They don't dream of gugging heim.

(March 1931)

Pennipomes Twoguineaseach

Sing a song of shillings
A guinea cannot buy,
Thirteen tiny pomikins
Bobbing in a pie.

The printer's pie was published
And the pomes began to sing
And wasn't Herbert Hughesius
As happy as a king!

(April 1932)

Pour la rîme seulement

A Pierre de Lanux
dit Valery Larbaud,
Prête moi un dux
qui peut conduire l'assault.
Mes pioupions sont fondus
et meurent de malaise.
Sois ton petit tondu
pour la gloire d'Arès.

Lanux de la Pierre
à Beaulard fit réplique,
Fous-moi la guerre
avec tes soldiqués.
Car pour l'Italie
presto fais tes malles,
tire ta bonne partie
avec quelques balles.

A ces mots Leryval
file en obobus,
et comme le vieux Hannibal
perce le blocus,
à peine atterre sa mine
qu'on crie à la foire,
un sous la Mursoline
pour l'arrats de gloire.

(May 1932)

A Portrait of the Artist as an Ancient Mariner

(1)   I met with a ancient scribelleer
       As I scoured the pirates' sea
       His sailes were alullt at nought coma null
       Not raise the wind could he.

(2)   The bann of Bull, the sign of Sam
       Burned crimson on his brow.
       And I rocked at the rig of his bricabrac brig
       With K.O. 11 on his prow

(3)   Shakefears & Coy danced poor old joy
       And some of their steps were corkers
       As they shook the last shekels like phantom freckels
       His pearls that had poisom porkers

(4)   The gnome Norbert read rich bills of fare
       The ghosts of his deep debauches
       But there was no bibber to slip that scribber
       The price of a box of matches

(5)   For all cried, Schuft! He has lost the Luft
       That made his U.boat go
       And what a weird leer wore that scribelleer
       As his wan eye winked with woe.

(6)   He dreamed of the goldest sands uprolled
       By the silviest Beach of Beaches
       And to watch it dwindle gave him Kugelkopfschwindel
       Till his eyeboules bust their stitches

(7)   His hold shipped seas with a drunkard's ease
      And its deadweight grew and grew
      While the witless wag still waived his flag
      Jemmyrend's white and partir's blue.

(8)   His tongue stuck out with a dragon's drouth
      For a sluice of schweppes and brandy
      And but for the glows on his roseate nose
      You'd have staked your goat he was Ghandi.

(9)   For the Yanks and Japs had made off with his traps!
      So that stripped to the stern he clung
      While, increase of a cross, an Albatross
      Abaft his nape was hung.

(October 1932)

Epilogue to Ibsen's Ghosts

Dear quick, whose conscience buried deep
The grim old grouser has been salving,
Permit one spectre more to peep.
I am the ghost of Captain Alving.

Silenced and smothered by my past
Like the lewd knight in dirty linen
I struggle forth to swell the cast
And air a long suppressed opinion.

For muddling weddings into wakes
No fool could vie with Parson Manders.

I, though a dab at ducks and drakes,
Let gooseys serve or sauce their ganders.

My spouse bore me a blighted boy,
Our slavey pupped a bouncing bitch.
Paternity, thy name is joy
When the wise child knows which is which.

Both swear I am that selfsame man
By whom their infants were begotten.
Explain, fate, if you care and can
Why one is sound and one is rotten.

Olaf may plod his stony path
And live as chastely as Susanna
Yet pick up in some Turkish bath
His *quantum sat* of *Pox Romana*.

While Haakon hikes up primrose way,
Spreeing and gleeing as he goes,
To smirk upon his latter day
Without a pimple on his nose.

I gave it up I am afraid
But if I loafed and found it fun
Remember how a coyclad maid
Knows how to take it out of one.

The more I dither on and drink
My midnight bowl of spirit punch
The firmlier I feel and think
Friend Manders came too oft to lunch.

Since scuttling ship Vikings like me
Reck not to whom the blame is laid,
Y.M.C.A., V.D., T.B.
Or Harbormaster of Port Said.

Blame all and none and take to task
The harlot's lure, the swain's desire.
Heal by all means but hardly ask
Did this man sin or did his sire.

The shack's ablaze. That canting scamp,
The carpenter, has dished the parson.
Now had they kept their powder damp
Like me there would have been no arson.

Nay more, were I not all I was,
Weak, wanton, waster out and out,
There would have been no world's applause
And damn all to write home about.

(April 1934)

Translation from Gottfried Keller's
Lebendig Begraben *Suite*

Now have I fed and eaten up the rose
Which then she laid within my stiffcold hand.
That I should ever feed upon a rose
I never had believed in liveman's land.

Only I wonder was it white or red
The flower that in this dark my food has been.
Give us, and if Thou give, thy daily bread,
Deliver us from evil, Lord. Amen.

(after April 1934)

A Come-all-ye, by a Thanksgiving Turkey

Come all you lairds and lassies and listen to my lay!
I'll tell you of my adventures upon last Thanksgiving Day
I was picked by Madame Jolas to adorn her barbecue
So the chickenchoker patched me till I looked as good as new.

I drove out, all tarred and feathered, from the Grand Palais
    Potin
But I met with foul disaster in the Place Saint Augustin.
My charioteer collided – with the shock I did explode
And the force of my emotions shot my liver on the road.

Up steps a dapper sergeant with his pencil and his book.
Our names and our convictions down in Lieber's code he took.
Then I hailed another driver and resumed my swanee way.
They couldn't find my liver but I hadn't time to stay.

When we reached the gates of Paris cries the boss at the
    Octroi:
Holy Poule, what's this I'm seeing? Can it be Grandmother
    Loye?
When Caesar got the bird she was the dindy of the flock
But she must have boxed a round or two with some old turkey
    cock.

I ruffled up my plumage and proclaimed with eagle's pride:
You jackdaw, these are truffles and not blues on my backside.
Mind, said he, that one's a chestnut. There's my bill and here's
    my thanks
And now please search through your stuffing and fork out that
    fifty francs.

At last I reached the banquet-hall – and what a sight to see!
I felt myself transported back among the Osmanli.
I poured myself a bubbly flask and raised the golden horn
With three cheers for good old Turkey and the roost where I
    was born.

I shook claws with all the hommes and bowed to blonde and
    brune
The mistress made a signal and the mujik called the tune.
Madamina read a message from the Big Noise of her State
After which we crowed in unison: That Turco's talking
    straight!

We settled down to feed and, if you want to know my mind,
I thought that I could gobble but they left me picked behind.
They crammed their chops till cockshout when like ostriches
    they ran
To hunt my missing liver round the Place Saint Augustin.

Envoi
Still I'll lift my glass to Gallia and augur that we may
Untroubled in her dovecote dwell till next Thanksgiving Day
So let every Gallic gander pass the sauceboat to his goose –
And let's all play happy homing though our liver's on the loose.

(November 1937)

LIMERICKS

John Quinn

There's a donor of lavish largesse
Who once bought a play in MS.
    He found out what it all meant
    By the final instalment
But poor Scriptor was left in a mess.

(September 1917)

Claude Sykes

There is a clean climber called Sykes
Who goes scrambling through ditches and dykes.
    To skate on his scalp
    Down the side of an alp
Is the kind of diversion he likes.

(September 1917)

Solomon
(*on Simeone Levi*)

There's a hairyfaced Moslem named Simon
Whose tones are not those of a shy man

When with cast iron lungs
He howls twentyfive tongues –
But he's not at all easy to rhyme on.

(September 1917)

D. L. G.
(on David Lloyd George)

There's a George of the Georges named David
With whose words we are now night and day fed.
    He cries: I'll give small rations
    To all the small nations.
Bully God made this world – but I'll save it.

(November 1917)

P. J. T.
(on Patrick Tuohy)

There's a funny facepainter dubbed Tuohy
Whose bleaklook is rosybud bluey
    For when he feels strong
    He feels *your* daub's all wrong
But when he feels weak he feels wooey.

(1925–7)

COLLECTED OCCASIONAL POEMS

The Holy Office

Myself unto myself will give
This name Katharsis-Purgative.
I, who dishevelled ways forsook
To hold the poets' grammar-book,
Bringing to tavern and to brothel
The mind of witty Aristotle,
Lest bards in the attempt should err
Must here be my interpreter:
Wherefore receive now from my lip
Peripatetic scholarship.
To enter heaven, travel hell,
Be piteous or terrible
One positively needs the ease,
Of plenary indulgences.
For every true-born mysticist
A Dante is, unprejudiced,
Who safe at ingle-nook, by proxy,
Hazards extremes of heterodoxy,
Like him who finds a joy at table
Pondering the uncomfortable.
Ruling one's life by common sense
How can one fail to be intense?
But I must not accounted be
One of that mumming company –
With him who hies him to appease
His giddy dames' frivolities
While they console him when he whinges
With gold-embroidered Celtic fringes –

Or him who sober all the day
Mixes a naggin in his play –
Or him who conduct 'seems to own',
His preference for a man of 'tone' –
Or him who plays the rugged patch
To millionaires in Hazelhatch
But weeping after holy fast
Confesses all his pagan past –
Or him who will his hat unfix
Neither to malt nor crucifix
But show to all that poor-dressed be
His high Castilian courtesy –
Or him who loves his Master dear –
Or him who drinks his pint in fear –
Or him who once when snug abed
Saw Jesus Christ without his head
And tried so hard to win for us
The long-lost works of Eschylus.
But all these men of whom I speak
Make me the sewer of their clique.
That they may dream their dreamy dreams
I carry off their filthy streams
For I can do those things for them
Through which I lost my diadem,
Those things for which Grandmother Church
Left me severely in the lurch.
Thus I relieve their timid arses,
Perform my office of Katharsis.
My scarlet leaves them white as wool
Through me they purge a bellyful.
To sister mummers one and all
I act as vicar-general

And for each maiden, shy and nervous,
I do a similar kind service.
For I detect without surprise
That shadowy beauty in her eyes,
The 'dare not' of sweet maidenhood
That answers my corruptive 'would'.
Whenever publicly we meet
She never seems to think of it;
At night when close in bed she lies
And feels my hand between her thighs
My little love in light attire
Knows the soft flame that is desire.
But Mammon places under ban
The uses of Leviathan
And that high spirit ever wars
On Mammon's countless servitors
Nor can they ever be exempt
From his taxation of contempt.
So distantly I turn to view
The shamblings of that motley crew,
Those souls that hate the strength that mine has
Steeled in the school of old Aquinas.
Where they have crouched and crawled and prayed
I stand the self-doomed, unafraid,
Unfellowed, friendless and alone,
Indifferent as the herring-bone,
Firm as the mountain-ridges where
I flash my antlers on the air.
Let them continue as is meet
To adequate the balance-sheet.
Though they may labour to the grave
My spirit shall they never have

Nor make my soul with theirs at one
Till the Mahamanvantara be done:
And though they spurn me from their door
My soul shall spurn them evermore.

(August 1904)

Gas from a Burner

Ladies and gents, you are here assembled
To hear why earth and heaven trembled
Because of the black and sinister arts
Of an Irish writer in foreign parts.
He sent me a book ten years ago
I read it a hundred times or so,
Backwards and forwards, down and up,
Through both the ends of a telescope.
I printed it all to the very last word
But by the mercy of the Lord
The darkness of my mind was rent
And I saw the writer's foul intent.
But I owe a duty to Ireland:
I hold her honour in my hand,
This lovely land that always sent
Her writers and artists to banishment
And in a spirit of Irish fun
Betrayed her own leaders, one by one.
'Twas Irish humour, wet and dry,
Flung quicklime into Parnell's eye;
'Tis Irish brains that save from doom
The leaky barge of the Bishop of Rome
For everyone knows the Pope can't belch
Without the consent of Billy Walsh.
O Ireland my first and only love
Where Christ and Caesar are hand in glove!
O lovely land where the shamrock grows!
(Allow me, ladies, to blow my nose)
To show you for strictures I don't care a button
I printed the poems of Mountainy Mutton

And a play he wrote (you've read it, I'm sure)
Where they talk of 'bastard' 'bugger' and 'whore'
And a play on the Word and Holy Paul
And some woman's legs that I can't recall
Written by Moore, a genuine gent
That lives on his property's ten per cent:
I printed mystical books in dozens:
I printed the table book of Cousins
Though (asking your pardon) as for the verse
'Twould give you a heartburn on your arse:
I printed folklore from North and South
By Gregory of the Golden Mouth:
I printed poets, sad, silly and solemn:
I printed Patrick What-do-you-Colm:
I printed the great John Milicent Synge
Who soars above on an angel's wing
In the playboy shift that he pinched as swag
From Maunsel's manager's travelling-bag.
But I draw the line at that bloody fellow,
That was over here dressed in Austrian yellow,
Spouting Italian by the hour
To O'Leary Curtis and John Wyse Power
And writing of Dublin, dirty and dear,
In a manner no blackamoor printer could bear.
Shite and onions! Do you think I'll print
The name of the Wellington Monument,
Sydney Parade and the Sandymount tram,
Downes's cakeshop and Williams's jam?
I'm damned if I do – I'm damned to blazes!
Talk about *Irish Names of Places*!
It's a wonder to me, upon my soul,
He forgot to mention Curly's Hole.

No, ladies, my press shall have no share in
So gross a libel on Stepmother Erin.
I pity the poor – that's why I took
A red-headed Scotchman to keep my book.
Poor sister Scotland! Her doom is fell;
She cannot find any more Stuarts to sell.
My conscience is fine as Chinese silk:
My heart is as soft as buttermilk.
Colm can tell you I made a rebate
Of one hundred pounds on the estimate
I gave him for his Irish Review.
I love my country – by herrings I do!
I wish you could see what tears I weep
When I think of the emigrant train and ship.
That's why I publish far and wide
My quite illegible railway guide.
In the porch of my printing institute
The poor and deserving prostitute
Plays every night at catch-as-catch-can
With her tight-breeched British artilleryman
And the foreigner learns the gift of the gab
From the drunken draggletail Dublin drab.
Who was it said: Resist not evil?
I'll burn that book, so help me devil.
I'll sing a psalm as I watch it burn
And the ashes I'll keep in a one-handled urn.
I'll penance do with farts and groans
Kneeling upon my marrowbones.
This very next lent I will unbare
My penitent buttocks to the air
And sobbing beside my printing press
My awful sin I will confess.

My Irish foreman from Bannockburn
Shall dip his right hand in the urn
And sign crisscross with reverent thumb
Memento homo upon my bum.

Flushing, September 1912

Ecce Puer

Of the dark past
A child is born;
With joy and grief
My heart is torn.

Calm in his cradle
The living lies.
May love and mercy
Unclose his eyes!

Young life is breathed
On the glass;
The world that was not
Comes to pass.

A child is sleeping:
An old man gone.
O, father forsaken,
Forgive your son!

(February 1932)

EXILES

(a play in three acts)

RICHARD ROWAN, a writer,
BERTHA,
ARCHIE, their son, aged eight years,
ROBERT HAND, journalist,
BEATRICE JUSTICE, his cousin, music-teacher,
BRIGID, an old servant of the Rowan family,
A FISHWOMAN

At Merrion and Ranelagh, suburbs of Dublin
Summer of the year 1912

FIRST ACT

[*The drawingroom in Richard Rowan's house at Merrion, a suburb of Dublin. On the right, forward, a fireplace before which stands a low screen. Over the mantelpiece a giltframed glass. Farther back in the right wall, folding doors leading to the parlour and kitchen. In the wall at the back to the right a small door leading to a study. Left of this a sideboard. On the wall above the sideboard a framed crayon drawing of a young man. More to the left double doors with glass panels leading out to the garden. In the wall at the left a window looking out on the road. Forward in the same wall a door leading to the hall and the upper part of the house. Between the window and door a lady's davenport stands against the wall. Near it a wicker chair. In the centre of the room a round table. Chairs, upholstered in faded green plush, stand round the table. To the right, forward, a smaller table with a smoking service on it. Near it an easychair and a lounge. Cocoanut mats lie before the fireplace, beside the lounge and before the doors. The floor is of stained planking. The double doors at the back and the folding doors on the right have lace curtains which are drawn halfway. The lower sash of the window is lifted and the window is hung with heavy green plush curtains. The blind is pulled down to the edge of the lifted lower sash. It is a warm afternoon in June and the room is filled with soft sunlight which is waning.*]

[BRIGID *and* BEATRICE JUSTICE *come in by the door on the left.* BRIGID *is an elderly woman, lowsized, with irongrey hair.* BEATRICE JUSTICE *is a slender dark young woman of twentyseven years. She wears a wellmade navyblue costume and an elegant simply trimmed black straw hat, and carries a small portfolioshaped handbag*]

BRIGID

The mistress and Master Archie is at the bath. They never expected you. Did you send word you were back, Miss Justice?

BEATRICE

No. I arrived just now.

BRIGID

(*points to the easychair*) Sit down and I'll tell the Master you are here. Were you long in the train?

BEATRICE

(*sitting down*) Since morning.

BRIGID

Master Archie got your postcard with the views of Youghal. You're tired out, I'm sure.

BEATRICE

O no. (*she coughs rather nervously*) Did he practise the piano while I was away?

BRIGID

(*laughs heartily*) Practise, how are you! Is it Master Archie? He's mad after the milkman's horse now. Had you nice weather down there, Miss Justice?

BEATRICE

Rather wet, I think.

BRIGID

(*sympathetically*) Look at that now. And there's rain overhead too. (*moving towards the study*) I'll tell him you're here.

BEATRICE

Is Mr Rowan in?

BRIGID

(*points*) He's in his study. He's wearing himself out about something he's writing. Up half the night he does be. (*going*) I'll call him.

BEATRICE

Don't disturb him, Brigid. I can wait here till they come back if
they are not long.

BRIGID

And I saw something in the letterbox when I was letting you in.
(*she crosses to the study door, opens it slightly and calls*) Master
Richard, Miss Justice is here for Master Archie's lesson.

[RICHARD ROWAN *comes in from the study and advances
towards* BEATRICE, *holding out his hand. He is a tall athletic
young man of a rather lazy carriage. He has light brown hair
and moustache and wears glasses. He is dressed in loose
lightgrey tweed*]

RICHARD

Welcome.

BEATRICE

(*rises and shakes hands, blushing slightly*) Good afternoon, Mr
Rowan. I did not want Brigid to disturb you.

RICHARD

Disturb me! My goodness!

BRIGID

There's something in the letterbox, sir.

RICHARD

(*takes a small bunch of keys from his pocket and hands them to
her*) Here.

[BRIGID *goes out by the door on the left and is heard
opening and closing the box. A short pause. She enters with
two newspapers in her hands*]

RICHARD

Letters?

BRIGID

No, sir. Only them Italian newspapers.

RICHARD

Leave them on my desk, will you?

[BRIGID *hands him back the keys, leaves the newspapers in the study, comes out again and goes out by the folding doors on the right*]

RICHARD

Please, sit down. Bertha will be back any moment.

[BEATRICE *sits down again in the easychair.* RICHARD *sits beside the table*]

RICHARD

I had begun to think you would never come back. It is twelve days since you were here.

BEATRICE

I thought of that too. But I have come.

RICHARD

Have you thought over what I told you when you were here last?

BEATRICE

Very much.

RICHARD

You must have known it before. Did you? (*she does not answer*) Do you blame me?

BEATRICE

No.

RICHARD

Do you think I have acted towards you – badly? No? Or towards anyone?

BEATRICE

(*looks at him with a sad puzzled expression*) I have asked myself that question.

RICHARD

And the answer?

BEATRICE

I could not answer it.

RICHARD

If I were a painter and told you I had a book of sketches of you you would not think it so strange, would you?

BEATRICE

It is not quite the same case, is it?

RICHARD

(*smiles slightly*) Not quite. I told you also that I would not show you what I had written unless you asked to see it. Well?

BEATRICE

I will not ask you.

RICHARD

(*leans forward resting his elbows on his knees, his hands joined*) Would you like to see it?

BEATRICE

Very much.

RICHARD

Because it is about yourself?

BEATRICE

Yes. But not only that.

RICHARD

Because it is written by me? Yes? Even if what you would find there is sometimes cruel?

BEATRICE

(*shyly*) That is part of your mind too.

RICHARD

Then it is my mind that attracts you? Is that it?

BEATRICE

(*hesitating, glances at him for an instant*) Why do you think I come here?

RICHARD

Why? Many reasons. To give Archie lessons. We have known one another so many years, from childhood, Robert, you and I – haven't we? You have always been interested in me. Before I went away and while I was away. Then our letters to each other. About my book. Now it is published. I am here again. Perhaps you feel that some new thing is gathering in my brain. Perhaps you feel you should know it. Is that the reason?

BEATRICE

No.

RICHARD

Why then?

BEATRICE

Otherwise I could not see you.

[*She looks at him for a moment and then turns aside quickly*]

RICHARD

(*after a pause repeats uncertainly*) Otherwise you could not see me?

BEATRICE

(*suddenly confused*) I had better go. They are not coming back. (*rising*) Mr Rowan, I must go.

RICHARD

(*extending his arms*) But you are running away! Remain. Tell me what your words mean. Are you afraid of me?

BEATRICE

(*sinks back again*) Afraid? No.

RICHARD

Have you confidence in me? Do you feel that you know me?

BEATRICE

(*again shyly*) It is hard to know anyone but oneself.

RICHARD

Hard to know me? I sent you from Rome the chapters of my book as I wrote them and letters. For nine long years. Well, eight years.

BEATRICE

Yes, it was nearly a year before your first letter came.

RICHARD

It was answered at once by you. And from that on you have watched me in my struggle. (*joins his hands earnestly*) Tell me, Miss Justice, did you feel that what you read was written for your eyes? Or that you inspired me?

BEATRICE

(*shakes her head*) I need not answer that question.

RICHARD

What then?

BEATRICE

(*is silent for a moment*) I cannot say it. You yourself must ask me, Mr Rowan.

RICHARD

(*with some vehemence*) Then that I expressed in those chapters and letters and in my character and life as well something in your soul which you could not – pride or scorn?

BEATRICE

Could not?

RICHARD

(*leans towards her*) Could not because you dared not. Is that why?

BEATRICE

(*bends her head*) Yes.

RICHARD

On account of others or for want of courage – which?

BEATRICE

(*softly*) Courage.

RICHARD

(*slowly*) And so you have followed me with pride and scorn also in your heart?

BEATRICE

And loneliness.

[*She leans her head on her hand, averting her face.* RICHARD *rises and walks slowly to the window on the left. He looks out for some moments and then returns towards her, crosses to the lounge and sits down near her*]

RICHARD

Do you love him still?

BEATRICE

I do not even know.

RICHARD

It was that that made me so reserved with you – then – even though I felt your interest in me, even though I felt that I too was something in your life.

BEATRICE

You were.

RICHARD

You separated me from you. I was a third person, I felt. Your names were always spoken together, Robert and Beatrice, as long as I can remember. It seemed to me, to everyone. . . .

BEATRICE

We are first cousins. It is not strange that we were often together.

RICHARD

He told me of your secret engagement with him. He had no secrets from me. I suppose you know that.

BEATRICE

(*uneasily*) What happened – between us – is so long ago. I was a child.

RICHARD

(*smiles maliciously*) A child? Are you sure? It was in the garden of his mother's house. No? (*he points towards the garden*) Over there. You plighted your troth, as they say, with a kiss. And you gave him your garter. Is it allowed to mention that?

BEATRICE

(*with some reserve*) If you think it worthy of mention.

RICHARD

I think you have not forgotten it. (*clasping his hands quietly*) I do not understand it. I thought too that after I had gone. . . . Did my going make you suffer?

BEATRICE

I always knew you would go some day. I did not suffer. Only I was changed.

RICHARD

Towards him?

BEATRICE

Everything was changed. His life, his mind even, seemed to change after that.

RICHARD

(*musing*) Yes. I saw that you had changed when I received your first letter after a year; after your illness too. You even said so in your letter.

BEATRICE

It brought me near to death. It made me see things differently.

RICHARD

And so a coldness began between you, little by little. Is that it?

BEATRICE

(*half closing her eyes*) No. Not at once. I saw in him a pale reflection of you. Then that too faded. Of what good is it to talk now?

RICHARD

(*with repressed energy*) But what is this that seems to hang over you? It cannot be so tragic.

BEATRICE

(*calmly*) O, not in the least tragic. I shall become gradually better, they tell me, as I grow older. As I did not die then they tell me I shall probably live. I am given life and health again – when I cannot use them. (*calmly and bitterly*) I am convalescent.

RICHARD
(*gently*) Does nothing then in life give you peace? Surely it exists for you somewhere.

BEATRICE
If there were convents in our religion perhaps there. At least I think so at times.

RICHARD
(*shakes his head*) No, Miss Justice, not even there. You could not give yourself freely and wholly.

BEATRICE
(*looking at him*) I would try.

RICHARD
You would try, yes. You were drawn to him as your mind was drawn towards mine. You held back from him. From me too in a different way. You cannot give yourself freely and wholly.

BEATRICE
(*joins her hands softly*) It is a terribly hard thing to do, Mr Rowan – to give oneself freely and wholly – and be happy.

RICHARD
But do you feel that happiness is the best, the highest that we can know?

BEATRICE
(*with fervour*) I wish I could feel it.

RICHARD
(*leans back, his hands locked together behind his head*) O, if you knew how I am suffering at this moment! For your case too. But

suffering most of all for my own. (*with bitter force*) And how I pray that I may be granted again my dead mother's hardness of heart! For some help within me or without, I must find. And find it I will.

[BEATRICE *rises, looks at him intently and walks away towards the garden door. She turns with indecision, looks again at him and, coming back, leans over the easychair*]

BEATRICE

(*quietly*) Did she send for you before she died, Mr Rowan?

RICHARD

(*lost in thought*) Who?

BEATRICE

Your mother.

RICHARD

(*recovering himself, looks keenly at her for a moment*) So that too was said of me here by my friends – that she sent for me before she died and that I did not go.

BEATRICE

Yes.

RICHARD

(*coldly*) She did not. She died alone, not having forgiven me and fortified by the rites of holy church.

BEATRICE

Mr Rowan, why do you speak to me in such a way?

RICHARD

(*rises and walks nervously to and fro*) And what I suffer at this moment you will say is my punishment.

BEATRICE

Did she write to you? I mean before. . . .

RICHARD

(*halting*) Yes. A letter of warning, bidding me break with the past and remember her last words to me.

BEATRICE

(*softly*) And does death not move you, Mr Rowan? It is an end. Everything else is so uncertain.

RICHARD

While she lived she turned aside from me and from mine. That is certain.

BEATRICE

From you and from . . .?

RICHARD

From Bertha and from me and from our child. And so I waited for the end as you say. And it came.

BEATRICE

(*covers her face with her hands*) O no. Surely no.

RICHARD

(*fiercely*) How can my words hurt her poor body that rots in the grave? Do you think I do not pity her cold blighted love for me? I fought against her spirit while she lived to the bitter end. (*he presses his hand to his forehead*) It fights against me still – in here.

BEATRICE

(*as before*) O, do not speak like that!

RICHARD

She drove me away. On account of her I lived years in exile and poverty too or near it. I never accepted the doles she sent me through the bank. I waited too. Not for her death but for some understanding of me, her own son, her own flesh and blood. That never came.

BEATRICE

Not even after Archie . . .?

RICHARD

(*rudely*) My son, you think? A child of sin and shame! Are you serious? (*she raises her face and looks at him*) There were tongues here ready to tell her all, to embitter her withering mind still more against me and Bertha and our godless nameless child. (*holding out his hands to her*) Can you not hear her mocking me while I speak? You must know the voice surely, the voice that called you the black protestant, the pervert's daughter. (*with sudden self-control*) In any case a remarkable woman.

BEATRICE

(*weakly*) At least you are free now.

RICHARD

(*nods*) Yes. She could not alter the terms of my father's will or live for ever.

BEATRICE

(*with joined hands*) They are both gone now, Mr Rowan. They both loved you, believe me. Their last thoughts were of you.

RICHARD

(*approaching, touches her lightly on the shoulder and points to the crayon drawing on the wall*) Do you see him there, smiling and handsome? His last thoughts! I remember the night he died. (*he pauses for an instant, then goes on calmly*) I was a boy of fourteen. He called me to his bedside. He knew I wanted to go to the theatre to hear *Carmen*. He told my mother to give me a shilling. I kissed him and went. When I came home he was dead. Those were his last thoughts so far as I know.

BEATRICE

The hardness of heart you prayed for. . . . (*she breaks off*)

RICHARD

(*unheeding*) That is my last memory of him. Is there not something sweet and noble in it?

BEATRICE

Mr Rowan, something is on your mind to make you speak like that. Something has changed you since you came back three months ago.

RICHARD

(*gazing again at the drawing, calmly, almost gaily*) He will help me perhaps. My smiling handsome father.

[*A knock is heard at the halldoor on the left*]

RICHARD

(*suddenly*) No, no. Not the smiler, Miss Justice. The old mother. It is her spirit I need. I am going.

BEATRICE

Someone knocked. They have come back.

RICHARD

No. Bertha has a key. It is he. At least I am going whoever it is.

[*He goes out quickly on the left and comes back at once with his straw hat in his hand*]

BEATRICE

He? Who?

RICHARD

O, probably Robert. I am going out through the garden. I cannot see him now. Say I have gone to the post. Goodbye.

BEATRICE

(*with growing alarm*) It is Robert you do not wish to see?

RICHARD

(*quietly*) For the moment, yes. This talk has upset me. Ask him to wait.

BEATRICE

You will come back?

RICHARD

Please God.

[*He goes out quickly through the garden.* BEATRICE *makes as if to follow him and then stops after a few paces.* BRIGID *enters by the folding doors on the right and goes out on the left. The halldoor is heard opening. A few seconds after* BRIGID *enters with* ROBERT HAND.
ROBERT HAND *is a middlesized, rather stout man between thirty and forty. He is cleanshaven with mobile features. His hair and eyes are dark and his complexion sallow. His gait and speech are rather slow. He wears a dark blue morning suit and carries in his hand a large bunch of red roses wrapped in tissue paper*]

ROBERT

(*coming towards her with outstretched hand which she takes*) My dearest coz! Brigid told me you were here. I had no notion. Did you send mother a telegram?

BEATRICE

(*gazing at the roses*) No.

ROBERT

(*following her gaze*) You are admiring my roses. I brought them to the mistress of the house. (*critically*) I am afraid they are not nice.

BRIGID

O, they are lovely, sir. The mistress will be delighted with them.

ROBERT

(*lays the roses carelessly on a chair out of sight*) Is nobody in?

BRIGID

Yes, sir. Sit down, sir. They'll be here now any moment. The master was here.

[*She looks about her and with a half curtsey goes out on the right*]

ROBERT

(*after a short silence*) How are you, Beatty? And how are all down in Youghal? As dull as ever?

BEATRICE

They were well when I left.

ROBERT

(*politely*) O but I'm sorry I did not know you were coming. I would have met you at the train. Why did you do it? You have some queer ways about you, Beatty, haven't you?

BEATRICE

(*in the same tone*) Thank you, Robert. I am quite used to getting about alone.

ROBERT

Yes, but I mean to say . . . . O, well, you have arrived in your own characteristic way.

[*A noise is heard at the window and a boy's voice is heard calling* Mr Hand! ROBERT *turns*]

By Jove, Archie, too, is arriving in a characteristic way!

[ARCHIE *scrambles into the room through the open window on the left and then rises to his feet, flushed and panting.*
ARCHIE *is a boy of eight years, dressed in white breeches, jersey and cap. He wears spectacles, has a lively manner and speaks with the slight trace of a foreign accent*]

BEATRICE

(*going towards him*) Goodness gracious, Archie! What is the matter?

ARCHIE

(*rising, out of breath*) Eh! I ran all the avenue.

ROBERT

(*smiles and holds out his hand*) Good evening, Archie. Why did you run?

ARCHIE

(*shakes hands*)Good evening. We saw you on the top of the tram and I shouted: *Mr Hand!* But you did not see me. But we saw you, mamma and I. She will be here in a minute. I ran.

BEATRICE

(*holding out her hand*) And poor me!

ARCHIE

(*shakes hands somewhat shyly*) Good evening, Miss Justice.

BEATRICE

Were you disappointed that I did not come last Friday for the lesson?

ARCHIE

(*glancing at her, smiles*) No.

BEATRICE

Glad?

ARCHIE

(*suddenly*) But today it is too late.

BEATRICE

A very short lesson?

ARCHIE

(*pleased*) Yes.

BEATRICE

But now you must study, Archie.

ROBERT

Were you at the bath?

ARCHIE

Yes.

ROBERT

Are you a good swimmer now?

ARCHIE

(*leans against the davenport*) No. Mamma won't let me into the deep place. Can you swim well, Mr Hand?

ROBERT

Splendidly. Like a stone.

ARCHIE

(*laughs*) Like a stone! (*pointing down*) Down that way?

ROBERT

(*pointing*) Yes, down: straight down. How do you say that over in Italy?

ARCHIE

That? *Giù.* (*pointing down and up*) That is *giù* and this is *sù.* Do you want to speak to my pappie?

ROBERT

Yes. I came to see him.

ARCHIE

(*going towards the study*) I will tell him. He is in there, writing.

BEATRICE

(*calmly, looking at* ROBERT) No, he is out. He is gone to the post with some letters.

ROBERT

(*lightly*) O, never mind. I will wait if he is only gone to the post.

ARCHIE

But mamma is coming. (*he glances towards the window*) Here she is!

[ARCHIE *runs out by the door on the left.* BEATRICE *walks slowly towards the davenport.* ROBERT *remains standing. A short silence.* ARCHIE *and* BERTHA *come in through the door on the left.*
BERTHA *is a young woman of graceful build. She has dark grey eyes, patient in expression, and soft features. Her manner is cordial and selfpossessed. She wears a lavender dress and carries her cream gloves knotted round the handle of her sunshade*]

BERTHA

(*shaking hands*) Good evening, Miss Justice. We thought you were still down in Youghal.

BEATRICE

(*shaking hands*) Good evening, Mrs Rowan.

BERTHA

(*bows*) Good evening, Mr Hand.

ROBERT

(*bowing*) Good evening, *signora!* Just imagine, I didn't know either she was back till I found her here.

BERTHA

(*to both*) Did you not come together?

BEATRICE

No. I came first. Mr Rowan was going out. He said you would be back any moment.

BERTHA

I'm sorry. If you had written or sent over word by the girl this morning. . . .

BEATRICE

(*laughs nervously*) I arrived only an hour and a half ago. I thought of sending a telegram but it seemed too tragic.

BERTHA

Ah? Only now you arrived?

ROBERT

(*extending his arms, blandly*) I retire from public and private life. Her first cousin and a journalist, I know nothing of her movements.

BEATRICE

(*not directly to him*) My movements are not very interesting.

ROBERT

(*in the same tone*) A lady's movements are always interesting.

BERTHA

But sit down, won't you? You must be very tired.

BEATRICE

(*quickly*) No, not at all. I just came for Archie's lesson.

BERTHA

I wouldn't hear of such a thing, Miss Justice, after your long journey.

ARCHIE

(*suddenly, to* BEATRICE) And besides you didn't bring the music.

BEATRICE

(*a little confused*) That I forgot. But we have the old piece.

ROBERT

(*pinching* ARCHIE's *ear*) You little scamp. You want to get off the lesson.

BERTHA

O, never mind the lesson. You must sit down and have a cup of tea now. (*going towards the door on the right*) I'll tell Brigid.

ARCHIE

I will, mamma. (*he makes a movement to go*)

BEATRICE

No, please, Mrs Rowan. Archie! I would really prefer. . . .

ROBERT

(*quietly*) I suggest a compromise. Let it be a halflesson.

BERTHA

But she must be exhausted.

BEATRICE

(*quickly*) Not in the least. I was thinking of the lesson in the train.

ROBERT

(*to* BERTHA) You see what it is to have a conscience, Mrs Rowan?

ARCHIE

Of my lesson, Miss Justice?

BEATRICE

(*simply*) It is ten days since I heard the sound of a piano.

BERTHA

O, very well. If that is it . . .

ROBERT

(*nervously, gaily*) Let us have the piano by all means. I know what is in Beatty's ears at this moment. (*to* BEATRICE) Shall I tell?

BEATRICE

If you know.

ROBERT

The buzz of the harmonium in her father's parlour. (*to* BEATRICE) Confess.

BEATRICE

(*smiling*) Yes. I can hear it.

ROBERT

(*grimly*) So can I. The asthmatic voice of protestantism.

BERTHA

Did you not enjoy yourself down there, Miss Justice?

ROBERT

(*intervenes*) She did not, Mrs Rowan. She goes there on retreat, when the protestant strain in her prevails – gloom, seriousness, righteousness.

BEATRICE

I go to see my father.

ROBERT

(*continuing*) But she comes back here to my mother, you see. The piano influence is from our side of the house.

BERTHA

(*hesitating*) Well, Miss Justice, if you would like to play something . . . . But please don't fatigue yourself with Archie.

ROBERT

(*suavely*) Do, Beatty. That is what you want.

BEATRICE

If Archie will come?

ARCHIE

(*with a shrug*) To listen.

BEATRICE

(*takes his hand*) And a little lesson too. Very short.

BERTHA

Well, afterwards you must stay to tea.

BEATRICE

(*to* ARCHIE] Come.

[BEATRICE *and* ARCHIE *go out together by the door on the left.* BERTHA *goes towards the davenport, takes off her hat and lays it with her sunshade on the davenport. Then taking a key from a little flower vase, she opens a drawer of the davenport, takes out a slip of paper and closes the drawer again.* ROBERT *stands watching her*]

BERTHA

(*coming towards him with the paper in her hand*) You put this into my hand last night. What does it mean?

ROBERT

Do you not know?

BERTHA

(*reads*) *There is one word which I have never dared to say to you.* What is the word?

ROBERT

That I have a deep liking for you.

[*A short pause. The piano is heard faintly from the upper room*]

ROBERT

(*takes the bunch of roses from the chair*) I brought these for you. Will you take them from me?

BERTHA

(*taking them*) Thank you. (*she lays them on the table and unfolds the paper again*) Why did you not dare to say it last night?

ROBERT

I could not speak to you or follow you. There were too many people on the lawn. I wanted you to think over it and so I put it into your hand when you were going away.

BERTHA

Now you have dared to say it.

ROBERT

(*moves his hand slowly past his eyes*) You passed. The avenue was dim with dusky light. I could see the dark green masses of the trees. And you passed beyond them. You were like the moon.

BERTHA

(*laughs*) Why like the moon?

ROBERT

In that dress, with your slim body, walking with little even steps. I saw the moon passing in the dusk till you passed and left my sight.

BERTHA

Did you think of me last night?

ROBERT

(*comes nearer*) I think of you always – as something beautiful and distant – the moon or some deep music.

BERTHA

(*smiling*) And last night which was I?

ROBERT

I was awake half the night. I could hear your voice. I could see your face in the dark. Your eyes . . . . I want to speak to you. Will you listen to me? May I speak?

BERTHA

(*sitting down*) You may.

ROBERT

(*sitting beside her*) Are you annoyed with me?

BERTHA

No.

ROBERT

I thought you were. You put away my poor flowers so quickly.

BERTHA

(*takes them from the table and holds them close to her face*) Is this what you wish me to do with them?

ROBERT

(*watching her*) Your face is a flower too – but more beautiful. A wild flower blowing in a hedge. (*moving his chair closer to her*) Why are you smiling? At my words?

BERTHA

(*laying the flowers in her lap*) I am wondering if that is what you say – to the others.

ROBERT

(*surprised*) What others?

BERTHA

The other women. I hear you have so many admirers.

ROBERT

(*involuntarily*) And that is why you too . . . .?

BERTHA

But you have, haven't you?

ROBERT

Friends, yes.

BERTHA

Do you speak to them in the same way?

ROBERT

(*in an offended tone*) How can you ask me such a question? What kind of person do you think I am? Or why do you listen to me? Did you not like me to speak to you in that way?

BERTHA

What you said was very kind. (*she looks at him for a moment*) Thank you for saying it – and thinking it.

ROBERT

(*leaning forward*) Bertha!

BERTHA

Yes?

ROBERT

I have the right to call you by your name. From old times – nine years ago. We were Bertha – and Robert – then. Can we not be so now too?

BERTHA

(*readily*) O, yes. Why should we not?

ROBERT

Bertha, you knew. From the very night you landed on Kingstown
pier. It all came back to me then. And you knew it. You saw it.

BERTHA

No. Not that night.

ROBERT

When?

BERTHA

The night we landed I felt very tired and dirty. (*shaking her head*)
I did not see it in you that night.

ROBERT

(*smiling*) Tell me what did you see that night – your very first im-
pression.

BERTHA

(*knitting her brows*) You were standing with your back to the
gangway, talking to two ladies.

ROBERT

To two plain middleaged ladies, yes.

BERTHA

I recognised you at once. And I saw that you had got fat.

ROBERT

(*takes her hand*) And this poor fat Robert – do you dislike him
then so much? Do you disbelieve all he says?

BERTHA

I think men speak like that to all women whom they like or
admire. What do you want me to believe?

ROBERT

All men, Bertha?

BERTHA

(*with sudden sadness*) I think so.

ROBERT

I too?

BERTHA

Yes, Robert. I think you too.

ROBERT

All then – without exception? Or with one exception? (*in a lower tone*) Or is he too – Richard too – like us all – in that at least? Or different?

BERTHA

(*looks into his eyes*) Different.

ROBERT

Are you quite sure, Bertha?

BERTHA

(*a little confused, tries to withdraw her hand*) I have answered you.

ROBERT

(*tenderly*) Bertha, may I kiss your hand? Let me. May I?

BERTHA

If you wish.

[*He lifts her hand to his lips slowly. She rises suddenly and listens*]

BERTHA

Did you hear the garden gate?

ROBERT

(*rising also*) No.

> [*A short pause. The piano can be heard faintly from the upper room*]

ROBERT

(*pleading*) Do not go away. You must never go away now. Your life is here. I came for that too today – to speak to him – to urge him to accept this position. He must. And you must persuade him to. You have a great influence over him.

BERTHA

You want him to remain here.

ROBERT

Yes.

BERTHA

Why?

ROBERT

For your sake because you are unhappy so far away. For his too because he should think of his future.

BERTHA

(*laughing*) Do you remember what he said when you spoke to him last night?

ROBERT

About . . .? (*reflecting*) Yes. He quoted the *Our Father* about our daily bread. He said that to take care for the future is to destroy hope and love in the world.

BERTHA

Do you not think he is strange?

ROBERT

In that, yes.

BERTHA

A little – mad?

ROBERT

(*comes closer*) No. He is not. Perhaps we are. Why, do you. . . .?

BERTHA

(*laughs*) I asked you because you are intelligent.

ROBERT

You must not go away. I will not let you.

BERTHA

(*looks full at him*) You?

ROBERT

Those eyes must not go away. (*he takes her hands*) May I kiss your eyes?

BERTHA

Do so.

[*He kisses her eyes and then passes his hand over his hair*]

ROBERT

Little Bertha!

BERTHA

(*smiling*) But I am not so little. Why do you call me little?

ROBERT

Little Bertha! One embrace? (*he puts his arm round her*) Look into my eyes again.

BERTHA

(*looks*) I can see the little gold spots. So many you have.

ROBERT

(*delighted*) Your voice! Give me a kiss, a kiss with your mouth.

BERTHA

Take it.

ROBERT

I am afraid. (*he kisses her mouth and passes his hand many times over her hair*) At last! At last I hold you in my arms!

BERTHA

And are you satisfied?

ROBERT

Let me feel your lips touch mine.

BERTHA

And then you will be satisfied?

ROBERT

(*murmurs*) Your lips, Bertha!

BERTHA

(*closes her eyes and kisses him quickly*) There. (*puts her hands on his shoulders*) Why don't you say: *Thanks*?

ROBERT

(*sighs*) My life is finished – over.

BERTHA

O don't speak like that now, Robert.

ROBERT

Over, over. I want to end it and have done with it.

BERTHA

(*concerned but lightly*) You silly fellow!

ROBERT

(*presses her to him*) To end it all – death. To fall from a great high cliff down, right into the sea.

BERTHA

Please, Robert. . . .

ROBERT

Listening to music and in the arms of the woman I love – the sea, music and death.

BERTHA

(*looks at him for a moment*) The woman you love?

ROBERT

(*hurriedly*) I want to speak to you, Bertha – alone. Not here. Will you come?

BERTHA

(*with downcast eyes*) I too want to speak to you.

ROBERT

(*tenderly*) Yes, dear, I know. (*he kisses her again*) I will speak to you, tell you all then. I will kiss you then, long long kisses – when you come to me – long long sweet kisses.

BERTHA

Where?

ROBERT

(*in the tone of passion*) Your eyes. Your lips. All your divine body.

BERTHA

(*repelling his embrace, confused*) I meant where do you wish me to come.

ROBERT

To my house. Not my mother's over there. I will write the address for you. Will you come?

BERTHA

When?

ROBERT

Tonight. Between eight and nine. Come. I will wait for you tonight. And every night. You will?

[*He kisses her with passion, holding her head between his hands. After a few instants she breaks from him. He sits down*]

BERTHA

(*listening*) The gate opened.

ROBERT

(*intensely*) I will wait for you.

[*He takes the slip from the table.* BERTHA *moves away from him slowly.* RICHARD *comes in from the garden*]

RICHARD

(*advancing, takes off his hat*) Good afternoon!

ROBERT

(*rises, with nervous friendliness*) Good afternoon, Richard!

BERTHA

(*at the table, taking the roses*) Look what lovely roses Mr Hand brought me.

ROBERT

I am afraid they are overblown.

RICHARD

(*suddenly*) Excuse me for a moment, will you?

[*He turns and goes into his study quickly.* ROBERT *takes a pencil from his pocket and writes a few words on the slip: then hands it quickly to* BERTHA]

ROBERT

(*rapidly*) The address. Take the tram at Lansdowne road and ask to be let down near there.

BERTHA

(*takes it*) I promise nothing.

ROBERT

I will wait.

[RICHARD *comes back from the study*]

BERTHA

(*going*) I must put these roses in water.

RICHARD

(*handing her his hat*) Yes, do. And please put my hat on the rack.

BERTHA

(*takes it*) So I will leave you to yourselves – for your talk. (*looking round*) Do you want anything? Cigarettes?

RICHARD

Thanks. We have them here.

BERTHA

Then I can go.

[*She goes out on the left with* RICHARD's *hat, which she leaves in the hall, returns at once; she stops for a moment at the davenport, replaces the slip in the drawer, locks it, and replaces the key, and, taking the roses, goes towards the right.* ROBERT *precedes her to open the door for her. She bows and goes out*]

RICHARD

(*points to the chair near the little table on the right*) Your place of honour.

ROBERT

(*sits down*) Thanks. (*passing his hand over his brow*) Good Lord, how warm it is today! The heat pains me here in the eye. The glare.

RICHARD

The room is rather dark, I think, with the blind down but if you wish. . . .

ROBERT

(*quickly*) Not at all. I know what it is – the result of nightwork.

RICHARD

(*sits on the lounge*) Must you?

ROBERT

(*sighs*) Eh, yes. I must see part of the paper through every night. And then my leading articles. We are approaching a difficult moment. And not only here.

RICHARD

(*after a slight pause*) Have you any news?

ROBERT

(*in a different voice*) Yes. I want to speak to you seriously. Today may be an important day for you – or rather tonight. I saw the vicechancellor this morning. He has the highest opinion of you, Richard. He has read your book, he said.

RICHARD

Did he buy it or borrow it?

ROBERT

Bought it, I hope.

RICHARD

I shall smoke a cigarette. Thirtyseven copies have now been sold in Dublin.

[*He takes a cigarette from the box on the table and lights it*]

ROBERT

(*suavely, hopelessly*) Well, the matter is closed for the present. You have your iron mask on today.

RICHARD

(*smoking*) Let me hear the rest.

ROBERT

(*again seriously*) Richard, you are too suspicious. It is a defect in you. He assured me he has the highest possible opinion of you – as everyone has. You are the man for the post, he says. In fact he told me that if your name goes forward he will work might and main for you with the senate and I . . . will do my part, of course. In the press and privately. I regard it as a public duty. The chair of romance literature is yours by right, as a scholar, as a literary personality.

RICHARD

The conditions?

ROBERT

Conditions? You mean about the future?

RICHARD

I mean about the past.

ROBERT

(*easily*) That episode in your past is forgotten. An act of impulse. We are all impulsive.

RICHARD

(*looks fixedly at him*) You called it an act of folly then – nine years ago. You told me I was hanging a weight about my neck.

ROBERT

I was wrong. (*suavely*) Here is how the matter stands, Richard.

Everyone knows that you ran away eight years ago with a young girl . . . . How shall I put it? . . . . With a young girl not exactly your equal. (*kindly*) Excuse me, Richard, that is not my opinion nor my language. I am simply using the language of people whose opinions I don't share.

RICHARD

Writing one of your leading articles, in fact.

ROBERT

Put it so. Well, it made a great sensation at the time. A mysterious disappearance. My name was involved too as best man, let us say, on that famous occasion. Of course they think I acted from a mistaken sense of friendship. Well, all that is known. (*with some hesitation*) But what happened afterwards is not known.

RICHARD

No?

ROBERT

Of course, it is your affair, Richard. However you are not so young now as you were then. The expression is quite in the style of my leading articles, isn't it?

RICHARD

Do you or do you not want me to give the lie to my past life?

ROBERT

I am thinking of your future life – here. I understand your pride and your sense of liberty. I understand their point of view also. However, there is a way out. It is simply this. Refrain from contradicting any rumours you may hear concerning what happened . . . or did not happen . . . . after you went away. Leave the rest to me.

RICHARD

You will set these rumours afloat?

ROBERT

I will. God help me.

RICHARD

(*observing him*) For the sake of social conventions?

ROBERT

For the sake of something else too – our friendship, our lifelong friendship.

RICHARD

Thanks.

ROBERT

(*slightly wounded*) And I will tell you the whole truth.

RICHARD

(*smiles and bows*) Yes. Do please.

ROBERT

Not only for your sake. Also for the sake of . . . your present partner in life.

RICHARD

I see.

> [*He crushes his cigarette softly on the ashtray and then leans forward, rubbing his hands slowly*]

RICHARD

Why for her sake?

ROBERT

(*also leans forward, quietly*) Richard, have you been quite fair to her? It was her own free choice, you will say. But was she really free to choose? She was a mere girl. She accepted all that you proposed.

RICHARD

(*smiles*) That is your way of saying that she proposed what I would not accept.

ROBERT

(*nods*) I remember. And she went away with you. But was it of her own free choice? Answer me frankly.

RICHARD

(*turns to him, calmly*) I played for her against all that you say or can say: and I won.

ROBERT

(*nodding again*) Yes, you won.

RICHARD

(*rises*) Excuse me for forgetting. Will you have some whisky?

ROBERT

All things come to those who wait.

[RICHARD *goes to the sideboard and brings a small tray with decanter and glasses to the table where he sets it down*]

RICHARD

(*sits down again, leaning back on the lounge*) Will you please help yourself?

ROBERT

(*does so*) And you? Steadfast? (RICHARD *shakes his head*) Lord, when I think of our wild nights long ago – talks by the hour, plans, carouses, revelry. . . .

RICHARD

In our house.

ROBERT

It is mine now. I have kept it ever since though I don't go there often. Whenever you like to come let me know. You must come some night. It will be old times again. (*he lifts his glass and drinks*) Prosit!

RICHARD

It was not only a house of revelry. It was to be the hearth of a new life. (*musing*) And in that name all our sins were committed.

ROBERT

Sins! Drinking and blasphemy (*he points*) by me. And drinking and heresy, much worse, (*he points again*) by you – are those the sins you mean?

RICHARD

And some others.

ROBERT

(*lightly, uneasily*) You mean the women. I have no remorse of conscience. Maybe you have. We had two keys on those occasions. (*maliciously*) Have you?

RICHARD

(*irritated*) For you it was all quite natural?

ROBERT

For me it is quite natural to kiss a woman whom I like. Why not? She is beautiful for me.

RICHARD

(*toying with the lounge cushion*) Do you kiss everything that is beautiful for you?

ROBERT

Everything – if it can be kissed. (*he takes up a flat stone which lies on the table*) This stone, for instance. It is so cool, so polished, so delicate, like a woman's temple. It is silent. It suffers our passion: and it is beautiful. (*he places it against his lips*) And so I kiss it because it is beautiful. And what is a woman? A work of nature too, like a stone or a flower or a bird. A kiss is an act of homage.

RICHARD

It is an act of union between man and woman. Even if we are often led to desire through the sense of beauty can you say that the beautiful is what we desire?

ROBERT

(*pressing the stone to his forehead*) You will give me a headache if you make me think today. I cannot think today. I feel too natural, too common. After all what is most attractive in even the most beautiful woman?

RICHARD

What?

ROBERT

Not those qualities which she has and other women have not but the qualities which she has in common with them. I mean . . . the commonest. (*turning the stone, he presses the other side to his forehead*) I mean how her body develops heat when it is pressed, the movement of her blood, how quickly she changes by digestion what she eats into . . . . what shall be nameless. (*laughing*) I am very common today. Perhaps that idea never struck you?

RICHARD

(*drily*) Many ideas strike a man who has lived nine years with a woman.

ROBERT

Yes. I suppose they do. . . . This beautiful cool stone does me good. Is it a paperweight or a cure for headache?

RICHARD

Bertha brought it home one day from the strand. She too says that it is beautiful.

ROBERT

(*lays down the stone quietly*) She is right.

[*He raises his glass and drinks. A pause*]

RICHARD

Is that all you wanted to say to me?

ROBERT

(*quickly*) There is something else. The vicechancellor sends you through me an invitation for tonight – to dinner at his house. You know where he lives? (RICHARD *nods*) I thought you might have forgotten. Strictly private, of course. He wants to meet you again and sends you a very warm invitation.

RICHARD

For what hour?

ROBERT

Eight: but like yourself he is free and easy about time. Now, Richard, you must go there. That is all. I feel tonight will be the turningpoint in your life. You will live here and work here and think here and be honoured here – among our people.

RICHARD

(*smiling*) I can almost see two envoys starting for the United States to collect funds for my statue a hundred years hence.

ROBERT

(*agreeably*) Once I made a little epigram about statues. All statues are of two kinds. (*he folds his arms across his chest*) The statue which says: *How shall I get down?* And the other kind. (*he unfolds his arms and extends his right arm, averting his head*) The statue which says: *In my time the dunghill was so high.*

RICHARD

The second one for me, please.

ROBERT

(*lazily*) Will you give me one of those long cigars of yours?

[RICHARD *selects a Virginia cigar from the box on the table and hands it to him with the straw drawn out*]

ROBERT

(*lighting it*) These cigars Europeanise me. If Ireland is to become a new Ireland she must first become European. And that is what you are here for, Richard. Some day we shall have to choose between England and Europe. I am a descendant of the dark foreigners. That is why I like to be here. I may be childish: but where else in Dublin can I get a bandit cigar like this or a cup of black coffee? The man who drinks black coffee is going to conquer Ireland. And now I will take just a half measure of that whisky, Richard, to show you there is no ill feeling.

RICHARD

(*points*) Help yourself.

ROBERT

(*does so*) Thanks (*he drinks and goes on as before*) Then you yourself, the way you loll on that lounge. Then your boy's voice and also – Bertha herself. Do you allow me to call her that, Richard? I mean as an old friend of both of you.

RICHARD

O, why not?

ROBERT

(*with animation*) You have that fierce indignation which lacerated the heart of Swift. You have fallen from a higher world, Richard, and you are filled with fierce indignation when you find that life is cowardly and ignoble. While I . . . . shall I tell you?

RICHARD

By all means.

ROBERT

(*archly*) I have come up from a lower world and I am filled with astonishment when I find that people have any redeeming virtue at all.

RICHARD

(*sits up suddenly and leans his elbows on the table*) You are my friend, then?

ROBERT

(*gravely*) I fought for you all the time you were away. I fought to bring you back. I fought to keep your place for you here. I will fight for you still because I have faith in you, the faith of a disciple in his master. I cannot say more than that. It may seem strange to you . . . . Give me a match.

RICHARD

(*lights and offers him a match*) There is a faith still stranger than the faith of the disciple in his master.

ROBERT

And that is?

RICHARD

The faith of a master in the disciple who will betray him.

ROBERT

The church lost a theologian in you, Richard. But I think you look too deeply into life. (*he rises, pressing* RICHARD's *arm slightly*) Be gay. Life is not worth it.

RICHARD

(*without rising*) Are you going?

ROBERT

Must. (*he turns and says in a friendly tone*) Then it is all arranged. We meet tonight at the vicechancellor's. I shall look in at about ten. So you can have an hour or so to yourselves first. You will wait till I come.

RICHARD

Good.

ROBERT

One more match and I am happy.

[RICHARD *strikes another match, hands it to him and rises also.* ARCHIE *comes in by the door on the left, followed by* BEATRICE]

ROBERT

Congratulate me, Beatty. I have won over Richard.

ARCHIE

(*crossing to the door on the right, calls*) Mamma, Miss Justice is going.

ROBERT

And Mr Hand is going.

BEATRICE

On what are you to be congratulated?

ROBERT

On a victory, of course. (*laying his hand lightly on* RICHARD's *shoulder*) The descendant of Archibald Hamilton Rowan has come home.

RICHARD

I am not a descendant of Hamilton Rowan.

ROBERT

What matter?

[BERTHA *comes in from the right with a bowl of roses*]

BEATRICE

Has Mr Rowan . . . .?

ROBERT

(*turning towards* BERTHA) Richard is coming tonight to the vicechancellor's dinner. The fatted calf will be eaten: roast, I hope. And next session will see the descendant of a namesake of Etcetera, Etcetera in a chair of the university. (*he offers his hand*) Good afternoon, Richard. We shall meet tonight.

RICHARD

(*touches his hand*) At Philippi.

BEATRICE

(*shakes hands also*) Accept my best wishes, Mr Rowan.

RICHARD

Thanks. But do not believe him.

ROBERT

(*vivaciously*) Believe me, believe me. (*to* BERTHA) Good afternoon, Mrs Rowan.

BERTHA

(*shaking hands, candidly*) I thank you too. (*to* BEATRICE) You won't stay to tea, Miss Justice?

BEATRICE

No, thank you. (*takes leave of her*) I must go. Good afternoon. Goodbye, Archie. (*going*)

ROBERT

Addio, Archibald.

ARCHIE

Addio.

ROBERT

Wait, Beatty. I shall accompany you.

BEATRICE

(*going out on the left with* BERTHA) O, don't trouble.

ROBERT

(*following her*) But I insist – as a cousin.

[BERTHA, BEATRICE *and* ROBERT *go out by the door on the left.* RICHARD *stands irresolutely near the table.* ARCHIE *closes the door leading to the hall and, coming over to him, plucks him by the sleeve*]

ARCHIE

I say, pappie.

RICHARD

(*absently*) What is it?

ARCHIE

I want to ask you a thing.

RICHARD

(*sitting on the end of the lounge, stares in front of him*) What is it?

ARCHIE

Will you ask mamma to let me go out in the morning with the milkman?

RICHARD

With the milkman?

ARCHIE

Yes. In the milkcar. He says he will let me drive when we get on to the roads where there are no people. The horse is a very good beast. Can I go?

RICHARD

Yes.

ARCHIE

Ask mamma now can I go. Will you?

RICHARD

(*glances towards the door*) I will.

ARCHIE

He said he will show me the cows he has in the field. Do you know how many cows he has?

RICHARD

How many?

ARCHIE

Eleven. Eight red and three white. But one is sick now. No, not sick. But it fell.

RICHARD

Cows?

ARCHIE

(*with a gesture*) Eh! Not bulls. Because bulls give no milk. Eleven cows. They must give a lot of milk. What makes a cow give milk?

RICHARD

(*takes his hand*) Who knows? Do you understand what it is to give a thing?

ARCHIE

To give? Yes.

RICHARD

While you have a thing it can be taken from you.

ARCHIE

By robbers? No?

RICHARD

But when you give it you have given it. No robber can take it
from you. (*he bends his head and presses his son's hand against
his cheek*) It is yours then for ever when you have given it. It will
be yours always. That is to give.

ARCHIE

But pappie?

RICHARD

Yes?

ARCHIE

How could a robber rob a cow? Everyone would see him. In the
night, perhaps.

RICHARD

In the night. Yes.

ARCHIE

Are there robbers here like in Rome?

RICHARD

There are poor people everywhere.

ARCHIE

Have they revolvers?

RICHARD

No.

ARCHIE

Knives? Have they knives?

RICHARD

(*sternly*) Yes, yes. Knives and revolvers.

ARCHIE

(*disengages himself*) Ask mamma now. She is coming.

RICHARD

(*makes a movement to rise*) I will.

ARCHIE

No, sit there, pappie. You wait and ask her when she comes back. I won't be here. I'll be in the garden.

RICHARD

(*sinking back again*) Yes. Go.

ARCHIE

(*kisses him swiftly*) Thanks.

[*He runs out quickly by the door at the back leading into the garden.* BERTHA *enters by the door on the left. She approaches the table and stands beside it fingering the petals of the roses, looking at* RICHARD]

RICHARD

(*watching her*) Well?

BERTHA

(*absently*) Well. He says he likes me.

RICHARD

(*leans his chin on his hand*) You showed him his note?

BERTHA

Yes. I asked him what it meant.

RICHARD

What did he say it meant?

BERTHA

He said I must know. I said I had an idea. Then he told me he liked me very much. That I was beautiful – and all that.

RICHARD

Since when?

BERTHA

(*again absently*) Since when – what?

RICHARD

Since when did he say he liked you?

BERTHA

Always, he said. But more since we came back. He said I was like the moon in this lavender dress. (*looking at him*) Had you any words with him – about me?

RICHARD

(*blandly*) The usual thing. Not about you.

BERTHA

He was very nervous. You saw that?

RICHARD

Yes. I saw it. What else went on?

BERTHA

He asked me to give him my hand.

RICHARD

(*smiling*) In marriage?

BERTHA

(*smiling*) No, only to hold.

RICHARD

Did you?

BERTHA

Yes. (*tearing off a few petals*) Then he caressed my hand and asked would I let him kiss it. I let him.

RICHARD

Well?

BERTHA

Then he asked could he embrace me – even once? ... And then. . . .

RICHARD

And then?

BERTHA

He put his arm around me.

RICHARD

(*stares at the floor for a moment: then looks at her again*) And then?

BERTHA

He said I had beautiful eyes. And asked could he kiss them. (*with a gesture*) I said: *Do so.*

RICHARD

And he did?

BERTHA

Yes. First one and then the other. (*she breaks off suddenly*) Tell me, Dick, does all this disturb you? Because I told you I don't want that. I think you are only pretending you don't mind. I don't mind.

RICHARD

(*quietly*) I know, dear. But I want to find out what he means or feels just as you do.

BERTHA

(*points at him*) Remember you allowed me to go on. I told you the whole thing from the beginning.

RICHARD

(*as before*) I know, dear . . . . And then?

BERTHA

He asked for a kiss. I said: *Take it*.

RICHARD

And then?

BERTHA

(*crumpling a handful of petals*) He kissed me.

RICHARD

Your mouth?

BERTHA

Once or twice.

RICHARD

Long kisses?

BERTHA

Fairly long. (*reflects*) Yes, the last time.

RICHARD

(*rubs his hands slowly: then*) With his lips? Or . . . the other way?

BERTHA

Yes, the last time.

RICHARD

Did he ask you to kiss him?

BERTHA

He did.

RICHARD

Did you?

BERTHA

(*hesitates: then looking straight at him*) I did. I kissed him.

RICHARD

What way?

BERTHA

(*with a shrug*) O, simply.

RICHARD

Were you excited?

BERTHA

Well, you can imagine. (*frowning suddenly*) Not much. He has not nice lips . . . . Still I was excited, of course. But not like with you, Dick.

RICHARD

Was he?

BERTHA

Excited? Yes, I think he was. He sighed. He was dreadfully nervous.

RICHARD

(*resting his forehead on his hand*) I see.

BERTHA

(*crosses towards the lounge and stands near him*) Are you jealous?

RICHARD

(*as before*) No.

BERTHA

(*quietly*) You are, Dick.

RICHARD

I am not. Jealous of what?

BERTHA

Because he kissed me.

RICHARD

(*looks up*) Is that all?

BERTHA

Yes, that's all. Except that he asked me would I meet him.

RICHARD

Out somewhere?

BERTHA

No. In his house.

RICHARD

(*surprised*) Over there with his mother, is it?

BERTHA

No, a house he has. He wrote the address for me.

[*She goes to the desk, takes the key from the flower vase, unlocks the drawer and returns to him with the slip of paper*]

RICHARD

(*half to himself*) Our cottage.

BERTHA

(*hands him the slip*) Here.

RICHARD

(*reads it*) Yes. Our cottage.

BERTHA

Your . . .?

RICHARD

No, his. I call it ours. (*looking at her*) The cottage I told you about so often – that we had the two keys for, he and I. It is his now. Where we used to hold our wild nights, talking, drinking, planning – at that time. Wild nights; yes. He and I together. (*he throws the slip on the lounge and rises suddenly*) And sometimes I alone. (*stares at her*) But not quite alone. I told you. You remember?

BERTHA

(*shocked*) That place?

RICHARD

(*walks away from her a few paces and stands still, thinking, holding his chin*) Yes.

BERTHA

(*taking up the slip again*) Where is it?

RICHARD

Do you not know?

BERTHA

He told me to take the tram at Lansdowne road and to ask the man to let me down there. Is it . . . is it a bad place?

RICHARD

O no. Cottages. (*he returns to the lounge and sits down*) What answer did you give?

BERTHA

No answer. He said he would wait.

RICHARD

Tonight?

BERTHA

Every night, he said. Between eight and nine.

RICHARD

And so I am to go tonight to interview – the professor. About the appointment I am to beg for. (*looking at her*) The interview is arranged for tonight by him – between eight and nine. Curious, isn't it? The same hour.

BERTHA

Very.

RICHARD

Did he ask you had I any suspicion?

BERTHA

No.

RICHARD

Did he mention my name?

BERTHA

No.

RICHARD

Not once?

BERTHA

Not that I remember.

RICHARD

(*bounding to his feet*) O yes! Quite clear!

BERTHA

What?

RICHARD

(*striding to and fro*) A liar, a thief and a fool! Quite clear! A common thief! What else? (*with a harsh laugh*) My great friend! A patriot too! A thief – nothing else! (*he halts, thrusting his hands into his pockets*) But a fool also!

BERTHA

(*looking at him*) What are you going to do?

RICHARD

(*shortly*) Follow him. Find him. Tell him. (*calmly*) A few words will do. Thief and fool.

BERTHA

(*flings the slip on the lounge*) I see it all!

RICHARD

(*turning*) Eh?

BERTHA

(*hotly*) The work of a devil!

RICHARD

He?

BERTHA

(*turning on him*) No, you! The work of a devil to turn him against me as you tried to turn my own child against me. Only you did not succeed.

RICHARD

How? In God's name, how?

BERTHA

(*excitedly*) Yes, yes. What I say. Everyone saw it. Whenever I tried to correct him for the least thing you went on with your folly, speaking to him as if he were a grownup man. Ruining the poor child or trying to. Then of course I was the cruel mother and only you loved him. (*with growing excitement*) But you did not turn him against me – against his own mother. Because why? Because the child has too much nature in him.

RICHARD

I never tried to do such a thing, Bertha. You know I cannot be severe with a child.

BERTHA

Because you never loved your own mother. A mother is always a mother, no matter what. I never heard of any human being that did not love the mother that brought him into the world except you.

RICHARD

(*approaching her: quietly*) Bertha, do not say things you will be sorry for. Are you not glad my son is fond of me?

BERTHA

Who taught him to be? Who taught him to run to meet you? Who told him you would bring him home toys when you were out on your rambles in the rain, forgetting all about him – and me? I did. I taught him to love you.

RICHARD

Yes, dear. I know it was you.

BERTHA

(*almost crying*) And then you try to turn everyone against me. All is to be for you. I am to appear false and cruel to everyone except to you. Because you take advantage of my simplicity as you did – the first time.

RICHARD

(*violently*) And you have the courage to say that to me!

BERTHA

(*facing him*) Yes, I have! Both then and now. Because I am simple you think you can do what you like with me. (*gesticulating*) Follow him now. Call him names. Make him be humble before you and make him despise me. Follow him!

RICHARD

(*controlling himself*) You forget that I have allowed you complete liberty – and allow you it still.

BERTHA

(*scornfully*) Liberty!

RICHARD

Yes, complete. But he must know that I know. (*more calmly*) I will speak to him quietly. (*appealing*) Bertha, believe me, dear! It is not jealousy. You have complete liberty to do as you wish – you and he. But not in this way. He will not despise you. You don't wish to deceive me or to pretend to deceive me – with him, do you?

BERTHA

No, I do not. (*looking full at him*) Which of us two is the deceiver?

RICHARD

Of us? You and me?

BERTHA

(*in a calm decided tone*) I know why you have allowed me what you call complete liberty.

RICHARD

Why?

BERTHA

To have complete liberty yourself with – that girl.

RICHARD

(*irritated*) But, good God, you knew about that this long time. I never hid it.

BERTHA

You did. I thought it was a kind of friendship between you – till we came back and then I saw.

RICHARD

So it is, Bertha.

BERTHA

(*shakes her head*) No, no. It is much more and that is why you give me complete liberty. All those things you sit up at night to write about. (*pointing to the study*) In there – about her. You call that friendship!

RICHARD

Believe me, Bertha dear. Believe me as I believe you.

BERTHA

(*with an impulsive gesture*) My God, I feel it! I know it! What else is between you but love?

RICHARD

(*calmly*) You are trying to put that idea into my head but I warn you that I don't take my ideas from other people.

BERTHA

(*hotly*) It is. It is! And that is why you allow him to go on. Of course! It doesn't affect you. You love her.

RICHARD

Love! (*throws out his hands with a sigh and moves away from her*) I cannot argue with you.

BERTHA

You can't because I am right. (*following him a few steps*) What would anyone say?

RICHARD

(*turns on her*) Do you think I care?

BERTHA

But I care. What would he say if he knew? You who talk so much of the high kind of feeling you have for me, expressing yourself in that way to another woman. If he did it or other men I could understand because they are all false pretenders. But you, Dick! Why do you not tell him then?

RICHARD

You can if you like.

BERTHA

I will. Certainly I will.

RICHARD

(*coldly*) He will explain it to you.

BERTHA

He doesn't say one thing and do another. He is honest in his own way.

RICHARD

(*plucks one of the roses and throws it at her feet*) He is, indeed! The soul of honour!

BERTHA

You may make fun of him as much as you like. I understand more than you think about that business. And so will he. Writing those long letters to her for years and she to you. For years. But since I came back I understand it – well.

RICHARD

You do not. Nor would he.

BERTHA

(*laughs scornfully*) Of course. Neither he nor I can understand it. Only she can. Because it is such a deep thing!

RICHARD

(*angrily*) Neither he nor you – nor she either! Not one of you!

BERTHA

(*with great bitterness*) She will! She will understand it! The diseased woman!

[*She turns away and walks over to the little table on the right.* RICHARD *restrains a sudden gesture. A short pause*]

RICHARD

(*gravely*) Bertha, take care of uttering words like that!

BERTHA

(*turning, excitedly*) I don't mean any harm. I feel for her more than you can because I am a woman. I do sincerely. But what I say is true.

RICHARD

Is it generous? Think.

BERTHA

(*pointing towards the garden*) It is she who is not generous. Remember now what I say.

RICHARD

What?

BERTHA

(*comes nearer: in a calmer tone*) You have given that woman very much, Dick. And she may be worthy of it. And she may understand it all too. I know she is that kind.

178

RICHARD

Do you believe that?

BERTHA

I do. But I believe you will get very little from her in return – or
from any of her clan. Remember my words, Dick. Because she is
not generous and they are not generous. Is it all wrong what I am
saying? Is it?

RICHARD

(*darkly*) No. Not all.

[*She stoops and picking up the rose from the floor places it in
the vase again. He watches her.* BRIGID *appears at the
folding doors on the right*]

BRIGID

The tea is on the table, ma'am.

BERTHA

Very well.

BRIGID

Is Master Archie in the garden?

BERTHA

Yes. Call him in.

[BRIGID *crosses the room and goes out into the garden.*
BERTHA *goes towards the doors on the right. At the lounge
she stops and takes up the slip*]

BRIGID

(*in the garden*) Master Archie! You are to come in to your tea.

BERTHA

Am I to go to this place?

179

RICHARD

Do you want to go?

BERTHA

I want to find out what he means. Am I to go?

RICHARD

Why do you ask me? Decide yourself.

BERTHA

Do you tell me to go?

RICHARD

No.

BERTHA

Do you forbid me to go?

RICHARD

No.

BRIGID

(*from the garden*) Come quickly, Master Archie! Your tea is waiting on you.

[BRIGID *crosses the room and goes out through the folding doors.* BERTHA *folds the slip into the waist of her dress and goes slowly towards the right. Near the door she turns and halts*]

BERTHA

Tell me not to go and I will not.

RICHARD

(*without looking at her*) Decide yourself.

BERTHA

Will you blame me then?

RICHARD

(*excitedly*) No, no! I will not blame you. You are free. I cannot blame you.

[ARCHIE *appears at the garden door*]

BERTHA

I did not deceive you.

[*She goes out through the folding doors.* RICHARD *remains standing at the table.* ARCHIE, *when his mother has gone, runs down to* RICHARD]

ARCHIE

(*quickly*) Well, did you ask her?

RICHARD

(*starting*) What?

ARCHIE

Can I go?

RICHARD

Yes.

ARCHIE

In the morning? She said yes?

RICHARD

Yes. In the morning.

[*He puts his arm round his son's shoulders and looks down at him fondly*]

SECOND ACT

[*A room in Robert Hand's cottage at Ranelagh. On the right, forward, a small black piano, on the rest of which is an open piece of music. Farther back a door leading to the street door. In the wall at back folding doors, draped with dark curtains, leading to a bedroom. Near the piano a large table on which is a tall oillamp with a wide yellow shade. Chairs, upholstered, near this table. A small cardtable more forward. Against the back wall a bookcase. In the left wall, back, a window looking out on the garden and, forward, a door and porch also leading to the garden. Easychairs here and there. Plants in the porch and near the draped folding doors. On the walls are many framed black and white designs. In the right corner, back, a sideboard: and in the centre of the room, left of the table, a group consisting of a standing Turkish pipe, a low oilstove which is not lit, and a rocking chair. It is the evening of the same day*].*

[ROBERT HAND, *in evening dress, is seated at the piano. The candles are not lit but the lamp on the table is lit. He plays softly in the bass the first bars of Wolfram's song in the last act of* Tannhäuser. *Then he breaks off and, resting an elbow on the ledge of the keyboard, meditates. Then he rises and, pulling out a pump from behind the piano, walks here and there in the room ejecting from it into the air sprays of perfume. He inhales the air slowly and then puts the pump back behind the piano. He sits down on a chair near the table and, smoothing his hair carefully, sighs once or twice. Then, thrusting his hands into his trouser pockets, he leans back, stretches out his legs and waits.*
A knock is heard at the street door. He rises quickly]

ROBERT

(*exclaims*) Bertha!

[*He hurries out by the door on the right. There is a noise of confused greeting. After a few moments* ROBERT *enters, followed by* RICHARD ROWAN, *who is in grey tweed as before but holds in one hand a dark felt hat and in the other an umbrella*]

ROBERT

First of all let me put these outside.

[*He takes the hat and umbrella, leaves them in the hall and returns*]

ROBERT

(*pulling round a chair*) Here you are. You are lucky to find me in. Why didn't you tell me today? You were always a devil for surprises. I suppose my evocation of the past was too much for your wild blood. See how artistic I have become. (*he points to the walls*) The piano is an addition since your time. I was just strumming out Wagner when you came. Killing time. You see I am ready for the fray. (*laughs*) I was just wondering how you and the vicechancellor were getting on together. (*with exaggerated alarm*) But are you going in that suit? O, well, it doesn't make much odds, I suppose. But how goes the time? (*he takes out his watch*) Twenty past eight already, I declare!

RICHARD

Have you an appointment?

ROBERT

(*laughs nervously*) Suspicious to the last!

RICHARD

Then I may sit down?

ROBERT

Of course, of course. (*they both sit down*) For a few minutes anyhow. Then we can both go on together. We are not bound for time. Between eight and nine he said, didn't he? What time is it, I wonder? (*is about to look again at his watch; then stops*) Twenty past eight, yes.

RICHARD

(*wearily, sadly*) Your appointment also was for the same hour. Here.

ROBERT

What appointment?

RICHARD

With Bertha.

ROBERT

(*stares at him*) Are you mad?

RICHARD

Are you?

ROBERT

(*after a long pause*) Who told you?

RICHARD

She.

[*A short silence*]

ROBERT

(*in a low voice*) Yes. I must have been mad. (*rapidly*) Listen to me, Richard. It is a great relief to me that you have come – the greatest relief. I assure you that ever since this afternoon I have thought and thought how I could break it off without seeming a fool. A great relief! I even intended to send word ... a letter, a few lines. (*suddenly*) But then it was too late ... (*passes his hand over his forehead*) Let me speak frankly, will you? Let me tell you everything.

RICHARD

I know everything. I have known for some time.

ROBERT

Since when?

RICHARD

Since it began between you and her.

ROBERT

(*again rapidly*) Yes, I was mad. But it was merely lightheadedness. I admit that to have asked her here this evening was a mistake. But only a mistake. I can explain everything to you. And I will. Truly.

RICHARD

Explain to me what is the word you longed and never dared to say to her. If you can or will.

ROBERT

(*looks down, then raises his head*) Yes. I will. I admire very much the personality of your ... of .... your wife. That is the word, I can say it. It is no secret.

RICHARD

Then why did you wish to keep secret your wooing?

ROBERT

Wooing?

RICHARD

Your advances to her, little by little, day after day, looks, whispers. (*with a nervous movement of the hands*) Insomma, wooing.

ROBERT

(*bewildered*) But how do you know all this?

RICHARD

She told me.

ROBERT

This afternoon?

RICHARD

No. Time after time, as it happened.

ROBERT

You knew? From her? (RICHARD *nods*) You were watching us all the time?

RICHARD

(*very coldly*) I was watching you.

ROBERT

(*quickly*) I mean, watching me. And you never spoke! You had only to speak a word – to save me from myself. You were trying me. (*passes his hand again over his forehead*) It was a terrible trial. Now also. (*desperately*) Well, it is past. It will be a lesson to me for all my life. You hate me now for what I have done and for. . . .

RICHARD

(*quietly, looking at him*) Have I said that I hate you?

ROBERT

Do you not? You must.

RICHARD

Even if Bertha had not told me I should have known. Did you not see that when I came in this afternoon I went into my study suddenly for a moment?

ROBERT

You did. I remember.

RICHARD

To give you time to recover yourself. It made me sad to see your eyes. And the roses too. I cannot say why. A great mass of overblown roses.

ROBERT

I thought I had to give them. Was that strange? (*looks at* RICHARD *with a tortured expression*) Too many, perhaps? Or too old or common?

RICHARD

That was why I did not hate you. The whole thing made me sad all at once.

ROBERT

(*to himself*) And this is real. It is happening – to us.

[*He stares before him for some moments in silence, as if dazed: then, without turning his head, continues*]

ROBERT

And she too was trying me. Making an experiment with me for your sake?

RICHARD

You know women better than I do. She says she felt pity for you.

ROBERT

(*brooding*) Pitied me because I am no longer ... an ideal lover. Like my roses. Common, old.

RICHARD

Like all men you have a foolish wandering heart.

ROBERT

(*slowly*) Well, you spoke at last. You chose the right moment.

RICHARD

(*leans forward*) Robert, not like this. For us two, no. Years, a whole life, of friendship. Think a moment. Since childhood, boyhood ... No, no. Not in such a way – like thieves – at night. (*glancing about him*) And in such a place. No, Robert, that is not for people like us.

ROBERT

What a lesson! Richard, I cannot tell you what a relief it is to me that you have spoken – that the danger is past. Yes, yes. (*somewhat diffidently*) Because . . . there was some danger for you too, if you think. Was there not?

RICHARD

What danger?

ROBERT

(*in the same tone*) I don't know. I mean if you had not spoken. If you had watched and waited on until. . . .

RICHARD

Until?

ROBERT

(*bravely*) Until I had come to like her more and more (because I can assure you it is only a lightheaded idea of mine), to like her deeply, to love her. Would you have spoken to me then as you have done just now? (RICHARD *is silent*. ROBERT *goes on more boldly*) It would have been different, would it not? For then it might have been too late while it is not too late now. What could I have said then? I could have said only: You are my friend, my dear good friend. I am very sorry but I love her. (*with a sudden fervent gesture*) I love her and I will take her from you however I can because I love her.

[*They look at each other for some moments in silence*]

RICHARD

(*calmly*) That is the language I have heard often and never believed in. Do you mean by stealth or by violence? Steal you could not in my house because the doors were open: nor take by violence if there were no resistance.

ROBERT

You forget that the kingdom of heaven suffers violence: And the kingdom of heaven is like a woman.

RICHARD

(*smiling*) Go on.

ROBERT

(*diffidently but bravely*) Do you think you have rights over her – over her heart?

RICHARD

None.

ROBERT

For what you have done for her? So much! You claim nothing?

RICHARD

Nothing.

ROBERT

(*after a pause strikes his forehead with his hand*) What am I saying? Or what am I thinking? I wish you would upbraid me, curse me, hate me as I deserve. You love this woman. I remember all you told me long ago. She is yours, your work. (*suddenly*) And that is why I too was drawn to her. You are so strong that you attract me even through her.

RICHARD

I am weak.

ROBERT

(*with enthusiasm*) You, Richard! You are the incarnation of strength.

RICHARD

(*holds out his hands*) Feel those hands.

ROBERT

(*taking his hands*) Yes. Mine are stronger. But I meant strength of another kind.

RICHARD

(*gloomily*) I think you would try to take her by violence.

[*He withdraws his hands slowly*]

ROBERT

(*rapidly*) Those are moments of sheer madness when we feel an intense passion for a woman. We see nothing. We think of nothing. Only to possess her. Call it brutal, bestial, what you will.

RICHARD

(*a little timidly*) I am afraid that that longing to possess a woman is not love.

ROBERT

(*impatiently*) No man ever yet lived on this earth who did not long to possess – I mean to possess in the flesh – the woman whom he loves. It is nature's law.

RICHARD

(*contemptuously*) What is that to me? Did I vote it?

ROBERT

But if you love . . . . what else is it?

RICHARD

(*hesitatingly*) To wish her well.

ROBERT

(*warmly*) But the passion which burns us night and day to possess her. You feel it as I do. And it is not what you said now.

RICHARD

Have you . . .? (*he stops for an instant*) Have you the luminous certitude that yours is the brain in contact with which she must think and understand and that yours is the body in contact with which her body must feel? Have you this certitude in yourself?

ROBERT

Have you?

RICHARD

(*moved*) Once I had it, Robert: a certitude as luminous as that of my own existence – or an illusion as luminous.

ROBERT

(*cautiously*) And now?

RICHARD

If you had it and I could feel that you had it – even now. . . .

ROBERT

What would you do?

RICHARD

(*quietly*) Go away. You and not I would be necessary to her. Alone as I was before I met her.

ROBERT

(*rubs his hands nervously*) A nice little load on my conscience!

RICHARD

(*abstractedly*) You met my son when you came to my house this afternoon. He told me. What did you feel?

ROBERT

(*promptly*) Pleasure.

RICHARD

Nothing else?

ROBERT

Nothing else. Unless I thought of two things at the same time. I am like that. If my best friend lay in his coffin and his face had a comic expression I should smile. (*with a little gesture of despair*) I am like that. But I should suffer too, deeply.

RICHARD

You spoke of conscience . . . . did he seem to you a child only – or an angel?

ROBERT

(*shakes his head*) No. Neither an angel nor an Anglo-Saxon. Two things, by the way, for which I have very little sympathy.

RICHARD

Never then? Never even . . . with her? Tell me. I wish to know.

ROBERT

I feel in my heart something different. I believe that on the last day (if it ever comes) when we are all assembled together that the Almighty will speak to us like this. We will say that we lived chastely with one other creature. . . .

RICHARD

(*bitterly*) Lie to Him?

ROBERT

Or that we tried to. And He will say to us: Fools! Who told you that you were to give yourselves to one being only? You were made to give yourselves to many freely. I wrote that law with My finger on your hearts.

RICHARD

On woman's heart too?

ROBERT

Yes. Can we close our heart against an affection which we feel deeply? Should we close it? Should she?

RICHARD

We are speaking of bodily union.

ROBERT

Affection between man and woman must come to that. We think

too much of it because our minds are warped. For us today it is of no more consequence than any other form of contact – than a kiss.

RICHARD

If it is of no consequence why are you dissatisfied till you reach that end? Why were you waiting here tonight?

ROBERT

Passion tends to go as far as it can. But, you may believe me or not, I had not that in my mind – to reach that end.

RICHARD

Reach it if you can. I will use no arm against you that the world puts in my hand. If the law which God's finger has written on our hearts is the law you say I too am God's creature.

[*He rises and paces to and fro for some moments in silence. Then he goes towards the porch and leans against the jamb.* ROBERT *watches him*]

ROBERT

I always felt it. In myself and in others.

RICHARD

(*absently*) Yes?

ROBERT

(*with a vague gesture*) For all. That a woman too has the right to try with many men until she finds love. An immoral idea, is it not? I wanted to write a book about it. I began it . . .

RICHARD

(*as before*) Yes?

ROBERT

Yes. Because I knew a woman who seemed to me to be doing that

– carrying out that idea in her own life. She interested me very much.

RICHARD

When was this?

ROBERT

O, not lately. When you were away.

[RICHARD *leaves his place rather abruptly and again paces to and fro*]

ROBERT

You see I am more honest than you thought.

RICHARD

I wish you had not thought of her now – whoever she was or is.

ROBERT

(*easily*) She was and is the wife of a stockbroker.

RICHARD

(*turning*) You know him?

ROBERT

Intimately.

[RICHARD *sits down again in the same place and leans forward, his head on his hands*]

ROBERT

(*moving his chair a little closer*) May I ask you a question?

RICHARD

You may.

ROBERT

(*with some hesitation*) Has it never happened to you in these years – I mean when you were away from her, perhaps, or travelling –

to .... betray her with another. Betray her, I mean, not in love. Carnally, I mean .... Has that never happened?

RICHARD

It has.

ROBERT

And what did you do?

RICHARD

I remember the first time. I came home. It was night. My house was silent. My little son was sleeping in his cot. She too was asleep. I wakened her from sleep and told her. I cried beside her bed: and I pierced her heart.

ROBERT

O, Richard, why did you do that?

RICHARD

Betray her?

ROBERT

No. But tell her, waken her from sleep to tell her. It was piercing her heart.

RICHARD

She must know me as I am.

ROBERT

But that is not you as you are. A moment of weakness.

RICHARD

(*lost in thought*) And I was feeding the flame of her innocence with my guilt.

ROBERT

(*brusquely*) O, don't talk of guilt and innocence. You have made her all that she is. A strange and wonderful personality – in my eyes, at least.

RICHARD

(*darkly*) Or I have killed her.

ROBERT

Killed her?

RICHARD

The virginity of her soul.

ROBERT

(*impatiently*) Well lost! What would she be without you?

RICHARD

I tried to give her a new life.

ROBERT

And you have. A new and rich life.

RICHARD

Is it worth what I have taken from her – her girlhood, her laughter, her young beauty, the hopes in her young heart?

ROBERT

(*firmly*) Yes. Well worth it. (*he looks at* RICHARD *for some moments in silence*) If you had neglected her, lived wildly, brought her away so far only to make her suffer . . . .

[*He stops.* RICHARD *raises his head and looks at him*]

RICHARD

If I had?

ROBERT

(*slightly confused*) You know there were rumours here of your life abroad – a wild life. Some persons who knew you or met you or heard of you in Rome. Lying rumours.

RICHARD

(*coldly*) Continue.

ROBERT

(*laughs a little harshly*) Even I at times thought of her as a victim. (*smoothly*) And of course, Richard, I felt and knew all the time that you were a man of great talent – of something more than talent. And that was your excuse – a valid one in my eyes.

RICHARD

Have you thought that it is perhaps now – at this moment – that I am neglecting her? (*he clasps his hands nervously and leans across towards* ROBERT) I may be silent still. And she may yield to you at last – wholly and many times.

ROBERT

(*draws back at once*) My dear Richard, my dear friend, I swear to you I could not make you suffer.

RICHARD

(*continuing*) You may then know in soul and body, in a hundred forms, and ever restlessly, what some old theologian, Duns Scotus, I think, called a death of the spirit.

ROBERT

(*eagerly*) A death. No: its affirmation! A death! The supreme instant of life from which all coming life proceeds, the eternal law of nature herself.

RICHARD

And that other law of nature, as you call it: change. How will it be when you turn against her and against me, when her beauty, or what seems so to you now, wearies you and my affection for you seems false and odious?

ROBERT

That will never be. Never.

RICHARD

And you turn even against yourself for having known me or trafficked with us both?

ROBERT

(*gravely*) It will never be like that, Richard. Be sure of that.

RICHARD

(*contemptuously*) I care very little whether it is or not because there is something I fear much more.

ROBERT

(*shakes his head*) You fear? I disbelieve you, Richard. Since we were boys together I have followed your mind. You do not know what moral fear is.

RICHARD

(*lays his hand on his arm*) Listen. She is dead. She lies on my bed. I look at her body which I betrayed – grossly and many times. And loved too and wept over. And I know that her body was always my loyal slave. To me, to me only she gave .... (*he breaks off and turns aside, unable to speak*)

ROBERT

(*softly*) Do not suffer, Richard. There is no need. She is loyal to you, body and soul. Why do you fear?

RICHARD

(*turns towards him, almost fiercely*) Not that fear. But that I will reproach myself then for having taken all for myself because I would not suffer her to give to another what was hers and not mine to give, because I accepted from her her loyalty and made her life poorer in love. That is my fear. That I stand between her and any moments of life that should be hers, between her and you, between her and anyone, between her and anything. I will not do it. I cannot and I will not. I dare not.

[*He leans back in his chair breathless, with shining eyes.* ROBERT *rises quietly and stands behind his chair*]

ROBERT

Look here, Richard. We have said all there is to be said. Let the past be past.

RICHARD

(*quickly and harshly*) Wait. One thing more. For you too must know me as I am – now.

ROBERT

More? Is there more?

RICHARD

I told you that when I saw your eyes this afternoon I felt sad. Your humility and confusion, I felt, united you to me in brotherhood. (*he half turns round towards him*) At that moment I felt our whole life together in the past and I longed to put my arm around your neck.

ROBERT

(*deeply and suddenly touched*) It is noble of you, Richard, to forgive me like this.

RICHARD

(*struggling with himself*) I told you that I wished you not to do anything false and secret against me – against our friendship, against her; not to steal her from me, craftily, secretly, meanly – in the dark, in the night – you, Robert, my friend.

ROBERT

I know. And it was noble of you.

RICHARD

(*looks up at him with a steady gaze*) No. Not noble. Ignoble.

ROBERT

(*makes an involuntary gesture*) How? Why?

RICHARD

(*looks away again: in a lower voice*) That is what I must tell you too. Because in the very core of my ignoble heart I longed to be betrayed by you and by her – in the dark, in the night – secretly, meanly, craftily. By you, my best friend, and by her. I longed for that passionately and ignobly, to be dishonoured for ever in love and in lust, to be . . . .

ROBERT

(*bending down, places his hands over* RICHARD's *mouth*) Enough. Enough. (*he takes his hands away*) But no. Go on.

RICHARD

To be for ever a shameful creature and to build up my soul again out of the ruins of its shame.

ROBERT

And that is why you wished that she . . . .

RICHARD

(*with calm*) She has spoken always of her innocence as I have spoken always of my guilt, humbling me.

ROBERT

From pride, then?

RICHARD

From pride and from ignoble longing. And from a motive deeper still.

ROBERT

(*with decision*) I understand you.

> [*He returns to his place and begins to speak at once, drawing his chair closer*]

ROBERT

May it not be that we are here and now in the presence of a
moment which will free us both – me as well as you – from the
last bonds of what is called morality? My friendship for you has
laid bonds on me.

RICHARD

Light bonds, apparently.

ROBERT

I acted in the dark, secretly. I will do so no longer. Have you the
courage to allow me to act freely?

RICHARD

A duel – between us?

ROBERT

(*with growing excitement*) A battle of both our souls, different as
they are, against all that is false in them and in the world. A battle
of your soul against the spectre of fidelity, of mine against the
spectre of friendship. All life is a conquest, the victory of human
passion over the commandments of cowardice. Will you, Richard?
Have you the courage? Even if it shatters to atoms the friendship
between us, even if it breaks up for ever the last illusion in your
own life? There was an eternity before we were born: another will
come after we are dead. The blinding instant of passion alone –
passion, free, unashamed, irresistible – that is the only gate by
which we can escape the misery of what slaves call life. Is not this
the language of your own youth that I heard so often from you in
this very place where we are sitting now? Have you changed?

RICHARD

(*passes his hand across his brow*) Yes. It is the language of my
youth.

ROBERT

(*eagerly, intensely*) Richard, you have driven me up to this point.

She and I have only obeyed your will. You yourself have roused these words in my brain. Your own words. Shall we? Freely? Together?

RICHARD

(*mastering his emotion*) Together no. Fight your part alone. I will not free you. Leave me to fight mine.

ROBERT

(*rises, decided*) You allow me then?

RICHARD

(*rises also, calmly*) Free yourself.

[*A knock is heard at the hall door*]

ROBERT

(*in alarm*) What does this mean?

RICHARD

(*calmly*) Bertha evidently. Did you not ask her to come?

ROBERT

Yes, but . . . (*looking about him*) Then I am going, Richard.

RICHARD

No. I am going.

ROBERT

(*desperately*) Richard, I appeal to you. Let me go. It is over. She is yours. Keep her and forgive me, both of you.

RICHARD

Because you are generous enough to allow me?

ROBERT

(*hotly*) Richard, you will make me angry with you if you say that.

RICHARD

Angry or not I will not live on your generosity. You have asked her to meet you here tonight and alone. Solve the question between you.

ROBERT

(*promptly*) Open the door. I shall wait in the garden. (*he goes towards the porch*) Explain to her, Richard, as best you can. I cannot see her now.

RICHARD

I shall go, I tell you. Wait out there if you wish.

[*He goes out by the door on the right.* ROBERT *goes out hastily through the porch but comes back the same instant*]

ROBERT

An umbrella! (*with a sudden gesture*) O!

[*He goes out again through the porch. The hall door is heard to open and close.* RICHARD *enters followed by* BERTHA, *who is dressed in a dark brown costume and wears a small dark red hat. She has neither umbrella nor waterproof*]

RICHARD

(*gaily*) Welcome back to old Ireland!

BERTHA

(*nervously, seriously*) Is this the place?

RICHARD

Yes, it is. How did you find it?

BERTHA

I told the cabman. I didn't like to ask my way. (*looking about her curiously*) Was he not waiting? Has he gone away?

RICHARD

(*points towards the garden*) He is waiting. Out there. He was waiting when I came.

BERTHA

(*selfpossessed again*) You see you came after all.

RICHARD

Did you think I would not?

BERTHA

I knew you could not remain away. You see, after all you are like all other men. You had to come. You are jealous like the others.

RICHARD

You seem annoyed to find me here.

BERTHA

What happened between you?

RICHARD

I told him I knew everything, that I had known for a long time. He asked how. I said from you.

BERTHA

Does he hate me?

RICHARD

I cannot read in his heart.

BERTHA

(*sits down helplessly*) Yes. He hates me. He believes I made a fool of him – betrayed him. I knew he would.

RICHARD

I told him you were sincere with him.

BERTHA

He does not believe it. Nobody would believe it. I should have told him first – not you.

RICHARD

I thought he was a common robber, prepared to use even violence against you. I had to protect you from that.

BERTHA

That I could have done myself.

RICHARD

Are you sure?

BERTHA

It would have been enough to have told him that you knew I was here. Now I can find out nothing. He hates me. He is right to hate me. I have treated him badly, shamefully.

RICHARD

(*takes her hand*) Bertha, look at me.

BERTHA

(*turns to him*) Well?

RICHARD

(*gazes into her eyes and then lets her hand fall*) I cannot read in your heart either.

BERTHA

(*still looking at him*) You could not remain away. Do you not trust me? You can see I am quite calm. I could have hidden it all from you.

RICHARD

I doubt that.

BERTHA

(*with a slight toss of her head*) O, easily if I had wanted to.

RICHARD

(*darkly*) Perhaps you are sorry now that you did not.

BERTHA

Perhaps I am.

RICHARD

(*unpleasantly*) What a fool you were to tell me! It would have been so nice if you had kept it secret.

BERTHA

As you do, no?

RICHARD

As I do, yes. (*he turns to go*) Goodbye for a while.

BERTHA

(*alarmed, rises*) Are you going?

RICHARD

Naturally. My part is ended here.

BERTHA

To her, I suppose?

RICHARD

(*astonished*) Who?

BERTHA

Her ladyship. I suppose it is all planned so that you may have a good opportunity. To meet her and have an intellectual conversation!

RICHARD

(*with an outburst of rude anger*) To meet the devil's father!

BERTHA

(*unpins her hat and sits down*) Very well. You can go. Now I know what to do.

RICHARD

(*returns, approaches her*) You don't believe a word of what you say.

206

BERTHA

(*calmly*) You can go. Why don't you?

RICHARD

Then you have come here and led him on in this way on account of me. Is that how it is?

BERTHA

There is one person in all this who is not a fool. And that is you. I am though. And he is.

RICHARD

(*continuing*) If so you have indeed treated him badly and shamefully.

BERTHA

(*points at him*) Yes. But it was your fault. And I will end it now. I am simply a tool for you. You have no respect for me. You never had because I did what I did.

RICHARD

And has he respect?

BERTHA

He has. Of all the persons I met since I came back he is the only one who has. And he knows what they only suspect. And that is why I liked him from the first and like him still. Great respect for me she has! Why did you not ask her to come away with you nine years ago?

RICHARD

You know why, Bertha. Ask yourself.

BERTHA

Yes, I know why. You knew the answer you would get. That is why.

RICHARD

That is not why. I did not even ask you.

BERTHA

Yes. You knew I would go, asked or not. I do things. But if I do one thing I can do two things. As I have the name I can have the gains.

RICHARD

(*with increasing excitement*) Bertha, I accept what is to be. I have trusted you. I will trust you still.

BERTHA

To have that against me. To leave me then. (*almost passionately*) Why do you not defend me then against him? Why do you go away from me now without a word? Dick, my God, tell me what you wish me to do?

RICHARD

I cannot, dear. (*struggling with himself*) Your own heart will tell you. (*he seizes both her hands*) I have a wild delight in my soul, Bertha, as I look at you. I see you as you are yourself. That I came first in your life or before him then – that may be nothing to you. You may be his more than mine.

BERTHA

I am not. Only I feel for him too.

RICHARD

And I do too. You may be his and mine. I will trust you, Bertha, and him too. I must. I cannot hate him since his arms have been around you. You have drawn us near together. There is something wiser than wisdom in your heart. Who am I that I should call myself master of your heart or of any woman's? Bertha, love him, be his, give yourself to him if you desire – or if you can.

BERTHA

(*dreamily*) I will remain.

RICHARD

Goodbye.

[*He lets her hands fall and goes out rapidly on the right.*
BERTHA *remains sitting. Then she rises and goes timidly
towards the porch. She stops near it and, after a little
hesitation, calls into the garden*]

BERTHA

Is anyone out there?

[*At the same time she retreats towards the middle of the
room. Then she calls again in the same way*]

BERTHA

Is anyone there?

[ROBERT *appears in the open doorway that leads in from the
garden. His coat is buttoned and the collar is turned up. He
holds the doorposts with his hands lightly and waits for*
BERTHA *to see him*]

BERTHA

(*catching sight of him, starts back: then quietly*) Robert!

ROBERT

Are you alone?

BERTHA

Yes.

ROBERT

(*looking towards the door on the right*) Where is he?

BERTHA

Gone. (*nervously*) You startled me. Where did you come from?

ROBERT

(*with a movement of his head*) Out there. Did he not tell you I
was out there – waiting?

BERTHA

(*quickly*) Yes, he told me. But I was afraid here alone. With the door open, waiting. (*she comes to the table and rests her hand on the corner*) Why do you stand like that in the doorway?

ROBERT

Why? I am afraid too.

BERTHA

Of what?

ROBERT

Of you.

BERTHA

(*looks down*) Do you hate me now?

ROBERT

I fear you. (*clasping his hands at his back, quietly but a little defiantly*) I fear a new torture – a new trap.

BERTHA

(*as before*) For what do you blame me?

ROBERT

(*comes forward a few steps, halts: then impulsively*) Why did you lead me on? Day after day, more and more. Why did you not stop me? You could have – with a word. But not even a word! I forgot myself and him. You saw it. That I was ruining myself in his eyes, losing his friendship. Did you want me to?

BERTHA

(*looking up*) You never asked me.

ROBERT

Asked you what?

BERTHA

If he suspected – or knew.

ROBERT

And would you have told me?

BERTHA

Yes.

ROBERT

(*hesitatingly*) Did you tell him – everything?

BERTHA

I did.

ROBERT

I mean – details?

BERTHA

Everything.

ROBERT

(*with a forced smile*) I see. You were making an experiment for his sake. On me. Well, why not? It seems I was a good subject. Still, it was a little cruel of you.

BERTHA

Try to understand me, Robert. You must try.

ROBERT

(*with a polite gesture*) Well, I will try.

BERTHA

Why do you stand like that near the door? It makes me nervous to look at you.

ROBERT

I am trying to understand. And then I am afraid.

BERTHA

(*holds out her hand*) You need not be afraid.

[ROBERT *comes towards her quickly and takes her hand*]

ROBERT

(*diffidently*) Used you to laugh over me – together? (*drawing his hand away*) But now I must be good or you may laugh over me again – tonight.

BERTHA

(*distressed, lays her hand on his arm*) Please listen to me, Robert .... But you are all wet, drenched! (*she passes her hands over his coat*) O you poor fellow! Out there in the rain all that time! I forgot that.

ROBERT

(*laughs*) Yes, you forgot the climate.

BERTHA

But you are really drenched. You must change your coat.

ROBERT

(*takes her hands*) Tell me, it is pity then that you feel for me, as he – as Richard – says?

BERTHA

Please change your coat, Robert, when I ask you. You might get a very bad cold from that. Do please.

ROBERT

What would it matter now?

BERTHA

(*looking round her*) Where do you keep your clothes here?

ROBERT

(*points to the door at the back*) In there. I fancy I have a jacket here. (*maliciously*) In my bedroom.

BERTHA

Well go in and take that off.

ROBERT

And you?

BERTHA

I will wait here for you.

ROBERT

Do you command me to?

BERTHA

(*laughing*) Yes I command you.

ROBERT

(*promptly*) Then I will. (*he goes quickly towards the bedroom door; then turns round*) You won't go away?

BERTHA

No. I will wait. But don't be long.

ROBERT

Only a moment.

[*He goes into the bedroom, leaving the door open.* BERTHA *looks curiously about her and then glances in indecision towards the door at the back*]

ROBERT

(*from the bedroom*) You have not gone?

BERTHA

No.

ROBERT

I am in the dark here. I must light the lamp.

[*He is heard striking a match and putting a glass shade on a lamp. A pink light comes in through the doorway.* BERTHA *glances at her watch at her wristlet and then sits at the table*]

ROBERT

(*as before*) Do you like the effect of the light?

BERTHA

O yes.

ROBERT

Can you admire it from where you are?

BERTHA

Yes, quite well.

ROBERT

It was for you.

BERTHA

(*confused*) I am not worthy even of that.

ROBERT

(*clearly, harshly*) Love's labour lost.

BERTHA

(*rising nervously*) Robert!

ROBERT

Yes?

BERTHA

Come here quickly! Quickly, I say!

ROBERT

I am ready.

[*He appears in the doorway, wearing a dark green velvet jacket. Seeing her agitation he comes quickly towards her*]

ROBERT

What is it, Bertha?

BERTHA

(*trembling*) I was afraid.

ROBERT

Of being alone?

BERTHA

(*catches his hands*) You know what I mean. My nerves are all upset.

ROBERT

That I . . .?

BERTHA

Promise me, Robert, not to think of such a thing. Never. If you like me at all. I thought that moment . . . .

ROBERT

What an idea!

BERTHA

But promise me if you like me.

ROBERT

If I like you, Bertha! I promise. Of course I promise. You are trembling all over.

BERTHA

Let me sit down somewhere. It will pass in a moment.

ROBERT

My poor Bertha! Sit down. Come.

[*He leads her towards a chair near the table. She sits down. He stands beside her*]

ROBERT

(*after a short pause*) Has it passed?

BERTHA

Yes. It was only a moment. I was very silly. I was afraid that . . . . I wanted to see you near me.

ROBERT

That . . . that you made me promise not to think of?

BERTHA

Yes.

ROBERT

(*keenly*) Or something else?

BERTHA

(*helplessly*) Robert, I feared something. I am not sure what.

ROBERT

And now?

BERTHA

Now you are here. I can see you. O, now it has passed.

ROBERT

(*with resignation*) Passed. Yes. Love's labour lost.

BERTHA

(*looks up at him*) Listen, Robert. I want to explain to you about that. I could not deceive Dick. Never. In nothing. I told him everything – from the first. Then it went on and on: and still you never spoke or asked me. I wanted you to.

ROBERT

Is that the truth, Bertha?

BERTHA

Yes, because it annoyed me that you could think I was like ... like the other women I suppose you knew that way. I think that Dick is right too. Why should there be secrets?

ROBERT

(*softly*) Still, secrets can be very sweet. Can they not?

BERTHA

(*smiles*) Yes, I know they can. But, you see, I could not keep things secret from Dick. Besides, what is the good? They always come out in the end. Is it not better for people to know?

ROBERT

(*softly and a little shyly*) How could you, Bertha, tell him everything? Did you? Every single thing that passed between us?

BERTHA

Yes. Everything he asked me.

ROBERT

Did he ask you – much?

BERTHA

You know the kind he is. He asks about everything. The ins and outs.

ROBERT

About our kissing too?

BERTHA

Of course. I told him all.

ROBERT

(*shakes his head slowly*) Extraordinary little person! Were you not ashamed?

BERTHA

No.

ROBERT

Not a bit?

BERTHA

No. Why? Is that terrible?

ROBERT

And how did he take it? Tell me. I want to know everything too.

BERTHA

(*laughs*) It excited him. More than usual.

ROBERT

Why? Is he excitable – still?

BERTHA

(*archly*) Yes, very. When he is not lost in his philosophy.

ROBERT

More than I?

BERTHA

More than you? (*reflecting*) How could I answer that? You both are, I suppose.

[ROBERT *turns aside and gazes towards the porch, passing his hand once or twice thoughtfully over his hair*]

BERTHA

(*gently*) Are you angry with me again?

218

ROBERT

(*moodily*) You are with me.

BERTHA

No, Robert. Why should I be?

ROBERT

Because I asked you to come to this place. I tried to prepare it for you. (*he points vaguely here and there*) A sense of quietness.

BERTHA

(*touching his jacket with her fingers*) And this too. Your nice velvet coat.

ROBERT

Also. I will keep no secrets from you.

BERTHA

You remind me of someone in a picture. I like you in it . . . . But you are not angry, are you?

ROBERT

(*darkly*) Yes. That was my mistake. To ask you to come here. I felt it when I looked at you from the garden and saw you – you, Bertha – standing here. (*hopelessly*) But what else could I have done?

BERTHA

(*quietly*) You mean because others have been here?

ROBERT

Yes.

[*He walks away from her a few paces. A gust of wind makes the lamp on the table flicker. He lowers the wick slightly*]

BERTHA

(*following him with her eyes*) But I knew that before I came. I am
not angry with you for it.

ROBERT

(*shrugs his shoulders*) Why should you be angry with me after all?
You are not even angry with him – for the same thing – or worse.

BERTHA

Did he tell you that about himself?

ROBERT

Yes. He told me. We all confess to one another here. Turn about.

BERTHA

I try to forget it.

ROBERT

It does not trouble you?

BERTHA

Not now. Only I dislike to think of it.

ROBERT

It is merely something brutal, you think? Of little importance?

BERTHA

It does not trouble me – now.

ROBERT

(*looking at her over his shoulder*) But there is something that
would trouble you very much and that you would not try to
forget.

BERTHA

What?

ROBERT

(*turning towards her*) If it were not only something brutal – with this person or that – for a few moments. If it were something fine and spiritual – with one person only – with one woman. (*smiles*) And perhaps brutal too. It usually comes to that sooner or later. Would you try to forget and forgive that?

BERTHA

(*toying with her wristlet*) In whom?

ROBERT

In anyone. In me.

BERTHA

(*calmly*) You mean in Dick.

ROBERT

I said in myself. But would you?

BERTHA

You think I would revenge myself? Is Dick not to be free too?

ROBERT

(*points at her*) That is not from your heart, Bertha.

BERTHA

(*proudly*) Yes, it is. Let him be free too. He leaves me free also.

ROBERT

(*insistently*) And you know why? And understand? And you like it? And you want to be? And it makes you happy? And has made you happy? Always? This gift of freedom which he gave you – nine years ago?

BERTHA

(*gazing at him with wideopen eyes*) But why do you ask me such a lot of questions, Robert?

ROBERT

(*stretches out both hands to her*) Because I had another gift to offer you then – a common simple gift – like myself. If you want to know it I will tell you.

BERTHA

(*looking at her watch*) Past is past, Robert. And I think I ought to go now. It is nine almost.

ROBERT

(*impetuously*) No, no. Not yet. There is one confession more. And we have the right to speak.

[*He crosses before the table rapidly and sits beside her*]

BERTHA

(*turning towards him, places her left hand on his shoulder*) Yes, Robert. I know that you like me. You need not tell me. (*kindly*) You need not confess any more tonight.

[*A gust of wind enters through the porch with a sound of moving leaves. The lamp flickers quickly*]

BERTHA

(*pointing over his shoulder*) Look! It is too high.

[*Without rising he bends towards the table and turns down the wick more. The room is half dark. The light comes in more strongly through the doorway of the bedroom*]

ROBERT

The wind is rising. I will close that door.

BERTHA

(*listening*) No, it is raining still. It was only a gust of wind.

ROBERT

(*touches her shoulder*) Tell me if the air is too cold for you. (*half rising*) I will close it.

BERTHA

(*detaining him*) No. I am not cold. Besides I am going now.
Robert. I must.

ROBERT

(*firmly*) No, no. There is no *must* now. We were left here for this.
And you are wrong, Bertha. The past is not past. It is present here
now. My feeling for you is the same now as it was then because
then – you slighted it.

BERTHA

No, Robert. I did not.

ROBERT

(*continuing*) You did. And I have felt it all these years without
knowing it – till now. Even while I lived – the kind of life you know
and dislike to think of – the kind of life to which you condemned me.

BERTHA

I?

ROBERT

Yes, when you slighted the common simple gift I had to offer you
– and took his gift instead.

BERTHA

(*looking at him*) But you never. . . .

ROBERT

No. Because you had chosen him. I saw that. I saw it on the first
night we met, we three together. Why did you choose him?

BERTHA

(*bends her head*) Is that not love?

ROBERT

(*continuing*) And every night when we two – he and I – came to

223

that corner to meet you I saw it and felt it. You remember the corner, Bertha?

BERTHA

(*as before*) Yes.

ROBERT

And when you and he went away together for your walk and I went along the street alone I felt it. And when he spoke to me about you and told me he was going away – then most of all.

BERTHA

Why then most of all?

ROBERT

Because it was then that I was guilty of my first treason towards him.

BERTHA

Robert, what are you saying? Your first treason? Against Dick?

ROBERT

(*nods*) And not my last. He spoke of you and himself. Of how your life would be together – free and all that. Free, yes! He would not even ask you to go with him. (*bitterly*) He did not. And you went all the same.

BERTHA

I wanted to be with him. You know . . . (*raising her head and looking at him*) You know how we were then – Dick and I.

ROBERT

(*unheeding*) I advised him to go alone – not to take you with him – to live alone in order to see if what he felt for you was a passing thing which might ruin your happiness and his career.

BERTHA

Well, Robert. It was unkind of you towards me. But I forgive you because you were thinking of his happiness and mine.

ROBERT

(*bending closer to her*) No, Bertha. I was not. And that was my treason. I was thinking of myself – that you might turn from him when he had gone and he from you. Then I would have offered you my gift. You know what it was now. The simple common gift that men offer to women. Not the best perhaps. Best or worst – it would have been yours.

BERTHA

(*turning away from him*) He did not take your advice.

ROBERT

(*as before*) No. And the night you ran away together – O, how happy I was!

BERTHA

(*pressing his hands*) Keep calm, Robert. I know you liked me always. Why did you not forget me?

ROBERT

(*smiles bitterly*) How happy I felt as I came back along the quays and saw in the distance the boat lit up, going down the black river, taking you away from me! (*in a calmer tone*) But why did you choose him? Did you not like me at all?

BERTHA

Yes. I liked you because you were his friend. We often spoke about you. Often and often. Every time you wrote or sent papers or books to Dick. And I like you still, Robert. (*looking into his eyes*) I never forgot you.

ROBERT

Nor I you. I knew I would see you again. I knew it the night you went away – that you would come back. And that was why I wrote and worked – to see you again – here.

BERTHA

And here I am. You were right.

ROBERT

(*slowly*) Nine years. Nine times more beautiful!

BERTHA

(*smiling*) But am I? What do you see in me?

ROBERT

(*gazing at her*) A strange and beautiful lady.

BERTHA

(*almost disgusted*) O, please don't call me such a thing!

ROBERT

(*earnestly*) You are more. A young and beautiful queen.

BERTHA

(*with a sudden laugh*) O Robert!

ROBERT

(*lowering his voice and bending nearer to her*) But do you not know that you are a beautiful human being? Do you not know that you have a beautiful body? Beautiful and young!

BERTHA

(*gravely*) Some day I will be old.

ROBERT

(*shakes his head*) I cannot imagine it. Tonight you are young and beautiful. Tonight you have come back to me. (*with passion*) Who knows what will be tomorrow? I may never see you again or never see you as I do now.

BERTHA

Would you suffer?

ROBERT

(*looks round the room, without answering*) This room and this hour were made for your coming. When you have gone – all is gone.

BERTHA

(*anxiously*) But you will see me again, Robert . . . As before.

ROBERT

(*looks full at her*) To make him – Richard – suffer.

BERTHA

He does not suffer.

ROBERT

(*bowing his head*) Yes, yes. He does.

BERTHA

He knows we like each other. Is there any harm then?

ROBERT

(*raising his head*) No, there is no harm. Why should we not? He does not know yet what I feel. He has left us alone here at night at this hour because he longs to know it – he longs to be delivered.

BERTHA

From what?

ROBERT

(*moves closer to her and presses her arm as he speaks*) From every law, Bertha, from every bond. All his life he has fought to deliver himself. Every chain but one he has broken and that one we are to break, Bertha – you and I.

BERTHA

(*almost inaudibly*) Are you sure?

ROBERT

(*still more warmly*) I am sure that no law made by man is sacred before the impulse of passion. (*almost fiercely*) Who made us for one only? It is a crime against our own being if we are so. There is no law before impulse. Laws are for slaves. Bertha, say my name! Let me hear your voice say it. Softly!

BERTHA

(*softly*) Robert!

ROBERT

(*puts his arm about her shoulders*) Only the impulse towards youth and beauty does not die. (*he points towards the porch*) Listen!

BERTHA

(*in alarm*) What?

ROBERT

The rain falling. Summer rain on the earth. Night rain. The darkness and warmth and flood of passion. Tonight the earth is loved – loved and possessed. Her lover's arms are round her: and she is silent. Speak, dearest!

BERTHA

(*suddenly leans forward and listens intently*) Hush!

ROBERT

(*listening, smiles*) Nothing. Nobody. We are alone.

> [*A gust of wind blows in through the porch with the sound of shaken leaves. The flame of the lamp leaps*]

BERTHA

(*pointing to the lamp*) Look!

ROBERT

Only wind. We have light enough from the other room.

[*He stretches his hand across the table and puts out the lamp. The light from the doorway of the bedroom crosses the place where they sit. The room is quite dark*]

ROBERT

Are you happy? Tell me.

BERTHA

I am going now, Robert. It is very late. Be satisfied.

ROBERT

(*caressing her hair*) Not yet, not yet. Tell me, do you love me a little?

BERTHA

I like you, Robert. I think you are good. (*half rising*) Are you satisfied?

ROBERT

(*detaining her, kisses her hair*) Do not go, Bertha! There is time still. Do you love me too? I have waited a long time. Do you love us both – him and also me? Do you, Bertha? The truth! Tell me. Tell me with your eyes. Or speak!

[*She does not answer. In the silence the rain is heard falling*]

THIRD ACT

[*The drawingroom of Richard Rowan's house at Merrion. The folding doors at the right are closed and also the double doors leading to the garden. The green plush curtains are drawn across the window on the left. The room is half dark.*

It is early in the morning of the next day. Bertha sits beside the window, looking out between the curtains. She wears a loose saffron dressing gown. Her hair is combed loosely over the ears and knotted at the neck. Her hands are folded in her lap. Her face is pale and drawn. BRIGID *comes in through the folding doors on the right with a featherbroom and duster. She is about to cross but, seeing* BERTHA, *she halts suddenly and blesses herself instinctively*]

BRIGID

Merciful hour, ma'am! You put the heart across me. Why did you get up so early?

BERTHA

What time is it?

BRIGID

After seven, ma'am. Are you long up?

BERTHA

Some time.

BRIGID

(*approaching her*) Had you a bad dream that woke you?

BERTHA

I didn't sleep all night. So I got up to see the sun rise.

BRIGID

(*opens the double doors*) It's a lovely morning now after all the rain we had. (*turns round*) But you must be dead tired, ma'am. What will the master say at your doing a thing like that? (*she goes to the door of the study and knocks*) Master Richard!

BERTHA

(*looks round*) He is not there. He went out an hour ago.

BRIGID

Out there, on the strand, is it?

BERTHA

Yes.

BRIGID

(*comes towards her and leans over the back of a chair*) Are you fretting yourself, ma'am, about anything?

BERTHA

No, Brigid.

BRIGID

Don't be. He was always like that, meandering off by himself somewhere. He's a curious bird, Master Richard, and always was. Sure there isn't a turn in him I don't know. Are you fretting now maybe because he does be in there (*pointing to the study*) half the night at his books? Leave him alone. He'll come back to you again. Sure he thinks the sun shines out of your face, ma'am.

BERTHA

(*sadly*) That time is gone.

BRIGID

(*confidentially*) And good cause I have to remember it – that time when he was paying his addresses to you. (*she sits down beside* BERTHA: *in a lower voice*) Do you know that he used to tell me all about you and nothing to his mother, God rest her soul? Your letters and all.

BERTHA

What? My letters to him!

BRIGID

(*delighted*) Yes. I can see him sitting on the kitchen table, swinging his legs and spinning out of him yards of talk about you and him and Ireland and all kinds of devilment – to an ignorant old woman like me. But that was always his way. But if he had to meet a grand highup person he'd be twice as grand himself. (*suddenly looks at* BERTHA) Is it crying you are now? Ah sure, don't cry. There's good times coming still.

BERTHA

No, Brigid, that time comes only once in a lifetime. The rest of life is good for nothing except to remember that time.

BRIGID

(*is silent for a moment: then says kindly*) Would you like a cup of tea, ma'am? That would make you all right.

BERTHA

Yes, I would. But the milkman has not come yet.

BRIGID

No. Master Archie told me to wake him before he came. He's going out for a jaunt in the car. But I've a sup left overnight. I'll have the kettle boiling in a jiffy. Would you like a nice egg with it?

BERTHA

No, thanks.

BRIGID

Or a nice bit of toast?

BERTHA

No, Brigid, thanks. Just a cup of tea.

BRIGID

(*crossing to the folding doors*) I won't be a moment. (*she stops, turns back and goes towards the door on the left*) But first I must waken Master Archie or there'll be ructions.

[*She goes out by the door on the left. After a few moments* BERTHA *rises and goes over to the study. She opens the door wide and looks in. One can see a small untidy room with many bookshelves and a large writingtable with papers and an extinguished lamp and before it a padded chair. She remains standing for some time in the doorway, then closes the door again without entering the room. She returns to her chair by the window and sits down.*
ARCHIE, *dressed as before, comes in by the door on the right, followed by* BRIGID]

ARCHIE

(*comes to her and, putting up his face to be kissed, says:*) *Buon giorno, mamma!*

BERTHA

(*kissing him*) *Buon giorno*, Archie! (*to* BRIGID) Did you put another vest on him under that one?

BRIGID

He wouldn't let me, ma'am.

ARCHIE

I'm not cold, mamma.

BERTHA

I said you were to put it on, didn't I?

ARCHIE

But where is the cold?

233

BERTHA

(*takes a comb from her head and combs his hair back at both sides*) And the sleep is in your eyes still.

BRIGID

He went to bed immediately after you went out last night, ma'am.

ARCHIE

You know he's going to let me drive, mamma.

BERTHA

(*replacing the comb in her hair, embraces him suddenly*) O what a big man to drive a horse!

BRIGID

Well, he's daft on horses anyhow.

ARCHIE

(*releasing himself*) I'll make him go quick. You will see from the window, mamma. With the whip. (*he makes a gesture of cracking a whip and shouts at the top of his voice*) Avanti!

BRIGID

Beat the poor horse, is it?

BERTHA

Come here till I clean your mouth. (*she takes her handkerchief from the pocket of her gown, wets it with her tongue and cleans his mouth*) You're all smudges or something, dirty little creature you are.

ARCHIE

(*repeats, laughing*) Smudges! What is smudges?

[*The noise is heard of a milkcan rattled on the railings before the window*]

BRIGID

(*draws aside the curtains and looks out*) Here he is!

ARCHIE

(*rapidly*) Wait. I'm ready. Goodbye, mamma! (*he kisses her hastily and turns to go*) Is pappie up?

BRIGID

(*takes him by the arm*) Come on with you now.

BERTHA

Mind yourself, Archie, and don't be long or I won't let you go any more.

ARCHIE

All right. Look out of the window and you'll see me. Goodbye.

[BRIGID *and* ARCHIE *go out by the door on the left.* BERTHA *stands up and drawing aside the curtains still more stands in the embrasure of the window, looking out. The halldoor is heard opening: then a slight noise of voices and cans is heard. The door is closed. After a moment or two* BERTHA *is seen waving her hand gaily in salute.* BRIGID *enters and stands behind her, looking over her shoulder*]

BRIGID

Look at the sit of him! As serious as you like.

BERTHA

(*suddenly withdrawing from her post*) Stand out of the window. I don't want to be seen.

BRIGID

Why, ma'am, what is it?

BERTHA

(*crossing towards the folding doors*) Say I'm not up, that I'm not well. I can't see anyone.

BRIGID

(*follows her*) Who is it, ma'am?

BERTHA

(*halting*) Wait a moment.

[*She listens. A knock is heard at the halldoor*]

BERTHA

(*stands a moment in doubt: then*) No, say I'm in.

BRIGID

(*in doubt*) Here?

BERTHA

(*hurriedly*) Yes. Say I have just got up.

[BRIGID *goes out on the left.* BERTHA *goes towards the double doors and fingers the curtains nervously as if settling them. The halldoor is heard to open. Then* BEATRICE JUS-TICE *enters and, as* BERTHA *does not turn at once, stands in hesitation near the door on the left. She is dressed as before and has a newspaper in her hand*]

BEATRICE

(*advances rapidly*) Mrs Rowan, excuse me for coming at such an hour.

BERTHA

(*turns*) Good morning, Miss Justice. (*she comes towards her*) Is anything the matter?

BEATRICE

(*nervously*) I don't know. That is what I wanted to ask you.

BERTHA

(*looks curiously at her*) You are out of breath. Won't you sit down?

BEATRICE

(*sitting down*) Thank you.

BERTHA

(*sits opposite her: pointing to her paper*) Is there something in the paper?

BEATRICE

(*laughs nervously: opens the paper*) Yes.

BERTHA

About Dick?

BEATRICE

Yes. Here it is. A long article, a leading article, by my cousin. All his life is here. Do you wish to see it?

BERTHA

(*takes the paper and opens it*) Where is it?

BEATRICE

In the middle. It is headed: *A Distinguished Irishman.*

BERTHA

Is it . . . for Dick or against him?

BEATRICE

(*warmly*) O, for him! You can read what he says about Mr Rowan. And I know that Robert stayed in town very late last night to write it.

BERTHA

(*nervously*) Yes. Are you sure?

BEATRICE

Yes. Very late. I heard him come home. It was long after two.

BERTHA

(*watching her*) It alarmed you? I mean to be awakened at that hour of the morning.

BEATRICE

I am a light sleeper. But I knew he had come from the office and then ... I suspected he had written an article about Mr Rowan and that was why he came so late.

BERTHA

How quick you were to think of that?

BEATRICE

Well, after what took place here yesterday afternoon – I mean what Robert said – that Mr Rowan had accepted this position. It was only natural I should think. . . .

BERTHA

Ah, yes. Naturally.

BEATRICE

(*hastily*) But that is not what alarmed me. But immediately after I heard a noise in my cousin's room.

BERTHA

(*crumples together the paper in her hands, breathlessly*) My God! What is it? Tell me.

BEATRICE

(*observing her*) Why does that upset you so much?

BERTHA

(*sinking back, with a forced laugh*) Yes, of course, it is very foolish of me. My nerves are all upset. I slept very badly too. That is why I got up so early. But tell me what was it then?

BEATRICE

Only the noise of his valise being pulled along the floor. Then I heard him walking about his room, whistling softly. And then locking it and strapping it.

BERTHA

He is going away!

BEATRICE

That was what alarmed me. I feared he had had a quarrel with Mr Rowan and that his article was an attack.

BERTHA

But why should they quarrel? Have you noticed anything between them?

BEATRICE

I thought I did. A coldness.

BERTHA

Lately?

BEATRICE

For some time past.

BERTHA

(*smoothing the paper out*) Do you know the reason?

BEATRICE

(*hesitatingly*) No.

BERTHA

(*after a pause*) Well, but if this article is for him, as you say, they have not quarrelled. (*she reflects a moment*) And written last night too.

BEATRICE

Yes. I bought the paper at once to see. But why then is he going away so suddenly? I feel that there is something wrong. I feel that something has happened between them.

BERTHA

Would you be sorry?

BEATRICE

I would be very sorry. You see, Mrs Rowan, Robert is my first cousin and it would grieve me very deeply if he were to treat Mr Rowan badly now that he has come back or if they had a serious quarrel, especially because. . . .

BERTHA

(*toying with the paper*) Because?

BEATRICE

Because it was my cousin who urged Mr Rowan always to come back. I have that on my conscience.

BERTHA

It should be on Mr Hand's conscience, should it not?

BEATRICE

(*uncertainly*) On mine too. Because – I spoke to my cousin about Mr Rowan when he was away and, to a certain extent, it was I. . . .

BERTHA

(*nods slowly*) I see. And that is on your conscience. Only that?

BEATRICE

I think so.

BERTHA

(*almost cheerfully*) It looks as if it was you, Miss Justice, who brought my husband back to Ireland.

BEATRICE

I, Mrs Rowan?

BERTHA

Yes, you. By your letters to him and then by speaking to your cousin as you said just now. Do you not think that you are the person who brought him back?

BEATRICE

(*blushing suddenly*) No. I could not think that.

BERTHA

(*watches her for a moment, then turns aside*) You know that my husband is writing very much since he came back.

BEATRICE

Is he?

BERTHA

Did you not know? (*she points towards the study*) He passes the greater part of the night in there writing. Night after night.

BEATRICE

In his study?

BERTHA

Study or bedroom. You may call it what you please. He sleeps there, too, on a sofa. He slept there last night. I can show you if you don't believe me.

[*She rises to go towards the study.* BEATRICE *half rises quickly and makes a gesture of refusal*]

BEATRICE

I believe you, of course, Mrs Rowan, when you tell me.

BERTHA

(*sitting down again*) Yes. He is writing. And it must be about something which has come into his life lately – since we came back to Ireland. Some change. Do you know that any change has come into his life? (*she looks searchingly at her*) Do you know it or feel it?

BEATRICE

(*answers her look steadily*) Mrs Rowan, that is not a question to ask me. If any change has come into his life since he came back you must know and feel it.

BERTHA

You could know it just as well. You are very intimate in this
house.

BEATRICE

I am not the only person who is intimate here.

[*They both look at each other coldly in silence for some
moments.* BERTHA *lays aside the paper and sits down on a
chair nearer to* BEATRICE]

BERTHA

(*placing her hand on* BEATRICE's *knee*) So you also hate me, Miss
Justice?

BEATRICE

(*with an effort*) Hate you? I?

BERTHA

(*insistently but softly*) Yes. You know what it means to hate a
person?

BEATRICE

Why should I hate you? I have never hated anyone.

BERTHA

Have you ever loved anyone? (*she puts her hand on* BEATRICE's
wrist) Tell me. You have?

BEATRICE

(*also softly*) Yes. In the past.

BERTHA

Not now?

BEATRICE

No.

BERTHA

Can you say that to me – truly. Look at me.

BEATRICE

(*looks at her*) Yes. I can.

> [*A short pause.* BERTHA *withdraws her hand and turns away her head in some embarrassment*]

BERTHA

You said just now that another person is intimate in this house. You meant your cousin . . . . Was it he?

BEATRICE

Yes.

BERTHA

Have you not forgotten him?

BEATRICE

(*quietly*) I have tried to.

BERTHA

(*clasping her hands*) You hate me. You think I am happy. If you only knew how wrong you are!

BEATRICE

(*shakes her head*) I do not.

BERTHA

Happy! When I do not understand anything that he writes, when I cannot help him in any way, when I don't even understand half of what he says to me sometimes! You could and you can. (*excitedly*) But I am afraid for him, afraid for both of them. (*she stands up suddenly and goes towards the davenport*) He must not go away like that. (*she takes a writing pad from the drawer and writes a few lines in great haste*) No, it is impossible! Is he mad to do such a thing? (*turning to* BEATRICE) Is he still at home?

BEATRICE

(*watching her in wonder*) Yes. Have you written to him to ask him to come here?

BERTHA

(*rises*) I have. I will send Brigid across with it. Brigid!

[*She goes out by the door on the left rapidly*]

BEATRICE

(*gazing after her, instinctively*) It is true then!

[*She glances towards the door of* RICHARD's *study and catches her head in her hands. Then, recovering herself, she takes the paper from the little table, opens it, takes a spectacle case from her handbag and, putting on a pair of spectacles, bends down reading it.*
RICHARD ROWAN *enters from the garden. He is dressed as before but wears a soft hat and carries a thin cane*]

RICHARD

(*stands in the doorway, observing her for some moments*) There are demons (*he points out towards the strand*) out there. I heard them jabbering since dawn.

BEATRICE

(*starts to her feet*) Mr Rowan!

RICHARD

I assure you. The isle is full of noises. Yours also. *Otherwise I could not see you*, it said. And her voice. And his voice. But, I assure you they are all demons. I made the sign of the cross upside down and that silenced them.

BEATRICE

(*stammering*) I came here, Mr Rowan, so early because . . . to show you this . . . Robert wrote it . . . . about you . . . last night.

RICHARD

(*takes off his hat*) My dear Miss Justice, you told me yesterday, I think, why you come here and I never forget anything. (*advancing towards her, holding out his hands*) Good morning.

BEATRICE

(*suddenly takes off her spectacles and places the paper in his hands*) I came for this. It is an article about you. Robert wrote it last night. Will you read it?

RICHARD

(*bows*) Read it now? Certainly.

BEATRICE

(*looks at him in despair*) O, Mr Rowan, it makes me suffer to look at you.

RICHARD

(*opens the paper and reads*) *Death of the Very Reverend Canon Mulhall.* Is that it?

[BERTHA *appears at the door on the left and stands to listen*]

RICHARD

(*turns over a page*) Yes, here we are! *A Distinguished Irishman.* (*he begins to read in a rather loud hard voice*) Not the least vital of the problems which confront our country is the problem of her attitude towards those of her children who, having left her in her hour of need, have been called back to her now on the eve of her longawaited victory, to her whom in loneliness and exile they have at last learned to love. In exile, we have said, but here we must distinguish. There is an economic and there is a spiritual exile. There are those who left her to seek the bread by which men live and there are others, nay, her most favoured children, who left her to seek in other lands that food of the spirit by which a nation of human beings is sustained in life. Those who recall the intellectual life of Dublin of a decade since will have many memories of Mr Rowan. Something of that fierce indignation which lacerated the heart. . . .

[*He raises his eyes from the paper and sees* BERTHA *standing in the doorway. Then he lays aside the paper and looks at her. A long silence*]

BEATRICE

(*with an effort*) You see, Mr Rowan, your day has dawned at last. Even here. And you see that you have a warm friend in Robert, a friend who understands you.

RICHARD

Did you notice the little phrase at the beginning: *those who left her in her hour of need?*

[*He looks searchingly at* BERTHA, *turns and walks into his study, closing the door behind him*]

BERTHA

(*speaking half to herself*) I gave up everything for him, religion, family, my own peace.

[*She sits down heavily in an armchair.* BEATRICE *comes towards her*]

BEATRICE

(*weakly*) But do you not feel also that Mr Rowan's ideas. . . .

BERTHA

(*bitterly*) Ideas and ideas! But the people in this world have other ideas or pretend to. They have to put up with him in spite of his ideas because he is able to do something. Me, no. I am nothing.

BEATRICE

You stand by his side.

BERTHA

(*with increasing bitterness*) Ah, nonsense, Miss Justice! I am only a thing he got entangled with and my son is – the nice name they give those children. Do you think I am a stone? Do you think I don't see it in their eyes and in their manner when they have to meet me?

BEATRICE

Do not let them humble you, Mrs Rowan.

BERTHA

(*haughtily*) Humble me! I am very proud of myself, if you want to know. What have they ever done for him? I made him a man. What are they all in his life? No more than the dirt under his boots! (*she stands up and walks excitedly to and fro*) He can despise me too like the rest of them – now. And you can despise me. But you will never humble me, any of you.

BEATRICE

Why do you accuse me?

BERTHA

(*going to her impulsively*) I am in such suffering. Excuse me if I was rude. I want us to be friends. (*she holds out her hands*) Will you?

BEATRICE

(*taking her hands*) Gladly.

BERTHA

(*looking at her*) What lovely long eyelashes you have! And your eyes have such a sad expression!

BEATRICE

(*smiling*) I see very little with them. They are very weak.

BERTHA

(*warmly*) But beautiful.

[*She embraces her quietly and kisses her. Then withdraws from her a little shyly.* BRIGID *comes in from the left*]

BRIGID

I gave it to himself, ma'am.

BERTHA

Did he send a message?

BRIGID

He was just going out, ma'am. He told me to say he'd be here after me.

BERTHA

Thanks.

BRIGID

(*going*) Would you like the tea and the toast now, ma'am?

BERTHA

Not now, Brigid. After perhaps. When Mr Hand comes show him in at once.

BRIGID

Yes, ma'am.

[*She goes out on the left*]

BEATRICE

I will go now, Mrs Rowan, before he comes.

BERTHA

(*somewhat timidly*) Then we are friends?

BEATRICE

(*in the same tone*) We will try to be. (*turning*) Do you allow me to go out through the garden? I don't want to meet my cousin now.

BERTHA

Of course. (*she takes her hand*) It is so strange that we spoke like this now. But I always wanted to. Did you?

BEATRICE

I think I did too.

BERTHA

(*smiling*) Even in Rome. When I went out for a walk with Archie I used to think about you, what you were like, because I knew about you from Dick. I used to look at different persons, coming out of churches or going by in carriages, and think that perhaps they were like you. Because Dick told me you were dark.

BEATRICE

(*again nervously*) Really?

BERTHA

(*pressing her hand*) Goodbye then – for the present.

BEATRICE

(*disengaging her hand*) Good morning.

BERTHA

I will see you to the gate.

> [*She accompanies her out through the double doors. They go down through the garden.*
> RICHARD ROWAN *comes in from the study. He halts near the doors, looking down the garden. Then he turns away, comes to the little table, takes up the paper and reads.* BERTHA, *after some moments, appears in the doorway and stands watching him till he has finished. He lays down the paper again and turns to go back to his study*]

BERTHA

Dick!

RICHARD

(*stopping*) Well?

BERTHA

You have not spoken to me.

RICHARD

I have nothing to say. Have you?

BERTHA

Do you not wish to know – about what happened last night?

RICHARD

That I will never know.

BERTHA

I will tell you if you ask me.

RICHARD

You will tell me. But I will never know. Never in this world.

BERTHA

(*moving towards him*) I will tell you the truth, Dick, as I always told you. I never lied to you.

RICHARD

(*clenching his hands in the air, passionately*) Yes, yes. The truth! But I will never know, I tell you.

BERTHA

Why then did you leave me last night?

RICHARD

(*bitterly*) In your hour of need.

BERTHA

(*threateningly*) You urged me to it. Not because you love me. If you loved me or if you knew what love was you would not have left me. For your own sake you urged me to it.

RICHARD

I did not make myself. I am what I am.

BERTHA

To have it always to throw against me. To make me humble before you as you always did. To be free yourself. (*pointing *towards the garden*) With her! And that is your love! Every word you say is false.

RICHARD

(*controlling himself*) It is useless to ask you to listen to me.

BERTHA

Listen to you! She is the person for listening. Why would you waste your time with me? Talk to her.

RICHARD

(*nods his head*) I see. You have driven her away from me now as you drove everyone else from my side – every friend I ever had, every human being that ever tried to approach me. You hate her.

BERTHA

(*warmly*) No such thing! I think you have made her unhappy as you have made me and as you made your dead mother unhappy and killed her. Womankiller! That is your name.

RICHARD

(*turns to go*) Arrivederci!

BERTHA

(*excitedly*) She is a fine and high character. I like her. She is everything that I am not – in birth and education. You tried to ruin her but you could not. Because she is well able for you – what I am not. And you know it.

RICHARD

(*almost shouting*) What the devil are you talking about her for?

BERTHA

(*clasping her hands*) O, how I wish I had never met you! How I curse that day!

RICHARD

(*bitterly*) I am in the way, is it? You would like to be free now. You have only to say the word.

BERTHA

(*proudly*) Whenever you like I am ready.

RICHARD

So that you could meet your lover – freely.

BERTHA

Yes.

RICHARD

Night after night?

BERTHA

(*gazing before her and speaking with intense passion*) To meet my lover! (*holding out her arms before her*) My lover! Yes! My lover!

[*She bursts suddenly into tears and sinks down on a chair, covering her face with her hands.* RICHARD *approaches her slowly and touches her on the shoulder*]

RICHARD

Bertha! (*she does not answer*) Bertha, you are free.

BERTHA

(*pushes his hand aside and starts to her feet*) Don't touch me! You are a stranger to me. You do not understand anything in me – not one thing in my heart or soul. A stranger! I am living with a stranger!

[*A knock is heard at the halldoor.* BERTHA *dries her eyes quickly with her handkerchief and settles the front of her gown.* RICHARD *listens for a moment, looks at her keenly and, turning away, walks into his study.*
ROBERT HAND *enters from the left. He is dressed in dark brown tweed and carries in his hand a brown Alpine hat*]

ROBERT

(*closing the door quietly behind him*) You sent for me.

BERTHA

(*rises*) Yes. Are you mad to think of going away like that –
without even coming here – without saying anything?

ROBERT

(*advancing towards the table on which the paper lies, glances at
it*) What I have to say I said here.

BERTHA

When did you write it? Last night – after I went away?

ROBERT

(*gracefully*) To be quite accurate. I wrote part of it – in my mind
– before you went away. The rest – the worst part – I wrote after.
Much later.

BERTHA

And you could write last night!

ROBERT

(*shrugs his shoulders*) I am a welltrained animal. (*he comes closer
to her*) I passed a long wandering night after . . . in my office, at
the vicechancellor's house, in a nightclub, in the streets, in my
room. Your image was always before my eyes, your hand in my
hand. Bertha, I will never forget last night. (*he lays his hat on the
table and takes her hand*) Why do you not look at me? May I not
touch you?

BERTHA

(*points to the study*) Dick is in there.

ROBERT

(*drops her hand*) In that case children be good.

BERTHA

Where are you going?

ROBERT

To foreign parts. That is, to my cousin Jack Justice, *alias* Doggy Justice, in Surrey. He has a nice country place there and the air is mild.

BERTHA

Why are you going?

ROBERT

(*looks at her in silence*) Can you not guess one reason?

BERTHA

On account of me?

ROBERT

Yes. It is not pleasant for me to remain here just now.

BERTHA

(*sits down helplessly*) But this is cruel of you, Robert. Cruel to me and to him also.

ROBERT

Has he asked . . . what happened?

BERTHA

(*joining her hands in despair*) No. He refuses to ask me anything. He says he will never know.

ROBERT

(*nods gravely*) Richard is right there. He is always right.

BERTHA

But, Robert, you must speak to him.

ROBERT

What am I to say to him?

BERTHA

The truth! Everything!

ROBERT

(*reflects*) No, Bertha. I am a man speaking to a man. I cannot tell him everything.

BERTHA

He will believe that you are going away because you are afraid to face him after last night.

ROBERT

(*after a pause*) Well, I am not a coward any more than he. I will see him.

BERTHA

(*rises*) I will call him.

ROBERT

(*catching her hands*) Bertha! What happened last night? What is the truth that I am to tell? (*he gazes earnestly into her eyes*) Were you mine in that sacred night of love? Or have I dreamed it?

BERTHA

(*smiles faintly*) Remember your dream of me. You dreamt that I was yours last night.

ROBERT

And that is the truth – a dream? That is what I am to tell?

BERTHA

Yes.

ROBERT

(*kisses both her hands*) Bertha! (*in a softer voice*) In all my life only that dream is real. I forget the rest. (*he kisses her hands again*) And now I can tell him the truth. Call him.

[BERTHA *goes to the door of* RICHARD's *study and knocks. There is no answer. She knocks again*]

BERTHA

Dick! (*there is no answer*) Mr Hand is here. He wants to speak to you, to say goodbye. He is going away. (*there is no answer. She beats her hand loudly on the panel of the door and calls in an alarmed voice*) Dick! Answer me!

[RICHARD ROWAN *comes in from the study. He comes at once to* ROBERT *but does not hold out his hand*)

RICHARD

(*calmly*) I thank you for your kind article about me. Is it true that you have come to say goodbye?

ROBERT

There is nothing to thank me for, Richard. Now and always I am your friend. Now more than ever before. Do you believe me, Richard?

[RICHARD *sits down on a chair and buries his face in his hands.* BERTHA *and* ROBERT *gaze at each other in silence. Then she turns away and goes out quietly on the right.* ROBERT *goes towards* RICHARD *and stands near him, resting his hands on the back of a chair, looking down at him. There is a long silence.*
A FISHWOMAN *is heard crying out as she passes along the road outside*]

THE FISHWOMAN

Fresh Dublin bay herrings! Fresh Dublin bay herrings! Dublin bay herrings!

ROBERT

(*quietly*) I will tell you the truth, Richard. Are you listening?

RICHARD

(*raises his face and leans back to listen*) Yes.

[ROBERT *sits on the chair beside him. The* FISHWOMAN *is heard calling out farther away*]

THE FISHWOMAN

Fresh herrings! Dublin bay herrings!

ROBERT

I failed, Richard. That is the truth. Do you believe me?

RICHARD

I am listening.

ROBERT

I failed. She is yours as she was nine years ago when you met her first.

RICHARD

When we met her first, you mean.

ROBERT

Yes. (*he looks down for some moments*) Shall I go on?

RICHARD

Yes.

ROBERT

She went away. I was left alone – for the second time. I went to the vicechancellor's house and dined. I said you were ill and would come another night. I made epigrams new and old – that one about the statues also. I drank claret cup. I went to my office and wrote my article. Then . . . .

RICHARD

Then?

ROBERT

Then I went to a certain nightclub. There were men there – and also women. At least they looked like women. I danced with one of them. She asked me to see her home. Shall I go on?

RICHARD

Yes.

ROBERT

I saw her home in a cab. She lives near Donnybrook. In the cab took place what the Subtle Duns Scotus calls a death of the spirit. Shall I go on?

RICHARD

Yes.

ROBERT

She wept. She told me she was the divorced wife of a barrister. I offered her a sovereign as she told me she was short of money. She would not take it and wept very much. Then she drank some melissa water from a little bottle which she had in her satchel. I saw her enter her house. Then I walked home. In my room I found that my coat was all stained with the melissa water. I had no luck even with my coats yesterday: that was the second one. The idea came to me then to change my suit and go away by the morning boat. I packed my valise and went to bed. I am going away by the next train, to my cousin Jack Justice in Surrey. Perhaps for a fortnight. Perhaps longer. Are you disgusted?

RICHARD

Why did you not go by the boat?

ROBERT

I slept it out.

RICHARD

You intended to go without saying goodbye – without coming here?

ROBERT

Yes.

RICHARD

Why?

ROBERT

My story is not very nice, is it?

RICHARD

But you have come.

ROBERT

Bertha sent me a message to come.

RICHARD

But for that . . .?

ROBERT

But for that I should not have come.

RICHARD

Did it strike you that if you had gone without coming here I should have understood it – in my own way?

ROBERT

Yes, it did.

RICHARD

What then do you wish me to believe?

ROBERT

I wish you to believe that I failed. That Bertha is yours now as she was nine years ago when you – when we – met her first.

RICHARD

Do you want to know what I did?

ROBERT

No.

RICHARD

I came home at once.

ROBERT

Did you hear Bertha return?

RICHARD

No. I wrote all the night. And thought. (*pointing to the study*) In there. Before dawn I went out and walked the strand from end to end.

ROBERT

(*shaking his head*) Suffering. Torturing yourself.

RICHARD

Hearing voices about me. The voices of those who say they love me.

ROBERT

(*points to the door on the right*) One. And mine?

RICHARD

Another still.

ROBERT

(*smiles and touches his forehead with his right forefinger*) True. My interesting but somewhat melancholy cousin. And what did they tell you?

RICHARD

They told me to despair.

ROBERT

A queer way of showing their love, I must say! And will you despair?

RICHARD

(*rising*) No.

[*A noise is heard at the window.* ARCHIE's *face is seen flattened against one of the panes. He is heard calling*]

ARCHIE

Open the window! Open the window!

ROBERT

(*looks at* RICHARD) Did you hear his voice too, Richard, with the others – out there on the strand? Your son's voice? (*smiling*) Listen! How full it is of despair!

ARCHIE

Open the window please, will you?

ROBERT

Perhaps there, Richard, is the freedom we seek – you in one way, I in another. In him and not in us. Perhaps . . .

RICHARD

Perhaps. . . .?

ROBERT

I said *perhaps*. I would say almost surely if . . .

RICHARD

If what?

ROBERT

(*with a faint smile*) If he were mine.

[*He goes to the window and opens it.* ARCHIE *scrambles in*]

ROBERT

Like yesterday – eh?

ARCHIE

Good morning, Mr Hand! (*he runs to* RICHARD *and kisses him*)
Buon giorno, babbo!

RICHARD

Buon giorno, Archie.

ROBERT

And where were you, my young gentleman?

ARCHIE

Out with the milkman. I drove the horse. We went to Booterstown.
(*he takes off his cap and throws it on a chair*) I'm very hungry.

ROBERT

(*takes his hat from the table*) Richard, goodbye. (*offering his
hand*) To our next meeting!

RICHARD

(*touches his hand*) Goodbye.

[BERTHA *appears at the door on the right*]

ROBERT

(*catches sight of her: to* ARCHIE) Get your cap. Come on with me.
I'll buy you a cake and I'll tell you a story.

ARCHIE

(*to* BERTHA) May I, mamma?

BERTHA

Yes.

ARCHIE

(*takes his cap*) I'm ready.

ROBERT

(*to* RICHARD *and* BERTHA) Goodbye to pappa and mamma. But
not a big goodbye.

ARCHIE

Will you tell me a fairy story, Mr Hand?

ROBERT

A fairy story? Why not? I am your fairy godfather.

[*They go out together through the double doors and down the garden. When they have gone* BERTHA *goes to* RICHARD *and puts her arm round his waist*]

BERTHA

Dick dear, do you believe now that I have been true to you? Last night and always.

RICHARD

(*sadly*) Do not ask me, Bertha.

BERTHA

(*pressing him more closely*) I have been, dear. Surely you believe me. I gave you myself – all. I gave up all for you. You took me – and you left me.

RICHARD

When did I leave you?

BERTHA

You left me: and I waited for you to come back to me. Dick dear, come here to me. Sit down. How tired you must be!

[*She draws him towards the lounge. He sits down, almost reclining, resting on his arm. She sits on the mat before the lounge, holding his hand*]

BERTHA

Yes, dear. I waited for you. Heavens, what I suffered then – when we lived in Rome! Do you remember the terrace of our house?

RICHARD

Yes.

BERTHA

I used to sit there, waiting, with the poor child with his toys, waiting till he got sleepy. I could see all the roofs of the city and the river, the *Tevere*. What is its name?

RICHARD

The Tiber.

BERTHA

(*caressing her cheek with his hand*) It was lovely, Dick, only I was so sad. I was alone, Dick, forgotten by you and by all. I felt my life was ended.

RICHARD

It had not begun.

BERTHA

And I used to look at the sky, so beautiful, without a cloud, and the city you said was so old: and then I used to think of Ireland and about ourselves.

RICHARD

Ourselves?

BERTHA

Yes. Ourselves. Not a day passes that I do not see ourselves, you and me, as we were when we met first. Every day of my life I see that. Was I not true to you all that time?

RICHARD

(*sighs deeply*) Yes, Bertha. You were my bride in exile.

BERTHA

Wherever you go I will follow you. If you wish to go away now I will go with you.

RICHARD

I will remain. It is too soon yet to despair.

BERTHA

(*again caressing his hand*) It is not true that I want to drive everyone from you. I wanted to bring you close together – you and him. Speak to me. Speak out all your heart to me: what you feel and what you suffer.

RICHARD

I am wounded, Bertha.

BERTHA

How wounded, dear? Explain to me what you mean. I will try to understand everything you say. In what way are you wounded?

RICHARD

(*releases his hand and, taking her head between his hands, bends it back and gazes long into her eyes*) I have a deep deep wound of doubt in my soul.

BERTHA

(*motionless*) Doubt of me?

RICHARD

Yes.

BERTHA

I am yours. (*in a whisper*) If I died this moment I am yours.

RICHARD

(*still gazing at her and speaking as if to an absent person*) I have wounded my soul for you – a deep wound of doubt which can never be healed. I can never know, never in this world. I do not wish to know or to believe. I do not care. It is not in the darkness of belief that I desire you. But in restless living wounding doubt. To hold you by no bonds, even of love, to be united with you in

265

body and soul in utter nakedness – for this I longed. And now I am tired for a while, Bertha. My wound tires me.

[*He stretches himself out wearily along the lounge.* BERTHA *holds his hand still, speaking very softly*]

BERTHA

Forget me, Dick. Forget me and love me again as you did the first time. I want my lover: to meet him, to go to him, to give myself to him. You, Dick. O, my strange wild lover come back to me again!

[*She closes her eyes*]

NOTES

PUBLISHED COLLECTIONS

Chamber Music (published 1907)

The relation between real-life and literary sources is discussed in the Introduction above. The girl who directly prompted Poems XII and XXV, and also perhaps Poem XX, was in real life Mary Sheehy, daughter of a schoolfriend whom Joyce came to know in his next to last year at Belvedere, and who was, according to Stanislaus, the first girl in whom Joyce took a romantic interest (*MBK* 156–8). She appears in *Stephen Hero* as Emma Clery (*SH* 70–73, 157–60, 192–4, 200–204), and in *Portrait* as E— C— and Emma (*P* 70, 116). Compare also Father Conmee's attitude towards the family in *Ulysses* (*U* 180–81). The relation was no less remote than it was intense, and the status of the girl in Joyce's writing derives from English, French and Irish literary backgrounds as much as from biography.

As described below, Mary Sheehy shaded into Nora as Nora replaced her in Joyce's affections, during which time the nature of Joyce's feelings underwent considerable change. Joyce later told Nora that the girl of the poems existed in his imagination as 'a girl fashioned into a curious grave beauty by the culture of generations before her', that is, before Nora outshone what he had put into his verses. The book of his verses held 'the desire of his youth' and she, Nora, became 'the fulfilment of that desire' (*L* II 237).

The composition of the poems dates from between 1901 and 1904. Joyce had written a sufficient number of new poems, and had a clear enough sense of what he wanted to carry over from previous work, to reckon he had a new sequence in hand by the time he first left Ireland in 1902 (compare with Poem II below and *L* II 16, 23). The last poem in the sequence to be written dates from the next time he left Ireland, in 1904 (compare with Poem XXI below). Most of the extensive manuscript and pre-publication material bearing on the text of *Chamber Music*, which dates from December 1902 onwards, is to be found in *Archive* I 23–186. It comprises the manuscript versions of Poems II–V and VII–XXXIII at

Cornell, the manuscript of Poems I–XXXIV and the final manuscript of Poems I–XXXVI at Yale, and the page proofs of Poems I–XXX and XXXV–XXXVI at Cornell. The only significant exception is the manuscript of thirty-three poems that Joyce gave to Sylvia Beach and was owned by James Gilvarry when the facsimile was made, which represents one of the earliest complete stages of the suite. However, Tindall's collation of the Beach–Gilvarry manuscript is said on good authority to be reasonably accurate (*Archive* I xxxiii).

The extant materials comprise fair copies of individual poems, copies of groups of poems and proofs. The texts of individual poems differ in wording and punctuation, but their main interest lies in the different ordering of groups. The Beach–Gilvarry manuscript comprises twenty-seven poems positioned at the centre of large, handsome sheets of laid paper, to which six other poems on 'inferior' paper have been added. The sequence of twenty-seven poems comprises Poems I, III, II, IV, V, VIII, VII, IX, XVII, XVIII, VI, X, XIII, XIV, XV , XIX, XXIII, XXII, XXIV, XVI, XXXI, XXVIII, XXIX, XXXII, XXX, XXXIII, XXXIV; Poems XXVII, XI, XII, XXVI, XXV and also XX, are the ones added later. The original twenty-seven-poem sequence, as well as the enlarged sequence of thirty-three poems, can be shown to be organized according to a rising and falling movement, apparently along the lines of *Shine and Dark*, turning around the present Poem XIV. The design is uncovered by Robert Boyle, 'The Woman Hidden in James Joyce's *Chamber Music*' in *Women in Joyce*, eds. Suzette Henke and Elaine Unkeless (Urbana, Ill., 1982) 3–30.

Subsequent or perhaps coterminous manuscripts experiment with differently ordered sequences. Their different composition and arrangement is set out in tabular form in Aubert 1336–7. It is not easy to be certain about the line of transmission, but Poem XXI emerges as the new turning-point, embodying as it does Joyce's fear of betrayal, which intensified after the break with Gogarty. Though the additions to the original sequence are few, they change the meaning of what was already written even more than the replacement of Emma Clery by Nora. For example, the meanings of Poem XVII accrue strong particular resonances in the light of the 1904 crisis – as do the two following poems, if less obviously.

In such ways the rather simple, programmatic tendency of the original sequence was overlaid by another, and it could be argued that the darker implications are not consonant with what Joyce previously wrote. It is easy enough to accept that the present Poems XXXV and XXXVI are tailpieces, just as Poems I and II are preludes, but it is still difficult to accept Poem XIV as 'central', 'after which the movement is all downwards' (*L* I 67). The movement of the poems that follow Joyce's celebratory 'Song of Songs', Poem XIV, is seriously disrupted. As clear a story of wooing, betrayal and desertion as can be disentangled is described by Francis Warner, 'The Poetry of James Joyce' in *James Joyce: An International Perspective*, eds. Suheil Badi Bushrei and Bernard Benstock (Gerrards Cross, Bucks, 1982) 115–27 (122–4 especially).

Joyce's increasing indifference to what he had written is undoubtedly connected with the loosening of the structure, though whether as result or cause is impossible to say. Eventually he left the final compromise to Stanislaus, as Stanislaus described to Tindall in 1953:

> The arrangement of the poems in 'Chamber Music' is not my brother's; it is mine. He sent the ms. to me from Rome, telling me 'to do what I liked with it'. He practically disowned the poems. . . . I arranged them, now, in their present order – approximately allegretto, andante cantabile, mosso – to suggest a closed episode of youth and love. . . .
>
> My brother accepted my arrangement of his poems without question and without comment. . . . In making my arrangement, I had, of course, in mind the last fateful year or so before he went into voluntary exile. I wished the poems to be read as a connected sequence, representing the closed chapter of that intensely lived life in Dublin, or more broadly, representing the withering of the Adonis garden of youth and pleasure. The arrangement begins on a rather subdued note, a kind of adagio. (Tindall 44; compare *L* II 172, 219; *MBK* 225; etc.)

Joyce tinkered with the phrasing and punctuation of individual poems in manuscript and proof, but not extensively. All the extant versions could be described as fair copies, as distinct from drafts. Six poems were published in book form or in periodicals from May 1904 onwards (Poems VI, VII, XII, XVIII, XXIV, XXVI) before the collection as a whole by Elkin Mathews in May 1907. This text is reproduced in *The Viking Portable James Joyce* (NY, 1947) with four minor variants and in *P&SW* with even fewer variants.

Though Joyce accepted some of changes made by the printer of the first edition – for instance, the patterns of indentation – he intervened to make changes in the second edition in 1918, and more extensively in the third English edition published by the Egoist Press in 1923 (Harriet

Weaver to Tindall, Tindall 100). The improvements affect punctuation and the removal of hyphens. Errors and corruptions crept into subsequent editions and collections, and the present edition therefore reproduces the 1923 Egoist Press text. I have indicated earlier manuscripts or versions in the notes below, but not texts from groups, whose bearing is more obviously on the ordering of the sequence.

Title The title was suggested to Joyce by Stanislaus, after an incident involving a whore and a chamber pot (*CDD* 28, and 26–7). Stephen recalls the Elizabethan sense of chambering as sexual indulgence in *P* 176, and the ambiguities clearly appealed to Joyce as an embodiment of his ambivalence towards the book as a whole (compare *U* 232). None the less, Tindall's interpretation largely in terms of micturation, based largely on Poems VII and XXVI, has left more readers complaining than convinced (73–9, 211–12, etc.; and compare his 'Joyce's Chambermade Music', *Poetry*, Chicago, LXXX:2, May 1952, 105–16).

I: 'Strings in the earth and air'

The poem is one of five that appear in a separate, rather scrappy group of manuscripts dating from about 1903 to 1904 (*Archive* I 32). Joyce described it as forming a prelude, along with Poem III (*L* I 67).

10: With head to the music bent Compare the recurrence of this pose of a lowered or inclined head in Poems II, IV, VII, XXVI. It had been made fashionable by Pre-Raphaelite writers and painters, and so continued in certain circles to the end of the century.

11–12 Tindall would have this to be a description of masturbation (63–5).

II: 'The twilight turns from amethyst'

Stanislaus Joyce told Tindall that the poem belonged to an earlier collection, and he transcribed it in a notebook as early as about 1902 under the title *Commonplace* (Tindall 7n, 183; *Archive* I 24–5). This was the title of one of the poems Joyce sent William Archer in the summer of 1901 (*MBK* 150). In short, the evidence points to it being one of the earliest-written poems in the sequence.

1: amethyst The quotation from Keats's *Endymion* in the relevant volume of the *OED* (1888) might have influenced Joyce's usage here:

'Western cloudiness, that takes/The semblance of gold rocks ...
palaces/And towers of amethyst.'

5: old piano Compare *SH* 47–8, 160–61 on Stephen visiting Mr Daniels's
house (Sheehy's) and playing such a piano. Tindall 27 suggests the
scene echoes Verlaine's 'Le piano que baisse une main frêle' in *Ro-
mances sans paroles* (1874).

11: twilight The reconciliation of night and day, as throughout Yeats's
Wind Among the Reeds (1899) for example.

III: 'At that hour when all things have repose'

As noted with reference to Poem I above, Joyce thought of the poem as
forming a prelude.

2: lonely watcher of the skies Echoing 'some watcher of the skies' in
Keats's sonnet 'On First Looking into Chapman's Homer'.

3–4: sighs/Of harps The 'zephyr-travell'd' Æolian harps of Romantic
poetry. Physical details are given in Stephen Bonner's article in *The
New Grove Dictionary of Music and Musicians*, ed. Stanley Sadie
(London, 1980) I 115–17; and among literary treatments the *locus
classicus* remains Coleridge's 'The Eolian Harp'.

   Did Joyce know that Tobias Smollett's smart adventurer, Ferdinand
Count Fathom, used such a harp to seduce a country girl (in Chapter
XXXIV of the eponymous novel of 1753)? He could not have known
that in *Jubilate Agno* (published 1939) Christopher Smart suggested it
was the biblical shawm: compare below on Fragment No. 9, in Poems
of Early Youth.

5: The pale gates of sunrise The phrase evokes several passages in Blake's
poetry, probably because of the use of 'gates' – a word Blake was fond of.

7: sweet harps Echoing 'sweethearts'; and compare 'the language of
sweet tarts' in *FW* 116.23.

9: in antiphon In the transferred general sense of 'response, answer',
another nineteenth-century revival of a seventeenth-century usage.
Skeat 27 discusses the word in a short article.

10: overgone In the intransitive sense of 'passed by' or 'passed away'.
Joyce was consciously reviving an older usage.

IV: 'When the shy star goes forth in heaven'

Sent to Stanislaus Joyce from Paris in 1903, along with Poem XXXVI (*L*
II 27–9; *Archive* I 29). The poem is a sort of response to Poem II, which it
follows in one manuscript – 'shy star' recalls 'Shy thoughts', and so on.

1: **shy star**   Venus, the Evening Star, which appears alone at twilight.

V: 'Lean out of the window'

The poem is one of five that appear in a separate, rather scrappy group of manuscripts dating from about 1903–4 (*Archive* I 33).

1: **Lean**   The position shadows the bending position of the girl in other poems, and compare specifically Poem XXVI.

2: **Goldenhair**   Compare the 'yellow hair' of Poem XI.

9–10   Tindall 187 records that in the Beach–Gilvarry manuscript an unknown hand inserted two lines from Tennyson's *The Lady of Shalott*:

> She left the web, she left the loom,
> She made three paces thro' the room.

It is not necessary to assume the echo, if intended, was meant originally as parody.

VI: 'I would in that sweet bosom be'

When the poem was printed in the *Speaker* (October 1904), it was titled *A Wish*.

1: **that**   Tindall 188, 205 suggests such a use of the demonstrative might owe something to Yeats. Compare Poem XXI for another good example. In fact, Joyce's use of 'that' in place of 'who' or 'which' is more conspicuous (see Poems IV, IX, X, XI, etc.) and anticipates a stylistic habit of Yeats. (Richard Ellmann, *The Identity of Yeats*, London, 1954, 140, holds Yeats acquired this from his father.)

1: **sweet bosom**   A phrase that appears also in Shakespeare's *Richard III*, I ii 124.

3: **rude wind**   Appears also in *King Lear*, IV ii 30.

4, 9: **austerities**   Skeat 43 has adjoining articles on 'austere' and 'austral', which would have alerted Joyce to the pun involving his parching or burning wind.

VII: 'My love is in a light attire'

1: **light attire**   Echoed in *The Holy Office* lines 69–72:

> At night when close in bed she lies
> And feels my hand between her thighs

My little love in light attire
Knows the soft flame that is desire.

2: appletrees   Compare Solomon 2:3 and 8:5.

7–8, 11–12   Tindall 74, 189–90 understands the woman to be urinating. In the Beach–Gilvarry manuscript, the poem is followed by the comment 'Yah!' in pencil, presumably in Joyce's hand. Compare with Poem XV.

VIII: 'Who goes amid the green wood'

1: green wood   'Pseudo-Elizabethan song, this poem owes something of its archaic air to "brave," "merry," and "green wood," and something to the use of "that" in the last line as a relative pronoun' (Tindall 191).

8: mien   Skeat 367 discusses the word fully.

12, 14: brave attire, rich apparel   The combination 'rich attire' occurs in both Milton's *Paradise Lost* VII 501 and Coleridge's *Ancient Mariner* line 278 to describe nature. In line 12 Joyce might also have been influenced by the discussion in Skeat 75, in which it is explained that Old Dutch *brauve* in itself means 'fine attire'.

IX: 'Winds of May, that dance on the sea'

1: May   Mary's month. The poem shares the mood of Poem VII, with its appletrees, and of Poem VIII, with its virginal mien.

2: ringaround   Not in any dictionary, I think, but on the model of 'ringaring' ('ring-a-ring-a-roses'). Compare Stephen's 'ringroundabout' in *U* 157.

7: Welladay   The word appears in Shakespeare, Herrick, Coleridge, Keats, etc.; but Joyce was undoubtedly aware of the lengthy discussion in Skeat 702 in which it is described as an unmeaning corruption of 'Wellaway'. (Compare also Skeat in his *Principles of English Etymology*, Oxford, 1892, 428, 462.)

9: Love is unhappy when love is away!   Joyce had the line engraved on an ivory necklace for Nora when he was in Dublin in 1909 (see *L* II 245–6 and the illustration facing 241).

X: 'Bright cap and streamers'

Tindall 193 compares Mangan's 'Noon-Day Dreaming' (*Poems*, Dublin, 1903); also Yeats's 'The Cap and Bells' (in *The Wind Among the Reeds*, 1899).

1: Bright cap and streamers The jester – like Mulligan in *Ulysses* – appears as fertilizer and incubator (*U* 328), and introduces themes of physical love directly into the sequence. Compare the 'rogue in red and yellow dress' of Poem XXXIII.

16: I come Echoing Cleopatra's climactic, 'Husband, I come' in *Antony and Cleopatra* V ii 290; but the innocent romantic meaning is shadowed by the meaning of sexual climax. Compare 'come into her little garden' in Poem XIII, etc.

XI: 'Bid adieu, adieu, adieu'

The manuscript of the poem at Yale is dated 18 September 1904 (*Archive* I 37), though it may be a fair copy of a poem written somewhat earlier, 'on a white Becker's tea-bag' (Patricia Hutchins, *James Joyce's Dublin*, London, 1950, 90). Joyce was particularly fond of it and set it to music, although or even because it was rejected by *Harper's* (*L* II 80). Tindall compares Yeats's 'Fasten your hair with a golden pin' in 'He gives his Beloved certain Rhymes' and 'loosen your hair' in 'He thinks of those who have Spoken Evil of his Beloved' (both in *The Wind Among the Reeds*, 1899).

4: Thee The present poem is the first in the sequence to employ conventional poetic diction (see also 'doth', 'hast'). Stephen comments on 'feudal terminology' as a distancing, ironizing device in *SH* 179. Compare Poems XII, XV, XXV, XXVI and XXVII.

6, 11: snood Compare Joyce's notes for *Exiles* (p. 348), where, referring to this poem, he mentions that a snood is worn by unmarried women as a sign of their condition. The sartorial rule appears to have been derived by Joyce from Walter Scott via Skeat. Skeat 569 gives the meaning simply as 'a filet, ribbon', from a root meaning to twist, twine or turn. Joyce must have looked up Skeat's illustration – 'Her satin snood' in Scott's *Lady of the Lake* I xix – and read on to the description of Alice's 'virgin snood' in III v.

The word appears to have been connected in Joyce's mind with his image of Mary Sheehy. Compare with Poem XII below for a connection between Emma Clery wearing her shawl 'cowlwise', capuchins and 'the hooded moon'. It is possible that it carries forward to *Ulysses*, where Bloom gives the virginal Milly a 'new tam', a 'new coquette cap', for her birthday (*U* 54, 331).

XII: 'What counsel has the hooded moon'

The poem was written at the end of an outing with Mary Sheehy (*MBK*

156–8). Tindall 195 suggests that, transposed, it might be the poem Stephen writes about Emma Clery on the step of the last tram, an incident that haunts him (*P* 222; *SH* 72–3).

1: hooded moon Tindall 197 compares the veiled moon-maiden of Dowson's 'Pierrot of the Minute'. Compare also the fragment of Shelley ('Art thou pale for weariness') quoted by Stephen in *P* 96 and alluded to in Joyce's notes for *Exiles* (p. 346), and with 'capuchin' below.

3: plenilune Full moon. Borrowed from Jonson's *Cynthia's Revels* V iii; or from line 28 of Swinburne's 'A Vision of Spring in Winter' ('Large nightfall, nor imperial plenilune'), *Poems and Ballads: Second Series* (1878).

6: capuchin A friar of the order of St Francis, so called from the sharp-pointed hood. Stephen confesses to being fascinated by the order in *SH* 181–2. Emma Clery is associated particularly with a shawl or hood (*P* 222, 248).

12: sentimentalist Compare Stephen's definition adapted from Meredith: '*The sentimentalist is he who would enjoy without incurring the immense debtorship for a thing done*' (*U* 164).

XIII: 'Go seek her out all courteously'

3: Wind of spices Compare the south wind blowing on the 'garden enclosed' of Solomon 4:12, 16, etc.

4: Epithalamium A genre of nuptial song cultivated by Renaissance poets – for instance, Spenser. Stephen gives his companions in Holles Street 'An exquisite dulcet epithalame of most mollificative suadency for juveniles amatory whom the odoriferous flambeaus of the paranymphs have escorted to the quadrupedal proscenium of connubial communion' in *U* 322.

11: little garden The *locus amoenus* as a traditional image of enclosure and love is as old as the Book of Genesis. Ernst Robert Curtius, *European Literature and the Latin Middle Ages* (NY, 1953) 192–200 gives plentiful examples.

14: at his noon The opposite to the sterile love of his 'plenilune' in Poem XII.

XIV: 'My dove, my beautiful one'

Stanislaus Joyce points out that the imagery recalls the Song of Solomon (*MBK* 251–2). Compare in particular Solomon 2:10 ('Rise up, my love, my fair one, ...', 2:14 ('O my dove, ...'), 5:2, etc. The strong concentration of allusions here increases the force of possible echoes in surrounding poems. Equally important, the irregular rhyme scheme is unusual, indeed, has no parallel. Each stanza is different, and only the continuity of the dominant *b* rhymes (arise, lies, eyes, sighs) holds the verses together.

According to Joyce himself, this poem of dawn would have occupied the central place in his original twenty-seven-poem sequence. See the headnote on the sequence as a whole for references and discussion.

1: **My dove**   Like the wading bird-girl on Dollymount Strand (*P 171*). Birds were associated with the creative and the feminine for Joyce. Compare the thrushes of Poem XVI and Stephen's wren of Poem XXIII.

XV: 'From dewy dreams, my soul, arise'

Written by 31 August 1904 as a 'matutine' to balance the nocturne in prose, 'She comes at night when the city is still' (*Epiphany* 34 *P&SW* 194; *CDD* 74–5). The prose epiphany was a dream-epiphany recorded by Joyce on his Paris sojourn in 1902–3 (*MBK* 226–7; compare *U* 473–5). Tindall 28–9 says it inescapably suggests Shelley's 'Indian Serenade', 'I arise from dreams of thee', etc., which Joyce admired and, as Eugene Sheehy reported, used to sing in his back parlour. Aubert 1347 remarks on the closeness of the poem to Stephen's villanelle (*P 223–34*).

1: **dewy dreams**   The notion of sleep vanishing like the dew is at least as old as Milton in English poetry (*Paradise Lost* IX 1044); but the word 'dewy' underwent something of a fashionable revival among Romantic poets from Collins onwards. Compare also Yeats's 'dew of the morn' in 'Into the Twilight' (in *The Wind Among the Reeds*, 1899), etc.
   There are overtones of a less innocent meaning, also, as at the close of Poem X.

1, 3: **arise, sighs**   The rhyme is carried forward from lines 2, 6, 7, 16 of the previous poem. Compare also the 'skies' and 'sighs' of Poem III, and the 'sigh' and 'deny' of Poem XIX.

11: **the wise choirs of faery**   Perhaps recalled from Keats's 'Ode to a Nightingale' ('in faery lands forlorn'), prompted by Shelley's reference to the 'nightingale's complaint' in line 14 of the 'Indian Serenade'. The dewiness, slumbrous death and bells of morn are also more redolent of the mood of Keats's poem than of Shelley's.

12: **innumerous**   Though used by Milton in *Paradise Lost* VII 455, Joyce

more likely intends an allusion to Newman in *Callista* (1855) Ch. 15 –
a book Stephen recalls in *SH* 198.

The poem is followed in the Beach–Gilvarry manuscript by a pen-
cilled comment, 'Yah!' (Tindall 200) – like Poem VII.

XVI: 'O cool is the valley now'

1, 5: the valley ... the thrushes   Joyce might be alluding to Glenasmole
– Irish 'Glen of the Thrush' – which is in the Dublin Mountains not far
from Pine Forest (compare with Poem XX below).

XVII: 'Because your voice was at my side'

Transcribed by Stanislaus Joyce in a commonplace book in about 1902
(*Archive* I 25–6), so, if it was introduced into the sequence to reflect
Joyce's break with Gogarty (*JJ* 175; compare *L* II 46), it is unlikely to
have been composed with this in mind. That is, the 'friend' of the last
line was indeterminate until the events of summer 1904. It originally
followed Poem IX in the sequence, and Tindall 201 points out that there
are Elizabethan precedents such as Thomas Campion's 'While another
holds your hand'. See Poem XXI below.

XVIII: 'O sweetheart, hear you'

13–16   Compare Solomon 2:6: 'His left hand is under my head, and his
right hand doth embrace me.'

14, 16: breast, rest   Yeats uses the same rhyme in 'The Lover asks
Forgiveness because of his Many Moods' (in *The Wind Among the
Reeds*, 1899).

XIX: 'Be not sad because all men'

2, 4; 5, 7: you; tears   Joyce similarly uses identical words instead of
rhyme in Poems VI, VIII, XVI and XXVIII; and compare the interlink-
ing of rhymes in Poem XIV. The feature is shared with Yeats's 'He
thinks of those who have Spoken Evil of his Beloved' (in *The Wind
Among the Reeds*, 1899), which Tindall 203 suggests is also comparable
in theme.

8: As they deny, deny.   The strong-lined effect is unusual in Joyce's
poetry, and not one he usually aimed for.

XX: 'In the dark pinewood'

A separate manuscript dating from about 1903 is preserved at Yale
(*Archive* I 30). Another manuscript, initialled and dated 1903, in the

possession of Stanislaus Joyce at the time Tindall was in correspondence with him, was subsequently lost (see Tindall 102, 146; and compare Aubert 1348), and is now published in *P&SW* 251.

1: the dark pinewood   Dubliners would find it difficult not to identify the locale as Pine Forest, a secluded yet convenient spot on the edge of the Dublin Mountains. Compare *MBK* 156–8 on an excursion to some such place with Mary Sheehy, which prompted Poems XII and XXV.

   Perhaps there is also an allusion to the 'dark wood' of Dante (*Inferno* I 3).

6, 8: kiss, is   Compare Poem XXIII for the same off-rhyme, which may owe something to the example of Yeats. Stephen contrives to introduce it into a misquoted version of Douglas Hyde, when he walks on Sandymount Strand (*U* 39).

8: Enaisled   The word is not in dictionaries. It is tempting to suspect a punning allusion to that unhappy English Victorian, Matthew Arnold, who wrote in 'To Marguerite':

> Yes! in the sea of life enisled,
> With echoing straits between us thrown . . .

11: tumult   The word also appears prominently in Yeats's 'He bids his Beloved be at Peace' (in *The Wind Among the Reeds*, 1899). Yeats was also drawn to describe tents of hair, as were others at the time. Compare Dante Gabriel Rossetti's 'The Blessed Damozel' lines 21–22:

> Surely she leaned o'er me – her hair
> Fell all about my face.

XXI: 'He who hath glory lost nor hath'

The manuscript fair copy Joyce gave his friend Constantine Curran was headed 'Dedication/To Nora'. It dates from September 1904, like another fragmentary manuscript (*Archive* I 36, 38), and the poem might well have been the last of the sequence to be written. Stanislaus Joyce records that it was added to the collection after the others, along with Poem XXXVI (*MBK* 246).

September 1904 was the month Joyce stayed with Gogarty in the Tower at Sandycove – as described in the first chapter of *Ulysses* – before he left Ireland with Nora. The present poem not surprisingly played a special part in the evolution of the sequence, and retrospectively adds meaning to Poems XVII, XVIII and XIX.

5: unconsortable   The negative form of the unusual seventeenth-century word is perhaps Joyce's own. It means 'not companionable, not consorting together'.

6: companion   A term that had some currency at the time for advanced sexual unions, according to Richard Brown, *James Joyce and Sexuality* (Cambridge, 1985) 14, who also cites *SH* 62 (compare 77). The relevant volume of the *OED* (1893) cites Shakespeare, *Antony and Cleopatra* I ii 30: 'Find me to marrie me with Octavius Caesar, and companion me with my mistress.'

XXII: 'Of that so sweet imprisonment'

4: detain   Stephen chooses Newman's use of the word for philological commentary in *SH* 33, *P* 188. The 1897 *OED* definition gives as the first meaning: 'To keep in confinement, or under restraint; to keep prisoner' – which has a bearing here on line 6.

7: interwoven   Tindall 206 points out that the word was dear to Yeats. Compare for instance 'Who Goes with Fergus?' and 'The Man who Dreamed of Faeryland' (both in *The Rose*, 1893).

XXIII: 'This heart that flutters near my heart'

1: flutters   The word is prominent in Keats – for instance, 'Ode to Psyche' line 42 – yet the grammatical movement and conceit of these opening lines is closer to Donne in 'The Sun Rising':

> She is all states, and all princes I,
>   Nothing else is.
> Princes do but play us; compared to this,
> All honour's mimic, all wealth alchemy.

2, 4: is, kiss   Compare the same rhyme in Poems XX and XXIX. It might owe something to the example of Yeats.

8: wrens   Associated in Irish folklore with St Stephen's Day, 26 December, as Joyce recalls in *U* 392 and *FW* 363.05. Compare the dove of Poem XIV and the thrushes of Poem XVI.

10   Tindall 207 remarks that the line gave Joyce trouble, as the manuscripts prove. Compare Tindall 152 and *Archive* I 63, 97, 137.

XXIV: 'Silently she's combing'

The poem is one of five that appear in a separate, rather scrappy group of manuscripts dating from about 1903–4 (*Archive* I 33). It was the first of the poems in the sequence to be published (on 14 May 1904 in the *Saturday Review*).

2, 4: hair, air   Yeats uses the rhyme in stanzas 5 and 7 of 'The Cap and Bells' (in *The Wind Among the Reeds*, 1899).

6: dappled grass   Perhaps deriving from Yeats's 'The Song of Wandering Aengus', which gives Stephen one of his nicknames in *Ulysses* (*U* 176, 179, 204).

8: lookingglass   The mirror metaphor recurs throughout a book Joyce is known to have been enthusiastic about while he was an undergraduate, Meredith's *The Egoist*, and Tindall 209 suggests he took it over as an image of narcissism and sterility. It recurs prominently as such in descriptions of Gerty MacDowell and Milly Bloom in *U* 288, 304, and especially of Isabel in *FW* 561–2.

16: many a negligence   Compare Herrick's 'A slight disorder in her dress', alluded to in *U* 340. Also Jonson's 'Still to be neat', which Joyce admired and sang (Padraic Colum, *Road Round Ireland*, 310, cited by Tindall 31 and 208).

XXV: 'Lightly come or lightly go'

Stanislaus Joyce records that the poem was inspired by Mary Sheehy, on the same outing reflected in Poem XII (*MBK* 156). A separate manuscript dating from about 1904 is preserved at Yale (*Archive* I 31).

4: Oread   Nymph of the mountain. Compare *SH* 42 on Stephen's pursuit of 'that One: arms of love that had not love's malignity, laughter running upon the mountains of the morning, an hour wherein might be encountered the incommunicable'.

9: evenstar   Recalling Venus, the Evening Star of Poem IV.

XXVI: 'Thou leanest to the shell of night'

1: leanest   The archaic form is undoubtedly used with parodic intent. Compare with Poem XI.

5: rivers rushing forth   Tindall 211–12 accumulates parallels of water and making water, combined images of purgation and creativity.

12: In Purchas or in Holinshed.   Samuel Purchas (1575?–1626) wrote his *Pilgrimage*, which Coleridge said prompted *Kubla Khan*. Joyce admired Coleridge (Budgen 182), and Alph the sacred river is an element of ALP in *Finnegans Wake*. Raphael Holinshed (d. 1580?) wrote the chronicles on which several of Shakespeare's plays are based – for instance, *Macbeth*, alluded to in Poem XXXIV below.

XXVII: 'Though I thy Mithridates were'

The manuscript fair copy that Joyce gave Constantine Curran is dated 30 September 1904 (*Archive* I 39). Stanislaus Joyce appears to have had a hand in the revision of the poem (*CDD* 75; compare *L* II 92, 220).

1: **Mithridates**   Mithridates VI, King of Pontius and Bythnia (120–63 BC), is said to have made himself immune to poisons by the constant use of antidotes.

4: **heart**   Thus – without punctuation – in the manuscripts and also the later printed editions. It is followed by a comma in the earlier printed editions only.

   The lack of punctuation and the consequent momentary uncertainty as to whether the next line begins a sentence (it surely does not) is matched by the ambiguity of 'unaware' in line 3. Does the word refer to him or her, the speaker or the person addressed?

8: **wise**   Compare the same word in Poems XII (line 7), XV (line 11) and XXIII (line 11), where, like here, it is charged with overtones of worldly-wise knowingness, bored familiarity. Elsewhere, too, Joyce uses the word in an unusually pejorative sense: for instance, to describe Mr Deasy or as part of a slur cast by Stephen's father (*U* 30, 73).

10: **piping poets**   With overtones of Blake's 'piping loud' ('Infant Sorrow') and 'Piping Songs' (Introduction to *Songs of Innocence*)? Or, more immediately, the 'piper piping away' throughout Yeats's 'The Host of the Air' (in *The Wind Among the Reeds*, 1899).

XXVIII: 'Gentle lady, do not sing'

The poem is one of five that appear in a separate, rather scrappy group of manuscripts dating from about 1903–4 (*Archive* I 34).

1–2: **do not sing/Sad songs about the end of love**   Follows the movement of Shakespeare's 'let us sit upon the ground/And tell sad stories of the death of kings' (*Richard II* III ii 155–6).

2, 4: **love, enough**   Tindall 214 remarks on Yeats's fondness for such imperfect rhymes in the period 1902–5. Compare with Poem XXIII above.

6–7: **how/In the grave all love shall sleep**   Vaguely but inextinguishably reminiscent of a conceit that recurs in early seventeenth-century poems. Compare Donne's 'bracelet of bright hair about the bone' and Marvell's 'The grave's a fine and private place'.

8: **aweary**   A *fin de siècle* emotional posture that was as conventional as the head bending physically downwards and sideways in Poems I, II, IV, VII, XXVI.

XXIX: 'Dear heart, why will you use me so?'

4: raimented   The word is a seventeenth-century coinage that was revived by Tennyson in the first, 1832 version of *The Lady of Shalott*. Since Tennyson removed the word in subsequent editions, one would have thought Joyce found it in the *OED* – except that the relevant volume, *Q–R*, was not published till 1914.

6, 8: kiss, is   The rhyme is shared with Poems XX and XXIII.

7, 8: Desolate winds, shadowy garden   Contrasting with the 'Wind of spices' and 'little garden' of earlier poems like Poem XIII.

12: use   A usage endemic in poets like Wyatt and Surrey.

XXX: 'Love came to us in time gone by'

5: grave lovers   A pun contrived to recall the 'lovers that are dead' of Poem XXVIII.

8: ways   The image or motif of journeying recurs with special force throughout Joyce's writings, from before the taking-flight of the *Portrait* to beyond the odyssey of *Ulysses*.

XXXI: 'O, it was out by Donnycarney'

1: Donnycarney   In Joyce's time, a pretty village on the Malahide Road where lovers went and were surprised by the likes of Father Conmee (*U* 199; compare 184, 339–40), now a suburb between Marino and Artane.

2: the bat   Tindall 217–18 gives references to bats and vampires in Joyce, the girl here having become a vampire. It forms a deliberate contrast to the imagery of birds in earlier poems.

4, 7: sweet, softer   The two nouns – with their adjectival and adverbial variants – recur more than any others in Joyce's sequence. Compare *A Concordance to the 'Collected Poems' of James Joyce*, ed. Paul A. Doyle (NY, 1966) 172–3, 164–5 and *passim*.

5: the summer wind   In Joyce's own, earlier arrangement, the present poem preceded Poem XXIX, where the winds are 'Desolate' and presumably autumnal.

XXXII: 'Rain has fallen all the day'

Surely echoing the poem of Verlaine that begins,

> Il pleure dans mon coeur
> Comme il pleut sur la ville,

in *Romances sans paroles* (1874).

XXXIII: 'Now, O now, in this brown land'

Stanislaus dates the composition of this poem and the three following to Joyce's first stay in Paris, in 1902–3 (*MBK* 222).

1: **brown** A word that recurs throughout *Dubliners* to image the dinginess of the city. Compare also *SH* 216: 'one of those brown brick houses which seem the very incarnation of Irish paralysis'. The other colours – 'red and yellow' in line 7 – also signify autumnal decay (compare yellow as Lynch's favourite word and the 'uncouth faces . . . stained yellow or red or livid' of the Christian Brothers in *P* 165, etc.) in contrast to the vital blues and greens of earlier poems.

7: **rogue in red and yellow dress** The same jester in 'bright cap and streamers' who entered the sequence in Poem X.

14: **vilanelle** The elaborate Renaissance verse form underwent a fashionable revival among English poets of the 1890s. The usual spelling is with two sets of double *l* (as in *P* 223), but Joyce deleted the second *l* in the Cornell manuscript and repeated this spelling in the two subsequent fair copies (*Archive* I 73, 110, 147). All the printed texts up to *Collected Poems* (1936) have only the one *l*.

Joyce must have been aware of the derivation of the word from the Latin *villa*, 'small village'. Why he should contrive to confuse it with *vilem*, meaning 'worthless or vile', is obscure – unless he intended an oblique comment on the worth of such fashionable verse forms, after indulging in them.

XXXIV: 'Sleep now, O sleep now'

The poem is one of five that appear in a separate, rather scrappy group of manuscripts dating from about 1903–4 (*Archive* I 35), and it forms the conclusion to the Beach–Gilvarry sequence. In a letter written to the composer, G. Molyneaux Palmer, Joyce described it as 'vitally the end of the book' (*L* I 67).

1: **Sleep now, O sleep now** An allusion to *Macbeth* II ii 34–43? Joyce alludes to the same passage in *FW* 250.16–18.

2, 12: **unquiet heart** Echoing the same phrase in Yeats's 'The Old Age of Queen Maeve' (1903) line 30, though Yeats derived it from Tennyson's *In Memoriam* V 5.

5–6: **The voice of the winter/Is heard at the door** Invoking for English readers 'the voices of children are heard on the green', in the 'Nurse's Songs' of William Blake's *Innocence* and *Experience*. Tindall 222 compares the whole paragraph with Solomon 2:11–12 – a passage that is parodied in *FW* 39.14.

following 12 There is a note in pencil at the end of this poem in the Beach–Gilvarry manuscript, 'r. from Y' – presumably a memorandum that the sequence had been lent to Yeats.

XXXV: 'All day I hear the noise of waters'

Joyce sent a version of the poem on a postcard to J. F. Byrne shortly before he returned to Dublin from Paris in December 1902 (*L* II 20–21, facing 32; *Archive* I 23). The title here was: 'Second Part – Opening which tells of the journeyings of the soul'. The reference appears to be to a planned contrast between Joyce's life before and after leaving Dublin for Paris (see also *L* II 27n). It was however included only in the last of the manuscript sequences – dating from October 1906 (*Archive* I 149) – and Joyce afterwards described it as a tailpiece (*L* I 67).

The poem appears to owe something to Verlaine's 'Chanson d'automne', which Joyce translated in 1900–1902 (quoted below on pp. 301–2). The word-as-line 'Monotone' at the close of the first stanza is borrowed directly, and the last stanza here might be compared with Arthur Symons's translation of the same Verlaine poem in *Knave of Hearts: Poems 1894–1908* (London, 1913; reprinted in *Poems: Volume III*, London, 1924, 113):

> And I go
> Where the winds know,
> Broken and brief,
> To and fro,
> As the winds blow
> A dead leaf.

3: the seabird Compare the prophecy of the 'hawklike man flying sunward above the sea' in *P* 169.

XXXVI: 'I hear an army charging upon the land'

Joyce sent the poem to Stanislaus along with Poem IV, from Paris, in 1903 (*L* II 27–9; *Archive* I 29 and compare 27), where he describes it as 'for the second part'. Like Poem XXXV, it was not included in any of the preliminary manuscript sequences, and Joyce afterwards described it as a tailpiece (*L* I 67).

Stanislaus says the poem was based on a dream (*MBK* 246). Compare also the image of the sea, 'Thundering like ramping hosts of warrior horse' in the last poem of Meredith's *Modern Love*; and Yeats's 'I hear the Shadowy Horses', etc., in 'He bids his Beloved be at Peace' and 'The clash of fallen horsemen and the cries/Of unknown perishing armies beat about my ears' in 'The Valley of the Black Pig' (both in *The Wind Among the Reeds*, 1899). In the light of these recollections, it is ironic that Yeats repeatedly singled out the poem for particular praise (*L* II 351, 356, 381, 405). It appears he was responsible for kindling Pound's enthusiasm for the poem, and therefore its inclusion in the important *Des Imagistes* anthology of 1914 (see *P/J* 18). Ellmann notes that it contains some slight echoes of Paul Gregan's 'Recreant' (*Sunset Town*, Kilkenny and Dublin, 1901, 46; *L* II 10n).

1: **hear** Carried forward from the previous poem, where the word echoes oppressively throughout.

8: **clanging upon the heart as upon an anvil** Compare Stephen as he goes 'to encounter for the millionth time the reality of experience and to forge in the smithy of [his] soul the uncreated conscience of [his] race' (*P* 252–3). In *Finnegans Wake*, Shem the Penman is also a forger.

12: **My love, my love, my love** Tindall 225 suggests the three loves are those from whom Stephen exiles himself in the *Portrait*: his religion, his country and his family.

— **why have you left me alone?** Recalling Jesus's cry at the ninth hour, from the cross, 'My God, my God, why hast thou forsaken me?' (Matthew 27:46).

Pomes Penyeach (published 1927)

The first version of the first poem in the sequence, *Cabra*, was written in Dublin as early as 1903, and the last poem, *A Prayer*, was written in Paris in spring 1924. The eleven other poems, beginning with *Watching the Needleboats at San Sabba*, were written between September 1913 and 1915–16 in Trieste and Zurich. They centre on Joyce's exploration of his feelings for his pupil, Amalia Popper, which he explored more explicitly in *Giacomo Joyce*. Joyce is further removed from the commotion he registers in the private context of the prose writings, and adds comments further removed by times and places. Whereas Signorina Popper in Trieste (and later Marthe Fleischmann in Zurich) helped create the conditions in which he entered the mind of Gerty MacDowell, the poems step back into Joyce's own mind, closer to the second half of *Nausikaa* and the mind of Bloom.

Separate manuscript versions of several of the poems are extant, as well as typed versions of groups of them at Cornell, Buffalo and the Huntington (*Archive* I 202–28, 229–40, 241–8 and 251–73). All but *Tilly* and *A Prayer* were published in magazines between 1913 and 1920, eight of them in two issues of *Poetry* (Chicago), several in versions that differ from the final texts. At one stage, about 1918–19, Joyce appears to have intended his Felix Beran translation, *Lament for the Yeomen*, to be part of the sequence (*Archive* I 239; compare p. 310 below); and it appears that *A Memory of the Players*, which had already been written (*Archive* I 194, 195), was substituted.

Joyce added dates and places in the later sequences as part of an attempt to clarify the relation between separate poems, and his changing sense of the relation explains why the dates and order of poems differ between sequences. The Zurich–Paris datelines of the last four poems mark them off from the poems that come before, and remained constant. However, a sequence that was put together as late as 1927, now at the Huntington Library, gives the order of the previous four poems in the central Trieste group – *On the Beach at Fontana* and *Simples*, and *Flood* and *Nightpiece* – differently from the final, published version, and appends different dates accordingly. The two arrangements are set out side by side in *Archive* I xl–xli, and also by Michael Groden, 'A Textual and Publishing History' in *A Companion to Joyce Studies*, eds. Zack Bowen and James F. Carens (Westport, Conn. 1984) 111, and in Aubert 1378–9.

Joyce was himself ambivalent about the public worth of the poems, and it can be argued that he published them as much for personal as for artistic reasons. Ezra Pound had disparaged *Finnegans Wake*, then appearing as *Work in Progress*, and the poems prove that at least Joyce was capable of simple, lyric expression (*L* I 255; compare III 154–55). As it is, the title attempts to strike the balance that was also Joyce's attitude towards *Chamber Music*: 'a title which to a certain extent repudiated the book, without altogether disparaging it' (*L* II 182). The twelve poems sold for a shilling (twelve old-pence), and Joyce glossed the title for Jacques Mercanton as 'like the cry of a woman who sells her wares in the street, a poem or pome, another old English word (derived from *pomme*), an *m* dropped, as the *n* in penny, to make it smaller. This little punning game amused him, and it is much like the games in "Work in Progress", if a bit simpler' (Potts 236). Joyce encouraged his daughter Lucia to design the initial letters for a special limited, facsimile edition in 1932, and was particularly gratified when the collection was set to music as *The Joyce Book* in 1933 (compare *Pennipomes Twoguineaseach* above p. 91).

The first publication that appeared in 1927 from Shakespeare and Company contained a good many misprints that had to be corrected on an errata slip. The corrections were taken in to the second edition published by Faber in 1933, when Joyce made two further improvements in punctuation. This is the version reproduced here. The text included in *The Viking Portable James Joyce* (NY, 1947) mixes the 1927 and 1933 versions, and omits the appended dates. *P&SW* provides a corrected version of 1927.

Tilly

Stanislaus Joyce refers to the poem as early as 1903 (*CDD* 2), and it was apparently considered for the *Chamber Music* collection in 1906 (*L* II 181), even though it is unrhymed and resembles only the final poem in the sequence in style. Joyce referred to it as 'the Cabra poem' in 1906 and made a copy under this title in 1915–16. He subsequently emended it under the title *Ruminants* in 1918–19. Texts of *Cabra* and *Ruminants* will be found in *Archive* I 202–4 and 229; *P&SW* 254. The present version of the poem under the present title appears to be late, perhaps as late as the year in which it was published.

In the earlier versions of the poem, the final stanza runs as follows:

> Herdsman [*or* O herdsman], careful of the herd,
> Tonight sleep well by the fire
> When the herd too is asleep
> And the door made fast.

The change confirms the direction of other changes in previous stanzas, so that the poet is separated from the drover he describes. The earlier poem of sympathetic identification with a pastoral idyll gives way to a complaint against the rabblement, an atmosphere of betrayal and alienation.

The poem has attracted more commentary than others in the collection, and the conclusions are less at odds than might appear. Ellmann suggests the original version was prompted by the death of Joyce's mother in August 1903, the 'bough' of the last line (*JJ* 136–7); Chester G. Anderson argues the emphasis in the revised versions falls on Joyce's relation with J. F. Byrne, Cranly in the *Portrait*, the 'boor' of line 9 ('James Joyce's "Tilly"', *Publications of the Modern Language Association of America* LXXIII, 1958, 285–98); Robert Scholes draws attention to Joyce's exploitation of literary tradition, making connections with themes that are endemic in his writing ('James Joyce, Irish Poet', *JJQ* II, Summer 1965, 255–70). One connection suggested by Scholes (264) is with Richard and Robert in *Exiles*, in whom one can see the 'torn bough', and 'bond of the herd', the tearing hand.

Title   The title of the poem as published means the small extra measure or gratuitous added portion. It is the thirteenth poem in the baker's dozen making up the collection.

4: Cabra   Joyce's father bought a house at 7 St Peter's Terrace, Cabra, in October 1902, and the family lived there until May 1905 (*JJ* 105–6). Cabra is situated between Glasnevin and the Phoenix Park, and was then at the northern margins of the city.

9: Boor, bond of the herd   Anderson 289–92 identifies the boor with J. F. Byrne on the basis of Lynch's role as betrayer in *Stephen Hero* and the *Portrait*, and of his association with cattle imagery in these books and in *Ulysses*. Drover-ploughman poets are endemic in Irish poetry, as F. R. Higgins and Patrick Kavanagh subsequently demonstrated.

12: my torn bough!   In support of the notion that the bough is a widely accepted literary symbol of betrayal, Scholes 263–4 cites Virgil, *Aeneid* III 22–48, Ovid, *Metamorphoses* VIII 761ff, Dante, *Inferno* XIII, Ariosto, *Orlando Furioso* VI 26–56, Spenser, *Faerie Queene* I ii 30–34.

Watching the Needleboats at San Sabba

Stanislaus Joyce told Ellmann that the poem was written as Joyce watched him take part in a sculling race at San Sabba, near Trieste. As the scullers pulled towards the shore, they began to sing Johnson's aria from the last act of Puccini's *La Fanciulla del West* (*The Girl of the Golden West*; *JJ* 347). Joyce's poem, which mourns the lost intensity of youth, is related to his involvement with Amalia Popper, but the word 'needleboat' and his revision of date aligns this with Nora's youthful love feelings in Galway (compare *She weeps over Rahoon*).

In short, the poem introduces a nexus of interests that subsequent poems enlarge on. It was the first serious poem Joyce had written since about the time he left Dublin in 1904. It was published in the *Saturday Review* (September 1913).

Title   Padraic Colum, presumably echoing what Joyce had told him, reported that the word 'needleboat' is used because the pointed prows of the boats at Sabba reminded Joyce of the shape of boats in Ireland;

this is why, he says, Joyce used 'a Galway term' ('James Joyce as Poet' in *The Joyce Book*, ed. Herbert Hughes, London, 1932, 14). The word does not appear in dictionaries, but Mr Tom Kenny of Kenny's Bookshop in Galway tells me that single sculls on the Corrib were known as 'needleboats' by the rivermen, because of the way they appeared to jump ahead of each other in races like shuttles or needles.

Fr. Eddie Diffely SJ, of Colaiste Iognaid in Galway, came up with another definition from Gerry Madden, who was about the Corrib all his life; this is that needleboat was a slang term for a single randan. The randan, known in England and on the Liffey as a rumtum, was a clinker-built single sculling boat used by beginners or as a pleasure boat, and it may also have been used in Galway for a pair-oared pleasure boat, or tub pair.

The research operation on which this note is based was mounted by Irish oarsman Michael Johnston of Sandycove, Co. Dublin.

4: No more, return no more! A lugubrious rendering of the last line of the Puccini aria:

> Aspetterà ch'io torni,
> E passeranno i giorni e passerannano i giorni
> ed io non tornerò ed io non tornerò.

('She will await my return,/And days will pass and days will pass/And I will not return and I will not return.') The music and libretto are conveniently to hand in Bauerle 125–6a.

6: loveblown bannerets The same associations were drawn upon by Yeats at about the same time: 'packed his marriage day/With banneret and pennon' ('That the Night Come' in *Responsibilities*, 1914).

following 9: 1912 The earliest manuscripts and typescripts are dated 7 September 1913 (*Archive* I 188, 205–13), and a copy was sent to Stanislaus for 'your young friends of the *Rowing Club* if they want them for a dinner programme or some such thing' two days later (*L* II 323–4). The 1912 date appears to have been substituted at a late stage before the publication of the sequence (compare *Archive* I xl, 255).

A Flower given to my Daughter

The flower was given to Lucia Joyce by Joyce's pupil, Amalia Popper, as he noted in *GJ* 3: 'A flower given to her by my daughter. Frail gift, frail giver, frail blue-veined child.' A fair copy made by Joyce for Lucia in 1917 is reproduced by Stelio Crise, *Epiphanies and Phadographs: Joyce e Trieste* (Milan, 1967) Appendix 41.

3: sere Macbeth's late, sad appropriation of the word is the one everyone remembers: 'my way of life/Is fall'n into the sere, the yellow leaf' (*Macbeth* V iii 22–3).

She weeps over Rahoon

Rahoon is the burial place in Galway City where Nora's early sweetheart, Michael Bodkin, was buried. In *The Dead*, Joyce transposed the burial-place of Bodkin's fictional counterpart, Michael Furey, to Oughterard, some seventeen miles away; but the present poem is a reworking of the same, even down to 'falls softly, softly falling' (compare *D* 223–4). Compare also Joyce's notes for *Exiles*, pp. 346–7.

One must suppose the speaker to be Nora/Gretta. The serious use of dramatic monologue is unusual in Joyce's verse, and, despite the existence of Gerty MacDowell and Molly Bloom in *Ulysses*, the adoption of a female lyric persona is unique. Tindall remarks, 'It is not easy to understand why after embodying the experience in a great story [Joyce] tried to recapture it in a minor lyric' (97n). The answer must surely be, to bring his involvement with Amalia Popper, which is a central theme of the *Pomes Penyeach* sequence, into alignment with the related situation – as he understood it – of Nora and Michael Bodkin. The changed dating of the present poem bears on this, and has the same integrating effect as the title and changed dating of *Needleboats* above.

following 12: 1913 In the manuscript at Buffalo and the typescript at the Huntington, the poem is dated 1914 (*Archive* I 232, 258). It is remotely possible that some version of the lines was sent to Nora from Galway in 1912 (*L* II 309).

Tutto è Sciolto

The title derives from Elvino's short but beautiful lament in the second act of Vincenzo Bellini's *La sonnambula* (*The Sleepwalker*). Elvino's bride-to-be has been caught sleepwalking in Rudolpho's room, and Elvino, not knowing her innocence, upbraids her and then in despair sings the song:

> Tutto è sciolto.
> Più per me non c'ha conforto
> Il mio cor per sempre è morto
> Alla gioia ed all'amor.

Bauerle 120–23 provides the complete libretto and score.

Ellmann quotes a 1916 notebook in which Joyce noted one of Nora's dreams – 'Prezioso weeping/I have passed him in the street/My book "Dubliners" in his hand' – and commented: 'The motive of *Tutto è sciolto* played back to the front. The point with which he tried to wound had been turned against him – by her . . .' (*JJ* 437; compare Scholes No. 52). In other words, the dream connects his insistent belief, in 1909 and after, that he had been betrayed by Nora ('all is lost'), with the reversal of the situation in his unfulfilled affair with Amalia Popper in Trieste in 1914. The same aria appears in *Ulysses* as a motif to express Bloom's feelings about Molly and Blazes Boylan. Richie Goulding mentions it by its English name, in *Sirens*, and Bloom immediately applies it to his own mood (*U* 223–4; compare other references at 210, 238, 339, 394, 426).

The manuscript now at the Fondation Martin Bodmer is reproduced in *English and American Autographs in the Bibliotheca Bodmeriana*, comp. Margaret Crum (Cologny-Geneva, 1977) 43.

On the Beach at Fontana

The poem was originally ninth in the preliminary arrangement of the poems in the typescript now at the Huntington, preceding *Alone* (*Archive* I xli, 268). It is based on an incident involving Giorgio Joyce, born 27 July 1905, recorded in the second of the following three paragraphs that constitute an entry in the Trieste notebook (in *The Workshop of Daedalus: James Joyce and the Raw Materials for 'A Portrait of the Artist as a Young Man'*, eds. Robert Scholes and Richard M. Kain, Evanston, Ill., 1965, 98–9):

> You were a few minutes old. While the doctor was drying his hands I walked up and down with you, humming to you. You were quite happy, happier than I.
>
> I held him in the sea at the baths of Fontana and felt with humble love the trembling of his frail shoulders: *Asperge[s] me, Domine, hyssopo et mundabor: lavabis me et super nivem dealbalor.*
>
> Before he was born I had no fear of fortune.

As Scholes and Kain explain, the Latin is a quotation from the Asperges, or the Sprinkling with Holy Water performed every Sunday immediately before the commencement of High Mass. It translates as 'Thou shalt sprinkle me with hyssop, O Lord, and I shall be cleansed: thou shalt wash me and I shall be made whiter than snow.'

Title Fontana is the familiar Triestine abbreviation of the imposing

Fontana de Continenti o delle Quattro Parti del Mondo, which stands in the enormous Piazza dell'Unita in the centre of Trieste, one side of which, across the road, fronts on to the Bacino S. Giusto. An old photograph of 'Il bagno *Fontano*', such as it is, is reproduced by Stelio Crise, *Epiphanies and Phadographs: Joyce e Trieste* (Milan, 1967) plate 13, and in *And Trieste, Ah Trieste: Exhibition Catalogue for the Third International James Joyce Symposium, Trieste 1971* (Milan, 1971) plate VII.

In other words, the title situates Joyce's poem at the edge of a working harbour in a large city, not on a holiday beach with buckets and sand.

Simples

The poem preceded *On the Beach* in the preliminary arrangement of the poems in a typescript now at the Huntington, that is, was number eight (*Archive* xli, 267). The epigraph and line eight adapt a folk-song from the Alpine (Trentino) area:

> Come porti i capelli,
> bella bionda!
> Tu li porti
> a la bella marinara!
> Tu li porti
> come l'onda,
> come l'onda,
> in mezzo al mar!
>
> In mezzo al mar
> ci stà un camin che fumano;
> saranno la mia bella
> che si consumano!

This translates as 'How you wear your hair,/beautiful blondè!/You wear it/ in a style which is beautiful and associated with the sea!/You wear it like the wave,/like the wave,/in the middle of the sea!//In the middle of the sea/there's a smoking chimney;/it'll be my beautiful girl/consuming herself!' (Italian text and translation supplied by Professor John Barnes, of University College Dublin; compare Francesco Gozzi, *La Poesia di James Joyce*, Bari, 1974, 163.)

Ellmann reports how Joyce brought the poem to a pupil, Oscar

Schwarz, explaining how it was addressed to Lucia and accepting Schwarz's response that it was 'pure music' (*JJ* 382). This is true in a particular sense. The girl who is addressed is his daughter, and the poem matches *On the Beach at Fontana*, which is concerned with his son. She is also at the same time less specific – an encompassing siren voice.

9: a waxen ear   Odysseus defended his crew from the lure of the Sirens' song by stopping their ears with wax (*Odyssey* XII).

12: simples   The meaning changes from not complicated and free from guile, innocent, to the medical sense of medicinal herbs (as Bloom uses it in *U* 69).

Flood

The poem is one of those that changed its date as well as its position as Joyce revised his poems as a sequence. It followed sixth in the sequence of poems at the Huntington, dated 1914, after *Tutto è Sciolto* (*Archive* I xli, 261).

The imagery and language are close to Stephen's meditation on the swirling, incoming seawater at the close of *Proteus* (*U* 41):

> In long lassoes from the Cock lake the water flowed full, covering greengoldenly lagoons of sand, rising flowing. . . . It flows purling, widely flowing, floating foampool, flower unfurling.
>
> Under the upswelling tide he saw the writhing weeds lift languidly and sway reluctant arms, hising up their petticoats, in whispering water swaying and upturning coy silver fronds. Day by day: night by night: lifted, flooded and let fall. . . .

The sexual connotations of Stephen's reverie are, however, more obvious. The tide mingles with his thoughts about the woman he has seen on the beach: 'Weary too in sight of lovers, lascivious men, a naked woman shining in her courts, she draws a toil of waters.' *P&SW* 239, 291 n71 lists parallels between a similar passage in *Giacomo Joyce*, and *Portrait* and *Exiles*. The same images in the poem work to communicate a more acute sense of isolation.

11: Lambent   From the Latin *lambere*, 'to lick', and so: gliding over a surface, shining with a soft clear light, softly radiant.

Nightpiece

The poem is another of those whose date and position Joyce changed as he revised the sequence. It followed seventh in the Huntington typescript, dated 1915 (*Archive* I xli, 266).

The poem constitutes a reworking of an entry in *Giacomo Joyce*, and is thereby associated with Joyce's feelings for Amalia Popper. It will be noticed that while the visual clarity of the prose gives way to less precise images, the feelings embodied therein are more complicated:

> In the raw veiled spring morning faint odours float of morning Paris: aniseed, damp sawdust, hot dough of bread: and as I cross the Pont Saint Michel the steelblue waking waters chill my heart. They creep and lap about the island whereon men have lived since the stone age ... Tawny gloom in the vast gargoyled church. It is cold as on that morning: *quia frigus erat*. Upon the steps of the far high altar, naked as the body of the Lord, the ministers lie prostrate in weak prayer. The voice of an unseen reader rises, intoning the lesson from Hosea. *Hæc dicit Dominus: in tribulatione sua mane consurgent ad me. Venite et revertamur ad Dominum* ... She stands beside me, pale and chill, clothed with the shadows of the sindark nave, her thin elbow at my arm. Her flesh recalls the thrill of that raw mist-veiled morning, hurrying torches, cruel eyes. Her soul is sorrowful, trembles and would weep. Weep not for me, O daughter of Jerusalem! (*GJ* 10; *P&SW* 235).

A manuscript at the British Museum (*Archive* I 196–7) links the poem with the Tristan and Isolde story as Joyce treated it in *FW* II 4.

1, 4: gloom, illume Stephen quotes a piece from Shelley with the same rhymes to Cranly, justifying the archaic form 'illume', in *SH* 133–4.

12: thurible A censer, that is, vessel in which incense is burnt in religious ceremonies. The word is common enough in contexts like that described in the *GJ* entry (and compare *U* 295), but unusual in verse. Joyce's style in verse builds on a heightened, poetic awareness of such isolated words.

17: Voidward A Joycean coinage that is not yet in the dictionaries. It literally means 'in the direction of the casting off', and is etymologically linked to 'Waste' in the following line.

Alone

In a letter to Herbert Gorman, Joyce's language-student, Georges Borach, a Zurich businessman, described how the poem was composed during a walk along the lake (compare Potts 72; Lund No. 251).

5: **The sly reeds whisper**   Tindall 210–11 identifies this as 'an allusion to Midas' that 'shadows forth the relationship of father and daughter'. I do not understand this, and think a more likely allusion is to Syrinx, pursued by Pan and changed into a reed – making the speaker appear more Pan-like, even goatish.

8: **A swoon of shame**   Compare Stephen's 'swoon of sin' at the close of *Portrait* Ch. 2 and his 'swooning' at the close of Ch. 4 (*P* 101, 172); also Gabriel Conroy at the close of *The Dead* ('His soul swooned slowly', etc. *D* 224). Joyce's interest in the word almost certainly owed something to Keats's 'swoon to death' at the close of the 'Bright star!' sonnet.

A Memory of the Players in a Mirror at Midnight

The background of the poem is explained by Frank Budgen. Joyce helped the English Players in their business arrangements and in a general advisory capacity, also with prompting and singing 'off', though he never appeared on stage with them. The present poem grew from his experience of singing 'off' in a performance of Browning's *In a Balcony* (Budgen 201).

The subject of Browning's closet drama (published in 1855) is the different love of men and women, how it is compromised by circumstance and yet how heroically it finds expression. The characters eventually overcome their inhibitions and state beliefs that are also Browning's:

> That woman yonder, there's no use in life
> But just to obtain her! Heap earth's woes in one
> And bear them – make a pile of all earth's joys
> And spurn them, as they help or help not this;
> Only, obtain her!

Browning's hero Norbert, with the help of the heroine Constance, states his love; Joyce, alone, meditates that he has not. His lines are an alienated reflection on high passion that translates itself into action for others but not for him, in a style that echoes Browning's vehement, elliptical manner. Curiously, Joyce appears to identify again with Browning's protagonist, Norbert, in *A Portrait of the Artist as an Ancient Mariner* line 13.

Bahnhofstrasse

Joyce suffered his first attack of glaucoma on this Zurich street the year before, and in the poem he takes such evidence of the ageing process to indicate the impossibility of recovering youth and young love. The poem was written shortly before he began an 'affair' with Marthe Fleischmann, one which recalled but lacked the innocence of his feelings for Amalia Popper in Trieste. See *JJ* 450, etc.

3: **Grey way whose violet signals are** In a letter to Harriet Weaver of September 1928 Joyce proves he was fully aware of the different consequences of secondary cataracts, German *grauer Star*, and glaucoma, German *grüner Star* (*L* I 269).

4: **the twining star** Fritz Gysling, 'A Doctor's Look at a Neglected Poem', *JJQ* VII (Spring 1970) 251–2, diagnoses double images, or diplopia, as symptomatic of Joyce's affliction.

5: **star of evil! star of pain!** The photosensibility of glaucoma patients is reduced to an extent that sources of light appear as sparkling dots.

A Prayer

The poem, dating from May 1924, is the first of its kind Joyce had written for six years. It is one of the very few whose beginnings in, and evolution through, early rough drafts can be traced (compare *Archive* I 198–200). Aubert 1392 compares the psychology of Joyce's letter to Nora of 13 December 1909 (*L* II 272–3).

2 The line is not in italics in the first-draft manuscript at Buffalo, and it is revised in a way that suggests it is not a quotation. (Thus: 'Come, [yield, *del*] give, yield all your [force *del*] strength to me,' *Archive* I 198). Nor is the second 'Come' (line 16) italicized in the same first-draft manuscript.

   Could the word 'Come' have any of the sexual overtones it possesses in the *Chamber Music* sequence (see Poems X, XIII, etc.)?

5: **Gentling** Joyce probably coined the word without reference to previous usage. The first use recorded by the *OED* is 1883 (and compare *Supplement*).

7: **Blind me ...** Dr Borsch had recently observed that a secretion was forming in the conjunctiva of Joyce's left eye, and advised an operation (*L* III 92; *JJ* 564; etc.).

POEMS OF EARLY YOUTH

Doyle No. 11 lists a four-line parody of Macaulay's 'Horatius' included in Patricia Hutchins, *James Joyce's Dublin* (London, 1950) 70, but the original undergraduate publication, *St Stephen's*, makes no connection with Joyce and the lines are not included here. Doyle No. 12 – two lines in German – are in fact quoted from Goethe's *Faust* (compare *L* II 24). Doyle No. 18 – a twisted quotation of Milton's *Lycidas* that Joyce supplied for Gogarty to use – is quoted in the next section of the Notes, in connection with the 'Satire on John Eglinton'. The parody of 'Salve Regina' Joyce mentioned in a letter to Stanislaus in 1907 (*L* II 210) has not come to light.

It is the nature of the case that there should be marginal instances. Eugene Sheehy quotes a refrain of an Irish love-song that Joyce appears to have invented, though he may have inherited it from his father (*May It Please the Court*, Dublin, 1951, 22–3). His version of 'The Yellow Ale' again appears to have contained invented elements (*JJ* 334n). It is also probable, given the way occasional poems circulate, that further examples will come to light as others unknown have been lost. The genre does not tolerate sharply defined limits.

Satire on George O'Donnell
(in the style of Goldsmith)

Joyce wrote the verses on the front page of a copy of P. W. Joyce's *A Concise History of Ireland* (1894), which belonged to a schoolfriend, George O'Donnell, headed by O'Donnell's name. They are reported by Colum 147n, who says: 'The class in Belvedere had been reading Goldsmith's "Retaliation," and the sixteen-year-old Joyce singled out one of his classmates for an address that echoes Goldsmith's mock epitaphs.' Joyce was able to quote the lines on Burke from the same poem many years afterwards (Colum 147–8). The copy of P. W. Joyce is reported now to be in private hands (*James Joyce's Manuscripts: An Index,* comp. Michael Groden, NY, 1980, 161).

O'Donnell (b. 26 February 1879) enrolled at Belvedere College on 1 September 1890. Little is recorded about his activities at the school other than that he was elected Secretary of the Sodality in his final year, 1895–6, the year in which Joyce was elected an ordinary member (Joyce was to hold the position of Prefect in the two years following, 1896–8). Dr Bruce Bradley SJ, the present Headmaster and the historian of Joyce's years at the school, thinks it unlikely that Joyce and O'Donnell were actually in the same class. It should also be noted that the poem was most likely written when Joyce was fourteen or fifteen.

O'Donnell is rumoured subsequently to have had a commission in the British Army and then a position in the Irish Post Office. It is significant that Colum was the only person to whom he showed the poem: friends who remember him from later days in the Dublin Arts Club have suggested he is likely to have been sensitive to Joyce's rather cruel humour.

2: **'murphies'** Potatoes, sold here in an 'everything' neighbourhood shop. The only O'Donnell listed in *Thom's Directory* in the relevant grocery-merchant category is Hugh O'Donnell, with business premises at 12 and 13 Queen Street, residing at Geraldine Cottage, Dalkey.

3-4 O'Donnell did in fact have sandy-red hair.

7: **Kilmainham** The gaol was completed in 1796 to house prisoners from Co. Dublin, but at once became famous as a high-security detention centre for nationalist activists. Robert Emmet and Napper Tandy, John O'Leary and O'Donovan Rossa, Michael Davitt and Charles Stuart Parnell, all spent time there.

9: **Drumcondra's production** O'Donnell's address when he entered Belvedere was 17 St Alphonsus Road, Drumcondra. The Joyces, with their declining fortunes, had lived in the same suburb for a brief period when Joyce entered the school.

12: **Portland Gaol** A prison in Dorset, which subsequently became a borstal and youth detention centre. It is unclear why Joyce singled it out. It was not particularly favoured by Irish felons; at the time, its occupants were engaged almost exclusively in quarrying stone for the building of the Portland breakwater.

Translation of Horace's 'O Fons Bandusiae'

The poem is an untitled school-exercise. Horace, *Odes* III 13, was on the Latin course during Joyce's last year at Belvedere (Bruce Bradley, *James Joyce's Schooldays*, Dublin, 1982, 138–9), and Jacques Mercanton records that Joyce 'delighted in Horace, whom he preferred to Virgil because of his minute perfections, his diverse meters, his rarest music', and that he was able to quote Horace from memory long afterwards (Potts 227–8). Compare *P* 179–80; also *FW* 280.31–2 ('that fount Bandusian shall play').

The only known text was printed by Gorman 45–6, and it is possible that Gorman's 'forms' in line 5 should be emended to 'horns'. Joyce's translation is discussed by Kevin Sullivan, *Joyce among the Jesuits* (NY, 1958) 75–7. His skill might be measured in a comparison with Milton's schoolboy translation of Horace, *Odes* I 5, beginning 'What slender youth bedewed with liquid odours'. The original Latin goes as follows:

O fons Bandusiae, splendidior vitro,
dulci digne mero non sine floribus,
   cras donaberis haedo,
      cui frons turgida cornibus

primis et venerem et proelia destinat.
frustra: nam gelidos inficiet tibi
   rubro sanguine rivos
      lascivi suboles gregis.

te flagrantis atrox hora Caniculae
nescit tangere, tu frigus amabile
   fessis vomere tauris
      praebes et pecori vago.

fies nobilium tu quoque fontium,
me dicente cavis impositam ilicem
   saxis, unde loquaces
      lymphae desiliunt tuae.

Fragments from Shine and Dark *(1900?)*
(perhaps also from the earlier collection Moods *and other sources)*

The first thirty fragments owe their preservation to the accident that Stanislaus Joyce used the blank sides of thirty pages for his commonplace book, which is now at Cornell. They are reproduced in *Archive* I 1–15 and are here derived from that source. Nos. V, XI, XVI, XX, XXIV, XXV, XXVI, XXVII and XXIX were previously published by Ellmann (*JJ* 80–82), and Stanislaus Joyce adds two more lines to No. X below (*MBK* 101). The numbers coincide with the *Archive* numbering, but it should be emphasized that they are an editorial insertion.

Stanislaus used only the lower halves of pages, and traces of preceding lines of poems (descenders, etc.) appear at the top of most leaves. What has been preserved does not have an overall title or description. No. VII is dated 29 June 1900, and Nos. VI and XXIX are described as deriving from unpublished or unfinished plays written at the same time. The fragments probably represent the bulk of Joyce's second collection, *Shine and Dark*. It is also possible that some poems from Joyce's first collection, *Moods*, were carried forward. It is likely that they were part of the collection sent to William Archer for possible publication around September 1901 (*L* II 9–10; *JJ* 83). No. XXXI is derived from *MBK* 101.

I   The punctuation at the end of most lines and perhaps some words might have been lost because the manuscript is worn.

II   A rendering in French of Arthur Symons's lyric 'Pastel'?

VI: **With the Rommany Rye**   That is, in the gypsy spirit or like a gypsy. 'Romany' means gypsy, from gypsy *rom*, 'man'; 'Rye' is gypsy for 'gentleman'. George Borrow used the phrase in *Lavengro* (1851) and made it the title of the sequel he published in 1857. Stephen reveals an interest in the language of gypsies in *Proteus* (*U* 39).

— *A Brilliant Career*   Stanislaus Joyce gives an account of the play (*MBK* 126–7), which can be supplemented by a letter from William Archer, to whom Joyce sent it (*JJ* 79–80). Compare also Leo Daly, *James Joyce and the Mullingar Connection* (Dublin, 1975) 57–8.

IX: **shawms**   An early woodwind instrument with a double reed, forerunner of the modern oboe. Joyce's description more probably rests on a sixteenth-century literary source (for instance Spenser's *Faerie Queene* I xii 13) rather than on first-hand musical experience.

X   Stanislaus Joyce described the poem as a half-humorous serenade in dialect: 'The dialect consisted mainly in omitting the g of the present participle' (*MBK* 101). He gives the title as 'Rebuking', and quotes two more lines that follow on directly from what is given here:

> To be listenin' to me mopin'
> Here and singin', lady mine?

XI: **ah, I am faint ... and, ah, I fall**   Compare Shelley's 'I fall upon the thorns of life, I bleed', etc.; Ellmann compares the 'Villanelle of the Temptress' used in the *Portrait* but dating from this same period (*JJ* 82). Could the fragment have anything to do with the 'ambitious effort ... on the Valkyrie' recalled but not quoted by Stanislaus Joyce in *MBK* 101?

XIII   Aubert 1330 compares the opening words of the prayer spoken before Communion: 'Domine non sum dignus ut intres sub tectum meum, sed tantum dic verbum et sanabitur anima mea' ('Lord, I am not worthy to receive you under my roof; say but the word and my soul shall be healed').

XX   As Ellmann notes, one of the few examples of *Shine* poems; the larger part of what was preserved represents *Dark* (*JJ* 82). Aubert 1331 suggests the second stanza opens with an allusion to Ernst Haeckel's *The Riddle of the Universe* (English version 1900).

XXIV   Latin for 'Lord, grant him eternal peace' from the Introit to the

Mass for the Dead. Ellmann remarks that the fallen seraphim and flames and cries of lines 7–8 appear again in Stephen's villanelle (*JJ* 81n; compare *P* 223–4; *P&SW* 72). He also compares Yeats's poem, 'To Some I have Talked with by the Fire' (in *The Rose*, 1893):

> And of the embattled flaming multitude
> Who rise, wing above wing, flame above flame,
> And, like a storm, cry the Ineffable Name,

XXVI–XXVII Ellmann suggests the two fragments are to be taken together as Joyce's version of a witches' sabbath, and that they perhaps derive from the orgiastic dance in Yeats's story *The Tables of the Law*, whole pages of which Joyce knew by heart (*JJ* 81–2).

XXIX: Joyce's note The present fragment is all that survives of Joyce's play. The 'following lyric' is not necessarily No. XXX in the sequence here, of course.

XXXI I have added this fragment to the Cornell sequence. It celebrates 'some joyous festival of youth', and was recalled by Stanislaus Joyce in *MBK* 101.

Translation of Verlaine's 'Chanson d'automne' (1900–1902)

The only known version of the poem was quoted by Herbert Gorman 59. In his essay on Mangan, Joyce compared the rhythmic expressiveness of Verlaine with that of Shakespeare (*CW* 75), and continued to admire him long afterwards (Dario de Tuoni and Georges Borach in Potts 34n, 72; Budgen 181). Verlaine was mentioned by Thomas Kettle in his review of *Chamber Music* (*CH* I 37), and Hugh Kenner analyses this translation as evidence of Joyce's developing poetical maturity (*Dublin's Joyce*, London, 1955, 27–35).

According to Stanislaus Joyce, this translation and the villanelle of the temptress in the *Portrait* were the only early poems that Joyce thought to preserve (unpublished letter cited in *JJ* 76n). Among other French poets, Joyce is known to have translated from Maeterlinck (Gorman 59).

The Verlaine original, from *Poèmes saturniens* (1866), is as follows:

> Les sanglots longs
> Des violons
>   De l'automne
> Blessent mon cœur
> D'une langueur
>   Monotone.

Tout suffocant
Et blême, quand
   Sonne l'heure,
Je me souviens
Des jours anciens
   Et je pleure;

Et je m'en vais
Au vent mauvais
   Qui m'emporte
Deçà, delà
Pareil à la
   Feuille morte.

Joyce's youthful effort stands up to a comparison with Arthur Symons's translation of the same original in *Knave of Hearts: Poems 1894–1908* (London, 1913; reprinted in *Poems: Volume III*, London, 1924, 113). Joyce made different use of the same Verlaine poem in *Chamber Music*, Poem XXXV. Stephen recalls line 13 in *P* 252.

'Alas, how sad the lover's lot' (1902)

These early verses in Joyce's holograph could not be located at Cornell (Scholes No. 21d) when the *Archive* was in preparation, or when a further search was made in October 1989. Fortunately, Richard Ellmann had made a transcript, which provides the text in *P&SW* 89.

'She is at peace where she is sleeping' (1902)

The poem exists in two versions, the priority of which is not known. The version given here is in Joyce's holograph at Cornell, on paper the same as that on which 'I said: I will go down to where' and 'Though we are leaving youth behind' are written. The other version was copied on to library slips from Joyce's dictation in March 1902 by J. F. Byrne; it is now at Texas (J. F. Byrne, *Silent Years*, NY, 1953, 64–5). Both versions are reproduced in *Archive* I 16–17, 20–21.

In the Byrne version, the poem opens differently, as follows:

> O, it is cold and still – alas! –
> The soft white bosom of my love,
> Wherein no mood of guile or fear
> But only gentleness did move.

In the second stanza, the order of lines 2 and 4 is reversed, and lines 5 and 6 read:

> I saw her passing like a cloud,
> Discreet and silent and apart.

Line 8 reads: 'the heart'. Finally, the last four lines of the concluding stanza read as follows:

> We lie upon the bed of love
> And lie together in the ground:
> To live, to love and to forget
> Is all the wisdom lovers have.

On the second library slip at the end of stanza 2, against the word 'sorrow', Joyce added a stress mark and the instruction: 'accent divided equally'.

It might be remarked that the poem has nothing to do with the death of Joyce's mother, which it predates. Its sources are literary, not obviously biographical. Like the poem that precedes and the three that follow, it is tangentially related to the *Chamber Music* sequence.

Some informative remarks on the version Joyce copied out for Byrne are made by Chester G. Anderson, 'Joyce's Verses' in *A Companion to Joyce Studies*, eds. Zack Bowen and James F. Carens (Westport, Conn., 1984) 136–8. He points out how the first line revises Shelley's 'My cheek is cold and still, alas!' from 'The Indian Serenade', on which the whole poem, too, depends; and possible echoes of Browning, Verlaine and others.

'I said: I will go down to where' (1902?)

The only known version is in Stanislaus Joyce's hand, on paper that also contains 'She is at peace where she is sleeping,' in Joyce's hand, which is now at Cornell (*Archive* I 18). This manuscript is Scholes No. 12; another manuscript, Scholes No. 21c, had been mislaid before the publication of *Archive* I.

'Though we are leaving youth behind' (1902?)

The only known version is in Stanislaus Joyce's hand, on paper that also contains 'She is at peace where she is sleeping', in Joyce's hand, now at Cornell (*Archive* I 19).

'Come out to where the youth is met' (1903–4?)

The holograph initialled fair copy at the Huntington is reproduced in

Archive I 22; published in *JJ* 150. The Elizabethan idiom is displayed on the surface, differently from the poems in the *Chamber Music* sequence.

12: psaltery   A musical instrument, the use of which Yeats had tried to revive. See his essay 'Speaking to the Psaltery' (1902).

Latin Poem of Questionable Authorship (1900–1904?)

This untitled Latin poem at Cornell (Doyle No. 8; Scholes No. 1443) is included as a doubtful attribution. It is not included by Aubert, nor in *P&SW*.

The poem is written in Joyce's hand on two paper slips of the size used by the National Library of Ireland. They were folded before they were written on, and the stanzas were afterwards numbered to make clear the sequence when they were unfolded. Line 2 of the text is smudged, other words have extra ligatures, and the photocopy I worked from has specks that might convert e's into i's or elsewhere might be punctuation. The transcript and line-by-line translation owe much to the suggestions of my former colleague, Dr Andrew Smith:

(1)

A soldier seduced a maiden, safe back in his winter quarters,
He rushed to escape as far as possible[?] from Hell –
He remained without food, but drank deeply,
And, aware of his crime, would shout out amidst his drinking:
　　'Poor Balia, unfortunate Balia,
　　Betrayed and abandoned, most wretched Balia.'

(2)

In burning passion when he crept to bed:
'O fine traitor, you have committed a foul deed.'
The night lamps glow – and look, a dreadful vision
Stood before the soldier's face, and smoking with anger said:
　　'Look on Balia, unfortunate Balia,
　　Betrayed and abandoned, most wretched Balia.'

(3)

'Be off – why have you scrutinized me with your pale body!
An all too treacherous gift have you given to whom you wanted.

I wander along the banks of Styx – the priest makes a just
objection –
The judge calls it suicide – but you are to blame, you rogue!
    You are to blame, who violated Balia,
    Betrayed and abandoned, most wretched Balia.'

(4)

'I have twenty sovereigns – how shining, how beautiful;
Take them and you can procure for me the honour of a tomb;
Then you do not make my shades angry as before.'
She counts out the money with a smile – her voice comes forth more
joyfully:
    'Goodbye, goodbye, my sweetheart, you deceived Balia by your
    word;
    Goodbye, goodbye, my sweetheart, now if you want deceive
    another.'

The lines are signed with a name that is not easy to read: it looks like G.
H. Glansi. Though the last three or four letters of the surname are
ambiguous, I could trace no one with the initials G.H.G. (or E.H.E. or
whatever) among Joyce's acquaintances or in university records of the
time. (George Clancy, who appears as Davin in the *Portrait*, did not have
H as his second initial. Clancy entered UCD in the same year as Joyce,
was awarded First Class Honours in his second-year exams in 1901,
but appears not to have graduated.)

   The poem itself is a puzzle: Balia might be a woman called Bailey, but
then why did Joyce commemorate her so? Was she from Dublin's
Nighttown district? Has the poem any connection with Gogarty, who
prided himself on his Classical attainments and his familiarity with fallen
women? Alternatively, might Balia be, as the Latin pronunciation could
suggest, the Irish Baile (Átha Cliath), the figure of Dublin, betrayed by the
British soldier on the model of Dark Rosaleen in Mangan and other Irish
poets? But then, could such a figure be represented as a suicide? Is the
language an instance of that peculiar kind described in *SH* 110–11, in
which Latin is filtered through Irish, French and German? Joyce's connec-
tion with the lines will remain in dispute until such questions are
answered.

UNCOLLECTED OCCASIONAL POEMS

I have not included the following scraps of verse, on the grounds that they are adapted quotations – flourishes *au courant* – as distinct from composition on independent grounds: Doyle No. 24, being two lines (mis)quoted from Milton's *Paradise Lost* that Gogarty records in *It Isn't This Time of Year at All* (NY, 1954) 95; Doyle No. 27, being a doggerel German formula on Professor Marckwardt's pedagogy at the Berlitz School in Pola (*JJ* 188); Doyle No. 62, being a misquotation of a well-known tag from Robert Louis Stevenson (*L* I 255); Doyle No. 66, being a mangled version of a German proverb in a letter to Miss Weaver (*L* I 280); Doyle No. 75, being an adapted quotation from a music-hall song (*L* I 351); Doyle No. 81, being a two-line jingle from a popular tune (*L* II 150); and Doyle No. 85, a variant of an old *devinette* (*L* III 416; though see Aubert 80, 1451).

Doyle No. 51 is a humorous couplet about Joyce's father, quoted in passing by Peter Spielberg, 'Take a Shaggy Dog by the Tale', *JJQ* I (Spring 1964) 42. It appears on p. 76 of an unpublished holograph workbook for *Finnegans Wake* at Buffalo (Spielberg No. VI.B.5), and is really part of that text (though Aubert 68, 1426–7 includes it). Likewise, four lines at Yale beginning 'Have you heard of one Humpty Dumpty' are, though they are given separately in *Archive* I 354, in fact part of the Ballad of Persse O'Reilly, *FW* 45.1–4 (though see Aubert 77, 1447–8; *P&SW* 145).

Doyle No. 80 – an eighty-line poem to an American girl in Paris described in Slocum No. E.17, b.xi – has still not come to light. Nor has Doyle No. 83, an epigram sent to Giorgio Joyce for his birthday mentioned in a letter to Lucia in 1932 (*L* III 255).

I am also unable to include, for copyright reasons, a number of poems that have now appeared in *P&SW* and a few others besides. See Foreword.

Satire on John Eglinton:
A Collaboration with Oliver St John Gogarty (1903–4)
(in the style of Burns)

From the typescript now at Yale, signed O.G. and J.A.J. (*Archive* I 275). Buck Mulligan sings the opening line in Eglinton's presence in *Scylla and Charybdis* (*U* 177). The extent and nature of Joyce's contribution is not known. It was Gogarty who appears to have had a particular animus against Eglinton as 'the horrible virgin' (*CDD* 11–12, 14; *MBK* 246–7). Joyce, on the other hand, wrote a limerick on him unaided in 1902 (*P&SW* 112). Apropos of the possible collaboration, this is as good a place as any to record that in 1903 Joyce contributed a line singled out for special praise by the judge of Gogarty's prize-winning poem, 'The Death of Shelley': 'Shines on thee, soldier of song, Leonidas' (*MBK* 178).

John Eglinton was the pen name of the librarian W. K. Magee. The lines closely follow Burns's 'John Anderson, My Jo', 'Jo' being a Scottish term of familiar endearment. The words and music of the original are given in Bauerle 338.

2, 5   The lacunae are probably intended – hovering pauses to be filled by lurid imagination. Their function is the same as the asterisks that fill Gogarty's collaboration with Seumas O'Sullivan, 'To George Moore on the Occasion of his Wedding' (*Secret Springs of Dublin Song*, ed. Susan L. Mitchell, Dublin, 1918, 49).

Satire on the Brothers Fay (June 1904)

The circumstances of the poem are described by Ellmann. Joyce had turned up drunk at a rehearsal of the National Theatre Society in the Camden Hall, and collapsed in the narrow passageway that led to it. An actress, Vera Esposito, and her mother had been startled by Joyce's grunts and had summoned help from the company's directors, Frank and William Fay. Joyce remonstrated when he was evicted, but he calmed down and agreed to go home quietly when he understood that he had upset the Espositos (*JJ* 160–61).

Joyce wrote the poem when he recovered his senses, and there is a holograph fair copy at Yale signed with his initials (*Archive* I 277). For more background on the Fays, who are important to an understanding of the Irish theatre and literary movement as Joyce perceived it, see William G. Fay and Catherine Carswell, *The Fays of the Abbey Theatre* (London, 1935) and Frank Fay, *Towards a National Theatre: Dramatic Criticism of Frank Fay*, ed. Robert Hogan (Dublin, 1970). William Fay directed *Exiles* for the Stage Society in 1926; compare Lund No. 645.

An interesting sidelight is thrown on the same incident by Beckett's allusion to it in his short story, 'Dante and the Lobster'. Beckett's protagonist, Belacqua, leaves a parcel in a hallway that causes a mild commotion and agitates two ladies (because it contains a live lobster). The original of one of the ladies was Beckett's Italian coach, Bianca

Esposito, sister of the lady Joyce upset in a Dublin hallway many years before.

'The flower I gave rejected lies' (1902–4?)

The only known version is a revised holograph on lined paper, written in pencil, at Cornell (*Archive* I 286). Ostensibly the speech of a lover to one who has spurned him, it is, as Robert Scholes remarks, 'in the mood of the two broadsides rather than *Chamber Music* and the earlier poetry' (Scholes No. 50). This may offer some clue to its date and occasion. *P&SW* 264 comments that 'the mood fits the *Giacomo Joyce* period'.

5: Alberic The Nibelung dwarf in Richard Wagner's *Das Rheingold*, who renounces love so that he may steal the Rhine gold, guarded by the Rhine maidens. Joyce's early enthusiasm for Wagner is echoed in the presentation of Stephen Dedalus (*CW* 37, 40, 43, 45, etc.; *P* 252–3; *U* 475–6) and resurfaces in *Exiles* (see the articles cited on pp. 357 and 376 below).

12: Vengeance is mine. I will repay Quoted from Romans 12:19.

On Rudolf Goldschmidt (November 1917?)
(to the tune of the 'Amorous Goldfish')

The text and its background are reported by Gorman 246–7; Lund No. 358. Claud Sykes had agreed to type the opening chapters of *Ulysses* if Joyce could find him a typewriter. Joyce sent him to Goldschmidt, an Austrian Jewish friend and pupil who worked in the Österreich-Ungarisches-Hilfsverein, that is, an organization that assisted Austro-Hungarian subjects resident in Switzerland. Though Sykes had difficulty in penetrating the outer offices of the Hilfsverein, he found Goldschmidt himself most friendly, and willing to lend the typewriter instantly. Joyce composed the poem when Sykes reported the incident to him, though Joyce's postcards to Sykes (*L* II 412–13, 416) suggest the loan-arrangement was not as simple and decisive as Gorman suggests.

Title Joyce undoubtedly meant readers to be aware of the literal German meaning of the name Goldschmidt, 'Goldsmith', which connects with his approach to the man. The 'Amorous Goldfish' is a song from *The Geisha* (1896), a popular light opera with libretto by Owen Hall, lyrics by Harry Greenbank and music by Sidney Jones. It was running through Joyce's head when he wrote *Ulysses* (*U* 177, 269, 335).

1: Kriegsverein Literally, 'war-syndicate', but, as Aubert 1411 points out, with some characteristic verbal topspin. The 'Hilfsverein' where Goldschmidt worked may be translated as a Benevolent Society, and a 'Kriegersverein' would be a Veterans' Association. Joyce's coinage gives the second on the model of the first, and therefore an emphasis like *Male*volent Society.

7: Schlachtfeld   German for 'battlefield'.

9: Kaiser Karl   Charles I of Austria and Charles IV of Hungary (1887–1922), the last ruler of the Austro-Hungarian Empire from 1916 to 1918.

Chorus   Joyce misunderstood Goldschmidt's status. He was actually a Swiss citizen, exempt from military service, who took on Hilfsverein duties in addition to his business as a grain merchant.

14: Donnerwet-wet-wetter   German for 'Blast-ast-ast'.

Dooleysprudence (1916–18)
(Air: 'Mr Dooley')

Though Joyce afterwards insisted on keeping his British passport, he maintained a stance of neutrality during the war that British consular officials found trying. The serious background of his position is described at length and sympathetically by Dominic Manganiello, *Joyce's Politics* (London, 1980). In the Museyroom episode of *Finnegans Wake*, Dooley is one of the three soldiers (*FW* 10.5, 6).

The popular song 'Mr Dooley' was written by William Jerome in 1901, with music by Jean Schwarz. The text here is taken from a typescript now at Yale (*Archive* I 310–13), whose unusually large number of small errors I have silently corrected. There is also the beginnings of a holograph text with five bars of a musical setting at Cornell (*Archive* I 318–19), and more music in another manuscript there (*Archive* II 624–5). The key, time and melody of Joyce's setting are quite changed from the original (compare Bauerle 64–7). The text was printed in *JJ* 424–5 and *CW* 246–8 without the concluding stanza.

stanza 3: the gospel of the German on the Mount   Aubert 1413 suggests Nietzsche, or alternatively his protagonist Zarathustra.

— the curse of Moses/On both your houses   Echoing Mercutio in *Romeo and Juliet* III i 102–3.

stanza 4: chibouk; pandect   Respectively, a Turkish tobacco pipe with a long stiff stem, sometimes four or five feet long; and the complete code of laws.

stanza 5: income tax   Ellmann remarks that Joyce was proud not to have paid a demand for 3/6d in tax in Dublin in 1904 (*JJ* 424n).

— **snout of unicorn**   The lion and the unicorn are part of the British coat of arms.

Lament for the Yeomen (1918)
(from the German of Felix Beran)

Joyce claimed not to care much for German verse, but singled out Beran's 'Des Weibes Klage' and praised it as the only good war poem he knew (Budgen 12–13). Beran's poem reads as follows:

> Und nun ist kommen der Krieg der Krieg
> Und nun ist kommen der Krieg der Krieg
> Und nun ist kommen der Krieg der Krieg
>   Krieg
>
> Nun sind sie alle Soldaten
> Nun sind sie alle Soldaten
> Nun sind sie alle Soldaten
>   Soldaten
>
> Soldaten müssen sterben
> Soldaten müssen sterben
> Soldaten müssen sterben
>   Sterben müssen sie
>
> Wer wird nun küssen
> Wer wird nun küssen
> Wer wird nun küssen
>   Meinen weissen Leib

Budgen records that the word 'Leib' moved Joyce to enthusiasm. 'It was a sound that created the image of a body in one unbroken mass. . . . He spoke of the plastic monosyllable as a sculptor speaks about a stone.' Beran became a personal friend (L III 255).

Joyce intended to include his translation in *Pomes Penyeach*, and it appears eleventh in the sequence of fair copies now at Buffalo between *Alone* and *Bahnhofstrasse*, where it is dated 'Zurich: 1916' (*Archive* I 239). Later, however, he struck through the translation, renumbering the pages and substituting *A Memory of the Players in a Mirror at Midnight*. The Buffalo fair copy is the version reproduced here. Ellmann prints from a separate copy in the possession of Frau Lisa Beran, which differs slightly in punctuation (*JJ* 432n; compare Lund No. 377).

To Budgen, Raughty Tinker (1918)

Joyce's convivial friendship with the painter Frank Budgen was one of the most significant in his career. Budgen described it in his *James Joyce and the Making of 'Ulysses'* (originally published 1934), and his singing of an obscene sea-shanty, 'The Raughty Tinker', particularly delighted Joyce (*JJ* 432). In the light of Nora's disapproval of Joyce's roistering, her signature appended to the present lines is worthy of remark. They exist in a transcript by Ethel Turner at Yale (*Archive* I 318). A fullstop should perhaps be inserted after 'clog' (line 6); Ellmann reads 'and Joghurt', in line 7 (*JJ* 433), but compare *P&SW* 124.

Title   'Raughty' is variant of the slang 'rorty', jolly. The word 'tinker' resonates with its meaning in Ireland, where it suggests more strongly a person living outside the limits of settled society than an itinerant craftsman; that is, Joyce pictures Budgen more like a character drawn by Jack B. Yeats than by Wordsworth.

7: **Roggenbrot**   German for 'rye-bread'.

8: **Paint and be damned**   Echoing a saying attributed to the Duke of Wellington, 'Publish and be damned', often repeated since by crusading or muckraking newspaper editors.

New Tipperary; or, The C.G. is Not Literary (October 1918)

The poem celebrates Joyce's first victory over the British Consul-General, Henry Carr, who had claimed expenses for clothes he had bought to play Algernon Moncrieff in Wilde's *The Importance of Being Earnest*. The quarrel became open soon after the play closed: Joyce sued Carr for the money owing on five tickets, Carr counter-claimed against Joyce, who had been the English Players' business manager. The court found against Carr, and ordered him to pay costs and also Joyce for his trouble and expenses.

This first lawsuit was followed by a second in February 1919, which proved to be equally inconclusive. Ellmann tells the story (*JJ* 425–8, 440–41, 445–7). Carr was taken into *Circe* as the British private who strikes Stephen in the face (*U* 491, etc.), and appears under several guises in *Finnegans Wake*.

I give the version of the poem in typescript at Cornell (*Archive* I 316–17). It differs in several particulars from that printed by Gorman and reprinted by Ellmann (*JJ* 445–6; note that the poem is printed in the 1939 American edition of Gorman, on 256, but not in the 1941 English edition, presumably for fear of libel action); also in *P&SW* 123–4. The Cornell typescript is headed, simply, 'New Tipperary'; Gorman's version, simply, 'The C.G. is Not Literary'.

Title The song that names the Irish county was written and composed by Jack Judge and Harry Williams for music-hall performance in 1912, and it became immensely popular among British soldiers during the First World War (Bauerle 575–6). Joyce's new version goes against the grain of its customary role. It is frequently alluded to in *Finnegans Wake*.

5: literary So spelled throughout the Cornell typescript, I assume deliberately. Whether 'bloddy' in line 16 is also echoic, I do not know, but compare the transliteration of cockney accent of the final line. 'Quid' and 'tin' (lines 14, 15) are cockney slang for 'pound' and '(coin) money'; the use of 'comrade', 'brother' and 'chummy' (lines 15, 26, 27), cockney idiom.

8: an Irish kish of brogues Basket of leggings or trousers (rather than shoes, here).

12: Private Carr Carr, seconded from the Black Watch on medical grounds, was in the ranks, not commissioned.

15: comrade Bennett See the limerick on Bennett (*P&SW* 122).

18: Norse solicitor Dr Georg Wettstein, who was Norwegian Vice-Consul in Zurich as well as a lawyer acting for Carr. Joyce makes him the second of the bruiser, Battling Bennett (no relation to the C.G.), in *Cyclops* (*U* 262).

20: Gerichtshof German for 'tribunal'.

20–21 Echoing the nursery rhyme, 'Jack and Jill' (as in Joyce's epigram on Dr Rosenbach, see *P&SW* 130).

28: If you put a beggar upon horseback A proverb current in all European languages. 'Set a beggar upon horseback and he'll ride to the devil'; that is, there is no one so arrogant as a beggar grown suddenly rich.

The Right Man in the Wrong Place (August 1920)
(Air: 'My heart's in my highlands')

Joyce sent the lines to his theatrical collaborator, Claud W. Sykes, on a postcard that is now at Yale (*Archive* I 320; *L* III 16–17); and made a copy to accompany *The Right Heart in the Wrong Place*, now at Cornell (*Archive* I 321).

Title: 'My heart's in my highlands' Ellmann on both occasions reads 'the' for 'my', which is the correct title of the old song best known in the version by Robert Burns, but Joyce on both occasions wrote 'my'. Compare *P&SW* 125. Joyce had moved to Paris in June, Sykes was still in the highlands of Zurich.

5: Jack Spratt Of the nursery rhyme of that name.

7: Rumbold Sir Horace Rumbold had been British Minister to Switzerland at the time Joyce was in dispute with Henry Carr (see above on *New Tipperary*) and was appointed Ambassador to Poland in 1919. Joyce resented his indifference to his problems and embedded his name in two chapters of *Ulysses* as a barber–hangman (*U* 249, 253; and 384, 484–5).

8 Joyce added afterwards as a postscript, 'For your next production of *Pippa Passes*.' The line itself comes directly from the song in Browning's play, indeed Joyce's lines altogether follow the movement of Browning's.

The Right Heart in the Wrong Place (August 1920)

The fair copy now at Cornell (*Archive* I 321), reproduced here, differs in some particulars from the version printed in *L* III 16 (and *JJ* 533), which was sent to Stanislaus Joyce. It was signed 'S.O.S.', which must indicate Save Our Souls rather than Seumas O'Sullivan. The typed copy at Southern Illinois was probably made for Gorman, who gives the same text as Ellmann (compare Gorman 271).

2: Bull John Bull, the British. Compare 'the bann of Bull' in *A Portrait of the Artist as an Ancient Mariner* line 5.

4: the mayor of Cork Terence MacSwiney, Lord Mayor of Cork, was arrested on 12 August 1920 on charges of subversion against British rule in Ireland. He went on hunger strike in Brixton Gaol and died after seventy-three days, on 25 October.

Joyce appears to have identified with MacSwiney's stand against British officialdom more than with Sinn Féin policy during the war of independence (Dominic Manganiello, *Joyce's Politics*, London, 1980, 163–6, etc.). He might also have believed that he and MacSwiney were distantly related (*JJ* 533; compare 13, 16).

8: Rumbold See above on *The Right Man in the Wrong Place* line 7.

Quatrain for Richard Wallace (c. 1921)

Richard Wallace (1870?–1927), the American book illustrator and advertising businessman, whose acquaintance Joyce made in Paris shortly before Christmas 1920 (*L* III 33; compare *Bis Dat Qui Cito Dat* in *P&SW* 126). Their friendship developed quickly in subsequent months (Lund Nos. 692ff), and Joyce addressed several sets of verses to him. His wife Lillian contributed the word 'yes' to Molly's monologue in *Ulysses* (*JJ* 516; though compare 521–2 for a rival claim).

The lines are printed out, initialled J.J., on an undated scrap among Wallace's papers in the Morris Library, Southern Illinois University at Carbondale (Collection No. VFM 1288; Lund No. 700). They were presumably written to express Joyce's sense of imposing on Wallace, who was reading *Ulysses* as it moved through the press. Compare Lund No. 692 for Joyce's sense of imposing, and also Nos. 693, 695. *P&SW* 267 suggests they were written for Sylvia Beach, as *Ulysses* neared publication.

Joyce's quatrain parodies the second stanza of Yeats's 'The Lake Isle of Innisfree':

> And I shall have some peace there, for peace comes dropping slow,
> Dropping from the veils of the morning to where the cricket sings;
> There midnight's all a glimmer, and noon a purple glow,
> And evening full of the linnet's wings.

3: midnight's Joyce spelled 'MIDNIGT'S', which is surely a mistake. *P&SW* introduces other readings ('tramp' in line 2, 'all of' in line 3), which I cannot explain, since the manuscript is unambiguous.

To Sylvia Beach (February 1922)
(following the publication of Ulysses)

Sylvia Beach, the young American proprietor of a Paris bookshop, had undertaken to publish *Ulysses* with as many copies as possible being subscribed in advance. Joyce had warned her no one would buy the book, at the time he accepted her proposal (*JJ* 504). He wrote and sent her the poem a few days after 2 February 1922, when the first copies of *Ulysses* became available.

Joyce's holograph is at Buffalo, and there is a copy in another hand at Princeton (*Archive* I 322, 323); the poem was printed with slight variations in Sylvia Beach's account of her Paris years, *Shakespeare and Company* (London, 1960) 94. Joyce's lines are 'after W.S.' because they are a line-for-line reworking of the song in *The Two Gentlemen of Verona* IV i 39–53, even while the name Shakespeare at the same time adverts to Sylvia Beach's bookshop.

Fréderic's Duck (June 1923)
(Air: 'Dougherty's Duck')

Joyce wrote the lines on a piece of writing-paper from the Terminus Hotel, Calais, dating them 21 June 1923. They are among the Wallace papers in the Morris Library, Southern Illinois University at Carbondale (Collection No. VFM 1288; Lund No. 703 misreads the date as 1929, though Wallace died in July 1927). Joyce was in Calais en route to London and Bognor, beginning to work in earnest on the project that became *Finnegans Wake*. Had the dinner for which he thanks Wallace been to celebrate the first anniversary of Bloomsday (16 June)? Or did it take place a few days later, on the eve of his departure from Paris?

Fréderic's Duck is the sobriquet of a well-known Paris restaurant, La Tour d'Argent (French for 'Tower of Money', 'Pile of Cash'). The original chef, Fréderic, died in 1913 at the age of seventy. Duck according to his recipe is still served at the restaurant, which is still expensive.

Title 'Dougherty's Duck' is not known to any Dublin authority on ballads and old songs I consulted, and it can only be Joyce's invention. (I must thank Mr Michael Bowles of Ballsbridge, Dublin 4, in particular, for giving his mind to this problem.) Joyce's title is modelled on the well-known 'Nell Flaherty's Drake', the words and music of which are given in *Irish Street Ballads,* ed. Colm O Lochlainn (Dublin, 1939) 134–5, 214.

The text of *Fréderic's Duck* shares only the eight-line stanza (here divided) with 'Nell Flaherty's Drake', ending with a reference to the bird itself, and the two texts move to quite different rhythms. The Cardinal's parodic rendering in *Circe* (U 427) is a good deal closer to the original ballad.

Adeline Glasheen says, in her *Third Census of 'Finnegans Wake'* (Berkeley, Calif., 1977) 77, that Dougherty was one of Joyce's early names for Gogarty. 'Dougherty's duckboard' crops up in *FW* 374.15. Did Joyce see Gogarty as the archetypal murderer of Nell Flaherty's Drake? Or associate his well-fed figure with overcharging restaurants?

1: **Cantus Plenus**   Latin for 'full voice', but normally *cantus planus*, that is, plainchant, or the monophonic unison chant of the Christian liturgies.

4–5: **Cantus Coenatorum**   Latin for 'chorus of the diners'.

On a Fountain Pen Given Him by Richard Wallace (February 1924)

The lines, so signed and dated 5 February 1924, are among the Wallace Papers in the Morris Library, Southern Illinois University at Carbondale (Collection No. VFM 1288; Lund No. 701). The pen might have been a present on his birthday, three days before.

The letters Joyce wrote to Wallace in the following months (Lund Nos. 697, 698) appear to make use of the same pen, which made his writing neither less nor more legible than otherwise. Shem is the brother closer to the Stephen figure in Joyce's then *Work in Progress*, which became *Finnegans Wake*. Joyce was working on the *Shem and Shaun* episode at the time, and offered to read it to Wallace in the following month (Lund. No. 698).

On Kellog's Bran Poultice (April 1925)

The lines are written in Joyce's enlarged handwriting, initialled and dated 5 April 1925, on a single leaf among the Richard Wallace papers in the Morris Library, Southern Illinois University at Carbondale (Collection No. VFM 1288; Lund No. 702). Joyce was at the time suffering both from his eyes and an embedded fragment of tooth (*JJ* 569–70); presumably the poultice was on the advice of the dentist, who removed the fragment in early April, though he was to undergo a seventh operation on his left eye later in the month. *P&SW* assumes the bran was ingested. A letter containing the epigram on Dr Borsch's clinic sent to Miss Weaver (see *P&SW* 133; *Archive* I 331) is in the same thick black-pencil handwriting.

The first two lines echo the opening of the nursery rhyme, 'Pat-a-cake, pat-a-cake, baker's man,/Bake me a cake as fast as you can'; the third, a line in the Lord's Prayer, 'Give us this day our daily bread'.

Fragment on Miss Moschos (1920s?)

The lines are recalled in Colum 121. They describe Miss Moschos as the younger sister of a Greek assistant at Shakespeare and Company (for whom see *L* III 60, 66, 85, 125, 171 and *FW* 84.1). She 'was very hushed and very retiring; she came forward only to deliver mail or bring proofs to Joyce'.

Schevingen, 1927 (July 1927)

Joyce had stayed at The Hague for a few days in late May 1927, spending most of his time lying on the beach at nearby Schevingen, but a dog attacked him and broke his glasses, and the Joyces left for a hotel in Amsterdam (*JJ* 592). Typically, Joyce assimilated the cur to Carr and to all his assailants (*Et Cur Heli!, FW* 73.19). The lines were written for Sylvia Beach after he returned to Paris, and appear to constitute a request for funds (compare *Dear Miss Minnehaha* in *SB* 197–8 but not included in *P&SW*). The card on which they are written is now at Buffalo (*Archive* I 338), and they were printed in Spielberg No. IV.B.5.

4: ón the rócks   Wrecked and broke, stranded high and dry and penniless.

Hue's Hue? or Dalton's Dilemma (*c.* 1928)

The second of two epigrams on Samuel Roth.

Roth published available fragments of *Work in Progress* in his magazine *Two Worlds* (NY) between September 1925 and September 1926, and then, from July 1926, he set about publishing a serialized version of *Ulysses* in *Two Worlds Monthly*. Joyce had protested from the first (*L* III 131, etc.), and an International Protest signed by 167 writers was issued on his birthday, 1927. Joyce's first epigram on Roth was included in a letter to Miss Weaver the day before the Protest was published (*L* I 249; *Archive* I 337; *P&SW* 135).

Joyce's second epigram, given here, exists in holograph, initialled, on a card preserved at Buffalo (*Archive* I 340), and is dated by Spielberg – who prints it (No. IV.B.7) – *c.* 1928. The last pirated passage published by Roth, *Oxen of the Sun*, appeared in October 1927, after which he was enjoined from using Joyce's name in any way (*JJ* 587). The title is Joyce's, and Dalton's dilemma is colour blindness, because it was first described (in 1794) by the scientist John Dalton, who suffered from it.

Epigram on the Ladyfriends of St James (January 1931)

The lines are recorded by Mary Colum, *Life and the Dream* (NY, 1947) 395. She describes how she reproved Joyce for his treatment of a young American college instructor. 'He stopped me. A slow fury mounted to his face, and he moved irritatedly in his chair. "I hate women who know anything," he said. "No, Joyce, you don't," said I. "You like them, and I

am going to contradict you about this in print when I get the chance."
After a few seconds of silent anger, a whimsical smile came upon his face,
and the rest of the afternoon with him was pleasant.' Joyce read the lines
to Mary Colum a few days later, 'with great gusto'. She admits the
possibility that she does not record them all. *P&SW* 270 notes that they
are a take-off of 'As I was going to St Ives'.

Father O'Ford (February 1931)
(Air: 'Father O'Flynn')

Ford lent Joyce his house in Toulon at the time Joyce agreed to be
godfather to his daughter (*L* III 175, 176, 177; compare *Crossing to the
Coast*, *P&SW* 137). Now, a few years later, he reappeared in Paris with a
new wife, 'an eighth or eighteenth', as Joyce told Miss Weaver (*JJ* 635n).
Joyce included the verses in his letter to Miss Weaver, which is now at
Yale (*Archive* I 342), ending them 'to be continued)'. The version here is
from a separate typed copy at Buffalo that contains improvements (*Archive* I 343; oddly, someone – Spielberg No. IV.B.8 conjectures Sylvia
Beach – has added the date 1930).

Alfred Percival Graves's sentimental ballad 'Father O'Flynn' insists on
its protagonist's spiritual and intellectual, not sexual, skills. The words
and music are given in Bauerle 142–9. The song is quoted three times in
Ulysses, sixteen times in *Finnegans Wake*, and it is not an accident that
Mulligan in *Ulysses* is transformed into Father Malachi O'Flynn (*U* 489;
compare 3). In a letter to Giorgio in 1935, Joyce claimed to dislike the
setting by Villiers Stanford, 'and the words, and most of all Father
O'Flynn himself, the so called soggarth aroon' (*L* I 361; compare 400).
The feelings Joyce attaches to the original somewhat qualify the tone of
his own composition.

Rhyme to Advertise Extract from Work in Progress (May 1931?)

Joyce wrote a set of rhymes to advertise *Anna Livia Plurabelle* when it
was published in booklet form by Faber & Faber, in a brown-paper
cover. A holograph headed *A. L. P.* that he wrote at Euston Station for T.
S. Eliot, a director of Faber, is in the collection of Ronald L. Dzierbicki
(*Archive* I 341) and is now published in *P&SW* 139. Joyce wrote another
set of rhymes to advertise *Haveth Childers Everywhere*, published in the
same series, which he first inscribed in Eliot's copy. The text of the
second set of verses, given here, is from a version Joyce copied for Sylvia
Beach in October 1931 and now at Buffalo (*Archive* I 346).

Joyce's verses echo the 'Humpty Dumpty' nursery rhyme. The word 'Sevensinns' in the first set incorporates the German *Sinn*, 'sense'. In the second set, 'Kinks english' mangles the King's English; and 'irishmanx brogues' combines traditional Irish footwear, Ireland and the Isle of Man, and traditional Irish speech. The booklet fitted into the finally published book at *FW* 532–54.

The sales manager of Faber & Faber was reluctant to use rhymes as promotional material, and Joyce was annoyed that, in the end, they were used only on a mimeographed publicity release (see *L* III 247n; *JJ* 616–17). The second set was published under the heading 'James Joyce, Ad-Writer' in *transition* (Paris) No. 21 (March 1932) 258.

To Mrs Herbert Gorman Who Complained That Her Visitors Kept Late Hours (March 1931)

Joyce's poem is a response to the complaint by the wife of his biographer, Jean Gorman, that John Holms, who often visited them with Peggy Guggenheim, always wanted to stay on, conversing and drinking. The text here is from a typescript at Buffalo (*Archive* I 345), which improves slightly on the holograph written two days before, now at Texas (*Archive* I 344). The earlier version was printed by Peggy Guggenheim in *Out of This Century* (NY, 1946) 130 (and again in *JJ* 622).

8: heim   German for 'home'.

Pennipomes Twoguineaseach (April 1932)

The poem celebrates the publication of *The Joyce Book*, compiled by Herbert Hughes for a limited edition in London, the previous month. The book is made up of musical settings of *Pomes Penyeach* and pleased Joyce very much.

An untitled, undivided version of the poem exists in Joyce's holograph, dated 20 April 1932 (*Archive* I xi, 348). The version reproduced here is from a typescript now at Buffalo (*Archive* I 349; compare Spielberg No. IV.B.12; *JJ* 619).

Joyce's verses follow the tune of the nursery rhyme, 'Sing a Song of Six-pence'.

Pour la rîme seulement (May 1932)

Joyce enclosed the verses in a letter from Paris to Valery Larbaud

(1881–1957), the French literary critic who became his friend and helper from the time *Ulysses* was published (*L* III 245; compare *JJ* 499, 520–24, etc.). Larbaud was also an informed and prodigious collector of toy soldiers, which he deployed in battle against and exchanged with his friend, Pierre de Lanux (b. 1887), previously secretary of *La Nouvelle Revue française* and subsequently a journalist and historian. Sylvia Beach describes their shared passion in *Shakespeare and Company* (London, 1960) 66.

In the letter to Larbaud, Joyce says: 'I talked about you a few days ago at lunch with de Lanux who is having a show here of his soldiers. The enclosed *bêtise*, written only for the sake of the rhymes, is the result.' The manuscript, now at Buffalo, was dictated over the telephone to Sylvia Beach, and is in her hand on three sheets of graph paper (*Archive* I 350–52; Spielberg No. IV.B.13). I have corrected some of Miss Beach's obvious errors, and supplied more punctuation than elsewhere to ease the reader's difficulties. *P&SW* 142 provides an uncorrected text, but differs in the reading of several words.

A translation is difficult because of the wordplay and reversals of meaning. For instance, lines 9 and 10 reverse lines 1 and 2; the last line of stanza 1 is reversed at the close of stanza 3. Aubert 1443 suggests that the lines move to the tune of 'Au clair de la lune, mon ami Pierrot', the second verse of which is particularly well suited to the two principals, 'Prête-moi ta plume pour écrire un mot'. The words *dux, soldiqués, obobus, Mursoline* and *arrats* do not appear in the dictionary. The difficulties are not more easy to resolve because Miss Beach may not have copied down the words correctly.

Light is thrown on the tendency of Joyce's references by the fact that Lanux was a known liberal; also that Joyce disliked Mussolini (Potts 149, 245) as well as war and soldiers in real life. Wars and skirmishes like those played out between Larbaud and Lanux preoccupied him during the composition of *Finnegans Wake*, which happened at a time when fascism and militarism were a rising tide in Europe (Aubert 1441–3 adds details).

> To Pierre de Lanux
> Said Valery Larbaud,
> Grant me a leader
> Who can conduct the assault.
> My footsoldiers are destroyed,
> And are dying of disaffection.

Be your little bobtail,
For the glory of Ares.

Lanux de la Pierre
To Beaulard made reply,
To hell with the war,
With your 'mercenaries'.
And for Italy
Quickly pack your bags,
Make the best of it
With a few bullets.

At these words, Leryval
Dashes off on an exploding coach,
And like old Hannibal
Breaks through the blockade,
Hardly changes his expression
When someone cries bedlam,
One beneath Mursoline
For the arrest of glory.

3: **un dux**   The non-French, Latin form alludes to *Il Duce*, Mussolini.

5: **pioupions**   The manuscript appears to read *pioux prion*, which is not grammatical and does not make sense. (Adding *s* to read *prions*, is it possible Joyce intended 'captured pawns'?) *P&SW* reads *pioux piou*, footsoldiers.

There is a play on *fondu* in the same line; it means literally 'cast', as in a lead mould.

7: **ton petit tondu**   I translate literally; it means a short haircut, like a soldier's. Le Petit Tondu was also the nickname of General Bonaparte, who is thereby brought into alignment with the *dux* above (Mussolini). It could be argued that Miss Beach misheard *ton* for *mon*.

8: **Arès**   Ares, the Greek god of war.

10: **Beaulard**   The word is not capitalized in the manuscript. As such, it means literally 'perky porker'. Larbaud was noticeably plump.

11: **Fous-moi**   The manuscript reads *Foute-moi*.

12: **soldiqués**   French *soldat*, 'soldier', + *être à la solde de*, 'to be in the pay of'.

13–14   Larbaud was well known as a constantly restless traveller. *Presto* inevitably recalls Swift in early editions of *Journal to Stella* – as Joyce was well aware (*FW* 289.17, 484.32, 613.4) – though I cannot fathom what difference this makes.

18: obobus A coinage made up of *autobus*, 'coach', + *obus*, 'shell'.

19: Hannibal Larbaud's generous proportions might be imagined as like an elephant's.

21 One would normally expect a subject to be (re)introduced for the verb.

22: foire The manuscript reading could be *forire* – perhaps intending *fou* + *rire*, 'wild laughter' (Aubert 1443).

23 The meaning of this line and the next is obscure. Joyce clearly intends to repeat the terms of lines 7–8 while turning around their meaning: Mussolini is to Napoleon, as the termination or withdrawing of *la gloire* is to its celebration. This becomes apparent to the impassive Larbaud when he crosses the Alps into turbulent Italy.

24: l'arrats de gloire French *arrêt*, 'halt' + *arracher*, 'wrest'?

A Portrait of the Artist as an Ancient Mariner (October 1932)

The typescript Joyce sent to Sylvia Beach is now at Buffalo, and was published by Ellmann (*Archive* I 353; *JJ* 654–5). The title, stanzaic scheme, details and 'events' depend on Coleridge's *Rime of the Ancient Mariner*. Joyce follows the narrative sequence of the first two parts of the original (only), sometimes stanza by stanza and at other times in a looser, syncopating paraphrase. It will be noticed that he never follows through the movement of any of Coleridge's stanzas in its entirety: he shadows the movement of a pair of lines, at which stage he turns and develops them differently on his own. Again, Joyce's narrative is shifted entirely into the third person.

1–2 The *Ancient Mariner* opens: 'It is an ancient Mariner/And he stoppeth one of three.'

5 John Bull and Uncle Sam, Britain and America, where *Ulysses* was banned (as well as – combined – Sam Coleridge, the British author).

5–8 The lines have no exact equivalent in Coleridge. They correspond to the description of the Mariner's 'glittering eye' by which the Wedding Guest is transfixed (*Ancient Mariner* lines 12–20).

8: K.O. 11 Knockout in the eleventh round, that is, in the eleventh year after *Ulysses* was published.

9: Shakefears & Coy Sylvia Beach of Shakespeare and Company first published *Ulysses* in 1922.

9–12 The lines are Joyce's equivalent for the music and 'merry din' that the Wedding Guest hears while he is being detained by the Mariner (*Ancient Mariner* lines 30–35).

12: **His pearls that had poisom porkers** The meaning is obscure. Poisom is a Joycean coinage, perhaps meaning weighty. Are there allusions to Matthew 6:6 ('Neither cast ye your pearls before swine') and to Shakespeare's *The Tempest* I ii 396 ('Those are pearls that were his eyes')?

13: **The gnome Norbert** I can only suggest Joyce refers to the protagonist of Browning's *In a Balcony*, a production of which he had helped with in Zurich (see *A Memory of the Players in a Mirror at Midnight*). The character Norbert is a minister of state in Browning's playlet, but Joyce might want to present himself – as in the *Pomes Penyeach* poem, but here more ironically – as a shrunken, aged, failed version of the same. Another, simpler explanation would be more satisfactory.

13–16 The auditor, as Norbert, is in the position of the Wedding Guest, aware of what he is missing, 'Yet he cannot choose but hear.' Compare *Ancient Mariner* lines 36–40.

17–18 Compare *Ancient Mariner* lines 95–6: 'Ah wretch! said they, the bird to slay,/That made the breeze to blow!'

17: **Schuft . . . Luft** German for 'rogue, scoundrel'; and 'breeze', referring directly to Coleridge's poem.

18: **his U. boat** Submarine (German *Unterseeboot*) and *Ulysses*. Joyce refers to previous supporters like Ezra Pound, who felt he had lost his way in the later chapters and in his writing since. Compare *Troppa Grazia, Sant' Antonio!, P&SW* 135.

20–24 The equivalent passage in the *Ancient Mariner* is debatable. Perhaps, given the pattern of reference in following stanzas, Joyce's lines 20–21 attempt to match the spirit of Coleridge's lines 101–5:

> The fair breeze blew, the white foam flew,
> The furrow followed free;
> We were the first that ever burst
> Into that silent sea.

22: **the silviest Beach of Beaches** Compare *Schevingen, 1927* line 3.

23: **Kugelkopfschwindel** German for 'Round-head-vertigo'. Ellmann fancifully suggests a reference to the Nazi theory that brachycephalic peoples (including the Celts) were inferior to dolichocephalic ones, 'though it could also be dizziness from eating too many cupcakes' (*JJ* 655n).

24 Alluding to Joyce's numerous eye operations.

25–8 The stanza is Joyce's equivalent for lines 106–30 in Coleridge, from 'Down dropped the breeze, the sails dropped down,' to 'blue and white'.

28 White and blue, the colours of the Greek flag, and the colours in which *Ulysses* first appeared (as well as the colour of the water-snakes in *Ancient Mariner* line 130).

29–30 Compare *Ancient Mariner* lines 135–6: 'And every tongue, through utter drought,/Was withered at the root.'

32: **You'd have staked your goat he was Ghandi** Because of his emaciated pallor: Gandhi's hunger strikes, accompanied by a staked goat, attracted wide publicity.

33 *Ulysses* had been pirated by American and Japanese publishers.

35–6 Compare the closing lines of Part II of Coleridge's poem: 'Instead of the cross, the Albatross/About my neck was hung.' It is also relevant that the Odyssey Press, Hamburg, took over the European publication of *Ulysses* from Sylvia Beach under the imprint of the Albatross Press.

Epilogue to Ibsen's Ghosts (April 1934)

Joyce wrote the epilogue in Zurich, 'after having seen for the nth time Ginette Faccone in . . . *Ghosts* at the Théâtre des Champs Elysées in Paris before leaving [for Switzerland]' (Gorman papers quoted in Potts 273n). He gave it to Gorman to publish, along with the dictated remark: 'This (which is in fact a grotesque amplification of Osvalt's own attempted defence of his father in the play) is not to be interpreted, however, in the sense that he does not consider Ibsen to be the supreme dramatic poet, basing his belief, however, on the later plays from the *Wild Duck* onwards, and of course does not mean that he considers *Ghosts* as anything but a great tragedy' (Gorman 224–5n; *JJ* 670n). There is a typescript at Yale and another, corrected typescript at Southern Illinois (*Archive* I 356–59; Lund No. 381).

The epilogue is supposed to be spoken by Captain Alving, and it moves forward by means of a parody of Ibsen's familiar devices of Spreading the Guilt and the Horrible Hint. The succinct summary in *CW* 271 cannot be improved upon:

Captain Alving points out that he is assumed to have fathered two children, one out of wedlock and one in, the first (Regina) healthy, the second (Oswald) congenitally sick. Pursuing the trail of guilt with the zeal of the ghost in *Hamlet*, and profiting from suggestions in *Ghosts* that Parson Manders and Mrs Alving were once in love, the captain wickedly implies that Manders was Oswald's begetter. He declares with equal effrontery that his own sins supplied incomparable material for a dramatic masterpiece. Joyce's interest in the profligate father, compounded of Shakespeare's dead king and Ibsen's dead rogue, is in the temper of *Finnegans Wake*.

Ellmann adds in *JJ* 670 that Joyce's interest in the profligate father recalls both his own father and himself, and that he too had one sick and one healthy child. The biographical parallels are not to be pressed, however, and the way Joyce exploits the comic dimension of Ibsen's techniques is more important. Harold Pinter's production of *Exiles* proved that Joyce's awareness of such a dimension was thoroughly assimilated at an earlier stage. B. J. Tysdahl has pointed out how the poem is reworked in the inquest scene in *Finnegans Wake* (FW 532.14–20 etc.; see *Joyce and Ibsen: A Study in Literary Influence*, Oslo/NY, 1968, 158). However, the comic potential is given a different, more robust airing in verse than in the play or the prose.

2: **The grim old grouser** Ibsen.

6: **the lewd knight in dirty linen** Falstaff in Shakespeare's *The Merry Wives of Windsor*.

11–12 That is, though the Captain acknowledges norms of sexual behaviour, he does not prescribe rules for their operation.

15: **thy name is joy** Echoes 'Frailty, thy name is woman!' in *Hamlet* I ii 146.

16: **child** Thus in both typescripts, though Gorman (followed by CW and P&SW) reads 'sire', which does not necessarily make better sense. Compare Mr Dedalus on 'the Goulding faction' and 'the wise child that knows her own father' in *U* 73.

21, 25: **Olaf, Haakon** Not characters in the play but opposite types, like Shaun and Shem in *Finnegans Wake*, or Peter and Paul.

24: **sat** Thus in both typescripts, though Gorman (followed by CW and P&SW) reads *est*. The line can be paraphrased in both cases as 'his fill of the pox', with play on the phrase *Pax Romana*, the peace existing between different members of the Roman Empire.

39 That is, Young Men's Christian Association, venereal disease, tuberculosis.

41 As Ibsen also implies, everyone is to blame; the guilt, as in *Finnegans Wake*, is pervasive.

45–6 Engestrand, the carpenter, sets the orphanage on fire towards the end of the play, but for purposes of blackmail makes Parson Manders feel responsible.

47 By excessive drinking.

Translation from Gottfried Keller's Lebendig Begraben *Suite* (after April 1934)

Though Joyce had been unimpressed by Keller's prose when friends like August Suter and Ottocaro Weiss tried to interest him in it in 1915–16, he was overwhelmingly impressed when, revisiting Zurich for a consultation concerning an eye operation, he heard Othmar Schoeck's Lied-Zyklus *Lebendig-Begraben* (German for 'buried alive'), opus 40, a suite of fourteen songs by Keller for male voice and orchestra (*JJ* 394, 669; Potts 62, 268, 272). Gorman implies that Joyce translated the complete suite, but he records only one of them (Gorman 342). Keller's original is as follows:

> Nun hab' ich gar die Rose aufgefressen
> Die sie mir in die starre Hand gegeben.
> Das ich nur einmal wuerde Rosen essen
> Das haett' ich nie geglaubt in meinem Leben.
>
> Nur moecht' ich wissen ob es eine rote
> Od' eine weisse Rose da gewesen.
> Gib taeglich uns, O Herr, von Deinem Brote
> Und, wenn Du willst, erloes uns von dem Boesen!

A Come-all-ye, by a Thanksgiving Turkey (November 1937)

Joyce had been invited to a Thanksgiving dinner at Neuilly by the Jolases. He was prompted to write the poem when he heard the turkey had been dropped on its way from market and had somehow lost its liver. A facsimile of the corrected holograph was reproduced in *Pastimes of James Joyce*, published by the Joyce Memorial Committee in 1941; also in *Archive* I 360–61 (the original cannot be located). Ellmann's transcription in *JJ* 705–6n and *P&SW* 149–50 differ in a few particulars.

Maria Jolas's autobiography has yet to be published in full, but fragments have appeared: see in particular 'James Joyce en 1939–40', *Mercure de France* No. 309 (May 1950) 45–58; and 'The Joyce I knew and the Women around him' in *James Joyce: New Perspectives*, ed. Colin MacCabe (Brighton, 1982) 184–94. Compare the letter from Constantine Curran's daughter in Curran 90–91, describing another wild dinner at the Jolases' with Joyce.

1: **lairds and lassies** Ellmann and *P&SW* read 'ladies'. Joyce first wrote 'lads' for 'lairds'. The Scottish words acknowledge the Scottish ancestry of Maria MacDonald Jolas.

5: **Grand Palais Potin** Félix Potin, a pre-war grocery chain.

10: **Lieber's code** Franz Lieber (1789–1872), political philosopher and jurist, drafted a *Code for the Government of Armies* (1863) during the American Civil War. It concerns the protection of civilians and regulates the treatment of prisoners of war, and it has provided the basis for present-day international conventions.

11: **swanee** The allusion to Stephen Foster's song, 'Old Folks at Home', also known as 'Swanee River', is a compliment to Mrs Jolas: see line 27 below.

13: **Octroi** Toll-house.

14: **Holy Poule** Holy Bird (in the sense of fast young woman, 'chick'), and echoing the Dublin exclamation 'Holy Paul'.

14: **Loye** *l'oie*, French for 'goose', alluding to Charles Perrault's *Contes de ma mère l'Oye* (1697).

15: **Caesar** When Caesar married Pompeia, she appeared above reproach ('the dindy of the flock'), but he divorced her on the suspicion of a scandal. Compare the saying that Caesar's wife must be above suspicion.

The word 'dindy' later in the same line is, besides English 'dandy', French *dinde* (fem.), turkey-hen.

17: **eagle's pride** Alluding to the bald eagle on the American coat of arms.

22: **Osmanli** Ottomans, that is, Turks. The 'golden horn' in the next line is, besides being a champagne glass, an inlet on the Bosporus at Istanbul.

25: **hommes** The word looks like 'hammers' in the manuscript, which is how Ellmann and *P&SW* read it.

26: **the mujik** The Jolases' Russian servant, Conrad, here acting as major domo.

27: **Madamina** The first word in a celebrated aria in *Don Giovanni*, as well as a combination of 'Madame' (Jolas) and 'Balamina' (a Southern song she used to sing).

27: a message from the Big Noise of her State Franklin D. Roosevelt's Thanksgiving Day message.

28: Turco Alluding also to *Turco the Terrible*, a pantomime that had been an instant hit in Dublin from the time of its first performance in 1873. Stephen recalls his mother's enjoyment of it in the opening chapter of *Ulysses* (*U* 8–9).

34: Thanksgiving Day Always the fourth Thursday in November.

35: sauceboat Containing cranberry sauce. Joyce omits to mention the other essential component of a Thanksgiving meal, pumpkin pie.

LIMERICKS

The limerick form was cultivated in the Gogarty–Joyce circle, expressing as it does a very different ambience from the verse forms cultivated by the circle round Yeats and AE (and indeed by Joyce himself in *Chamber Music*). Joyce's college friend, C. P. Curran, gives examples of Gogarty's productions, including one on Joyce, in Curran 75–6. Further examples are given by James F. Carens, *Surpassing Wit: Oliver St John Gogarty, His Poetry and His Prose* (Dublin, 1979) 22, 24–5.

Another college friend, Eugene Sheehy, recalled Joyce and Gogarty engaging in a limerick competition and also composing dialogic-limericks extempore (in O'Connor 28–9; this anecdote was added to the memories Sheehy published in 1951). Those known only in versions reported by Gogarty might well have been revised by him in the retelling, and the authorship of at least one – on Admiral Togo, in *P&SW* 111 – might seem more likely to be his on internal grounds.

This section of the present collection has been curtailed with particular severity due to the decision of the copyright-holders. This is regrettable on several counts, not least because the annotation in *P&SW* is restricted and not always correct. As a sample of what has been jettisoned, the reader might compare the annotation of the limerick 'There was a young priest named Delaney' (*P&SW* 110 and 263) with the commentary that follows.

On Father Delany (1904)

When Gogarty published the limerick in *Start from Somewhere Else* (NY, 1955), 84, he described it as having a scabrous origin:

There was a Jesuit father, a convert, who, in spite of his name, was an Englishman. Joyce wrote to him from 4 Faithful Place, one of four or five houses that stood at the back of the red-light district of the city. A very dangerous place for anyone who was not well known as a medico or a pal of the medicos on whom the whores depended for first aid.

When C. P. Curran copied the limerick from Gogarty into his commonplace book (153; UCD, CUR MS 6), he demurred and described it as having been written by Joyce during the controversy over admitting women fully to the college – that is, with reference to Fr William Delany SJ, the President, who was commonly held to be resistant to change.

There were no obstacles to women in the statutes of the Royal University, and women were full members of other constituent colleges, but University College Dublin pleaded that shortage of space made restrictions on their entry necessary. The campaign for full admittance escalated in 1904, following Trinity's decision to admit women, which led to the resignation of the UCD Registrar, Francis Sheehy-Skeffington. Though the relevant decisions were taken by the Academic Council of the college, Delany was generally held to be responsible. See The Fathers of the Society of Jesus, *A Page of Irish History: The Story of University College Dublin 1883–1909* (Dublin, 1930) 465–6; Thomas J. Morrissey, *Towards a National University: William Delany SJ (1835–1924)* (Dublin, 1983) 279–87.

Curran's identification is confirmed by the fact that, though there was another Jesuit in Ireland at the time, Charles, he was neither a convert nor an Englishman. (I gratefully acknowledge the help of Br John Maguire of Loyola House, Dublin 4, and Fr Fergus O'Donoghue of Milltown Park, Dublin 6, who checked Jesuit records on my behalf.) In Gogarty's story, Delany has merged with English converts at UCD like Fr Darlington and Fr Browne, though of course Joyce might have sent the limerick to the President of UCD from the Faithful Place address. Joyce alludes to the admittance controversy in *SH* 71, and perhaps anticipates his verses in the following description of Delany: 'The President gathered in his soutane for the ascent with a slow hermaphroditic gesture' (*SH* 103).

JJ 88n prints the limerick from the Curran papers. Joyce repeated it for Dr Rosenbach in Paris in 1928, who copied it into his pocket book. See Clive Driver in *James Joyce, 'Ulysses': A Facsimile of the Manuscript*

(NY, Philadelphia, 1975) I 31. The three known versions differ only in punctuation.

John Quinn (September 1917)

Joyce sent this and the following limerick to Claud Sykes (*L* II 406; *Archive* I 308); the titles are his. They were published in Gorman 247.

John Quinn (1870–1924), the New York lawyer and patron, was introduced to Joyce's work by Pound and sent money in March 1917 in return for the manuscript of *Exiles*, which was dispatched in two instalments. He afterwards purchased the *Ulysses* manuscript, but Joyce thought his defence of the *Little Review* against obscenity charges had been halfhearted. See the biography by B. L. Reid, *The Man from New York: John Quinn and His Friends* (NY, 1968).

Claude Sykes (September 1917)

Joyce enclosed the limerick with the previous one on a card to Sykes (*L* II 406; *Archive* I 308). The title is his (Sykes normally spelled his first name without an *e*). It was published in Gorman 247.

Sykes (1883–1964), a professional actor then resident in Zurich with his actress wife, agreed to type *Ulysses* for Joyce at this time, and he and Joyce later founded the English Players (see above *New Tipperary, The Right Man in the Wrong Place*, etc.). Joyce was detached from Sykes's enthusiasm for mountains and walking, but they shared an enjoyment of humorous verse, especially limericks.

Solomon (September 1917)
(on Simeone Levi)

Joyce's title derives from the comic song 'Solomon Levi', the verses being concerned with his Zurich pupil, Simeone or Simon Levi. Levi had come from Trieste, but Joyce thought he was a Turkish subject, hence a Muslim. He sent the limerick on a card to Sykes (*L* II 406; *Archive* 309), and it was published in Gorman 247. Levi remained on good terms, and asked Joyce to arrange his subscription to the *Egoist* (*L* II 417).

D. L. G. (November 1917)
(on David Lloyd George)

Joyce sent this limerick about Lloyd George to Sykes on a postcard from Locarno (*L* II 410; *Archive* I 309). It was published in Gorman 247. For 'Bully God' understand 'John Bull's or the British God'. Joyce's sympathy was with 'the small nations' to whom Lloyd George had decreed 'small rations'.

Lloyd George had avoided becoming involved in Joyce's dispute with the Zurich consular officials, when Joyce appealed to him directly. It turned out that he was to send in the Black and Tans in 1919 at the beginning of the Anglo-Irish war, and to be the instrument of Partition in 1921, thus causing civil war in the Irish Free State.

P. J. T. (1925—7)
(on Patrick Tuohy)

Joyce had commissioned Patrick Tuohy, the Dublin painter, to paint John Stanislaus Joyce in 1923. Tuohy came to Paris the following May and asked Joyce if he would sit for a portrait himself. Joyce found the sittings tedious, but liked Tuohy's treatment of his tie and jacket (*JJ* 565–6). There is an undated reworked holograph of the limerick at Buffalo dating from *c.* 1925 (*Archive* I 334; printed in Spielberg No. IV.B.3), and Joyce gave a copy to a friend of Tuohy's as a valentine in 1927 (quoted in *JJ* 565n).

COLLECTED OCCASIONAL POEMS

The Holy Office (August 1904)

Joyce submitted the poem to Constantine Curran for inclusion in the UCD magazine, *St Stephen's* (*JJ* 165; compare Curran 46–7), and, when it was rejected, took steps to get it printed himself. It was printed as a broadside over the signature James A. Joyce later in August 1904 in Dublin, and then, having been destroyed when Joyce could not afford to pay, it was printed again in Pola between November 1904 and March 1905. Stanislaus Joyce was given the job of distributing the fifty copies of the Pola printing to the butts of his brother's satire. See Slocum 4–5; *JJ* 200.

No copies of the Dublin printing have survived, and the present text reproduces the Pola printing. There is a manuscript fair copy at Yale, which differs in a few details of phrasing and punctuation, a fragment of the final manuscript with the printer's slip at Cornell, and a typescript copy in the Sylvia Beach Collection at Princeton (*Archive* I 278–85). The poem was reprinted in Joyce's lifetime only in Gorman's biography (NY, 1939, 138–41).

Joyce had already lampooned or parodied in verse the separate figures who made up the Dublin literary scene. See poems on John Eglinton (W. K. Magee) and the Fay brothers (above pp. 77–8); on Lady Gregory, George Russell, Magee, Seumas O'Sullivan (*P&SW* 109, 110, 112); on W. B. Yeats (O'Connor 28–9; omitted by *P&SW*). But his form here is no longer limerick, parody or epigram. He lumps them together as he leaves them behind; and, in an inclusive monologue or *flyting*, he castigates their timidity, hypocrisy and introversion. The service he performs in bringing forward truths they would prefer to conceal is both confessional and purgative; and the monologue builds to an assertion of his own embattled position. The notes that follow are much indebted to *CW* 149–52.

Title Referring ironically to (a) the office of confession and (b) the department of the Church that launched the Inquisition and that today (after 1917) exercises the function of censorship. There are also overtones of 'the holy office an ostler does for the stallion' (*U* 166).

4: the poets' grammar-book Joyce collected the solecisms of his eminent contemporaries in a notebook called *Memorabilia* (*JJ* 124–5). Joyce might also refer to his own departure from a dishevelled Dublin in 1904, to devote himself to poetry in the widest sense.

6: witty Aristotle Joyce identified with Aristotle at the expense of Dublin Platonism, to bolster his stand on behalf of hard empirical reasoning that brought dreams to the bar of fact. 'Katharsis' in line 2 is a central concept in Aristotle's *Poetics*. 'Peripatetic' in line 10 is used with specific reference to the Lyceum colonnade where Aristotle walked and taught.

16: A Dante is, unprejudiced Alluding to a sentence in Joyce's own review of Ibsen's *Catilina*, in which he defends the system of Dante's belief against imprecise, confused modern prejudice (*CW* 101).

22: intense A fashionable concept in the aesthetic of Art for Art's Sake. Compare for instance Walter Pater on the need to cast off inertia and to burn always with a hard, gem-like flame, in *The Renaissance* (1873). There are connections with Stephen's theorizing on art as 'the enchantment of the heart' in *P* 213.

24: that mumming company The Abbey Theatre, which had received its patent in August 1904, and grew out of the Irish National Theatre. Since all the young Irish writers of the time were in some way involved in it, it stands for Irish literary and cultural, as well as theatrical life, at the time. Yeats wrote, in his 'To Ireland in the Coming Times':

> Know, that I would accounted be
> True brother of a company
> That sang, to sweeten Ireland's wrong,

In a more Joycean spirit, compare Mulligan's use of the word 'mummers' in *U* 5, 164, 177, 178).

25–6: him . . . His giddy dames' W. B. Yeats, along with Miss Horniman, who provided financial support for the Abbey Theatre, Lady Gregory, who managed and wrote for it, perhaps Maude Gonne MacBride and the host of other women surrounding Yeats, including his sisters. The dames are singular in the manuscript.

28: gold-embroidered Celtic fringes Alluding to the gilt decorations on the books Yeats published in the 1890s, or perhaps to tasselled bookmarks.

29–30: him who sober . . . John Millington Synge (1871–1909), the principal dramatist of the Abbey, wrote sympathetically about drinking but did not himself indulge.

31–2: him who conduct . . . Oliver St John Gogarty (1878–1972), the original of Buck Mulligan in *Ulysses*. The poem caused Gogarty to decide to break with Joyce (*JJ* 167).

33–6: him who plays . . . Padraic Colum (1881–1972). In 1903 Colum had been promised a three-year subsidy by an American millionaire living near Celbridge, on condition that he live among and write about country people. Joyce tried and failed to get in on the scheme (*JJ* 141). Despite this early resentment, he and Colum became good friends.

37–40: him who will his hat unfix . . . W. K. Magee, 'John Eglinton', poet and librarian. See 'Satire on John Eglinton' in Uncollected Occasional Poems, p. 77, and the limerick on Magee in *P&SW* 112.

41: him who loves . . . George Roberts, a devoted follower of George Russell (also known as AE), who addressed Russell in this way in a poem. Joyce afterwards entered into a protracted dispute with Roberts in his role as manager of Maunsel & Co.: compare with *Gas from a Burner*, below.

42: him who drinks . . . James Sullivan Starkey, 'Seumas O'Sullivan' (1879–1958). See the parody on Starkey in *P&SW* 112.

43–6: him who once . . . George Russell (1867–1935), also known as AE, visionary artist and poet, who was at the centre of Dublin cultural life alongside Yeats. See Joyce's two-stanza limerick in *P&SW* 110.

48: sewer In the obsolete sense of servant who arranges the seating, as well as the other, modern sense of drains?

49: That they may dream their dreamy dreams The 'mumming' Yeats responded to Joyce in the first epigraph to his volume *Responsibilities* (1914), pretending to derive it from an 'Old Play': *'In dreams begins responsibility.'*

57: My scarlet leaves them white as wool Compare Isaiah 1:18: 'Though your sins be as scarlet, they shall be as white as snow.' Joyce sets his crude realism against the mystical hypocrisy of the Celtic Twilight.

60: vicar-general A bishop's assistant, who handles operational details in the diocese.

65–6: 'dare not', 'would' Compare *Macbeth* I vii 44–5: 'Letting "I dare not" wait upon "I would",/Like the poor cat i' the adage.'

69–71: Light attire The phrase overlaps *Chamber Music*, Poem VII, whose tone is thereby modified. Compare also 'the soft flame that is desire' (line 72) with the 'soft and golden fire' of *Chamber Music*, Poem VIII, the floor reflected in the fire of Poem V, 'the softly burning fires' of Poem XV.

74: Leviathan The solitary, heroic, individualistic Satan (compare Isaiah 27:1) – here Joyce – who opposes those who worship Mammon and are compromised by their desire for material recognition.

82: Steeled in the school of old Aquinas Joyce championed the close-connected thinking of Aquinas and others against what he considered the vague posturings of the mainly Protestant Anglo-Irish Revivalists. Compare Stephen's aesthetic in the *Portrait*, and also William T. Noon, *Joyce and Aquinas* (New Haven, Conn., 1957).

87–8: I flash my antlers on the air The image of himself as a hunted deer was a favourite form of self-portrayal for Joyce. Compare *SH* 39: 'There was his ground and he flung them disdain from flashing antlers'; Stephen in the *Proteus* episode: 'I just simply stood pale, silent, bayed about' (*U* 38); *JJ* 438; *P&SW* 212; and compare *CW* 227; *D* 134 on Parnell.

94: Mahamanvantara Sanskrit for 'great year', associated with the great thousand-year cycles of the theosophical concepts of history; Stephen recalls the word in *Proteus* (*U* 34). Ellmann suggests the closing lines might owe something to Ibsen in poems like 'On the Vidda':

> Now I am steel-set: I follow the call
> To the height's clear radiance and glow.
> My lowland life is lived out: and high

On the vidda are God and Liberty –
Whilst wretches live fumbling below.
(M. C. Bradbrook's translation; *JJ* 167n)

Gas from a Burner (September 1912)

The following summary by Mason and Ellmann provides the background of the poem (CW 242):

> In September 1909, Joyce, then on a visit to Dublin, signed a contract with the Dublin firm of Maunsel & Co. to publish *Dubliners*. But George Roberts, the manager of the firm, began to find reasons first for delaying and then for censoring the manuscript. Negotiations dragged along for three years, until finally Joyce returned to Dublin in July 1912, and brought the matter to a head. Both Joyce and Roberts consulted solicitors; Roberts was advised that the use of actual names for public houses and the like was libellous, and began to demand so many changes that there was no possibility of agreement. At length he decided to accept Joyce's offer to purchase the sheets for the book, which John Falconer, a Dublin printer, had finished. But Falconer, hearing of the dispute, decided he wanted nothing to do with so unpleasant a book, and guillotined the sheets. Joyce left Dublin full of bitterness, which he vented by writing this broadside on the back of his contract with Maunsel & Co. for the publication of *Dubliners* . . .

The poem was printed in Trieste as a broadside over the signature James Joyce and distributed in Dublin (somewhat reluctantly) by Joyce's brother, Charles. It was reprinted in Joyce's lifetime only in Gorman's biography (NY, 1939, 217–19). See Slocum 11–12; *JJ* 337. The early drafts, now at Cornell, are written on the back of the forms and typescripts of the *Dubliners* agreement with Maunsel & Co., and there is a copy of the printed broadside with an inscribed explanatory note by Joyce at Kansas (*Archive* I 288–304a). The explanatory note reads: 'This pasquinade was written in the railway station waiting room at Flushing Holland, on the way to Trieste from Dublin after the malicious burning of the 1st edition of *Dubliners* (1,000 copies less one in my possession) by the printer Messrs John Falconer. Upper Sackville Street Dublin in July 1912.'

As for the previous poem, I am much indebted to CW 242–5 in the notes that follow; also to the notes in Oliver St John Gogarty, *Mourning Became Mrs Spendlove* (NY, 1948) 58–61. The later draft of the manuscript at Cornell is marked in ornate script. 'The/Dean Swift/Rote'. This dimension of the poem is ably discussed by Thomas F. Staley, 'The Poet Joyce and the Shadow of Swift' in *Jonathan Swift: Tercentenary Essays*, eds. Winston Weathers and Thomas F. Staley (Tulsa, Okla., 1967) 39–52.

Title Joyce claimed the sheets of his book were burnt; Roberts always insisted they were guillotined (see *JJ* 335). Conflagration better fits Joyce's early identification with Giordano Bruno, who 'was terribly burned' by the censoring forces of the Inquisition (*SH* 175; *P* 249). Compare line 86.

6: I The first draft of the poem is described in the margin as 'Falconer addresses the Vigilance Committee' (*Archive* I 289); the second draft, at the end, as 'Falconer on "Dubliners"' (*Archive* I 295). The speaker of the present, final version is a blend of Roberts and Falconer, though at times his voice is overtaken by that of Joyce (the 'He' of line 5). The invective is a good deal more personal, less controlled, than in *The Holy Office*.

13–24: But I owe ... Gogarty remarks that 'Here the sentiments are obviously out of character and the voice becomes that of Joyce, who has not yet won to his prerogative of speaking twice-tongued.'

14: I hold her honour in my hand Ellmann records that Joyce claimed Falconer had been paid £70 by someone unidentified to burn the book (*JJ* 336n).

19–20: 'Twas Irish humour This incident occurred at Castlecomer in the summer of 1891, according to Parnell's biographer and friend, R. Barry O'Brien. It was on Joyce's mind earlier in 1912, in a newspaper article he wrote on Parnell in Trieste (*CW* 227).

24: Billy Walsh His Grace the Most Reverend William J. Walsh, DD, Archbishop of Dublin from 1885 to 1921. He took a prominent part in the downfall of Parnell, for which he was held in contempt by Joyce's father (compare *P* 33, where Walsh is described as 'Billy with the lip').

27: shamrock Aubert 1370 suggests a pun on the flower that is the emblem of Ireland and the sham rock – false foundation – on which the Christian Church is founded.

29 The first draft of the poem begins here (*Archive* I 288).

30: Mountainy Mutton Joseph Campbell (1881–1944), author of *The Mountainy Singer*, published by Maunsel in 1909.

32: 'bastard', etc. Campbell's *Judgment: A Play in Two Acts*, published by Maunsel in 1912, contains the words 'bastard' and 'whore' (25).

33—6: a play on the Word ... *The Apostle*, published by Maunsel in 1911. Moore's play, in which Christ (the Word) and Paul meet after Christ's death, includes a dialogue between Christ and Mary in which Mary laments her lost beauty. In a long preface Moore surveys the Bible for evidence of sensuality and remarks (9), 'In Samuel we read how David was captured by the sweetness of Bathsheba's legs while bathing' and (26) 'It may be doubted whether Paul always succeeded in subduing these infirmities of the flesh, but we would not love him less, even if we knew that he had loved St Eunice not wisely but too well.'

38: the table book of Cousins James H. Cousins, one of George Russell's (AE's) circle and a member of the Hermetic Society. Joyce stayed with him occasionally in Dublin, and Mrs Cousins lent her first name to Gretta in *The Dead* (*JJ* 162, 171, 247n). Joyce sent him a copy of *The Holy Office* in 1905 (*JJ* 200), and the 'table book' is probably his *Etain the Beloved and Other Poems*, published by Maunsel in 1912.

40: 'Twould give you a heartburn on your arse An expression of Joyce's father. Compare *U* 102.

42: Gregory of the Golden Mouth Maunsel published Lady Gregory's *Kiltartan History Book* in 1909 and *The Kiltartan Wonder Book* in 1910. If 'Golden Mouth' connects her with the eloquence of St John Chrysostom (*c.* 347–407), the allusion must be ironic and must be literally to her dental fillings.

44: Patrick What-do-you-Colm Padraic Colum.

45–8: the great John Milicent Synge The word 'shift' spoken by a character in John Millington Synge's *Playboy of the Western World* caused a week of rioting at the Abbey Theatre in 1907. Maunsel published the play in the same year, as Roberts reminded Joyce in the course of their dispute (*JJ* 328). It is difficult to say if the single *l* in 'Milicent' is deliberate; compare Joyce's omission of a medial *l* in a word in Poem XXXII of *Chamber Music*. Meanwhile, Roberts was a traveller in ladies' underwear, and Joyce and Gogarty had played a practical joke with his samples in a raid on the rooms of the Hermetic Society in 1904 (*JJ* 174).

Gogarty's comment is also worth remark, that the speaker who is compounded of Maunsel's manager cannot pillory himself in this way if the device of the speaker is interpreted literally.

50–51: dressed in Austrian yellow ... Joyce, from Austrian Trieste, where he naturally spoke Italian. Aubert 1372 points out that those condemned by the Inquisition were marked by a yellow badge.

52: O'Leary Curtis A Dublin journalist, and one of the recipients of *The Holy Office* in 1905 (*JJ* 200).

— **John Wyse Power** An official in the Royal Irish Constabulary in Dublin Castle, and a man of considerable cultivation. He figures as Mr Power in *Grace* (*D* 152, etc.), and in *Ulysses* in the characters of Jack Power and John Wyse Nolan.

53: dirty and dear The phrase 'dear, dirty Dublin' is proverbial and accurate. It appears to have been coined by Lady Sydney Morgan, and it provides a caption in *Aeolus* (*U* 119).

55: Shite and onions! An expression of Joyce's father. Compare *U* 104.

56–8: Wellington Monument,/Sydney Parade ... Localities in Dublin that appear in *D* 202 and 113 respectively. Downes's Cakeshop appears on 102, though Williams's jam was omitted from the published text.

60: Irish Names of Places *The Origin and History of Irish Names of Places* (Dublin, 1869) by Patrick Weston Joyce – no relation of James Joyce.

62: Curly's Hole A bathing pool at Dollymount, Clontarf. Compare Jack's Hole in Co. Wicklow.

64: Stepmother Erin Roberts was an Ulster Scot, so Erin is only his stepmother. Pointing to the lines that follow, Aubert 1373 suggests Falconer is in Joyce's mind here, as well as Roberts. Compare line 95 below.

66: a red-headed Scotchman Roberts himself, who was his own bookkeeper.

70: My heart is as soft as buttermilk An allusion to his remark to Joyce that the Giant's Causeway was soft putty compared to him (recorded in *JJ* 337n).

73: Irish Review Edited by Colum from March 1912 to July 1913.

78: railway guide Maunsel & Co. were indeed the official publishers of both railway and sailing timetables.

82: tight-breeched artilleryman Written when a British garrison in Dublin supported a vibrant red-light district. The breeches are of the trousers and of the gun.

85: Resist not evil? Christ, in the Sermon on the Mount (Matthew 5:39).

86: I'll burn that book It was important for Joyce's sense of martyrdom to maintain that his book had been burned. Compare note on title above.

95: Bannockburn Not in Ireland, but famously in Scotland, where Robert Bruce fought the English in 1314.

98: Memento homo 'Memento, homo, quia pulvis est' are the words of the priest on Ash Wednesday as he marks the sign of the cross of ashes on the penitent's forehead.

Ecce Puer (February 1932)

The poem was written on 15 February 1932, the day of the birth of Joyce's grandson who was named after him, Stephen James Joyce. The birth followed a difficult pregnancy for Helen Joyce and followed only nine days after the death of Joyce's father. It therefore reaches before and after, spanning three generations. Joy is counterpointed by grief, the darkness of the past by the light of the future, the spirit of welcome by a mood of farewell. It draws on allusions to the Crucifixion as well as to the Nativity. 'Each of us crucifies and is crucified, each forsakes and is forsaken, and each must forgive much, just as each asks forgiveness' (Lawrence Richard Holmes, 'Joyce's *Ecce Puer*', *The Explicator*, XIII:2, November 1954, No. 12).

The poem was published in the *New Republic* (NY) LXXIII:939 (30 November 1932) 70, and included in Joyce's *Collected Poems* (NY, 1936). I have corrected the 1936 punctuation with reference to the earlier typescript at Princeton (*Archive* I 347). The wording does not vary between these versions. C. P. Curran noted an autograph copy with pencil corrections among the Leon papers, in his commonplace book now at University College Dublin (CUR MS 6) 90.

Title Latin for 'behold the boy'. Alluding to Pilate's words when he introduced Jesus wearing the crown of thorns, 'Behold the man!' (John 19:5). The title *Ecce homo* is applied to countless paintings of Christ's Passion, including one by Munkacsy on which Joyce wrote a youthful essay (CW 31–7). It sums up a poem that is a cry for atonement, made too late, to ears that cannot hear it (as I believe someone said before me, though I cannot remember who).

2 Verbatim from Isaiah 9:6, and the burden of many Christmas hymns.

3: **joy and grief** Coincident with Edgar on the death of Gloucester in Shakespeare's *King Lear* V iii 198. Lines 9–10 below might echo the dying Lear, contemplating his daughter, later in the same scene (lines 261–3).

8 The child's eyes' blinded by sin and also blind like Joyce's. Compare also St Paul's 'now we see through a glass, darkly' (I Corinthians 13:12).

15: **O, father forsaken** Compare Jesus's final cry: 'my God, my God, why hast thou forsaken me?' (Matthew 27:46; Mark 15:34).

16: **Forgive your son!**   Compare Jesus on the cross before his death:
'Father, forgive them; for they know not what they do' (Luke 23:34).

EXILES

The play *Exiles* draws in an obvious way on events in Joyce's own life. It
is set in the 'Summer of the year 1912', when he brought Nora and the
children to Ireland in a vain attempt to secure the publication of *Dublin-
ers*. Its gestation dates from the two years following his return to Trieste,
as he brooded on the state of his marriage and career. It registers his
realization that he did not want to live in Ireland – in fact, he never
afterwards returned, even for a visit – and it explores the nature of the
independent life he had chosen in terms of the relationship that was most
important in it. The exploration anticipates themes that are central to
Ulysses: Envy, Jealousy, Abnegation, Equanimity (*U* 602–3).

Exiles returns to the very beginning of Joyce's relationship with Nora
when they eloped, and even to Nora's life in Galway before. It embodies
feelings of jealousy he had been plagued with on his first return-visit to
Ireland in 1909, when his friend Vincent Cosgrave pretended previously
to have had an affair with Nora – feelings that had been reawakened on
his second visit and by an over-attentive admirer of Nora's in Trieste.
Such themes are worked out in ways coterminous with his state of
mind, as *Dubliners* awaited publication and the revision of *Stephen Hero*
into the *Portrait* was completed. The first chapters of *Ulysses* were in
process of being drafted, even as he considered his next step as a writer.
It was a time when he was particularly vulnerable, almost alienated, but
out of which he won towards a significantly, indeed dramatically ambi-
tious starting-point.

The materials for the play in Vol. XI of the *Archive* comprise a
notebook at Buffalo (1–61), separate fragments of dialogue at Cornell
(64–85), a holograph of the complete manuscript at Yale (87–262), and a
near-complete set of uncorrected galley proofs of the English edition at
Cornell (264–389). Two entries in the Buffalo notebook, about two thirds
through, are dated 12 and 13 November 1913 (p. 346); in another entry
that follows (p. 353) Joyce speaks as if the First Act were already drafted,
while the 'dialogue notes' mentioned in this same entry could refer to the
fragments at Cornell. Though the Cornell fragments are not dated, they
all relate to the two later acts. In other words, the First Act appears to

have been roughed out by autumn 1913, as Joyce pondered how to make use of other material that was either to hand or evolving.

The preliminary writing appears to have continued in the spring of 1914, and then in earnest after August 1914. Joyce says he brought the manuscript with him to Zurich the following summer, where it was completed (*L* I 78, 83, 104–5; II 338, 353; III 508, etc.). An intervening typescript has not survived, but the manuscript at Yale – the one Joyce sold to Quinn in 1917 – appears to be a fair copy from which the typescript was made. A good many changes were made between this stage and the proof, and English and American editions were published simultaneously on 25 May 1918.

The evolution of the text, from its beginnings through its various revisions and stages of publication, is analysed and very clearly presented by MacNicholas (27–47). He provides further references and details that enlarge on the bald summary above. MacNicholas's analysis also provides the basis for the text that appears in this edition. It derives from his collation of the fair-copy manuscript, the first English edition and the galley proofs at Cornell. A number of small errors are thereby corrected, and a number of omissions from Joyce's stage directions are restored. Another difference from all previous versions is that the text here conforms to Joyce's practice in capitalization, punctuation, spelling and word division. Any one such adjustment may appear trivial, but they accumulate to create a different overall effect.

In addition, the relevant entries from the Buffalo notebook and the fragments of dialogue at Cornell are given following this headnote, headed A and B. With respect to the notes headed A, it is important that Joyce wrote them after he had written a version of the First Act, but apparently before he drafted the remaining two acts. That is, they should be interpreted as a commentary on the play at an interim stage – *reculer pour mieux sauter*. They are prompted by feelings that are neither wholly preparatory nor purely retrospective. Material for future use is set down alongside reflections and excursions prompted by material that might have been preserved in a different form. The entries are separated by lines across the page (here represented by rules), though it is clear that groups of entries were written on the same occasion.

It is likewise important to be clear about the status of the fragments headed B. They are not drafts; they are fair copies on paper that for Joyce is unusually small and leaves little room for revision. MacNicholas 32 speculates that they were copied for Stanislaus between January and March 1915, perhaps from a (lost) notebook version made the previous year. Whether or not this is the case, the fragments bear an oblique relation to the finished text; they do not necessarily relate to the play as we know it, even though they are arranged here in a sequence that parallels the action. Their arrangement and numbering is an editorial intervention.

The chronological relation of the materials at Buffalo and Cornell is undetermined. The *cf* that appears in the Buffalo notebook followed by a passage of dialogue (p. 348) strongly suggests that Joyce had other such passages to hand that have not survived. It is unclear whether the notebook reference to 'dialogue notes prepared' refers to the Cornell fragments or to the lost original they were copied from. In other words, the two sets of materials presented alongside one another here should be interpreted with considerable circumspection. They are connected with a basic shift of focus in the structuring of the First Act that can be traced in the fair-copy manuscript – and that indeed can only be guessed at (MacNicholas 33–42).

As I have said, the present text puts into operation the recommendations made by MacNicholas, and I have departed from them on only a few trivial occasions. The notes, however, differ in that I have corrected what has been borrowed and I have added a good deal more. Even so, the larger and more important backgrounds of the play cannot adequately be annotated. The way in which characters as different as Nora's childhood loves, Gogarty, Roberto Prezioso, Thomas Kettle and Vincent Cosgrave, combine with literary influences in the character of Robert Hand can be explained only with reference to the continuous history of Joyce's thoughts and feelings.

Similarly, Beatrice Justice combines distant memories of Eileen Vance (Stephen's Protestant neighbour in *Portrait*), Mary Sheehy, Joyce's reading in Dante, and his infatuation with the Triestine language-student, Amalia Popper, which is celebrated in *Giacomo Joyce* and which establishes links between *Exiles* and *Pomes Penyeach*. Such backgrounds are not composed of isolable details that can be parcelled into discrete footnotes. The play stands at a crossroads in Joyce's life and career, and traces of it are threaded through the length of Ellmann's large biography.

(A) ENTRIES IN A NOTEBOOK, NOW AT BUFFALO

Richard – an automystic
Robert – an automobile

The soul like the body may have a virginity. For the woman to yield it or for the man to take it is the act of love. Love (understood as the desire of good for another) is in fact so unnatural a phenomenon that it can scarcely repeat itself, the soul being unable to become virgin again and not having energy enough to cast itself out again into the ocean of another's soul. It is the repressed consciousness of this inability and lack of spiritual energy which explains Bertha's mental paralysis.

Her age: 28. Robert likens her to the moon because of her dress. Her age is the completion of a lunar rhythm. Cf Oriani on menstrual flow – *la malattia sacra che in un rituo lunare prepara la donna per il sacrificio.*

Robert wishes Richard to use against him the weapons which social conventions and morals put in the hands of the husband. Richard refuses. Bertha wishes Richard to use these weapons also in her defence. Richard refuses also and for the same reason. His defence of her soul and body is an invisible and imponderable sword.

As a contribution to the study of jealousy Shakespeare's *Othello* is incomplete. It and Spinoza's analysis are made from the sensationalist standpoint – Spinoza speaks of *pudendis et excrementis alterius jungere imaginem rei amatae.* Bertha has considered the passion in itself – apart from hatred or baffled lust. The scholastic definition of jealousy as a *passio irascibilis* comes nearer – its object being a difficult good. In this play Richard's jealousy is carried one step nearer to its own heart. Separated from hatred and having its baffled lust converted into an erotic stimulus and moreover holding in its own power the hindrance, the difficulty which has excited it it must reveal itself as the very immolation of the pleasure of possession on the altar of love. He is jealous, wills and knows his own dishonour and the dishonour of her, to be united with every phase of whose being is love's end as to achieve that union in the region of the difficult, the void and the impossible is its necessary tendency.

It will be difficult to recommend Beatrice to the interest of the audience, every man of which is Robert and would like to be Richard – in any case Bertha's. The note of compassion can be struck when she takes the spectacles from her pocket in order to read. Critics may say what they like, all these persons – even Bertha – are suffering during the action.

Why the title *Exiles*? A nation exacts a penance from those who dared to leave her payable on their return. The elder brother in the fable of the Prodigal Son is Robert Hand. The father took the side of the prodigal. This is probably not the way of the world – certainly not in Ireland: but Jesus' Kingdom was not of this world nor was or is his wisdom.

Bertha's state when abandoned spiritually by Richard must be expressed by the actress by a suggestion of hypnosis. Her state is like that of Jesus in the garden of olives. It is the soul of woman left naked and alone that it may come to an understanding of its own nature. She must appear also to be carried forward to the last point consistent with her immunity by the current of the action and must show even a point of resentment against the man who will not hold out a hand to save her. Through these experiences she will suffuse her own reborn temperament with the wonder of her soul at its own solitude and at her beauty, formed and dissolving itself eternally amid the clouds of mortality.

The secondary and lower phase of Robert's position is the suspicion that Richard is a cunning adventurer using Bertha's body as a bait to gain Robert's friendship and support. The corresponding phase in Richard's attitude is the suspicion that Robert's admiration and friendship for him is simulated in order to lull and stupefy the vigilance of his mind. Both these suspicions are borne in upon the characters from purely external evidence and do not in either case spring into existence spontaneously from the soils of their natures.

It is an irony of the play that while Robert not Richard is the apostle of beauty, beauty in its visible and invisible being is present under Richard's roof.

Since the publication of the lost pages of *Madame Bovary* the centre of sympathy appears to have been esthetically shifted from the lover or fancyman to the husband or cuckold. This displacement is also rendered more stable by the gradual growth of a collective practical realism due to changed economic conditions in the mass of the people who are called to hear and feel a work of art relating to their lives. This change is utilised in *Exiles* although the union of Richard and Bertha is irregular to the extent that the spiritual revolt of Richard which would be strange and ill-welcomed otherwise can enter into combat with Robert's decrepit prudence with some chance of fighting before the public a drawn battle. Praga in *La Crisi* and Giacosa in *Tristi Amori* have understood and profited by this change but have not used it, as is done here, as a technical shield for the protection of a delicate, strange and highly sensitive conscience.

Robert is convinced of the non-existence, of the unreality of the spiritual facts which exist and are real for Richard. The action of the piece should however convince Robert of the existence and reality of Richard's mystical defence of his wife. If this defence be a reality how can those facts on which it is based be then unreal?

It would be interesting to make some sketches of Bertha if she had united her life for nine years to Robert – not necessarily in the way of drama but rather impressionist sketches. For instance, Mrs Robert Hand (because he intended to do it decently) ordering carpets in Grafton Street, at Leopardstown races, provided with a seat on the platform at the unveiling of a statue, putting out the lights in the drawingroom after a social evening in her husband's house, kneeling outside a confessional in the jesuit church.

Richard has fallen from a higher world and is indignant when he discovers baseness in men and women. Robert has risen from a lower world and so far is he from indignation that it surprises him that men and women are not baser and more ignoble.

Robert

(*nods*) Yes, you won. I saw your triumph.

Richard

(*rising suddenly*) Excuse me. I forgot. Will you have some whisky?

Robert

All things come to those who wait.

[*Richard goes to the sideboard and fills out a glass of whisky from the decanter, brings it with a small carafe of water to the table*]

Richard

(*lolling back on the couch*) Will you add the water yourself?

Robert

(*does so*) And you?

Richard
(*shakes his head*) Nothing.

Robert
(*holding his glass*) I think of our wild nights long ago, our nights of revelry and talk and carousing.

Richard
In our house.

Robert
(*raising his glass*) Prosit!

When Richard left the church he met many men of the same type as Robert.

Problem. Archie, Richard's son, is brought up on Robert's principles.

Beatrice has had an interview with her mother before she enters in the first act.

Bertha alludes to Beatrice as her ladyship.

N.(B) – 12 Nov. 1913
    Garter: precious, Prezioso, Bodkin, music, palegreen, bracelet, cream
        sweets, lily of the valley, convent garden (Galway), sea.
    Rat: Sickness, disgust, poverty, cheese, woman's ear, (child's ear?)
    Dagger: heart, death, soldier, war, band, judgment, king.

N.(B) – 13 Nov. 1913
    Moon – Shelley's grave in Rome. He is rising from it: blond. She
    weeps for him. He has fought in vain for an ideal and died killed by
    the world. Yet he rises. Graveyard at Rahoon by moonlight where
    Bodkin's grave is. He lies in the grave. She sees his tomb (family
    vault) and weeps. The name is homely. Shelley's is strange and wild.
    He is dark, unrisen, killed by love and life, young. The earth holds
    him.
        Bodkin died. Kearns died. In the convent they called her the
    man-killer. (Womankiller was one of her names for me). I live in
    soul and body.
        She is the earth, dark, formless, mother, made beautiful by the

346

moonlit night, darkly conscious of her instincts. Shelley whom she has held in her womb or grave rises: the part of Richard which neither love nor life can do away with: the part for which she loves him: the part she must try to kill, never be able to kill, and rejoice at her impotence. Her tears are of worship, Magdalen seeing the rearisen Lord in the garden where He had been laid in the tomb. Rome is the strange world and strange life to which Richard brings her. Rahoon her people. She weeps over Rahoon too, over him whom her love has killed, the dark boy whom, as the earth, she embraces in death and disintegration. He is her buried life, her past. His attendant images are the trinkets and toys of girlhood (bracelet, cream sweets, palegreen lily of the valley, the convent garden). His symbols are music and the sea, liquid formless earth in which are buried the drowned soul and body. There are tears of commiseration. She is Magdalen who weeps remembering the loves she could not return.

If Robert really prepares the way for Richard's advance and hopes for it while he tries at the same time secretly to combat this advance by destroying at a blow Richard's confidence in himself the position is like that of Wotan who in willing the birth and growth of Siegfried longs for his own destruction. Every step advanced by humanity through Richard is a step backwards by the type which Robert stands for.

Richard fears the reaction inevitable in Robert's temperament: and not for Bertha's sake only, that is, not to feel that he by standing aside has allowed her to go her way through a passing love to neglect but to feel that a woman chosen by him has been set aside for another not chosen by him.

Beatrice's mind is an abandoned cold temple in which hymns have risen heavenward in a distant past but where now a doddering priest offers alone and hopelessly prayers to the Most High.

Richard having first understood the nature of innocence when it had been lost by him fears to believe that Bertha, to understand the chastity of her nature, must first lose it in adultery.

Blister – amber – silver – oranges – apples – sugarstick – hair – spongecake – ivy – roses – ribbon.

The blister reminds her of the burning of her hand as a girl. She sees her own amber hair and her mother's silver hair. This silver is the crown of age but also the stigma of care and grief which she and her lover have laid upon it. This avenue of thought is shunned completely: and the other aspect, amber turned to silver by the years, her mother a prophecy of what she may one day be, is hardly glanced at. Oranges, apples, sugarstick – these take the place of the shunned thoughts and are herself as she was, being her girlish joys. Hair: the mind turns again to this without adverting to its colour, adverting only to a distinctive sexual mark and to its growth and mystery rather than to its colour. The softly growing symbol of her girlhood. Spongecake, a weak flash again of joys which now begin to seem more those of a child than those of a girl. Ivy and roses: she gathered ivy often when out in the evening with girls. Roses grew then. A sudden scarlet note in the memory which may be a dim suggestion of the roses of the body. The ivy and the roses carry on and up, out of the idea of growth, through a creeping vegetable life into ardent perfumed flower life the symbol of mysteriously growing girlhood, her hair. Ribbon for her hair. Its fitting ornament for the eyes of others, and lastly for his eyes. Girlhood becomes virginity and puts on 'the snood that is the sign of maidenhood'. A proud and shy instinct turns her mind away from the loosening of her bound-up hair – however sweet or longed for or inevitable – and she embraces that which is hers alone and not hers and his also – happy distant dancing days, distant, gone for ever, dead. Or killed? *cf*

Robert

You have made her all that she is. A strange and wonderful personality.

Richard

(*darkly*) Or I have killed her.

Robert

Killed her?

Richard

The virginity of her soul.

Richard must not appear as a champion of woman's rights. His language at times must be nearer to that of Schopenhauer against women and he must show at times a deep contempt for the long-haired, short-legged sex. He is in fact fighting for his own hand, for his own emotional dignity and liberation in which Bertha, no less and no more than Beatrice or any other woman is coinvolved. He does not use the language of adoration and his character must seem a little unloving. But it is a fact that for nearly two thousand years the women of Christendom have prayed to and kissed the naked image of one who had neither wife nor mistress nor sister and would scarcely have been associated with his mother had it not been that the Italian church discovered, with its infallible practical instinct, the rich possibilities of the figure of the Madonna.

Snow:

frost; moon; pictures, holly and ivy, currantcake, lemonade, Emily Lyons, piano, windowsill

tears:

ship, sunshine, garden, sadness, pinafore, buttoned boots, bread and butter, a big fire.

In the first the flow of ideas is tardy. It is Christmas in Galway, a moonlit Christmas eve with snow. She is carrying picture almanacs to her grandmother's house to be ornamented with holly and ivy. The evenings are spent in the house of a friend where they give her lemonade. Lemonade and currantcake are also her grandmother's Christmas fare for her. She thumps the piano and sits with her dark-complexioned gipsy-looking girl friend Emily Lyons on the windowsill.

In the second the ideas are more rapid. It is the quay of Galway harbour on a bright morning. The emigrant ship is going away and Emily, her dark friend, stands on deck going out to America. They kiss and cry bitterly. But she believes that some day her friend will come back as she promises. She cries for the pain of separation and for the dangers of the sea that threaten the girl who is going away. The girl is older than she and has no lover. She too has no lover. Her sadness is brief. She is alone, friendless, in her grandmother's garden and can see the garden, lonely now, in which the day before she played with her friend. Her grandmother consoles her, gives her a clean new pinafore to wear and buttoned boots, a present from her uncle, and nice bread and butter to eat and a big fire to sit down to.

Homesickness and regret for dead girlish days are again strongly marked. A persistent and delicate sensuality (visual: pictures, adorned with holly and ivy; gustatious: currant cake, bread and butter, lemonade; tactual: sunshine in the garden, a big fire, the kisses of her friend and grandmother) runs through both series of images. A persistent and delicate vanity also, even in her grief; her pinafore and buttoned boots. No thought of a more recent admiration, which is strong even to the point of being fetishism and has been well observed by her, crosses her mind now. The boots suggest their giver, her uncle and she feels vaguely the forgotten cares and affections among [which] she grew up. She thinks of them kindly, not because they were kind to *her* but because they were kind to her girlself which is now gone and because they are part of it, hidden away even from herself in her memory. The note of regret is ever present and finds utterance at last in the tears which fill her eyes as she sees her friend go. A departure. A friend, her own youth, going away. A faint glimmer of lesbianism irradiates this mind. This girl too is dark, even like a gipsy, and she too, like the dark lover who sleeps in Rahoon, is going away from her, the man-killer and perhaps also the love-killer, over the dark sea which is distance, the extinction of interest and death. They have no male lovers and are moved vaguely one towards the other. The friend is older, stronger, can travel alone, braver, a prophecy of a later dark male. The passiveness of her character to all that is not vital to its existence, and yet a passiveness which is suffused with tenderness. The assassin is alone and quiet amid the mild sunlight and the mild cares and ministrations of her grandmother, happy that the fire is warm, toasting her toes.

What then is this tenderness and regard to give which is death, or discontent, or distance or the extinction of interest? She has no remorse for she [knows] what she can give when she reads desire in dark eyes. Have they not need of it since they long and ask? To refuse it, her heart tells her, would be to kill more cruelly and pitilessly those whom the waves or a disease or the passing of the years will bear surely away from her life towards distance, early death and that extinction of personality which is death in life.

In the incertitude of the two female characters Bertha has the advantage of her beauty – a fact behind which even an evil woman's character can safely hide much less a character not morally evil.

Act II:
Bertha wishes for the spiritual union of Richard and Robert and *believes* (?) that union will be effected only through her body and perpetuated thereby.

Richard accepts Robert's homage for Bertha as by so doing he robs it from Bertha's countrywomen and revenges himself and his forbidden love upon them.

The play is three cat and mouse acts.

The bodily possession of Bertha by Robert, repeated often, would certainly bring into almost carnal contact the two men. Do they desire this? To be united, that is carnally through the person and body of Bertha as they cannot, without dissatisfaction and degradation – be united carnally man to man as man to woman?

Exiles – also because at the end either Robert or Richard must go into exile – perhaps the new Ireland cannot contain both. Robert will go. But her thoughts will they follow him into exile as those of her sister-in-love Isolde follow Tristan?

All believe that Bertha is Robert's mistress. This *belief* rubs against his own *knowledge* of what has been: but he accepts the belief as a bitter food.

Of Richard's friends Robert is the only one who has entered Richard's mind through the gate of Bertha's affection.

The play: a rough and tumble between the Marquis de Sade and Freiherr v. Sacher Masoch. Had not Robert better give Bertha a little bite when they kiss? Richard's Masochism needs no example.

In the last act (or second) Robert can also suggest that he knew from the first that Richard was aware of his conduct and that he himself was being watched and that he persisted because he had to and because he wished to see to what length Richard's silent forbearance would go.

Bertha is reluctant to give the hospitality of her womb to Robert's seed. For this reason she would like more a child of his by another woman than a child of him by her. Is this true? For him the question of child or no child is immaterial. Is her reluctance to yield (even when the possibility of a child is removed) this same reluctance or a survival of it or a survival of the fears (purely physical) of a virgin? It is certain that her instinct can distinguish between concessions and for her the supreme concession is what the fathers of the church call *emissio seminis inter vas naturale.* As for the accomplishment of the act otherwise externally, by friction, or in the mouth the question needs to be scrutinised still more. Would she allow her lust to carry her so far as to receive his emission of seed in any other opening of the body where it could not be acted upon, when once emitted, by the forces of her secret flesh?

Bertha is fatigued and repelled by the restless curious energy of Richard's mind and her fatigue is soothed by Robert's placid politeness.

Her mind is a grey seamist amid which common objects – hillsides, the masts of ships, and barren islands – loom with strange and yet recognisable outlines.

The sadism in Robert's character – his wish to inflict cruelty as a necessary part of sensual pleasure – is apparent only or chiefly in his dealings with women towards whom he is unceasingly attractive because unceasingly aggressive. Towards men, however, he is meek and humble of heart.

Europe is weary even of the Scandinavian women (Hedda Gabler, Rebecca Rosmer, Asta Allmers) whom the poetic genius of Ibsen created when the slav heroines of Dostoievsky and Turgenev were growing stale. On what woman will the light of the poet's mind now shine? Perhaps at last on the Celt. Vain question. Curl the hair how you will and undo it again as you will.

Richard, unfitted for adulterous intercourse with the wives of his friends because it would involve a great deal of pretence on his part rather than because he is convinced of any dishonourableness in it wishes, it seems, to feel the thrill of adultery vicariously and to possess a bound woman Bertha through the organ of his friend.

Bertha at the highest pitch of excitement in Act III enforces her speech with the word 'Heavens'.

The doubt which clouds the end of the play must be conveyed to the audience not only through Richard's questions to both but also from the dialogue between Robert and Bertha.

All Celtic philosophers seemed to have inclined towards incertitude or scepticism – Hume, Berkeley, Balfour, Bergson.

The dialogue notes prepared are altogether too diffuse. They must be sifted in the sieve of the action. Possibly the best way to do this is to draft off the next act (II) letting the characters express themselves. It is not necessary to bind them to the expressions in the notes.

The greatest danger in the writing of this play is tenderness of speech or of mood. In Richard's case it does not persuade and in the case of the other two it is equivocal.

During the second act as Beatrice is not on the stage, her figure must appear before the audience through the thoughts or speech of the others. This is by no means easy.

The character of Archie in the third act carries on the light-heartedness of Richard, which has been apparent at intervals in the first and second acts. However, as Richard's spiritual affection for his son (also his filial feeling towards his own father) has been adequately represented in the former acts to balance this, the love of Bertha for her child must be brought out as strongly and as simply and as early as possible in the third act. It must, of course, be accentuated by the position of sadness in which she finds herself.

Perhaps it would be well to make a separate sketch of the doings of each of the four chief persons during the night, including those whose actions are not revealed to the public in the dialogue, namely Beatrice and Richard.

Robert is glad to have in Richard a personality to whom he can pay the tribute of complete admiration, that is to say, one to whom it is not necessary to give always a qualified and half-hearted praise. This he mistakes for reverence.

A striking instance of the changed point of view of literature towards this subject is Paul de Kock – a descendant surely of Rabelais, Molière and the old *souche gauloise*. Yet compare *George Dandin* or *Le Cocu Imaginaire* of Molière with *Le Cocu* of the later writer. Salacity, humour, indecency, liveliness were certainly not wanting in the writer yet he produces a long, hesitating, painful story – written also in the first person. Evidently that spring is broken somewhere.

The relations between Mrs O'Shea and Parnell are not of vital significance for Ireland – first, because Parnell was tongue-tied and secondly because she was an Englishwoman. The very points in his character which could have been of interest have been passed over in silence. Her manner of writing is not Irish – nay, her manner of loving is not Irish. The character of O'Shea is much more typical of Ireland. The two greatest Irishmen of modern times – Swift and Parnell – broke their lives over women. And it was the adulterous wife of the King of Leinster who brought the first Saxon to the Irish coast.

ANNOTATION OF (A) ENTRIES IN A NOTEBOOK, NOW AT BUFFALO

Title The entries are titled on a separate page of the notebook: '*Exiles/* (a play in three acts)/by/James Joyce'/.

p. 343: Love (understood as the desire of good for another) A commonplace of scholastic discussions of love and the will, many of which cite Aquinas, *Summa Contra Gentiles* I 91, *Summa Theologiae* Ia, q. 20, a. 1, ad. 3, etc., and which go back to Aristotle, *Nicomachean Ethics* Bks VIII and IX and *Rhetoric* 1380b33–1381c. (I owe these references to the kindness of Dr Gerard Casey, of University College Dublin.)

p. 343: 28 ... the moon ... lunar rhythm Aubert 1772 suggests that such correspondences anticipate the twenty-eight 'rainbow girls' of *Finnegans Wake*.

p. 343: Oriani on menstrual flow – *la malattia sacra che in un rituo lunare prepara la donna per il sacrificio* Alfredo Oriani, *La Rivolta ideale* (1908) 148; this translates as 'a sacred malady seems within a lunar rhythm to prepare her for the sacrifice'. The translation is by Dominic Manganiello, 'The Italian Sources for *Exiles*: Giacosa, Praga, Oriani and Joyce' in *Myth and Reality in Irish Literature*, ed. Joseph Ronsley (Waterloo, Ontario, 1977) 227–37 (232 specifically), who provides further discussion.

p. 343: Spinoza speaks of *pudendis* ... *amatae*. Joyce's phrases draw on the discussion of jealousy in Spinoza's 'On the Origin and Nature of Emotions'. Spinoza concludes that 'he who thinks, that a woman whom he loves prostitutes herself to another, will feel pain, not only because his own desire is restrained, but also because, being compelled to associate the image of her he loves with the parts of shame and the excreta of another, he therefore shrinks from her' (trans. R. H. M. Elwes, *Ethics* III xxxvn).

p. 343: The scholastic definition of jealousy as a *passio irascibilis* ... In Scholastic philosophy, an irascible passion must overcome impediments to achieve a sensible good, whereas a concupiscible passion leads easily to good. The irascible passions are hope, despair, courage, fear, anger; and jealousy is more often classified as a sin.

p. 343: a difficult good Compare Stephen on the distinction between *bonum simpliciter* and *bonum arduum* in *SH* 185.

p. 343: In this play ... its necessary tendency Dominic Manganiello, 'The Italian Sources for *Exiles*: Giacosa, Praga, Oriani and Joyce' in *Myth and Reality in Irish Literature*, ed. Joseph Ronsley (Waterloo, Ontario, 1977) 235–6, suggests these sentences derive from a novel by Oriani, *Gelosia: Vortice* (1894), a copy of which Joyce possessed. The novel treats of a lover's jealousy of his mistress's husband, and it would appear that Mario, the lover, is yet another model for the jealousy of Richard, the husband.

p. 344: the fable of the Prodigal Son Luke 15:11–32.

p. 344: Jesus in the garden of olives Gethsemene on the Mount of Olives, where Christ suffered 'the agony in the garden' before he was arrested, tried and crucified (Luke 22:39–46; Mark 14:32–42; Matthew 26:38–46).

p. 344: the soul of woman left naked Aubert 1773 remarks this is the title of a story, 'Animo a nude', by Marco Praga, to whom Joyce refers on the next page.

p. 344: amid the clouds of mortality Joyce's language is curiously close to Hermetic sources, such as were current in circles surrounding George Russell (AE), on which he poured scorn at the time he left Dublin.

p. 344: publication of the lost pages of *Madame Bovary* The deletions Flaubert was forced to make when his novel was published in serial form in 1856, which were restored when it was published entire in 1857, are indicated in the Louis Conard edition of 1910. They were not as extensive as Joyce suggests, however; nor do they much alter the perception of Charles Bovary as a cuckold. Joyce's interest, as his subsequent citation of Praga and Giacosa makes clear, is on the shift of interest effected by Flaubert from lover to husband, from action to re-action.

p. 345: Praga in *La Crisi* Marco Praga (1862–1929), the main theme of whose naturalist plays was adultery. In his masterpiece, *La Crisi* (1901), the husband willingly tolerates his wife's affair for fear of losing her altogether. Michael Mason shows that Joyce singled out this play and Giacosa's (below) because of their protagonists' unusual toleration of their wives' adultery ('Why is Leopold Bloom a Cuckold?', *English Literary History* XLIV, 1977, 171–88).

p. 345: Giacosa in *Tristi Amori* The later plays of Guiseppe Giacosa (1847–1906) are naturalistic. *Tristi Amori* (1888) focuses on a wife who decides to resist an extramarital affair for the sake of her child and on a husband who, though unforgiving, also decides the family must be preserved.

An adaptation, under the title *The Wife of Scarli*, was performed in Dublin at the Gaiety Theatre, 22 October 1897. Molly refers to the adaptation in *Penelope* (*U* 633).

p. 345: Grafton Street ... Leopardstown races ... the jesuit church A fashionable shopping street in central Dublin; horse-races in a well-heeled southside suburb; and perhaps the Jesuit church on Gardiner Street, where the retreats of *Grace* and the *Portrait* take place (*D* 163–74, *P* 107ff).

pp. 345–6 The dialogue was worked out as Joyce wrote it down. I have not recorded deletions, and I have supplied some italics and some punctuation. It ends at the bottom of a page (*Archive* XI 15) and I have supplied a rule.

p. 346: N. (B) – 12 Nov. 1913 Nora (Bertha) or Nota (Bene). The chain of associations and semantic transfers that follows takes off from the 'garter' incident referred to in the First Act (p. 123).

p. 346: Prezioso Roberto Prezioso, an Italian journalist and friend of the Joyces in Trieste. When he attempted to seduce Nora, Joyce remonstrated with and publicly humiliated him (*JJ* 316–17). His stylish dressing influenced the presentation of Buck Mulligan and Blazes Boylan as well as Robert Hand. Compare above with the Third Act, p. 231.

p. 346: Bodkin ... bracelet, cream sweets ... convent garden Michael 'Sonny' Bodkin was a young man who gave Nora a bracelet and courted her in Galway. He contracted tuberculosis and died on 11 February 1900, at the age of twenty. The cream sweets are associated with Willie Mulvey, who courted Nora after Bodkin died. See *JJ* 158–9.

Nora was first attracted to Joyce, she said, because he reminded her of Bodkin (*JJ* 243). The same materials are reworked in *The Dead* and, differently, in *Penelope*.

p. 346: Moon – Shelley's grave in Rome A tablet commemorating Shelley was the first thing that struck Joyce when he arrived in Rome in 1906 (*LL* II 144). It is not known if he visited Shelley's tomb, but compare Shelley's 'To the Moon' (1824), quoted in *P* 96.

This reworking of Joyce's previous note, in the form of continuous hallucination, assimilates Shelley to Bodkin to Richard the 'automystic'.

p. 346: Graveyard at Rahoon Michael Bodkin was actually buried at Rahoon on the edge of Galway City, though in *The Dead* Joyce imagines Michael Furey buried seventeen miles away, at Bodkin's home-village, Oughterard. Compare *Pomes Penyeach* and *JJ* 324–5; also below on Kearns (Keany).

p. 346: Kearns died Untraced. Brenda Maddox identifies Kearns with the real-life Michael Feeny, the first boy Nora loved, who died at the age of sixteen and a half and was buried at Rahoon – like Michael Bodkin, only some years earlier (*Nora: A Biography of Nora Joyce*, London, 1988, 25–8). The name in the manuscript could be construed as Keany, which reinforces her suggestion. Did Joyce conflate Feeny with the more-widespread Galway name, Kenny?

p. 346: the earth, dark, formless, mother Compare Joyce on Molly Bloom as the 'perfectly sane full amoral fertilisable untrustworthy engaging shrewd limited prudent indifferent *Weib. Ich bin das Fleisch das stets bejaht*' (*L* I 170); also *U* 606 on Molly, 'in the attitude of Gea-Tellus, fulfilled, recumbent, big with seed'.

p. 347: Wotan ... Siegfried In Wagner's *Der Ring des Nibelungen*, Wotan, chief of the Gods, is the grandfather of Siegfried. Joyce responded particularly to the moment of Siegfried's death (*L* II 214).

The parallel themes of betrayal, conspiracy and marital exchange in the *Ring* and *Exiles* are explored by John MacNicholas, 'Joyce contra Wagner', *Comparative Drama* IX (1975) 29–43.

p. 347: birth and growth ... destruction Compare Temple's comment in *P* 231: 'Reproduction is the beginning of death'; also the nexus of ideas contained in the phrase 'death of the spirit' in the text of the play on pp. 197 and 258.

p. 347: the nature of innocence Compare Stephen's reflections on Emma in *P* 222–3.

p. 348: 'the snood that is the sign of maidenhood' From *Chamber Music*, Poem XI, above p. 14.

p. 348: Schopenhauer against women Arthur Schopenhauer, 'On Women', *Essays*, trans. Mrs Rudolf Dircks (London, 1897) 64–79, a much underlined copy of which was in Joyce's Trieste library. The description 'long-haired, short-legged' is from the same essay.

p. 349: the rich possibilities of the figure of the Madonna   Joyce believed as much in the mystery of fatherhood as of motherhood, and that the too easy and unsubtle worship of Mary as madonna was characteristic of 'mob' worship (*CW* 35–6, *U* 170).

p. 349: Emily Lyons   A childhood friend of Nora's, whose departure from Galway to America left her wholly disconsolate (Brenda Maddox, *Nora: A Biography of Nora Joyce*, London, 1988, 20). Compare with the 'emigrant ship', etc., in the next paragraph.

p. 349: Her grandmother consoles her   Nora's maternal grandmother, Catherine Mortimer Healy, at whose house she was fostered from the age of two or five, thereby experiencing what Maddox calls her 'first exile and the one which most shaped her personality' (20).

p. 349: her uncle   Michael Healy, Nora's uncle, was relatively well-off and continued to give assistance to the Joyces after they were married.

p. 350: lesbianism . . . The friend   Aubert 1780 compares Molly's relationship with Hester, which is recalled in *Penelope* (*U* 622; compare 643).

p. 350: desire in dark eyes   Aubert 706 compares the effect on Stephen of 'dark womanish eyes' in *P* 178 (also *P* 221), and he notes the significance of Stephen's particular response to Cranley's 'dark eyes' in *SH* 113; *P* 194, 245.

p. 350: *believes* (?)   The question mark in brackets is Joyce's own.

p. 351: cat and mouse   The customary phrase possessed an added, particular meaning at the time Joyce wrote. In 1913 the British Parliament passed a law by which suffragettes were released from custody conditionally on their good behaviour and which was popularly known as the Cat and Mouse Act. The added meaning applies with special force to Bertha's situation throughout the play.

p. 351: sister-in-love Isolde   In Wagner's opera, *Tristan und Isolde* (1865), the wounded Tristan is sent into exile when his love for Isolde is revealed. The story is partly Irish in origin and, mediated by Joseph Bédier's *The Romance of Tristan and Iseult* (1910), it pervades *Finnegans Wake*.

p. 351: Marquis de Sade and Freiherr v. Sacher Masoch   The French and Austrian writers (1740–1814; 1835–95) from whom sadism and masochism take their name. Joyce appears to have been more impressed by Leopold von Sacher-Masoch, several of whose books he owned and to whom he also refers in *U* 193, 380, 461.

p. 351: *emissio seminis inter vas naturale*   Latin, 'emission of semen within the natural organ', a version of the canon law definition of a consummated act of intercourse. The Latin phrase forms the title of a chapter in Richard Brown's *James Joyce and Sexuality* (Cambridge, 1985), in which he suggests that Joyce's discussion in these *Exiles* notes derives from Paul Garnier, *Onanisme seul et à deux sous toutes ses formes et leurs consequences* (Paris, 1885; see Brown 56–7 especially). Versions of the same phrase recur in *U* 183, 605.

p. 352: Hedda Gabler, Rebecca Rosmer, Asta Allmers Ibsen heroines, though Miss West, the heroine of *Rosmersholm*, becomes Rebecca Rosmer only figuratively in death. Asta Allmers is the heroine of *Little Eyolf*. Brown (*James Joyce and Sexuality* 95) suggests the list here was prompted by Joyce's reading of Havelock Ellis, *The New Spirit* (1892), which he owned in Trieste.

p. 353: Paul de Kock Charles-Paul de Kock (1794–1871), a prolific and popular Parisian novelist, is mentioned twice in *Ulysses* (*U* 53, 380). Kock's *Le Cocu* was among Joyce's books in Trieste.

p. 353: *souche gauloise* French for 'Gallic root' – that is, that native, earthy tradition from which polite letters derive.

p. 354: Mrs O'Shea and Parnell Charles Stewart Parnell (1846–1891) conducted a markedly successful campaign on behalf of Irish Home Rule in the British Parliament; but the revelation in 1889 that he had lived for many years with Katherine O'Shea, wife of one of his aides, brought his political career to a dramatic, contentious end.

Joyce's first publication is said to have been a broadside attacking those responsible for Parnell's downfall (*MBK* 65; *P&SW* 71). Compare *D* 118–35, *P* 31–2, etc., for Joyce's early identification with Parnell, as well as multiple references, and allusions in *Ulysses* and *Finnegans Wake*. Compare also *The Holy Office*, lines 87–8, and note (above pp. 105, 334).

p. 354: Her manner of writing is not Irish Katherine O'Shea's biography of Parnell, published in 1914, is written in a rather high-minded style. It was one of two biographies of Parnell in Joyce's Trieste library.

p. 354: Swift Swift's relations with women – his Stella and Vanessa – have always been more important in Irish folklore than other readers might understand. Allusions to the two relationships pervade *Finnegans Wake*; and, during the time the book was being written, the Abbey staged plays by Arthur Power and by Yeats on the theme, Denis Johnston and Sybil Le Brocquy began researches that were later published as books, Beckett incorporated some of the folklore into his short story, 'Fingal', and so on.

p. 354: the adulterous wife of the King of Leinster Devorghil, wife of Tiernan O'Rourke, Prince of Breffni, deserted her husband for Dermot MacMurrough, King of Leinster, in 1152. Some fifteen years later,

MacMurrough was defeated by the joint forces of O'Rourke and Roderick O'Connor, High King of Ireland. He sought the assistance of Henry II and thereby occasioned the Anglo-Norman invasion of Ireland in 1169.

Mr Deasy's reference to the same episode in *Nestor* (*U* 29) suggests the present note might be intended to be read dramatically – that is, be intended to display muddled or facile recollection. The same characters reappear in *FW*.

p. 354 Two words that are difficult to decipher – 'moorsta = midista'? – have been added after the last rule on some other occasion. Whatever they mean, they appear to have nothing to do with *Exiles*.

(B) FRAGMENTS OF DIALOGUE, NOW AT CORNELL

I

Richard

But in such a way – like thieves – at night – in such a place. It is not for people like us. It is not for me nor for her: it is not even for you.

Robert

Yes, you are right. You are so young and yet you seem to be her father and mine. I have acted like a common man.

Richard

When I met her first she was eighteen and since that time I have watched. I have felt her soul unfolding. Sometimes I turn to look at her in our room. I mean when I am writing. She is lying on the bed reading some book I have given her – Wagner's Letters or a novel of Jacobsen. She is struggling with sleep. You say I am like her father. Do you know what I feel then when I look at her?

Robert

What?

Richard

I feel as if I had carried her within my own body, in my womb.

Robert

Can a man feel like that.

Richard

Her books, her music, the fire of thought stolen from on high out of whose flames all ease and culture have come, the grace with which she tends the body we desire – whose work is that? I feel that it is mine. It is my work and the work of others like me now or in other times. It is we who have conceived her and brought her forth. Our minds flowing together are the womb in which we have bourne her.

II

Richard

You spoke of our boyhood. Since our boyhood together our ways have been different.

Robert

(*sighs*) Ah, yes.

Richard

You have taken the smooth path, accepting ironically everything in which you disbelieved and building for your body and for that function of it which I suppose you call your soul a peace of prudence, irony and pleasure.

Robert

Are those things bad?

Richard

I have not chosen them.

Robert

I know that. As it was in my character to choose them it was in yours to reject them.

Richard

I have lived without prudence, risking everything, destroying everything in order to create again.

Robert

You will. I feel that you will.

Richard

I have done something already. I have destroyed and recreated in my own image a woman.

Robert

Bertha?

Richard

I carried her away with me into exile and now, after years, I carry her back again remade in my own image. And this I did for you.

Robert

For me?

Richard

Yes, for you who risked nothing and lived prudently.

Robert

(*smiling weakly*) It is a queer kind of present, Richard, like the giver. You see of course that I have no intention of accepting it. No, you have made her new and strange. She is yours. Keep her.

Richard

Because you are generous enough to allow me?

III

Robert

Then it was not jealous you felt.

Richard

I felt what I tell you – longing.

Robert

No hatred of me? But how?

Richard

And for all I know jealousy, as you call it, may be this longing.

IV

Bertha

No, thank you, Brigid. Just a cup of tea will do.

Brigid

Or a bit of toast?

Bertha

No, thanks.

Brigid

Maybe it was them greengages yesterday upset your stomach, ma'am. They upsets some people that way.

Bertha

I suppose so.

[*Brigid goes out*]

V

Bertha

I wish I had never met you.

Richard

You would like to be freer now than you are.

Bertha

Yes.

Richard

(*pained*) So that you could go to that house at night more freely to meet your lover.

Bertha

(*putting her arms about his neck*) Yes, dear. I wish I had never met you. I wish you were my lover waiting for me there.

Richard

Or he?

Bertha

(*shaking her head*) You, dear. I want to love you over again. I want to forget you. (*kissing him*) Love me, Dick. Forget me and love me.

Richard

Have you forgotten me for him?

Bertha

No. I remember you. You have a different way of giving yourself to a woman – a more beautiful way than he has. (*she smooths back his hair*) Dick, never embrace her the way men do.

Richard

Her? Who?

Bertha

Beatrice. Never do. Let her remember you always as I can see you now.

Richard

And if she does will you not envy her?

Bertha

No. I want her to remember you always and to think of you. But not like others. Because she is a fine kind of person too.

VI

Robert

Jealousy. Not that of common men of course. (*with a smile*) That of Richard Rowan.

Richard

I effaced myself. I gave you both your freedom. I tried to feel for you and for her, to consider you both. I had only to forbid her: and I did not. I had only to say a tender word to her of – of our own past life: and I did not. I left you both free.

Robert

For our sakes?

Richard

For my own sake, do you think?

Robert

Would you have left us free then – nine years ago?

Richard

You met her often then with me and without me.

Robert

Would you have allowed us the same freedom then? Answer me that.

Richard

If she had desired you then I should have left her to you. She did not.

Robert

(*quietly*) No, she did not. If she had you would not have left her to me. At least that is not exactly the way to put it.

Richard

(*simply*) No?

364

Robert

She would not have been yours to leave but mine – then. Am I right?

Richard

(*turns towards him*) Yes.

Robert

(*waves his hand*) That is past. But I ask you, knowing that she was yours then, would you *then* have given us the freedom you gave now – for our sakes?

Richard

Then no.

Robert

(*bends across the table*) Then no. Because then only one woman was in your heart. That is why.

Richard

You think that now . . . ?

Robert

Yes, I do think it.

Richard

Has Bertha told you?

Robert

I saw it without being told. I know you and I know (*he points with his thumb over his shoulder*) my interesting if somewhat melancholy cousin.

[*He leans back in his chair, smiling. Richard rises slowly and walks to and fro, his hands at his back*]

VII

Robert

(*after a long silence*) Appearances are against me.

Richard

You mean I judge by them?

Robert

I mean you cannot enter into my mind. It is I who have won freedom for myself.

Richard

Speak out your mind. What freedom?

Robert

I will. Of us two it is I who am free. I have never really believed, not even as a boy. I have never wept, as you did, for my sins. I do not know what sin is. I have never believed in truth of man or woman. I have never been true myself. To what or to whom since all is chance and change? I have freed myself within and without. I care nothing for human or legal bonds or laws or moral prejudices. I do not even care to make my life fit my ideas. I live by what I disbelieve in. I do not even feel the excitement of revolt against it. And that is my greatest freedom. It is you, Richard, with all your talent who are still the slave.

Richard

(*shaken but calm*) How well I know the tempter's voice!

Robert

(*nearer*) The voice of reality. She was not free even last night. The shadow of her fear of you was over her. You have not healed your soul. You have wounded it – a deep wound of doubt which neither her words nor mine can heal completely.

Richard

Is it not at least as noble to fight on in doubt as in faith?

Robert

It may be nobler. I still admire the noble friend in you and love him all the more since I see that he also is the victim of a delusion.

Richard

Delusion? Because I believe in myself – and in her?

Robert

Because, Richard, I see that your type is not, as you wish to believe, the type of the humanity which will come after us.

Richard

But you are that type – is that your delusion?

Robert

I am not – wholly.

Richard

Who then?

Robert

Perhaps – your son. Your creedless lawless fearless son.

Richard

(*slowly*) Archie! . . . And you?

Robert

I am his godfather.

[*He takes his hat from the table*]

Richard

(*repeats*) Perhaps.

Robert

I said *perhaps* because he is yours. I could say *almost surely* if . . . .

Richard

If . . . ?

Robert

(*with a smile*) If he were mine.

VIII

Bertha

(*putting her arm about his waist*) I have been true to you, Dick, have I not?

Richard

(*smiling*) You know that best yourself.

Bertha

(*averting her eyes*) I have been. Very true. I gave you myself. You took me and you left me.

Richard

Left you!

Bertha

You left me: and I waited for you to come back to me.

Richard

(*disturbed*) Yes, I know what you mean.

Bertha

O, Dick, those long evenings in Rome, what I went through! Do you remember the terrace on the top of the house where we lived?

Richard

Yes.

Bertha

I used to sit there, waiting, with the poor child playing with his toys, waiting until he got sleepy. I could see all over the city, the sun setting and right under me the river, the *Tevere*. What is it called in English? I forget.

Richard

The Tiber.

Bertha

Yes. It was lovely, Dick, only for I was so sad. I was alone, forgotten by you and by all. You had grown tired of me because I was too simple and uneducated for a person like you. I thought my life was over and yours too.

Richard

It had not begun.

Bertha

And I used to look at the sky, so beautiful, without a cloud and at the city you said was so old. It was all something high and beautiful. But it made me cry.

Richard

Why, dear?

Bertha

Because I was so uneducated. I knew nothing about all those things. And still I was moved by them.

IX

Richard

I suffered too.

Bertha

But not like I did, Dick.

Richard

Yes. I know what you felt. That I was giving to another the finer part of myself and only what was gross to you.

Bertha

I could not bear that. I tried to understand everything in your strange character. But that no.

368

Richard

I saw it in your eyes, a vague fear, the fear of life. I heard it in your voice, your wonder. You were asking yourself what was this thing in life, in love itself; and you were praying almost in your heart that it might not come, even that life or love might die before it came.

Bertha

(*pointing to her breast*) In there, dear. In my heart I felt something breaking. That you saw in my eyes.

Richard

(*seizing her hands, kisses her passionately*) O, how I loved you then! My little bride! My little bride in exile!

Bertha

Am I useful to you in your life, dear, in something?

Richard

(*laughing, shakes his head*) No, quite useless!

Bertha

Ah, tell me! I want to know.

X

Bertha

When you said goodnight to me I knew by your voice you wanted to be alone. I felt so sad then, Richard. Your lips when you kissed me were so soft and cold. I could not speak to you as if the world were between us. And when I was in bed, alone in the room, in the silence and saw the little lamp burning on the washstand I thought of my girlhood.

Richard

(*tenderly*) Tell me more, dearest.

Bertha

I thought I was in the room I used to sleep in when I was a girl, that I had never been in a man's arms, that I was still innocent and young. I was innocent when I met you first, Richard, was I not?

Richard

(*touching her sleeve with his lips*) Always, always.

Bertha

I thought I was in that room and I could see it, the little oil-lamp burning quietly near my bed and on the wall I could see the picture of Robert Emmet that used to be on the wall. You know? In a green uniform, with his hat off, with dark eyes. Then . . . . . .

Richard

Then?

Bertha

Then I thought of Robert. I felt you were gone away and would never come back to me. I felt you were not thinking of me but of her and perhaps he was. I felt lonely for someone.

Richard

How did you think of him?

Bertha

His name, his eyes and how his voice is when he says my name. I was glad to think that he sleeps alone: and I said his name to myself softly thinking perhaps he might hear me someway.

Richard

(*walks to and fro a little in silence, then standing near her*) Bertha!

Bertha

What?

Richard

Did you feel then that you were beginning to love him? Tell me the truth.

Bertha

(*simply*) No. I loved you.

Richard

Even then?

Bertha

I felt I had lost you. I could not understand why. It was useless to think what it meant. You were lost for me.

XI

Richard

What you wished has taken place – and what I wished. In this case when events were in our power we cannot blame them.

370

ANNOTATION OF (B) FRAGMENTS OF DIALOGUE, NOW AT CORNELL

p. 360: she was eighteen Nora Barnacle was born on 21 or 22 March 1884. Compare 'her age: 28', (A) Entries in a Notebook, Now at Buffalo, p. 343 above.

p. 360: Wagner's Letters or a novel of Jacobsen The only explicit trace of the Wagnerian references in the Buffalo notebook among these fragments.

Joyce placed the Danish novelist, Jens Peter Jacobsen, in the line between Flaubert and D'Annunzio in *The Day of the Rabblement* (CW 71) and was reading him in the months following his first departure from Dublin (*L* II 83). He resumed Danish lessons in Rome in 1906–7 (*JJ* 235, 240). However, his copy of Wagner's letters to Minna Wagner – *Letters to His First Wife*, in the English translation (Michael Patrick Gillespie, *James Joyce's Trieste Library*, Austin, Texas, 1986, No. 533) – was not published till 1909.

To the extent that Gretta is modelled on Nora, therefore, the choice of titles muddles biographical with thematic reasons. Nora is known to have made an effort to keep up with Joyce's intellectual interests at the time – reading *Hedda Gabler* with interest twice before forgetting it, as well as Seumas O'Kelly's stories, Joyce reported (*L* II 196).

p. 361: the smooth path Compare the smooth, or gentle, or primrose, paths of numerous proverbs and quotations.

p. 363: kissing him; she smooths back his hair The manuscript does not have punctuation at the end of either of the previous sentences, leaving unclear whether the actions described are meant to accompany the preceding or the following words. I follow MacNicholas 171, 182 here. I have accepted other of MacNicholas's emendations (supplying full stops at the end of sentences, etc.), but not all of them.

p. 366: the type of humanity which will come after us Robert is indulging in Nietzsche-talk, which was something of a fashion in Dublin literary circles at the turn of the century (Yeats called him 'that strong enchanter'). It is probably significant that Gogarty–Mulligan thought of the Sandycove Tower as a temple of Nietzschean neo-paganism, and Joyce himself was not unaffected. See *JJ* 142, 162, 172; and compare *U* 19, 42 on Kinch the Superman.

The association of Robert with Nietzsche illuminates a phrase in the Buffalo notebook (p. 346 above): 'Archie, Richard's son, is brought up on Robert's principles.' That is, it explains why attention is drawn to

Archie's 'wildness', which is otherwise puzzling. Joyce acquired several titles by Nietzsche in Trieste, at the time *Exiles* was on the verge of and was being written (Gillespie Nos. 350–52).

p. 367: godfather   The full stop is again editorially supplied, and Joyce may have intended to indicate that the words accompanied, not preceded, the action.

p. 367: those long evenings in Rome   The Joyces' depressing sojourn in Rome was a time when they found themselves in the position of emigrants rather than exiles. Compare Carla de Petris in *Joyce in Rome: The Genesis of 'Ulysses'*, ed. Giorgio Melchiori (Rome, 1984) 73–96; and also *JJ* Ch. XIV. Bertha goes on to describe the view from the window of the fourth-floor apartment on Via Monte Brianzo.

p. 370: the picture of Robert Emmet   Emmet (1778–1803), one of the last of the United Irishmen, had been executed for his part in a failed uprising. His centenary in 1903 was widely celebrated in nationalist circles.

To Joyce's mind, Emmet's uprising was 'foolish' and the Emmet cult of sacrificial idealism was sentimental. Compare *CW* 189 and the *Cyclops* episode of *Ulysses*, where Emmet's speech from the dock and his execution are parodied, among others (*U* 247–8, 251–5). Bloom examines such a picture as Bertha describes, and comments on it, at the close of *Sirens* (*U* 238–9).

ANNOTATION OF THE TEXT OF *EXILES*

Characters

Rowan   Ruth Bauerle, 'Two Unnoticed Musical Allusions', *JJQ* IX (Fall 1971) 140–2, and 'Some *Mots* on a Quickbeam in Joyce's Eye', *JJQ* X (Spring 1973) 346–8, discusses the origins of the name in Lady Nairne's song, 'O, Rowan Tree' and in Irish history and folklore. Aubert 1785 notes that the rowan tree is associated with the month of February in Irish folklore, which for Joyce had special, personal associations.

Archie   See below on p. 375, on Archibald Hamilton Rowan.

Robert Hand   While the first name is associated with Robert Prezioso (see note on Entries in a Notebook, now at Buffalo, p. 356 above), Sheldon R. Brivic connects the surname with the Hand of Blake's *Jerusalem* in 'Structure and Meaning in Joyce's *Exiles*', *JJQ* VI (Fall 1968) 94–122. Might the name also – against the background of

Carson's unionism and Joyce's nationalism – pick up associations of the denying Red Hand of Ulster?

Beatrice The Dantean associations of the name are discussed in relation to the play as a whole, with its theme of reversed exile, by Mary T. Reynolds, *Joyce and Dante: The Shaping Imagination* (Princeton, NJ, 1981) 166–74 (and compare 266–9).

First Act

p. 115: Merrion, a suburb of Dublin Merrion is a somewhat indeterminate area south and inland from Sandymount that was undergoing suburban development.

Other references suggest Joyce had a Blackrock address in mind (see notes on pp. 373–4, 374). Blackrock, however, was an existing village with its own character, whereas Merrion better suggests the bourgeois values that impinge on Richard.

p. 115: at the bath The swimming bath at nearby Blackrock? Compare p. 133.

p. 116: Youghal A pretty seaside town south of Cork, possessed of Protestant or Planter associations since the time of Elizabeth Tudor.

p. 120: Why ... I could not see you Richard's question and Beatrice's answer are repeated from *Giacomo Joyce* (*P&SW* 241). The 'book of sketches' Richard refers to earlier in the dialogue (p. 119) undoubtedly recalled, for Joyce, the same record of his feelings for Amalia Popper.

Compare below p. 244 and note.

p. 127: While she lived Aubert 1786 compares Stephen to Cranly: 'Whatever else is unsure in this stinking dunghill of a world a mother's love is not' (*P* 241–2).

p. 128: our godless nameless child Joyce had to endure the gossip of his Dublin acquaintances when his son, Giorgio, was born in 1905 because he refused to have him baptized or to marry his mother (both took place eventually). See *JJ* 204.

p. 128: Carmen The opera by Georges Bizet (1875). The anecdote derives from one told of Joyce's own grandfather, as he lay dying in 1866 (*MBK* 45).

p. 130: My dearest coz From *Macbeth* IV ii 14, a context resonant with false welcomes and betrayals.

p. 132: the avenue Either Mount Merrion Avenue or Carysfort Avenue, where Joyce lived between 1892 and 1893. Both connect with the

Blackrock baths; compare 'the avenue' of *P* 63. Compare also p. 132, from which it appears the Rowans' house is situated on or near the avenue.

p. 139: I think of you always – Aubert 1786 compares Gabriel in *The Dead*: 'He asked himself what is a woman standing on the stairs in the shadow, listening to distant music, a symbol of' (*D* 210).

p. 140: A wild flower blowing in a hedge Joyce used the same expression several times to Nora in letters written during his absence in 1909 (*L* II 269, 273, 281).

p. 142: Kingstown pier Where the Holyhead ferry berths (since renamed Dun Laoghaire).

p. 149: Lansdowne road Midway between Merrion and central Dublin, where Bertha would have to change from the Dalkey to the Kenilworth tram line. Compare p. 171 and the map in MacNicholas ii.

p. 150: the paper Most likely *The Daily Express*, for which Gabriel Conroy in *The Dead* and Joyce himself wrote reviews. The paper was unionist in a more Dublin-professional, less Ascendancy-oriented way than *The Irish Times*. Bloom is associated with the third Dublin morning paper, the *Freeman's Journal*.

p. 150: a difficult moment In April 1912, just months before the supposed action of the play, John Redmond succeeded in tabling a Home Rule Bill before the House of Commons. Compare Robert's description in the newspaper of how certain of Ireland's children 'have been called back to her now on the eve of her longawaited victory' (p. 245).

Though Redmond claimed to be Parnell's heir, Joyce thought of him as a time-server ('fatuous', *CW* 209). Robert's support manifests his inclination to compromise.

p. 150: the vicechancellor In Irish terms, signifying the National University, of which University College Dublin forms a part. Compare pp. 157, 159, 253. Dublin University – Trinity College – has always had a provost and vice-provost.

p. 151: chair As Joyce emphasized to Stanislaus, it was in real life a lecturership, not a chair, and only in 'commercial Italian' (*L* II 234, 238).

p. 155: *Prosit!* German equivalent of 'Your health!'

p. 156: the strand Merrion Strand, which connects with Sandymount Strand, on which Stephen and Bloom appear in separate episodes of *Ulysses*.

p. 157: All statues are of two kinds MacNicholas xvii–xix provides photographs of well-known Dublin statues, both of the folded-arms and the arm-extended varieties. Eugene Sheehy, *May It Please the Court* (Dublin, 1951) 24 reports other, early epigrams by Joyce on Dublin statues.

p. 158: I am a descendant of the dark foreigners Robert implies that his credentials as a native Irishman are impeccable. In fact, *dubhgaill* (dark foreigners or pagans) was the name given to the Viking invaders, and there is little reason for him to distinguish them from the group of *fionnghaill* (fair or pale foreigners) other than to communicate a knowing sense of belonging.

p. 158: that fierce indignation which lacerated the heart of Swift Phrases that translate Swift's epitaph in St Patrick's Cathedral – 'ubi saeva indignatio ulterius cor lacerare nequit' – and almost commonplace in Dublin talk. Robert repeats them in his newspaper article (p. 245).

p. 160: Archibald Hamilton Rowan 1751–1834; see the *Dictionary of National Biography*. Reneging on a privileged upbringing in England, Rowan joined Napper Tandy, Wolfe Tone and others to found the United Irishmen. He was convicted for sedition in 1794, escaped via Clongowes to France and then to America. He subsequently came to approve the Act of Union, win a pardon and return to Ireland.

The youthful Stephen recalls him at Clongowes (*P* 10). In Irish history, from one point of view, he appears as a well-heeled turncoat.

p. 161: At Philippi Where the spectre that appears to Brutus tells him they will meet again and where Brutus meets his doom (Plutarch, *Lives: Caesar* LXIX vii; Shakespeare, *Julius Caesar* IV iii 282, 285).

p. 164: robbers here like in Rome Joyce had been robbed of his last salary the day before he left Rome in February 1907 (*JJ* 241–2).

p. 170: cottage With implications of a poorer as well as smaller house: compare 'the rough tribes from the cottages' in *Araby* (*P* 30). Robert kept on the cottage for himself after Richard's departure, just as Mulligan/Gogarty stayed on at the Sandycove Tower, thereby exacerbating Stephen's/Joyce's sense of dispossession.

p. 173: The work of a devil Robert M. Adams, 'Light on Joyce's *Exiles*? A New MS, A Curious Analogue, and Some Speculations', *Studies in Bibliography* XVII (1964) 83–105 (98–102 especially) glosses the connections between the writer, the devil and the theme of exile.

Second Act

p. 182: *Ranelagh* A suburb of Dublin that is closer to the centre and older than Merrion.

p. 182: *the first bars of Wolfram's song in the last act of* Tannhäuser 'O du mein holder Abendstern': Wolfram sings this greeting to the Evening Star and to Elizabeth, in the role of God-fearing rival to Tannhäuser, who is the slave of lust. As Zack Bowen comments, 'Robert, about to consummate a liaison with Bertha, should be singing Tannhäuser's songs instead of the chaste and good Wolfram's. The aria is part of the false picture he presents of himself and his own motivations' (*Musical Allusions in the Works of James Joyce*, Albany, NY, 1975, 10). Compare also Joseph Kestner, 'Joyce, Wagner, Bizet: *Exiles, Tannhäuser* and *Carmen*', *Modern British Literature* V (Spring and Fall 1980) 53–62.

p. 192: Neither an angel nor an Anglo-Saxon Alluding to Bede's story of Gregory the Great meeting the Saxons at Rome. Gregory, struck by their fair complexions, described them as not Angles but angels (*Historia Ecclesiastica* II i).

p. 192: Affection . . . must come to that As Mr Duffy also believes, in *A Painful Case* (D 112).

p. 197: a man of great talent – of something more than talent Joyce's college contemporary, Thomas Kettle, praised *Chamber Music* in a tone that was similarly ambiguous (*CH* I 37). *JJ* 63, 261 describes further connections between Kettle and Hand; compare the limerick in *P&SW* 110.

p. 197: what some old theologian, Duns Scotus, I think, called death of the spirit The phrase is not in Scotus (*c.* 1264–1308), and it is not characteristic of his writing. Alessandro Francini recalled Joyce discussing the ideas of the 'Irishman' Scotus in Trieste (Potts 37), and the misattribution here, to the first great theologian to defend the Immaculate Conception, must be ironic.

Arthur Power recalls Joyce attributing the phrase 'the death of the soul' to Aquinas, to define the act of copulation (*Conversations with James Joyce*, 1974, 108). This squares with Robert's confident appropriation of it in the Third Act (p. 258) to refer to a little death of a carnal sort. It seems unlikely that Joyce was codding Power and very likely that Power misremembered or misheard the name Augustine. Augustine used the colourful phrase *mors animae* many times; for instance, in *De Trinitate* IV 3, *De Verbis Domini* VI 1.

p. 203: cabman On the tram, that is.

p. 214: Love's labour lost Alluding to the title of Shakespeare's play; compare p. 216.

p. 225: the quays . . . the black river North Wall, on the Liffey quays, from where passengers departed for the Continent. Compare p. 142 on the Kingstown ferry operating within these islands.

Third Act

p. 231: Sure he thinks the sun shines out of your face Something Roberto Prezioso said to Nora when he tried to seduce her, 'Il sole s'è levato per Lei' (*JJ* 316). Compare (A) Entries in a Notebook, Now at Buffalo, p. 346 above.

p. 244: The isle is full of noises Caliban in Shakespeare's *The Tempest* III ii 133.

p. 244: *Otherwise I could not see you* Quoted from the First Act (p. 120) and deriving ultimately from *Giacomo Joyce* (*P&SW* 241).

p. 254: my cousin Jack Justice, *alias* Doggy Justice, in Surrey Because of Dogberry, the master constable, in Shakespeare's *Much Ado About Nothing*? (In the manuscript, *Archive* XI 246, Joyce first gave the English county as Sussex.)

p. 257: that one about the statues also See above, p. 157 and note.

p. 258: Donnybrook An inner suburb of Dublin adjacent to Ranelagh, en route to Merrion.

p. 258: what the Subtle Duns Scotus calls a death of the spirit Robert borrows the phrase from Richard: see p. 197.

p. 258: melissa water A herbal infusion possessed of a supposedly exhilarating effect.

p. 260: Before dawn Aubert 1798 remarks that Joyce translated Gerhard Hauptmann's *Vor Sonnenaufgang* in his youth.

p. 262: *babbo!* Italian 'daddy' (by which Joyce was known to his own son, Giorgio).

p. 262: Booterstown A suburb north of Blackrock, along the coast. In *P* 53 Stephen Dedalus and a friend ride with the milkman in the other direction, to Stradbrook and Carrickmines.

COPYRIGHT ACKNOWLEDGEMENTS

The publishers would like to thank the following institutions for permission to reproduce copyright material in their possession: Cornell University (Department of Rare Books); Southern Illinois University at Carbondale (Richard Wallace Collection of James Joyce, Special Collections, Morris Library); University of Buffalo; Yale University Library (The Beinecke Rare Book and Manuscript Library).

Thanks are also due to Máire Colum O'Sullivan for permission to quote from the 'Epigram on the Ladyfriends of St James' from *Life and the Dream* by Mary Colum; and to Peter Smith Publisher, Inc. for the 'Satire on George O'Donnell (in the style of Goldsmith)' and 'Fragment on Miss Moschos' from *Our Friend James Joyce* by Mary and Padraic Colum.

INDEX OF TITLES*

* Joyce's own titles are printed in italic, with his own collection titles in italic caps;
editorial titles are in roman.

INDEX OF FIRST LINES

FOR THE BEST IN PAPERBACKS, LOOK FOR THE

In every corner of the world, on every subject under the sun, Penguin represents quality and variety – the very best in publishing today.

For complete information about books available from Penguin – including Puffins, Penguin Classics and Arkana – and how to order them, write to us at the appropriate address below. Please note that for copyright reasons the selection of books varies from country to country.

In the United Kingdom: Please write to *Dept E.P., Penguin Books Ltd, Harmondsworth, Middlesex, UB7 0DA.*

If you have any difficulty in obtaining a title, please send your order with the correct money, plus ten per cent for postage and packaging, to *PO Box No 11, West Drayton, Middlesex*

In the United States: Please write to *Dept BA, Penguin, 299 Murray Hill Parkway, East Rutherford, New Jersey 07073*

In Canada: Please write to *Penguin Books Canada Ltd, 2801 John Street, Markham, Ontario L3R 1B4*

In Australia: Please write to the *Marketing Department, Penguin Books Australia Ltd, P.O. Box 257, Ringwood, Victoria 3134*

In New Zealand: Please write to the *Marketing Department, Penguin Books (NZ) Ltd, Private Bag, Takapuna, Auckland 9*

In India: Please write to *Penguin Overseas Ltd, 706 Eros Apartments, 56 Nehru Place, New Delhi, 110019*

In the Netherlands: Please write to *Penguin Books Netherlands B.V.. Postbus 3507, 1001 AH, Amsterdam*

In West Germany: Please write to *Penguin Books Ltd, Friedrichstrasse 10–12, D–6000 Frankfurt/Main 1*

In Spain: Please write to *Alhambra Longman S.A., Fernandez de la Hoz 9, E–28010 Madrid*

In Italy: Please write to *Penguin Italia s.r.l., Via Como 4, I-20096 Pioltello (Milano)*

In France: Please write to *Penguin Books Ltd, 39 Rue de Montmorency, F-75003 Paris*

In Japan: Please write to *Longman Penguin Japan Co Ltd, Yamaguchi Building, 2–12–9 Kanda Jimbocho, Chiyoda-Ku, Tokyo 101*

BY THE SAME AUTHOR

A Portrait of the Artist as a Young Man
Edited with an Introduction and Notes by Seamus Deane

A Portrait of the Artist as a Young Man (1916) portrays Stephen's Dublin childhood and youth and in doing so, provides an oblique self-portrait of the young James Joyce. At its centre are questions of origin and source, authority and authorship and the relationship of an artist to his family, culture and race. Exuberantly inventive in its style, the novel subtly and beautifully orchestrates the patterns of quotation and repetition instrumental in its hero's quest to create his own character, his own language, life and art.

'He is a postmodernist besides Yeats's modernism,' writes Seamus Deane, 'It is the imagined future, not the re-imagined future, not the re-imagined past of Ireland that Stephen seeks.'

Dubliners
With an Introduction and Notes by Terence Brown

In *Dubliners*, completed when Joyce was only twenty-five, he produced a definitive group portrait. Extensive notes to this new edition fill in the rich network of local and historical references. And yet, beyond its brilliant and almost brutal realism, it is also a book full of enigmas, ambiguities and symbolic resonances. *Dubliners* remains an undisputed masterpiece, a work that, in Terence Brown's words, 'compels attention by the power of its unique vision of the world, its controlling sense of the truths of human experience as its author discerned them in a defeated, colonial city'.

Ulysses

With an Introduction by Declan Kiberd

'It is the book to which we are all indebted and from which none of us can escape' – *T. S. Eliot*

Ulysses is unquestionably one of the supreme masterpieces, in any artistic form, of the twentieth century. A modernist classic, its ceaseless verbal inventiveness and astonishingly wide-ranging allusions confirm its standing as an imperishable monument to the human condition. As Declan Kiberd writes in his stimulating and provocative introduction, '*Ulysses* is an endlessly open book of utopian epiphanies. It holds a mirror up to the colonial capital that was Dublin on 16 June 1904, but it also offers redemptive glimpses of a future world which might be made over in terms of those utopian moments.'

Published to coincide with the fiftieth anniversary of Joyce's death, this edition returns to the standard Random House/Bodley Head text that first appeared in 1960.

'His standing is now second to none among writers of our own century ... He was witty, difficult, subtle and perhaps the greatest genius among the many who have come from Ireland to bewilder the world with the magic of art' – *Irish Independent*

CLASSICS OF THE TWENTIETH CENTURY

The Outsider Albert Camus

Meursault leads an apparently unremarkable bachelor life in Algiers, until his involvement in a violent incident calls into question the fundamental values of society. 'The protagonist of *The Outsider* is undoubtedly the best achieved of all the central figures of the existential novel' – *Listener*

Another Country James Baldwin

'Let our novelists read Mr Baldwin and tremble. There is a whirlwind loose in the land' – *Sunday Times*. *Another Country* draws us deep into New York's Bohemian underworld of writers and artists as they betray, love and test each other – men and women, men and men, black and white – to the limit

I'm Dying Laughing Christina Stead

A dazzling novel set in the 1930s and 1940s when fashionable Hollywood Marxism was under threat from the savage repression of McCarthyism. 'The Cassandra of the modern novel in English' – Angela Carter

Christ Stopped at Eboli Carlo Levi

Exiled to a barren corner of southern Italy for his opposition to Mussolini, Carlo Levi entered a world cut off from history, hedged in by custom and sorrow, without comfort or solace, where, eternally patient, the peasants lived in an age-old stillness, and in the presence of death – for Christ did stop at Eboli.

The Expelled and Other Novellas Samuel Beckett

Rich in verbal and situational humour, these four stories offer the reader a fascinating insight into Beckett's preoccupation with the helpless individual consciousness.

Chance Acquaintances and Julie de Carneilhan Colette

Two contrasting works in one volume. Colette's last full-length novel, *Julie de Carneilhan* was 'as close a reckoning with the elements of her second marriage as she ever allowed herself'. In *Chance Acquaintances*, Colette visits a health resort, accompanied only by her cat.

Petersburg   Andrei Bely

'The most important, most influential and most perfectly realized Russian novel written in the twentieth century' (*The New York Times Book Review*), *Petersburg* is an exhilarating search for the identity of the city, presaging Joyce's search for Dublin in *Ulysses*.

The Miracle of the Rose   Jean Genet

Within a squalid prison lies a world of total freedom, in which chains become garlands of flowers – and a condemned prisoner is discovered to have in his heart a rose of monstrous size and beauty. Of this profoundly shocking novel Sartre wrote: 'Genet holds the mirror up to us: we must look at it and see ourselves.'

Labyrinths   Jorge Luis Borges

Seven parables, ten essays and twenty-three stories, including Borges's classic 'Tlön, Uqbar; Orbis Tertius', a new world where external objects are whatever each person wants, and 'Pierre Menard', the man who rewrote *Don Quixote* word for word without ever reading the original.

The Vatican Cellars   André Gide

Admired by the Dadaists, denounced as nihilist, defended by its author as a satirical farce: five interlocking books explore a fantastic conspiracy to kidnap the Pope and place a Freemason on his throne. *The Vatican Cellars* teases and subverts as only the finest satire can.

The Rescue   Joseph Conrad

'The air is thick with romance like a thunderous sky...' 'It matters not how often Mr Conrad tells the story of the man and the brig. Out of the million stories that life offers the novelist, this one is founded upon truth. And it is only Mr Conrad who is able to tell it us' – Virginia Woolf

Southern Mail/Night Flight   Antoine de Saint-Exupéry

Both novels in this volume are concerned with the pilot's solitary struggle with the elements, his sensation of insignificance amid the stars' timelessness and the sky's immensity. Flying and writing were inextricably linked in the author's life and he brought a unique sense of dedication to both.

CLASSICS OF THE TWENTIETH CENTURY

Victory Joseph Conrad

Victory is both a tale of rescue and adventure and a perceptive study of a complex relationship and the power of love. Its hero Axel Heyst was described by Jocelyn Baines as 'perhaps the most interesting and certainly the most complex' of Conrad's characters.

The Apes of God Wyndham Lewis

'It is so immense, I have no words for it,' commented T. S. Eliot on this blistering satire on twenties Bohemianism. Lewis's prose is as original and exciting as Joyce's, and the verbal savagery of his lampooning reads like a head-on collision between Swift and the Machine Age.

Despair Vladimir Nabokov

With shattering immediacy, Nabokov takes us into a deranged world, yet one full of an impudent, startling humour, dominated by the egotistical and scornful figure of a murderer who thinks himself an artist.

The Rainbow D. H. Lawrence

Suppressed by outraged moralists within six weeks of publication, *The Rainbow* is today seen as a great work of the metaphysical imagination that, despite its meticulous attention to detail and local colour, is both visionary and prophetic.

Tales of the Pacific Jack London

Shattered by tropical disease, London spent the last months of his life writing in Hawaii. Springing from his desire to reconcile the dream of an unfallen world with the harsh reality of twentieth-century materialism, these stories combine the power of Hemingway with a mastery of the short story form equal to Conrad's.

Clayhanger Arnold Bennett

The first book in the Clayhanger trilogy is a vivid portrayal of English provincial life at the turn of the century, revealing Bennett's fascination with the romance of manufacturing industry and also its slovenly ugliness. 'There is ... a complete lack of contrivance on the part of the author; Bennett follows the grain of life' – Walter Allen

FOR THE BEST IN PAPERBACKS, LOOK FOR THE

CLASSICS OF THE TWENTIETH CENTURY

Thirst for Love   Yukio Mishima

Before her husband's death Etsuko had already learnt that jealousy is useless unless it can be controlled. Love, hatred, and a new, secret passion – she can control them all as long as there is hope. But as that hope fades, her frustrated desire gathers a momentum that can be checked only by an unspeakable act of violence.

The Collected Dorothy Parker

Dorothy Parker, more than any of her contemporaries, captured in her writing the spirit of the Jazz Age. Here, in a single volume, is the definitive Dorothy Parker: poetry, prose, articles and reviews.

Remembrance of Things Past (3 volumes)   Marcel Proust

'What an extraordinary world it is, the universe that Proust created! Like all great novels, *À la Recherche* has changed and enlarged our vision of the "real" world in which we live' – Peter Quennell

The Sword of Honour Trilogy   Evelyn Waugh

A glorious fusion of comedy, satire and farcical despair, Waugh's magnificently funny trilogy is also a bitter attack on a world where chivalry and nobility were betrayed at every hand.

Buddenbrooks   Thomas Mann

Published in 1902, Mann's 'immortal masterpiece' was already a classic before it was banned and burned by Hitler. 'The richness and complexity ... the interplay of action and ideas ... has never been surpassed in German fiction' – J. P. Stern

A Clergyman's Daughter   George Orwell

The rector's daughter's submissive routine shatters, and Dorothy finds herself down and out in London. She is wearing silk stockings, has money in her pocket and cannot remember her name. Among unemployment, poverty and hunger, her faith is challenged by a social reality that changes her life.

WITHDRAWN

CLASSICS OF THE TWENTIETH CENTURY

Memoirs of a Dutiful Daughter Simone de Beauvoir

The first of her four volumes of autobiography takes Simone de Beauvoir from her early childhood to her meeting with Jean-Paul Sartre at the Sorbonne. Her intellectual honesty leads inevitably to a rebellion that she charts with moving sincerity.

Arrival and Departure Arthur Koestler

'Koestler is one of the very few novelists who attacks the most difficult and troubling issues of private and public morality and who, having raised serious questions, never tries to satisfy us with ready-made answers or evasions' – Saul Bellow

The Heart is a Lonely Hunter Carson McCullers

Set in a small town in the American South, Carson McCullers's first novel deals with isolation, the need for human understanding and the search for love. 'A poet's sensitivity interlocks with a novelist's gifts' – Cyril Connolly

Howards End E. M. Forster

'"Only connect..." Such is the epigraph of a novel much concerned with the relationships, and the possibility of reconciliation, between certain pairs of opposites' – Oliver Stallybrass. *Howards End* expresses, more perhaps than any other of his novels, themes close to Forster's heart.

Gertrude Hermann Hesse

A sensitive young composer, the narrator is drawn to Gertrude through their mutual love of music. Gradually, he is engulfed by an enduring and hopeless passion for her. 'It would be a pity to miss this book – it has such a rare flavour of truth and simplicity' – Stevie Smith

Eva Trout Elizabeth Bowen

Monolithic, rich, unloved, and with a genius for unreality, Eva Trout has an endless 'capacity for making trouble, attracting trouble, strewing trouble around her'. In her last completed novel, Elizabeth Bowen's elegant style and intense sensibility combine with her gift for social comedy to create one of her most formidable – and moving – heroines.

DEAD LIKE YOU

Peter James was educated at Charterhouse then at film school. He lived in North America for a number of years, working as a screenwriter and film producer before returning to England. His novels, including the *Sunday Times* number one bestselling Roy Grace series, have been translated into thirty-six languages, with worldwide sales of fifteen million copies. Three of his earlier novels have been filmed. His novella *The Perfect Murder* and his first Roy Grace novel, *Dead Simple*, have both been adapted for the stage. James has also produced numerous films, including *The Merchant of Venice*, starring Al Pacino, Jeremy Irons and Joseph Fiennes. He divides his time between his homes in Notting Hill, London, and near Brighton in Sussex.

Visit his website at www.peterjames.com
Or follow him on Twitter @peterjamesuk
Or Facebook: facebook.com/peterjames.roygrace

By Peter James

The Roy Grace Series

DEAD SIMPLE   LOOKING GOOD DEAD
NOT DEAD ENOUGH   DEAD MAN'S FOOTSTEPS
DEAD TOMORROW   DEAD LIKE YOU
DEAD MAN'S GRIP   NOT DEAD YET
DEAD MAN'S TIME   WANT YOU DEAD

Other Novels

DEAD LETTER DROP   ATOM BOMB ANGEL
BILLIONAIRE   POSSESSION   DREAMER
SWEET HEART   TWILIGHT   PROPHECY
ALCHEMIST   HOST   THE TRUTH
DENIAL   FAITH   PERFECT PEOPLE

Short Stories

SHORT SHOCKERS: COLLECTION ONE
SHORT SHOCKERS: COLLECTION TWO

Children's Novel

GETTING WIRED!

Novella

THE PERFECT MURDER

DEAD LIKE YOU

PETER JAMES

PAN BOOKS

First published 2010 by Macmillan

This edition published 2014 by Pan Books
an imprint of Pan Macmillan, a division of Macmillan Publishers Limited
Pan Macmillan, 20 New Wharf Road, London N1 9RR
Basingstoke and Oxford
Associated companies throughout the world
www.panmacmillan.com

ISBN 978-1-4472-7266-3

3 5 7 9 8 6 4

A CIP catalogue record for this book is available from the British Library.

Typeset by SetSystems Ltd, Saffron Walden, Essex
Printed and bound by CPI Group (UK) Ltd, Croydon, CR0 4YY

Visit www.panmacmillan.com to read more about all our books
and to buy them. You will also find features, author interviews and
news of any author events, and you can sign up for e-newsletters
so that you're always first to hear about our new releases.

TO ANNA-LISA LINDEBLAD-DAVIES

1997

1

We all make mistakes, all of the time. Mostly trivial stuff, like forgetting to return a phone call, or to put money in a parking meter, or to pick up milk at the supermarket. But sometimes – luckily very rarely – we make the big one.

The kind of mistake that could cost us our life.

The kind of mistake Rachael Ryan made.

And she had a long time to reflect on it.

If . . . she had been less drunk. If . . . it hadn't been so sodding freezing cold. If . . . it hadn't begun to rain. If . . . there hadn't been a queue of a hundred equally drunk revellers at the taxi rank in Brighton's East Street at 2 a.m. on Christmas Eve, or, rather, Christmas morning. If . . . her flat had not been within walking distance, unlike her equally drunk companions, Tracey and Jade, who lived far away, on the other side of the city.

If . . . she had listened to Tracey and Jade telling her not to be so bloody stupid. That there were plenty of taxis. That it would only be a short wait.

*

His whole body stiffened with excitement. After two hours of watching, finally the woman he had been waiting for was turning into the street. She was on foot and alone. Perfect!

3

She was wearing a miniskirt with a shawl around her shoulders and looked a little unsteady on her legs, from drink and probably from the height of the heels. She had nice legs. But what he was really looking at was her shoes. His kind of shoes. High-heeled with ankle straps. He liked ankle straps. As she came closer, approaching beneath the sodium glare of the street lights, he could see, through his binoculars, through the rear window, that they were shiny, as he had hoped.

Very sexy shoes!

She was his kind of woman!

*

God, was she glad she had decided to walk! What a queue! And every taxi that had gone past since was occupied. With a fresh, windy drizzle on her face, Rachael tottered along past the shops on St James's Street, then turned right into Paston Place, where the wind became stronger, batting her long brown hair around her face. She headed down towards the seafront, then turned left into her street of Victorian terraced houses, where the wind and the rain played even more havoc with her hairdo. Not that she cared any more, not tonight. In the distance she heard the wail of a siren, an ambulance or a police car, she thought.

She walked past a small car with misted windows. Through them she saw the silhouette of a couple snogging, and she felt a twinge of sadness and a sudden yearning for Liam, whom she had dumped almost six months ago now. The bastard had been unfaithful. OK, he had pleaded with her to forgive him, but she just knew he would stray again, and again – he was that sort. All the same, she missed him a lot at times, and she wondered where he was now. What he was doing tonight. Who he was with. He'd be with a girl for sure.

Whereas she was on her own.

She and Tracey and Jade. *The Three Saddo Singles*, they jokingly called themselves. But there was a truth that hurt behind the humour. After two and a half years in a relationship with the man she had really believed was the one she would marry, it was hard to be alone again. Particularly at Christmas, with all its memories.

God, it had been a shitty year. In August, Princess Diana had died. Then her own life had fallen apart.

She glanced at her watch. It was 2.35. Tugging her mobile phone from her bag, she rang Jade's number. Jade said they were still waiting in the queue. Rachael told her she was almost home. She wished her a merry Christmas. Told her to wish Tracey a merry Christmas too, and said she'd see them New Year's Eve.

'Hope Santa's good to you, Rach!' Jade said. 'And tell him not to forget the batteries if he brings you a vibrator!'

She heard Tracey cackling in the background.

'Sod off!' she said with a grin.

Then she slipped the phone back into her bag and stumbled on, nearly coming a purler as one high heel of her incredibly expensive Kurt Geigers, which she'd bought last week in a sale, caught between two paving stones. She toyed for a moment with the idea of taking them off, but she was almost home now. She tottered on.

The walk and the rain had sobered her up a little, but she was still too drunk, and too coked up, not to think it was odd that at almost three on Christmas morning a man in a baseball cap a short distance in front of her was trying to lug a fridge out of a van.

He had it half out and half in as she approached. She

could see he was struggling under its apparent weight and suddenly he cried out in pain.

Instinctively, because she was kind, she ran, stumbling, up to him.

'My back! My disc! My disc has gone! Oh, Jesus!'

'Can I help?'

It was the last thing she remembered saying.

She was hurled forward. Something wet slapped across her face. She smelt a sharp, acrid reek.

Then she blacked out.

NOW

2

Yac spoke into the metal thing on the tall brick wall.
'Taxi!' he said.

Then the gates opened, swanky wrought-iron ones,
painted black, with gold spikes along the top. He climbed
back into his white and turquoise Peugeot estate and
drove up a short, twisting drive. There were bushes on
either side, but he did not know what kind they were. He
hadn't got to bushes in his learning yet. Only trees.

Yac was forty-two. He wore a suit with a neatly
pressed shirt and a carefully chosen tie. He liked to dress
smart for work. He always shaved, combed his short dark
hair forward to a slight peak and rolled deodorant under
his armpits. He was aware that it was important not to
smell bad. He always checked his fingernails and his
toenails before leaving home. He always wound up his
watch. He always checked his phone for messages. But he
had only five numbers stored on the phone and only four
people had his, so it wasn't often that he received any.

He glanced at the clock on the dashboard: 6.30 p.m.
Good. Thirty minutes to go before he needed to have any
tea. Plenty of time. His Thermos sat on the seat beside
him.

At the top the drive became circular, with a low wall
in the middle enclosing a fountain that was lit up in

green. Yac steered carefully around it, past a quadruple garage door and one wall of the huge house, coming to a halt by steps leading up to the front door. It was a big, important-looking door and it was closed.

He began to fret. He didn't like it when passengers weren't already outside, because he never knew how long he would have to wait. And there were so many decisions.

Whether to switch the engine off. And if he switched the engine off, should he switch the lights off? But before he switched the engine off he needed to do some checks. *Fuel.* Three-quarters of a tank. *Oil.* Pressure normal. *Temperature.* Temperature was good. So much to remember in this taxi. Including to switch the meter on if they did not come out in five minutes. But most important of all, his drink of tea, on the hour, every hour. He checked the Thermos was still there. It was.

This wasn't actually *his* taxi, it belonged to someone he knew. Yac was a journeyman driver. He drove the hours the guy who owned it did not want to drive. Mostly nights. Some nights longer than others. Tonight was New Year's Eve. It was going to be a very long one and he had started early. But Yac didn't mind. Night was good. Much the same as day to him, but darker.

The front door of the house was opening. He stiffened and took a deep breath, as he had been taught by his therapist. He didn't really like passengers getting into his taxi and invading his space – except ones with nice shoes. But he had to put up with them until he could deliver them to their destination, then get them out again and be free.

They were coming out now. The man was tall and slim, his hair slicked back, wearing a tuxedo with a bow tie and holding his coat over his arm. She had a furry-looking jacket on, red hair all done nicely, flowing around her head. She looked beautiful, as if she might be a famous actress, like the ones he saw pictures of in the papers that people left in his taxi or on television of stars arriving at premieres.

But he wasn't really looking at her; he was looking at her shoes. Black suede, three ankle straps, high heels with glinting metal around the edges of the soles.

'Good evening,' the man said, opening the door of the taxi for the woman. 'Metropole Hotel, please.'

'Nice shoes,' Yac said to the woman, by way of reply. 'Jimmy Choo. Uh-huh?'

She squealed in proud delight. 'Yes, you're right. They are!'

He recognized her intoxicating scent too, but said nothing. *Oscar de la Renta Intrusion*, he thought to himself. He liked it.

He started the engine and quickly ran through his mental checks. *Meter on. Seat belts. Doors closed. Into gear. Handbrake off.* He had not checked the tyres since dropping off the last fare, but he had done so half an hour ago, so they might still be all right. *Check in mirror.* As he did, he caught another glimpse of the woman's face. Definitely beautiful. He would like to see her shoes again.

'The main entrance,' the man said.

Yac did the calculation in his head as he steered back down the drive: 2.516 miles. He memorized distances. He knew most of them within this city because he had memorized the streets. It was 4,428 yards to the Hilton Brighton Metropole, he recalculated; or 2.186 nautical miles, or 4.04897 kilometres, or 0.404847 of a Swedish mile. The fare would be approximately £9.20, subject to traffic.

'Do you have high-flush or low-flush toilets in your house?' he asked.

After a few moments of silence while Yac pulled out into the road, the man glanced at the woman, raised his eyes and said, 'Low flush. Why?'

'How many toilets do you have in your house? I bet you've got a lot, right? Uh-huh?'

'We have enough,' the man said.

'I can tell you where there's a good example of a high-flush toilet – it's in Worthing. I could take you there to see it if you're interested.' Hope rose in Yac's voice. 'It's a really good example. In the public toilets, near the pier.'

'No, thank you. They're not my thing.'

The couple in the back fell silent.

Yac drove on. He could see their faces in the glow of the street lights, in his mirror.

'With your low-flush toilets, I bet you have some push-button ones,' he said.

'We do,' the man said. 'Yes.' Then he put his mobile phone to his ear and answered a call.

Yac watched him in the mirror before catching the woman's eyes. 'You're a size five, aren't you? In shoes.'

'Yes! How did you know?'

'I can tell. I can always tell. Uh-huh.'

'That's very clever!' she said.

Yac fell silent. He was probably talking too much. The guy who owned the taxi told him there had been complaints about him talking too much. The guy said people didn't always like to talk. Yac did not want to lose his job. So he kept quiet. He thought about the woman's shoes as he headed down to the Brighton seafront and turned left. Instantly the wind buffeted the taxi. The traffic was heavy and it was slow going. But he was right about the fare.

As he pulled up outside the entrance to the Metropole Hotel, the meter showed £9.20.

The man gave him £10 and told him to keep the change.

Yac watched them walk into the hotel. Watched the woman's hair blowing in the wind. Watched the Jimmy Choo shoes disappearing through the revolving door. Nice shoes. He felt excited.

Excited about the night ahead.

There would be so many more shoes. Special shoes for a very special night.

3

Detective Superintendent Roy Grace stared out of his office window into the dark void of the night, at the lights of the ASDA superstore car park across the road and the distant lights of the city of Brighton and Hove beyond, and heard the howl of the gusting wind. He felt the cold draught that came though the thin pane on his cheek.

New Year's Eve. He checked his watch: 6.15. Time to go. Time to quit his hopeless attempt at clearing his desk and head home.

It was the same every New Year's Eve, he reflected. He always promised himself that he would tidy up, deal with all his paperwork and start the next year with a clean slate. And he always failed. He would be coming back in tomorrow to yet another hopeless mess. Even bigger than last year's. Which had been even bigger than the one the year before.

All the Crown Prosecution files of the cases he had investigated during this past year were stacked on the floor. Next to them were small, precarious tower blocks of blue cardboard boxes and green plastic crates crammed with unresolved cases – as cold cases were now starting to be called. But he preferred the old title.

Although his work was predominantly concerned with current murders and other major crimes, Roy Grace

14

cared about his cold cases very much, to the point that he
felt a personal connection with each victim. But he had
been unable to dedicate much time to these files, because
it had been a strangely busy year. First, a young man had
been buried alive in a coffin on his stag night. Then a vile
snuff-movie ring had been busted. This had been followed
by a complex case of a homicidal identity thief, before
he'd successfully potted a double-killer who had faked his
disappearance. But he'd had precious little acknowledge-
ment for getting these results from his departing boss,
Assistant Chief Constable Alison Vosper.

Perhaps next year would be better. Certainly it was
filled with promise. A new ACC, Peter Rigg, was starting
on Monday – five days' time. Also starting on Monday,
which would greatly relieve his workload, was a brand-
new Cold Case Team comprising three former senior
detectives under his command.

But most important of all, his beloved Cleo was due
to give birth to their child in June. And some time before
then, at a date still to be sorted out, they would be getting
married, so long as the one obstacle standing in their way
could be removed.

His wife, Sandy.

She had disappeared nine and a half years ago, on
his thirtieth birthday, and, despite all his efforts, no word
had been heard from her since. He did not know whether
she had been abducted or murdered, or had run off with
a lover, or had had an accident, or had simply, elabo-
rately, faked her disappearance.

For the past nine years, until his relationship with
Cleo Morey had begun, Roy had spent almost all of his
free time in a fruitless quest to discover what had hap-
pened to Sandy. Now he was finally putting her into the

past. He had engaged a solicitor to have her declared legally dead. He hoped the process could be fast-tracked so they would be able to get married before the baby was born. Even if Sandy did turn up out of the blue, he would not be interested in resuming a life with her, he had decided. He had moved on in his own mind – or so he believed.

He shovelled several piles of documents around on his desk. By stacking one heap on top of another, it made the desk look tidier, even if the workload remained the same.

Strange how life changed, he thought. Sandy used to hate New Year's Eve. It was such an artifice, she used to tell him. They always spent it with another couple, a police colleague, Dick Pope, and his wife, Leslie. Always in some fancy restaurant. Then afterwards Sandy would invariably analyse the entire evening and pull it apart.

With Sandy, he had come to view the advent of New Year's Eve with decreasing enthusiasm. But now, with Cleo, he was looking forward to it hugely. They were going to spend it at home, alone together, and feast on some of their favourite foods. Bliss! The only downer was that he was the duty Senior Investigating Officer for this week, which meant he was on twenty-four-hour call – which meant he could not drink. Although he had decided he would allow himself a few sips of a glass of champagne at midnight.

He could hardly wait to get home. He was so in love with Cleo that there were frequent moments in every day when he was overcome by a deep yearning to see her, hold her, touch her, hear her voice, see her smile. He had that feeling now, and wanted nothing more than to leave and head for her house, which had now, to all intents and purposes, become his home.

Just one thing stopped him.

All those damned blue boxes and green crates on the floor. He needed to have everything in order for the Cold Case Team on Monday, the first official working day of the New Year. Which meant several hours of work still ahead of him.

So instead he sent Cleo a text with a row of kisses.

For a time, this past year, he had managed to delegate all these cold cases to a colleague. But that hadn't worked out and now he had inherited them all back. Five unsolved major crimes out of a total number of twenty-five to be reinvestigated. Where the hell did he begin?

The words of Lewis Carroll's *Alice's Adventures in Wonderland* came into his head suddenly: 'Begin at the beginning and go on till you come to the end: then stop.'

So he began at the beginning. Just five minutes, he thought, then he would quit for the year and head home to Cleo. As if echoing his thoughts, his phone pinged with an incoming text. It was an even longer row of kisses.

Smiling, he opened the first file and looked at the activity report. Every six months the DNA labs they used would run checks on the DNA from their cold-case victims. You just never knew. And there had been several offenders who must have long thought they had got away with their crimes but who had successfully been brought to trial and were now in prison because of advances in DNA extraction and matching techniques.

The second file was a case that always touched Roy Grace deeply. Young Tommy Lytle. Twenty-seven years ago, at the age of eleven, Tommy had set out from school on a February afternoon to walk home. The one lead in the case was a Morris Minor van, spotted near the scene of the boy's murder, which was later searched. From the files, it was obvious that the Senior Investigating Officer at the time was convinced the owner of the van was the offender, but they were unable to find that crucial forensic evidence that would have linked the boy to the van. The man, a weirdo loner with a history of sexual offences, was released – but, Grace knew, still very much alive.

He turned to the next file: *Operation Houdini.*
Shoe Man.

Names of operations were thrown up randomly by the CID computer system. Occasionally they were apt. This one was. Like a great escapologist, this particular offender had so far avoided the police net.

The Shoe Man had raped – or attempted to rape – at least five women in the Brighton area over a short period of time back in 1997, and in all likelihood had raped and killed a sixth victim whose body had never been found. And it could have been a lot more – many women are too embarrassed or traumatized to report an attack. Then suddenly the attacks appeared to have stopped. No DNA evidence had been recovered from any of the victims who had come forward at the time. But techniques for obtaining it were less effective then.

All they had to go on was the offender's MO. Almost every criminal had a specific modus operandi. A way of doing things. His or her particular 'signature'. And the Shoe Man had a very distinct one: he took his victim's panties and one of her shoes. But only if they were classy shoes.

Grace hated rapists. He knew that everyone who became a victim of crime was left traumatized in some way. But most victims of burglaries and street crimes could eventually put it behind them and move on. Victims of sexual abuse or sexual assault, particularly child victims and rape victims, could never ever truly do that. Their lives were changed forever. They would spend the rest of their days living with the knowledge, struggling to cope, to hold down their revulsion, their anger and their fear.

It was a harsh fact that most people were raped by someone they knew. Rapes by total strangers were exceedingly rare, but they did happen. And it was not uncommon for these so-called 'stranger rapists' to take a souvenir – a trophy. Like the Shoe Man had.

Grace turned some of the pages of the thick file, glancing through comparisons with other rapes around the country. In particular, there was one case further north, from the same time period, that bore striking similarities. But that suspect had been eliminated, as evidence had established that it definitely could not have been the same person.

So, Shoe Man, Grace wondered, *are you still alive? If so, where are you now?*

4

Nicola Taylor was wondering when this night of hell would end, little knowing that the hell had not yet even begun.

'Hell is other people', Jean-Paul Sartre once wrote, and she was with him on that. And right now hell was the drunken man with the wonky bow tie on her right who was crushing every bone in her hand, and the even drunker man on her left, in a green tuxedo jacket, whose sweaty hand felt as slimy as pre-packed bacon.

And all the other 350 noisy, drunken people around her.

Both men were jerking her arms up and down, damned nearly pulling them out of their sockets as the band in the Metropole Hotel function room struck up 'Auld Lang Syne' on the stroke of midnight. The man on her right had a plastic Groucho Marx moustache clipped to the inside of his nostrils and the one on her left, whose slimy hand had spent much of the evening trying to work its way up her thigh, kept blowing a whistle that sounded like a duck farting.

She so totally did not want to be here. So wished to hell she had stuck to her guns and stayed home, in her comfort zone, with a bottle of wine and the television – the way she had most evenings this past year, since her husband had dumped her in favour of his twenty-four-year-old secretary.

But oh no, her friends Olivia and Becky and Deanne had all insisted there was *no way* they were going to allow her to get away with spending New Year's Eve moping at home on her own. Nigel was not coming back, they assured her. The slapper was pregnant. Forget him, kiddo. There were plenty more fish in the sea. Time to get a life.

This was getting a life?

Both her arms were jerked up in the air at the same time. Then she was dragged forward in a huge surge, her feet almost falling out of her insanely expensive Marc Jacobs heels. Moments later she found herself being dragged, tripping, backwards.

Should auld acquaintance be forgot ... the band played.

Yes, they bloody well should. And current ones too!

Except she could not forget. Not all those midnights on New Year's Eve when she had stared into Nigel's eyes and told him she loved him, and he'd told her he loved her as well. Her heart was heavy, too damned heavy. She wasn't ready for this. Not now, not yet.

The song finally ended and Mr Pre-packed Bacon now spat his whistle out, gripped both her cheeks and planted a slobbery, lingering kiss on her lips. 'Happy New Year!' he burbled.

Then balloons fell from the ceiling. Paper streamers rained down on her. Jolly smiling faces surrounded her. She was hugged, kissed, fondled from every direction she turned. It went on and on and on.

Nobody would notice, she thought, if she escaped now.

She struggled across the room, weaving through the

sea of people, and slipped out into the corridor. She felt a cold draught of air and smelt sweet cigarette smoke. God, how she could do with a fag right now!

She headed along the corridor, which was almost deserted, turned right and walked along into the hotel foyer, then crossed over to the lifts. She pressed the button and, when the door opened, stepped in and pressed the button for the fifth floor.

Hopefully, they'd all be too drunk to notice her absence. Maybe she should have drunk more too and then she'd have been in a better party mood. She was feeling stone cold sober and could easily have driven home, but she'd paid for a room for the night and her stuff was in there. Perhaps she'd call up some champagne from room service, watch a movie and get quietly smashed on her own.

As she stepped out of the lift, she pulled her plastic room key-card out of her silver lamé Chanel evening bag – a copy she'd bought in Dubai on a trip there with Nigel two years ago – and made her way along the corridor.

She noticed a slender blonde woman – in her forties, she guessed – a short distance ahead. She was wearing a full-length, high-necked evening dress with long sleeves and appeared to be struggling to open her door. As she drew level with her, the woman, who was extremely drunk, turned to her and slurred, 'I can't get this sodding thing in. Do you know how they work?' She held out her key-card.

'I think you have to slip it in and then out quite quickly,' Nicola said.

'I've tried that.'

'Let me try for you.'

Nicola, helpfully, took the card and slipped it into the

slot. As she pulled it out, she saw a green light and heard a click.

Almost instantaneously, she felt something damp pressed across her face. There was a sweet smell in her nostrils and her eyes felt as if they were burning. She felt a crashing blow on the back of her neck. Felt herself stumbling forward. Then the carpet slammed into her face.

1997

5

Rachael Ryan heard the snap of the man's belt buckle in the darkness. A clank. The rustle of clothes. The sound of his breathing – rapid, feral. She had a blinding pain in her head.

'Please don't hurt me,' she begged. 'Please don't.'

The van was rocking in the frequent gusts of wind outside and occasionally a vehicle passed, bright white light strobing through the interior from its headlamps, as terror strobed through her. It was in those moments that she could see him most clearly. The black mask tight over his head, with tiny slits for his eyes, nostrils and mouth. The baggy jeans and the tracksuit top. The small, curved knife that he gripped in his left, gloved hand, the knife he said he would blind her with if she shouted out or tried to get away.

A musty odour, like old sacks, rose from whatever thin bedding she was lying on. It mingled with the faint smell of old plastic upholstery and the sharper reek of leaking diesel oil.

She saw his trousers come down. Stared at his white underpants, his lean, smooth legs. He pushed his pants down. Saw his small penis, thin and stumpy like the head of a snake. Saw him rummage in his pocket with his right hand and pull something out which glinted. A square foil packet. He sliced it open with his knife, breathing even harder and squeezed something out. A condom.

Her brain was racing with wild thoughts. A condom? Was he being considerate? If he was considerate enough to use a condom, would he really use his knife on her?

'We're going to get the rubber on,' he panted. 'They can get DNA now. They can get you from DNA. I'm not leaving you a present for the police. Make me hard.'

She shuddered with revulsion as the head of the snake moved closer to her lips and saw his face suddenly lit up brightly again as another car passed. There were people outside. She heard voices in the street. Laughter. If she could just make a noise – bang on the side of the van, scream – someone would come, someone would stop him.

She wondered for a moment whether she should just try to arouse him, to make him come, then maybe he would let her go and he would disappear. But she felt too much revulsion, too much anger – and too much doubt.

Now she could hear his breathing getting even deeper. Hear him grunting. See that he was touching himself. He was just a pervert, just a weirdo fucking pervert and this was not going to happen to her!

And suddenly, fuelled by the courage from the alcohol inside her, she grabbed his sweaty, hairless scrotum and crushed his balls in both hands as hard as she could. Then, as he recoiled, gasping in pain, she tore the hood off his head and jammed her fingers into his eyes, both eyes, trying to gouge them out with her nails, screaming as loudly as she could.

Except, in her terror, as if she were trying to scream in a nightmare, only a faint croak came out instead.

Then she felt a crashing blow on the side of her head.

'You bitch!'

He smashed his fist into her again. The mask of pain and fury that was his face, all blurred, was inches from her own. She felt the fist again, then again.

Everything swam around her.

And suddenly she felt her panties being pulled off, and then he was entering her. She tried to move back, to push away, but he had her pinned.

This is not me. This is not my body.

She felt totally detached from herself. For an instant she wondered if this was a nightmare from which she could not wake. Lights flashed inside her skull. Then fused.

NOW

6

Thursday 1 January

Today was New Year's Day. And the tide was in!

Yac liked it best when the tide was in. He knew the tide was in because he could feel his home moving, rising, gently rocking. Home was a Humber keel coaler called *Tom Newbound,* painted blue and white. He did not know why the boat had been given that name, but it was owned by a woman called Jo, who was a district nurse, and her husband, Howard, who was a carpenter. Yac had driven them home one night in his taxi and they had been kind to him. Subsequently they'd become his best friends. He adored the boat, loved to hang about on it and to help Joe with painting, or varnishing, or generally cleaning her up.

Then one day they told him they were going to live in Goa in India for a while, they did not know how long. Yac was upset at losing his friends and his visits to the boat. But they told him they wanted someone to look after their houseboat, and their cat, for them.

Yac had been here for two years now. Just before Christmas he'd had a phone call from them, telling him they were going to stay for another year at least.

Which meant he could stay here for another year at least, which made him very happy. And he had a prize from last night, a new pair of shoes, which also made him very happy . . .

Red leather shoes. Beautifully curved with six straps and a buckle and six-inch stilettos.

They lay on the floor beside his *bunk*. He had learned nautical terms. It was a bed, really, but on a ship it was called a bunk. Just like the way the toilet wasn't called a toilet, but the *heads*.

He could navigate from here to any port in the UK – he had memorized all the Admiralty charts. Except the boat had no engine. One day he would like to have a boat of his own, with an engine, and then he would sail to all those places that he had stored inside his head. Uh-huh.

Bosun nuzzled his hand, which was hanging over the side of his bunk. Bosun, the big, slinky ginger tom, was the boss here. The true master of this boat. Yac knew that the cat regarded him as its servant. Yac didn't mind. The cat had never thrown up in his taxi, like some people had.

The smell of expensive new shoe leather filled Yac's nostrils. Oh yes. Paradise! To wake up with a new pair of shoes.

On a rising tide!

That was the best thing of all about living on the water. You never heard footsteps. Yac had tried to live in the city, but it had not worked for him. He could not stand the tantalizing sound of all those shoes clacking all around him when he was trying to sleep. There were no shoes here, out on the moorings on the River Adur at Shoreham Beach. Just the slap of water, or the silence of the mudflats. The cry of gulls. Sometimes the cry of the eight-month-old baby on the boat next door.

One day, hopefully, the infant would fall into the mud and drown.

But for now, Yac looked forward to the day ahead. To getting out of bed. To examining his new shoes. Then to cataloguing them. Then perhaps to looking through his collection, which he stored in the secret places he had found and made his own on the boat. It was where he kept, among other things, his collection of electrical wiring diagrams. Then he would go into his little office up in the bow and spend time on his laptop computer, online.

What better way could there be to start a New Year?

But first he had to remember to feed the cat.

But before doing that he had to brush his teeth.

And before that he had to use the *heads.*

Then he would have to run through all the checks on the boat, ticking them off from the list the owners had given him. First on the list was to check his fishing lines. Then he had to check for leaks. Leaks were not good. Then he needed to check the mooring ropes. It was a long list and working through it made him feel good. It was good to be needed.

He was needed by Mr Raj Dibdoon, who owned the taxi.

He was needed by the nurse and the carpenter, who owned his home.

He was needed by the cat.

And this morning he had a new pair of shoes!

This was a good start to a New Year.

Uh-huh.

7

Thursday 1 January

Carlo Diomei was tired. And when he was tired he felt low, as he did right now. He did not like these long, damp English winters. He missed the crisp, dry cold of his native Courmayeur, high up in the Italian Alps. He missed the winter snow and the summer sunshine. He missed putting on his skis on his days off and spending a few precious hours alone, away from the holidaying crowds on the busy pistes, making his own silent tracks down parts of the mountains that only he and a few local guides knew.

He had just one more year of his contract to run and then, he hoped, he would return to the mountains and, with luck, to a job managing a hotel there, back among his friends.

But for now the money was good here and the experience in this famous hotel would give him a great step up his career ladder. But, shit, what a lousy start to the New Year this was!

Normally as Duty Manager of the Brighton Metropole Hotel he worked a day shift, which enabled him to spend his precious evenings at home in his rented sea-view apartment with his wife and children, a two-year-old son and a four-year-old daughter. But the Night Manager had picked yesterday, New Year's Eve of all nights, to go down with flu. So he'd had to come back and take over, with just a two-hour break in which to dash home, put his kids to bed, toast his wife a Happy New Year with mineral water, instead of the champagne night at home they had planned, and hurry back to work to supervise all the New Year celebrations the hotel had been hosting.

He'd now been on duty for eighteen hours straight and was exhausted. In half an hour he would hand over to his deputy and would finally go home, and celebrate by smoking a badly needed cigarette, then falling into bed and getting some even more badly needed sleep.

The phone rang in his tiny, narrow office on the other side of the wall to the front desk.

'Carlo,' he answered.

It was Daniela de Rosa, the Housekeeping Manager, another Italian, from Milano. A room maid was concerned about room 547. It was 12.30, half an hour past check-out time, and there was a *Do Not Disturb* sign still hanging on the room door. There had been no response when she knocked repeatedly, nor when she phoned the room.

He yawned. Probably someone sleeping off a night of overindulgence. Lucky them. He tapped his keyboard to check on the room's occupant. The name was Mrs Marsha Morris. He dialled the room number himself and listened to it ringing, without answer. He called Daniela de Rosa back.

'OK,' he said wearily, 'I am coming up.'

Five minutes later, he stepped out of the lift on the fifth floor and walked along the corridor, to where the Housekeeping Manager was standing, and knocked hard on the door. There was no response. He knocked again. Waited. Then, using his pass key, he opened the door slowly and stepped in.

'Hello!' he said quietly.

The heavy curtains were still drawn, but in the semi-darkness he could make out the shape of someone lying on the wide bed.

'Hello!' he said again. 'Good morning!'

He detected the faintest movement on the bed. 'Hello!' he said again. 'Good morning, Mrs Morris. Hello! Happy New Year!'

There was no response. Just a little more movement.

He felt on the wall for the light switches and pressed one. Several lights came on at once. They revealed a slender, naked woman with large breasts, long red hair and a dense triangle of brown pubic hair, spread-eagled on the bed. Her arms and legs were outstretched in a crucifix position and held in place with white cords. The reason there was no response from her was instantly clear as he stepped closer, feeling a growing spike of unease in his gullet. Part of a face towel protruded either side of duct tape pulled tight across her mouth.

'Oh, my God!' the Housekeeping Manager cried out.

Carlo Diomei hurried over to the bed, his tired brain trying to make sense of what he was looking at and not entirely succeeding. Was this some strange sex game? Was her husband, or boyfriend or whoever, lurking in the bathroom? The woman's eyes looked at him in desperation.

He ran to the bathroom and flung open the door, but it was empty. He'd seen some strange things going on in hotel rooms and had to deal with some weird shit in his time, but for a moment, for the first time in his career to date, he was uncertain what he should do next. Had they interrupted some kinky sex game? Or was something else going on?

The woman looked at him with small, frightened eyes. He felt embarrassed looking down at her nakedness. Overcoming it, he tried to remove the duct tape, but as he gave the first tentative pull the woman's head thrashed violently. Clearly it was hurting her. But he had to get it off, he was certain. Had to speak to her. So he pulled it away from her skin as gently as he could, until he was able to pluck the towel out of her mouth.

Instantly the woman began burbling and sobbing incoherently.

8

It had been a long time, Roy Grace reflected, since he had felt this good on a New Year's Day. For as far back as he could remember, except for the times when he had been on duty, the New Year always began with a blinding headache and the same overwhelming sensation of doom that accompanied his hangovers.

He had drunk even more heavily on those first New Year's Eves since Sandy's disappearance, when their close friends Dick and Leslie Pope would not hear of him being on his own and insisted he join in their celebrations. And, almost as if it was a legacy from Sandy, he had started to intensely dislike the festivity too.

But now, this particular New Year's Eve had been totally different. Last night's had been the most sober – and the most enjoyable – he could remember in his entire life.

For a start, Cleo passionately loved the whole idea of celebrating the New Year. Which made it all the more ironic that she was pregnant and therefore could not really drink very much. But he hadn't minded; he was just happy to be with her, celebrating not just the coming year, but their future together.

And, quietly, he celebrated the fact that his irascible boss, Alison Vosper, would no longer be there to dampen his spirits on an almost daily basis. He looked forward to his first meeting with his new boss, Assistant Chief Constable Peter Rigg, on Monday.

All he had managed to glean about the man so far was that he was a stickler for detail, liked to be hands-on involved and had a short fuse with fools.

To his relief, it had been a quiet morning in the CID HQ at Sussex House, so he'd spent the time steadily working through his paperwork and making brisk progress, while keeping a regular eye on the serials – the log of all reported incidents in the city of Brighton and Hove – on the computer.

As expected, there had been a few incidents in the bars, pubs and clubs, mostly fights and a few handbag thefts. He noted a couple of minor road traffic collisions, a *domestic* – a couple fighting – a complaint about noise from a party, a lost dog, a stolen moped and a naked man reported running down Western Road. But now a serious entry had appeared. It was a reported rape, at Brighton's smart Metropole Hotel, which had popped on to the screen a few minutes ago, at 12.55 p.m.

There were four principal categories of rape: *stranger, acquaintance, date* and *partner.* At this moment there was no mention on the serial of which this might be. New Year's Eve was the kind of time when some men got blind drunk and forced themselves on their dates or partners, and in all likelihood this incident would be in one of those categories. Serious enough, but not something likely to involve Major Crime.

Twenty minutes later he was about to head across the road to the ASDA supermarket, which doubled as the CID HQ canteen, to buy himself a sandwich for lunch, when his internal phone rang.

It was David Alcorn, a detective inspector he knew and liked a lot. Alcorn was based at the city's busy main police station in John Street, where Grace himself had spent much of his early career as a detective, before moving to the CID HQ at Sussex House.

'Happy New Year, Roy,' Alcorn said in his usual blunt, sardonic voice. From the tone of his voice, *happy* had just fallen off a cliff.

'You too, David. Did you have a good night?'

'Yeah. Well, it was all right. Had to keep off the booze a bit to be here for seven this morning. You?'

'Quiet, but nice – thanks.'

'Thought I'd better give you a heads-up, Roy. Looks like we might have a stranger rape at the Metropole.'

He filled him in on the sketchy details. A Uniform Response Team had attended the hotel and called in CID. A Sexual Offences Liaison Officer or SOLO was now on her way over to accompany the victim to the recently opened specialist rape unit, the Sexual Assault Referral Centre or SARC, in Crawley, a post-war town located in the geographical centre of Sussex.

Grace jotted down the details, such as Alcorn could give him, on a notepad. 'Thanks, David,' he said. 'Keep me updated on this. Let me know if you need any help from my team.'

There was a slight pause and he sensed the hesitation in the DI's voice. 'Roy, there's something that could make this a bit politically sensitive.'

'Oh?'

'The victim had been at a do last night at the Metropole. I'm informed that a number of police brass were at a table at this same function.'

'Any names?'

'The Chief Constable and his wife, for starters.'

Shit, Grace thought, but did not say.

'Who else?'

'The Deputy CC. And one assistant chief constable. You get my drift?'

Grace got his drift.

'Maybe I should send someone from Major Crime up to accompany the SOLO. What do you think? As a formality.'

'I think that would be a good plan.'

Grace quickly ran through his options. In particular he was concerned about his new boss. If ACC Peter Rigg was truly a stickler for detail, then he damned well had to start off on the right footing – and to cover himself as best he could.

'OK. Thanks, David. I'll send someone up there right away. In the meantime, can you get me a list of all attendees of that event?'

'That's already in hand.'

'And all the guests staying there, plus all the staff – I would imagine there might have been extra staff drafted in for last night.'

'I'm on to all of that.' Alcorn sounded just slightly miffed, as if Grace was doubting his abilities.

'Of course. Sorry.'

Immediately after he ended the call, he rang DC Emma-Jane Boutwood, one of the few members of his team who was in today. She was also one of the detectives he had tasked with working through the mountains of bureaucracy required by the Crown Prosecution Service for *Operation Neptune*, a large and harrowing human-trafficking investigation he had been running in the weeks before Christmas.

It took her only a few moments to reach him from her desk in the large, open-plan Detectives' Room just beyond his door. He noticed she was limping a little as she came into his office – still not fully recovered from the horrific injuries she had sustained in a pursuit last summer, when she had been crushed against a wall by a van. Despite multiple fractures and losing her spleen, she had insisted on cutting short her advised convalescence period to get back to work as quickly as possible.

'Hi, E-J,' he said. 'Have a seat.'

Grace had just begun to run through the sketchy details David Alcorn had given him and to explain the delicate political situation when his internal phone suddenly rang again.

'Roy Grace,' he answered, raising a finger to E-J to ask her to wait.

'Detective Superintendent Grace,' said a chirpy, friendly voice with a posh, public-school accent. 'How do you do? This is Peter Rigg here.'

Shit, Grace thought again.

'Sir,' he replied. 'Very nice to – er – um – hear from you. I thought you weren't actually starting until Monday, sir.'

'Do you have a problem with that?'

Oh boy, Roy Grace thought, his heart sinking. The New Year was barely twelve hours old and they had their first serious crime. And the new ACC hadn't even officially started and he'd managed to piss him off already.

He was conscious of E-J's eyes on him, and her ears scooping this all up.

'No, sir, absolutely not. This is actually fortuitous timing. It would seem we have our first critical incident of

44

the year. It's too early to tell at this moment, but it has potential for a lot of unwelcome media coverage.'

Grace then signalled to E-J that he needed privacy and she left the room, closing the door.

For the next couple of minutes he ran through what was happening. Fortunately, the new Assistant Chief Constable continued in a friendly vein.

When Grace had finished, Rigg said, 'You're going up there yourself, I take it?'

Roy hesitated. With the highly specialized and skilled team at Crawley, there was no actual need for him to be there at this stage, and his time would be far better employed here in the office, dealing with paperwork and keeping up to speed on the incident via the phone. But he decided that was not what the new ACC wanted to hear.

'Yes, sir. I'm on my way shortly,' he replied.

'Good. Keep me informed.'

Grace assured him he would.

As he hung up, thinking hard, his door opened and the morose face and shaven dome of Detective Sergeant Glenn Branson appeared. His eyes, against his black skin, looked tired and dulled. They reminded Grace of the eyes of fish that had been dead too long, the kind Cleo had told him he should avoid on a fishmonger's slab.

'Yo, old-timer,' Branson said. 'Reckon this year's going to be any less shitty than last?'

'Nope!' Grace said. 'The years never get less shitty. All we can do is try to learn to cope with that fact.'

'Well, you're a sack-load of goodwill this morning,' Branson said, slumping his huge frame down into the chair E-J had just vacated.

Even his brown suit, garish tie and cream shirt looked

tired and rumpled, as if they'd also been on a slab too long, which worried Grace about his friend. Glenn Branson was normally always sharply dressed, but in recent months his marriage breakup had sent him on a downward spiral.

'Wasn't the best year for me last year, was it? Halfway through I got shot and three-quarters of the way through my wife threw me out.'

'Look on the bright side. You didn't die and you got to trash my collection of vinyls.'

'Thanks a bunch.'

'Want to take a drive with me?' Grace asked.

Branson shrugged. 'A drive? Yeah, sure. Where?'

Grace was interrupted by his radio phone ringing. It was David Alcorn calling again to give him an update.

'Something that might be significant, Roy. Apparently some of the victim's clothes are missing. Sounds like the offender might have taken them. In particular her shoes.' He hesitated a moment. 'I seem to remember there was someone doing that a few years back, wasn't there?'

'Yes, but he took just one shoe and the underwear,' Grace replied, his voice quiet all of a sudden. 'What else has been taken?'

'We haven't got much out of her. I understand she's in total shock.'

No surprise there, he thought grimly. His eyes went down to one of the blue boxes on the floor – the one containing the cold-case file on the Shoe Man. He pondered for a moment.

That was twelve years ago. Hopefully it was just a coincidence.

But even as he thought that a wintry gust rippled through his veins.

1997

9

Thursday 25 December

They were moving. Driving somewhere. Rachael Ryan could hear the steady, dull boom of the exhaust and she was breathing in lungfuls of its fumes. She could hear the sound of the tyres sluicing on the wet road. Could feel every bump jarring her through the sacking on which she lay trussed up, arms behind her back, unable to move or speak. All she could see was the top of the back of his baseball cap in the driver's cab up front and his ears sticking out.

She was frozen with cold, with terror. Her mouth and throat were parched and her head ached terribly from when he had hit her. Her whole body hurt. She felt nauseous with disgust – dirty, filthy. She desperately wanted a shower, hot water, soap, shampoo. Wanted to wash herself inside and out.

She felt the van going around a corner. She could see daylight. Grey daylight. Christmas morning. She should be in her flat, opening the stocking her mother had posted to her. Every year of her childhood and still now, at twenty-two, she had a Christmas stocking.

She began crying. She could hear the clunk-clop of windscreen wipers. Suddenly, Elton John's 'Candle in the Wind' began playing loudly and crackly on the radio. She could see the man's head swaying to the music.

Elton John had sung that song at Princess Diana's funeral, with new lyrics. Rachael remembered that day so vividly. She had been one of the hundreds of thousands of mourners outside Westminster Abbey, listening to that song, watching the funeral on one of the huge television screens. She had camped the night on the pavement, and the day before had spent a big part of her week's wages from her job on the help desk in the customer relations department of American Express in Brighton on a bouquet of flowers that she had placed, alongside the thousands of others, in front of Kensington Palace.

She had idolized the Princess. Something had died inside her the day Diana died.

Now a new nightmare had begun.

The van braked sharply to a halt and she slid forward a few inches. She tried again to move her hands and her legs, which were agonizingly cramped. But she could move nothing.

It was Christmas morning and her parents were expecting her for a glass of champagne and then Christmas lunch – followed by the Queen's speech. A tradition, every year, like the stocking.

She tried again to speak, to plead with the man, but her mouth was taped shut. She needed to pee and had already once, some time ago, soiled herself. She could not do that again. There was a ringing sound. Her mobile phone; she recognized the Nokia ringtone. The man turned his head for an instant, then looked to the front again. The van moved forward. Through her blurry eyes and the smeared windscreen she saw a green traffic light pass by. Then she saw buildings on her left that she recognized. Gamley's, the toyshop. They were on Church Road, Hove. Heading west.

Her phone stopped. A short while later she heard a beep-beep, signalling a message.

From whom?

Tracey and Jade?

Or her parents calling to wish her Happy Christmas? Her mother anxious to know if she liked her stocking?

How long before they started to worry about her?

Oh, Christ! Who the hell is this man?

She rolled over to her left as the van made a sharp right turn. Then a left turn. Then another turn. And stopped.

The song stopped. A cheery male voice began talking about where the wonderful Elton John was spending his Christmas.

The man got out, leaving the engine running. The fumes and her fear were making her more and more nauseous. She was desperate for water.

Suddenly he came back into the van. They moved forward, into increasing darkness. Then the engine was switched off and there was a moment of complete silence as the radio went off too. The man disappeared.

There was a metallic clang as the driver's door shut.

Then another metallic clang, cutting out all light.

She lay still, whimpering in fear, in total darkness.

10

Suited and booted and proudly wearing the smart red paisley tie that Sandy had given him yesterday for Christmas, Roy passed on his left the blue door marked *Superintendent* and on his right the one marked *Chief Superintendent*. Roy often wondered whether he'd ever get to make Chief Superintendent.

The whole building felt deserted this Boxing Day morning, apart from a few members of the *Operation Houdini* team in the Incident Room on the top floor. They were still working around the clock to try to catch the serial rapist known as the Shoe Man.

As he waited for the kettle to boil, he thought for a moment about the Chief Superintendent's cap. With its band of silver to distinguish it from the lesser ranks, it was, no question, very covetable. But he wondered if he was smart enough to rise to such a rank – and doubted it.

One thing Roy Grace had learned about Sandy, in their years of marriage, was that she had at times a perfectionist view of how she wanted her particular world to be – and a very short fuse if any aspect failed her expectations. On a number of occasions, her sudden flare of temper at an inept waiter or shop assistant had left him feeling acutely embarrassed. But that spirit in her was part of what had attracted him to her in the first place.

She had all the support and enthusiasm in the world for success, however big or small, but he just had to remember that, for Sandy, failure was never an option.

Which explained, in part, her deep resentment, and occasional outbursts of anger, that, after years of trying almost every fertility treatment possible, she was still unable to conceive the baby they both so desperately wanted.

Humming the words of Eric Clapton's 'Change the World' – which for some reason had popped into his head – Roy Grace carried his mug of coffee down to his desk in the deserted open-plan Detectives' Room on the second floor of Brighton's John Street police station, with its rows of partitioned desks, its manky blue carpet, its crammed pigeonholes and its view to the east of the white walls and gleaming blue windows of the American Express headquarters. Then he logged on to the clunky, slow computer system to check the overnight serials. While he waited for it to load, he took a sip of coffee and fancied a cigarette, silently cursing the ban on smoking in police offices which had recently been introduced.

An attempt had been made, as it was every year, to bring some Christmas cheer into the place. There were paper-chains hanging from the ceiling. Bits of tinsel draped along the tops of the partitions. Christmas cards on several desks.

Sandy was deeply unimpressed that this was the second Christmas in three years that he had found himself on duty. And, as she quite rightly pointed out, it was a lousy week to be working. Even most of the local villains, off their trolleys with drink or off their faces with drugs, were in their homes or their lairs.

Christmas was the peak period for sudden deaths and for suicides. It might be a happy few days for those with friends and families, but it was a desperate, wretched time for the lonely, particularly the elderly lonely ones who didn't even have enough money to heat their homes properly. But it was a quiet period for serious crimes – the kind that could get an ambitious young detective sergeant like himself noticed by his peers and give him the chance to show his abilities.

That was about to change.

Very unusually, the phones had been quiet. Normally they rang all around the room constantly.

As the first serials appeared, his internal phone suddenly rang.

'CID,' he answered.

It was a Force Control Room operator, from the centre which handled and graded all enquiries.

'Hi, Roy. Happy Christmas.'

'You too, Doreen,' he said.

'Got a possible misper,' she said. 'Rachael Ryan, twenty-two, left her friends on Christmas Eve at the cab rank on East Street to walk home. She did not show up for Christmas lunch at her parents and did not answer her home phone or mobile. Her parents visited her flat in Eastern Terrace, Kemp Town, at 3 p.m. yesterday and there was no response. They've informed us this is out of character and they are concerned.'

Grace took down the addresses of Rachael Ryan and her parents and told her he would investigate.

The current police policy was to allow several days for a missing person to turn up before assigning any resources, unless they were a minor, an elderly adult or someone identified as being vulnerable. But with today promising to be quiet, he decided he'd rather be out doing something than sitting here on his backside.

The twenty-nine-year-old Detective Sergeant got up and walked along a few rows of desks to one of his colleagues who was in today, DS Norman Potting. Some fifteen years his senior, Potting was an old sweat, a career detective sergeant who had never been promoted, partly because of his politically incorrect attitude, partly because of his chaotic domestic life, and partly because, like many police officers, including Grace's late father, Potting preferred frontline work rather than taking on the bureaucratic responsibilities that came with promotion. Grace was one of the few here who actually liked the man and enjoyed listening to his 'war stories' – as police tales of past incidents were known – because he felt he could learn something from them; and besides, he felt a little sorry for the guy.

The Detective Sergeant was intently pecking at his keyboard with his right index finger. 'Bloody new technology,' he grumbled in his thick Devon burr as Grace's shadow fell over him. A reek of tobacco smoke rose from the man. 'I've had two lessons, still can't make sodding head nor tail of this. What's wrong with the old system we all know?'

'It's called progress,' Grace said.

'Hrrr. Progress like allowing all sorts into the force?'

Ignoring this, Grace replied, 'There's a reported misper that I'm not very happy about. You busy? Or got time to come with me to make some enquiries?'

Potting hauled himself to his feet. 'Anything to break the mahogany, as my old auntie would say,' he replied. 'Have a good Christmas, Roy?'

'Short and sweet. All six hours of it that I spent at home, that is.'

'At least you *have* a home,' Potting said morosely.

'Oh?'

'I'm living in a bedsit. Threw me out, didn't she? Not much fun, wishing your kids a merry Christmas from a payphone in the corridor. Eating an ASDA Christmas Dinner for One in front of the telly.'

'I'm sorry,' Grace replied. He genuinely was.

'Know why women are like hurricanes, Roy?'

Grace shook his head.

'Because when they arrive they're wet and wild. When they leave they take your house and car.'

Grace humoured him with a thin, wintry smile.

'It's all right for you – you're happily married. Good luck to you. But just watch out,' Potting went on. 'Watch out for when they turn. Trust me, this is my second bloody disaster. Should have learned my lesson first time around. Women think coppers are dead sexy until they marry 'em. Then they realize we're not what they thought. You're lucky if yours is different.'

Grace nodded but said nothing. Potting's words were uncomfortably close to the truth. He had never been interested in opera of any kind. But recently Sandy had dragged him to an amateur operatic society performance of *The Pirates of Penzance*. She had nudged him continually during the song 'A Policeman's Lot is not a Happy One'.

Afterwards she had asked him, teasing, if he thought those words were wrong.

He'd replied that yes, they were wrong. He was very happy with his lot.

Later, in bed, she'd whispered to him that perhaps the lyrics needed to be changed. That they should have sung, 'A policeman's *wife's* lot is not a happy one.'

NOW

11

Several of the houses in the residential street outside the hospital had Christmas lights in the windows and wreaths on the front door. They'd be coming down soon for another year, Grace thought a little sadly, slowing as they approached the entrance to the squat slab of stained concrete and garishly curtained windows of Crawley Hospital. He liked the magical spell that the Christmas break cast on the world, even when he had to work through it.

The building had no doubt looked a lot more impressive under the sunny blue sky of the architect's original impression than it did on a wet January morning. Grace thought that the architect had probably failed to take into account the blinds blocking half of its windows, the dozens of cars parked higgledy-piggledy outside, the plethora of signs and the weather stains on the walls.

Glenn Branson normally liked to terrify him by showing off his driving skills, but today he had allowed his colleague to drive here, freeing him to concentrate on giving Roy the full download on his lousy Christmas week. Glenn's marriage, which had hit new lows in the weeks building up to Christmas, had deteriorated even further on Christmas Day itself.

Already livid that his wife, Ari, had changed the locks on their house, his temper had boiled over on Christmas morning when he'd arrived laden with gifts for his two young children and she'd refused to let him in. A massively powerful former nightclub bouncer, Glenn kicked open the front door, to find, as he suspected, her new lover ensconced in *his* house, playing with *his* children, in front of *his* Christmas tree, for God's sake!

She had dialled the nines and he had narrowly escaped being arrested by the Response Team patrol car that had turned up from East Brighton Division – which would have put paid to his career.

'So what would you have done?' Glenn said.

'Probably the same. But that doesn't make it OK.'

'Yeah.' He was quiet for a moment, then said, 'You're right. But when I saw that dickhead personal trainer playing the X-Box with *my* kids, I could have fucking ripped his head off and played basketball with it.'

'You're going to have to keep a lid on it somehow, matey. I don't want you screwing your career up over this.'

Branson just stared through the windscreen at the rain outside. Then he said bleakly, 'What does it matter? Nothing matters any more.'

Roy Grace loved this guy, this big, well-meaning, kind-hearted man-mountain. He'd first encountered him some years back, when Glenn was a freshly promoted detective constable. He had recognized in him so many aspects of himself – drive, ambition. And Glenn had that key element it took to make a good policeman – high emotional intelligence. Since then, Grace had mentored him. But now, with his disintegrating marriage and his failing control of his temper, Glenn was dangerously close to losing the plot.

He was also dangerously close to damaging their deep

friendship. For the past few months Branson had been his lodger, at his home just off the Hove seafront. Grace did not mind about that, as he was now effectively living with Cleo in her town house in the North Laine district of central Brighton. But he did mind Branson's meddling with his precious record collection and the constant criticism of his taste in music.

Such as now.

In the absence of having his own car – his beloved Alfa Romeo, which had been destroyed in a chase some months earlier and was still the subject of an insurance wrangle – Grace was reduced to using pool cars, which were all small Fords or Hyundai Getzs. He had just mastered an iPod gadget that Cleo had given him for Christmas which played his music through any car's radio system and had been showing off to Branson on the way here.

'Who's this?' Branson asked, in a sudden change of focus as the music changed.

'Laura Marling.'

He listened for a moment. 'She's so derivative.'

'Of whom?'

Branson shrugged.

'I like her,' Grace said defiantly.

They listened in silence for a few moments, until he spotted an empty slot and steered into it. 'You're soft in the head for women vocalists,' Branson said. 'That's your problem.'

'I do actually like her. OK?'

'You're sad.'

'Cleo likes her too,' he retorted. 'She gave me this for Christmas. Want me to tell her you think she's sad?'

Branson raised his huge, smooth hands. 'Whoahhhh!'

'Yeah. Whoahhhh!'

'Respect!' Branson said. But his voice was almost quiet and humourless.

All three spaces reserved for the police were taken, but as today was a public holiday there were plenty of empty spots all around. Grace pulled into one, switched off the ignition and they climbed out of the car. Then they hurried through the rain around the side of the hospital.

'Did you and Ari ever argue over music?'

'Why?' Branson asked.

'Just wondering.'

Most visitors to this complex of buildings would not even have noticed the small white sign with blue lettering saying SATURN CENTRE, pointing along a nondescript pathway bordered by the hospital wall on one side and bushes on the other. It looked as if it might be the route to the dustbins.

In fact it housed Sussex's first Sexual Assault Referral Centre. A dedicated unit, recently opened by the Chief Constable, like others around England it showed a marked change in the way rape victims were treated. Grace could remember a time, not so long ago, when traumatized rape victims had to walk through a police station and frequently be interviewed by cynical male officers. All that had now changed and this centre was the latest development.

Here the victims, who were in a deeply vulnerable state, would be seen by trained same-sex officers and psychologists – professionals who would do their very best to comfort them and put them at their ease, while at the same time having to go through the brutal task of establishing the truth.

One of the hardest things facing Sexual Offences

Liaison Officers was the fact that the victims actually had to be treated as crime scenes themselves, their clothes and their bodies potentially containing vital trace evidence. Time, as in all investigations, was crucial. Many rape victims took days, weeks or even years before they went to the police, and many never reported their attacks ever, not wanting to relive their most tormented experience.

*

Branson and Grace hurried past a black wheelie bin, then a row of traffic cones incongruously stacked there, and reached the door. Grace pressed the bell and moments later the door was opened. They were ushered in, and out of the elements, by a woman staff member he knew, but whose name he had momentarily forgotten.

'Happy New Year, Roy!' she said.

'You too!'

He saw her looking at Glenn and desperately racked his brains for her name. Then it came to him!

'Glenn, this is Brenda Keys – Brenda, this is DS Glenn Branson, one of my colleagues in the Major Crime Branch.'

'Nice to meet you, Detective Sergeant,' she said.

Brenda Keys was a trained interviewer who had processed victims in Brighton and other parts of the county before this facility was established. A kind, intelligent-looking woman with short brown hair and large glasses, she was always dressed quietly and conservatively, as she was today, in her black slacks and a grey V-neck over a blouse.

You could tell you were inside one of the modern generation of interview suites with your eyes shut, Grace thought. They all smelt of new carpets and fresh paint and had a deadened, soundproofed atmosphere.

This one was a labyrinth of rooms behind closed pine doors, with a central reception area carpeted in beige. The cream-painted walls were hung with framed, brightly coloured and artily photographed prints of familiar Sussex scenes – beach huts on the Hove promenade, the Jack and Jill windmills at Clayton, Brighton Pier. It all felt well intentioned, but as if someone had tried just a bit too hard to distance the victims who came here from the horrors they had experienced.

They signed themselves in and Brenda Keys brought them up to speed. As she did so, a door opened along the corridor and a heavily built female uniformed constable with spikes of short black hair rising from her head, as if she had stuck her fingers into an electrical socket, ambled towards them with a genial smile

'Constable Rowland, sir,' she said. 'Detective Superintendent Grace?'

'Yes – and this is DS Branson.'

'They're in Interview One – only just started. The SOLO, DC Westmore, is talking to the victim and DS Robertson's observing. Would you like to go into the observation room?'

'Is there room for us both?'

'I'll put another chair in. Can I get you anything to drink?

'I'd murder a coffee,' Grace said. 'Muddy, no sugar.'

Branson asked for a Diet Coke.

They followed the constable down the corridor, past doors marked *Medical Examination Room*, *Meeting Room*, then *Interview Room*.

A short distance along she opened another door with

no sign on it and they went in. The observation room was a small space, with a narrow white worktop on which sat a row of computers. A flat-screen monitor was fixed to the wall, displaying the CCTV feed from the adjoining interview room. The Detective Sergeant who had first attended at the Metropole Hotel, a boyish-looking man in his late twenties with a shaven fuzz of fair hair, was seated at the desk, an open notebook in front of him and a bottle of water with the cap removed. He was wearing an ill-fitting grey suit and a purple tie with a massive knot, and he had the clammy pallor of a man fighting a massive hangover.

Grace introduced himself and Glenn, then they sat down, Grace on a hard secretarial swivel chair which the Constable had wheeled in.

The screen gave a static view of a small, windowless room furnished with a blue settee, a blue armchair and a small round table on which sat a large box of Kleenex. It was carpeted in a cheerless dark grey and the walls were painted a cold off-white. A second camera and a microphone were mounted high up.

The victim, a frightened-looking woman in her thirties, in a white towelling dressing gown with the letters MH monogrammed on the chest, sat, hunched up like a ball on the sofa, arms wrapped around her midriff. She was thin, with an attractive but pale face, and streaked mascara. Her long red hair was in a messy tangle.

Across the table from her sat DC Claire Westmore, the Sexual Offences Liaison Officer. She was mirroring the victim, sitting with the same posture, arms wrapped around her midriff too.

The police had learned, over the years, the most effective ways to obtain information from victims and witnesses during interviews. The first principle concerned dress code. Never wear anything that might distract the subject, such as stripes or vivid colours. DC Westmore was dressed appropriately, in a plain blue open-neck shirt beneath a navy V-neck jumper, black trousers and plain black shoes. Her shoulder-length fair hair was swept back from her face and cinched with a band. A simple silver choker was the only jewellery she was wearing.

The second principle was to put the victim or witness in the dominant position, to relax them, which was why the interviewee – Nicola Taylor – was on the sofa, while the DC was on the single chair.

Mirroring was a classic interview technique. If you mirrored everything that the subject did, sometimes it would put them at ease to such an extent that they began to mirror the interviewer. When that happened, the interviewer then had control and the victim would acquiesce, relating to the interviewer – and, in interview parlance, start to *cough*.

Grace jotted down occasional notes as Westmore, in her gentle Scouse accent, slowly and skilfully attempted to coax a response from the traumatized, silent woman. A high percentage of rape victims suffer immediate post-traumatic stress disorder, their agitated state limiting the time they are able to concentrate and focus. Westmore was intelligently making the best of this by following the guidelines to go to the most recent event first and then work backwards.

Over his years as a detective Grace had learned, from numerous interviewing courses he had attended, something that he was fond of telling team members: there is no such thing as a bad witness – only a bad interviewer.

But this DC seemed to know exactly what she was doing.

'I know this must be very difficult for you to talk about, Nicola,' she said. 'But it would help me to understand what's happened and really help in trying to find out who has done this to you. You don't have to tell me today if you don't want to.'

The woman stared ahead in silence, wringing her hands together, shaking.

Grace felt desperately sorry for her.

The SOLO began wringing her hands too. After some moments, she asked, 'You were at a New Year's Eve dinner at the Metropole with some friends, I understand?'

Silence.

Tears were rolling down the woman's cheeks.

'Is there anything at all you can tell me today?'

She shook her head suddenly.

'OK. That's not a problem,' Claire Westmore said. She sat in silence for a short while, then she asked, 'At this dinner, did you have very much to drink?'

The woman shook her head.

'So you weren't drunk?'

'Why do you think I was drunk?' she snapped back suddenly.

The SOLO smiled. 'It's one of those evenings when we all let our guard down a little. I don't drink very much. But New Year's Eve I tend to get wrecked! It's the one time of year!'

Nicola Taylor looked down at her hands. 'Is that what you think?' she said quietly. 'That I was wrecked?'

'I'm here to help you. I'm not making any assumptions, Nicola.'

'I was stone cold sober,' she said bitterly.

'OK.'

Grace was pleased to see the woman reacting. That was a positive sign.

'I'm not judging you, Nicola. I'd just like to know what happened. I honestly do understand how difficult it is to speak about what you have been through and I want to help you in any way I can. I can only do that if I understand exactly what's happened to you.'

A long silence.

Branson drank some of his Coke. Grace sipped his coffee.

'We can end this chat whenever you want, Nicola. If you would rather we leave it until tomorrow, that's fine. Or the next day. Whatever you feel is best. I just want to help you. That's all I care about.'

Another long silence.

Then Nicola Taylor suddenly blurted out the word, 'Shoes!'

'Shoes?'

She fell silent again.

'Do you like shoes, Nicola?' the SOLO probed. When there was no response she said chattily, 'Shoes are my big weakness. I was in New York before Christmas with my husband. I nearly bought some Fendi boots – they cost eight hundred and fifty dollars!'

'Mine were Marc Jacobs,' Nicola Taylor said, almost whispering.

'Marc Jacobs? I love his shoes!' she replied. 'Were they taken with your clothes?'

Another long silence.

Then the woman said, 'He made me do things with them.'

'What kind of things? Try – try to tell me.'

Nicola Taylor started to cry again. Then, in between her sobs, she began talking in graphic detail, but slowly, with long periods of silence in between, as she tried to compose herself, and sometimes just plain let go, waves of nausea making her retch.

As they listened in the observation room, Glenn Branson turned to his colleague and winced.

Grace acknowledged him, feeling very uncomfortable. But as he listened now, he was thinking hard. Thinking back to that cold-case file on his office floor, which he had read through only very recently. Thinking back to 1997. Recalling dates. A pattern. An MO. Thinking about statements given by victims back then, some of which he had re-read not long ago.

That same wintry gust he had felt earlier was rippling through his veins again.

1997

12

'Thermometer says *tonight*!' Sandy said, with that twinkle in her brilliant blue eyes that got to Roy Grace every time.

They were sitting in front of the television. Chevy Chase's *Christmas Vacation* had become a kind of ritual, a movie they traditionally watched every Boxing Day night. The sheer stupidity of the disasters normally made Roy laugh out aloud. But tonight he was silent.

'Hello?' Sandy said. 'Hello, Detective Sergeant! Anyone home?'

He nodded, crushing out his cigarette in the ashtray. 'I'm sorry.'

'You're not thinking about work, are you, my darling? Not tonight. We didn't have a proper Christmas, so let's at least enjoy what's left of Boxing Day. Let's make something special out of it.'

'I know,' Roy said. 'It's just—'

'It's always, *It's just . . .*' she said.

'I'm sorry. I had to deal with a family who didn't have a Christmas or a Boxing Day celebration, OK? Their daughter left her friends early on Christmas morning and never arrived home. Her parents are frantic. I – I have to do what I can for them. For her.'

'So? She's probably busy shagging some bloke she met in a club.'

'No. Not her pattern.'

'Oh, sod it, Detective Sergeant Grace! You told me yourself about the number of people who get reported missing by loved ones every year. Around two hundred and thirty thousand in the UK alone, you said, and most of them turn up within thirty days!'

'And eleven thousand, five hundred don't.'

'So?'

'I have a feeling about this one.'

'Copper's nose?'

'Uh-huh.'

Sandy stroked his nose. 'I love yours, Copper!' She kissed it. 'We have to make love tonight. I checked my temperature and it seems like I might be ovulating.'

Roy Grace grinned and stared into her eyes. When colleagues, off duty, got wrecked in the bar upstairs at Brighton nick or out in pubs, and talk turned, as it always did among men, to football – something in which he had little interest – or to birds, the girls got divided fifty-fifty into those that blokes fancied because of their tits and those that blokes fancied because of their legs. But Roy Grace could honestly say that the first thing he had fancied about Sandy was her mesmerizing blue eyes.

He remembered the first time they met. It was a few days after Easter and his father had just been diagnosed with terminal bowel cancer. His mother had just been diagnosed with secondaries from breast cancer. He was a probationary police officer and feeling about as low as it was possible to feel. Some colleagues had encouraged him to join them for an evening at the dogs.

With little enthusiasm he'd turned up to the Brighton and Hove greyhound stadium and found himself seated across from a beautiful, bubbly young woman whose name he failed to clock. After some minutes busily chatting to a guy sitting beside her, she had leaned across the table to Grace and said, 'I've been given a tip! Always bet on any dog that does its business before it races!'

'You mean watch and see if it has a crap?'

'Very sharp,' she'd said. 'You must be a detective!'

'No,' he'd replied, 'not yet. But I'd like to be one day.'

So, while eating his prawn cocktail, he'd carefully watched the dogs for the first race being paraded out towards the starting gate. No. 5 had stopped for a serious dump. When the woman from the Tote had come round, the girl had bet a fiver on it and, to show off, he'd bet a tenner on it that he could ill afford to lose. The dog had romped home last by about twelve lengths.

On their first date, three nights later, he had kissed her in the darkness to the sound of the echoing roar of the sea beneath Brighton's Palace Pier. 'You owe me a tenner,' he'd then said.

'I think I got a bargain!' she replied, fumbling in her handbag, pulling out a banknote and dropping it down the inside of his shirt.

*

He looked at Sandy now, in front of the television. She was even more beautiful than when they had first met. He loved her face, the smells of her body and of her hair; he loved her humour, her intelligence. And he loved the way she took all life in her stride. Sure, she had been angry that he'd been on duty over Christmas, but she understood because she wanted him to succeed.

That was his dream. Their dream.

Then the phone rang.

Sandy answered it, said coldly, 'Yes he is,' and handed the receiver to Roy.

He listened, jotted down an address on the back of a Christmas card, then said, 'I'll be there in ten minutes.'

Sandy glared at him and shook a cigarette out of the packet. Chevy Chase continued his antics on the screen.

'It's *Boxing Night*, for Christ's sake!' she said, reaching for the lighter. 'You don't make it easy for me to quit, do you?'

'I'll be back as quickly as I can. I have to go and see this witness – a man who claims he saw a man pushing a woman into a van in the early hours.'

'Why can't you see him tomorrow?' she demanded petulantly.

'Because this girl's life may be at risk, OK?'

She gave him a wry smile. 'Off you go, Detective Sergeant Grace. Go and save the sodding world.'

NOW

13

'You seem very distracted tonight. Are you OK, my love?'
Cleo said.

Roy Grace was sitting on one of the huge red sofas in
the living room of her town house in a converted ware-
house development, and Humphrey, getting larger and
heavier by the day, was sitting on him. The black puppy,
nestled comfortably in his lap, was pulling surreptitiously
at the strands of wool of his baggy jumper as if his game
plan was to unravel it entirely before his master noticed.
The plan was working, because Roy was so engrossed in
the pages of case-file notes on *Operation Houdini* he was
reading that he had not noticed what the dog was doing.

The first reported sexual assault in *Operation Houdini*
had been on 15 October 1997. It was a botched attack on
a young woman late one evening in a twitten – a narrow
alleyway – in the North Laine district of Brighton. A man
walking his dog had come to her rescue before her assail-
ant had removed her panties, but he had run off with one
of her shoes. The next was, unfortunately, more success-
ful. A woman who had attended a Halloween ball at the
Grand Hotel at the end of the month had been seized in
the corridor of the hotel by a man dressed as a woman
and was not found by hotel staff until the morning, bound
and gagged.

Cleo, curled up on the sofa opposite him, wrapped in a camel poncho over woollen black leggings, was reading a tome on the ancient Greeks for her Open University philosophy degree studies. Pages of her typed and hand-written notes, all plastered with yellow Post-its, were spread out around her. Her long blonde hair tumbled across her face and every few minutes she would sweep it back with her hand. Grace always loved watching her do that.

A Ruarri Joseph CD was playing on the hi-fi and on the muted television screen Sean Connery, in *Thunderball*, held a beautiful woman in an urgent clinch. During the past week, since Christmas, Cleo had developed a craving for king prawn kormas and they were waiting for the delivery of tonight's meal – their fourth curry in five days. Grace didn't mind, but tonight he was giving his system a rest with some plain tandoori chicken.

Also on the table sat one of Grace's Christmas presents to Cleo, a big new goldfish bowl, replacing the one that had been smashed by an intruder the previous year. Its incumbent, which she had named Fish-2, was busily exploring its environment of weed and a miniature submerged Greek temple in sharp, nervy darts. Next to it was a stack of three books that had been Glenn Branson's Christmas present to him. *Bloke's 100 Top Tips for Surviving Pregnancy, The Expectant Father* and *You're Pregnant Too, Mate!*

'Yup, I'm fine,' he said, looking up with a smile.

Cleo smiled back and he felt a sudden rush of such intense happiness and serenity that he wished he could just stop the clock now and freeze time. Make this moment last forever.

'And I'd rather share your company,' Ruarri Joseph was singing to his acoustic guitar, and yes, Grace thought,

I'd rather share your company, my darling Cleo, than anyone else's on this planet.

He wanted to stay here, on this sofa, in this room, staring longingly at this woman he loved so deeply, who was carrying their child, and never, ever leave it.

'It's New Year's Day,' Cleo said, raising her glass of water and taking a tiny sip. 'I think you should stop working now and relax! We'll all be back in the fray on Monday.'

'Right, like the example you're setting, working on your degree. Is that relaxing?'

'Yes, it is! I love doing this. It's not work for me. What you're doing *is* work.'

'Someone should tell criminals they're not permitted to offend during public holidays,' he said with a grin.

'Yep, and someone should tell old people they shouldn't die over the Christmas break. It's very antisocial! Morticians are entitled to holidays too!'

'How many today?'

'Five,' she said. 'Poor sods. Well, actually three of them were yesterday.'

'So they had the decency to wait for Christmas.'

'But couldn't face the prospect of another year.'

'I hope I never get like that,' he said. 'To the point where I can't face the prospect of another year.'

'Did you ever read Ernest Hemingway?' she asked.

Grace shook his head, acutely aware of how ignorant he was compared to Cleo. He'd read so little in his life.

'He's one of my favourite writers. I'm going to make you read him one day! He wrote, "The world breaks everyone and afterward many are strong at the broken places." That's you. You're stronger, aren't you?'

'I hope so – but I sometimes wonder.'

'You have to be stronger than ever now, Detective Superintendent.' She patted her stomach. 'There are two of us who need you.'

'And all the dead people who need you!' he retorted.

'And the dead who need you too.'

That was true, he thought ruefully, glancing at the file again. All those blue boxes and green crates on his office floor. Most of them representing victims who were waiting from beyond the grave for him to bring their assailants to justice.

Would today's rape victim, Nicola Taylor, get to see the man who did this brought to justice? Or would she end up one day as just a name on a plastic tag on one of those cold-case files?

'I'm reading about a Greek statesman called Pericles,' she said. 'He wasn't really a philosopher, but he said something very true. "What you leave behind is not what is engraved in stone monuments, but what is woven into the lives of others." That's one of the many reasons I love you, Detective Superintendent Grace. You're going to leave good things woven into the lives of others.'

'I try,' he said, and looked back down at the files on the Shoe Man.

'You poor love, your mind really is somewhere else tonight.'

He shrugged. 'I'm sorry. I hate rapists. It was pretty harrowing today up in Crawley.'

'You haven't really talked about it.'

'Do you want to hear about it?'

'Yes, I do. I really do want to hear about it. I want to know everything you learn about the world that our child is going to be born into. What did this man do to her?'

Grace picked up his bottle of Peroni from the floor,

took a long pull on it, draining it, and could have done with another. But instead he put it down and thought back to this morning.

'He made her masturbate with the heel of her shoe. It was some expensive designer shoe. Marc Joseph or something.'

'Marc Jacobs?' she asked.

He nodded. 'Yes. That was the name. Are they expensive?'

'One of the top designers. He made her masturbate? You mean using the heel like a dildo?'

'Yes. So, do you know much about shoes?' he asked, a little surprised.

He loved the way Cleo dressed, but when they were out together she rarely looked in shoe-shop or fashion-shop windows. Whereas Sandy used to all the time, sometimes driving him to distraction.

'Roy, darling, *all* women *know* about shoes! They're part of a woman's femininity. When a woman puts on a great pair of shoes, she feels sexy! So, he just watched her doing this to herself?'

'Six-inch stilettos, she said,' he replied. 'He made her push the heel all the way in repeatedly, while he touched himself.'

'That's horrible. Sick bastard.'

'It gets worse.'

'Tell me.'

'He made her turn over, face down, then he pushed the heel right up her back passage. OK? Enough?'

'So he didn't actually rape her? In the sense that I understand it?'

'Yes, he did, but that was later. And he had problems getting an erection.'

After some moments' silent thought she said, 'Why, Roy? What makes someone like that?'

He shrugged. 'I talked to a psychologist this afternoon. But he didn't tell me anything I didn't already know. Stranger rape – which this one looks like – is rarely about sex. It's more about hatred of women and power over them.'

'Do you think there's a connection between whoever did this and your file on the Shoe Man?'

'That's why I'm reading it. Could be coincidence. Or a copycat. Or the original rapist reoffending.'

'So what do you think?'

'The Shoe Man did the same things to some of his victims. He also had problems getting an erection. And he always took one of his victim's shoes.'

'This woman today – did he take one of her shoes?'

'He took both, and all her clothes. And from what the victim has said so far, it sounds like he might be a transvestite.'

'So there's a slight difference.'

'Yes.'

'What's your instinct? What does your copper's nose tell you?'

'Not to jump to conclusions. But . . .' He fell silent.

'But?'

He stared at the file.

14

Ask people to recall where they were and what they were doing at the moment – *the exact moment* – they heard about the planes striking the Twin Towers on 9/11, or about Princess Diana's death, or that John Lennon had been shot or, if they are old enough, that John F. Kennedy had been assassinated in Dallas, Texas, and most will be able to tell you, with crystal clarity.

Roxy Pearce was different. The defining moments in her life came on those days when she finally bought the shoes that she had been lusting after. She could tell you exactly what was happening in the world on the day she acquired her first Christian Louboutins. Her first Ferragamos. Her first Manolo Blahniks.

But today, all those gleaming leather treasures languishing in her cupboards paled into insignificance as she strutted around the grey-carpeted floor of Brighton's Ritzy Shoes emporium.

'Oh yes! Oh, God, yes!'

She looked at her ankles. Pale, slightly blue from the veins beneath the surface, they were too thin and bony. Never before her best feature, today they were transformed. They were, she had to admit, one pair of drop-dead-beautiful ankles. The thin black straps wrapped themselves like sensuous, living, passionate fronds around the white skin either side of the protruding bone.

She was sex on legs!

She stared in the mirror. Sex on legs stared back at her! Sleek black hair, a great figure, she definitely looked a lot younger than a woman three months short of her thirty-seventh birthday.

'What do you think?' she said to the assistant, staring at her reflection again. At the tall stilettos, the curved sole, the magical black gloss of the leather.

'They were made for you!' the confident thirty-year-old salesgirl said. 'They were just absolutely made for you!'

'I think so!' Roxy squealed. 'You think so too?'

She was so excited that several people in the shop glanced round at her. Brighton was busy this first Saturday morning of the new year. The bargain hunters were out in force as the Christmas sales headed into their second week and some prices came down even more.

One customer in the shop did not glance round. Anyone looking would have seen an elegantly dressed middle-aged woman with a long dark coat over a high roll-neck jumper and expensive-looking high-heeled boots. Only if they peeled back the top of the roll-neck would they have spotted the giveaway Adam's apple.

The man in drag did not glance round, because he was already looking at Roxy. He had been observing her discreetly from the moment she'd asked to try on those shoes.

'Jimmy Choo just has it!' the assistant said. 'He really knows what works.'

'And you really do think these look good on me? They're not very easy to walk in.'

Roxy was nervous. Well, £485 was a lot of money, particularly at the moment, when her husband's software solutions business was in near meltdown and her own small PR agency was barely washing its face.

But she had to have them!

OK, £485 could buy an awful lot of things.

But none would give her the pleasure of these shoes!

She wanted to show them off to her friends. But more than anything she wanted to wear them for Iannis, her crazily sexy lover of just six weeks. OK, not the first lover she'd had in twelve years of marriage, but the best, oh yes. Oh yes!

Just thinking about him brought a big grin to her face. Then a twist of pain in her heart. She had been through it all twice before and knew she should have learned from experience. Christmas was the worst time for lovers having an affair. It was when workplaces shut down and most people got drawn into family stuff. Although they had no kids of their own – neither she nor Dermot had ever wanted any – she'd been forced to accompany her husband to his family in Londonderry for four whole days over Christmas, and then another four, following straight on, with her parents – *the ageing Ps*, as Dermot called them – in the remote wilds of Norfolk.

On the one day they had planned to meet, before the end of the year, Iannis, who owned two Greek restaurants in Brighton and a couple more in Worthing and East-bourne, had had to fly unexpectedly to Athens to visit his father, who'd had a heart attack.

This afternoon they were going to be seeing each other for the first time since the day before Christmas Eve – and it felt more like a month. Two months. A year. Forever! She longed for him. Yearned for him. Craved him.

And, she had now decided, she wanted to wear these shoes for him!

Iannis was into feet. He loved to take off her shoes, breathe in their scents, smell them all over, then inhale, as if he was tasting a fine wine in front of a proud sommelier. Maybe he'd like her to keep her Jimmy Choos on today! The thought was turning her on so much she was feeling dangerously moist.

'You know the great thing with these shoes is you can dress up or down with them,' the assistant continued. 'They look terrific with your jeans.'

'You think so?'

It was a stupid question. Of *course* the assistant thought so. She was going to say they looked good on her if she came in wrapped in a bin liner full of sardine heads.

Roxy was wearing these leg-hugging, ripped DKNYs because Iannis said she had a great arse in jeans. He liked to unzip them and pull them slowly down, telling her in that rich, deep accent of his that it was like unpeeling beautiful ripe fruit. She liked all the romantic tosh he spoke. Dermot never did anything sexy these days. His idea of foreplay was to walk across the bedroom in his socks and Y-fronts and fart twice.

'I do!' the assistant said earnestly.

'I don't suppose there's any discount on these? Not part of the sale or anything?'

'I'm afraid not, no. I'm sorry. They are new stock, only just in.'

'That's my luck!'

'Would you like to see the handbag that goes with them?'

'I'd better not,' she said. 'I daren't.'

But the assistant showed it to her anyway. And it was

gorgeous. Roxy rapidly reached the conclusion that, having seen the two together, the shoes now looked quite naked without the bag. If she didn't buy that bag, she would regret it later, she knew.

Because the shop was so busy, and because her thoughts were totally on how she could keep the receipt concealed from Dermot, she took no notice at all of any of the other customers, including the one in the roll-neck jumper, who was examining a pair of shoes a short distance behind her. Roxy was thinking she'd have to grab her credit card statement when it came in and burn it. And anyway, it was her own money, wasn't it?

'Are you on our mailing list, madam?' the assistant asked.

'Yes.'

'If you could let me have your postcode I'll bring your details up.'

She gave it to the assistant, who tapped it into the computer beside the till.

Behind Roxy, the man jotted something down quickly on a small electronic notepad. Moments later her address appeared. But the man didn't need to read the screen.

'Mrs Pearce, 76 Droveway Avenue?'

'That's right,' Roxy said.

'Right. That's a total of one thousand, one hundred and twenty-three pounds. How would you like to pay?'

Roxy handed over her credit card.

The man in drag slipped out of the shop, swinging his hips. He actually had developed, with much practice, quite a sexy walk, he thought. He was absorbed into the teeming mass of shoppers in the Brighton Lanes within moments, his heels clicking on the dry, cold pavement.

15

It was always quiet in these anticlimactic days following New Year's Eve. It was the end of the holidays, people were back to work, and more broke this year than usual. It was hardly surprising, thought PC Ian Upperton of the Brighton and Hove Road Policing Unit, that there weren't many people out and about on this freezing January Saturday afternoon, despite the sales being in full swing.

His colleague, PC Tony Omotoso, was behind the wheel of the BMW estate, heading south in the falling darkness, past Rottingdean pond and then on down towards the seafront, where he turned right at the lights. The south-westerly wind, straight off the Channel, buffeted the car. It was 4.30 p.m. One final cruise along above the cliffs, past St Dunstan's home for blind servicemen and Roedean school for posh girls, then along the seafront and back up to their base for a cup of tea, and wait there on the radio for the remainder of their shift.

There were some days, Upperton felt, when you could almost feel electricity in the air and you knew things were going to happen. But he felt nothing this afternoon. He looked forward to getting home, seeing his wife and kids, taking the dogs for a walk, then a quiet evening in front of the telly. And to the next three days, which he had off.

As they drove up the hill, where the 30-mph limit

gave way to a 50-mph one, a little Mazda MX-2 sports car roared past them in the outside lane, way too fast.

'Is the driver effing blind?' Tony Omotoso said.

Drivers usually braked when they saw a police patrol car, and not many dared to pass a police car, even when it was being driven at several miles per hour under the limit. The Mazda driver had either stolen it, was a head-case or had simply not seen them. It was pretty hard not to see them, even in the gloom, with the luminous Battenberg markings and POLICE in high-visibility lettering covering every panel of the car.

The tail lights were rapidly pulling away into the distance.

Omotoso floored the accelerator. Upperton leaned forward, switched on the flashing lights, siren and onboard speed camera, then tugged on his shoulder strap, to take the slack out of it. His colleague's pursuit-driving always made him nervous.

They caught up with the Mazda rapidly, clocking it at 75 mph before it slowed going down the dip towards the roundabout. Then, to their astonishment, it accelerated away again, hard, as it left the roundabout. The ANPR fixed to the dashboard, which automatically read all number plates in front of it and fed the information into the government-licensing computer, remained silent, indicating that the car had not been reported stolen and that its paperwork was in order.

This time the speed camera dial showed 81 mph.

'Time for a chat,' said Upperton.

Omotoso accelerated directly behind the Mazda, flashing his headlights. This was a moment when they always wondered whether a car would try to do a runner, or be sensible and stop.

Brake lights came on sharply. The left-hand indicator began winking, then the car pulled over. From the silhouette they could see through the rear window, there appeared to be just one occupant, a female driver. She was looking over her shoulder anxiously at them.

Upperton switched the siren off, left the blue lights flashing and switched on the emergency red hazard flashers. Then he got out of the car and, pushing against the wind, walked around to the driver's door, keeping a wary eye out for cars coming along the road behind them.

The woman wound down the window part-way and peered out at him nervously. She was in her early forties, he guessed, with a mass of frizzed hair around a rather severe, but not unattractive, face. Her lipstick seemed to have been put on clumsily and her mascara had run, as if she had been crying.

'I'm sorry, Officer,' she said, her voice sounding edgy and slurred. 'I think I might have been going a bit fast.'

Upperton knelt to get as close to her face as possible, in order to smell her breath. But he didn't need to. If he'd lit a match at this moment, flames would have probably shot out of her mouth. There was also a strong smell of cigarette smoke in the car.

'Got bad eyesight, have you, madam?'

'No – er – no. I had my eyes tested quite recently. My vision's near perfect.'

'So you always overtake police cars at high speed, do you?'

'Oh, bugger, did I? I didn't see you! I'm sorry. I've just had a row with my ex-husband – we've got a business together, you see. And I—'

'Have you been drinking, madam?'

'Just a glass of wine – at lunchtime. Just one small glass.'

It smelt more like she'd drunk an entire bottle of brandy to him.

'Could you switch your engine off, madam, and step out of the car. I'm going to ask you to take a breath test.'

'You're not going to book me, are you, Officer?' She slurred even more than before now. 'You see – I need the car for my business. I've already got some points on my licence.'

No surprise there, he thought.

She unclipped her seat belt, then clambered out. Upperton had to put his arm out to stop her staggering further into the road. It was unnecessary to get her to blow into the machine, he thought. All he needed to do was hold it within a twenty-yard radius and the reading would go off the scale.

1979

16

'Johnny!' his mother bellowed from her bedroom. 'Shut up! Shut that noise up! Do you hear me?'

Standing on the chair in his bedroom, he removed another of the nails clenched between his lips, held it against the wall and struck it with his claw hammer. *Blam! Blam! Blam!*

'JOHNNY, BLOODY WELL STOP THAT NOISE! NOW! STOP IT!' She was screaming now.

Lying neatly on the floor, exactly the same distance apart, were each of his prized collection of high-flush lavatory chains. All fifteen of them. He'd found them in skips around Brighton – well, all except two, which he had stolen from toilets.

He took another nail from his mouth. Lined it up. Began hammering.

His mother ran into the room, reeking of Shalimar perfume. She wore a black silk camisole, fish-net stockings with suspenders not yet fastened, harsh make-up and a wig of blonde ringlets that was slightly askew. She was standing on one black stiletto-heeled shoe and holding the other in her hand, raised, like a weapon.

'DO YOU HEAR ME?'

Ignoring her, he began hammering.

'ARE YOU BLEEDIN' DEAF? JOHNNY?'

'I'm not Johnny,' he mumbled through the nails, continuing to hammer. 'I am *Yac*. I have to hang my chains up.'

Holding the shoe by the toe, she slammed the stiletto into his thigh. With a yelp like a whipped dog, he fell sideways and crashed to the floor. Instantly she was kneeling over him, raining down blows on him with the sharp tip of the heel.

'You are not Yac, you are Johnny! Understand? Johnny Kerridge.'

She hit him again, then again. And again.

'I am Yac! The doctor said so!'

'You stupid boy! You've driven your father away and now you're driving me crazy. The doctor did not say so!'

'The doctor wrote Yac!'

'The doctor wrote *YAC – Young Autistic Child* – on his sodding notes! That's what you are. Young, *useless*, sodding pathetic autistic child! You are Johnny Kerridge. Got it?'

'I am Yac!'

He curled himself up in a protective ball as she brandished the shoe. His cheek was bleeding from where she had struck him. He breathed in her dense, heady perfume. She had a big bottle on her dressing table and she once told him it was the classiest perfume a woman could wear, and that he should appreciate he had such a high-class mother. But she wasn't being classy now.

Just as she was about to strike him again the front doorbell rang.

'Oh shit!' she said. 'See what you've done? You've made me late, you stupid child!' She hit him again on the thigh, so hard it punctured his thin denim trousers. 'Shit, shit, shit!'

She ran out of the room, shouting, 'Go and let him in. Make him wait downstairs!'

She slammed her bedroom door.

Yac picked himself up, painfully, from the floor and limped out of his room. He walked slowly, deliberately, unhurriedly down the staircase of their terraced two-up, two-down on the edge of the Whitehawk housing estate. As he reached the bottom step, the doorbell rang again.

His mother shouted, 'Open the door! Let him in! I don't want him going away. We need it!'

With blood running down his face, seeping through his T-shirt in several places and through his trousers, Yac grumpily limped up to the front door and reluctantly pulled it open.

A plump, perspiring man in an ill-fitting grey suit stood there, looking awkward. Yac stared at him. The man stared back and his face reddened. Yac recognized him. He'd been here before, several times.

He turned and shouted back up the stairs, 'Mum! It's that smelly man you don't like who's come to fuck you!'

1997

17

Rachael was shivering. A deep, dark terror swirled inside her. She was so cold it was hard to think. Her mouth was parched and she was starving. Desperate for water and for food. She had no idea what the time was: it was pitch black in here, so she could not see her watch, could not tell whether it was night or day outside.

Had he left her here to die or was he coming back? She had to get away. Somehow.

She strained her ears for traffic noise that might give her a clue as to whether it was day or night, or for the caw of a gull that might tell her if she was still near the sea. But all she could hear was the occasional, very faint wail of a siren. Each time her hopes rose. Were the police out looking for her?

They were, weren't they?

Surely her parents would have reported her missing? They would have told the police that she hadn't turned up for Christmas lunch. They'd be worried. She knew them, knew they would have gone to her flat to find her. She wasn't even sure what day it was now. Boxing Day? The day after?

Her shivering was getting worse, the cold seeping deep inside her bones. It was all right, though, she thought, so long as she was shivering. Four years ago, when she had left school, she'd worked for a season as a washer-upper in a ski resort in France. A Japanese skier had taken the last chairlift up one afternoon in a snowstorm. There was a mistake by the lift attendants, who thought the last person had already gone up and been counted at the top, so they turned the lift off. In the morning, when they switched it back on, he arrived at the top, covered in ice, dead, stark naked, with a big smile on his face.

No one could understand why he was naked or smiling. Then a local ski instructor she'd had a brief fling with explained to her that during the last stages of hypothermia people hallucinated that they were too hot and would start removing their clothes.

She knew that somehow she had to keep warm, had to ward off hypothermia. So she did the only movements she could, rolling, left and then right on the hessian matting. Rolling. Rolling. Totally disoriented by the darkness, there were moments when she lay on her side and toppled on to her face and others when she fell on to her back.

She had to get out. Somehow. Had to. How? Oh, God, how?

She couldn't move her hands or her feet. She couldn't shout. Her naked body was covered in goose pimples so sharp they felt like millions of needle points piercing her flesh.

Oh, please God, help me.

She rolled again and crashed into the side of the van. Something fell over with a loud, echoing clangggggg.

Then she heard a gurgling noise.

Smelt something foul, rancid. Diesel oil, she realized. Gurgling. Glug . . . glug . . . glug.

She rolled again. And again. Then her face pressed into it, the sticky, stinking stuff, stinging her eyes, making her cry even more.

But, she figured, it must be coming from a can!

If it was pouring out, then the top had come off. The neck of the can would be round and thin! She rolled again and something moved through the stinking wet slimy stuff, clattering, scraping.

Clatter . . . clatter . . . clangggg.

She trapped it against the side of the van. Wriggled around it, felt it move, made it turn, forced it to turn until it was square on, spout outwards. Then she pressed against the sharpness of the neck. Felt its rough edge cutting into her. She wormed her body against it, jigging, slowly, forcefully, then felt it spin away from her.

Don't do this to me!

She wriggled and twisted until the can moved again, until she felt the rough neck of the spout again, then she pressed against it, gently at first, then applying more pressure, until she had it wedged firmly. Now she moved slowly, rubbing right, left, right, left, for an eternity at whatever was binding her wrists. Suddenly, the grip around them slackened, just a fraction.

But enough to give her hope.

She kept on rubbing, twisting, rubbing. Breathing in and out through her nose. Breathing in the noxious, dizzying stink of the diesel oil. Her face, her hair, her whole body soaked in the stuff.

The grip on her wrists slackened a tiny bit further.

Then she heard a sudden loud metallic clang and she froze. *No, please no.* It sounded like the garage door opening. She rolled on to her back and held her breath. Moments later she heard the rear doors of the van opening. A flashlight beam suddenly blinded her. She blinked into it. Felt his stare. Lay in frozen terror wondering what he was going to do.

He just seemed to be standing in silence. She heard heavy breathing. Not her own. She tried to cry out, but no sound came.

Then the light went out.

She heard the van doors clang shut. Another loud clang, like the garage door closing.

Then silence.

She listened, unsure whether he was still in here. She listened for a long time before she began to rub against the neck once more. She could feel it cutting into her flesh, but she didn't care. Each time she rubbed now, she was certain the bonds holding her wrists were slackening more and more.

NOW

18

Garry Starling and his wife, Denise, had gone to the China Garden restaurant most Saturday nights for the past twelve years. They favoured the table just up the steps, to the right of the main part of the restaurant, the table where Garry had proposed to Denise almost twelve years ago.

Separated from the rest of the room by a railing, it had a degree of privacy, and with Denise's increasingly heavy drinking, they could sit here without the rest of the diners being privy to her frequent tirades – mostly against him.

She was usually drunk before they had even left home, particularly since the smoking ban, when she would quaff the best part of a bottle of white wine and smoke several cigarettes, despite his nagging her for years to quit, before tottering out to the waiting taxi. Then, at the restaurant, Denise would polish off one and often two Cosmopolitans in the bar area before they got to their table.

At which point she usually kicked off and began complaining about defects she perceived in her husband. Sometimes the same old ones, sometimes new ones. It was water off a duck's back to Garry, who remained placid and unemotional, which usually wound her up even

109

more. He was a control freak, she told her girlfriends. As well as being a sodding fitness freak.

The couple they normally came here with, Maurice and Ulla Stein, were heavy drinkers too and, long used to Denise's tirades, they tended to humour her. Besides, there were plenty of undercurrents in their own relationship.

Tonight, the first Saturday of the New Year, Denise, Maurice and Ulla were in particularly heavy drinking mode. Their hangovers from New Year's Eve, which they had celebrated together at the Metropole Hotel, were now distant memories. But they were also a little tired and Denise was in an uncharacteristically subdued mood. She was even drinking a little water – which, normally, she rarely touched.

The third bottle of Sauvignon Blanc had just been poured. As she picked her glass up, Denise watched Garry, who had stepped out to take a phone call, walking back towards them and slipping his phone into his top pocket.

He had a slight frame and a sly, studious face topped with short, tidy black hair that was thinning and turning grey. His big, round, staring eyes, set beneath arched eyebrows, had earned him the nickname *Owl* at school. Now, in middle age, wearing small, rimless glasses, a neat suit over a neat shirt and sober tie, he had the air of a scientist quietly observing the world in front of him with a look of quizzical disdain, as if it was an experiment he had created in his laboratory with which he was not entirely happy.

In contrast to her husband, Denise, who had been a slender blonde with an hourglass figure when they had first met, had ballooned recently. She was still blonde, thanks to her colourist, but years of heavy drinking had taken their toll. With her clothes off, in Garry's opinion – which he had never actually voiced to her because he was too reserved – she had the body of a flabby pig.

'Lizzie – my sister,' Garry announced apologetically, sitting down again. 'She's been at the police station for the last few hours – she's been done for drink-driving. I was just checking that she's seen a solicitor and that she's getting a lift home.'

'Lizzie? Stupid woman, what's she gone and done that for?' said Denise.

'Oh, sure,' Garry said. 'She did it deliberately, right? Give her a break, for God's sake! She's been through the marriage from hell and now she's going through the divorce from hell from that bastard.'

'Poor thing,' said Ulla.

'She's still way over the limit. They won't let her drive home. I wonder if I should go and—'

'Don't you dare!' Denise said. 'You've been drinking too.'

'You have to be so damned careful, drinking and driving now,' Maurice slurred. 'I just won't do it. I'm afraid I don't have much sympathy with people who get caught.' Then, seeing his friend's darkening expression, he said, 'Of course, except for Lizzie.' He smiled awkwardly.

Maurice had made gazillions out of building sheltered homes for the aged. His Swedish wife, Ulla, had become heavily involved in animal rights in recent years and not long ago had led a blockade of Shoreham Harbour – Brighton's main harbour – to stop what she considered to be the inhumane way that sheep were exported. Garry had noticed, particularly in the past couple of years, that the two of them had less and less in common.

Garry had been Maurice's best man. He'd secretly lusted after Ulla in those days. She had been the classic flaxen-haired, leggy Swedish blonde. In fact he'd continued to lust after her until quite recently, when she had begun to let her looks go. She too had put on weight, and had taken to dressing like an Earth Mother, in shapeless smocks, sandals and hippy jewellery. Her hair was wild and she seemed to apply make-up as if it was warpaint.

'Do you know about the Coolidge effect?' Garry said.

'What's that?' Maurice asked.

'When Calvin Coolidge was president of the United States he and his wife were being taken around a chicken farm. The farmer got embarrassed when a rooster began shagging a hen right in front of Mrs Coolidge. When he apologized the President's wife asked him how many times a day the rooster did this and the farmer replied that it was dozens. She turned to him and whispered, "Would you mind telling my husband?"'

Garry paused while Maurice and Ulla laughed. Denise, who had heard it before, remained stony-faced.

He continued, 'Then a little later Coolidge asked the farmer more about the rooster. "Tell me, does it always screw the same hen?" The farmer replied, "No, Mr President, always a different one." Coolidge whispered to the man, "Would you mind telling my wife?"'

Maurice and Ulla were still laughing when crispy duck and pancakes arrived.

'I like that one!' Maurice said, then winced as Ulla kicked him under the table.

'A bit close to home for you,' she said acidly.

Maurice had confided to Garry, over the years, about a string off affairs. Ulla had found out about more than one of them.

'At least the rooster has proper sex,' Denise said to her husband. 'Not the weird stuff you get off on.'

Garry's mask smiled implacably at her, humouring her. They sat in awkward silence as the pancakes and spring onions and hoisin sauce appeared, and while the waiter shredded the duck before retreating.

Helping himself to a pancake and rapidly changing the subject, Maurice asked, 'So, how's business looking going into the New Year, Garry? Think people are going to cut down?'

'How would he know?' Denise butted in. 'He's always on the sodding golf course.'

'Of course I am, my darling!' Garry retorted. 'That's where I get my new leads. That's how I built my business. I got the police as customers through playing golf with an officer one day.'

Garry Starling had started in life as an electrician, working for Chubb Alarms, doing installations. Then he had left and taken the gamble of forming his own company, operating at first from a tiny office in central Brighton. His timing had been perfect, as it was just when the security business began to boom.

It was a winning formula. He used his membership of his golf club, of the Round Table and then the Rotary Club to work on everyone he met. Within a few years of opening his doors, he had built up Sussex Security Systems and its sister company, Sussex Remote Monitoring Services, into one of the major security businesses in the Brighton area for home and commercial premises.

Turning back to Maurice, he said, 'Actually, business is OK. We're holding our own. How about you?'

'Booming!' Maurice said. 'Incredible, but it is!' He raised his glass. 'Well, cheers, everyone! Here's to a brilliant year! Never actually got to toast you on New Year's Eve, did we, Denise?'

'Yep, well, sorry about that. Don't know what came over me. Must be the bottle of champagne we had in our room while we were getting changed!'

'That *you* had,' Garry corrected her.

'Poor thing!' Ulla said.

'Still,' Maurice said, 'Garry did his best to make up for you by drinking your share, didn't you, old son?'

Garry smiled. 'I made a sterling effort.'

'He did,' Ulla said. 'He was well away!'

'Hey, did you see the *Argus* today?' Maurice said with an abrupt change of tone.

'No,' Garry said. 'Haven't read it yet. Why?'

'A woman was raped in the hotel! Right while we were partying! Incredible!'

'In the Metropole?' Denise said.

'Yes! In a bedroom. Can you believe it?'

'Great,' she said. 'Terrific to know your caring husband is getting shit-faced while his wife's in bed alone, with a rapist at large.'

'What did it say in the paper?' Garry said, ignoring the comment.

'Not much – just a few lines.'

'Don't look so guilty, darling,' Denise said. 'You couldn't keep it up long enough to rape a flea.'

Maurice busied himself with his chopsticks, lifting strands of duck on to his pancake.'

'Unless of course she was wearing some high – ouch!' she cried out.

Garry had kicked her hard under the table. Silencing her.

1997

19

Rachael was beyond caring about the pain she was in. Her wrists, behind her back, were numb from cold as she sawed, desperately, back and forward against the sharp rim of the fuel can spout. Her bum was numb and a sharp, cramping pain shot down her right leg every few moments. But she ignored it all. Just sawing. Sawing. Sawing in utter desperation.

It was desperation that kept her going. Desperation to get free before he came back. Desperation for water. Desperation for food. Desperation to speak to her parents, to hear their voices, to tell them she was OK. She was crying, shedding tears as she sawed, writhed, wriggled, struggled.

Then, suddenly, to her utter joy, the gap between her wrists widened a fraction. She could feel the bonds slackening. She sawed even harder and now they were becoming slacker by the second.

Then her hands were free.

Almost in disbelief, she moved them further and further apart in the darkness, as if they might suddenly be propelled back together and she would wake to find it was all an illusion.

Her arms ached terribly, but she did not care. Thoughts were racing through her mind.

I'm free.

He's going to come back.

My phone. Where's my phone?

She needed to phone for help. Except, she realized, she did not know where she was. Could they locate you from where your phone was? She didn't think so. Which meant all she could tell them, until she got out of the door and found her bearings, was that she was in a van in a garage somewhere in Brighton or Hove, perhaps.

He might come back at any moment. She needed to free her legs. In the darkness she felt the area around her for her phone, her bag, anything. But there was just slimy, stinky diesel oil. She reached forward, to her ankles, and felt the PVC tape around them, wound so tight it was as hard as a plaster cast. Then she reached up to her face, to see if she could free her mouth and at least shout for help.

But would that be smart?

The tape was just as tight around her mouth. She got a grip on it with difficulty, her fingers slippery with the diesel oil, and tore it off, almost oblivious to the pain in her urgency. Then she tried to get a grip on an edge of the tape around her legs, but her fingers were shaking so much she couldn't find one.

Panic rose.

Must escape.

She tried to get to her feet but, with them bound together, at her first attempt she fell over sideways, striking her forehead hard on something. Moments later she felt liquid trickle down into her eye. Blood, she guessed. Snorting air, she rolled over, sat back against the side of the van and then, trying to grip the floor with her bare feet, began pushing herself up the side. But her feet kept slipping on the damned diesel oil, which had turned the floor into a skating rink.

She scrabbled around until she found the hessian she had been lying on, then put her feet on that and tried again. This time she got more grip. Steadily, she began to rise. She made it all the way up on to her feet, her head striking the roof of the van. Then, totally disoriented by the pitch darkness, she fell sideways with a jarring crash. Something slammed into her eye with the force of a hammer.

NOW

20

There was a ping from the data unit on the dashboard. It startled Yac, who was parked up in a meter bay on the blustery seafront, close to Brighton Pier, drinking a mug of tea. His 11 p.m. mug of tea. He was actually ten minutes late drinking it, because he had been so absorbed reading the newspaper.

He looked at the screen. It was a call from the dispatcher that read:

> China Garden rest. Preston St. 2 Pass. Starling. Dest.
> Roedean Cresc.

The China Garden restaurant was just around the corner. He knew the destination. He could visualize it now, the way he could visualize every street and every dwelling in Brighton and Hove. Roedean Crescent sat high up above the cliffs to the east of the city. All the houses were big, detached and individual, with views out across the Marina and the Channel. Rich people's homes.

The sort of people who could afford nice shoes.

He hit the acknowledge button, confirming that he would make the pick-up, then continued to sip his tea and read the newspaper that had been left in his taxi.

They'd be finishing their meal still. When people ordered a taxi in a restaurant, they expected to wait a

123

while, certainly a quarter of an hour or so on a Saturday night in downtown Brighton. And besides, he could not stop reading and then re-reading the story about the rape of the woman in the Metropole on New Year's Eve. He was riveted.

In his mirrors he could see the twinkly lights of the pier. He knew all about those lights. He used to work on the pier as an electrical engineer, part of the team maintaining and repairing the rides. But he got the sack. It was for the same reason he usually got the sack, because he lost his temper with someone. He hadn't yet lost his temper with anyone in his taxi, but he had once got out and shouted at another driver who'd pulled on to a rank in front of him.

He finished his tea, reluctantly folded the newspaper and put the mug back in the plastic bag alongside his Thermos, then placed the bag on the front seat.

'Vocabulary!' he said aloud. Then he began his checks.

First check the tyres. Next start the engine, then switch on the lights. Never the other way around, because if the battery was low, the lights might drain the energy that the starter motor needed. The owner of the taxi had taught him that. Especially in winter, when there were heavy loads on the battery. It was winter now.

As the engine idled, he checked the fuel gauge. Three-quarters of a tank. Then the oil pressure. Then the temperature gauge. The interior temperature was set to twenty degrees, as he had been instructed. Outside, a digital display told him, it was two degrees Celsius. Cold night.

Uh-huh.

He looked in his mirror, checked his seat belt was on,

indicated, pulled out into the road and drove up to the junction, where the lights were red. When they changed to green he turned right into Preston Street and almost immediately pulled over to the kerb, halting outside the front door of the restaurant.

Two very drunk yobs staggered down the hill towards him, then knocked on his window and asked if he was free to take them to Coldean. He wasn't free, he was waiting for passengers, he told them. As they walked away he wondered whether they had high-flush or low-flush toilets in their homes. It suddenly became very important to him to know. He was about to get out and hurry after them, to ask them, when finally the restaurant door opened.

Two people emerged. A slim man in a dark coat, with a scarf wound around his neck, and a woman who was clinging to him, teetering on her heels; she looked like she'd fall over if she let go. And from the height of the stilettos she was wearing, that would be a long fall.

They were nice heels. Nice shoes.

And he had their address! He always liked to know where women who had nice shoes lived.

Uh-huh.

Yac lowered his window. He didn't want the man knocking on it. He didn't like people knocking on his window.

'Taxi for Starling?' the man said.

'Roedean Crescent?' Yac replied.

'That's us!'

They climbed in the back.

'Sixty-seven Roedean Crescent,' the man said.

'Sixty-seven Roedean Crescent,' Yac repeated. He had been told always to repeat the address clearly.

The car filled with smells of alcohol and perfume. *Shalimar,* he recognized instantly. The perfume of his childhood. The one his mother always wore. Then he turned to the woman.

'Nice shoes,' he said. 'Bruno Magli.'

'Yesh,' she slurred.

'Size four,' he added.

'An expert on shoes, are you?' the woman asked him sourly.

Yac looked at the woman's face in the mirror. She was all uptight. She did not have the face of a woman who had had a good time. Or who was very nice. The man's eyes were closed.

'Shoes,' Yac said. 'Uh-huh.'

1997

21

Saturday 27 December

Rachael woke with a start. Her head was throbbing. Disoriented, for a cruel, fleeting instant she thought she was at home in bed with a mighty hangover. Then she felt the hard metal floor. The hessian matting. Breathed in the stink of diesel oil. And reality gate-crashed her consciousness, kicking her wide awake, sending dark dread spiralling through her.

Her right eye hurt like hell. God, it was agony. How long had she been lying there? He could come back at any moment, and if he did he would see that she'd freed her wrists. He would tape them up again and probably punish her. She had to free her legs and run, now, while she had the chance.

Oh, God. Please help me.

Her lips were so parched they cracked painfully when she tried to move them. Her tongue felt like a ball of fur in her mouth. She listened for an instant, to make sure she was still alone in here. All she could hear was a distant siren and again she wondered, with the faintest uplift of hope, whether that might be the police out looking for her.

But how would they find her in here?

She rolled over until she felt the side of the van, then hauled herself upright and began picking at the tape binding her ankles with her fingernails. Trying to find a join on the slippery, diesel-coated PVC where she could get a grip.

Finally she found one and slowly, carefully, worked it free, until she had a whole wide strip of it. She began to unwind it, jerking it free with a series of sharp ripping noises. Then she winced in pain as the last of it came away from the skin of her ankles.

Grabbing the sodden hessian matting, she got to her feet, stretched and rubbed her legs to get feeling back into them, and stumbled her way, weakly, to the back of the van, crying out in pain, suddenly, as she stood on something sharp in her bare feet – a nut or a bolt. Then she felt her way across the rear doors for the handle. She found a vertical metal rod and ran her hands up it until she reached the handle. She tried to pull it down. Nothing happened. She tried to move it upwards and it would not budge.

It was locked, she realized, her heart sinking.

No. Please, no. Please, no.

She turned and made her way down to the front, her fast, rasping breaths echoing in the metallic cavern of the van's interior. She found the back of the passenger seat, climbed over clumsily, then ran her finger along the sill of the passenger window until she found the lock pin. She gripped it as hard as she could with her slippery fingers and pulled.

To her relief, it popped up easily.

Then she groped for the handle, pulled it and shoved as hard as she could on the door, almost tumbling out on to the concrete floor as it opened, and simultaneously the interior light in the van came on.

Now, in its dim glow, she could see the inside of her prison. But there wasn't much. Just some tools hanging on hooks on the bare wall. A tyre. Grabbing the matting, she hurried along the side of the van towards the garage door, her heart thudding with fear. Suddenly the matting snagged on something and, when she tugged it, there was a loud metallic crash as several objects fell to the floor. She winced but carried on, until she reached the up-and-over door.

There was a two-sided handle in the centre, attached to wires to the mechanism at the top of the door. She tried to turn the handle, first to the right, then to the left, but it would not move. It must be locked from the outside, she realized. With panic increasing inside her, she grabbed the wire and pulled. But her fingers slipped on it, not getting any purchase.

In desperation, Rachael bashed the door with her shoulder, oblivious to the pain. But nothing happened. Whimpering in fear and increasing desperation, she tried again. There was a loud, echoing, metallic booommmmm.

Then another.

And another.

Please, God, somebody must hear this. Please, God. Please.

Then suddenly the door swung up, startling her, almost knocking her over backwards.

In the stark glare of the street lighting outside he stood there, looking at her inquisitively.

She stared back at him in utter terror. Her eyes darted, desperately hoping there might be a passer-by, wondering if she could find the strength to dodge by him and run.

But before she had a chance, he hit her, slamming his fist up beneath her chin, snapping her head back so hard it bashed with a loud crack against the rear of the van.

22

Detective Sergeant Roy Grace was surprised at the number of people packed into the top-floor conference room of Brighton's John Street police station, on this December morning. Despite the cold outside, it was feeling stuffy in here.

Mispers never usually attracted much attention, but this was a quiet time of the year for news. A bird flu epidemic in Hong Kong was one of the few big stories that the national headline writers could use as a shocker in between the Christmas festivities and the upcoming New Year's celebrations.

But the story of the missing young woman, Rachael Ryan, in the wake of the series of rapes that had occurred in the city in the past couple of months, had caught the imagination of the press and media not only locally but nationally. And the *Argus*, of course, was having a field day with Brighton heading into a new year with the Shoe Man still at large.

Newspaper, radio and television reporters occupied all the chairs, and the standing room as well, in the cramped windowless space. Grace sat suited and booted behind a table on the raised platform facing them, next to Chief Inspector Jack Skerritt, in full dress uniform, reeking of pipe tobacco, and the Police Press Officer, Tony Long.

A blue back board carrying the Sussex Police crest stood behind them, next to which was a blow-up photograph of Rachael Ryan, and the table was covered in microphones and tape recorders. Cables led down from the table and across the floor to TV cameras from BBC South Today and Meridian.

With cameras clicking and the constant strobing of flash, Skerritt first introduced his colleagues on the top table, then read in his blunt voice from a prepared statement: 'A twenty-two-year-old resident of Brighton, Ms Rachael Ryan, was reported missing by her family on the evening of Christmas Day, after she failed to turn up for Christmas dinner. No word has been heard from her since. Her parents have informed us that this is completely uncharacteristic behaviour. We are concerned for the safety of this young lady and would ask her, or anyone with information about her, to contact the Incident Room at Brighton police station urgently.'

A tenacious, balding, bespectacled crime reporter from the *Argus*, Phil Mills, dressed in a dark suit, sitting hunched over his notepad, asked the first question. 'Chief Inspector, do Brighton police suspect that the disappearance of this young lady might be connected with *Operation Houdini* and the rapist you have nicknamed the Shoe Man?'

Both Skerritt and Grace reacted to this in silent fury. Although the police knew him as the Shoe Man, his MO had been kept secret from the public, as was usual. This was in order to weed out time-wasters who either confessed to the crime or phoned in purporting to have knowledge of the perpetrator. Grace could see Skerritt wrestling with whether or not to deny the nickname. But he clearly decided that it was out in the open now and they were stuck with it.

'We have no evidence to suggest that,' he replied curtly and dismissively.

Jack Skerritt was a popular and diligent member of the CID. A tough, blunt, no-nonsense copper of nearly twenty years' experience, he had a lean military bearing and a hard face, topped with a slick of brown hair clipped short. Grace liked him, although Skerritt made him a little nervous because he was intensely demanding of his officers and did not treat mistakes lightly. But he had learned a lot working under him. Skerritt was the kind of detective he would like to be himself one day.

A female reporter immediately raised her hand. 'Chief Inspector, can you explain more about what you mean by "Shoe Man"?'

'We believe the offender who has been preying on women in the Brighton area for several months now has an abnormal interest in women's shoes. It is one of a number of lines of enquiry we are pursuing.'

'But you haven't mentioned this publicly before.'

'We haven't, no,' Skerritt replied. 'As I said, it is one line.'

Mills came straight back at him. 'The two friends Rachael was out with on Christmas Eve say that she had a particular obsession with shoes and spent a disproportionate amount of her income on them. I understand that the Shoe Man specifically targets women wearing so-called *designer* shoes.'

'On a night like Christmas Eve, every young lady in Brighton and Hove would have been out in her finery,' Skerritt retorted. 'I repeat that, at this stage of our investigations, we have no evidence to suggest there is any connection to the so-called Shoe Man rapes that have occurred in this vicinity.'

A woman reporter Grace did not recognize raised her hand. Skerritt nodded at her.

'You have assigned the name *Operation Sundown* to Rachael Ryan's disappearance. Creating a formal operation tells us you are taking this more seriously than a normal missing persons inquiry. Is that correct?'

'We take all missing persons inquiries seriously. But we have elevated the status of this particular inquiry to a major incident.'

A local radio reporter raised his hand. 'Chief Inspector, do you have any leads in your search for the Shoe Man?'

'At this stage, as stated, we are pursuing several lines of enquiry. There has been a substantial response from the public and all calls to our Incident Room are being followed up by my team.'

'But you are not close to an arrest?'

'At this stage, that is correct.'

Then a journalist Grace recognized as a stringer for several national papers raised his hand. 'What steps are Brighton police currently taking to find Rachael Ryan?'

'We have forty-two officers deployed in the search for her. They are carrying out house-to-house enquiries in her immediate neighbourhood and along the route we believe she took home. We are searching all garages, warehouses and empty buildings in the vicinity. We have been given particularly good information by a witness who lives near Ms Ryan's residence in Kemp Town, who believes he saw a young lady forced into a white van in the early hours of Christmas morning,' Skerritt said, then studied the journalist for some moments, as if eyeing him up as a suspect, before once more addressing everyone present.

'Unfortunately we have only part of the registration number for this van, which we are working on, but we would urge anyone who thinks they might have seen a white van in the vicinity of Eastern Terrace on Christmas Eve or early Christmas morning to contact us. I will give out the Incident Room phone number at the end of this briefing. We are also anxious to hear from anyone who may have seen this young lady on her way home.' He pointed at the screen behind him, on which were displayed a series of photographs of Rachael Ryan, obtained from her parents.

He paused for a moment and patted his pocket, as if checking his pipe was there, then continued: 'Rachael was wearing a black mid-length coat over a miniskirt, and black patent-leather shoes with high heels. We are trying to trace her precise route home from the time she was last seen, at the taxi rank in East Street, shortly after 2 a.m.'

A diminutive, rotund man, his face largely obscured by an unkempt beard, raised a stubby, chewed finger. 'Chief Inspector, do you actually have any suspects in your Shoe Man enquiries?'

'All I can say at this stage is that we are following some good leads and we are grateful to the public for their response.'

The tubby man got in a second question quickly. 'Your enquiry into Rachael Ryan seems to be a departure from police policy,' he said. 'You don't normally react so quickly to missing-person reports. Would I be correct in assuming you think there may be a link here to the Shoe Man – *Operation Houdini* – even if you are not publicly announcing this?'

'No, you would not be correct,' Skerritt said bluntly.

A woman reporter raised her hand. 'Can you tell us some of the other lines of enquiry you are pursuing on Rachael Ryan, Chief Inspector?'

Skerritt turned to Roy Grace. 'My colleague DS Grace is organizing a reconstruction of the parts of Rachael's journey home that we can be reasonably certain of. This will take place at 7 p.m. on Wednesday.'

'Does this mean you don't believe you are going to find her before then?' Phil Mills asked.

'It means what it says,' retorted Skerritt, who had had several run-ins with this reporter before. Then he nodded at his colleague.

Roy Grace had never spoken at a press briefing before and suddenly he was nervous as all hell. 'We have a WPC who is of similar height and build to Rachael Ryan, who will be dressed in similar clothing and will walk the route we believe Rachael took on the night – or rather early morning – of her disappearance. I would urge all people who might have been out early on Christmas morning to spare the time to retrace their steps and see if it jogs their memories.'

He was perspiring when he finished. Jack Skerritt gave him a brief nod of approval.

These reporters were after a story that would sell their papers, or bring listeners to their radio stations or viewers to their channels. He and Skerritt had a different agenda. To keep the streets of Brighton and Hove safe. Or at least to make the citizens *feel* they were safe in a world that never had been safe and never would be. Not with the kind of human nature he had come to know as a police officer.

There was a predator out on the streets of this town. As a result of the Shoe Man's reign of terror, there was not a woman in Brighton who felt comfortable right now. Not a single woman who did not look over her shoulder, did not ram home her door chain, did not wonder if she might be next.

Roy Grace was not involved in the Shoe Man investigation. But he had an increasingly certain feeling that *Operation Houdini* and the search for Rachael Ryan were one and the same thing.

We're going to get you, Shoe Man, he promised silently.

Whatever it takes.

23

Rachael was in a helicopter with Liam. With his long, spiky hair and his sulky, boyish face he looked so much like Liam Gallagher of Oasis, her favourite group. They were swooping low through the Grand Canyon. Crimson rocks of the cliff face were passing either side, so close, dangerously close. Below them, a long, long way down, the metallic blue water snaked along through jagged grey-brown contours.

She gripped Liam's hand. He gripped hers back. They couldn't speak to each other because they had headsets on, listening to the pilot's commentary. She turned and mouthed *I love you* to him. He grinned, looking funny with the microphone partially obscuring his mouth, and mouthed *I love you* back.

Yesterday they'd walked past a wedding chapel. For a joke he'd suddenly dragged her through the door, into the tiny golden-coloured interior. There were rows of pews either side of the aisle and two tall vases of flowers acting as a kind of cheesy non-denominational altar. Fixed to the wall behind was a glass display cabinet containing on one shelf a bottle of champagne and a white handbag with a floral handle, and on another an empty white basket and big white candles.

'We could get married,' he said. 'Right now. Today!'

'Don't be daft,' she'd replied.

'I'm not being daft. I'm serious! Let's do it! We'll go back to England as Mr and Mrs Hopkirk!'

She wondered what her parents would think. They'd be upset. But it was tempting. She felt so intensely happy. This was the man she wanted to spend the rest of her life with.

'Mr Liam Hopkirk, are you proposing to me?'

'No, not exactly – but I'm thinking, you know, screw all the crap and bridesmaids and stuff that goes with a wedding. It would be fun, wouldn't it? Surprise them all?'

He was being serious and that shocked her. He meant it! Her parents would be devastated. She remembered sitting on her father's knee when she was a child. Her father telling her how beautiful she was. How proud he would be one day to walk her down the aisle on her wedding day.

'I couldn't do this to my parents.'

'They mean more to you than me?'

'No. It's just . . .'

His face darkened. Sulking again.

The sky darkened. Suddenly the helicopter was sinking. The walls turning dark and rushing past the big bubble window. The river beneath rushing up towards them.

She screamed.

Total darkness.

Oh, Christ.

Her head was pounding. Then a light came on. The feeble glow of the dome lamp of the van. She heard a voice. Not Liam, but the man, glaring down at her.

'You stink,' he said. 'You're making my van stink.'

Reality crashed through her. The coils of terror spiralling through every cell in her body. *Water. Please. Water.* She stared up at him, parched and weak and dizzy. She tried to speak but could only make a feeble deep whine in her throat.

'I can't have sex with you. You revolt me. Know what I'm saying?'

A faint ray of hope lifted her. Perhaps he would let her go. She tried again to make a coherent sound. But her voice was just a hollow rumbling mumble.

'I should let you go.'

She nodded. *Yes. Yes, please. Please. Please.*

'I can't let you go, because you saw my face,' he said.

She pleaded with her eyes. *I won't tell anyone. Please let me go. I won't tell a soul.*

'You could put me behind bars for the rest of my life. Do you know what they do to people like me in prison? It's not nice. I can't take that chance.'

The knot of fear in her stomach spread like poison through her blood. She was trembling, quaking, whimpering.

'I'm sorry,' he said, and he really did sound sorry. Really apologetic, like a man in a crowded bar who had just accidentally stepped on her foot. 'You're in the papers. You are on the front page of the *Argus*. There's a photograph of you. *Rachael Ryan.* That's a nice name.'

He stared down at her. He looked angry. And sulky. And genuinely apologetic. 'I'm sorry you saw my face,' he said. 'You shouldn't have done that. It wasn't clever, Rachael. It could all have been so very different. Know what I'm saying?'

NOW

24

The newly formed Cold Case Team was part of Roy Grace's Major Crime Branch responsibility. It was housed in an inadequate office within the Major Incident Suite on the first floor of Sussex House, with views across a yard cluttered with wheelie bins, emergency generator housings and SOCO vehicles to the custody block, which cut out much of the natural light.

There were few things in the world, Roy Grace always thought, that could create as much paperwork as a Major Crime investigation. The grey-carpeted floor was piled high with stacks of large green crates and blue cardboard boxes, all labelled with operation names, as well as reference books, training manuals and a doorstop of a tome sitting on its own, *Practical Homicide*.

Almost every inch of the desktop space of the three workstations was covered by computers, keyboards, phones, racks of box files, crammed in trays, Rolodex files, mugs and personal effects. Post-it notes were stuck on just about everything. Two free-standing tables visibly sagged beneath the weight of files piled on them.

The walls were plastered with news cuttings of some of the cases, and photographs and old wanted posters of suspects still at large. One was a picture of a smiling dark-haired teenager, with the wording above:

HAVE YOU SEEN THIS WOMAN?

£500 reward

Another was a black-and-white Sussex Police poster featuring an amiable-looking man with a big smile and a shock of unruly hair. It was captioned:

SUSSEX POLICE

MURDER of JACK (John) BAKER.

Mr Baker was murdered at Worthing, Sussex
on 8/9 January 1990.

Did you know him? Have you seen him before?

IF YOU HAVE ANY INFORMATION
PLEASE CONTACT THE MURDER INCIDENT ROOM

telephone no. 0903-30821,

OR ANY POLICE STATION.

There were hand-drawn sketches of victims and suspects, computer-generated E-Fits, one of a rape suspect shown with different hats and hoods, with and without glasses.

In charge of this entire new cold case initiative, and answering to Roy Grace, was Jim Doyle, a former detective chief superintendent with whom Grace had worked many years back. Doyle was a tall, studious-looking man, whose appearance belied his mental – and physical – toughness. He had about him more the courteous air of a distinguished academic than a police officer. Yet with his firm, unflappable manner, his enquiring mind and a precision in the way he approached everything, he had been a devastatingly effective detective, involved in solving many of the county's most serious violent crimes during his thirty-year career. His nickname in the force had been *Popeye*, after his namesake, Jimmy 'Popeye' Doyle in the film *The French Connection.*

Doyle's two colleagues were similarly experienced. Eamon Greene, a quiet, serious man, was a former Sussex under-16 chess champion and was now a grand master, still playing and winning tournaments. Before retiring at just forty-nine, and then returning to the force as a civilian, he had reached the rank of detective superintendent in Sussex CID, Major Crime Branch. Brian Foster, a former detective chief inspector known as *Fossy*, was a lean sixty-three-year-old, with close-cropped hair and still, despite his age, boyishly handsome features. In the previous year he had run four marathons in four consecutive weeks in different countries. Since retiring from Sussex CID at the age of fifty-two, he had worked for the past decade in the prosecutor's office of the International War Crimes Tribunal in The Hague, and had now returned home eager to start a new phase in his career.

Roy Grace, wearing a suit and tie for his first meeting with the new Assistant Chief Constable later that morning, cleared a space on one of the work surfaces and sat down on it, cradling his second mug of coffee of the day. It was 8.45 a.m.

'OK,' he said, swinging his legs. 'It's good to have the three of you. Actually, let me rephrase that – it is bloody brilliant!'

They all grinned.

'Popeye, you taught me just about everything I know, so I don't want to sit here and teach you how to suck eggs. The "Chief" – ' by which he meant Chief Constable Tom Martinson – 'has given us a generous budget, but we're going to have to deliver if we want the same again next year. Which is shorthand for saying if you guys still want your jobs next year.'

Turning to the others, he said, 'I'm just going to tell you something Popeye told me when I first worked with him. As part of his work-load back in the 1990s he had just been given responsibility for cold cases – or whatever they were called then!'

That raised a titter. All three retired officers knew the headaches caused by the ever-changing police terminology.

Grace pulled a sheet of paper from his pocket and read from it. 'He said, and I quote, "Cold-case reviews utilize the forensic technology of today to solve the crimes of the past, with a view to preventing the crimes of the future."'

'Glad all those years with you weren't wasted, Roy,' Jim Doyle said. 'At least you remembered something!'

'Yep. Impressive to have learned anything from an *old sweat*!' quipped Foster.

Doyle did not rise to the bait.

Roy Grace went on: 'You've probably seen it on the serials or in the *Argus* that a woman was raped on New Year's Eve.'

'In the Metropole Hotel?' Eamon Greene said.

'That's the one.'

'I attended the initial interview of the victim last Thursday, New Year's Day,' Grace said. 'The offender, apparently disguised in drag, appears to have forced the victim into a hotel room on the pretext of asking for help. Then, wearing a mask, he tied her up and sexually assaulted her vaginally and anally with one of her stiletto shoes. He then attempted to penetrate her himself, with only partial success. This has similarities to the MO of the

Shoe Man cold case back in 1997. In those cases, the Shoe Man adopted a series of different disguises and pretexts for requiring help to lure his victims. Then he stopped offending – in Sussex at any rate – and was never apprehended. I have a summary of this case file which I'd like you all to read as a priority. You will each have your own individual cases to review, but for now I want you all to work on this one, as I think it could help with the case I'm investigating now.'

'Was there any DNA evidence, Roy?' Jim Doyle asked.

'There was no semen from any of the women, but three of his victims said that he wore a condom. There were clothing fibres, but nothing conclusive from those. No nail scrapings, no saliva. A couple of his victims reported that he had no pubic hair. This man was clearly very forensically aware, even back then. No DNA was ever found. There was just one common link – each of the victims was seriously into shoes.'

'Which covers about 95 per cent of the female population – if my wife is anything to go by,' Jim Doyle said.

'Precisely.' Grace nodded.

'What about descriptions?' asked Brian Foster.

'Thanks to the way in which rape victims were treated back then, not much. We have a slightly built man, with not a lot of body hair, a classless accent and a small dick.

'I've spent the weekend reading through the files of those victims, and all other major crimes committed during this same period,' Grace went on. 'There is one more person that I suspect might have been a victim of the Shoe Man – possibly the last victim. Her name is Rachael Ryan. She disappeared in the early hours of Christmas Eve – or rather Christmas Day, 1997. What has brought her to my attention is that I was a DS back then on the day she was reported missing. I went to interview her parents. Respectable people, completely mystified that she never turned up for Christmas dinner. By all accounts she was a decent young woman of twenty-two, sensible, although low after having split up with a boy-friend.'

He nearly added, but did not, that she had vanished off the face of the earth, just like his own wife, Sandy, had vanished.

'Any theories?' asked Foster.

'Not from the family,' Grace said. 'But I interviewed the two friends she was out with on Christmas Eve. One of them told me that she was a bit obsessed with shoes. That she bought shoes which were way beyond her means – designer shoes at upwards of a couple of hundred quid a pop. All the Shoe Man's victims wore expensive shoes.' He shrugged.

'Not much of a peg to hang your coat on there, Roy,' said Foster. 'If she'd split up with her boyfriend she could have topped herself. Christmas, you know, that's a time when people feel pain like this. I remember my ex walking out on me three weeks before Christmas. I damned near topped myself over that Christmas holiday – 1992, it was. Had Christmas dinner on my own in a bloody Angus Steak House.'

Grace smiled. 'It's possible, but from all I learned about her at that time I don't think so. Something I do think is significant is that one of her neighbours happened to be looking out of his window at three o'clock on Christmas morning – the timing fits perfectly – and saw a man pushing a woman into a white van.'

'Did he get the registration?'

'He was shit-faced. He got part of it.'

'Enough to trace the vehicle?'

'No.'

'You believed him?'

'Yes. I still do.'

'Not a lot to go on, is it, Roy?' said Jim Doyle.

'No, but there's something strange. I came in early this morning to look up that particular file before this meeting – and do you know what?' He stared at each of them.

They all shook their heads.

'The pages I was looking for were missing.'

'Who would remove them?' Brian Foster said. 'I mean – who would have access to them to be able to remove them?'

'You used to be a copper,' Grace said. 'You tell me. And then tell me why?'

25

Maybe it was time to quit.

Prison aged you. Ten years it put on – or took off – your life, depending on which way you looked at it. And right now Darren Spicer wasn't too happy about either of the ways he was looking at it.

Since he was sixteen, Spicer had spent much of his life inside. *Doing bird.* A *revolving-door prisoner*, they called him. A career criminal. But not a very successful one. He'd only once, since becoming an adult, spent two consecutive Christmases as a free man, and that had been in the early years of his marriage. His birth certificate – his real one – told him he was forty-one. His bathroom mirror told him he was fifty-five – and counting. Inside he felt eighty. He felt dead. He felt . . .

Nothing.

Lathering up, he stared at the mirror with dull eyes, grimacing at the lined old geezer staring back at him. He was naked, his gangly, skinny body – which he liked to think of as just plain lean – toned up from daily workouts in the prison gym.

Then he set to work on his hard stubble with the same blunted blade he had been using for weeks in prison before his release and which he had taken with him. When he had finished, his face was as clean-shaven as the rest of his body, which he had shaved last week. He always did that when he came out of prison, as a way of cleansing himself. One time, in the early days of his now long-dead marriage, he'd come home with lice in his pubes and chest hair.

He had two small tattoos, at the top of each arm, but no more. Plenty of his fellow inmates were covered in the things and had a macho pride in them. Macho pride equalled mucho stupidity, in his view. Why make it easy for someone to identify you? Besides, he had enough identifying marks already – five scars on his back, from stab wounds when he'd been set on in prison by mates of a drug dealer he'd done over some years back.

This last sentence had been his longest yet – six years. He was finally out on licence now after three of them. Time to quit, he thought. Yeah, but.

The big *but*.

You were supposed to feel free when you left prison. But he still had to report to his probation officer. He had to report for retraining. He had to obey the rules of the hostels he stayed in. When you were released, you were supposed to go home.

But he had no home.

His dad was long dead and he'd barely spoken a dozen words to his mum in twenty-five years – and that was too many. His only sibling, his sister Mags, had died from a heroin overdose five years back. His ex-wife was living in Australia with his kid, whom he hadn't seen in ten years.

Home was wherever he could find a place to doss down. Last night it was a room in a halfway house just off the Old Steine in Brighton. Shared with four pathetic, stinking winos. He'd been here before. Today he was going to try to get into a better place. St Patrick's night shelter. They had decent grub, a place you could store things. You had to sleep in a big dormitory but it was clean. Prison was meant to help your rehabilitation back into the community after serving your time. But the reality was that the community didn't want you, not really. Rehabilitation was a myth. Although he played the game, went along with the concept.

Retraining!

Ha! He wasn't interested in retraining, but he had shown willing while he had been at Ford Open Prison these past six months in preparation for his release, because that had enabled him to spend days out of prison on their work placement scheme. *Working Links*, they were called. He had chosen the hotel handyman course, which enabled him to spend time in a couple of different Brighton hotels. Working behind the scenes. Understanding the layouts. Getting access to the room keys and to the electronic room-key software. Very useful indeed.

Yeah.

His regular prison visitor at Lewes, a pleasant, matronly lady, had asked him if he had a dream. If he could ever see a life for himself beyond the prison walls. And what was it?

Yeah, sure, he'd told her, he had a dream. To be married again. To have kids. To live in a nice house – like one of those fancy homes he burgled for a living – and drive a nice car. Have a steady job. Yep. Go fishing at the weekends. That was his dream. But, he told her, that was never going to happen.

'Why not?' she had asked him.

'I'll tell you why not,' Darren had replied. 'Cos I've got one hundred and seventy-two *previous*, right? Who's gonna let me stay in a job when they find that out? And they always do find out.' He'd paused before adding, 'Anyhow, it's all right here. Got me mates. The grub's good. The electricity's paid for. Got me television.'

Yeah, it was all right. Except . . .

No women. That's what he missed. Women and cocaine were what he liked. Could get the drugs in prison, but not the women. Not very often, anyway.

The Guv had let him stay in over Christmas, but he'd been released two days after Boxing Day. To what?

Shit.

Tomorrow hopefully he'd move. If you played by the rules at St Patrick's for twenty-eight days, you could get yourself into one of their MiPods. They had these strange plastic pods in there, like space capsules, taken from some Japanese hotel idea. You could stay in a MiPod for another ten weeks. They were cramped, but they gave you privacy; you could keep your things safe.

And he had things he needed to keep safe.

His mate, Terry Biglow – if he could call the shifty little weasel a mate – was safeguarding the only possessions he owned in the world. They were inside a suitcase, with three padlocked chains holding its contents a secret – the chains and padlocks were a mark of how much he could trust Biglow not to open it up.

Maybe this time he could stay out of jail. Get enough money together, from burgling and drug dealing, to buy himself a little flat. And then what? A woman? A family? One moment that seemed attractive, the next it was all too much. Too much hassle. Truth was, he had grown used to his way of life. His own company. His own secret kicks.

His dad had been a roofer and as a kid he'd helped

him out. He'd seen some of the posh houses in Brighton and Hove his dad worked on – and the tasty women with their beautiful clothes and their flash cars who lived in them. His dad fancied that kind of lifestyle. Fancied a posh house and a classy-looking woman.

One day his dad fell through a roof, broke his back and never worked again. Instead he just drank his compensation money all day and night. Darren didn't fancy roofing, that wasn't ever going to make you rich, he figured. Studying could. He liked school, was good at maths and science and mechanical things, loved all that. But he had problems at home. His mother was drinking too. Some time around his thirteenth birthday she clambered into his bed, drunk and naked, told him his father couldn't satisfy her any more, now it was his job as the man in the family.

Darren went to school every day, ashamed, increasingly disconnected from his friends. His head was all messed up and he couldn't concentrate any more. He didn't feel a part of anything, and took to spending more and more time alone, fishing, or in really bad weather hanging about in his uncle's locksmith's shop, watching him cut keys, or running errands, and occasionally standing behind the counter while his uncle nipped along to the bookie. Anything to escape from home. From his mother.

He liked his uncle's machinery, liked the smell, liked the mystery of locks. They were just puzzles, really. Simple puzzles.

When he was fifteen his mother told him it was time he started supporting her and his dad, that he needed to learn a skill, get a job. His uncle, who had no one to take over the business when he retired, offered him an apprenticeship.

Within a couple of months, Darren could solve any problem anyone had with a lock. His uncle told him he was a bloody genius!

There was nothing to it, Darren figured. Anything that was made by a man could be figured out by another man. All you had to do was think your way inside the lock. Imagine the springs, the tumblers – imagine the inside of the lock, put yourself into the mind of the man who designed it. After all, there were basically only two kinds of domestic lock – a Yale, which operated with a flat key, and a Chubb, which operated with a cylindrical key. Mortises and rim locks. If you had a problem, you could see inside most locks with a simple bit of medical kit, a proctoscope.

Then he graduated to safes. His uncle had developed a bit of a niche business, opening safes for the police. Given a bit of time, there wasn't any mechanical safe his nephew could not open. Nor any door lock.

He'd burgled his first house, up in Hollingdean, when he was sixteen. He got busted and spent two years in an approved school. That was where he developed a taste for drugs for the first time. And where he learned his first valuable lesson. It was the same risk to burgle a shitty little house for a stereo system as it was to burgle a ritzy pad where there might be jewellery and cash.

When he came out his uncle didn't want him back – and he had no inclination to get a low-paid labouring job, which was his only choice. Instead he burgled a house in Brighton's secluded Withdean Road. Took seven grand from a safe. Blew three of it on cocaine, but invested four of it in heroin, which he traded and made a twenty-grand profit.

He did a string of large houses after then, made himself almost a hundred Gs. Sweet. Then he met Rose in a club. Married her. Bought a little flat in Portslade. Rose didn't approve of him burgling, so he tried going straight. Through a bloke he knew, he faked a new ID and got a job working for a company that installed alarm systems called Sussex Security Systems.

They had a top-end clientele. Half of the city's big homes. Being in them was like being a kid in a sweetshop. It did not take him long to miss the buzz of burgling. Particularly the kick he got out of it. But even more particularly the money he could make.

The best of all of it was being alone in a posh bedroom. Smelling the scent of a rich woman. Inhaling her perfumes, the perspiration on her underwear in the wash baskets, her expensive clothes hanging in her wardrobe, her silks, cottons, furs, leathers. He liked rifling through her things. Particularly her underwear and her shoes. Something about these places aroused him.

These women were from a different world to the one he knew. Women beyond his means. Beyond his social skills.

Women with their stuffy husbands.

These kinds of women were gagging for it.

Sometimes a scent of cologne or a sour odour on a soiled garment would remind him of his mother, and something erotic would burn inside him for a brief instant, before he suppressed it with a flash of anger.

For a while he'd been able to fool Rose by telling her he was going fishing – night fishing, mostly. Rose asked him why he never took the kid fishing. Darren told her he would, when the kid was older. And he would have done, he really would.

But then one February evening, burgling a house in Tongdean, the owner came home, surprising him. He legged it out the back, across the garden and straight into the deep end of an empty sodding swimming pool, breaking his right leg, his jaw and his nose, and knocking himself out cold.

Rose only visited him once in prison. That was to tell him she was taking the kid to Australia and she never wanted to see him again.

Now he was out and free again, he had nothing. Nothing but his suitcase at Terry Biglow's place – if, of course, Terry was still there and not dead or back inside. And nothing else but his hard, scarred body, and the urges from three years of lying on his narrow bunk, dreaming of what he would do when he was back out . . .

1997

26

'I *can* forget that I saw your face,' Rachael said, staring up at him.

In the yellow glow of the interior light he looked jaundiced. She tried to make eye contact, because in the dim, distant, terror-addled recesses of her mind, she remembered reading somewhere that hostages *should* try to make eye contact. That people would find it harder to hurt you if you established a bond.

She was trying, through her parched voice, to bond with this man – this monster – this *thing*.

'Sure you can, Rachael. When do you think I was born? Yesterday? Last week on Christmas fucking Day? I let you go, right, and one hour later you'll be in a police station with one of those E-Fit guys, describing me. Is that about the size of it?'

She shook her head vigorously from side to side. 'I promise you,' she croaked

'On your mother's life?'

'On my mother's life. Please can I have some water? Please, something.'

'So I could let you go, and if you do cheat me and go to the police, it would be OK for me to go round to your mother's house, in Surrenden Close, and kill her?'

Dimly, Rachael wondered how he knew where her

mother lived. Perhaps he had read it in the papers? That gave her a glimmer of hope. *If* he had read it in the papers, then it meant she was in the news. People would be out looking for her. Police.

'I know everything about you, Rachael.'

'You can let me go. I'm not going to risk her life.'

'I can?'

'Yes.'

'In your dreams.'

NOW

27

He liked to be inside nice big houses. Or, more accurately, to be inside the *inside* of these houses.

Sometimes, squeezed into narrow cavities, it felt as if he was wearing the house like a second skin! Or squeezed into a wardrobe, surrounded by hanging dresses and the tantalizing smells of the beautiful woman who owned them, and of the leather of her shoes, he would feel on top of the world, as if he owned the woman.

Like the one who owned the dresses all around him now. And who owned racks and racks full of some of his favourite designer shoes.

And for a while, soon now, he would own her! Very soon.

He already knew a lot about her – far more than her husband did, he was sure about that. It was Thursday. He'd watched her for the past three nights. He knew the hours she came home and went out. And he knew the secrets on her laptop – so obliging of her to have no password! He'd read the emails to and from the Greek man she was sleeping with. The files with the photographs she had taken of him, some of them very rude indeed.

But for a while, if he got lucky, *he* would be her lover tonight. Not Mr Hairy Designer Stubble, with his massive, indecently big pole.

He would have to be careful not to move an inch when she came home. The hangers were particularly clanky – they were mostly those thin metal ones that came from dry-cleaners. He'd removed some, the worst offenders, and laid them on the wardrobe floor, and he'd wrapped tissues around the ones nearest him. Now all he had to do was wait. And hope.

It was like fishing. A lot of patience was required. She might not come home for a long time, but at least there was no danger of her husband returning tonight.

Hubby had gone on a jet plane far, far away. To a software conference in Helsinki. It was all there on the kitchen table, the note from him to her telling her he'd see her on Saturday, and signed off, *Love you XXXX*, with the name of the hotel and the phone number.

Just to be sure, as he'd had time to kill, he'd phoned the hotel using the kitchen phone and asked to speak to Mr Dermot Pearce. He was told in a slightly sing-song voice that Mr Pearce was not picking up and asked if he would like to leave a message on his voicemail.

Yes, I am about to have sex with your wife, he was tempted to say, getting caught up in the thrill of the moment, the joy at the way it was all dropping into his lap. But sensibly he hung up.

The photographs of two teenage children, a boy and a girl, displayed downstairs in the living room were a slight worry. But their two bedrooms were immaculate. Not the bedrooms of children who were living here. He concluded they were the husband's children by a former marriage.

There was a cat, one of those nasty-looking Burmese things that had glared at him in the kitchen. He'd given it a kick and it had disappeared through the flap. All was quiet. He was happy and excited.

He could feel some houses living and breathing around him. Especially when the boilers rumbled into life and the walls vibrated. Breathing! Yes, like him now, breathing so hard with excitement he could hear the sound of it in his ears, and he could hear the pounding of his heart, the roaring of his blood coursing through his veins like it was in some kind of a race.

Oh, God, this felt so good!

28

Roxy Pearce had been waiting all week for tonight. Dermot was away on a business trip and she had invited Iannis over for a meal. She wanted to make love to him here in her own home. The idea felt deliciously wicked!

She hadn't seen him since Saturday afternoon, when she'd strutted around his apartment naked in her brand-new Jimmy Choos, and they'd screwed with her still wearing them, which had driven him wild.

She'd read somewhere that the female mosquito gets so crazed for blood that she will do anything, even if she knows she will die in the process, to get that blood.

That's how she felt about being with Iannis. She had to see him. *Had* to have him, whatever the cost. And the more she had him, the more she needed him.

I am not a good person, she thought guiltily, as she drove home, accelerating her silver Boxster through the street-lit darkness up swanky Shirley Drive, past the Hove recreation ground. She turned right into Droveway Avenue, then right again into their drive and up to the big, square, modern house they'd had built, a secluded paradise within the city, with its rear garden backing on to the playing fields of a private school. The security lights popped on as she headed along the short drive.

I am SO not a good person.

This was the kind of thing you could rot in hell for. She'd been brought up a good Catholic girl. Brought up to believe in sin and eternal damnation. And she'd got herself both the T-shirt and the one-way ticket to damnation with Dermot.

He had been married when they'd met. She'd lured him away from his wife, and the kids he adored, after an intensely passionate affair that had become stronger and stronger over two years. They'd been crazily in love. But then, when they'd got together, the magic between them had steadily evaporated.

Now those same deep passions had exploded inside her all over again with Iannis. Just like Dermot, he was married, with two much younger children. Her best friend, Viv Daniels, had not approved, warning her she was going to get a reputation as a marriage wrecker. But she couldn't help it, could not switch off those feelings.

She reached up to the sun visor for the garage clicker, waited for the door to rise, drove into the space which seemed cavernous without Dermot's BMW and switched off the engine. Then she grabbed the Waitrose bags off the passenger seat and climbed out.

She had first met Iannis when Dermot had taken her to dinner at Thessalonica in Brighton. Iannis had come and sat at their table when their meal was finished, plying them with ouzo on the house and staring constantly at her.

It was his voice she'd fallen for first. The passionate way he spoke about food and about life, in his broken English. His handsome, unshaven face. His hairy chest, visible through a white shirt opened almost to the navel. His ruggedness. He seemed to be a man without a care in the world, relaxed, happy in his skin.

And so intensely sexy!

As she opened the internal door, then tapped out the code on the touch pad to silence the beeping alarm warning, she did not notice that a different light on the panel was on from the usual one. It was the night-setting warning for downstairs only, isolating the upstairs. But she was totally preoccupied in an altogether different direction. Would Iannis like her cooking?

She'd opted for something simple: mixed Italian hors d'oeuvres, then rib-eye steak and salad. And a bottle – or two – from Dermot's prized cellar.

Shutting the door behind her she called out to the cat, 'Sushi! Yo Sushi! Yo! Mummy's home!'

The cat's stupid name had been Dermot's idea – taken from the first restaurant they had gone to, in London, on their first date.

Silence greeted her, which was unusual.

Normally the cat would stride over to meet her, rub against her leg and then look up at her expectantly, waiting for dinner. But he wasn't there. Probably out in the garden, she thought. Fine.

She looked at her watch, then at the kitchen clock: 6.05. Less than an hour before Iannis was due to arrive.

It had been another shitty day at the office, with a silent phone and the overdraft on fast-track towards its limit. But tonight, for a few hours, she was not going to care. Nothing mattered but her time with Iannis. She would savour every minute, every second, every nano-second!

She emptied the contents of the bags on to the kitchen table, sorted them out, grabbed a bottle of Dermot's prized Château de Meursault and put it in the fridge to chill, then she opened a bottle of his Gevrey

Chambertin 2000 to let it breathe. Next she prised the lid off a can of cat food, scooped its contents into the bowl and placed it on the floor. 'Sushi!' she called out again. 'Yo Sushi! Supper!'

Then she hurried upstairs, planning to shower, shave her legs, spray on some Jo Malone perfume, then go back down and get the meal ready.

*

From inside her wardrobe, he heard her calling out, and he pulled his hood on over his head. Then he listened to her footsteps coming up the stairs. Everything inside him tightened with excitement. With anticipation.

He was in a red mist of excitement. Hard as hell! Trying to calm his breathing. Watching her from behind the silk dresses, through the curtained glass-fronted wardrobe doors. She looked so beautiful. Her sleek black hair. The careless way she kicked off her black court shoes. Then stepped wantonly out of her navy two-piece. As if she was doing it for him!

Thank you!

She removed her white blouse and her bra. Her breasts were smaller than he had imagined they might be, but that did not matter. They were OK. Quite firm, but with small nipples. It didn't matter. Breasts were not his thing.

Now her undies!

She was a shaver! Bald and white, down to a thin strip of a Brazilian! Very hygienic.

Thank you!

He was so aroused he was dripping perspiration.

Then she walked, naked, through into the bathroom. He listened to the hiss of the shower. This would be a good moment, he knew, but he didn't want her all wet and slippery with soap. He liked the idea that she dried herself for him and perhaps put on some perfume for him.

After a few minutes she came back out into the bedroom, swathed in a big towel, a smaller white towel wrapped around her head. Then suddenly, as if she was giving him a private performance, she let the towel drop from her body, opened a wardrobe door, and selected from the racks a pair of elegant, gleaming black shoes with long stiletto heels.

Jimmy Choos!

He could barely contain his excitement as she slipped them on, placed one foot, then the other on the small armchair beside the bed and tied the straps, four on each shoe! Then she paraded around the room eyeing herself, naked, pausing to pose from every angle in the large mirror on the wall.

Oh yes, baby. Oh yes! Oh yes! Thank you!

He stared at the trim narrow strip of black pubic hair beneath her flat stomach. He liked it trim. He liked women who looked after themselves, who took care of the details.

Just for him!

She was coming towards the wardrobe now, towel still around her head. She reached out a hand. Her face was inches from his own, through the curtained glass.

He was prepared.

She pulled open the door.

His surgically gloved hand shot out, slamming the chloroform pad into her nose.

Like a striking shark, he glided out through the hanging dresses, grabbing the back of her head with his free arm, keeping up the pressure against her nose for a few seconds until she went limp in his arms.

1997

29

Rachael Ryan lay motionless on the floor of the van. His fist hurt from where he had hit her on the head. It hurt so damned much he worried he had broken both his thumb and a finger. He could hardly move them.

'*Shit,*' he said, shaking it. '*Shit, fuck, shit. Bitch!*'

He peeled off his glove so he could examine them, but it was hard to see anything in the feeble glow of the van's interior light.

Then he knelt beside her. Her head had gone back with a loud snap. He didn't know if it was a bone breaking in his own hand or her jaw. She did not seem to be breathing.

He laid his head against her chest anxiously. There was movement, but he wasn't sure if it was his movement or hers.

'Are you OK?' he asked, feeling a sudden surge of panic. 'Rachael? Are you OK? Rachael?'

He worked his glove back on, gripped her shoulders and shook her. 'Rachael? Rachael? Rachael?'

He pulled a small torch out of his pocket and shone it in her face. Her eyes were closed. He pulled one lid open and it closed again when he let go.

His panic was increasing. 'Don't die on me, Rachael! Do not die on me, do you hear me? Do you fucking hear me?'

Blood was trickling from her mouth.

'Rachael? Do you want something to drink? Want me to get you something to eat? You want a McDonald's? A Big Mac? A Cheeseburger? Or maybe a submarine? I could get you a submarine. Yeah? Tell me, tell me what filling you'd like in it. Spicy sausage? Something with melted cheese? They're really good those. Tuna? Ham?'

NOW

30

Thursday 8 January

Yac was hungry. The chicken-n-melted cheese submarine had been tantalizing him for over two hours. The bag rolled around on the passenger seat, along with his Thermos flask every time he braked or went around a corner.

He'd been planning to pull over and eat it during his on-the-hour tea break, but there were too many people around. Too many fares. He'd had to drink his 11 p.m. cup while driving. Thursday nights were normally busy, but this was the first Thursday after the New Year. He had expected it to be quiet. However, some people had recovered and were out partying again. Taking taxis. Wearing nice shoes.

Uh-huh.

That was fine by him. Everyone had their own way of partying. He was happy for them all. Just so long as they paid what was on the meter and didn't try to do a runner, as someone did every now and then. Even better when they tipped him! All tips helped. Helped towards his savings. Helped towards building up his collection.

That was growing steadily. Very nicely. Oh yeah!

A siren wailed.

He felt a sudden prick of alarm. Held his breath.

Flashing blue lights filled his mirrors, then a police car shot past. Then another police car moments later, as if following in its wake. Interesting, he thought. He was out all night most nights and it wasn't often he saw two police cars together. Must be something bad.

He was approaching his regular spot on Brighton seafront, where he liked to pull over every hour, on the hour, during the night and drink his tea, and now, also, to read his paper. Since the rape in the Metropole Hotel last Thursday he had started to read the paper every night. The story excited him. The woman's clothes had been taken. But what excited him most of all was reading that her shoes had been taken.

Uh-huh!

He brought the taxi to a halt, switched off the engine and picked up the carrier bag with the submarine inside, but then he put it down again. It did not smell good any more. The smell made him feel sick.

His hunger was gone.

He wondered where those police cars were headed.

Then he thought about the pair of shoes in the boot of his taxi and he felt good again.

Really good!

He tossed the submarine out of the window.

Litter lout! he chided himself. *You bad litter lout!*

31

One good thing, or rather, one of the *many* good things about Cleo being pregnant, Grace thought, was that he was drinking a lot less. Apart from the occasional glass of cold white wine, Cleo had been dutifully abstemious, so he had cut down too. The bad thing was her damned craving for curries! He wasn't quite sure how many more of those his system could take. The whole house was starting to smell like an Indian fast-food joint.

He longed for something plain. Humphrey was unimpressed too. After just one lick, the puppy had decided that curries were not going to provide him with any tasty leftover scraps in his bowl that he would want to eat.

Roy endured them because he felt duty-bound to keep Cleo company. Besides, in one of the pregnancy-formen books Glenn Branson had given him, there was a whole passage about indulging and sharing your partner's cravings. It would make your partner feel happy. And if your partner felt happy, then the vibes would be picked up by your unborn child, and it would be born happy and not grow up to become a serial killer.

Normally, he liked to drink lager with curry, Grolsch preferably or his favourite German beer, Bitberger, or the weissbier he'd developed a taste for through his acquaintance with a German police officer, Marcel Kullen, and from his visits last year to Munich. But this week it was his rota turn to be the Major Crime Branch's duty Senior Investigating Officer, which meant he was on call 24/7, so he was reduced to soft drinks.

Which explained why he felt bright as a button, sitting in his office at 9.20 a.m. this Friday, sipping his second coffee, switching his focus from the serials to the emails that poured in as if they were coming out of a tap that had been left running, then to the paper mountain on his desk.

Just two and a bit more days to go until midnight Sunday, then another detective superintendent or detective chief inspector on the rota would take over the mantle of Senior Investigating Officer and it would be another six weeks before his turn came round again. He had so much work to get through, preparing cases for trial, as well as supervising the new Cold Case Team, that he really did not need any new cases to consume his time.

But he was out of luck.

His phone rang and as soon as he answered he instantly recognized the blunt, to-the-point voice of DI David Alcorn from Brighton CID.

'Sorry, Roy. Looks like we've got another stranger rape on our hands.'

Up until now, Brighton CID had been handling the Metropole Hotel rape, although keeping Roy informed. But now it sounded as if the Major Crime Branch was going to have to take over. Which meant him.

And it was a sodding Friday. Why on Fridays? What was it about Fridays?

'What do you have, David?'

Alcorn summed up briefly and succinctly: 'The victim is deeply traumatized. From what Uniform, who attended, have been able to glean, she arrived home alone last night

– her husband is away on a business trip – and was attacked in her house. She rang a friend, who went around this morning, and she was the one who called the police. The victim was seen by an ambulance crew but did not need medical attention. She's been taken up to the rape centre at Crawley accompanied by a SOLO and a CID constable.'

'What details do you have?'

'Very sketchy, Roy. As I said, I understand she's deeply traumatized. It sounds like a shoe was involved again.'

Grace frowned. 'What do you have on that?'

'She was violated with one of her shoes.'

Shit, Grace thought, scrabbling through the mess of papers on his desk for a pen and his notepad. 'What's her name?'

'Roxanna – or Roxy – Pearce.' Alcorn spelled the surname out in full. 'Address 76 Droveway Avenue, Hove. She has a PR agency in Brighton and her husband's in IT. That's all I really know at this stage. I've been in contact with Scenes of Crime and I'm going to the house now. Want me to pick you up on the way?'

His office was hardly on the way to the address for someone at Brighton nick, Roy thought, but he didn't argue. He could use the time in the car to get any more information on the Metropole rape that might have surfaced and to discuss the transfer of all information to the Major Crime Branch.

'Sure, thanks.'

When he terminated the call, he sat still for a moment, collecting his thoughts.

In particular, his mind went back to the Shoe Man. All this week, the Cold Case Team had been focusing on him as a priority to see what links, if any, they could establish in the MOs between the known cases, back in 1997, and the assault on Nicola Taylor at the Metropole on New Year's Eve.

Her shoes had been taken. That was the first possible link. Although back in 1997 the Shoe Man took just one shoe and the woman's panties. Both Nicola Taylor's shoes had been taken, along with all her clothes.

Somewhere beneath his paper mountain was the massively thick folder containing the offender profile, or rather, as these were now known, the Behavioural Investigator Report. It had been written by a distinctly oddball forensic psychologist, Dr Julius Proudfoot.

Grace had been sceptical of the man when he first encountered him back in 1997 on his investigations into Rachael Ryan's disappearance, but had consulted him on a number of cases since.

He became so absorbed in the report that he did not notice the click of his door opening and the footfalls across the carpet.

'Yo, old-timer!'

Grace looked up with a start to see Glenn Branson standing in front of his desk and said, 'What's your problem?'

'Life. I'm planning to end it all.'

'Good idea. Just don't do it here. I've got enough shit to deal with.'

Branson walked around his desk and peered over his shoulder, reading for some moments before saying, 'You know that Julius Proudfoot's seriously off his trolley, don't you? His reputation, right?'

'So what's new? You have to be seriously off your trolley to join the police force.'

'And to get married.'

'That too.' Grace grinned. 'What other great pearls of wisdom do you have for me?'

Branson shrugged. 'Just trying to be helpful.'

What would be really helpful, Grace thought, but did not say, would be if you were about a thousand miles from here right now. If you stopped trashing my house. If you stopped trashing my CD and vinyl collections. That's what would be *really* helpful.

Instead, he looked up at the man he loved more than any man he had ever met before and said, 'Do you want to fuck off, or do you want to really help me?'

'Sweetly put – how could I resist?'

'Good.' Grace handed him Dr Julius Proudfoot's file on the Shoe Man. 'I'd like you to summarize that for me for this evening's briefing meeting, into about two hundred and fifty words, in a form that our new ACC can absorb.'

Branson lifted the file up, then flipped through the pages.

'Shit, two hundred and eighty-two pages. Man, that's a fucker.'

'Couldn't have put it better myself.'

32

Roy Grace's father had been a true copper's copper. Jack Grace told his son that to be a police officer meant that you looked at the world differently from everyone else. You were part of a *healthy culture of suspicion*, he'd called it.

Roy had never forgotten that. It was how he looked at the world, always. It was how he looked, at this moment, at the posh houses of Shirley Drive on this fine, crisp, sunny January morning. The street was one of hilly Brighton and Hove's backbones. Running almost into the open countryside at the edge of the city, it was lined with smart detached houses way beyond the pocket of most police officers. Wealthy people lived here: dentists, bankers, car dealers, lawyers, local and London business people, and of course, as with all the smartest addresses, a smattering of successful criminals. It was one of the city's aspirational addresses. If you lived in Shirley Drive – or one of its tributaries – you were a *somebody*.

At least, you were to anyone driving by who did not have a copper's jaundiced eye.

Roy Grace did not have a jaundiced eye. But he had a good, almost photographic memory. As David Alcorn, in a smart grey suit, drove the small Ford up past the recreational ground, Grace clocked the houses one by one. It was routine for him. The London protection racketeer's Brighton home was along here. So was the Brighton brothel king's. And the crack cocaine king's was just one street away.

In his late forties, short, with cropped brown hair and smelling permanently of cigarette smoke, David Alcorn looked outwardly hard and officious, but inside he was a gentle man.

Turning right into Droveway Avenue he said, 'This is the street the missus would like to live in.'

'So,' Grace said, 'move here.'

'I'm just a couple of hundred grand short of being a couple of hundred grand short of the down payment,' he replied. 'And then some.' He hesitated briefly. 'You know what I reckon?'

'Tell me.'

Grace watched each of the detached houses slide by. On his right, they passed a Tesco convenience store. On his left, a dairy with an ancient cobbled wall.

'Your Cleo would like it here. Suit a classy lady like her, this area would.'

They were slowing now. Then Alcorn braked sharply. 'That's it there on the right.'

Grace looked for any signs of a CCTV camera as they drove down the short, laurel-lined driveway, but saw none. He clocked the security lights.

'All right, isn't it?' David Alcorn said.

It was more than sodding all right, it was totally stunning. If he had the money to design and build his dream house, Grace decided, this might be one he'd copy.

It was like a piece of brilliant white sculpture. A mixture of crisp, straight lines and soft curves, some played off against each other in daring geometric angles.

The place seemed to be built on split levels, the windows were vast and solar panels rose from the roof. Even the plants strategically placed around the walls looked as if they had been genetically modified just for this property. It wasn't a huge house; it was on a liveable scale. It must be an amazing place to come home to every night, he thought.

Then he focused on what he wanted to get from this crime scene, running through a mental checklist as they pulled up behind a small marked police car. A uniformed constable, a solid man in his forties, stood beside it. Behind him, a chequered blue-and-white crime scene tape closed off the rest of the driveway, which led up to a large integral garage.

They climbed out and the Constable, a respectful old-school officer, briefed them pedantically on what he had found earlier this morning when he had attended, and informed them that SOCO was on its way. He was not able to add much more to the details Alcorn had already given Grace, other than the fact that the woman had arrived home and apparently had deactivated the burglar alarm when she entered.

While they were talking, a small white van pulled up and a senior SOCO, a Crime Scene Manager called Joe Tindall with whom Grace had worked many times and found more than a tad tetchy, climbed out.

'Friday,' the Crime Scene Manager muttered by way of a greeting. 'What's with you and sodding weekends, Roy?' He gave Grace a smile that was incubating a leer.

'I keep asking offenders to stick to Mondays, but they're not an obliging lot.'

'I've got tickets to Stevie Wonder at the O$_2$ Arena tonight. If I miss that my relationship is kaput.'

'Every time I see you, you've got tickets to something, Joe.'

'Yeah. I like to think I have a life outside of this job, unlike half my colleagues.'

He gave the Detective Superintendent a pointed stare, then produced a clutch of white paper suits and blue overshoes from the rear of the van and handed them out.

Roy Grace sat on the rear sill of the van and slowly levered himself into the one-piece. Every time he did this, he cursed the designer as he wriggled to get his feet down through the trousers without tearing them, then worked himself into the arms. He was glad not to be in a public place, because the suit was almost impossible to put on without making a spectacle of yourself. Finally, grunting, he stooped down and pulled on the protective overshoes. Then he snapped on some latex gloves.

The Constable led the way inside and Grace was impressed that he'd had the good sense to mark on the ground with tape a single entry and exit route.

The open-plan hall, with polished parquet flooring, elegant metal sculptures, abstract paintings and tall, lush plants, was something that Cleo would love, he thought. There was a strong, pleasant smell of pine and a slightly sweeter, muskier scent, probably from pot-pourri, he thought. It made a refreshing change not to walk into a house that smelt of curry.

The Constable said he would come upstairs, to be available to answer questions, but he would not enter the bedroom, to minimize the disturbance in there.

Grace hoped that the officer, being this forensically aware, hadn't trampled all over it when he had responded to the emergency call earlier. He followed Alcorn and Tindall up a glass spiral staircase, along a short galleried landing and into a huge bedroom that smelt strongly of perfume.

The windows had curtains like a fine white gauze and the walls were lined with fitted wardrobes with curtained glass panels. The double doors of one of them were open and several dresses on their hangers lay fallen on the carpeted floor.

The centrepiece of the room was a king-sized bed with four tapered wooden columns rising from it. An unwound dressing gown cord lay around one of them, and a striped man's tie, knotted to a plain tie, around another. Four more ties, knotted together into two doubles, lay on the floor. The cream satin duvet was badly rumpled.

'Mrs Pearce was left gagged and tied by her wrists and ankles to each of those posts,' the Constable said from the doorway. 'She managed to free herself at about half past six this morning, and then she called her friend.' He checked his notebook. 'Mrs Amanda Baldwin. I have her number.'

Grace nodded. He was staring at a photograph on a glass-topped dressing table. It was of an attractive woman, with sleek black hair clipped up, wearing a long evening dress, standing next to a sharp-looking guy in a dinner suit.

Pointing at it, he said, 'Presume this is her?'

'Yes, chief.'

David Alcorn studied her too.

'What state was she in?' Grace asked the Constable.

'Pretty bad shock,' he replied. 'But quite compos mentis, considering her ordeal, if you know what I mean.'

'What do we know about her husband?'

'He went away yesterday on a business trip to Helsinki.'

Grace thought for a moment, then looked at David Alcorn. 'Interesting timing,' he said. 'Might be significant. I'd like to find out how often he goes away. It could be someone who knows her, or who's been stalking her.'

Turning to the Constable, he said, 'He was wearing a mask, right?'

'Yes, sir, he was – a hood with slits cut in.'

Grace nodded. 'Has the husband been contacted?'

'He's going to try to get a flight back today.'

Alcorn went out to check the other rooms.

Joe Tindall was holding a compact camera up to his eye. He took a 360-degree video of the scene, then zoomed in on the bed.

'Did you attend alone?' Grace asked the Constable.

He cast his eyes around the room as he spoke. On the floor lay a pair of cream undies, a white blouse, a navy skirt and top, tights and a bra. They weren't strewn around the room as if they had been torn off the woman; they looked as if they had been stepped out of carelessly and left where they fell.

'No, sir, with Sergeant Porritt. He's accompanied her and the SOLO to the Saturn Centre.'

Grace made a brief sketch plan of the room, noting the doors – one to the hallway, one to the en-suite bathroom – and the windows, all as possible entry/exit areas. He would require careful combing of the room for fingerprints, hair, fibres, skin cells, saliva, semen, possible lubricant traces from a condom, if one had been used, and footprints. The outside of the house would need to be searched carefully also, especially for footprints, and for clothing fibres that might have come off on a wall or a frame if the offender escaped via a window, as well as for cigarette butts.

He would need to write out and give Tindall his recovery policy on how much of the contents of the room and the house and surroundings he might want bagged and tagged for lab testing. The bedding, for sure. Towels in the bathroom in case the offender had dried his hands or any parts of his body. The soap.

He made notes, padding around the room, looking for anything out of the ordinary. There was a huge fixed mirror facing the bed, put there for kinky purposes he thought, not disapprovingly. On one bedside table were a diary and a chick-lit novel and on the other a pile of IT magazines. He opened each of the wardrobe doors in turn. There were more dresses hanging here than he had ever seen in his life.

Then he opened another and, breathing in a luxurious rich scent of leather, he encountered an Aladdin's cave of shoes. They were racked floor-to-ceiling on slide-out drawers. Grace was no expert on ladies' footwear, but he could tell at a glance that these were serious and classy. There had to be more than fifty pairs in here. The next door he opened revealed another fifty pairs. Followed by the same behind the third door.

'Looks like she's a high-maintenance lady!' he commented.

'I understand she has her own business, Roy,' David Alcorn said.

Grace silently chided himself. It had been a stupid comment, the kind of sexist assumption he might have expected from someone like Norman Potting.

'Right.'

He walked over to the window and peered out at the rear garden, a handsomely landscaped plot, with an oval swimming pool, beneath its winter cover, as its centrepiece.

Beyond the garden, visible through dense shrubs and young trees, were school playing fields. Rugby posts were up on two pitches and netted football goals on a third. This would have made a possible access route for the offender, he thought.

Who are you?

The Shoe Man?

Or just another creep?

33

'Yer could have fucking knocked,' Terry Biglow whined.

Knocking had never been Darren Spicer's style. He stood in the small room, in the semi-darkness from the drawn window blind, clutching his holdall and trying to breathe in as little as possible of the fetid air. The room reeked of ingrained cigarette smoke, old wood, dusty carpet and rancid milk.

'Thought you was still inside.' The elderly villain's voice was small and reedy. He lay, blinking into Spicer's torch beam. 'Anyhow, what the fuck you doing here at this hour?'

'Been shagging,' Spicer replied. 'Thought I'd pop by and tell you all about her, and pick up my stuff while I was at it.'

'Like I need to know. My days of shagging are over. Can hardly get it to piss. What do you want? Stop shining that bleedin' thing in my face.'

Spicer flicked the beam around the walls, found a wall switch and clicked it on. A gloomy overhead light in an even gloomier tasselled shade came on. He wrinkled his face in disgust at the sight of this room.

'You gone over the wall again?' Biglow said, still blinking.

He looked terrible, Spicer thought. Seventy, going on ninety.

'Good behaviour, mate, yeah? I'm on early release licence.' He tossed a wristwatch on to Biglow's chest. 'Brought you a present.'

Biglow grabbed it with his gnarled little hands and peered at it greedily. 'Wossis? Korean?'

'It's real. Nicked it last night.'

Biglow hauled himself up a little in the bed, scrabbled on the table beside him and put on some reading glasses that were unfashionably large. Then he studied the watch. 'Tag Heuer Aquaracer,' he announced. 'Nice one. Thieving and shagging?'

'Other way around.'

Biglow gave him a thin smile, revealing a row of sharp little teeth the colour of rusty tin. He was wearing a filthy-looking T-shirt that might once have been white. Beneath it he was all skin and bone. He smelt of old sacks.

'Nice,' he said. 'Very nice. Wot yer want for it?'

'A grand.'

'Yer having a laugh. Might get yer a monkey if I can find a buyer – and if it's kosher and not some copy. Otherwise, a one-er now. I could give yer a one-er now.'

A monkey was £500; a one-er £100.

'It's a two-grand watch,' Spicer said.

'And we're in a bleedin' recession and all.' Biglow looked at the watch again. 'You're lucky you didn't come out much later.' He fell silent, then when Spicer said nothing he went on. 'I ain't got long, see?' He coughed, a long, harsh, racking cough that made his eyes water, and spat some blood into a grimy handkerchief. 'Six months they gimme.'

'Bummer.'

Darren Spicer cast his eyes around the basement bedsit. It shook as a train thundered close by outside, emitting an eerie howl. A cold draught of air blew through the room. The place was a tip, just like he remembered it when he had last been here, over three years ago. A threadbare carpet covered some of the floorboards. Clothes hung from the dado rail on wire hangers. An old wooden clock on a shelf said it was 8.45. A crucifix was nailed to the wall just above the bed and a Bible lay on the table beside Biglow, along with several labelled bottles of medication.

This is going to be me in thirty years' time, if I get that far.

Then he shook his head. 'This it, Terry? This where you're ending your days?'

'It's all right. It's convenient.'

'Convenient? Convenient for what? The fucking funeral parlour?'

Biglow said nothing. A short distance away, across the Lewes Road, adjacent to the cemetery and the mortuary, was a whole line of undertakers.

'Ain't yer got running water?'

'Course I have,' Biglow spluttered, through another fit of coughing. He pointed across the room at a wash-basin.

'Don't you ever wash? It smells like a toilet in here.'

'You want a cup of tea? Coffee?'

Spicer looked at a corner shelf on which sat a kettle and some cracked mugs. 'No thanks. Not thirsty.'

He shook his head as he looked down at the old villain. *You were a big player in this city. Even I was shit scared of you as a lad. Just the name Biglow put the fear into most people. Now look at you.*

The Biglows had been a crime family to be reckoned with, running one of the major protection rackets, controlling half of Brighton and Hove's drug scene, and Terry had been one of the scions. He wasn't a man you messed with, not if you didn't want a razor scar across your cheek or acid thrown in your face. He used to dress mean and sharp, with big rings and watches, and drive fancy cars. Now, ruined by booze, his face was all sallow and shrunken. His hair, which used to be freshly coiffed, even at midnight, now looked more worn than the carpet, and was the colour of nicotine from some off-the-shelf dye.

'On the nonce's wing, were you, in Lewes, Darren?'

'Screw you. I was never no *nonce*.'

'Not what I heard.'

Spicer looked at him defensively. 'I told you it all before, right? She was gagging for it. You can tell a woman that's gagging for it. Threw herself at me, didn't she? I had to push her away.'

'Funny the jury didn't believe yer.'

Biglow pulled a packet of cigarettes out of a drawer, shook out a cigarette and put it in his mouth.

Spicer shook his head. 'Lung cancer and you're lighting up?'

'Big lot of difference that's going to make now, nonce.'

'Fuck you.'

'Always nice to see yer, Darren.'

He lit his cigarette using a plastic lighter, inhaled and was then lost in a coughing fit.

Spicer knelt down, rolled back the carpet, removed some floorboards, then extricated the old, square leather suitcase which had three chains around it, each secured with a heavy-duty padlock.

Biglow held up the watch. 'Tell you what. I always been a fair man and don't want you thinkin' ill of me

after I gone. We got three years' left-luggage fee to nego-
tiate and all. So what I'll do is give you thirty quid for the
watch. Can't say fairer than that.'

'A fucking carpet?'

In a fit of fury, Spicer grabbed Terry Biglow's hair
with his left hand and jerked him up, out of bed, and held
him in front of his face, dangling him like a ventriloquist's
dummy. He was surprised how light the man was. Then
he slammed a rising punch under his chin as hard as he
could, with his right hand. So hard it hurt like hell.

Terry Biglow went limp. Spicer released him and he
fell to the floor in a crumpled heap. He took a few steps
forward and trampled out the cigarette that was burning.
Then he looked around the squalid bedsit for anything
that might be worth taking. But other than recovering the
watch, there was nothing. Nothing at all. There really
wasn't.

Lugging the heavy suitcase under one arm, and his
holdall containing all his basics, he let himself out of the
door, hesitating for one moment, in which he turned back
to the crumpled heap.

'See you at your funeral, mate.'

He closed the door behind him, then climbed the
stairs and went out into the freezing, blustery Brighton
Friday morning.

34

For the second time in just over a week, the Sexual Offences Liaison Officer, DC Claire Westmore, was back at the Saturn Centre, the Sexual Assault Referral Centre attached to Crawley Hospital.

She knew from experience that no two victims ever reacted the same way, and nor did their conditions remain static. One of the difficult tasks facing her right now was to keep abreast of the changing state of mind of the woman she was with. But while treating her sensitively and sympathetically, and trying to make her feel as safe as possible, she could not lose sight of the cruel fact that Roxy Pearce, like it or not, was a crime scene from whom every possible scrap of forensic evidence needed to be obtained.

When that was completed, she would let the woman rest – safe here in this suite – and with the help of medication get some sleep. Tomorrow, when hopefully the woman would be in a better state, the interview process could start. For Roxy Pearce, as with most victims, that was likely to mean three gruelling days of reliving what had happened, with Westmore extracting from her a harrowing narrative that would eventually fill thirty pages of her A4 notebook.

At this moment she was going through the most

201

distressing part of all for the victim – and for herself. They were alone with a female Forensic Medical Examiner, or FME, as Police Surgeons were now called, in the sterile Forensic Room. Roxy Pearce was wearing only the white towelling dressing gown and pink slippers in which she had travelled here. She'd had a blanket wrapped around her for warmth in the police car, but now that had been removed. She sat, hunched and silent and forlorn, on the blue examining couch, her head bowed, eyes staring blankly at nothing, her long black hair matted and partially obscuring her face. From being hyper-talkative when the police had first arrived at her house, she had now become almost catatonic.

Claire Westmore had heard victims say that being raped was like having their souls murdered. Just as with murder, there was no going back. No amount of therapy would restore Roxy Pearce to the person she had previously been. Yes, in time she would recover a little, enough to function, to live a seemingly normal life. But it would be a life constantly stalked by the shadow of fear. A life in which she would find it hard ever to trust anyone or any situation.

'You're safe here, Roxy,' Claire said to her with a bright smile. 'You're in the safest possible place. He can't get to you here.'

She smiled again. But there was no response. It was like talking to a waxwork.

'Your friend Amanda is here,' she went on. 'She just went out for a ciggie. She's going to stay with you all day.' Again she smiled.

Again the blank expression. The dead eyes. Blank. As blank as everything in here around her. As blank and numb as her insides.

Roxy Pearce's eyes registered the magnolia-coloured walls of the small room. Recently painted. The round, institutional clock showing the time as 12.35. A rack of boxes containing blue latex gloves. Another rack of blue and red crates containing syringes, swabs and vials, all sealed in sterile wrappers. A pink chair. Weighing scales. A basin with a moisturizer dispenser on one side and sterile handwash on the other. A telephone sitting on a bare white work-surface like some unused lifeline in a television quiz game. A foldaway screen on castors.

Tears welled in her eyes. She wished Dermot was here. She wished, in her addled mind, that she hadn't been unfaithful to him, hadn't had this crazy thing with Iannis.

Then suddenly she blurted out, 'It's all my fault, isn't it?'

'Why do you think that, Roxy?' the SOLO asked, jotting down her words in the log she was keeping in her notepad. 'You mustn't blame yourself at all. That's not right.'

But the woman lapsed back into silence.

'OK, my love. Don't worry. You don't have to say anything to me. We don't have to talk today if you don't want to, but what I do need to do is obtain forensic evidence from you, to help us try to catch the man who did this to you. Is that all right with you?'

After some moments, Roxy said, 'I feel dirty. I want to take a shower. Can I do that?'

'Of course, Roxy,' the Forensic Medical Examiner said. 'But not just yet. We don't want to wash away any evidence, do we?' She had a slightly bossy tone, Claire Westmore thought, a little too officious for the victim's fragile state.

Silence again. Roxy's mind went off on a tangent. She had taken out two of Dermot's best bottles. Left them somewhere. One open on the kitchen table, the other in the fridge. She would have to buy a bottle somewhere to replace the opened one, and go to the house before Dermot came back and replace them in the cellar. He'd go loopy otherwise.

The FME snapped on a pair of latex gloves, walked over to the plastic crates and removed the first item from its sterile wrapping. A small, sharp implement for taking scrapings from underneath fingernails. It was possible the woman had scratched her attacker and that crucial skin cells containing his DNA might be trapped beneath her nails.

This was just the start of a long ordeal for Roxy Pearce in this room. Before she would be permitted to take a shower, the FME would have to take swabs from every part of her body where contact with her assailant might have occurred, looking for saliva, semen and skin cells. She would comb her pubic hair, take her blood alcohol and a urine sample for toxicology tests, and sketch in the Medical Examination Book any damage to the genital area.

As the FME worked her way through each of the woman's nails, bagging the scrapings separately, the SOLO tried to reassure Roxy.

'We're going to get this man, Roxy. That's why we're doing this. With your cooperation, we'll be able to stop him from doing this to anyone else. I know it must be hard for you, but try to hold on to that.'

'I don't know why you're bothering,' Roxy suddenly said. 'Only 4 per cent of rapists ever get convicted. Right?'

Claire Westmore hesitated. She'd heard that nationwide it was actually only 2 per cent, because just 6 per cent of rapes were ever reported. But she didn't want to make things worse for the poor woman.

'Well, that's not entirely true,' she answered. 'But the figures are low, yes. That's because so few victims have your guts, Roxy. They don't have the courage to come forward like you are doing.'

'Guts?' she retorted bitterly. 'I don't have *guts.*'

'Yes, you do. You really do have guts.'

Roxy Pearce shook her head bleakly. 'It's my fault. If I'd had guts, I'd have stopped him. Everyone'll think I must have wanted him to do this, that I must have encouraged him somehow. Anyone else might have managed to stop him, knee him in the nuts or something, but I didn't, did I? I just lay there.'

35

Darren Spicer's morning was getting better. He'd recovered his things from Terry Biglow and now he had a place to store them, a tall, cream metal locker with a key of his own at St Patrick's night shelter. And he hoped, in a few weeks, he'd get a MiPod there.

The big Neo-Norman church at the end of a quiet residential street in Hove had adapted to the changing world. With its shrinking congregation, much of St Patrick's cavernous interior had been partitioned off and placed in the hands of a charity for the homeless. Part of it was a fourteen-bed dormitory where people could doss down for a maximum of three months. Another part, the MiPod Room, was a sanctuary. It was where people who showed real intentions of retraining could stay for a further ten weeks in the hope of giving them a stable base.

The MiPod Room was modelled on Japanese capsule hotels. It was a self-contained space, with six plastic pods, a kitchen area and a living area with television. Each of the pods was large enough to sleep in and to store a couple of suitcases.

To become eligible for one, first Spicer had to convince the management here that he was a model resident. He hadn't thought beyond those ten weeks in the pod, but by then, with luck, he'd have plenty of cash to rent a flat or house again.

Being a model resident meant obeying the rules, such as having to be out by 8.30 a.m. and not returning until dinnertime at 7.30 p.m. During the hours in between he was meant to be retraining. Yeah, well, that's what they would all think he was doing. He'd report to the retraining centre and sign on, and hopefully get a job in the maintenance department of one of Brighton's posh hotels. There'd be some easy pickings in the rooms from that. Should be able to build himself a nice stash. And stumble across a willing woman or two, like he had last night.

Shortly after midday, dressed in a windcheater over a sweater, jeans and sneakers, he left the retraining centre. The interview had gone fine and he now possessed a stamped form and the address of the swanky Grand Hotel on the seafront, where he would start on Monday. He had the rest of today to kill.

As he mooched along Western Road, the wide shopping street connecting Brighton with Hove, his hands were dug into his pockets against the cold. He had just £7 in his pocket – all that was left from his £46 prison discharge allowance, plus the small amount of cash he'd had on him when he'd last been arrested. And he had his emergency stash in the suitcase he had retrieved from Terry Biglow.

In his head he was making out a shopping list of stuff he needed. He was given basic necessities here, like new razor blades, shaving cream, toothpaste. But he needed a few treats. He walked past a bookshop called City Books, then stopped, turned back and peered at the display in the window. Dozens of books, some by authors whose names he knew, others by authors he'd never heard of.

It was still a novelty being out. To smell the salty sea air. To walk freely among women. To hear the hum and buzz and roar of vehicles and occasional snatches of music. Yet although he felt free, he felt vulnerable and exposed too. Life *inside*, he realized, had become his comfort zone. He didn't know this other world so well any more.

And this street seemed to have changed in the past three years. It was much more vibrant than he remembered. As if the world, three years on, was a party he had not yet been invited to.

It was lunchtime and the restaurants were starting to get busy. Filling up with strangers.

Just about everyone was a stranger to him.

Sure, there were a few friends he could contact, and would in time. But he didn't have a lot to say to them at the moment. Same old same old. Yeah. He'd call them when he needed to score some coke. Or when he had some brown to sell.

A police car was coming past in the opposite direction and automatically he turned and peered in through an estate agent's window, pretending to be interested.

Most of the police in this city knew his face. Half of them had nicked him at one time or another. He had to remind himself that he was permitted to walk down this street now. That he wasn't a fugitive. He was a citizen of Brighton and Hove. He was like everyone else!

He stared at some of the houses on display. A nice one opposite Hove Park caught his eye. It looked familiar and he had a feeling he'd burgled it some years ago. Four bedrooms, conservatory, double garage. A nice price too: £750,000. Yeah, a bit above his bracket. Like £750,000 above his bracket.

The huge Tesco supermarket was a short distance ahead of him now. He crossed the road and walked in past the queue of waiting cars at the car-park barriers. Plenty of smart ones. A convertible Beemer, a nice Merc sports and several huge, in-your-face off-roader jobs – Brighton and Hove ladies doing their shopping. Yummy mummies with infants strapped smugly into their child seats in the rear.

People with folding money, with credit cards, debit cards, Tesco Club Cards.

How obliging some of them were!

He stopped outside the front entrance, watching the stream of people coming out with their bags or with laden trolleys. He ignored the ones holding just a couple of bags; they were of no interest to him. It was the laden trolleys he focused on. The mummies and daddies and rest-home proprietors doing their big shop for the week-end ahead. The ones who would have had £200 and more swiped from their MasterCards, or Barclaycards, or Amex.

Some had infants strapped into the buggy seats in their trolleys, but he wasn't interested in those. Who the fuck wanted baby food?

Then he saw her coming out.

Oh yes! Perfect!

She looked rich. She looked arrogant. She had the kind of figure he'd lain on the top bunk of his cell dreaming about for three years. She had a trolley piled so high that the top layer defied gravity. And she was wearing really nice boots. Snakeskin, with five-inch heels, he guessed.

But it wasn't the shoes that interested him at this moment. It was the fact that she paused by the dustbins, screwed up her receipt and tossed it in. He strolled nonchalantly over to the bin, keeping an eye on her, while she pushed her trolley towards a black Range Rover Sport.

Then he slipped his hand inside the top of the bin and pulled out a clutch of receipts. It only took a moment to find hers – it was a good two feet long, with a checkout time of just two minutes ago.

Well, well – £185! And, a real bonus, it was a cash receipt, which meant he would not have to produce any credit card or ID. He read down the items: wine, whiskey, prawn cocktail, moussaka, apples, bread, yoghurt. So much stuff. Razor blades! Some of the stuff he didn't want, but hey, this was not the time to be fussy ... Fantastic! He gave her a little wave, which she never saw. At the same time, he clocked her car's registration number – well, she was a looker with nice shoes, you never knew! Then, grabbing a trolley, he entered the store.

*

It took Spicer half an hour to go through her list, item by item. He was aware of the checkout time printed at the bottom, but he had his story ready, that one of the eggs was broken so he'd gone to replace it, and then he'd stopped for a coffee.

There was some stuff, such as a dozen tins of cat food, that he really did not need, and two tins of smoked oysters he could have done without, but he decided it was better to match the items on the list exactly, in case he was challenged. Six frozen steak and kidney pies he truly blessed her for. His kind of grub! And the half a dozen tins of Heinz Baked Beans. He had no stomach for fancy stuff. He approved of her choice of Jameson's Irish Whiskey, but wished she had chosen something more to his taste than Baileys. She was big into organic eggs and fruit. He could live with that.

He would take his shopping home and chuck or maybe flog or barter for cigarettes the stuff he did not want. Then he would go out on the hunt.

Life was looking good. Only one thing could improve it for him at the moment. Another woman.

1998

36

Friday 2 January

It was now eight days since Rachael Ryan had been reported missing by her parents.

Eight days in which there had been no proof of life.

Roy Grace had worked doggedly on the case since Christmas Day, increasingly certain something was very wrong, until Chief Inspector Jack Skerritt had insisted that the Detective Sergeant take New Year's Eve off to spend with his wife.

Grace had done so reluctantly, torn between his concern to find Rachael and his need to keep the peace at home with Sandy. Now, after a two-day absence, he returned on this Friday morning to a briefing update by Skerritt. The Chief Inspector told his small team of detectives of his decision, made in consultation with his ACC, to upgrade *Operation Sundown* to an Incident Room. A HOLMES – Home Office Large Major Enquiry System team – had been requisitioned, and six additional detectives from other parts of the county were being drafted in.

The Incident Room was set up on the fourth floor of John Street police station, next to the CCTV department and across the corridor from the busy *Operation Houdini* Incident Room, where the investigation into the Shoe Man continued.

Grace, who was convinced that the two operations

215

should be merged, was allocated his present desk, where he was to be based for the duration of the inquiry. It was by the draughty window, giving him a bleak view across the car park and the grey, rain-soaked rooftops towards Brighton Station and the viaduct.

Seated at the next desk along was DC Tingley, a bright, boyish-looking twenty-six-year-old police officer whom he liked. In particular, he liked the man's energy. Jason Tingley, sleeves rolled up, was on the phone, pen in hand, dealing with one of the dozens of calls that had come in following their reconstruction, three days earlier, of Rachael's journey from the East Street taxi rank back home.

Grace had a thick file on Rachael Ryan on his desk. Already, despite the holidays, he had her bank and her credit-card details. There had been no transactions during the past week, which meant he could effectively rule out that she had been mugged for the contents of her handbag. There had been no calls from her mobile phone since 2.35 on Christmas morning.

However, there was something useful he had gleaned from the mobile phone company. There were mobile phone base stations, or mini masts, located around Brighton and Hove, and every fifteen minutes, even in standby mode, the phone would send a signal to the nearest mast, like a plane radioing its current position, and receive one back.

Although no further calls had been made from Rachael Ryan's phone, it had remained switched on for three more days, until the battery died, he guessed. According to information he'd received from the phone company, shortly after her last phone call, she had suddenly moved two miles east of her home – in a vehicle of some kind, judging from the speed at which it had happened.

She had remained there for the rest of the night, until 10 a.m. on Christmas Day. Then she had travelled approximately four miles west, into Hove. Again the speed of the journey indicated that she was travelling in a vehicle. Then she had stopped and remained static until the last signal received, shortly after 11 p.m. on Saturday.

On a large-scale map of Brighton and Hove on the Incident Room wall, Grace had drawn a red circle around the maximum area that would be covered by this particular beacon's range. It included most of Hove as well as part of Brighton, Southwick and Portslade. Over 120,000 people lived within its radius – an almost impossible number for house-to-house enquiries.

Besides, the information was only of limited value, he realized. Rachael could have been separated from her phone. It was just an indicator of where she *might* be, but no more. But so far it was all they had. One line he would try, he decided, was to see if anything had been picked up on CCTV cameras on the routes matching the signal information. But there was only coverage on major routes and that was limited.

Rachael did not own a computer and there was nothing on the one in her office at American Express to give any clue as to why she might have disappeared.

At the moment it was if she had fallen through a crack in the earth.

Tingley put down the phone and drew a line through the name he had written a couple of minutes earlier on his pad. 'Tosser!' he said. 'Time waster.' Then he turned to Roy. 'Good New Year's Eve, mate?'

'Yeah, it was all right. Went with Dick and Leslie Pope to Donatello's. You?'

'Went up to London with the missus. Trafalgar

Square. It was brilliant – until it started pissing with rain.'
He shrugged. 'So what do you think? She still alive?'

'Not looking good,' he replied. 'She's a homebody.
Still sore about the bust-up with her ex. Into shoes, big
time.' He looked at his colleague and shrugged. 'That's
the bit I keep coming back to.'

Grace had spent an hour earlier in the day with
Dr Julius Proudfoot, the behavioural analyst *Operation
Houdini* had drafted into their team. Proudfoot told him
that, in his view, Rachael Ryan's disappearance could not
be connected to the Shoe Man. He still did not under-
stand how the arrogant psychologist had arrived at that
conclusion, since he had so little evidence.

'Proudfoot insists this isn't the Shoe Man's style. He
says the Shoe Man attacks his victims and then leaves
them. Because he's used the same MO for five victims,
Proudfoot doesn't accept that he would suddenly have
changed and kept one.'

'Similar MO, Roy,' Jason Tingley said. 'But he takes
them in different places, right? He tried that first one in
an alley. One in a hotel room. One in her home. One
under the pier. One in a multi-storey car park. Clever if
you want to look at it that way – makes it hard for anyone
to second-guess him.'

Grace looked down at his notes, thinking hard. There
was one common denominator with each of the Shoe
Man's victims. All of them were into designer shoes. Each
one had bought a new pair of shoes, from different shops
in Brighton, shortly before they were attacked. But so far
interviews with staff in the shops had revealed nothing
helpful.

Rachael Ryan had bought a new pair of shoes too.
Three days before Christmas. Expensive for a girl of her

means – £170. She had been wearing them the night she vanished.

But Proudfoot had dismissed that.

Grace turned to Tingley and told him this.

Tingley nodded, looking pensive suddenly. 'So if it isn't the Shoe Man, who's taken her? Where has she gone? If she's OK, why isn't she contacting her parents? She must have seen the appeal in the *Argus* or heard it on the radio.'

'Doesn't make any sense. She normally phones her parents every day and chats to them. Eight days of silence? And at this time of year – Christmas and New Year? No call to wish them Happy Christmas or Happy New Year? Something's happened to her, for sure.'

Tingley nodded. 'Abducted by aliens?'

Grace looked back down at his notes. 'The Shoe Man took his victims in a different place each time, but what he did to them was consistent. And even more important was what he did to his victims' lives. He didn't need to kill them. They were already dead inside by the time he had finished with them.'

Are you a victim of the Shoe Man, Rachael? Or has some other monster got you?

NOW

37

MIR-1, the larger of the two Major Incident Rooms at Sussex House, had an atmosphere that Roy Grace always found energizing.

Located in the heart of the Major Crime Suite at the CID headquarters, it would have looked to a casual observer like any other large administrative office. It had cream walls, functional grey carpeting, red chairs, modern wooden workstations, filing cabinets, a water dispenser and several large whiteboards on the walls. The windows were high up, with permanently closed blinds across them, as if to discourage anyone from wasting one second of their time looking out of them.

But to Roy Grace this was much more than an office. MIR-1 was the very nerve centre of his current investigation, as it had been with the previous ones he had run from here, and to him it had an almost hallowed atmosphere. Many of the worst crimes committed in Sussex in the past decade had been solved, and the offenders locked up, thanks to the detective work that had been carried out in this room.

The red, blue and green marker-pen scrawlings on the whiteboards in any other office out in the commercial world might have been performance figures, sales targets, market penetrations. Here they were timelines of the crimes, family trees of the victims and suspects, along with photographs and any other key information. When they got an E-Fit of the offender, hopefully soon, that would go up too.

The place instilled in everyone a sense of purpose, of racing against a clock, and, except during briefings, there was little of the chat and banter between colleagues that was usual in police offices.

The only frivolity was a photocopied cartoon of a fat blue fish from the film *Finding Nemo* which Glenn Branson had stuck on the inside of the door. It had become a tradition in Sussex CID for a jokey image to be found for each operation, to provide a little light relief from the horrors that the team had to deal with, and this was the movie-buff Detective Sergeant's contribution to *Operation Swordfish.*

There were three other dedicated Major Crime Suites around the county, also housing similar rooms, the most recent being the purpose-built one at Eastbourne. But this location was more convenient for Roy Grace, as well as being well sited, because the two crimes he was now investigating had occurred only a couple of miles away.

There were all kinds of repeating patterns in life, he had noticed, and it seemed that recently he was on a run of crimes that took place – or were discovered – on Fridays, thus ensuring his and everyone else's weekend was wiped out.

He was meant to be going to dinner with Cleo at one of her oldest friend's tomorrow night – Cleo wanted to show him off, as she grinningly told him. He had been looking forward to a further insight into the life of this woman he was so deeply in love with and still knew so little about. But that was now down the khazi.

Fortunately for him, unlike Sandy, who had never understood or got used to his frequent crazy working hours, Cleo was regularly on call herself 24/7, having to go out at all hours to recover bodies from wherever they were found. Which made her much more sympathetic – although not always totally forgiving.

It was the case in the early stages of any major crime investigation that everything else had to be instantly dropped. The first task of the Senior Investigating Officer's assistant was to clear the SIO's diary.

It was the first twenty-four hours after the crime had been discovered that were the most crucial. You needed to protect the crime scene to preserve the forensic evidence as much as possible. The perpetrator would be at his most heightened state of anxiety, the *red mist* that people tended to be in after committing a serious crime, in which they might behave erratically, drive erratically. There would be possible eyewitnesses for whom it was all fresh in their minds, and a chance to reach them quickly through the local press and media. And all CCTV cameras within a reasonable radius would still retain footage for those past twenty-four hours.

Grace looked down at the notes typed by his assistant – his MSA – which lay beside his fresh Policy Book for this case.

'It is 6.30 p.m., Friday, 9 January,' he read out. 'This is the first briefing of *Operation Swordfish*.'

The Sussex Police computer threw up operation names at random, most of them totally irrelevant to the case on which they were working. But here, he thought wryly, it was just a tad appropriate, fish being slippery creatures.

Grace was pleased that all but one of the trusted key CID members he wanted for his core team were available. Seated around the workstation with him were DC Nick Nicholl, still looking bleary-eyed from recent fatherhood, DC Emma-Jane Boutwood, highly effective DS Bella Moy, an open box of Maltesers, as ever, in front of her, belligerent DS Norman Potting, and Grace's mate and protégé DS Glenn Branson. Absent was DS Guy Batchelor, who was away on annual leave. Instead he had a detective constable he'd worked with some while back and had been very impressed with, Michael Foreman, a lean, quietly authoritative man, with gelled dark hair, who had an air of calm about him that made people naturally turn to him, even when he wasn't the senior officer present at a situation. For the past year, with a temporary promotion to acting sergeant, Foreman had been on secondment to the team at the Regional Intelligence Office. Now he was back at Sussex House, in his old rank, but Grace did not think it would be long before the man became a full sergeant. And, no question, he was heading for a much higher things than that.

Also present among Grace's regulars was HOLMES analyst John Black, a mild, grey-haired man who could have been a backroom accountant, and DC Don Trotman, a Public Protection Officer, who would be tasked with checking on MAPPA, the Multi-Agency Public Protection Arrangements, whether any recently released prisoners who were sexual offenders fitted the MO of the current offender.

New to the team was an analyst, Ellen Zoratti, who would be working closely with Brighton division and the

HOLMES analyst, progressing the intelligence leads, checking with the National Police Crime Database and SCAS, the Serious Crime Analysis Section, as well as carrying out instructions from Roy Grace.

Also new was a female press officer, Sue Fleet, from the revamped Police Public Relations Team. The pleasant thirty-two-year-old redhead, who had been a trusted and popular member of the Central Brighton John Street team, had replaced the previous public relations officer, Dennis Ponds, a former journalist who had never had an easy relationship with many members of this force, including Grace himself.

Grace wanted Sue Fleet present to organize an immediate media strategy. He needed to get a quick public response to help in the task of finding the offender and to alert the female population to the possible dangers they now faced, but at the same time he did not want to throw the city into panic. It was a delicate PR balance and would be a challenging task for her.

'Before I start,' Grace said, 'I want to remind you all of some statistics. In Sussex we have a good clear-up rate for homicide – with 98 per cent of all murders in the past decade solved. But in rape we've fallen behind the national average of 4 per cent to just above 2 per cent. This is not acceptable.'

'Do you think that's down to the attitude of some police officers?' asked Norman Potting, dressed in one of the tired old tweedy jackets that reeked of pipe smoke that he always seemed to wear. In Grace's view they made him look more like an elderly geography teacher than a detective. 'Or that some victims are just not reliable witnesses – because of other agendas?'

'Other agendas, Norman? Like that old attitude police

officers used to have that women who got raped asked for it? Is that what you mean?'

Potting grunted, non-committally.

'For God's sake, what planet are you on?' Bella Moy, who had never liked him, rounded on him furiously. 'It's like living a real *Life on Mars* working with you.'

The DS shrugged defensively and then mumbled, barely audibly, as if he wasn't convinced enough to say whatever he had on his mind more boldly, 'We know that some women cry rape out of guilt, don't they? It does make you wonder.'

'Makes you wonder what?' Bella demanded.

Grace was glaring at him, scarcely able to believe his ears. He was so angry he was tempted to kick the man off his investigation right now. He was beginning to think he had made a mistake bringing this tactless man in on such a sensitive case. Norman Potting was a good policeman, with a range of detective skills that were, unfortunately, not matched by his social skills. Emotional intelligence was one of the major assets of a good detective. On a scale of one to a hundred, Potting would have rated close to zero on this score. Yet he could be damned effective, particularly on outside enquiries. Sometimes.

'Do you want to stay on this investigation, Norman?' Grace asked him.

'Yes, Chief, I do. I think I could contribute to it.'

'Really?' Grace retorted. 'Then let's get something straight, from the start.' He glanced around the assembled company. 'I hate rapists as much as I hate murderers. Rapists destroy their victims' lives. Whether it is a stranger rape, a date rape or a rape by someone the victim knew and thought they trusted. And there's no difference in that, whether it's female rape or male rape, OK? But at this moment we happen to be dealing with attacks on women, which are more common.'

He stared pointedly at Norman Potting, then went on: 'Being raped is like being in a bad car crash that leaves you disabled for life. One moment a woman is going about her day or her night, in her comfort zone, the next moment she is shattered, and she's all smashed up in the wreckage. She faces years of counselling, years of terror, nightmares, mistrust. No matter how much help she receives, she will never be the same again. She will never lead what we know as a *normal* life again. Do you understand what I'm saying, Norman? Some women who are raped end up maiming themselves afterwards. They scrub their vaginas with wire wool and bleach because they have such a need to get rid of what happened. That's just a small part of what being raped can do to someone. Do you understand?' He looked around. 'Do you all understand?'

'Yes, chief,' Potting mumbled in his thick burr. 'I'm sorry. I didn't mean to be insensitive.'

'Does a man with four failed marriages know the meaning of the word *insensitive*,' Bella Moy asked, angrily snatching a Malteser from the box, popping it in her mouth and crunching it.

'OK, Bella, thank you,' Grace said. 'I think Norman knows where I'm coming from.'

Potting stared at his notepad, his face a dark shade of beetroot, and nodded, chastened.

Grace looked back down at his notes. 'We have another slightly sensitive issue. The Chief Constable, the Deputy Chief Constable and two of our four Assistant Chief Constables were all at the same dinner dance at the Metropole Hotel on New Year's Eve which Nicola Taylor, the first rape victim, attended.'

There was a moment of silence as everyone reflected on this.

'Are you saying that makes them suspects, boss?' DC Michael Foreman asked.

'Everyone who was in the hotel is a potential suspect, but I think I'd prefer to call them at this point *material witnesses to be eliminated from our enquiries,*' Grace replied. 'They're going to have to be interviewed along with everyone else. Any volunteers?'

No one raised a hand.

Grace grinned. 'Looks like I'll have to allocate that task to one of you. Could be a good opportunity to get noticed for promotion, or screw up your career permanently.'

There were a few uncomfortable smiles in the room.

'Perhaps I can recommend our master of tact, Norman Potting,' Bella Moy said.

There was a titter of laughter.

'I'd be happy to take that on,' Potting said.

Grace, deciding that Potting was the last person in this room he would allocate that task to, scribbled a note in his Policy Book, then studied his briefing notes for a moment.

'We have two stranger rapes within eight days, with enough similarity in the MO to assume for the moment it is the same offender,' he went on. 'This charmer made both his victims perform sexual acts on themselves with their shoes, then penetrated them anally with the heels of their shoes, then raped them himself. From what we have been able to establish – and the second victim has so far only given us a little information – he was unable to maintain an erection. This may have been due to premature ejaculation or because he is sexually dysfunctional.

There is one significant difference in his MO. Back in 1997, the Shoe Man took only one shoe, and his victim's panties. In the Metropole rape of Nicola Taylor he took all her clothes, including both her shoes. With Roxy Pearce, he took just her shoes.'

He paused to look down at his notes again, while several members of his team made notes also.

'Our offender appears to be forensically aware. In each case he wore a black hood and surgical gloves and used a condom. He either shaved his bodily hair or naturally had none. He is described as being of medium to small height, thin and softly spoken, with a neutral accent.'

Potting put up his hand and Grace nodded.

'Chief, you and I were both involved with *Operation Sundown*, the disappearance of a woman back in 1997 which may or may not have been connected to a similar case then, the Shoe Man – *Operation Houdini*. Do you think there's a possible link?'

'Apart from the differences in the trophies he took, the Shoe Man's MO is remarkably similar to the current offender's.' Grace nodded at the Analyst. 'This is one reason I've brought Ellen in.'

Sussex CID employed forty analysts. All but two of them were female, most of them with social sciences backgrounds. Male analysts were so rare that they were nicknamed *manolysts*. Ellen Zoratti was a very bright woman of twenty-eight, with dark hair just off her shoulders, cut in a sharp, modern style, and was elegantly dressed in a white blouse, black skirt and zebra-striped tights.

She would alternate round-the-clock twelve-hour shifts with another analyst and could play a crucial role over the coming days. Between them they would carry out subject profiles on the two victims, providing the team with information on their family backgrounds, their lifestyles, their friends. They would be researching them with the same depth of detail as if they were offenders.

Additional and possibly crucial information would be provided by the High-Tech Crime Unit, down on the ground floor, which had begun the process of analysing the mobile phones and computers of the two victims. They would be studying all the calls and texts made and received by the two women, from information on their phones and from their phone companies. They would look at their emails and at any chatlines either of them might have engaged with. Their address files. The websites they visited. If they had any electronic secrets, Grace's investigation team would soon know of them.

In addition, the High-Tech Crime Unit had deployed a Covert Internet Investigator to log into shoe- and foot-fetish chat rooms and build up relationships with other visitors, in the hope of finding some with extreme views.

'Do you think it could be a copycat, Ellen?' Michael Foreman asked her. 'Or the same offender from 1997 again?'

'I've started work on a comparative case analysis,' she replied. 'One of the crucial pieces of information withheld from the press and the public in *Operation Houdini* was the MO of the offender. It's too early to give you anything definitive, but from what I have so far – and it is very early days – it's looking possible that it's the same offender.'

'Do we have any information on why the Shoe Man stopped offending, sir?' Emma-Jane Boutwood asked.

'All we do know from *Operation Houdini*,' Grace said,

232

'is that he stopped offending at the same time as Rachael Ryan – possibly his sixth victim – disappeared. I was involved in her case, which is still open. We have no proof – or even evidence – that she was a victim, but she fitted one of his patterns.'

'Which was?' Michael Foreman asked.

'She had bought an expensive pair of shoes from a shop in Brighton approximately a week before she disappeared. Each of the Shoe Man's victims had bought a new, expensive pair of shoes shortly before they were attacked. One line of enquiry that *Operation Houdini* pursued at the time was questioning customers in Brighton and Hove's shoe shops. But no leads came from that.'

'Was there CCTV analysis then?' Bella Moy asked.

'Yes,' Grace replied. 'But the quality wasn't so good, and the city didn't have anything like the networked coverage it has now.'

'So what are the theories on why the Shoe Man stopped?' Michael Foreman asked.

'We don't know. The profiler – behavioural analyst – at the time, Julius Proudfoot, told us he might have moved away, to a different county or overseas. Or that he could be in prison for some other offence. Or that he could have died. Or it was possible he could have entered into a relationship that satisfied his needs.'

'If it is the same person, why would he stop for twelve years and then start offending again?' Bella Moy asked. 'And with a slightly different MO?'

'Proudfoot doesn't attach much importance to the difference in the trophies from 1997 to now. He is more interested that the overall MO is so similar. His view is that there could be a number of explanations why someone starts to reoffend. If it is the Shoe Man, he could simply have moved back into the area, thinking enough time has lapsed. Or the relationship he got into has changed and no longer satisfies his desires. Or he has been released from prison, where he's been for some other offence.'

'A pretty serious one if he's done twelve years,' Glenn Branson said.

'And easy to research,' Grace said. Then he turned to Ellen Zoratti. 'Ellen, have you found any other rapes with similar MOs around the country? Or where someone has been banged up for twelve years?'

'Nothing matching the Shoe Man other than a character in Leicester called James Lloyd, who raped women and then took their shoes, sir. He's currently doing life. I've checked back on all his offences and his movements, and eliminated him. He was in Leicester at the time these offences in Brighton were committed, and I have confirmation that he is currently in prison.' She paused and glanced at her notes. 'I have made a list of all sexual offenders who went inside no earlier than January 1998 and who were released prior to this past New Year's Eve.'

'Thanks, Ellen, that's very helpful,' Grace said. Then he addressed his whole team. 'It's a fact that a high percentage of stranger rapists tend to start with more minor offences. Flashing, frotting – rubbing themselves up against women – masturbating in public. That sort of thing. It's quite possible our offender was arrested for some minor offence at quite a young age. I've asked Ellen to check the local and national police databases for offenders and offences that might fit with this timeline before his first rapes in 1997 – and during the period in between. Checking for instances of theft or acts of indecency with ladies' shoes, for example. I also want every prostitute and dominatrix in the area questioned about any clients they might have with foot or shoe fetishes.'

Then he turned to Glenn Branson. 'Related to this, DS Branson's been studying Dr Proudfoot's report on the Shoe Man. What do you have for us, Glenn?'

'It's a real page-turner!' Glenn picked up a heavy-looking document. 'Two hundred and eighty-two pages of behavioural analysis. I've only had a chance to speed read it, since the chief tasked me with it earlier today, but there is something very interesting. There were five reported offences linked directly to the Shoe Man but Dr Proudfoot believes he could have committed a lot more that weren't reported.'

He paused for a moment. 'Many rape victims are so traumatized they cannot face the process of reporting it. But here's the really interesting thing: the first of the Shoe Man's reported rapes, back in 1997, occurred in the Grand Hotel, following a Halloween ball there. He lured a woman into a room. Does that sound familiar?'

There was an uncomfortable silence in the room. The Grand Hotel was next door to the Metropole.

'There's more,' Branson went on. 'The room at the Grand was booked by a woman – in the name of Marsha Morris. She paid cash and all efforts to trace her at the time failed.'

Grace absorbed the information in silence, thinking hard. The room at the Metropole, where Nicola Taylor was raped on New Year's Eve, was booked by a woman, according to the manager. Her name was Marsha Morris too. She paid in cash. The address she wrote in the register was false.

'Someone's having a laugh,' Nick Nicholl said.

'So does this mean it's the same perp,' Emma-Jane

Boutwood said, 'or a copycat with a sick sense of humour?'

'Was any of this information released to the public?' Michael Foreman asked.

Grace shook his head. 'No. The name Marsha Morris was never public knowledge.'

'Not even to the *Argus*?'

'Especially not to the *Argus*.' Grace nodded for Branson to continue.

'Here's where it gets even more interesting,' the DS said. 'Another of the victims was raped in her home, in Hove Park Road, exactly two weeks later.'

'That's a very smart address,' Michael Foreman said.

'Very,' Grace agreed.

Branson continued. 'When she arrived home, the burglar alarm was switched on. She deactivated it, went up into her bedroom and the offender struck – coming at her from out of a wardrobe.'

'Just like Roxy Pearce's attacker last night,' Grace said. 'From what we know so far.'

No one spoke for several moments.

Then Branson said, 'The Shoe Man's next victim was raped on the beach, beneath the Palace Pier. The one after that in the Churchill Square car park. His final one – if the chief's assumption is right – was taken walking home from a Christmas Eve piss-up with her friends.'

'So what you're saying, Glenn,' Bella said, 'is that we should be taking a close look at car parks in a week's time.'

'Don't go there, Bella,' Grace said. 'We're not going to let this get that far.'

He put on a brave, confident smile for his team. But inside he felt a lot less sure.

1998

38

'Does it work?' he asked.

'Yeah, course it works. Wouldn't be selling it other-
wise, would I?' He glared at the lean man in the brown
boiler suit as if he had just insulted his integrity. 'Every-
thing in here works, mate, all right? If you want rubbish
I can point you up the street. In here I only do quality.
Everything works.'

'It had better.' He stared down at the white chest
freezer that was tucked away between the upturned desks,
swivel office chairs and upended settees at the rear of
the vast second-hand furniture emporium in Brighton's
Lewes Road.

'Money-back guarantee, all right? Thirty days, any
problems, bring it back, no quibble.'

'Fifty quid you're asking?'

'Yeah.'

'What's your trade price?'

'Everything here's trade price.'

'Give you forty.'

'Cash?

'Uh-huh.'

'Taking it away with you? I'm not delivering for t
price.'

'Gimme a hand out with it?'

'That your van outside?'

'Yeah.'

'Better get a move on. There's a warden coming.'

*

Five minutes later he jumped into the cab of the Transit, a few seconds ahead of the traffic warden, started the engine and drove it with a bump off the pavement and away from the double yellow lines. He heard the clang of his new purchase bouncing on the hessian matting on the otherwise bare metal floor behind him and moments later heard it sliding as he braked hard, catching up the congested traffic around the gyratory system.

He crawled passed Sainsbury's, then made a left turn at the lights, up under the viaduct, and then on, heading towards Hove, towards his lock-up garage, where the young woman lay.

The young woman whose face stared out at him from the front page of the *Argus*, on every news-stand, beneath the caption HAVE YOU SEEN THIS PERSON? Followed by her name, Rachael Ryan.

He nodded to himself. 'Yes. Yep. I've seen her!'

I know where she is!

She is waiting for me!

39

Shoes are your weapons, ladies, aren't they? You use them to hurt men in so many ways, don't you?

Know what I'm saying? I'm not talking about the physical, about the bruises and cuts you can make on a man's skin by hitting him with them. I'm talking about the sounds you make with them. The clack-clack-clack of your heels on bare floorboards, on concrete paving stones, on floor tiles, on brick paths.

You're wearing those expensive shoes. That means you're going somewhere – and you're leaving me behind. I hear that clack-clack-clack getting fainter. It's the last sound of you I hear. It's the first sound of you I hear when you come back. Hours later. Sometimes a whole day later. You don't talk to me about where you've been. You laugh at me, sneer at me.

Once when you came back and I was upset, you walked over to me. I thought you were going to kiss me. But you didn't, did you? You just stamped your stiletto down hard on my bare foot. You drilled it right through the flesh and bone and into the floorboard.

NOW

40

He'd forgotten how good it had felt. How addictive it had been! He'd thought that maybe just one, for old times' sake. But that *one* had immediately given him the taste for *another*. And now he was raring to go again.

Oh yes!

Make the most of these winter months, when he could wear a coat and a scarf, hide that Adam's apple, strut around freely, just like any other elegant Brighton lady! He liked the dress he had chosen, Karen Millen, and the camel Prada coat, the Cornelia James shawl around his neck, the big shiny shoulder bag and the slinky black leather gloves on his hands! But most of all he liked the feel of his wet-look boots. Yep. He felt soooooo good today! Almost, dare he say it, *sexy*!

He made his way through the Lanes, through the light drizzle that was falling. He was all wrapped up and snug against the rain and the cold wind, and, yes, sooooo *sexy*! He cast constant sideways glances at himself in shop windows. Two middle-aged men strode towards him, and one gave him an appreciative glance as they passed. He gave a coy smile back, snaking his way on through the throng of people in the narrow streets. He passed modern jewellery shop, then an antiques shop that a reputation for paying good prices for stolen valual

He walked down past the Druid's Head pub, the Pump House, then English's restaurant, crossed East Street and turned right towards the sea, heading towards Pool Valley. Then he turned left in front of the restaurant that had once been the ABC cinema and arrived outside his destination.

The shoe shop called Last.

It was a specialist designer-shoe shop and stocked a whole range of labels to which he was particularly partial: Esska, Thomas Murphy, Hetty Rose. He stared at Last's window display. At pretty, delicate, Japanese patterned Amia Kimonos. At a pair of Thomas Murphy Genesis petrol court shoes with silver heels. At brown suede Esska Loops.

The shop had wooden floorboards, a patterned sofa, a footstool and handbags hanging from hooks. And, at the moment, one customer. An elegant, beautiful woman in her forties with long, flyaway blonde hair who was wearing Fendi snakeskin boots. Size five. A matching Fendi handbag hung from a shoulder strap. She was dressed to kill, or to shop!

She had on a long black coat, with a high collar turned up and a fluffy white wrap around her neck. A pert snub nose. Rosebud lips. No gloves. He clocked her wedding band and her big engagement rock. She might still be married, but she could be divorced. Could be anything. Difficult to tell from here. But he knew one thing.

She was his type. Yep!

She was holding up a Tracey Neuls TN_29 Homage button shoe. It was in white perforated leather with a ~upe trim. Like something Janet Leigh might have worn ~he office before she stole the money in the original ~o. But they weren't sexy! They were sort of retro

Miss America preppy, in his view. *Don't buy them*, he urged silently. *No, no!*

There were so many other much sexier shoes and boots on display. He cast his eye over them, looking appreciatively at each of their shapes, their curves, their straps, their stitches, their heels. He imagined this woman naked, wearing just these. Doing what he told her to do with them.

Don't buy those!

Good as gold, she put the shoe back. Then she turned and walked out of the shop.

He smelt her dense cloud of Armani Code perfume, which was like her own personal ozone layer, as she walked past him. Then she stopped, pulled a small black umbrella from her bag, held it up and popped it open. She had style, this lady. Confidence. She really, very definitely, could be his kind of lady. And she was holding up an umbrella, like a tour guide, just for him, so he could more easily spot her through the crowd!

Oh yes, my kind of lady!

The thoughtful kind!

He followed her as she set off at a determined stride. There was something predatory about her walk. She was on the hunt for shoes. No question. Which was good.

He was on the hunt too!

She stopped briefly in East Street to peer in the window of Russell and Bromley. Then she crossed over towards L.K. Bennett.

An instant later he felt a violent blow, heard a loud oath and he crashed, winded, down on to the wet pavement, feeling a sharp pain across his face, as if a hundred bees had stung him all at once. A steaming polysty Starbucks cup, its dark brown liquid spewing out, past him. His head felt a rush of cold air and he realized, with panic, that his wig had become dislodged.

He grabbed it and jammed it back on his head, not caring for a moment how it looked, and found himself staring up at a shaven-headed tattooed man-mountain.

'Faggot! Why don't you look where you're frigging going?'

'Screw you!' he shouted back, totally forgetting for an instant to mask his voice, scrambled to his feet, one hand clutching his blonde wig, and stumbled on, aware of the smell of hot coffee and the unpleasant sensation of hot liquid running down his neck.

'Fucking fairy!' the voice called after him as he broke into a run, weaving through a group of Japanese tourists, fixated on the bobbing umbrella of the woman striding into the distance. To his surprise, she did not stop to look in L.K. Bennett, but headed straight into the Lanes.

She took a left fork and he followed her. Past a pub and then another jewellery shop. He dug into his hand-bag, pulled out a tissue and dabbed the coffee from his smarting face, hoping it had not smeared his make-up.

Blondie crossed busy Ship Street and turned right, then immediately left into the pedestrian precinct of expensive clothes shops: Duke's Lane.

Good girl!

She entered Profile, the first shop on the right.

He peered into the window. But he wasn't looking at the row of shoes and boots displayed on the shelves, he was looking at his own reflection. As subtly as he could, he adjusted his wig. Then he peered more closely at his face, but it seemed all right; no big, weird smears.

Then he checked on Blondie. She was sitting on a hunched over her BlackBerry, pecking away at the keys. An assistant appeared with a shoebox, opened it the way a proud waiter might lift the lid from a tureen, and presented the contents for her inspection.

Blondie nodded approvingly.

The assistant removed a tall, high-heeled, blue satin Manolo Blahnik shoe with a square diamanté buckle.

He watched Blondie put the shoe on. She stood up and walked around the carpeted floor, peering at her foot's reflection in the mirrors. She seemed to like it.

He entered the shop and began browsing, breathing in the heady cocktail of tanned leather and Armani Code. He watched Blondie out of the corner of his eye, watched and *listened.*

The assistant asked her if she would like to try on the left foot as well. Blondie said she would.

As she strutted around the deep-pile carpeting, he was approached by the assistant, a young, slender girl with a dark fringe of hair and an Irish accent, asking if she could help her. He told her in his softest voice that he was *just looking, thank you.*

'I have to give an important speech next week,' Blondie said, in an American accent, he noticed. 'It's an after-lunch thing. I've bought the most divine blue dress. I think blue's good for daytime. What do you think?'

'Blue's a good colour on you, madam. I can tell from the shoes. Blue's a very good colour for daytime.'

'Yeah, um-umm. I think so too. Um-umm. I should have brought the dress along, but I know these are going to match.'

'They'll go with a wide range of blues.'

'Um-umm.'

Blondie stared down at the reflection of the shoes the mirror for some moments and tapped her teeth her fingernail. Then she said the magic words, *'I'll take these!'*

Good girl! Manolos were cool. They were beautiful. They were just so much a class act. Most importantly, they had five-inch heels.

Perfect!

And he liked her accent. Was it Californian?

He sidled up towards the counter as the purchase took place, listening intently, while pretending to study a pair of brown mules.

'Are you on our mailing list, madam?'

'I don't think so, no.'

'Would you mind if I entered you on it – we can let you know in advance of our sales. You can get some privileged bargains.'

She shrugged. 'Sure, why not?'

'If I could have your name?'

'Dee Burchmore. Mrs.'

'And your address?'

'Fifty-three Sussex Square.'

Sussex Square. In *Kemp Town*, he thought. One of the city's most beautiful squares. Most of its terraced houses were divided into flats. You had to be rich to have a whole house there. You had to be rich to buy the Manolos. And the handbag that went with it, which she was now fondling. Just the way he would soon be fondling her.

Kemp Town, he thought. That was an old stomping ground!

Happy memories.

41

Every time she bought a pair of shoes, Dee Burchmore got a guilty thrill. There was no need to feel guilty, of course. Rudy encouraged her to dress smart, to look great! As a senior executive of American & Oriental Banking, over here at its lavish new Brighton headquarters on a five-year posting to establish a foothold for the company in Europe, money was no object at all to her husband.

She was proud of Rudy and she loved him. She loved his ambitions to show the world that, in the wake of the financial scandals that had dogged US banking in recent years, it was possible to show a caring face. Rudy was attacking the UK mortgage market with zeal, offering deals to first-time buyers that none of the British lenders, still smarting from the financial meltdown, was prepared to consider. And she had an important role in this, in public relations.

In the time Dee had in between taking their two children, Josh, aged eight, and Chase, aged six, to school and then collecting them, Rudy had tasked her with networking as hard as she could within the city. He wanted her to find charities to which American & Oriental could make significant contributions – and, of course gain significant publicity as benefactors to the city. It w a role she relished.

A respectable golfer, she had joined the ladies' section of the city's most expensive golf club, the North Brighton. She had become a member of what she had gleaned was the most influential of Brighton's numerous Rotary Clubs and she had volunteered for the committees of several of the city's major charitable institutions, including the Martlet's Hospice. Her most recent appointment was to the fund-raising committee of Brighton and Hove's principal hostel for the homeless, St Patrick's, where they had a unique facility, offering Japanese-style pods to homeless people, including prisoners out on licence who were actively involved in retraining.

She stood in the small shop, watching the assistant wrap her beautiful blue Manolos in tissue, then carefully lay them in the box. She could not wait to get home and try her dress on with these shoes and bag. She knew they were going to look sensational. Just the thing to give her confidence next week.

Then she glanced at her watch: 3.30. Shit! It had taken longer than she thought. She was late for her appointment at the Nail Studio in Hove, on the other side of the city. She hurried out of the shop, barely clocking the weird-looking woman with lopsided blonde hair who was staring at something on display in the shop window.

She never once looked behind her all the way to the car park.

If she had, she might just have noticed this same woman following her.

1998

42

It was shortly after 10 p.m. when Roy Grace flicked the right-turn indicator. Driving faster than was sensible in the pelting rain because he was so late, he nearly lost the back end of the car on the slippery tarmac as he swung off wide, quiet New Church Road into the even quieter residential street that led down to Hove seafront, where he and Sandy lived.

The elderly 3-Series BMW creaked and groaned, and the brakes made a scraping noise in protest. The car was months overdue for a service, but he was even more broke than ever, thanks in part to an insanely expensive diamanté tennis bracelet he had bought Sandy for a surprise for Christmas, and the service was going to have to wait a few more months yet.

Out of habit, he clocked each of the vehicles parked in the driveways and on the street, but there was nothing that seemed out of place. As he neared his home, he carefully checked those isolated patches of darkness where the orange haze of the street lighting did not quite reach.

One thing about being a copper, arresting villains and usually facing them in court months later, you never knew who might harbour a grudge against you. It was rare that revenge attacks happened, but Grace knew a cou

255

colleagues who had received anonymous hate mail, and one whose wife had found a death threat against her carved on a tree in her local park. It was not a worry you lost sleep over, but it was an occupational hazard. You tried to keep your address a secret, but villains had ways of finding out such things. You could never, ever totally let your guard down, and that was something Sandy resented about him.

It particularly irked her that Roy always picked a pub or restaurant table that gave him the best possible view of the room and the door, and that he always tried to sit with his back against the wall.

He smiled as he saw the downstairs lights of his house were on, which meant Sandy was still up, although he was a little sad to see the Christmas lights were now gone. He turned right on to the driveway and stopped in front of the integral garage door. Sandy's even more clapped-out little black Golf would be parked inside, in the dry.

This house was Sandy's dream. Shortly before she had found it, she had missed a period and their hopes had risen, only to be dashed a few weeks later. It had plunged her into a deep depression – so much so that he had become seriously worried about her. Then she rang him at the office, to say she had found a house. It was beyond their budget, she'd told him, but it had such great potential. He would love it!

They'd bought the four-bedroom semi just over a year ago. It was a big jump up the property ladder from the small flat in Hangleton where they had first lived after their marriage, and a financial stretch for both of them. But Sandy had set her heart on the house, and she'd convinced Roy they should go for it. He'd agreed against his better judgement, and knew the real reason he had said yes. It was because he could see how desperately unhappy Sandy was because of her inability to conceive and he wanted so much to please her, somehow.

Now he switched off the engine and climbed out into the freezing, pelting rain, feeling exhausted. He leaned in again, lifted the bulging attaché case containing a ton of files he needed to read through tonight off the passenger seat, hurried up to the front door and let himself in.

'Hi, darling!' he called out as he entered the hallway. It looked strangely bare without the Christmas decorations.

He heard the sound of voices from the television. There was a tantalizing aroma of cooking meat. Ravenous, he shrugged off his mackintosh, hung it on an antique coat rack they'd bought from a stall on the Kensington Street market, plonked his case down and walked into the living room.

Sandy, in a thick dressing gown and covered in a blanket, was lying on the sofa, cradling a glass of red wine and watching the news. A reporter was standing, holding a microphone, in a gutted, torched village.

'I'm sorry, darling,' he said.

He smiled at her. She looked so beautiful, with her damp hair carelessly hanging around her face, and no make-up. That was one of the things he loved most of all about her, that she looked just as good without make-up as with it. Always an early riser, he loved some mornings to lie awake in bed for a few minutes, just watching her face.

'Sorry about what's happening in Kosovo?' she retorted.

He bent down and kissed her. She smelt of soap shampoo.

'No, for being so late. I was going to help you with the decorations.'

'Why aren't you sorry about Kosovo?'

'I am sorry about Kosovo,' he said. 'I'm also sorry about Rachael Ryan, who's still missing, and I'm sorry for her parents and her sister.'

'Are they more important to you than Kosovo?'

'I need a drink,' he said. 'And I'm starving.'

'I've already eaten, I couldn't wait any longer.'

'I'm sorry. I'm sorry I'm late. I'm sorry about Kosovo. I'm sorry about every damned problem in the world that I can't deal with.'

He knelt and pulled a bottle of Glenfiddich from the drinks cabinet, then, as he carried it out to the kitchen, she called after him, 'I've left you a plate of lasagne in the microwave and there's salad in the fridge.'

'Thanks,' he called back.

In the kitchen he poured himself four fingers of whisky, popped in some ice cubes, retrieved his favourite glass ashtray from the dishwasher and went back into the living room. He pulled off his jacket, then removed his tie and plonked himself down in his armchair as she was taking up the whole sofa. He lit a Silk Cut cigarette.

Almost instantly, like a Pavlovian reaction, Sandy batted away imaginary smoke.

'So, how was your day?' he asked. Then he reached down and picked a pine needle off the floor.

A young, attractive woman with spiky black hair and wearing battle fatigues appeared on the screen, against a background of burnt buildings. She was holding a microphone and talking to camera about the terrible human of the war in Bosnia.

'That's the Angel of Mostar,' Sandy said, nodding at

the screen. 'Sally Becker – she's from Brighton. She's doing something about the war there. What are you doing about it, Detective Sergeant, hoping soon to be *Detective Inspector*, Grace?'

'I'll start dealing with the war in Bosnia, and all the other problems of the world, when we've won the war in Brighton, which is the one I'm paid to fight.' He put the pine needle in the ashtray.

Sandy shook her head. 'You don't get it, do you, my love? That young woman, Sally Becker, is a hero – rather, a *heroine*.'

He nodded. 'She is, yes. The world needs people like her. But—'

'But what?'

He dragged on his cigarette and then sipped his whisky, feeling the burning, warming sensation deep in his gullet.

'No one person can solve all the problems in the world.'

She turned towards him. 'OK, so talk me through the one you've been solving.' She turned the volume on the television down.

He shrugged.

'Come on, I want to hear. You never tell me about your work. You always ask me about my day and I tell you about all the weirdo people I have to deal with who come into the medical centre. But every time I ask you, I get some crap about confidentiality. So, *soon-to-be Detective Inspector*, tell me about *your* day for a change. Tell me why for ten nights running you've left me to eat on my own, yet again. Tell me. Remember our wedding vows. Wasn't there something about not having secrets

'Sandy,' he said. 'Come on! I don't need this!'

'No, you *come on* for a change. Tell me about your day. Tell me how the search for Rachael Ryan is going.'

He took another deep drag on his cigarette. 'It's going bloody nowhere,' he said.

Sandy smiled. 'Well, there's a first! Don't think I've ever heard you be so honest in all the years we've been married. Thank you, *soon-to-be Detective Inspector!*'

He grinned. 'Shut up about that. I might not get through.'

'You will. You're the force's blue-eyed boy. You'll get the promotion. You know why?'

'Why?'

'Because it means more to you than your marriage.'

'Sandy! Come on, that's—'

He laid his cigarette in the ashtray, jumped up from his chair, sat on the edge of the sofa and tried to put an arm around her, but she resisted.

'Go on. Tell me about your day,' she said. 'I want every detail. If you truly love me, that is. I've never actually heard a minute-by-minute account of your day before. Not once.'

He stood up again and crushed the cigarette out, then moved the ashtray to the table beside the sofa and sat back down.

'I've spent the whole day looking for this young woman, all right? Just as I've been doing for the past week.'

'Yeah, fine, but what did that entail?'

'You really want to know the details?'

'Yes, I do. I really want to know the details. You have a problem with that?'

He lit another cigarette and inhaled. Then, with the ~~e~~ jetting from his mouth, he said, 'I went round with a detective sergeant – a guy called Norman Potting, he's not the most tactful officer in the force – to see the missing woman's parents again. They're in a terrible state, as you can imagine. We tried to reassure them about all we were doing, and took down every detail they could give us about their daughter that they might not already have done. Potting managed to upset them both.'

'How?'

'By asking a lot of awkward questions about her sex life. They needed to be asked – but there are ways of doing it . . .'

He took another sip of his drink and another drag, then laid the cigarette down in the ashtray. She was looking at him inquisitively.

'And then?'

'You really want to hear everything else?'

'I do, I really want to hear everything else.'

'OK, so we've been trying to prise out of them everything about Rachael's life. Did she have any friends or close work colleagues we haven't already talked to? Had anything like this ever happened before? We tried to build up a picture of her habits.'

'What were her habits?'

'Phoning her parents every day, without fail. That's the most significant one.'

'And now she hasn't phoned them for ten days?'

'That's right.'

'Is she dead, do you think?'

'We've checked her bank accounts to see if any money's been withdrawn and it hasn't. She has a credit card and debit card, and no transactions have taken place since the day before Christmas Eve.'

He drank some more whisky and was surpris

find that he'd emptied the glass. Ice cubes tumbled against his lips as he drained the last drops.

'She's either being held against her will or she's dead,' Sandy said flatly. 'People don't just vanish off the face of the earth.'

'They do,' he said. 'Every day. Thousands of people every year.'

'But if she had that close connection to her parents, she wouldn't want to hurt them deliberately, like this, surely?'

He shrugged.

'What does your copper's nose tell you?'

'That it doesn't smell good.'

'What happens next?'

'We're widening the search, the house-to-house enquiries are expanding to cover a bigger area, we're drafting in more officers. We're searching the parks, the waste dumps, the surrounding countryside. CCTV footage is being examined. Checks are being made at all stations, harbours and airports. Her friends are being questioned and her ex-fiancé. And we're using a criminal psychologist – a profiler – to help.'

After some moments Sandy asked, 'Is this the shoe rapist again, do you think? The Shoe Man?'

'She's mad about shoes, apparently. But this is not his MO. He's never taken one of his victims.'

'Didn't you once tell me that criminals get bolder and more violent – that it's an escalating thing?'

'That's true. The guy who starts out as a harmless flasher can turn into a violent rapist. So can a burglar, as he gets bolder.'

Sandy sipped her wine. 'I hope you find her quickly that she's OK.'

Grace nodded. 'Yup,' he said quietly. 'I hope so too.'
'Will you?'
He had no answer. Not, at least, the one she wanted to hear.

CHAPTER XXXIX

George A. talk: Voglio, ma ... mia father, I beg pardon,
I'm sorry.

Do robota I know, Naif, I'm sure amount women
salvator.

NOW

43

Yac did not like drunk people, especially drunk slappers, especially drunk slappers who got into his taxi. Especially this early on a Saturday night, when he was busy reading the latest on the Shoe Man in the *Argus*.

There were five drunk girls, all without coats, all in skimpy dresses, all legs and flesh, displaying their breasts and tattoos and pierced belly buttons. It was January! Didn't they feel the cold?

He was only licensed to carry four of them. He'd told them that, but they'd been too drunk to listen, all piling in at the rank on East Street, shouting, chattering, giggling, telling him to take them to the pier.

The taxi was full of their scents: Rock 'n Rose, Fuel for Life, Red Jeans, Sweetheart, Shalimar. He recognized them all. Uh-huh. In particular, he recognized the Shalimar.

His mother's perfume.

He told them it was only a short walk, that with the Saturday-night traffic they'd be quicker to walk. But they insisted he take them.

'It's bleedin' freezing, for Christ's sake!' one of them said.

She was a plump little thing, wearing the Shalim with a mass of fair hair and half-bared breasts that lo

267

like they'd been inflated with a bicycle pump. She reminded him a little of his mother. Something in the coarseness, the shape of her figure and the colour of her hair.

'Yeah,' said another. 'Sodding bleedin' freezing!'

One of them lit a cigarette. He could smell the acrid smoke. That was against the law too, he told her, staring at her crossly in the mirror.

'Want a drag, gorgeous?' she said, pouting, holding out the cigarette to him.

'I don't smoke,' he said.

'Too young, are you?' said another, and they broke into peals of squeaky laughter.

He nearly took them to the skeletal remains of the West Pier, half a mile further along the coast, just to teach them a lesson not to risk a taxi driver's livelihood. But he didn't, for one reason only.

The shoes and the perfume the plump one was wearing.

Shoes that he particularly liked. Black and silver sparkly Jimmy Choos. Size four. Uh-huh. His mother's size.

Yac wondered what she would look like naked, just wearing those shoes. Would she look like his mother?

At the same time, he wondered if she had a high- or low-flush loo in her home. But the problem with people who were drunk was that you couldn't have a proper conversation with them. Waste of time. He drove in silence, thinking about her shoes. Smelling her perfume. Watching her in the mirror. Thinking more and more how much she looked like his mother had once looked.

He made a right turn into North Street and crossed Steine Gardens, waited at the lights, then turned right and queued at the roundabout before coming to a halt in front of the gaudy lights of Brighton Pier.

Just £2.40 showed on the meter. He'd been sitting in the queue at the cab rank for thirty minutes. Not much for it. He wasn't happy. And he was even less happy when someone handed him £2.50 and told him to keep the change.

'Huh!' he said. 'Huh!'

The man who owned the taxi expected big money on a Saturday night.

The girls disgorged themselves, while he alternated between watching the Jimmy Choos and glancing anxiously around for any sign of a police car. The girls were cursing the cold wind, clutching their hair, tottering around on their high heels, then, still holding the rear door of the taxi open, began arguing among themselves about why they'd come here and not stayed in the bar they'd just left.

He reached across, called out, 'Excuse me, ladies!' then pulled the door shut and drove off along the seafront, the taxi reeking of Shalimar perfume and cigarette smoke and alcohol. A short distance along, he pulled over on to the double yellow lines, beside the railings of the promenade, and switched off the engine.

A whole bunch of thoughts were roaring around inside his head. Jimmy Choo shoes. Size four. His mother's size. He breathed deeply, savouring the Shalimar. It was coming up to 7 p.m. His on-the-hour, every hour, mug of tea. That was very important. He needed to have that.

But he had something else on his mind that he needed more.

Uh-huh.

44

Despite the cold and the biting wind, several groups of people, mostly youngsters, milled around the entrance to the pier. Garish lights sparkled and twinkled all along the structure, which stretched almost a third of a mile out into the inky darkness of the English Channel. A Union Jack crackled in the wind. A giant sandwich-board hoarding in the middle of the entrance advertised a live band. The ice-cream stall wasn't doing much business, but there were ragged queues at the Southern Fried Chicken, Doughnut, Meat Feast and Fish and Chips counters.

Darren Spicer, wearing a donkey jacket, jeans, woollen mittens and a baseball cap pulled low, was flying high, totally oblivious to the cold, as he stood in the queue to buy a bag of chips. The aroma of frying batter was tantalizing and he was hungry. He stuck his bent roll-up in his mouth, rubbed his hands together and checked his watch. Eight minutes to seven. He needed to be back at the St Patrick's night shelter by 8.30, lock-up time, or he would lose his bed, and it was a brisk twenty-five minutes' walk from here, unless he jumped on a bus or, more extravagantly, took a taxi.

Tucked into one of his big inside poacher's pockets as a copy of the *Argus* he'd pulled out of a wheelie bin e Grand Hotel, where he had registered earlier, to start work on Monday, doing a job that would utilize his electrical skills. The hotel was replacing its wiring, a lot of which did not appear to have been touched for decades. On Monday he would be in the basement, running new cables from the emergency generator to the laundry room.

It was a big area and they were short-staffed. Which meant not many people would be there to keep an eye on him. Which meant he'd pretty much have the run of the place. And all its rich pickings. And he'd have access to the computer system. Now all he needed was a pay-as-you-go mobile phone. That wouldn't be a problem.

He felt good! He felt terrific! At this moment he was the most powerful man in this whole city! And probably the horniest!

A gaggle of scantily clad girls disgorging from a taxi caught his eye. One of them was a plump little thing, with her tits almost falling out of her blouse and pouting, bee-stung lips. She tottered around on the tiles at the entrance in sparkly high heels, clutching at her hair, which was being batted by the wind. She looked as if she was a little the worse for wear from alcohol.

Her miniskirt blew up and he saw a sudden flash of the top of her thigh. It gave him a sharp prick of lust. She was his kind of girl. He liked a bit of flesh on a woman. Yeah, she was definitely his kind of tottie.

Yeah.

He liked her.

Liked her shoes.

He took a deep drag of his cigarette.

The taxi drove off.

The girls were arguing about something. Then th
all headed to the back of the queue behind him.

He got his bag of chips, then stepped away a short distance, leaned against a stanchion and watched the girls in the queue, still arguing and joshing each other. But in particular he watched the plump one, that prick of lust growing inside him, thinking again and again of the flash of her thigh he had seen.

He had finished his chips and lit another cigarette by the time the girls had all got their bags and had fumbled in their purses for the right change to pay for them. Then they set off up the pier, the plump one trailing behind them. She was hurrying to catch up but struggling on her heels.

'Hey!' she called out to the two at the rear. 'Hey, Char, Karen, not so fast. I can't keep up with yer!'

One of the four turned round, laughing, keeping up her pace, staying level with her friends. 'Come on, Mandy! It's cos yer too bleedin' fat, in't yer!'

Mandy Thorpe, her head spinning from too many Sea Breezes, broke into a run and caught up with her friends briefly. 'Sod off about my weight! I am so not fat!' she shouted in mock anger. Then, as the tiled entrance gave way to the wooden boardwalk of the pier itself, both her heels stuck in a slat, her feet came flying out of them and she fell flat on her face, her handbag striking the ground and spewing out its contents, her chips scattering across the decking.

'Shit!' she said. 'Shit, shit, shit!'

Scrambling back upright, she ducked down and jammed each of her feet back into the shoes, bending down even lower to lever them in with her fingers, cursing these cheap, ill-fitting Jimmy Choo copies which she had bought on holiday in Thailand and which pinched her

'Hey!' she called out. 'Char, Karen, hey!'

Leaving the mess of ketchup-spattered chips, she stumbled on after them, watching the slats in the decking carefully now. She followed her friends past a toy locomotive and into the bright lights and noise of the amusement arcade. Music was playing, and there were chimes from machines and the clatter of coins, and shouts of joy and angry cusses. She passed a giant illuminated pink cracker, then a glass-fronted machine filled with teddy bears, a sign flashing £35 CASH JACKPOTS, and a cash booth in the shape of a Victorian tram shelter.

Then they were outside in the biting cold again. Mandy caught up with her friends just as they passed a row of stalls, each blaring out music. HOOK A DUCK! LOBSTER POT – 2 BALLS FOR £1! HENNA TATTOOS!

In the distance to her left, across the black void of the sea, were the lights of the elegant town houses of Kemp Town. They walked on past the DOLPHIN DERBY, heading towards the carousel, helter-skelter, dodgems, the CRAZY MOUSE rollercoaster and the TURBO SKYRIDE, which Mandy had been on once – and it had left her feeling sick for days.

To their right now were the ghost train and the HORROR HOTEL.

'I want to go on the ghost train!' Mandy said.

Karen turned, pulling a cigarette pack out of her handbag. 'It's pathetic. The ghost train's shit. It's like nothing. I need another drink.'

'Yeah, me too!' said Char. 'I need a drink.'

'What about the Turbo?' said another girl, Joanna.

'No fear!' Mandy said. 'I want to go on the ghost train.'

Joanna shook her head. 'I'm scared of that.'

'It's not *really* scary,' Mandy said. 'I'll go on me own if you won't come.'

'You're not brave enough!' Karen taunted. 'You're a scaredy cat!'

'I'll show you!' Mandy said. 'I'll bloody show you!'

She tottered over to a booth that sold tokens for the rides. None of them noticed the man standing a short distance back from them, carefully crushing his cigarette out underfoot.

1998

45

He had never seen a dead body before. Well, apart from his mum, that was. She'd been all skeletal, wasted away from the cancer that had been on a feeding frenzy inside her, eating up just about everything except her skin. The little bastard cancer cells would probably have eaten that too if the embalming fluid hadn't nuked them.

Although they were welcome to her. It had seemed a shame to hurt them.

His mum had looked like she was asleep. She was all tucked into bed, in her nightdress, in a room in the undertaker's Chapel of Rest. Her hair all nicely coiffed. A bit of make-up on her face to give her some colour, and her skin had a slightly rosy hue from the embalming fluid. The funeral director had told him that she'd come up really nice.

Much nicer in death.

Dead, she couldn't taunt him any more. Couldn't tell him, as she climbed into his bed, that he was as useless as his drunken father. That his *thing* was pathetic, that it was shorter than the heels of her shoes. Some nights she brought a stiletto-heeled shoe into the bed with her and made him pleasure her with that instead.

She began calling him *Shrinky*. It was a name that quickly got around at his school. 'Hey, Shrinky,' o boys and girls would call out to him. 'Has it grown any longer today?'

He'd sat beside her, on the chair next to her bed, the way he'd sat beside her in the ward of the hospital in the days when her life was slipping away. He'd held her hand. It was cold and bony, like holding the hand of a reptile. But one that couldn't harm you any more.

Then he'd leaned over and whispered into her ear, 'I think I'm supposed to tell you that I love you. But I don't. I hate you. I've always hated you. I can't wait for your funeral, because afterwards I'm going to get that urn with your ashes and throw you into a fucking skip, where you belong.'

But this new woman now was different. He didn't hate Rachael Ryan. He looked down at her, lying naked on the bottom of the chest freezer he had bought this morning. Staring up at him through eyes that were steadily frosting over. That same glaze of frost that was forming all over her body.

He listened for a moment to the hum of the freezer's motor. Then he whispered, 'Rachael, I'm sorry about what happened, you know? Really I am. I never wanted to kill you. I've never killed anything. That's not me. I just want you to know that. Not me at all. Not my style. I'll look after your shoes for you, I promise.'

Then he decided he didn't like her eyes looking at him all hostile like that. As if she was still able to accuse him, even though she was dead. Able to accuse him from some other place, some other dimension she'd now arrived at.

He slammed the lid shut.

His heart was thumping. He was running with perspi-
on.

He needed a cigarette.

Needed to think very, very calmly.

He lit a cigarette and smoked it slowly, thinking. Thinking. Thinking.

Her name was everywhere. Police were looking for her all over the city. All over Sussex.

He was shaking.

You stupid dumb woman, taking off my mask!

Look what you've done. To both of us!

They mustn't find her. They'd know who she was if they found the body. They had all kinds of techniques. All kinds of science. If they found her, then at some point they were going to find him.

At least by keeping her cold he'd stopped the smell that had started to come from her. Frozen stuff didn't smell. So now he had time. One option was just to keep her here, but that was dangerous. The police had put in the paper that they were looking for a white van. Someone might have seen his van. Someone might tell the police that there was a white van that sometimes drove in and out of here.

He needed to get her away.

Throwing her in the sea might be an option, but the sea might wash her body ashore. If he dug a grave somewhere out in a wood, someone's dog might sniff her. He needed a place where no dog would sniff.

A place where no one was going to come looking.

NOW

46

Maybe this wasn't such a good idea after all, Mandy thought to herself, her courage suddenly deserting her as she handed her token to the man in the booth of the ghost train ride.

'Is it scary?' she asked him.

He was young and good-looking, with a foreign accent – maybe Spanish, she thought.

'No, is not really scary. Just a little!' He smiled. 'Is OK!'

'Yeah?'

He nodded.

She tottered along inside the railings to the first car. It looked like a wood-panelled Victorian bathtub on rubber wheels. She clambered in unsteadily, her heart in her throat suddenly, and sat down, putting her bag on the seat beside her.

'Sorry, you can't take bag. I look after for you.'

Reluctantly she handed it to him. Then he pulled down the metal safety bar and clicked it home, committing her.

'Smile!' he said. 'Enjoy! Is OK, really!'

Shit, she thought. Then she called out to her friends. 'Char! Karen!'

But the wind whipped her voice away. The car rumbled

283

forward, without warning crashing through double doors into darkness. The doors banged shut behind her and the darkness was total. In contrast to the blustery sea air, in here it was dry and smelt faintly of hot electrical wiring and dust.

The darkness pressed in all around her. She held her breath. Then the car swung sharply right, picking up speed. She could hear the roar of its wheels echoing around the walls; it was like being on a tube train. Streaks of light shot past her on both sides. She heard a ghostly laugh. Tendrils brushed her forehead and her hair, and she screamed in terror, clenching her eyes shut.

This is dumb, she thought. *This is so stupid. Why? Why did I do this?*

Then the car crashed through more double doors. She opened her eyes to see a long-dead, dusty old man rise up from behind a writing desk and swing head first towards her. She ducked, covering her eyes, her heart pounding, all the courage the alcohol had given her deserting her now.

They went down a sharp incline. She uncovered her eyes to see that the light was fading rapidly and she was back in pitch darkness again. She heard a hissing sound. A hideous, luminous, skeletal snake reared out of the darkness and spat at her, cold droplets of water striking her face. Then a brightly lit skeleton swung out of the darkness and she ducked in terror, convinced it would hit her.

They crashed through more doors. *Oh, God, how long was this going to go on for?*

They were travelling fast, downhill, in darkness. She heard a screech, then a horrible cackle of laughter. More tendrils touched her, like a spider crawling through her hair. They crashed through more doors, swung sharply left and, quite suddenly, stopped. She sat for a moment in the pitch darkness, shaking. Then suddenly she felt an arm around her neck.

A human arm. She smelt warm breath on her cheek. Then a voice whispered into her ear. A voice she had never heard before.

She froze in blind panic.

'Got a little extra for you, darling.'

Was this some prank from Char and Karen? Were they in here messing around?

Her brain was racing. Something was telling her this was not part of the ride. That something was badly wrong. The next instant she heard a clang as the safety bar jerked up. Then, whimpering in terror, she was jerked out of the car and dragged quickly over a hard surface. Something sharp bashed into her back and she was pulled through curtains into a room which smelt of oil. She was dropped on her back on to a hard surface. Then she heard the door clang shut. Heard a click that sounded like a switch, followed almost immediately by the grinding sound of heavy machinery. Then a torch was shining into her face, temporarily blinding her.

She stared up, almost paralysed by utter terror and confusion. Who was this? The ride operator she'd met outside?

'Please don't hurt me,' she said.

Through the beam of light she saw the silhouette of a man's face inside what looked like a nylon stocking with slits in it.

As she opened her mouth and tried to scream, something soft and foul-tasting was rammed into it. She heard a ripping sound and the next instant felt sticky tape being pressed over her lips and around each side of her face. She tried to scream again, but all that came out was a muffled choking sound that seemed to shimmy around inside her head.

'You're gagging for it, aren't you, doll? Dressed like that? Dressed in those shoes!'

She lashed out at him with her fists, pummelling him, trying to scratch him. Then she saw something glint in the darkness. It was the head of a large claw hammer. He was holding it in a latex-gloved hand.

'Keep still or I'll fucking hit you.'

She still in terror, staring at the dull metal.

Suddenly she felt a crashing blow to the side of her head. Her brain filled with sparks.

Then silence.

She never felt him entering her or removing her shoes afterwards.

47

Garry Starling entered the packed China Garden restaurant shortly after 9 p.m. and hurried towards his table, pausing only to order a Tsingtao beer from the manager, who stepped across to greet him.

'You are late tonight, Mr Starling!' the jovial Chinese man said. 'I don't think your wife is a very happy lady.'

'Tell me something new!' Garry replied, palming him a £20 note.

Then he hurried up the steps to his regular table and noticed that the gannets had almost finished the mixed starters. There was one solitary spring roll left in the huge bowl, and the tablecloth was littered with shreds of seaweed and stains from the spilt sauces. All three of them looked like they'd had a good few drinks.

'Where the sodding hell have you been?' his wife, Denise, said, greeting him with her customary acidic smile.

'Actually I've been *sodding* working, my darling,' he said, giving Maurice's barmy-looking Earth Mother wife, Ulla, a perfunctory kiss, shaking Maurice's hand and then sitting in the empty seat between them. He didn't kiss Denise. He'd stopped greeting her with a kiss back in the year dot.

Turning and staring pointedly at his wife, he said,

'Working. Right? *Working.* A word that's not in your lexicon. Know what it means? To pay for the sodding mortgage. Your sodding credit-card bill.'

'And your sodding camper van!'

'Camper van?' said Maurice, sounding astonished. 'That's not your style, Garry.'

'It's a VW. The original split-windscreen one. They're fine investments, very collectable. Thought it would be good for Denise and me to experience the open road, sleeping out in the wild every now and then, get back to nature! I would have bought a boat, but she gets seasick.'

'It's midlife crisis, that what it is,' Denise said to Maurice and Ulla. 'If he thinks he's taking me on holiday in a sodding van he can think again! Just like last year, when he tried to get me on the back of his motorbike to go on a blooming camping holiday in France!'

'It's not a sodding van!' Garry said, grabbing the last spring roll before anyone else could get it, dipping it by mistake in the hot sauce and cramming it into his mouth.

A small thermonuclear explosion took place inside his head, rendering him temporarily speechless. Denise took good advantage of it.

'You look like shit!' she said. 'How did you get that scratch on your forehead?'

'Crawling up in a sodding loft, trying to replace an alarm wire bloody mice had eaten. A nail sticking out of a rafter.'

Denise suddenly leaned closer to him and sniffed. 'You've been smoking!'

'I was in a taxi where someone had been smoking,' he mumbled a little clumsily, chewing.

'Oh, really?' She gave him a disbelieving look, then turned to their friends. 'He keeps pretending he's quit, but he thinks I'm stupid! He goes out to take the dog for a walk, or a bike ride, or to take his motorbike for a spin, and comes back hours later stinking of fags. You can always smell it on someone, can't you?' She looked a Ulla, then at Maurice and swigged some Sauvignon Blanc.

Garry's beer arrived and he took a long pull, glancing first at Ulla, thinking that her mad hair looked even madder than usual tonight, and then at Maurice, who looked more like a toad than ever. Both of them, and Denise as well, looked strange, as if he was seeing them through distorting glass. Maurice's black T-shirt stretched out over his pot belly, his eyes bulged out of their sockets and his expensive, hideous checked jacket, with its shiny Versace buttons, was too tight. It looked like a hand-me-down from an older brother.

Defending his friend, Maurice shook his head. 'Can't smell anything.'

Ulla leaned across and sniffed Garry, like a dog on heat. 'Nice cologne!' she said evasively. 'Smells quite feminine, though.'

'Chanel Platinum,' he replied.

She sniffed again, giving a dubious frown, and raised her eyebrows at Denise.

'So where the hell have you been?' Denise demanded. 'You look a mess. Couldn't you at least have brushed your hair?'

'It's blowing a hooley out there, in case you haven't noticed!' Garry replied. 'I had to deal with an irate client – we're short-staffed tonight – one down with flu, one down with something else, and a bolshy Mr Graham Lewis in Steyning, whose alarm keeps going off for no reason, was threatening to change suppliers. So I had to go and sort him out. OK? Turns out it was damned mice.'

She tilted her glass into her mouth, to drain it, then realized it was already empty. At that moment a waiter appeared with a fresh bottle. Garry pointed at his own wine glass, draining his beer at the same time. His nerves were shot to hell and he needed drink right now. Lots of it.

'Cheers, everyone!' he said.

Maurice and Ulla raised their glasses. 'Cheers!'

Denise took her time. She was glaring at Garry. She just did not believe him.

But, Garry thought, when had his wife last believed him about anything? He drained half of the sharp white wine in just one gulp, momentarily relieving the burning sensation in the roof of his mouth. If the truth be known, the last time she had believed him was probably on the day they got married, when he said his vows.

Although . . . he hadn't even been sure then. He could still remember the look she had given him in front of the altar, as he'd slipped the ring on to her finger and got prompted through the wording by the vicar. It was not the love in her eyes that he might have expected, more the smug satisfaction of a hunter returning home with a dead animal over their shoulder.

He had nearly bailed out then.

Twelve years later, there was not a day that went by when he didn't wish he had.

But hey. There were advantages to being married. It was important never to forget that.

Being married gave you respectability.

48

'I've had a go at the wording on the wedding invites,' Cleo called out from the kitchen.

'Great!' Roy Grace said. 'Want me to take a look?'

'We'll go through it when you've had supper.'

He smiled. One thing he was learning about Cleo was that she liked to plan things well in advance. It was going to be touch and go for the wedding to take place before their child was born. They couldn't even set a firm date yet because of all the bureaucracy that had to be dealt with to have Sandy declared legally dead first.

Humphrey lay contentedly beside him now on Cleo's living-room floor with a goofy grin, head flopped over, his tongue half out. Roy ran his palm back and forward across the happy creature's soft, warm belly, while a Labour politician on the flat-screen TV on the wall pontificated on *News at Ten*.

But he wasn't listening. With his suit jacket removed and his tie loosened, his thoughts were on the evening briefing and the pages of work he had brought home, which were spread out on the sofa beside him. In particular, he was poring over the similarities between the Shoe Man and the new offender. A number of unanswered questions were going around his mind.

If the Shoe Man was back, where had he been for the

past twelve years? Or if he had remained in the city, why had he stopped offending for so long? Was it possible that he had raped other victims who had not reported it?

Grace doubted that he could have raped repeatedly for twelve years without someone reporting it. Yet so far there were no rapists showing up on the national database with a comparable MO. He could of course have gone abroad, which would take a massive amount of time and resourcing to establish.

However, this evening it emerged that there was one potential suspect in the city, following the Analyst's search of the ViSOR and MAPPA databases, ViSOR being the Violent and Sex Offender Register and MAPPA the Multi-agency Public Protection Arrangements.

Having been set up to manage the release of violent and sexual offenders back into the community after their release from prison on licence, MAPPA graded these offenders into three categories. Level 1 was for released prisoners who were considered to have a low risk of reoffending and were monitored to ensure that they complied with the terms of their licence. Level 2 was for those considered to be in need of moderately active inter-agency monitoring. Level 3 was for those considered to have a high risk of reoffending.

Zoratti had discovered that there was a Level 2 who had been released on licence, from Ford Open Prison, having served three years of a six-year sentence, mostly at Lewes, for burglary and indecent assault – a career burglar and drugs dealer, Darren Spicer. He'd attempted to kiss a woman in a house he had broken into, then run off when she'd fought back and had pressed a hidden panic button. Later, she'd picked him out in an identity parade.

Spicer's current place of residence was being traced

urgently tonight through the Probation Service. But while he was worth interviewing, Grace wasn't convinced Darren Spicer ticked many boxes. He had been in and out of jail several times in the past twelve years, so why had he not offended in the interim? More important, in his view, was the fact that the man had no previous record of sexual assaults. The last offence that had contributed to Spicer's sentence appeared to be a one-off – although, of course, there was no certainty of that. With the grim statistic that only 6 per cent of rape victims ever reported the crimes, it was quite possible he had committed previous such offences and got away with them.

Next he turned his mind to the copycat theory. One thing that was deeply bothering him was the missing pages from the Rachael Ryan file. Sure, it was possible that they had simply been misfiled somewhere else. But there could be a much darker reason. Could it be that the Shoe Man himself had accessed the file and removed something that might incriminate him? If he had access to that file, he would have had access to all the Shoe Man's files.

Or was it someone else altogether who had gained access to them? Someone who had decided, for whatever sick reason, to copy the Shoe Man's MO.

Who?

A member of his trusted team? He didn't think so, but of course he couldn't discount that. There were plenty of other people who had access to the Major Crime Suite – other police officers, support staff and cleaning staff. Solving that mystery, he realized, was now a priority for him.

'Are you nearly ready to eat, darling?' Cleo called out.

Cleo was grilling him a tuna steak. Roy took this as a

sign that maybe, finally, she was starting to wean herself off curries. The reek of them had gone and there was now a strong smell of wood smoke from the crackling fire that Cleo had lit in the grate some time before he had arrived, and the welcoming aroma of scented candles burning in different parts of the room.

He took another long sip of the deliciously cold vodka martini she had mixed, enviously, for him. He now had to drink for both of them, she'd told him – and tonight he did not have a problem with that. He felt the welcoming buzz of the alcohol and then, still mechanically stroking the dog, he lapsed back into his thoughts.

A car had been seen leaving the Pearce house in Droveway Avenue at 9 p.m. on Thursday, which fitted perfectly with the timing of the attack. It had been travelling at speed and nearly ran over a local resident. The man was so angry he tried to take a note of the number plate, but could only be certain of two digits and one letter of the alphabet. Then he did nothing about it until he read of the attack in the *Argus*, which prompted him to phone the Incident Room this evening.

According to him, the driver was male, but with the vehicle's tinted windows he had not been able to get a clear look at his face. Somewhere in his thirties or forties with short hair was the extent of his description. He did much better with the car, asserting it was a light-coloured old-model Mercedes E-Class saloon. Just how many of those Mercedes were there around, Grace wondered? Loads of them. It was going to take a while to sift through all the registered keepers when they didn't have a full registration number to work from. And he did not have the luxury of time.

With the rising frenzy in the media after two stranger

rapes in the city in a little over a week, the news stories were ramping up fear in the public. The call handlers were being inundated with queries from anxious women about whether it was safe to go out and he was aware that his immediate superiors, Chief Superintendent Jack Skerritt and ACC Peter Rigg, were anxious to see rapid progress with this case.

The next press conference was scheduled for midday on Monday. It would calm everything down greatly if he could announce they had a suspect and, even better, that they had made an arrest. OK, they had Darren Spicer as a possible. But nothing made the police look more inefficient than having to release a suspect because of lack of evidence, or because it was the wrong person. The Mercedes was more promising. But the driver wasn't necessarily the offender. There could be an innocent explanation – perhaps a family friend who had popped round for a visit to the Pearce household, or simply someone delivering a package?

The fact that the car was being driven recklessly was a good indicator that it might have been the suspect. It was a known fact that offenders often drove badly immediately after committing a crime – because they were in a heightened state of anxiety, the *red mist*.

He'd sent all his team home for the night to get some rest, except for the two Analysts, who were working a 24/7 rota between them. Glenn Branson had asked him for a quick pint on the way home, but he'd apologetically excused himself, having barely seen Cleo this weekend. With his mate's marital woes spiralling from bad to worse, he was running out of sympathetic things to say to Glenn. Divorce was a grim option, especially for someone with young kids. But he could no longer see much alternative for his friend – and wished desperately that he could. Glenn was going to have to bite the bullet and move on. An easy thing to tell someone else, but an almost impossible thing to accept oneself.

He felt a sudden craving for a cigarette, but resisted, with difficulty. Cleo was not bothered if he smoked in here, or anywhere, but he was mindful of the baby she was carrying, and all the stuff about passive smoke, and the example he needed to try to set. So he drank some more, ignoring the craving.

'Ready in about five minutes!' she called out from the kitchen. 'Need another drink?' She popped her head around the door.

He raised his glass to show it was nearly empty. 'I'll be under the table if I have another!'

'That's the way I like you!' she replied, coming over to him.

'You're just a control freak!' he said with a big grin.

He would take a bullet for this woman. He would die for Cleo gladly, he knew. Without an instant's hesitation.

Then he felt a sudden strange pang of guilt. Wasn't this how he'd felt once about Sandy?

He tried to answer himself truthfully. Yes, it had been total hell when she disappeared. That morning on his thirtieth birthday, they had made love before he went to work, and that same evening, when he returned home, looking forward to their celebration, she had not been there – that had been total hell.

So had the days, weeks, months and then years after. Imagining all the terrible things that might have happened to her. And sometimes imagining what might still be happening to her in some monster's lair. But that was just one of many scenarios. He'd lost count of the number of psychics he'd had consultations or sittings with over these past ten years – and not one of them had said she was in the spirit world. Despite all of them, he was reasonably certain that Sandy was dead.

In a few months' time it would be ten years ago that she had disappeared. An entire decade, in which he'd gone from a young man to a middle-aged fart.

In which he'd met the loveliest, smartest, most incredible woman in the world.

Sometimes he woke up and imagined he must have dreamed it all. Then he would feel Cleo's warm, naked body beside him. He would slip his arms around her and hold her tightly, the way someone might try to hold on to their dreams.

'I love you so much,' he would whisper.

'Shit!' Cleo broke away from him, breaking the spell.

There was a smell of burning as she dashed back over to the hob. 'Shit, shit, shit!'

'It's OK! I like it well done. I don't like fish with its heart still beating!'

'Just as well!'

The kitchen filled with black smoke and the stink of burning fish. The smoke alarm started beeping. Roy opened the windows and the patio door and Humphrey raced outside, barking furiously at something in his squeaky puppy bark, then raced back inside and tore around barking at the alarm.

A few minutes later, Grace sat at the table and Cleo placed a plate in front of him. On it lay a blackened tuna steak, a lump of tartare sauce, some limp-looking mangetout, and a mess of disintegrated boiled potatoes.

'Eat that,' she said, 'and you are proving it's true love!'

The television above the table was on, with the sound turned down. The politician had gone and now Jamie Oliver was energetically demonstrating how to slice the coral from scallops.

Humphrey nudged his right leg, then tried to jump up.

'Down! No begging!' he said.

The dog looked at him uncertainly, then slunk away.

Cleo sat down beside him and gave him a wide-eyed frown.

'You don't have to eat it if it's really horrible.'

He forked some fish into his mouth. It tasted even worse than it looked, but only marginally. No question, Sandy was a better cook than Cleo. A thousand times better. But it did not matter to him one jot. Although he did glance a tad enviously at the dish Jamie Oliver was preparing.

'So how was your day?' he asked, dubiously forking another section of burnt fish into his mouth, thinking that the curries really had not been so bad after all.

She told him about the body of a forty-two-stone man she'd had to recover from his home. It had required the help of the fire brigade.

He listened in astounded silence, then ate some salad, which she put down on a side plate. At least she had managed not to burn that.

Switching subjects she said, 'Hey, something occurred to me about the Shoe Man. Do you want my thoughts?'

He nodded.

'OK, your Shoe Man – *if* it is the same offender as before and *if* he stayed in this area – I can't see that he would have just totally stopped getting his kicks.'

'Meaning what?'

'If he stopped offending, for whatever reason, he must still have had urges. He would need to satisfy them. So maybe he'd go to dominatrix dungeons – or places like that – weird sex places, fetishes and stuff. Put yourself in his shoes, as it were – forgive the pun! You're a creep who gets off on women's shoes. OK?'

'That's one of our lines of enquiry.'

'Yes, but listen. You've found a fun way of doing it – raping strangers in classy shoes and then taking those shoes. OK?'

He stared at her, without reacting.

'Then, oooops! You go a bit too far. She dies. The media coverage is intense. You decide to lie low, ride it out. But . . .' She hesitated. 'You want the *but*?'

'We don't know for sure that anyone died. All we know is that he stopped. But tell me?' he said

'You still get your rocks off on women's feet. OK? You following me?'

'In your footsteps? In your shoes?'

'Sod off, Detective Superintendent!'

He raised his hand. 'No disrespect!'

'None taken. OK, so you are the Shoe Man, you are still turned on by feet, or by shoes. Sooner or later that thing inside you, that *urge*, is going to ride to the top. You're going to need that. Where do you go? The Internet, that's where you go! So you type in *feet* and *fetish* maybe and *Brighton*. Do you know what you come up with?'

Grace shook his head, impressed with Cleo's logic. He tried to ignore the horrible stench of burnt fish.

'A whole bunch of massage parlours and dominatrix dens – just like the ones I sometimes have to recover bodies from. You know – old geezers who get too excited—'

Her mobile phone rang.

Apologizing to Roy, she answered it. Instantly her expression switched to work mode. Then, when she ended the call, she said to him, 'Sorry, my love. There's a dead body in a shelter on the seafront. Duty calls.'

He nodded.

She kissed him. 'I'll be as quick as I can. See you in bed. Don't die on me.'

'I'll try to stay alive.'

'Just one part of you anyway. The bit that matters to me!' She touched him gently, just below his belt.

'Slapper!'

'Horny bastard!'

Then she put a printout in front of him. 'Have a read – make any amendments you want.'

He glanced at the paper.

Mr and Mrs Charles Morey
request the pleasure of your company
at the marriage of their daughter
Cleo Suzanne
to Roy Jack Grace
at All Saints' Church, Little Bookham

'Don't forget to let Humphrey out for a pee and a dump before you go up!' she said.

Then she was gone.

Moments after she closed the door, his own phone rang. He pulled it from his pocket and checked the display. The number was withheld, which meant almost certainly it was someone calling from work.

It was.

And it was not good news.

49

In another part of the city, just a couple of miles away in a quiet, residential Kemp Town street, another couple were also discussing their wedding plans.

Jessie Sheldon and Benedict Greene were ensconced opposite each other in Sam's restaurant, sharing a dessert.

Anyone looking at them would have seen two attractive people, both in their mid-twenties, clearly in love. It was evident from their body language. They sat oblivious of their surroundings, and anyone else, their foreheads almost touching over the tall glass dish, each taking it in turn to dig a long spoon in and feed the other tenderly and sensually.

Neither was dressed up, even though it was Saturday night. Jessie, who had come straight from a kick-boxing class at the gym, wore a grey tracksuit with a large Nike tick across it. Her shoulder-length bleached hair was scooped up into a ponytail, with a few loose strands hanging down. She had a pretty face and, if it weren't for her nose, she would be almost classically beautiful.

Jessie had had a complex about her nose throughout her childhood. In her view, it wasn't so much a nose as a *beak*. In her teens she was forever glancing sideways to catch her reflection in mirrors or shop windows. She had been determined that one day she would have a nose job.

But that was then, in her life before Benedict. Now, at twenty-five, she didn't care about it any more. Benedict told her he loved her nose, that he would not hear of her changing it and that he hoped their children would inherit that same shape. She was less happy about that thought, about putting them through the same years of misery she had been through.

They would have nose jobs, she promised herself silently.

The irony was that neither of her parents had that nose, nor did her grandparents. It was her great-grand-father's, she had been told by her mother, who had a framed and fading sepia photograph of him. The damned hooked-nose gene had managed to vault two generations and fetch up in her DNA strand.

Thanks a lot, great-grandpa!

'You know something, I love your nose more every day,' Benedict said, holding up the spoon she had just licked clean and handing it to her.

'Is it *just* my nose?' she teased.

He shrugged and looked pensive for a moment. 'Other bits too, I suppose!'

She gave him a playful kick under the table. 'Which other bits?'

Benedict had a serious, studious face and neat brown hair. When she had first met him, he had reminded her of those clean-cut, almost impossibly perfect-looking boy-next-door actors who seemed to star in every US television mini series. She felt so good with him. He made her feel safe and secure, and she missed him every single second that they were apart. She looked forward with intense happiness to a life with him.

But there was an elephant in the room.

It stood beside their table now. Casting its own massive shadow over them.

'So, did you tell them, last night?' he asked.

Friday night. The Shabbat. The ritual Friday night with her mother and father, her brother, her sister-in-law, her grandmother, that she never missed. The prayers and the meal. The gefilte fish that her mother's appalling cooking made taste like cat food. The cremated chicken and shrivelled sweetcorn. The candles. The grim wine her father bought that tasted like boiled tarmac – as if drinking alcohol on a Friday night was a mortal sin, so he had to ensure that the stuff tasted like a penance.

Her brother, Marcus, was the big success of the family. He was a lawyer, married to a good Jewish girl, Rochelle, who was now irritatingly pregnant, and they were both irritatingly smug about that.

She had fully intended breaking the news, the same way she had intended breaking it for the past four Friday nights. That she was in love with and intended to marry a *goy*. And a *poor goy* to boot. But she had funked it yet again.

She shrugged. 'I'm sorry, I – I was going to – but – it just wasn't the right moment. I think they should meet you first. Then they'll see what a lovely person you are.'

He frowned.

She put down the spoon, reached across the table and took his hand. 'I've told you – they're not easy people.'

He put his free hand over hers and stared into her eyes. 'Does that mean you're having doubts?'

She shook her head vigorously. 'None. Absolutely none. I love you, Benedict, and I want to spend the rest of my life with you. I don't have one shred of doubt.'

And she didn't.

But she had a problem. Not only was Benedict not Jewish or wealthy, but he wasn't ambitious in the sense that her parents could – or would ever – understand: the *monetary* sense. He did have big ambitions in a different direction. He worked for a local charity, helping homeless people. He wanted to improve the plight of underprivileged people throughout his city. He dreamed of the day when no one would ever have to sleep on the streets of this rich city again. She loved and admired him for that.

Her mother had dreamed of her becoming a doctor, which had once been Jessie's dream too. When, with lower sights, she'd opted instead to go for a nursing degree at Southampton University, her parents had accepted it, her mother with less good grace than her father. But when she graduated she decided that she wanted to do something to help the underprivileged, and she got a job that was low-paid but she loved, as a nurse/ counsellor at a drug addict drop-in centre at the Old Steine in central Brighton.

A job with no prospects. Not something either of her parents could easily get their heads around. But they admired her dedication, no question of that. They were proud of her. And they were looking forward to a son-in-law, one day, they would be equally proud of. It was a natural assumption that he would be a big earner, a provider, to keep Jessie in the manner to which she was accustomed.

Which was a problem with Benedict.

'I'm happy to meet them any time. You know that.'

She nodded and gripped his hand. 'You're going to meet them next week at the ball. You'll charm them then, I'm sure.'

Her father was chair of a large local charity that raised money for Jewish causes around the world. He had booked a table at a fund-raising ball at the Metropole Hotel to which she had been invited to bring a friend.

She'd already bought her outfit and what she needed now was a pair of shoes to go with it. All she had to do was ask her father for the money, which she knew would please him no end. But she just could not bring herself to do that. She'd spotted some Anya Hindmarch shoes earlier today, in the January sale at a local store, Marielle Shoes. They were dead sexy but classy at the same time. Black patent leather, five-inch heels, ankle straps and open toe. But at £250 they were still a lot of money. She hoped that perhaps, if she waited, there might be a further reduction on them. If someone else bought them in the interim, well, too bad. She'd find something else. Brighton had no shortage of shoe shops. She'd find something!

The Shoe Man agreed with her.

He'd stood right behind her at the counter of Deja Shoes in Kensington Gardens earlier today. He'd listened to her telling the shop assistant that she wanted something classy and sexy to wear for her fiancé at an important function next week. Then he'd stood behind her at Marielle Shoes, just along the road.

And he had to admit she looked really sexy in those strapped black patent shoes she had tried on but not bought. So very sexy.

Much too sexy for them to be wasted on her fiancé.

He sincerely hoped she would return and buy them.

Then she could wear them for him!

50

Saturday 10 January

The words on the data unit's screen in Yac's taxi read:

> **China Garden rest. Preston St. 2 Pass. Starling. Dest.
> Roedean Cresc.**

It was 11.20 p.m. He had been parked up for some minutes now and had started the meter running. The man who owned the taxi said he should only wait for five minutes and then start the meter. Yac wasn't sure how accurate his watch was and he wanted to be fair to his passengers. So he always allowed twenty seconds' grace.

Starling. Roedean Crescent.

He had picked these people up before. He never forgot a passenger and especially not these people. The address: 67 Roedean Crescent. He had memorized that. She wore Shalimar perfume. The same perfume as his mother. He had memorized that too. She had been wearing Bruno Magli shoes. Size four. His mother's size.

He wondered what shoes she would be wearing tonight.

Excitement rose inside him as the restaurant door opened and he saw the couple emerge. The man was holding on to the woman and looked unsteady. She helped him negotiate the step down to the pavement, then he still clung to her as they walked the short distance, through the blustery wind, over to Yac.

But Yac wasn't looking at him. He was looking at the woman's shoes. They were nice. Tall heels. Straps. His kind of shoes.

Mr Starling peered in through the window, which Yac had opened.

'Taaxish for Roedean Chresshent? Shtarling?'

He sounded as drunk as he looked.

The man who owned the taxi said he did not have to take drunk passengers, especially ones who might be likely to throw up. It cost a lot of money to clear vomit out of the taxi, because it went everywhere, into the vents, down the windows into the electric motors, into the cracks down the sides of the seats. People didn't like getting into a taxi that smelt of stale sick. It wasn't nice to drive one either.

But it had been a quiet night. The man who owned the taxi would be angry with the poor takings. He had already complained about how little Yac had taken since New Year and he'd told Yac that he'd never known any taxi driver take so little on New Year's Eve itself.

He needed all the fares he could get, because he didn't want to risk the man who owned the taxi firing him and having someone else drive. So he decided to take a risk.

And he wanted to smell her perfume. Wanted those shoes in the taxi with him!

The Starlings climbed into the back and he drove off. He adjusted the mirror so he could see Mrs Starling's face, then he said, 'Nice shoes! Alberta Ferretti, I'll bet those are!'

'You a fucking pervert or shomething?' she said,

sounding almost as sloshed as her husband. 'I think you drove us before, didn't you, quite recently? Last week? Yesh?'

'You were wearing Bruno Maglis.'

'You're too fucking pershonal! None of your damned fucking business what shoes I'm wearing.'

'Into shoes, are you?' Yac asked.

'Yesh, she is into fucking shoes,' Garry Starling butted in. 'Spends all my money on them. Every penny I make ends up on her sodding feet!'

'That's because, my darling, you can only get it up when – ouch!' she cried out loudly.

Yac looked at her again in the mirror. Her face was contorted in pain. She'd been rude to him last time she had been in his taxi.

He liked seeing that pain.

1998

51

He'd spent the whole of the past few days thinking about Rachael Ryan lying in his chest freezer in his lock-up. It was hard to avoid her. Her face stared out at him from every damned newspaper. Her tearful parents spoke to him personally, and to him alone, from every damned television news broadcast.

'Please, whoever you are, if you have taken our daughter, give her back to us. She's a sweet, innocent girl and we love her. Please don't harm her.'

'It was your daughter's damned fault!' he whispered back at them. 'If she hadn't taken my mask off she'd be fine. Fine and dandy! She'd still be your loving daughter and not my damned problem.'

Slowly, steadily, the idea he had last night took hold more and more inside him. It could just be the perfect solution! He risk-assessed it over and over again. It stood up to each problem he tested it against. It would be riskier to delay than to act.

In almost every paper the white van was mentioned. It was referred to in big headlines on the front page of the *Argus*: DID ANYONE SEE THIS VAN? The caption beneath read: *Similar to the one seen in Eastern Terrace.*

The police said they had been overwhelmed with calls. How many of those calls were about white vans?

About his white van?

White Transit vans were a dime a dozen. But the police were not stupid. It was only a matter of time before a phone call led them to his lock-up. He had to get the girl out of there. And he had to do something about the van – they were getting smart with forensics these days. But deal with one problem at a time.

Outside, the rain was torrenting down. It was now 11 p.m. on Saturday. Party night in this city. But not so many people as usual would be out and about in this dreadful weather.

He made his decision and left the house, hurrying out to his old Ford Sierra runabout.

Ten minutes later, he pulled down the garage door behind the dripping-wet car, closing it with a quiet metallic clang, then switched on his torch, not wanting to risk putting on the overhead lights.

Inside the freezer, the young woman was completely frosted over, her face translucent in the harsh beam of light.

'We're going to take a little drive, Rachael. Hope you're cool with that?'

Then he smirked at his joke. Yeah. *Cool.* He felt OK. This was going to work. He just had to stay cool too. How did that saying go that he had read somewhere: *If you can keep your head while all about you are losing theirs . . .*

He pulled out his packet of cigarettes and tried to light one. But his damned hand was shaking so much, first he couldn't strike the wheel of the lighter, then he couldn't get the flame near the tip of the cigarette. Cold sweat was pouring down his neck as if it was coming from a busted tap.

*

At a few minutes to midnight, with his toolkit clipped to his belt, he drove around the Lewes Road gyratory system, past the entrance to the Brighton and Hove Borough Mortuary, wipers clunk-clunking away the rain, and then turned left on to the hard driveway of his destination, J. Bund and Sons, funeral directors.

He was shaking, all knotted up inside and perspiring heavily. *Stupid woman, stupid bloody Rachael, why the hell did you have to take my mask off?*

Up on the wall, above the curtained shop window of the premises, he clocked the burglar alarm box. Sussex Security Systems. Not a problem, he thought, pulling up in front of the padlocked steel gates. The lock was also not a problem.

Directly across the road was a closed estate agent's, with flats on the two storeys above. There was a light on in one of them. But they would be used to seeing vehicles come and go at a funeral parlour around the clock.

He switched the lights off, then climbed out of the Sierra into the rain to deal with the padlock. A trickle of cars and taxis drove past along the road. One of them was a police patrol car, its blue lights flashing and siren wailing. He held his breath, but its crew paid him no attention, just swishing straight past to some emergency or other. Moments later he drove through into the rear yard and parked between two hearses and a van. Then he hurried back through the rain and closed the gates, pulling the chain around them, but leaving the padlock dangling open. So long as no one came, all would be fine.

It took him less than a minute to pick the Chubb on the double rear receiving doors, then he entered the dark entrance hallway, wrinkling his nose at the smells of embalming fluid and disinfectant. The alarm was beeping.

Just the internal warning signal. He had sixty precious seconds before the external bells would kick off. It took him less than thirty to remove the front casing of the alarm panel. Another fifteen and it fell silent.

Too silent.

He closed the door behind him. And now it was even more silent. The faint click-whirr of a fridge. A steady tick-tick-tick of a clock or a meter.

These places gave him the creeps. He remembered the last time he had been in here; he had been alone then, and shit-scared. They were dead, all of the people in here, dead like Rachael Ryan. They couldn't hurt you, or tell tales on you.

Couldn't leap out at you.

But that didn't make it any better.

He flashed his torch beam along the corridor ahead, trying to orient himself. He saw a row of framed Health and Safety notices, a fire extinguisher and a drinking-water dispenser.

Then he took a few steps forward, his trainers silent on the tiled floor, listening intently for any new sounds inside or out. There was a staircase up to his right. He remembered it led to the individual rooms – or Chapels of Rest – where friends and relatives could visit and mourn their loved ones in privacy. Each room contained a body laid out on a bed, men in pyjamas, women in nightgowns, their heads poking out from beneath the sheets, hair tidy, faces all rosy from embalming fluid. They looked like they were checked into some tacky hotel for the night.

But for sure they wouldn't be doing a runner without paying their bills in the morning, he thought, and grinned despite his unease.

Then, flashing his torch through an open doorway to his left, he saw a prostrate white marble statue. Except, as he took a closer look, he saw it wasn't a statue. It was a dead man on a slab. Two handwritten tags hung from his right foot. An old man, he lay with his mouth open like a landed fish, embalming-fluid lines cannulated into his body, his penis lying uselessly against his thigh.

Close to him was a row of coffins, open and empty, just one of them with its lid closed. There was a brass plaque on the lid, engraved with the name of its occupant.

He stopped for a moment, listening. But all he could hear was the thudding of his own heart and the blood coursing through his veins louder than the roar of a river in flood. He could not hear the traffic outside. All that entered here from the world beyond the walls was a faint, eerie orange glow leaking in from a street light on the pavement.

'Hi, everyone!' he said, feeling very uncomfortable as he swung the beam around until it struck what he was looking for. The row of duplicated white A4 forms hanging on hooks from the wall.

Eagerly, he walked over to them. These were the registration forms for each of the bodies in here. All the information was on them: name, date of death, place of death, funeral instructions, and a whole row of optional disbursement boxes to be ticked – organist's fee, cemetery fee, churchyard burial fee, clergy's fee, church fee, doctor's fee, removal of pacemaker fee, cremation fee, gravedigger's fee, printed service sheets fees, flowers, memorial cards, obituary notices, coffin, casket for remains.

He read quickly through the first sheet. No good: the *Embalming* box had been ticked. The same applied to the next four. His heart began to sink. They were embalmed and their funerals were not until later in the week.

But on the fifth it looked like he might have struck gold:

Mrs Molly Winifred Glossop

D. 2 January 1998. Aged 81.

And further down:

Funeral on: 12 January 1998, 11 a.m.

Monday morning!

His eyes raced down the form to the words *Committal*. Not so good. He would have preferred a cremation. Done and dusted. Safer.

He turned to the remaining six forms. But none of them was any good at all. They were all funerals to be held later in the week – too risky, in case the family came to view. And all but one had requested embalming.

No one had requested that Molly Winifred Glossop be embalmed.

Not having her embalmed meant her family was probably too mean. Which might be an indication that they weren't going to care too much about her body. So hopefully no distraught relative was going to rush in tonight or first thing in the morning, wanting to have one last peep at her.

He shone his beam down on the plaque on the one closed coffin, trying hard to ignore the corpse lying just a few feet away.

Molly Winifred Glossop, it confirmed. *Died 2 January 1998, aged 81.*

The fact that it was closed, with the lid screwed down,

was a good indicator that no one was coming along tomorrow to see her.

Unclipping a screwdriver from his belt, he removed the shiny brass screws holding down the lid, lifted it away and peered inside, breathing in a cocktail of freshly sawn wood, glue and new fabric and disinfectant.

The dead woman nestled in the cream satin lining of the coffin, her head poking out of the white shroud that wrapped the rest of her. She did not look real; she looked like some kind of weird *granny* doll, that was his first reaction. Her face was emaciated and bony, all wrinkles and angles, the colour of a tortoise. Her mouth was sewn shut; he could see the threads through her lips. Her hair was a tidy bob of white curls.

He felt a lump in his throat as a memory came back to him. And another lump, this time of fear. He slipped his hands down either side of her and began to lift. He was startled by how light she was. He could feel the weightlessness of her frame in his arms. There was nothing on her, no flesh at all. She must have been a cancer victim, he decided, laying her down on the floor. Shit, she was a lot lighter than Rachael Ryan. Several stones lighter. But hopefully the pall-bearers would never realize.

He hurried back outside, popped open the boot of the Sierra and removed Rachael Ryan's body, which he had wrapped in two layers of heavy-duty plastic sheeting to prevent any water leaking out as she thawed.

*

Ten minutes later, with the alarm casing replaced, the system reset and the padlock again locked shut on the chain around the gate, he pulled the Ford Sierra out into the busy Saturday-night traffic on the rain-lashed road. A whole weight was gone from his mind. He accelerated recklessly, swinging out across the lanes, halting at a red light on the far side of the road.

He needed to keep calm, did not want to risk attracting the attention of the police, not with Molly Winifred Glossop lying in the boot of his car. He switched on the radio and heard the sound of the Beatles: 'We Can Work It Out'.

He thumped the steering wheel, almost elated with relief. *Yes! Yes! Yes! We* can *work it out!*

Oh yes!

Stage one had gone to plan. Now he just had stage two to worry about. It was a big worry; there were unknown factors. But it was the best of his limited options. And, in his view, quite cunning.

NOW

52

Sunday 11 January

St Patrick's night shelter relaxed the rules on Sundays that it applied for the rest of the week. Although the residents still had to vacate the premises by 8.30 a.m., they could return at 5 p.m.

Even so, Darren Spicer thought that was a bit harsh, since it was a church and all that, and wasn't a church supposed to give you sanctuary at any time? Especially when the weather was crap. But he wasn't going to argue, as he didn't want to blot his copybook here. He wanted one of the MiPods. Ten weeks of personal space and you could come and go as you pleased. Yeah, that would be good. That would enable him to get his life together – though not in the kind of way the people who ran this place had in mind.

It was pissing down outside. And sodding freezing. But he did not want to stay in all day. He'd showered and eaten a bowl of cereal and some toast. The television was on and a couple of the residents were watching a replay of a football match on its slightly fuzzy screen.

Football, yeah. Brighton and Hove Albion was his home team. He remembered that magical day, when he was a teenager, they'd played at Wembley in the FA Cup Final and drawn. Half the home-owners of Brighton and Hove had gone up there to watch the game, while the other half were in their sitting rooms, glued to their tellies. It had been one of the best day's burgling of his whole career.

Yesterday he'd actually been along to the Withdean Sports Stadium for a game. He liked football, not that he was much of an Albion supporter. He preferred Manchester United and Chelsea, but he had his reasons yesterday. He needed to score some charlie – as cocaine was known on the street – and the best way was to show his face. His dealer was there, in his usual seat. Nothing had changed there, apart from the price, which had gone up, and the quality, which had gone down.

After the game he'd acquired himself an eight ball for £140, dipping deep into his meagre savings. He'd washed down two of the three and a half grams with a couple of pints and a few whisky chasers almost straight away. The last gram and a half he'd saved to see himself through the tedium of today.

He pulled his donkey jacket on and his baseball cap. Most of the rest of his fellow residents were lazing around, talking in groups or lost in their thoughts or watching the TV. Like himself, none of them had anywhere to go, particularly on a Sunday, when the libraries were shut – the only warm places where they could hang out for hours for free without being hassled. But he had plans.

The round clock on the wall above the now closed food hatch said 8.23. Seven minutes to go.

It was at times like this that he missed being in prison. Life was easy in there. You were warm and dry. You had routine and companionship. You had no worries. But you had dreams.

He reminded himself of that now. His dreams. The

promise he had made himself. To make himself some kind of a future. Get a stash and then go straight.

Lingering in the dry for those last few minutes, Spicer read some of the posters stuck to the walls:

MOVING ON?

FREE CONFIDENCE BUILDING COURSE FOR MEN

FREE FOOD SAFETY COURSE

FREE NEW COURSE –
FEELING SAFER AT HOME AND IN THE COMMUNITY

INJECTING INTO MUSCLE? PLEASE BE AWARE

DO YOU THINK YOU MIGHT HAVE A PROBLEM
WITH COCAINE OR OTHER DRUGS?

He sniffed. Yeah, he did have a problem with cocaine. Not enough of it, that was the problem right now. He didn't have cash spare for any more and that was going to be a real problem. That's what he needed, he realized. Yeah. The coke he'd scored yesterday had made him fly, had put him in a great mood, made him horny, danger-ously so. But what the hell?

Now he was down with a bang this morning. A deep trough. He'd get himself a few drinks, take the rest of his charlie and then he wouldn't care about the crap weather – he'd set off around a few parts of the city he'd decided to target.

Sunday was a dangerous day to break into houses. Too many people were at home. Even if someone was out, their neighbours might not be. He would spend today on research, casing. He had a list of properties from contacts in insurance companies that he'd been steadily building up while in prison so as not to squander his precious time there. A whole list of houses and flats where the owners had quality jewellery and silverware. In some cases, he had the complete list of their valuables. Some very rich pickings to be had. If he was careful, enough to set him up for his new life.

'Darren?'

He turned, startled to hear his name. It was one of the volunteer workers here, a man of about thirty in a blue shirt and jeans, with short hair and long sideburns. His name was Simon.

Spicer looked at him, wondering what was wrong. Had someone reported him last night? Seen his enlarged pupils? If they caught you taking drugs or you were even just high on them in here, you could be thrown straight out.

'There are two gentlemen to see you outside.'

The words were like a sudden sideways pull of gravity deep inside him. As if all his innards had turned to jelly. It was the same feeling he always had when he realized the game was up and he was being arrested.

'Oh, right,' he said, trying to sound nonchalant and uninterested.

Two gentlemen could only mean one thing.

He followed the young man out into the corridor, his stomach really churning now. His brain was racing. Wondering which of the things he had done in the past few days they had come to get him for.

It felt more like a church out here. A long corridor with a pointed arch at the end. The reception office was next to it, glassed in. Outside it stood two men. From the way they were suited and booted, they could only be coppers.

One of them was thin and tall as a beanpole, with short, spiky hair that was a mess; he looked like he hadn't had a decent night's sleep in many months. The other was black, with his head shaven as bald as a meteorite. Spicer vaguely recognized him.

'Darren Spicer?' the black one said.

'Yeah.'

The man held up a warrant card, which Spicer barely bothered to glance at.

'DS Branson, Sussex CID, and this is my colleague, DC Nicholl. Wonder if we could have a chat.'

'I got a pretty busy schedule,' Spicer said. 'But s'pose I could fit you in.'

'Very accommodating of you.'

'Yeah, well, I like to be accommodating, with the police and all that.' He nodded. 'Yeah.' He sniffed.

The volunteer worker opened a door and indicated for them to walk through.

Spicer entered a small meeting room containing a table and six chairs, with a large stained-glass window on the far wall. He sat down and the two detectives sat opposite him.

'We've met before, haven't we, Darren?' DS Branson said.

Spicer frowned. 'Yeah, maybe. You look familiar. Trying to think where.'

'I interviewed you about three years ago, when you were in custody – about some house break-ins. You'd just been arrested for burglary and indecent assault. Remember now?'

'Oh yeah, rings a bell.'

He grinned at each of the detectives, but neither of

them smiled back. The mobile phone of the one with ragged hair rang suddenly. He checked the number, then answered it quietly.

'I'm tied up. I'll call you back,' he murmured, before sticking the phone back into his pocket.

Branson pulled out a notebook and flipped it open. He studied it for a moment.

'You were released from prison on 28 December, correct?'

'Yeah, that's right.'

'We'd like to talk to you about your movements since then.'

Spicer sniffed. 'Well, the thing is, I don't keep a diary, you see. Got no secretary.'

'That's all right,' the spiky-haired one said, pulling out a small black book. 'I've got one here. This one is for last year and I've got another for this year. We can help you on dates.'

'Very obliging of you,' Spicer replied.

'That's what we're here for,' Nick Nicholl said. 'To be obliging.'

'Let's start with Christmas Eve,' Branson said. 'I understand you were on day release at Ford Open Prison, working in the maintenance department of the Metropole Hotel up until your release on licence. Is that correct?'

'Yeah.'

'When was the last time you were at the hotel?'

Spicer thought for a moment. 'Christmas Eve,' he said.

'What about New Year's Eve, Darren?' Glenn Branson went on. 'Where were you then?'

Spicer scratched his nose, then sniffed again.

'Well, I had been invited to spend it up at Sandring-ham with the royals, but then I thought, nah, can't be spending all my time with toffs—'

'Cut it out,' Branson said sharply. 'Remember you're out on licence. We can do this chat the easy way or the hard way. The easy way is here, now. Or we can bang you back up and do it there. It's no sweat to us either way.'

'We'll do it here,' Spicer said hastily, sniffing again.

'Got a cold, have you?' Nick Nicholl asked.

He shook his head.

The two detectives caught each other's eye, then Branson said, 'Right, New Year's Eve. Where were you?'

Spicer laid his hands on the table and stared down at his fingers. All his nails were badly bitten, as was the skin around them.

'Drinking up at the Neville.'

'The Neville pub?' Nick Nicholl asked. 'The one near the greyhound stadium?'

'Yeah, that's right, by the dogs.'

'Can anyone vouch for you?' Branson queried.

'I was with a few – you know – acquaintances – yeah. Can give you some names.'

Nick Nicholl turned to his colleague. 'Might be able to verify that on CCTV if they've got it in there. I seem to remember they have, from a past inquiry.'

Branson made a note. 'If they haven't wiped it – a lot of them only keep seven-day records.' Then he looked at Spicer. 'What time did you leave the pub?'

Spicer shrugged. 'I don't remember. I was shit-faced. One, one-thirty maybe.'

'Where were you staying then?' Nick Nicholl asked.

'The Kemp Town hostel.'

'Would anyone remember you coming home?'

'That lot? Nah. They're not capable of remembering nothing.'

'How did you get home?' Branson asked.

'Had the chauffeur pick me up in the Roller, didn't I?'

He said it so innocently that Glenn had to struggle to stop himself from grinning. 'So your chauffeur can vouch for you?'

Spicer shook his head. 'I walked, didn't I? Shanks's pony.'

Branson flipped a few pages back in his notebook. 'Let's move on to this past week. Can you tell us where you were between 6 p.m. and midnight on Thursday 8 January?'

Spicer answered quickly, as if he had already known what the question would be. 'Yeah, I went to the dogs. Ladies' night. Stayed there till about 7.30 and then came back here.'

'The greyhound stadium? Your local pub, then, is that the Neville?'

'One of 'em, yeah.'

Branson made a mental note that the greyhound stadium was less than fifteen minutes' walk from Droveway Avenue, where Roxy Pearce was raped on Thursday night.

'Do you have anything to prove you were there? Betting stubs? Anyone with you?

'There was a bird I picked up.' He stopped.

'What was her name?' Branson asked.

'Yeah, well, that's the thing. She's married. Her husband was away for the night. I don't think she'd be too happy, you know, having the Old Bill asking questions.'

'Gone all moral, have we, Darren?' Branson asked. 'Suddenly developed a conscience?'

He was thinking, but did not say, that it was rather a strange coincidence that Roxy Pearce's husband had been away that night too.

'Not moral, but I don't want to give you her name.'

'Then you'd better deliver us some other proof that you were at the dogs, and during that time period.'

Spicer looked at them. He needed a smoke badly.

'Do you mind telling me what this is about?

'A series of sexual assaults have been committed in this city. We're looking to eliminate people from our enquiries.'

'So I'm a suspect?'

Branson shook his head. 'No, but your release date on licence makes you a possible Person of Interest.'

He did not reveal to Spicer that his records had been checked for 1997–8, and they showed he had been released from prison just six days before the Shoe Man's first suspected attack back then.

'Let's move on to yesterday. Can you account for where you were between 5 p.m. and 9 p.m.?'

Spicer was sure his face was burning. He felt boxed in, didn't like the way these questions kept on coming. Questions he couldn't answer. Yes, he could say exactly where he was at 5 p.m. yesterday. He was in a copse behind a house in Woodland Drive, Brighton's so-called Millionaire's Row, buying charlie from one of its residents. He doubted he'd live to see his next birthday if he so much as mentioned the address.

'I was at the Albion game. Went for some drinks with a mate afterwards. Until curfew here, right? Came back and had me dinner, then went to bed.'

'Crap game, wasn't it?' Nick Nicholl said.

'Yeah, that second goal, like ...' Spicer raised his hands in despair and sniffed again.

'Your mate got a name?' Glenn Branson asked.

'Nah. You know, that's a funny thing. See him about, known him for years – yet I still don't know his name. Not the sort of thing you can ask someone after you've been drinking with them on and off for ten years, is it?'

'Why not?' Nicholl asked.

Spicer shrugged.

There was a long silence.

Branson flipped his notebook over a page. 'Lock-up here is 8.30 p.m. I'm told you arrived back at 8.45 p.m., your voice was slurred and your pupils dilated. You were lucky they let you back in. Residents are forbidden to take drugs.'

'I don't take no drugs, Detective, sir.' He sniffed again.

'I'll bet you don't. You've just got a bad head cold, right?'

'Right. Must be what it is. Exactly right. A bad head cold!'

Branson nodded. 'I'll bet you still believe in Father Christmas, don't you?'

Spicer gave him a sly grin, unsure quite where this was going. 'Father Christmas? Yeah. Yeah, why not?'

'Next year write and ask him for a sodding handkerchief.'

53

Yac did not drive the taxi on Sundays because he was *otherwise engaged.*

He had heard people use that expression and he liked it. *Otherwise engaged.* It had a nice ring to it. He liked, sometimes, to say things that had a nice ring to them.

'Why don't you ever take the cab out on Sunday nights?' the man who owned the taxi had asked him recently.

'Because I'm otherwise engaged,' Yac replied importantly.

And he was. He had important business that filled his Sundays from the moment he got up until late into the night.

It was late at night now.

His first duty every Sunday morning was to check the houseboat for leaks, both from below the waterline and from the roof. Then he cleaned the houseboat. It was the cleanest floating home in all of Shoreham. Then he fastidiously cleaned himself. He was the cleanest, best-shaven taxi driver in the whole of Brighton and Hove.

When the owners of *Tom Newbound* finally came back from living in India, Yac hoped they would be proud of him. Maybe they would continue to let him live here

331

with them, if he agreed to clean the boat every Sunday morning.

He so much hoped that. And he had nowhere else to go.

One of his neighbours told Yac the boat was so clean he could eat off the deck, if he wanted to. Yac didn't understand that. Why would he want to? If he put food on the deck, gulls would come and eat it. Then he'd have the mess of food and gulls on the deck, and he'd have to clean all that up as well. So he ignored that suggestion.

He had learned over the years that it was wise to ignore suggestions. Most suggestions came from idiots. Intelligent people kept their thoughts to themselves.

His next task, in between making his hourly cups of tea and eating his Sunday dinner – always the same meal, microwaved lasagne – was removing his childhood collection of high-flush toilet chains from their hiding place in the bilges. *Tom Newbound*, he had discovered, provided him with several good hiding places. His collection of shoes was in some of them.

He liked to take his time laying the chains out on the floor of the saloon. First, he would count them to make sure that no one had been on the boat when he was out and stolen any of them. Then he would inspect them, to check there were no rust spots. Then he would clean them, lovingly rubbing each of the chain links with metal polish.

After he had put the chains carefully away, Yac would go on the Internet. He would spend the rest of the afternoon on Google Earth, checking for changes from his maps. That was something he had realized. Maps changed, just like everything else. You couldn't depend on them. You couldn't depend on anything. The past was shifting sand. Stuff that you read and learned and stored away in your head could – and did – get changed. Just because you knew something once did not mean it was still true today. Like with maps. You couldn't be a good taxi driver just from relying on maps. You had to keep up to date, up to the minute!

It was the same with technology.

Things you knew five or ten or fifteen years ago weren't always any good today. Technology changed. He had a whole filing cabinet on the boat filled with wiring diagrams of burglar alarm systems. He liked to work them out. He liked to find the flaws in them. A long time ago he had figured out that if a human being designed something, there would be a flaw in it somewhere. He liked to store those flaws away in his head. Information was knowledge and knowledge was power!

Power over all those people who thought he was no good. Who sneered or laughed at him. He could tell, sometimes, that people in his cab were laughing at him. He could see them in the mirror, sitting on the back seat smirking and whispering to each other about him. They thought he was a bit soft in the head. Potty. Doolally. Oh yes.

Uh-huh.

The way his mother did.

She made the same mistake. She thought he was stupid. She did not know that some days, or nights, when she was home, he watched her. She was unaware that he had made a small hole in the ceiling of her bedroom. He used to lie silently in the loft above her, watching her hurting a man with her shoes. He would watch her screwing her stiletto heels into the naked men's backs.

Other times she would lock Yac in his bedroom with a tray of food and a bucket, leaving him alone in the house for the night. He would hear the thunk of the lock, then he would hear her footsteps, her heels clicking on the floorboards, getting fainter and fainter.

She never knew that he understood locks. That he had read and memorized every specialist magazine and every instruction manual he could lay his hands on in the reference library. He knew just about everything there was to know about bored cylindrical locks, tumbler locks, lever locks. There wasn't a lock or alarm system on the planet, Yac reckoned, that could defeat him. Not that he had tried all of them. He thought that would be hard work and would take too long.

When she went out, leaving him alone, with the *clack-clack-clack* of her shoes fading into silence, he would pick the lock of his bedroom door and go into her room. He liked to lie naked on her bed, breathing in the heady, musky smells of her Shalimar perfume, and the air that still smelt of her cigarette smoke, holding one of her shoes in his left hand, safe from her, and then relieve himself with his right hand.

It was the way he liked to end each of his Sunday evenings now.

But tonight was better than ever! He had newspaper articles on the Shoe Man. He had read and re-read them, and not just the *Argus*, but other papers too. Sunday papers. The Shoe Man raped his victims and took their shoes.

Uh-huh.

He sprayed Shalimar around the interior of his room in the houseboat, short bursts into each corner, then a longer one towards the ceiling, directly above his head, so that tiny, invisible droplets of the fragrance would fall all around him.

He then stood, aroused, starting to shake. In moments he became drenched in perspiration, breathing with his eyes closed, as the smell brought back so many memories. Then he lit a Dunhill International cigarette and inhaled the sweet smoke deeply, holding it in his lungs for some moments before jetting it out through his nostrils, the way his mother did.

It was smelling like her room in here now. Yes.

In between puffs, getting more and more deeply aroused, he began unbuttoning his trousers. Then, lying back on his bunk, he touched himself and whispered, *Oh, Mummy! Oh, Mummy! Oh yes, Mummy, I'm such a bad boy!*

And all the time he was thinking of the really bad thing he had just done. Which aroused him even more.

54

Roy Grace was in a sombre mood at 7.30 a.m. The New Year was not even a fortnight old and he now had three violent stranger rapes on his hands.

He was seated in the office that always made him feel uncomfortable, even though its previous incumbent, the sometimes tyrannical Alison Vosper, was no longer there. Replacing her behind the large rosewood desk, which was now a lot more cluttered, was Assistant Chief Constable Peter Rigg, starting his second week here. And for the first time ever, Grace had actually been offered a drink in this office. He was now gratefully sipping strong coffee from an elegant china cup.

The ACC was a dapper, rather distinguished-looking man, with a healthy complexion, fair hair neatly and conservatively cut, and a sharp, posh voice. Although several inches shorter than Grace, he had fine posture, giving him a military bearing which made him seem taller than his actual height. He was dressed in a navy suit with discreet pinstripes, an elegant white shirt and a loud tie. From a row of photographs on his desk, and new pictures now hanging on the walls, the man was evidently keen on motor racing, which pleased Grace because that was something they would have in common, although he'd not had a chance to bring this up yet.

'I've had the new Chief Executive of the City Corporation on the phone,' said Rigg – his manner pleasant but no-nonsense. 'This was before the ghost train attack. Stranger rape is a very emotive subject. Brighton's already lost the Labour Party Conference for many years to come – not that that's connected to these rapes in any way – and he feels it would greatly help the future chances of this city to attract top-end conference trade if we can show how safe it is to come here. Fear of crime seems to have become a major issue in the competitive conference business.'

'Yes, sir, I appreciate that.'

'Our New Year's resolution should be to focus on the crimes that cause fear in the community – fear among ordinary decent people. That's where I think we should be maximizing our resources. Our subliminal message should be that people are as safe anywhere in Brighton and Hove as they are in their own homes. What do you think?'

Grace nodded his agreement, but privately he was concerned. The ACC's intentions were right, but his timing was not great. Roxy Pearce had clearly not been safe in her own home. Also, what he had just said wasn't new. He was merely reinforcing what, in Grace's view, had always been the police force's main role. Certainly, at any rate, his own main goal.

When he had first been promoted to the rank of detective superintendent, his immediate boss, the then head of CID, Gary Weston, had explained his philosophy to him very succinctly: 'Roy, I try as a boss to think what it is the public expect from me and would like me to do. What does my wife want? My elderly mum? They want to feel safe, they want to go about their lawful business unhindered, and they want me to lock up all the bad guys.'

Grace had used that as a mantra ever since.

Rigg held up a typewritten document, six sheets of paper clipped together, and Grace knew immediately what it was.

'This is the twenty-four-hour review from the Crime Policy and Review Branch on *Operation Swordfish*,' the ACC said. 'I had it dropped round last night.' He gave the Detective Superintendent a slightly worried smile. 'It's positive. You've ticked all the boxes – something I would have expected, from all the good things I've heard about you, Roy.'

'Thank you, sir!' Grace said, pleasantly surprised. Clearly the man hadn't spoken too much to the now departed Alison Vosper, his big fan – not.

'I think the political ride's going to get a lot rougher when the news on this third rape gets out. And, of course, we don't know how many more our offender might commit before we lock him up.'

'Or before he disappears again,' Grace replied.

The ACC looked as if he had just bitten a red-hot chilli.

55

Sussex Security Systems and Sussex Remote Monitoring Services were housed in a large 1980s building on an industrial estate in Lewes, seven miles from Brighton.

As the business which Garry Starling had started in a small shop in Hove fifteen years earlier expanded into two separate fields, he knew he would have to move into bigger premises. The perfect opportunity presented itself when the building in Lewes became vacant following a bankruptcy, with the receiver keen to do a deal.

But what attracted him even more than the favourable terms was the location itself, less than a quarter of a mile from Malling House, the headquarters of Sussex Police. He'd already secured two contracts with them, installing and maintaining alarms in a couple of small-town police stations that were closed at night, and he was sure that being so close to the hub of the whole force could do no harm.

He had been right. A combination of knocking on doors, schmoozing on the golf course and some very competitive pricing had brought a lot more work his way, and when, just over a decade ago, the CID moved into their new headquarters, Sussex House, it had been SSS that had secured the contract for the internal security system.

Despite his success, Garry Starling was not into flash,

expensive cars. He never drove them because in his view all you did was draw attention to yourself – and the flashier your wheels, the more your customers would think you were overcharging. Success to him meant freedom. The ability to hire people to do the stuff you didn't want to be stuck in the office doing. The freedom to be out on the golf course when you wanted. And to do other things you wanted too. He left it to Denise to be the spender. She could spend for England.

When they'd first met she'd been sex on legs. She liked everything that turned him on and she was randy as hell, with few limits. Now she just sat on her fat arse, letting it get fatter by the hour, and she didn't want to know about sex – at least, not any of the things that he enjoyed.

He drove his small grey Volvo along the industrial estate, passing a Land Rover dealer, the entrance to Tesco and then Homebase. He made a right, then a left and ahead, at the end of the cul-de-sac, he saw his twin single-storey building and a row of nine white vans, each bearing the company logo, outside.

Ever mindful about costs, the vans were plain white and the company name was on magnetic panels stuck to their sides. It meant he didn't have to pay sign-writing costs each time he purchased a new van; he could simply pull the panels off and use them again.

It was 9 a.m. and he wasn't happy to see so many vans still parked up. They should have been out doing installations or making service calls on customers. That was thanks to the recession.

Not many things made him happy these days.

*

Dunstan Christmas's butt was itching, but he did not dare scratch it. If he took his weight off this chair for more than two seconds during his shift, without first properly logging off, the alarm would sound and his supervisor would come running in.

You had to hand it to the guy who had thought of this, Christmas grudgingly admitted to himself, it was a damned good system. Foolproof, just about.

Which of course it needed to be, because that was what the customers of Sussex Remote Monitoring Services paid for: trained CCTV operators like himself to sit, in a uniform, and watch the images of their homes and business premises, in real time, around the clock. Christmas was thirty-six years old and weighed twenty stones. Sitting on his butt suited him well.

He couldn't much see the point of the uniform, as he never left the room, but the Big Cheese, Mr Starling, had everyone on the premises, even the receptionists, wear uniform. It gave people a sense of pride and purpose, Mr Starling said, and it impressed visitors. Everyone did what Mr Starling said.

Alongside the camera selection button on the panel in front of him was a microphone. Even though some of the houses and business premises on the twenty screens in front of him were many miles away, one click of the microphone button and he could scare the shit out of any intruder by talking straight to them. He liked that part of the job. Didn't happen too often, but when it did, boy, was it fun to see them jump! That was a perk.

Christmas worked an eight-hour shift, alternating between day, evening and night, and he was happy enough with the pay he got, but the job itself, Jesus, sometimes, particularly during the night, it could be mind-numbingly boring. Twenty different programmes on television and nothing happening on any of them! Just a picture of a factory gate on one. A domestic driveway on another. The rear of a big Dyke Road Avenue mansion on another. Occasionally a cat would slink across, or an urban fox, or a badger, or a scurrying rodent.

Screen no. 17 was one he had a bit of an emotional connection with. It showed images of the old Shoreham cement works that had been shut down for the past nineteen years. Twenty-six CCTV cameras were sited around the vast premises, one for the front entrance, the rest covering all key internal access points. At the moment the image was of the front, a high steel fence topped with razor wire, and chained gates.

His dad used to work there, as a cement tanker driver, and sometimes Dunstan would ride up front in the cab when his dad was making a collection. He loved the place. He always thought it was like being on the set of a Bond film, with its huge cement clinker kilns, grinding mills and storage silos, the bulldozers, dumptrucks and diggers, and activity around the clock.

The cement works sat in a huge quarried bowl in isolated countryside, a few miles inland and just to the north-west of Shoreham. The site covered several hundred acres and was now full of vast, derelict buildings. Rumour had it there were plans to reactivate it all, but since the last lorry had driven out of there, nearly two decades ago, it had lain derelict, a grey ghost village of mostly windowless structures, rusting components, old vehicles and weed-strewn tracks. The only visitors were the occasional vandals and thieves who had systematically stolen some of the electric motors, cables and lead piping, which was why the elaborate security system had been put in place.

But this particular Monday morning was more interesting than usual. Certainly on one particular screen, no. 11.

Each of the screens had feeds to ten different properties. Motion-sensor software would instantly bring a property up if there was any movement, such as a vehicle arriving or leaving, someone walking, or even a fox or large dog prowling. There had been constant activity on screen no. 11 since he had come on shift at 7 a.m. That was the front view of the Pearce house. He could see the crime scene tape, a Police Community Support Officer scene guard. A POLSA and three Police Search Officers in protective blue oversuits and rubber gloves, on their hands and knees, were searching inch by inch for any clues left behind by the intruder who had assaulted Mrs Pearce inside the house last Thursday night, and sticking small numbered markers here and there in the ground.

He dug his hand into the large packet of Kettle crisps beside the control panel on his workstation, shovelled the crisps into his mouth, then washed them down with a swig of Coke. He needed to pee, but decided to hang on for a while. He could log off the system to take a comfort break, as they were called, but it would be noted. An hour and a half was too soon after starting his shift; he needed to give it a bit longer, as he wanted to impress his boss.

The voice right behind him startled him.

'I'm glad to see the feed to Droveway Avenue has been fixed.'

Dunstan Christmas turned to see his boss, Garry Starling, the owner of this company, looking over his shoulder.

Starling had a habit of doing this. He was always snooping on his employees. Creeping silently up behind them, sometimes in working clothes of a white shirt, jeans and trainers, sometimes in a neat business suit. But always stealthily, silently, on rubber-soled shoes like some weirdo stalker. His big, owl-like eyes were peering at the bank of screens.

'Yes, Mr Starling. It was working when I came on shift.'

'Do we know what the problem was yet?'

'I haven't spoken to Tony.'

Tony was the chief engineer of the company.

Starling watched the activity at the Pearce house for some moments, nodding.

'Not good, is it, sir?' Christmas said.

'It's incredible,' Garry Starling said. 'The worst thing that's ever happened on any of the properties we monitor and the fucking system wasn't working. Incredible!'

'Bad timing.'

'You could say that.'

Christmas moved a toggle switch on the panel and zoomed in on one SOCO, who was bagging something of interest that was too small for them to see.

'Kind of interesting, watching how thorough these guys are,' he said.

There was no reply from his boss.

'Like something out of *CSI*.'

Again there was no reply.

He turned his head and discovered, to his astonishment, that Garry Starling had left the room.

56

Wearing expensive high heels makes you feel sexy, doesn't it? You think spending money on these things is an investment, don't you? All part of your trap. Do you know what you are like? All of you? Venus fly traps! That's what you are like.

Have you ever looked closely at the leaves of a Venus fly trap? They are all pink inside. Do they remind you of something? I'll tell you what they remind me of: vaginas with teeth. Which is of course exactly what they are. Nasty incisors all the way around, like prison cell bars.

The moment an insect enters and touches one of the tiny hairs in those inviting, sensual pink lips, the trap snaps shut. It seals out all the air. Just like you all do. Then the digestive juices set to work, slowly killing the prey if it hasn't been lucky enough to have suffocated first. Just like you all do! The soft, inner parts of the insect are dissolved, but not the tough outer part, the exoskeleton. At the end of the digestive process, after several days, sometimes a couple of weeks, the trap reabsorbs the digestive fluid and then reopens. The remains of the insect are blown away in the wind or washed away by the rain.

That's why you put those shoes on, isn't it? To trap us, suck all the fluids out of us, then excrete our remains.

Well, I've got news for you.

57

MIR-1 was capable of housing up to three Major Incident investigations at the same time. But with Roy Grace's rapidly expanding team, *Operation Swordfish* needed the entire room. Fortunately he'd always kept on the right side of the Senior Support Officer, Tony Case, who controlled all four Major Incident Suites in the county.

Case obligingly moved the only other major investigation currently taking place in Sussex House at the moment – the late-night street murder of an as yet unidentified man – to the smaller MIR-2 along the corridor.

Although Grace had held two briefings yesterday, several of his team had been absent on outside inquiries, for a number of important reasons. He had ordered full attendance this morning.

He sat down at a free space at one of the workstations, placing his agenda and Policy Book in front of him. Beside them sat his third coffee of the day, so far. Cleo was constantly reproaching him for the amount he consumed, but after his early pleasant but testy meeting with ACC Rigg, he felt in need of another strong caffeine hit.

Although MIR-1 had not been redecorated or refurbished for some years, the room always had a sterile, faintly anodyne modern-office smell. A big contrast to police offices before the smoking ban had been imposed, he thought. Almost all of them reeked of tobacco and had a permanently fuggy haze. But it gave them atmosphere and in some ways he missed that. Everything in life was becoming too sterile.

He nodded greetings to various members of his team as they filed into the room, most of them, including Glenn Branson, who appeared to be having yet another of his endless arguments with his wife, talking on their phones.

'Morning, old-timer,' Branson greeted him when he ended his call. He pocketed his phone, then tapped the top of his own shaven dome and frowned.

Grace frowned back. 'What?'

'No gel. Did you forget?'

'I was seeing the new ACC first thing, so thought I ought to be a little conservative.'

Branson, who had given Roy Grace a major fashion makeover some months ago, shook his head. 'You know what? Sometimes you're just plain sad. If I was the new ACC, I'd want officers with a bit of zing – not ones who looked like my grandfather.'

'Sod you!' Grace said with a grin. Then he yawned.

'See!' Branson said gleefully. 'It's your age. You can't take the pace.'

'Very funny. Look, I have to concentrate for a few minutes, OK?'

'You know who you remind me of?' Branson said, ignoring him.

'George Clooney? Daniel Craig?'

'Nah. Brad Pitt.'

For a moment Grace looked quite pleased. Then the Detective Sergeant added, 'Yeah, in *Benjamin Button* –

like at the point where he looks a hundred and hasn't started getting younger yet.'

Grace shook his head, stifling a grin, then another yawn. Monday was a day most normal people dreaded. But most *normal* people at least started the week feeling rested and fresh. He had spent the whole of his Sunday at work, first going to the pier, to the maintenance room of the ghost train, where Mandy Thorpe had been raped and seriously injured, and then visiting her at the Royal Sussex County Hospital, where she was under police guard. Despite a bad head injury, the young woman had managed to give a detailed initial statement to the SOLO allocated to her, who had in turn relayed this information to him.

Quite apart from the trauma to these poor victims, Roy Grace was feeling a different kind of trauma of his own, from the pressure to solve this and make an arrest. To compound matters, the head crime reporter of the *Argus*, Kevin Spinella, had now left three messages on his mobile phone asking him to call back urgently. Grace knew if he wanted the cooperation of his main local paper in this inquiry, rather than just a sensational headline in tomorrow's edition, he was going to have to manage Spinella carefully. That would mean giving him an exclusive extra titbit to the information he would release at the midday press conference – and at the moment he didn't have anything for the man. At least, nothing he wanted the public to know.

He gave the reporter a quick call back and got connected straight through to his voicemail. He left Spinella a message asking him to come to his office ten minutes before the press conference. He'd think of something for him.

And one day soon he was going to think of a suitable trap. Someone inside the police regularly leaked information to Spinella. The same person, Grace was sure, who had leaked every major crime story this past year to the sharp young crime reporter within minutes of the police being called to the scene. It had to be someone in either the Call Handling Centre or the IT department who had access to the minute-by-minute updated serials. It could be a detective, but he doubted that, because the leaked information was on *every* serious crime, and no one detective got early information on anything other than his own cases.

The only positive was that Kevin Spinella was savvy, a newspaper reporter with whom the police could do business. So far they had been lucky, but one day he might not be there, and a lot of damage could be done by someone less cooperative in his shoes.

'Bloody Albion – what is going on with them?' Michael Foreman strutted in, smartly suited as ever, with gleaming black Oxford shoes.

In the early stages of an inquiry, most detectives wore suits because they never knew when they might have to rush out to interview someone – particularly close relatives of a major crime victim, to whom they needed to show respect. Some, like Foreman, dressed sharply all the time.

'That second goal!' DC Nick Nicholl, who was normally quietly spoken, was talking animatedly, shaking his balled fists in the air. 'Like, what was all that about? Hello!'

'Yeah, well, Chelsea's my team,' said the HOLMES analyst, John Black. 'Gave up on the Albion a long time ago. The day they left the Goldstone Ground.'

'But when they move – the new stadium – that'll be something, right!' Michael Foreman said. 'Give them a chance to settle into that – they'll get their pride back.'

'Gay Pride, that's all they're good for,' grumbled Norman Potting, who shambled in last, shaking his head, reeking of pipe smoke.

He sat down heavily in a chair opposite Grace. 'Sorry I'm late, Roy. Women! I tell you, I've had it. I'm not getting married again. That's it. Four and out!'

'Half the female population of the UK will be very relieved to hear that,' Bella Moy murmured, loudly enough for everyone to hear.

Ignoring her, Potting stared gloomily at Grace. 'You know that chat we had before Christmas, Roy?'

Grace nodded, not wanting to be distracted by the latest in the long saga of disasters of the Detective Sergeant's love life.

'I'd appreciate a bit more of your wisdom – some time over the next week or so, if that's all right with you, Roy. When you've got a minute.'

When I've got a minute I want to spend it sleeping, Grace thought wearily. But he nodded at Potting and said, 'Sure, Norman.' Despite the fact that the DS frequently irritated him, he felt sorry for the man. Potting had remained in the force long past the age when he could have taken his pension, because, Grace suspected, his work was all he had in life that gave him purpose.

The last to enter the room was Dr Julius Proudfoot, a tan-leather man bag slung from his shoulder. The forensic psychologist – as behavioural analysts were now called – had worked on a large number of high-profile cases during the past two decades, including the original Shoe Man case. For the past decade he had been enjoying minor media celebrity status, and the spoils of a lucrative publishing deal. His four autobiographical books, charting his career to date, boasted of his achievements in playing a crucial role in bringing many of the UK's worst criminals to justice.

A number of senior police officers had privately said the books should be on the fiction rather than non-fiction shelves in the bookshops. They believed he had wrongly taken the credit in several cases where he had actually only played a bit part – and then not always successfully.

Grace did not disagree, but felt that because of Proudfoot's earlier involvement in the Shoe Man case, *Operation Houdini*, the man could bring something to the table on *Operation Swordfish*. The psychologist had aged in the twelve years since they had last met, and put on a considerable amount of weight, he thought, as he introduced him to his team members. Then he turned to his agenda.

'First, I want to thank you all for giving up your weekends. Second, I'm pleased to report that we have no issues from the Crime Policy and Review Branch. They are satisfied to date with all aspects of our investigation.' He looked down quickly at his agenda. 'OK, it is 8.30 a.m., Monday 12 January. This is our sixth briefing of *Operation Swordfish*, the investigation into the stranger rape of two persons, Mrs Nicola Taylor and Mrs Roxy Pearce, and maybe now a third victim, Miss Mandy Thorpe.'

He pointed to one of the whiteboards, on which were stuck detailed descriptions of the three women. To protect their privacy, Grace chose not to display their photographs openly, which he felt would be disrespectful. Instead he said, 'Victim photographs are available for who those who need them.'

Proudfoot raised a hand and wiggled his pudgy fingers. 'Excuse me, Roy, why do you say *maybe* now a third victim? I don't think there's much doubt about Mandy Thorpe, from what I have on this.'

Grace looked across to the workstation where Proudfoot was seated.

'The MO is significantly different,' Roy Grace replied. 'But I'll come on to that a bit later, if that's OK – it's on the agenda.'

Proudfoot opened and closed his tiny rosebud lips a couple of times, fixing his beady eyes on the Detective Superintendent and looking disgruntled at being put back in his box.

Grace continued. 'First, I want to review our progress to date into the rape of Nicola Taylor on New Year's Eve, and of Roxy Pearce, last Thursday. We have six hundred and nineteen possible suspects at this moment. That number is made up of the staff of the Metropole Hotel and guests staying there that night, plus partygoers at the hotel on New Year's Eve, including, as we know, several senior police officers. We also have names phoned in by the public, some directly to us, some through *Crimestoppers*. The suspects for the moment include all registered sex offenders in the Brighton and Hove area. And two different perverts who have been making nuisance calls to Brighton shoe shops, who have now been identified through phone records by the Outside Inquiry Team.'

He sipped some coffee.

'One suspect on this list is particularly interesting. A local repeat burglar and small-time drugs dealer, Darren Spicer. I should think he's known to a number of you here.'

'That piece of shit!' Norman Potting said. 'I nicked

him twenty years ago. Did a series of burglaries around Shirley Drive and Woodland Drive.'

'He has one hundred and seventy-three previous,' the Analyst, Ellen Zoratti, said. 'A regular charmer. He's out on licence after indecently assaulting a woman in a house in Hill Brow that he broke into. He tried to snog her.'

'Which is unfortunately a regular pattern,' Grace said, looking at Proudfoot. 'Burglars turning into rapists.'

'Exactly,' Proudfoot said, seizing his cue. 'You see, they start off penetrating houses, then they graduate to penetrating any woman they happen to find in the house.'

Grace clocked the frowns on the faces of several of his colleagues, who clearly thought this was mere psycho-babble. But he knew that, sadly, it was true.

'Spicer was released from Ford Open Prison on licence, on 28 December. DS Branson and DC Nicholl interviewed him yesterday morning.'

He nodded at Glenn.

'That's right, boss,' Branson replied. 'We didn't get much – just a lot of lip, really. He's a wily old trout. Claims he's got alibis for the times all three offences were committed, but I'm not convinced. We told him we want them substantiated. He was apparently seeing a married woman last Thursday night, and refuses to give us her name.'

'Has Spicer got any form for sex offences, apart from the last one?' DS Bella Moy asked. 'Or domestic violence, or fetishes?'

'No,' replied the Analyst.

'Wouldn't our offender be likely to have some *previous* as a pervert, Dr Proudfoot, on the assumption that rapists taking shoes is not a regular occurrence?' Bella Moy asked.

'Taking trophies of some kind is not uncommon for serial offenders,' Proudfoot said. 'But you are right, it is very unlikely these are the only offences he's committed.'

'There's something that could be very significant regarding Spicer,' Ellen Zoratti said. 'Last night I studied the victim statement – the one given by the woman Spicer indecently assaulted in her home just over three years ago – Ms Marcie Kallestad.' She looked at Roy Grace. 'I don't understand why no one's made the connection, sir.'

'Connection?'

'I think you'd better have a read of it. After Marcie Kallestad fought Spicer off, he knocked her to the floor, grabbed the shoes from her feet – and ran off with them. They were high-heeled Roberto Cavallis which had cost her three hundred and fifty quid. She'd only bought them that day, from a shop in Brighton.'

58

There was a palpable change of mood in the briefing room. Roy Grace could sense the sudden, intangible buzz of excitement. It happened every time there was a possible breakthrough in an inquiry. Yet he was the least excited member of his team at this moment.

'Shame we didn't know about this yesterday,' Glenn Branson said. 'We could have potted Spicer then.'

Nick Nicholl nodded in agreement.

'We've got enough to arrest him now, boss, haven't we?' said Michael Foreman.

Grace looked at Ellen. 'Do we know whether the shoes were recovered subsequently?'

'No, I'm afraid not,' she replied. 'I don't have that information.'

'Would they have had a cash value for him?' Nick Nicholl asked.

'Absolutely,' Bella Moy said. 'Brand-new Roberto Cavalli shoes like that – there are loads of second-hand clothes shops in the city that would buy them – at a knockdown price. I buy things from some of them. You can get brilliant bargains.'

Grace looked at Bella for a moment. In her early thirties, single and living at home, caring for her aged mother, he felt a little sorry for her, because she was not an unattractive woman but appeared to have no real life beyond her work.

'Ten per cent of their cost, Bella?' he asked.

'I don't know – but they wouldn't pay much. Twenty quid, perhaps, max.'

Grace thought hard. This new information was certainly enough to justify arresting Darren Spicer. And yet ... it didn't feel right. Spicer seemed almost too obvious to him. Sure, the villain was conveniently out of prison in time to have committed the first rape, on New Year's Day. Even more conveniently, he had been working at the Metropole Hotel, where it occurred. And now they had just learned that he'd taken his last burglary victim's shoes. But, Grace fretted, could the man really be so stupid?

More significantly, Spicer's past form was as a career burglar and drugs dealer. He made his living, such as it was, breaking into properties and into safes inside them, taking jewellery, watches, silverware, cash. Neither Nicola Taylor nor Roxy Pearce had, so far, reported any property stolen other than their shoes and, in Nicola's case, her clothes as well. It was the same with Mandy Thorpe on Saturday night. Just her shoes were gone. Unless Spicer had come out of prison a changed man – which, with his history, he doubted – this did not seem like Spicer's MO.

On the other hand, how could he be sure that Spicer had not committed other sexual offences for which he had not been caught? Could he possibly be the Shoe Man? The records produced by Ellen showed that he had been out of jail at the time of the Shoe Man offences. But the Shoe Man raped and assaulted his victims in vile ways. He didn't just try to kiss them, as Spicer had done. Again, the MO did not match.

Yes, they could bring him into custody. It would please the brass to get such a quick arrest, but that pleasure could be short-lived. Where would he go from there with Spicer? How would he get the proof needed for a conviction? The offender wore a mask and barely spoke, so there was no facial description or voice to go on. They hadn't even got an estimate of the offender's height that they were happy with. Medium seemed to be the best guess. Slight build. Few bodily hairs.

The forensic examination results showed that the offender had left no semen in any of the three victims. So far there were no DNA hits on any hairs or fibres or nail scrapings taken – although it was very early days. It would be a couple of weeks before everything taken was examined, and they couldn't hold Spicer for that length of time without charging him. For certain the Crown Prosecution Service would not consider there was enough to bring any charge on what they had.

They could question him about why he had taken Marcie Kallestad's shoes, but if he really was the Shoe Man that would alert him. Just as getting a search warrant for his locker at the night shelter would. From what Glenn and Nick had reported, Spicer thought he'd been clever and answered their questions to their satisfaction. Now he might not be worried about offending again. If they showed too much interest in him, it could drive him to ground – or out of the city. And what Grace needed more than anything was a result – not another twelve years of silence.

He thought for another moment, then said to Glenn Branson, 'Does Spicer have a car, or access to one?'

'I didn't get the impression he's got anything. I doubt it, boss, no.'

'He said he walks everywhere to save the bus fares, chief,' Nick Nicholl added.

'He can probably get one when he needs it,' Ellen Zoratti said. 'He's got a couple of previous convictions for vehicle theft – one for a van and one for a private car.'

That was good he had no transport, Grace thought. It would make the task of keeping him under observation much simpler.

'I think we'll get more chance of a result by watching him than pulling him, at the moment. We know where he is between 8.30 p.m. and 8.30 a.m., thanks to the curfew at the night shelter. He's got his retraining job at the Grand Hotel, so we'll know where he is during the day on weekdays. I'm going to get Surveillance to watch him when he leaves work and to see he doesn't leave the shelter at night.'

'If he's a real *Person of Interest*, Roy, which seems to be the case,' said Proudfoot, 'then I think you'd better move quickly on this.'

'I hope to get them started today,' Grace replied. 'This would be a good point to tell us your thoughts.'

The forensic psychologist stood up and walked over to a whiteboard on which there was a wide sheet of graph paper. Several spiking lines had been drawn on it in different-coloured inks. He took his time before speaking, as if to demonstrate he was so important he didn't need to hurry.

'The offender matrix of the Shoe Man and your current offender are very similar,' he said. 'This graph shows the linking factors to date between the two. Each colour is a different aspect: the geography, time of day, his approach to his victims, the form of his attack, appearance of the offender.'

He pointed each out, then stepped aside and continued: 'There are a number of characteristics of the Shoe Man offences that were never made public, but which nonetheless are apparent in your current offender's MO. This leads me to say with some certainty that there are sufficient linking factors for us to be able to assume at this stage we are dealing with the same person. One of the most significant is that the same name, Marsha Morris, was used in the hotel register both at the Grand in 1997 and at the Metropole on this past New Year's Eve – and this name was never made public knowledge.'

He now moved over to a blank whiteboard.

'I am also fairly certain that the offender is a local man, or at least a man with good local knowledge who has lived here in the past.'

He quickly drew some small squares in the top half of the whiteboard in black ink and numbered them 1 to 5, talking as he drew.

'The Shoe Man's first reported sexual assault was a botched one on 15 October 1997. I'm going to discount that for our purposes and just concentrate on the successful ones. His first successful one was at the Grand Hotel, in the early hours of 1 November 1997.' He wrote GH above the first square. 'His second was in a private house in Hove Park Road two weeks later.' He wrote HPR above the second square. 'The third was beneath the Palace Pier a further two weeks later.' He wrote PP over the third square. 'The fourth was in the Churchill Square car park another two weeks later.' He wrote CS above that one. 'A possible fifth attack was on Christmas morning, again two weeks later, in Eastern Terrace – although unconfirmed.' He wrote ET above the fifth box. Then he turned back to face the team, but fixed his gaze on Roy Grace.

'We know that all five of these women had bought an expensive pair of shoes at one of Brighton's shoe shops immediately prior to the attacks. I think it is likely the offender was familiar with these locations. It could have been a stranger coming into town, of course, but I really don't think so. Historically, strangers don't stick around. They attack, then move on.'

Grace turned to Michael Foreman, who was heading the Outside Inquiry Team. 'Michael, have you been on to the shoe shops where our current victims bought their shoes, to find out if they have CCTV?'

'It's being covered, boss.'

Julius Proudfoot then drew a circle around all five boxes. 'It is worth noting the relatively small geographical area within the city where these attacks took place. Now we come to the current series of attacks.'

Changing to a red pen, he drew three boxes on the lower half of the whiteboard, numbering them 1 to 3. He turned briefly to his audience, then back to the board.

'The first attack took place in the Metropole Hotel, which, as you know, is next door to the Grand.' He wrote MH above the first box. 'The second attack, approximately one week later, occurred in a private residence in a smart residential street, Droveway Avenue.' He wrote TD above the second box. 'The third attack – and I accept there are differences in the MO – took place just two days later on the Palace Pier – or *Brighton* Pier, as I understand it now calls itself.' He wrote BP above the third box, then turned back to face the team again.

'Droveway Avenue is the next street along from Hove Park Road. I don't think any of us need a degree in rocket science to see the geographical similarities in these attacks.'

DC Foreman raised a hand. 'Dr Proudfoot, this is a very smart observation. What can you tell us about the offender himself, from your very considerable experience?'

Proudfoot smiled, the flattery hitting his ego's G-spot. 'Well,' he said, flapping his arms expansively, 'he will almost certainly have had a dysfunctional childhood. Very likely a single-parent child, or possibly a repressively religious upbringing. He may have been subjected to childhood sexual abuse from one or more parent or a close relative. He will probably have been involved in low-level crime in the past, starting with cruelty to animals in childhood and perhaps minor thieving from classmates at school. He will definitely have been a loner with few if any childhood friends.'

He paused for a moment and cleared his throat before continuing: 'From early adolescence, he is likely to have been obsessed with violent pornography, and probably committed a range of minor sexual offences – exposure, indecent assaults, that sort of thing. He will have graduated to using prostitutes and quite likely become involved with those offering sadomasochistic services. And he's very likely to be a drug user – probably cocaine.'

He paused for a moment. 'His use of female clothing as a disguise is indicative to me of both a fantasy world he inhabits and the fact that he is intelligent, and he may have a perverse sense of humour which might be significant – in his choice of locations in 1997 and now and in his timings. The fact that he is so forensically aware is another indication that he is clever – and has knowledge or direct experience of police methodology.'

DC Emma-Jane Boutwood raised her hand. 'Are you able to suggest any theories, if he is the Shoe Man, why he might have stopped for twelve years, then restarted?'

'It's not uncommon. There was a sexual serial killer named Dennis Rader in the US who stopped offending for twelve years after getting married and starting a family. He was on the brink of starting again when he tired of the relationship, but fortunately he was caught before that happened. This could be the scenario for our offender. But it is equally possible that he moved elsewhere in the country, or even went overseas and continued offending there, and now has returned.'

*

When the briefing ended, Grace asked the forensic psychologist to come to his office for a few minutes. Grace closed the door. It was a stormy day and rain rattled against the windows as he sat behind his desk.

'I didn't want to have an argument with you in front of the team, Dr Proudfoot,' he said firmly, 'but I'm really concerned about the third attack, on the ghost train. Everything about the MO is different.'

Proudfoot nodded, with a smug smile, like a parent humouring a child.

'Tell me what you think the key differences are, Detective Superintendent.'

Grace found his tone patronizing and irritating, but tried not to rise to it. Instead, raising a finger, he said, 'First, unlike all the other victims, Mandy Thorpe had not recently bought the shoes that were used in the assault on her – and I'm including Rachael Ryan, about whom we still have an open mind. All five of those women back then had bought a brand-new pair of expensive designer shoes in the hours or days before they were attacked. As did the first two of our current victims, Nicola Taylor and

Roxy Pearce. Mandy Thorpe was different. She'd bought them months ago on holiday in Thailand.'

He raised another finger. 'Second, and I think this could be significant, unlike all the others, Mandy Thorpe was wearing fake designer shoes – copies of Jimmy Choos.'

'With respect, I'm no expert in these matters, but I thought the whole point about fakes was that people couldn't tell the difference.'

Grace shook his head. 'It's not about telling the difference. It's in shoe shops where he finds his victims. Third, and very importantly, he did not make Mandy Thorpe abuse herself with her shoes. That's how he gets his kicks, through his power over his victims.'

Proudfoot gave a shrug that indicated he might or might not agree with Grace. 'The young woman was unconscious, so we don't really know what he did.'

'Vaginal swabs taken show she was penetrated by someone wearing a condom. There was no indication vaginally or anally of penetration with part of a shoe.'

'He might have been disturbed and left hurriedly,' Proudfoot replied.

Grace raised another finger and continued. 'Perhaps. Fourth, Mandy Thorpe is plump – fat to be blunt. Obese. All the previous victims have been slim.'

The psychologist shook his head. 'Her figure isn't the significant factor. He's on the hunt. What is significant is the time frame. Previously with the Shoe Man it was two-week gaps. This new spate started off as one week, now it is down to two days. Neither of us knows what he was up to in the intervening twelve years, but his appetite could have become stronger – either from being bottled up if he repressed it for that length of time, or from confidence if he's continued to offend and got away with it. One thing I am certain about, the more an offender like this gets away with things, the more invincible he feels – and the more he's going to want.'

'I have a press conference at midday, Dr Proudfoot. What I say then could come home to roost. I want to put out accurate information that will help us catch our man, and give the public some degree of assurance. Presumably for your reputation, you want me putting the most accurate information out there too – you don't want to be shown up for getting something wrong.'

Proudfoot shook his head. 'I'm seldom mistaken, Detective Superintendent. You won't go far wrong if you listen to me.'

'I'm comforted to hear that,' Grace said coolly.

'You're an old pro, like me,' Proudfoot continued. 'You've got all kinds of political and commercial pressures on you – I know you have, every SIO I've ever worked with has. Here's the thing: which is worse for public consumption? For them to believe there's one violent sexual offender out there, preying on your women, or that there are two?' The psychologist stared hard at Grace and raised his eyebrows. 'I know which I'd go for if I was trying to protect the reputation of my city.'

'I'm not going to be driven by politics into making the wrong decision,' Grace replied.

'Roy – if I can call you that?'

Grace nodded.

'You're not dealing with Mr Norman Normal here, Roy. This is a clever guy. He's hunting victims. Something in his head is driving him to do the same as he did before, but he knows, because he's not stupid, that he needs to vary his routine or his methods. He'd be having a laugh if he could hear this conversation between us now. It's not just power over women that he enjoys; it's power over the police too. All part of his sick game.'

Grace thought for some moments. His training as an SIO told him to listen to experts, but not to be influenced by them, and always to form his own opinions.

'I hear what you are saying,' he said.

'I hope it's loud and clear, Roy. Just look at my past record if you've any doubts. I'm going to put a marker down about this offender. He's someone who needs a comfort zone, a bit of routine. He's sticking to the same pattern that he had before. That's his comfort zone. He'll take his victims from the same, or at least similar, places. Someone is going to be seized and raped in a car park in the centre of this city before the end of this week and their shoes will be taken. You can tell them that at your press conference from me.'

The smugness of the man was beginning to irritate Grace beyond belief. But he needed him. He needed every straw he could grasp at this moment.

'I can't stake out the whole damned city centre – we just don't have the surveillance resources. If we cover the city centre with uniform it won't help us catch him. It will just drive him somewhere else.'

'I think your man is smart enough and bold enough to do it right under your nose. He might even get a kick from that. You can cover the city wall to wall in police and he'll still get his victim.'

'Very reassuring,' Grace said. 'So what do you suggest?'

'You're going to have to make some guesses – and hope you get lucky. Or . . .' He fell silent for a moment, thinking. 'The case of Dennis Rader in the US – a particularly nasty individual who styled himself BTK – initials that stood for Bind, Torture, Kill. He was caught after twelve years of silence when the local paper wrote something about him that he didn't like. It was just a speculation . . .'

'What kind of thing?' Grace said, very curious suddenly.

'I think it was questioning the perpetrator's manhood. Something along those lines. You can be sure of one thing: that your current offender is going to be keeping a hawk-eye on the media, reading every word your local paper prints. The ego goes with the territory.'

'You don't think inflaming him will provoke him into offending even more?'

'No, I don't. He got away with those attacks twelve years ago. God knows what he's got away with since then. And now these new attacks. I imagine he thinks he's invincible – all-clever, all-powerful. That's how the press coverage to date has made him seem. Create a demon of our Shoe Man, make him the Monster of Brighton and Hove, and, *bingo*, newspaper sales shoot up across the nation, and so do news audience ratings. And all the time in reality we're dealing with a nasty, warped misfit with a screw loose.'

'So we get the local paper to say something demeaning about his manhood? That he's got a tiny dick or something?'

'Or how about the truth, that he can't get it up – or keep it up? No man's going to like reading that.'

'Dangerous,' Grace said. 'It could send him on a rampage.'

'He's dangerous enough already, Roy. But at the

moment he's clever, calculating, taking his time, not making any mistakes. Put him in a rage, provoke him into losing his cool – that way he'll make a mistake. And then you'll get him.'

'Or *them.*'

59

Monday 12 January

Sussex Square was one of the jewels in Brighton's architectural crown. Comprising one straight row and two magnificent crescents of Regency houses, each with views across five acres of private gardens and the English Channel beyond, the square had originally been built to provide weekend seaside homes for fashionable, rich Londoners. Now most of the buildings were divided up into apartments, but none of their grandeur had been lost in the process.

He drove the van slowly, passing the tall, imposing façades that were all painted a uniform white, checking out the numbers. Looking for no. 53.

He knew that it was still a single-dwelling home on five floors, with servants' quarters at the top. A fine residence, he thought, to reflect the status of a man like Rudy Burchmore, the Vice-President, Europe, of American & Oriental Banking, and of his socialite wife, Dee. A perfect home for entertaining in style. For impressing people. For wearing expensive shoes in.

He drove around the square again, quivering and clammy with excitement, and this time stopped short of the house, pulling into a gap on the garden side of the road. This was a good place to stop. He could see her car and he could see her front door, but she wouldn't notice him, regardless of whether she was looking out of her window or coming out of her front door.

He was invisible!

He had learned that certain things were invisible to the inhabitants of the affluent world. There were invisible people, like road sweepers and office cleaners and navvies. And there were invisible vehicles, like milk floats and white vans and taxis. Drug dealers used taxis a lot, because they never aroused suspicion driving around late at night. But the van suited his purposes better than a taxi at the moment.

He smiled, increasingly aroused, his breathing quickening. He could still smell her Armani Code fragrance. He could smell it so strongly, as if his whole van was filled with it now.

Oh yes, you bitch! he thought. *Oh yes! Oh yes! Oh yes!*

He would enjoy breathing that in while he made her do things to herself with those shoes, and then when he did things to her too. Fear would make her perspire and her perspiration would make the scent even stronger.

He could imagine her coming out of her front door wearing those blue Manolos and smelling of Armani Code. He could imagine her sliding into the driving seat of her car. Then parking somewhere safe, like she had done on Saturday, in an underground car park.

He knew exactly when she would be wearing those shoes. He'd heard her in the shop on Saturday when she bought them. *For an important speech*, she'd told the assistant. The *after-lunch thing* for which she had bought *a divine blue dress* and now had the shoes to match.

It would be nice if Dee Burchmore came out of her front door now, he thought, except she would not be wearing those new blue Manolos today.

Very conveniently, she had a section on her website for all her social engagements. In addition, she had a Facebook site where she announced them. And she told the world her movements, sometimes hour by hour, on Twitter. She was so helpful to him!

She had confirmed on her website and on Facebook that her next big social engagement was on Thursday, when she was giving a speech at a luncheon in aid of the local hospice, the Martlets. She had already started Tweeting it. The great and the good of the city of Brighton and Hove's female society would be attending. One of the guests of honour would be the wife of the current Lord Lieutenant of Sussex.

The luncheon was being held at the Grand Hotel, which had a big car park behind it.

That really could not be more convenient!

60

There was an insolence about the way Kevin Spinella entered Roy Grace's office, shortly before ten minutes to midday, pulled up a chair, uninvited, and sat down. Spinella always irked him and yet at the same time there were qualities about the young, ambitious reporter that Grace couldn't help, privately, liking.

Spinella lounged nonchalantly back in his chair on the other side of Grace's desk, hands in the pockets of his raincoat. Beneath it he wore a suit, with a slack, clumsily knotted tie. A slight, thin-faced man, Spinella was in his mid-twenties, with alert eyes and thin black hair gelled into tiny spikes. His sharp incisors, as always, were busily working on a piece of gum.

'So, what do you have for me, Detective Super-intendent?'

'You're the man in the know,' Grace replied, testing him. 'What do you have for me?'

The reporter cocked his head to one side. 'I hear that the Shoe Man's back.'

'Tell me, Kevin, what's your source?'

The reporter smiled and tapped the side of his nose.

'I will find out. You know that, don't you?' Grace said, his tone serious.

371

'I thought you asked me to come and see you because you want to do business.'

'I do.'

'So?'

Grace held his cool with difficulty and decided to let the subject of the leaks drop for the moment. Changing tack, he said, 'I want your help. If I tell you something off the record, can I have your word you'll keep it that way until I tell you otherwise? I need to trust you absolutely on this.'

'Can't you always?'

No, not always, actually, Grace recalled. Although, he had to admit, Spinella had been good as gold during this past year.

'Usually,' he conceded.

'What's in it for the *Argus*?'

'Possibly a credit for helping us to catch the offender. I'd certainly give an interview on that.'

'Just one offender, is there?' Spinella asked pointedly.

Shit, Grace thought, wondering where the hell he had got *that* from. Who had speculated about that outside of the briefing meeting earlier this morning? Was it one of his team members? Just where had that come from? Anger rose inside him. But it was clear from Spinella's expression he would get nothing from him. For the moment he had to park it.

'At this stage we believe there is one offender responsible for all the attacks.'

Spinella's shifty eyes said he did not believe him.

Grace ignored that and went on: 'OK, here's the deal.' He hesitated for an instant, knowing he was taking a massive gamble. 'I have two exclusives for you. The first I don't want you to print until I tell you, the second I'd like you to print right away. I'm not giving either of these to the press conference.'

There was a brief silence as the two men stared at each other. For a moment Spinella stopped chewing.

'Deal?' Grace asked.

Spinella shrugged. 'Deal.'

'OK. The first, not for you to print, is that we think there could be another attack this week. It's likely to be somewhere in the town centre, possibly in a car park.'

'Hardly rocket science if there have been three in the past two weeks already,' Spinella retorted sarcastically.

'No, I agree with you.'

'Not much of an exclusive. I could have predicted that off my own bat.'

'It'll make you look good if it does happen – you can write one of those *A senior detective had forewarned the* Argus *this attack was likely* kind of pieces that you've been good at inventing in the past.'

Spinella had the decency to blush. Then he shrugged. 'Car park? So you think he's mirroring the same sequence as before?'

'The forensic psychologist does.'

'Dr Proudfoot's got a bit of a reputation as a tosser, hasn't he?'

'You said that, not me.' Grace's eyes twinkled.

'So what are you doing to prevent the next attack?'

'All we can, short of closing down the centre of Brighton to the public. We're going to throw as much resourcing as we can behind it – but invisible. We want to catch him, not drive him away and lose him.'

'How are you going to warn the public?'

'I hope we can get the support of the press and media at the conference we're about to have – and warn them in a general but not specific way.'

Spinella nodded, then pulled out his notebook. 'Now tell me the one I can print.'

Grace smiled, then said, 'The offender has a small dick.'

The reporter waited, but Grace said nothing more.

'That's it?' Spinella asked.

'That's it.'

'You're joking?'

The Detective Superintendent shook his head.

'That's my exclusive? That the offender has a small dick?'

'Hope I'm not touching a nerve,' Grace replied.

1998

61

The old lady sat in the driver's seat of the stolen van, at the start of the steep hill, with her seat belt on as tight as it would go. Her hands rested on the steering wheel, with the engine idling, but the lights switched off.

He stood beside her, holding the driver's door open, nervous as hell. It was a black night, the sky densely lagged with clouds. He could have used some moonlight, but there was nothing to be done about that.

His eyes scanned the darkness. It was 2 a.m. and the country road, a few hundred yards to the north of the entrance to the Waterhall Golf Club, two miles from the outskirts of Brighton, was deserted. There was a half-mile steep descent, with a sharp left-hander at the bottom, the road winding on through the valley between the hills of the South Downs. The beauty of this location, he figured, was that he could see from the headlights if anything was coming, for over a mile in either direction. It was all clear for the moment.

Time to rock and roll!

He reached across her lap, released the handbrake, then jumped clear as the van immediately rolled forward, picking up speed rapidly, the driver's door swinging shut with a dull clang. The van veered worryingly into the oncoming lane, and stayed there, as it continued to pick up speed.

It was just as well no vehicle was coming up the hill towards the van, because the old lady would have been incapable of taking any avoiding action, or reacting in any way at all, on account of the fact that she had been dead for ten days.

He jumped on his bike and, with the boost of additional weight from his backpack, pedalled, then freewheeled down the hill after her, rapidly picking up speed.

Ahead of him he saw the silhouette of the van, which he had stolen from a construction site, veering towards the offside verge and, for one heart-in-his-mouth moment, he was sure it was going to crash into the thick gorse hedge, which might have stopped it. But then, miraculously, it veered briefly left, made a slight correction and careered on down the hill on a dead straight path, as if she really was steering it. As if she was having the ride of her life. Or rather, he thought, of her death!

'Go, baby, go! Go for it, Molly!' he urged. 'Enjoy!'

The van, which had the name *Bryan Barker Builders* emblazoned all over it, was continuing to pick up speed. Going so fast now he was feeling dangerously out of control, he touched the brakes of the mountain bike and slowed a little, letting the van pull away. It was hard to gauge distances. The hedgerows flashed by. Something flapped close to his face. What the fuck was it? A bat? An owl?

The cold, damp wind was streaming into his eyes, making them water, half-blinding him.

He braked harder. They were coming towards the bottom, approaching the left-hander. The van went straight on. He heard the crunching, tearing, screeching of barbed wire against paintwork as it ploughed through the hedge and the farmer's fence. He brought the bike to a skidding halt, his trainers bouncing along on the tarmac for several yards, narrowly avoiding going head over heels.

Through his watering eyes, more accustomed to the darkness now, he saw a massive black shape disappear. Then he heard a dull, rumbling metallic booming sound.

He leapt off his bike, tossing it into the hedge, pulled out his torch and switched it on, then scrambled through the hole in the hedge. The beam found its mark.

'Perfect! Oh yes, perfect! Sweet! Oh yes, baby, yes! Molly, you doll! You did it, Molly! You did it!'

The van was lying on its roof, all four of its wheels spinning.

He ran up to it, then stopped, switched the torch off and looked in every direction. Still no sign of any headlights. Then he shone the beam inside. Molly Glossop lay upside down, suspended from her lap-strap, her mouth still closed from the stitches through her lips, her hair hanging untidily down in short grey clumps.

'Thanks!' he whispered, as if his voice might travel ten miles. 'Well driven!'

He shrugged his backpack off and clumsily fumbled the buckles open with his trembling, gloved fingers. Then he lifted out the plastic five-litre container of petrol, hurried through the sodden winter wheat and the sticky mud up to the driver's door and tried to open it.

It would not budge.

Cursing, he put down the container and pulled the handle with both hands, with all his strength, but it only yielded a couple of inches, the buckled metal shrieking in protest.

It didn't matter because the window was open; that

would do. He shot another nervous glance in both directions. Still no sign of any vehicle.

He unscrewed the cap of the container, which came away with a hiss, and poured the contents in through the window, shaking as much of the petrol over the old lady's head and body as he could.

When it was empty he replaced the lid and returned the container to his backpack, retied the buckles and put it over his shoulders.

Next, he stepped several yards away from the upturned van, pulled out a packet of cigarettes, removed one and stuck it in his mouth. His hands were shaking so much he found it hard to flick the lighter wheel. Finally a flame erupted, briefly, then the wind blew it out.

'Shit! Fuck! Don't do this!'

He tried again, shielding it with his palm, and finally got the cigarette alight. He took two long drags on it and once more checked for headlights.

Shit.

A vehicle was coming down the hill.

Don't see us. Please don't see us.

He flattened himself in the wheat. Heard the roar of the engine. Felt the glare of the headlights wash over him, then darkness returned.

The roar of the engine was fading.

He stood up. Red tail lights were briefly visible, then vanished. He saw them again a few seconds later. Then they were gone for good.

He waited a few more seconds before walking towards the van, then tossed the cigarette in through the open window of the driver's door, turned and ran for several yards. He stopped and looked back.

Nothing happened. No flicker of a flame. Nothing at all.

He waited for what felt like an eternity. Still nothing happened.

Don't do this to me!

Headlights were coming from the other direction now.

Don't let this be the vehicle that passed, now turned round to come and look through the hole in the hedge!

To his relief, it wasn't. It was a car, sounding like it wasn't firing on all cylinders, blat-blatting its way up the hill. Its weak tail lights told him it was an old banger of some kind, its electrical system not liking the damp.

He waited another full minute, breathing in the increasingly strong reek of petrol in the air, but still nothing happened. Then he lit a second cigarette, stepped cautiously across and tossed that in. The result was the same. Nothing.

Panic started to grip him. Was the petrol dud?

A third vehicle came down the hill and passed by.

He pulled his handkerchief out, stepped cautiously up to the van, shone his flashlight in and saw both cigarettes, soggy and extinguished, lying in the pool of petrol on the cab roof. What the fuck was this? Cigarettes always lit petrol tanks in movies! He dabbed the handkerchief into the pool of petrol on the roof of the van, then stepped back and lit it.

There was such a violent explosion of flame that he dropped it, from shock, on to the ground. The handkerchief burned so intensely that all he could do was watch the flames consume it.

Now another bloody vehicle was coming down the

hill! He hastily stamped on the burning handkerchief, stamping again and again, extinguishing it. His heart thumping, he waited for the sweep of lights to pass and the roar of the engine to fade.

He removed the backpack, took his anorak off, squashed it into a ball, leaned in through the window and dunked it into the pool of petrol for a couple of seconds. Then he stepped back, holding it at arm's length, and shook it open. He clicked the lighter and there was a massive WHUMPH.

Flames leapt at him fiercely, searing his face. Ignoring the pain, he hurled the blazing anorak through the window, and this time the result was instant.

The whole interior of the van lit up like a furnace. He could see Molly Glossop clearly for some seconds before her hair disappeared and her colour darkened. He stood mesmerized, watching the flames, watching her get darker and darker still. Then, suddenly, what he had hoped for happened. The fuel tank exploded, turning the entire van into a blazing inferno.

Grabbing his backpack, he stumbled back to where he had flung his bike, mounted it and pedalled away from the scene as fast as he could, in the beautifully cool, silent air, taking his planned, circuitous route back to Brighton.

No vehicles passed him all the way back to the main road. He listened intently for the wail of a siren. But heard nothing.

NOW

62

Tuesday 13 January

Billy No Mates was seated in a window table of the café, digging her fork into a mountainous veggie salad, with watercress and frisée lettuce overflowing all around the rim of the bowl. It looked like she was eating a hairdo.

She chewed pensively, picking up her iPhone and staring at something on the screen in between mouthfuls. Her shoulder-length bleached hair was scooped up into a ponytail, with a few loose strands hanging down, just the way it had been the last time he had seen her, in Marielle Shoes, on Saturday.

She had a pretty face, despite her curiously hooked nose, and was dressed casually, almost sloppily, in a shapeless, sleeveless grey tunic over a black roll neck, jeans and sparkly trainers. He would have to get her to change out of those! Trainers on women just did not do it for him.

Clearly Jessie Sheldon didn't bother with her appearance for work, or maybe her look was deliberate. Her albums on Facebook showed she could look very pretty with her hair down and in nice clothes. Beautiful in some. Stunning. A very sexy lady indeed!

And she wasn't really Billy No Mates at all, although she did look like that at this moment, just sitting there all on her own. She actually had 251 friends, as of earlier today, when he'd last checked out her Facebook site. And one of them, Benedict Greene, was her fiancé – well, as good as, although they were not formally engaged, yet, she'd explained on the site. *Sssshh! Don't tell my parents!*

She was a good networker. She kept all her friends updated daily on her activities. Everyone knew what she would be doing in three hours' time, in six hours' time, in twenty-four hours' time, and for the next several weeks. And just like Dee Burchmore, she Tweeted. Mostly, at the moment, about her diet. *Jessie is thinking of eating a KitKat ... Jessie resisted the KitKat ... Lost a pound today! ... Rats, put on a pound today! Only eating vegetarian for rest of this week!*

She was a good girl, so helpful to him! She Tweeted far more than Dee Burchmore. Her latest was sent just an hour ago: *Keeping to diet! Lunching vegetarian today at Lydia, my current fave!*

She was tapping away on the iPhone now. Maybe she was Tweeting again?

He liked to keep an eye on his women. This morning, Dee Burchmore was at the spa at the Metropole Hotel, having a Thalgo Indocéane Complete Body Ritual. He wondered whether to have one too. But thought better of it. He had things to do today; in fact he should not be here at all. But it felt so good! How could he resist?

Billy No Mates had Tweeted earlier: *Going to look at those shoes again at lunchtime – hope they'll still be there!*

They were! He'd watched her take a photo of them with her iPhone, then tell the assistant she was going to have a think about them over lunch. She asked the shop assistant if she would keep them aside for her until 2 p.m. The assistant said she would.

They were dead sexy! The black ones, with the ankle

straps and the five-inch steel-coloured heels. The ones she wanted to wear, she had told the assistant, when she went to a function with her boyfriend, who would be meeting her parents for the first time.

Billy No Mates tapped out something on the keyboard, then raised the phone to her ear. Moments later her face lit up, animated. 'Hi, Roz! I just sent you a photo of the shoes! Have you got it? Yeah! What do you think? You do? Really? OK! I'm going to get them! I'll bring them over and show them to you tonight, after my squash game! What film are we going to see? You got *The Final Destination*? Great!'

He smiled. She liked horror movies. Maybe she might even enjoy the little show he had planned for her! Although it was not his intention to give pleasure.

'No, the car's fine now, all fixed. I'll pick up the takeaway. I'll tell him not to charge us for the seaweed. He forgot it last week,' she continued. 'Yeah, OK, soy sauce. I'll make sure he puts extra in.'

His own mobile rang. He looked at the display. Work. He pressed the red button, sending it to voicemail.

Then he looked down at the copy of the *Argus* he had just bought. The front page headline shouted:

POLICE STEP UP VIGILANCE AFTER THIRD CITY RAPE

He frowned, then began to read. The third attack, over the weekend, was in the ghost train on the pier. There was hot speculation that the so-called Shoe Man, who in 1997–8 had committed four and perhaps five rapes – and possibly many more that had never been reported – was back. Detective Superintendent Roy Grace, the Senior Investigating Officer, stated it was too soon for such speculation. They were pursuing a number of lines of enquiry, he said, and gave assurances that every possible resource Sussex Police had at their disposal was being harnessed. The safety of the city's women was their number-one priority.

Then the next paragraph hit him with a jolt.

> In an exclusive interview with the *Argus*, Detective Superintendent Grace stated that the offender had a physical sexual deformity. He declined to be specific, but told this reporter that it included an exceptionally diminutive manhood. He added that any woman who had had previous relations with him would remember this feature. A psycho-sexual therapist said that such an inadequacy could lead a person to attempt to compensate via violent means. Anyone who believed they might know such a person was urged either to phone 0845 6070999 and ask for the *Operation Swordfish* Incident Room or to call the Crimestoppers number anonymously.

His phone beeped twice with a voicemail message. He ignored it, glaring down at the print with rising fury. *Sexual deformity?* Was that what everyone was thinking of him? Well, maybe Detective Superintendent Grace was not very well endowed in another department, his brain. The detective hadn't caught him twelve years ago and he was not going to catch him now.

Little dick, big brain, Mr Grace.

He read the article again, every word of it, word by word. Then again. Then again.

A friendly female voice with a South African accent startled him. 'Are you ready to order, madam?'

He looked up at the young waitress's face. Then across to the table next to him by the window.

Billy No Mates had left.

It didn't matter. He knew where to find her later. In the car park at Withdean Sports Stadium after her game of squash this evening. It was a good car park, open air and large. It should be quiet at that time of day and pitch dark. With luck he'd be able to park right alongside the bitch's little black Ka.

He looked up at the waitress. 'Yes, I'll have a rump steak and chips, bloody.'

'I'm afraid this is a vegetarian restaurant.'

'Then what the fuck am I doing here?' he said, totally forgetting his ladylike voice.

He got up and flounced out.

63

At the end of Kensington Place he turned left and walked down Trafalgar Street, looking for a payphone. He found one at the bottom and went in. Several cards featuring half-naked ladies offering *French Lessons, Oriental Massage, Discipline Classes* were stuck in the window frames. 'Bitches,' he said, casting his eye across them. It took him a moment to work out what he had to do to make a call. Then he dug in his pocket for a coin and shoved the only thing he had, a pound, into the slot. Then, still shaking with rage, he looked at the first number in the *Argus* article and dialled it.

When it was answered, he asked to be put through to the Incident Room for *Operation Swordfish*, then waited.

After three rings, a male voice answered. 'Incident Room, Detective Constable Nicholl.'

'I want you to give a message to Detective Superintendent Grace.'

'Yes, sir. May I say who's calling?'

He waited for a moment, as a police car raced past, its siren wailing, then he left his message, hung up and hurried away from the booth.

64

All the team at the 6.30 p.m. briefing of *Operation Sword-fish*, gathered in MIR-1, were silent as Roy Grace switched on the recorder. The tape that had been sent over from the Call Handling Centre began to play.

There was a background rumble of traffic, then a man's voice, quiet, as if he had been making an effort to stay calm. The roar of traffic made it hard to hear him distinctly.

'I want you to give a message to Detective Superintend-ent Grace,' the man said.

Then they could hear Nick Nicholl's voice replying. *'Yes, sir. May I say who's calling?'*

Nothing for some moments, except the almost deaf-ening wail of a passing siren, then the man's voice again, this time louder: *'Tell him it's not small, actually.'*

It was followed by a loud clattering sound, a sharp click and the line went dead.

No one smiled.

'Is this real or a hoax?' Norman Potting asked.

After a few moments Dr Julius Proudfoot said, 'I'd put my money on that being real, from the way he spoke.'

'Can we hear it again, boss?' Michael Foreman asked.

Grace replayed the tape. When it finished, he turned to Proudfoot. 'Anything you can tell us from that?'

The forensic psychologist nodded. 'Well, yes, quite a bit. The first thing, assuming it is him, is that you've clearly succeeded in rattling his cage. That's why I think it's real, not a hoax. There's genuine anger in the voice. Full of emotion.'

'That was my intention, to rattle his cage.'

'You can hear it in his voice, in the way the cadence rises,' the forensic psychologist went on. 'He's all bottled up with anger. And the fact that it sounded like he fumbled replacing the receiver – probably shaking so much with rage. I can tell also that he's nervous, feeling under pressure – and that you've struck a chord. Is that information about him true? Something that's been obtained from statements by the victims?'

'Not in so many words, but yes, reading between the lines of the witness statements from back in 1997 and now.'

'What's your reasoning for giving that to the *Argus*, Roy?' Emma-Jane Boutwood asked.

'Because I suspect this creep thinks he's very clever. He got away with his attacks before and now he's confident he's going to get away with these new ones too. If Dr Proudfoot is right and he committed the ghost train rape as well, then he's clearly stepping up both the speed and the brazenness of his attacks. I wanted to lance his ego a little and hopefully get him into a strop. People who are angry are more likely to make mistakes.'

'Or be more brutal to their victims,' Bella Moy said. 'Isn't that a risk?'

'If he killed last time, Bella, which I think is likely,' Grace replied, 'there's a high risk he'll kill again, strop or no strop. When someone has taken a life once, they've crossed a personal Rubicon. It's far easier the second time. Particularly if they found they enjoyed it the first time. We're dealing with a nasty, warped freak here – and someone who's not stupid. We need to find ways to trip him up. I don't just want him not being more brutal to a victim – I want him not to have another victim, full stop. We have to catch him before he attacks again.'

'Anyone figure out his accent?' Nick Nicholl asked.

'Sounds local to me,' DC Foreman said, 'but difficult with that background noise. Can we get the recording enhanced?'

'That's being worked on now,' Grace replied. Then he turned to Proudfoot. 'Can you estimate the man's age from this?'

'That's a hard one – anywhere between thirty and fifty, I'd guess,' he said. 'I think you need to run this through a lab, somewhere like J. P. French, which specializes in speaker profiling. There's quite a bit of information they could get us from a call like this. Probably the man's regional and ethnic background, for a start.'

Grace nodded. He'd used the specialist firm before and the results had been helpful. He could also get a voiceprint from the lab that would be as unique as a fingerprint or DNA. But could they do it in the short amount of time he believed he had?

'There have been mass DNA screenings in communities,' Bella Moy said. 'What about trying something like that in Brighton with the voiceprint?'

'So all we'd have to do, Bella,' Norman Potting said, 'is get every bloke in Brighton and Hove to say the same words. There's only a hundred and forty thousand or so males in the city. Shouldn't take us more than about ten years.'

'Could you play it again, boss, please,' said Glenn

Branson, who'd been very quiet. 'Wasn't it that movie, *The Conversation*, with Gene Hackman, where they worked out where someone was from the traffic noise in the background on the tape?'

He played the tape again.

'Have we been able to trace the call, sir?' Ellen Zoratti asked.

'The number was withheld. But it's being worked on. It's a big task with the amount coming through the Call Centre every hour.' Grace played the tape again.

When it finished, Glenn Branson said, 'Sounds like somewhere in the centre of Brighton. If they can't trace the number we've still got the siren and the time of day – that vehicle sounds like it went right past very close to him. We need to check what emergency vehicle was on its blues and twos at exactly 1.55 p.m., and we'll get its route and know he was somewhere along it. A CCTV might have picked up someone on their mobile – and possibly bingo.'

'Good thinking,' Grace said. 'Although it sounded more like a landline than a mobile from the way he hung up.'

'Yes,' Michael Foreman said. 'That clunking sound – that's like an old-fashioned handset being replaced.'

'He might have just dropped his phone, if he was as nervous as Dr Proudfoot suggests,' said DC Boutwood. 'I don't think we should rule out a mobile.'

'Or it could be a public phone booth,' Foreman said. 'In which case there may be fingerprints.'

'If he's angry,' Proudfoot said, 'then I think it's even more likely he'll strike again quickly. And a racing certainty is that he'll copy his pattern from last time. He'll know that worked. He'll be fine if he sticks to the same again. Which means he's going to strike in a car park next – as I've said before.'

Grace walked over to a map of central Brighton and stared at it, looking at each of the main car parks. The station, London Road, New Road, Churchill Square, North Road. There were dozens of them, big and small, some run by the council, some by NCP, some part of supermarkets or hotels. He turned back to Proudfoot.

'It would be impossible to cover every damned car park in the city – and even more impossible to cover every level of every multi-storey,' he said. 'We just don't have the number of patrols. And we can hardly close them down.'

He was feeling anxious suddenly. Maybe it had been a mistake telling Spinella that yesterday. What if it pushed the Shoe Man over the edge into killing again? It would be his own stupid fault.

'The best thing we can do is get plain-clothes officers into the CCTV control rooms of those car parks that have it, step up patrols and have as many undercover vehicles drive around the car parks as we can,' Grace said.

'The one thing I'd tell your team to watch out for, Detective Superintendent, is someone on edge tonight. Someone driving erratically on the streets. I think our man is going to be in a highly wired state.'

65

You think you've been clever, don't you, Detective Superintendent Roy Grace? You think you're going to make me angry by insulting me, don't you? I can see through all that shit.

You should accept you are just a lame duck. Your colleagues didn't catch me before and you won't catch me now. I'm so much smarter than you could ever dream of being. You see, you don't realize I'm doing you a favour!

I'm getting rid of the poison in your manor! I'm your new best friend! One day you'll come to realize that! One day you and I will walk along under the cliffs at Rottingdean and talk about all of this. That walk you like to take with your beloved Cleo on Sundays! She likes shoes too. I've seen her in some of the shops I go in. She's quite into shoes, isn't she? You are going to need saving from her, but you don't realize that yet. You will do one day.

They're all poison, you see. All women. They seduce you with their Venus fly trap vaginas. You can't bear to be apart from them. You phone them and text them every few minutes of your waking day, because you need to know how much they still love you.

Let me tell you a secret.

No woman ever loves you. All she wants to do is control you. You might sneer at me. You might question the size of my manhood. But I will tell you something, Detective Superintendent. You'll be grateful to me, one day. You'll walk with me arm in arm along the Undercliff Walk at Rottingdean and thank me for saving you from yourself.

66

Tuesday 13 January

Jessie felt a deep and constant yearning all the time she was away from Benedict. It must be an hour now since she had texted him, she thought. Tuesdays were their one night apart. She played squash with a recently married friend, Jax, then after would pick up a takeaway Chinese and go round to Roz's and watch a DVD – something they had done almost every Tuesday night for as long as she could remember. Benedict, who liked to compose guitar music, had a similar long-standing Tuesday evening commitment – working late into the night with his co-writing partner, coming up with new songs. At the moment they were putting together an album they hoped might be their breakthrough.

Some weekends Benedict played gigs in a band in a variety of Sussex pubs. She loved watching him on stage. He was like a drug she just could not get enough of. Still, after eight months of dating, she could make love to him virtually all day and all night – on the rare opportunities they had such a length of time together. He was the best kisser, the best lover by a million, million miles – not that she'd had that many for comparison. Four, to be precise, and none of them memorable.

Benedict was kind, thoughtful, considerate, generous, and he made her laugh. She loved his humour. She loved the smell of his skin, his hair, his breath and his perspiration. But the thing she loved most of all about him was his mind.

And of course she loved that he really, truly, genuinely did seem to like her nose.

'You don't really like it, do you?' she'd asked him in bed, a few months ago.

'I do!'

'You can't!'

'I think you're beautiful.'

'I'm not. I've got a hooter like Concorde.'

'You're beautiful to me.'

'Have you been to an optician lately?'

'Do you want to hear something I read that made me think of you?' he asked.

'OK, tell me.'

'It's beauty that captures your attention, personality that captures your heart.'

She smiled now at the memory as she sat in the traffic jam in the sodium-lit darkness, the heater of her little Ford Ka whirring noisily, toasting her feet. She was half listening to the news on the radio, tuned to Radio 4, Gordon Brown being harangued over Afghanistan. She didn't like him, even though she was a Labour supporter, and she switched over to Juice. Air were playing, 'Sexy Boy'.

'Yayyyy!' She grinned, nodding her head and drumming the steering wheel for a few moments, in tune to the music. *Sexy Boy, that's what you are, my gorgeous!*

She loved him with all her heart and soul, of that she was sure. She wanted to spend the rest of her life with him – she had never ever been so certain of anything. It was going to hurt her parents that she wasn't marrying a

Jewish boy, but she couldn't help that. She respected her family's traditions, but she was not a believer in any religion. She believed in making the world a better place for everyone who lived in it, and she hadn't yet come across a religion that seemed capable of or interested in doing that.

Her iPhone, lying beside her on the passenger seat, pinged with an incoming text. She smiled.

The rush-hour gridlock up the London Road was being made worse than usual by new roadworks. The traffic light ahead had gone from green to red, to green to red again now, and they hadn't moved in inch. She was still alongside the brightly lit window display of British Bookshops. She had time to look at her phone safely, she decided.

Hope you win! XXXXXXXXXXXXXX

She smiled. The engine idled and the wipers alternated between a scraping and a screeching sound, flattening the droplets of rain that landed on the windscreen into an opaque smear. Benedict told her she needed new wiper blades and was going to get her some. She could have done with them now, she thought.

She looked at her watch: 5.50. *Shit.* Normally, the half an hour she allowed to get from the charity's offices in the Old Steine, where she had a free parking space, to the Withdean Sports Stadium was more than adequate. But this evening she had not moved an inch for over five minutes. She was due on court at 6 p.m. Hopefully it would be better once she was past the roadworks.

Jessie wasn't the only person being made anxious by the bad traffic. Someone waiting for her at the Withdean Sports Stadium, someone who was not her squash partner, was in a very bad mood. And it was worsening by the second.

67

Tuesday 13 January

It was meant to be dark here! It had been dark when he'd
checked it out last night. It was less than a month since
the longest night of the year – only 13 January, for Christ's
sake! At 6 p.m. it should be totally dark. But the sodding
car park of Withdean Sports Stadium was lit up like a
sodding Christmas Tree. Why did they have to pick
tonight to have bloody outdoor athletics practice? Hadn't
anyone told the stadium about global warming?

And where the fuck was she?

The car park was a lot fuller than he had expected.
He'd already driven around it three times, checking that
he had not missed the little black Ka. It definitely wasn't
here.

She distinctly said on Facebook that she would meet
Jax here at 5.45. The court was booked for 6 p.m. *As usual.*

He'd looked up pictures of Roz on Facebook, too.
*View photos of Roz (121). Send Roz a message. Poke Roz.
Roz and Jessie are friends.* Roz was quite a sexy vixen, he
thought. She rocked! There were some photos of her all
dressed up for a prom night.

He focused on the task in hand as his eyes hunted
through the windscreen. Two men hurried across in front
of him, each carrying sports bags, heads ducked low
against the rain, going into the main building. They didn't

see him. White vans were always invisible! He was tempted to follow them inside, to check in case somehow he had missed Jessie Sheldon and she was already on court. She'd said something about her car, that it had been fixed. What if something had gone wrong with it again and she'd got a lift from someone instead, or taken a bus or a taxi?

He stopped the van alongside a row of parked vehicles, in a position that gave him a clear view of the entrance ramp to the car park, switched the engine off and killed the lights. It was a God-awful cold, rainy night, which was perfect. No one was going to take any notice of the van, floodlights or no sodding floodlights. Everyone had their heads down, dashing for the cover of the buildings or their cars. All except the stupid athletes on the track.

He was prepared. He was already wearing his latex gloves. The chloroform pad was in a sealed container in his anorak pocket. He slipped his hand inside, to check again. His hood was in another pocket. He checked that again too. Just one thing concerned him: he hoped that Jessie would have a shower after her game, because he didn't like sweaty women. He didn't like some of the unwashed smells women had. She must shower, surely, because she was going straight on to pick up a Chinese takeaway and then to watch a horror film with Roz.

Headlights approached up the ramp. He stiffened. Was this her? He switched on the ignition to sweep the wipers over the rain-spattered screen.

It was a Range Rover. Its headlights momentarily blinded him, then he heard it roar past. He kept the wipers going. The heater pumped in welcoming warm air.

A guy in baggy shorts and a baseball cap was trudging

across the car park, with a sports bag slung over his shoulders, engrossed in a conversation on his mobile. He heard a faint beep-beep and saw lights wink on a dark-coloured Porsche, then the man opened the door.

Wanker, he thought.

He stared again at the ramp. Looked at his watch: 6.05 p.m. *Shit.* He pounded the wheel with his fists. Heard a faint, high-pitched whistling sound in his ears. He got that sometimes when he was all tensed up. He pinched the end of his nose shut and blew hard, but it had no effect and the whistling grew louder.

'Stop it! Fuck off! Stop it!'

It grew louder still.

Exceptionally diminutive manhood!

Jessie would be the judge of that.

He looked at his watch again: 6.10 p.m.

The whistling was now as loud as a football referee's whistle.

'Shut up!' he shouted, feeling all shaky, his eyes blurring with anger.

Then he heard voices, suddenly, and the scrunch of shoes.

'I told her he's an absolute waste of space.'

'She said she loves him! I told her, like, I mean, what??????'

There was a sharp double beep. He saw a flash of orange over to his left. Then he heard car doors click open and, a few moments later, slam shut. The brief whir of a starter motor, then the rattle of a diesel. The interior of the van suddenly stank of diesel exhaust. He heard the blast of a horn.

'Sod off,' he said.

The horn blasted again, twice, to his left.

'Sod off! Screw you! Fuck you! Fuck off!'

There was a mist in front of his eyes, inside his head. The wipers screeched, clearing the rain. More came. They cleared that too. More came.

Then the horn blasted again.

He turned in fury and saw reversing lights on. And then realized. A big, ugly people carrier was trying to reverse and he was parked right in front of it, blocking it.

'Fuck you! Screw you!' He started the van, crunched it into gear, jerked forward a few inches and stalled. His head was shaking, the whistling even louder, slicing his brain to bits like a cheese-wire. He started the van again. Someone knocked on the passenger door window. 'Fuck you!' He rammed the gear lever into first and shot forward. He carried on, almost blind with fury now, and hurtled down the ramp.

In his haze of fury he was utterly oblivious of the headlights of the little black Ford Ka racing up the ramp, in the opposite direction, and passing him.

1998

68

'I'm sorry I'm late, my darling,' Roy Grace said, coming through the front door.

'If I had a pound for every time you've said that, I'd be a millionaire!' Sandy gave him a resigned smile, then kissed him.

There was a warm smell of scented candles in the house. Sandy lit them most evenings, but there seemed more than usual tonight, to mark the special occasion.

'God, you look beautiful,' he said.

She did. She'd been to the hairdresser's and her long fair hair was in ringlets. She was wearing a short black dress that showed every curve of her body and she had sprayed on his favourite perfume, Poison. She raised her wrist to show him the slim silver bracelet he'd bought her from a modern jeweller in the Lanes.

'It looks great!' he said.

'It does!' She admired it in the mirror on the Victorian coat-stand in the hall. 'I love it. You have great taste, Detective Sergeant Grace!'

He held her in his arms and nuzzled her bare neck. 'I could make love to you right now, here on the hall floor.'

'Then you'd better be quick. There's a taxi coming in thirty minutes!'

'Taxi? We don't need a taxi. I'll drive.'

'You're not going to drink on my birthday?'

She helped him out of his coat, slung it on a hook on the stand and led him by the hand into the sitting room. The juke box they'd bought a couple of years earlier in the Saturday morning Kensington Gardens market, and had restored, was playing one of his favourite Rolling Stones tracks, their version of 'Under the Boardwalk'. The lights were dimmed and candles were burning all around. On the coffee table sat an open bottle of champagne, two glasses and a bowl of olives.

'I had thought we might have a drink before we went out,' she said wistfully. 'But it's OK. I'll put it in the fridge and we can have it when we get back! You could drink it off my naked body.'

'Mmmm,' he said. 'It's a lovely idea. But I'm on duty, darling, so I can't drink.'

'Roy, it's my *birthday*!'

He kissed her again, but she pulled away from him. 'You're not on duty on my birthday. You were on duty all over Christmas. You've been at work all day today since very early. Now you're switching off!'

'Tell Popeye that.'

Popeye was his immediate boss, Detective Chief Inspector Jim 'Popeye' Doyle. The DCI had been appointed the Senior Investigating Officer on *Operation Sundown*, the investigation into the disappearance of Rachael Ryan, which was currently consuming all Grace's working hours – and keeping him awake every night, his brain racing.

'Give me his number and I will!'

Grace shook his head. 'My darling, all leave has been cancelled. We're on this case around the clock. I'm sorry.

But if you were Rachael Ryan's parents, that's what you'd expect of us.'

'You're not telling me you can't have a drink on my birthday?'

'Let me nip up and change.'

'You're not going anywhere until you promise me you're going to drink with me tonight!'

'Sandy, if I get called out and someone smells alcohol on my breath, I could lose my job and get kicked off the force. Please understand.'

'*Please understand!*' she mimicked. 'If I had a pound for every time you said that as well, I'd be a *multi-millionaire!*'

'Cancel the cab. I'm going to drive.'

'You are not bloody driving!'

'I thought we were trying to save money for the mortgage and for all the work on the house.'

'I don't think one taxi's going to make much bloody difference!'

'It's two taxis actually – one there and one back.'

'So?' She placed her hands on her hips defiantly.

At that moment, his radio phone crackled into life with an incoming call. He tugged it from his pocket and answered.

'Roy Grace.'

She looked at him, giving him a *Don't you dare, whatever it is*, glare.

It was his DCI.

'Good evening, sir,' he said.

The reception was poor, Jim Doyle's voice crackly.

'Roy, there's a burnt-out van just been found in a field by a farmer out lamping for rabbits. The index shows it was stolen yesterday afternoon. There's a body in it which he thinks is female – he was in the Tank Corps of the army out in Iraq and knows a bit about these things apparently. Sounds possible it could be our missing Rachael Ryan – we need to secure the vehicle immediately. It's off the Saddlescombe Road, half a mile south of the Waterhall Golf Club. I'm on my way over now. Can you meet me there? How long would it take you?'

Grace's heart sank. 'You mean *now*, sir?'

'What do you think? Three weeks' time?'

'No, sir – it's just – it's my wife's birthday.'

'Wish her Happy Birthday from me.'

NOW

69

Norman Potting entered MIR-1 carrying a coffee he had just made in the kitchenette along the corridor. He was stooping, holding the steaming mug out at arm's length, as if mistrustful of it. He grunted a couple of times as he crossed the room, seeming to be about to say something, then changing his mind.

Like most of the team, Potting had been at his desk since before 7 a.m. It was now coming up to 8.30 a.m., and the morning briefing. Temporarily absent from the room was Roy Grace, who had an early appointment with the ACC, Peter Rigg, and Julius Proudfoot, who was due at any moment.

A phone rang, loudly, to the sound of a trumpet fanfare. Everyone looked around. Embarrassed, Nick Nicholl plucked his offending machine out and silenced it.

As Roy Grace entered the room another phone went off. The ring tone was the *Indiana Jones* theme. Potting had the decency to blush. It was his.

Mouthing an apology to Roy Grace, he yanked it out of his pocket and checked the display. Then he raised a finger. 'I'll just take this quickly ... Someone who may have a lead.'

Another phone rang. It was Julius Proudfoot's. The

forensic psychologist entered the room, extricating his mobile from his man bag as he walked, answered it and sat down, holding it to his ear.

The last to arrive was the Sexual Offences Liaison Officer, Claire Westmore, who had been interviewing and spending time with each of the three rape victims. This was the first of the briefings she had attended.

Potting, wedging his phone to his ear with his shoulder, was writing on his notepad. 'Thank you. That's very helpful. Thank you.'

He replaced his phone and turned to Roy, looking pleased with himself. 'We have another suspect, chief!'

'Tell me?'

'It's from a bloke I know, one of my *contacts*.' Potting tapped the side of his nose. 'Drives for Streamline Taxis. Told me there's a bloke – he's a bit of a joke among the other cabbies apparently – name of John Kerridge. But he calls himself by a funny nickname: Yac. Well, apparently this Yac fellow drives a journeyman night shift and is always going on about strange stuff – ladies' shoes is one of his things.'

Now he had the full attention of the room.

'There have been a few complaints about him by passengers – he gets a bit too personal about things, in particular the toilets in their homes and their footwear. I've spoken to the Hackney Carriage officer in the council. He tells me this driver hasn't actually propositioned anyone, but he's a bit more personal than some of his passengers like. The council want people – particularly women – to feel safe in licensed taxis, not vulnerable. He says he's planning to have a word with him.'

'Do you have an address for Kerridge?' Grace asked.

Potting nodded. 'Lives on a houseboat at Shoreham.'

'Good work,' Grace said. 'I've got *Suspects* on the agenda, so we'll add him to the list when we get to it.' He put his briefing notes down on the work surface in front of him, along with his Policy Book. 'OK, it is 8.30 a.m., Wednesday 14 January. This is our tenth briefing of *Operation Swordfish*, the investigation into the stranger rape of three persons, Mrs Nicola Taylor, Mrs Roxy Pearce and Miss Mandy Thorpe. I've asked the SOLO, Claire Westmore, to attend in order to update us on her interviews with the victims.'

He nodded at her.

'All three of them are, as you would expect, deeply traumatized by what they have been through – the assaults, and the intrusive procedures afterwards,' the SOLO said in her soft Scouse accent. 'I'll start with the first victim, Nicola Taylor, who still has only very limited recall of the attack at the Metropole. Her trauma has deepened since the original interview with her, part of which you and DS Branson witnessed. At the moment she is under sedation at her home in Brighton, being cared for around the clock by a female friend, and has attempted twice to self-harm. She may have to be taken into psychiatric care for a while before we can start a full interview process.'

She paused to look at her notes. 'I think we are making some progress with Mrs Roxanna Pearce, who was attacked in her home in Droveway Avenue last Thursday night. What is interesting in her situation is that when the offender struck, she was in the process of getting dressed up – while her husband was away on a business trip in Scandinavia. SOCO found evidence in her kitchen that she was expecting a guest.'

There were a few raised eyebrows. Then Bella said,

'She could simply have invited a girlfriend round. Why the innuendo?'

'Well,' Claire Westmore said, 'I don't think the signs indicate an *innocent* evening with a mate. There were Italian hors d'oeuvres in a carrier bag on the kitchen table. Two steaks on plates. An open bottle of a very expensive wine and another bottle in the fridge. I've asked her who she was going to be cooking these steaks for and she goes very defensive. She keeps repeating that she'd bought them to give her husband a treat when he came home. But he wasn't due home until the next day.'

'You don't let a wine breathe that long. It would be kaput,' Michael Foreman said. 'It's one of my interests. Doesn't matter what the quality, an hour or two perhaps. But that long? Never. I've had a look at the report. That opened bottle would cost over a hundred quid. That's not plonk you drink over a casual supper.'

'Yep, well, I don't know much about wine,' Westmore said, 'but I would have to agree with you. I think she was expecting someone.'

'You mean a lover?' Nick Nicholl asked.

'You don't open a bottle of wine for someone who's going to rape you,' Emma-Jane Boutwood said.

'Maybe she was planning a kinky sex session,' Norman Potting interjected.

'In your dreams,' Bella Moy retorted.

'She's obviously not going to tell you the truth if she was up to something while her husband was away,' Potting went on. 'And she's not going to want him finding out now, is she?'

'Could we be looking at a kinky sex game gone wrong?' Proudfoot asked.

'I don't think so,' Claire Westmore said. 'Not from the way I'm reading her.'

'So who was her mystery dinner guest?' Nick Nicholl asked.

'She's denying there was one.'

Glenn Branson spoke. 'The Mercedes car that was seen leaving her house at around the time of the attack, for which we only have two digits and one letter of the alphabet. We've now narrowed that down to eighty-three vehicles registered in the Brighton and Hove area. All the registered keepers are being contacted and interviewed. Of course, we've no way of being sure this was a local car, but it seems probable.'

'How many have been eliminated so far?' Roy Grace asked.

'Seventy-one, sir,' said a young DC, Alan Ramsay. 'We should have the rest covered in the next twenty-four hours.'

'So it could be the offender – or her dinner guest,' Grace said.

'If it was her guest, why did he drive away, do you think, boss?' Michael Foreman asked.

'Sounds like, if Claire is right, we might get a chance to ask him that directly.' Grace looked at her. 'Any more on the third victim?'

'Mandy Thorpe is still in hospital, under observation for her head injury, but she's improving – physically if not mentally, sir,' the SOLO said. 'But she's responding well to questioning.'

'Anything new from her?'

'No, sir.'

'I'm still not happy about the link with the first two

and her. I'm just not convinced it is the same offender.'
Grace looked at Proudfoot, who said nothing. 'OK, let's
move on to the suspect list. First, can I have an update on
where we are with Darren Spicer?'

Glenn Branson spoke again. 'Me and DC Nicholl
interviewed him again last night at the St Patrick's shelter
– we checked first he had been at work all that day at the
Grand Hotel, just to see if he was keeping his word about
wanting to go straight. We asked him why he'd taken the
shoes of his last victim – Marcie Kallestad – after sexually
assaulting her.'

'And?'

'He said it was to stop her chasing him.'

There was a titter of laughter.

'Did you believe him?' Grace asked.

'Not as far as I could throw him. He'll tell you
whatever he wants you to hear. But I didn't get the
impression he took them for any kinky reason.'

He turned towards Nick Nicholl, who shook his head
and said, 'I agree.'

'Did he say what he did with them?'

Nicholl nodded. 'He said he flogged them to a shop
down Church Street.'

'Is it still there?' Grace asked. 'Could we get them to
verify that?'

'Think they're going to remember a pair of shoes that
long ago, sir?'

Grace nodded. 'Good point. OK. Norman, what can
you tell us about this taxi driver, Johnny Kerridge – Yac?'

'He's a piece of work, from what I've gathered. I'm
planning to go and have a chat with him this morning.'

'Good. If you have enough for an arrest, bring him in.

The ACC's blowing smoke up my backside. But only if you really feel you have enough, understand?'

'Yes, chief.'

'What about a search warrant? Take him by surprise and stop him getting rid of any evidence.'

'I don't know if we have enough, chief,' Potting said.

'From what I've heard we've enough to justify. We're going in hard on all suspects now, so that's your next action, Norman.' Grace looked down at his notes. 'OK, where are we with other sex offenders on the register? Has anyone moved up the offender status?'

'No, sir,' Ellen Zoratti said. 'We're working through the list. I've got a possible in Shrewsbury four years ago – very similar MO and no suspect ever apprehended, and another in Birmingham six years ago. I'm waiting for more details.'

Grace nodded. 'One important question, Ellen, is have we captured all offences so far in our territory? Are we sure we haven't missed any? We know for a fact that only 6 per cent of rapes get reported. How are we going to get crucial information from the other 94 per cent? We've talked so far to our neighbouring forces, Kent, Surrey, Hampshire and the Met as well. That hasn't yielded anything.' He thought for a moment. 'You've been trawling SCAS for stranger rapes – any joy there?'

SCAS was the Serious Crime Analysis Section, which covered every county in the UK except for the London Metropolitan Police, who were not linked in on it.

'Nothing so far, sir,' she said, 'but I'm waiting on several forces to get back to me.'

'Let me know as soon as you have anything.'

Proudfoot coughed and then spoke. 'As I said, I'd be

very surprised if our man hasn't offended elsewhere in these past twelve years. Very surprised indeed. You can take it as a given that he has.'

'Offended as in *rape*?' Emma-Jane Boutwood asked.

'Urges don't just go away,' Proudfoot said. 'He'll have needed outlets for his urges.' His phone rang again. After a quick look at the display, he silenced it. 'I presume you're in contact with *Crimewatch*, Roy? They could be helpful here.'

'We have an excellent relationship with them, Julius,' Grace replied. 'Unfortunately, it's two weeks until they are on air again. I want to have our offender potted long before then.'

He could have added, but did not, that so did the ACC, Peter Rigg, the Chief Constable, Tom Martinson, and the Chief Executive of Brighton and Hove Corporation.

Suddenly, his own phone rang.

It was his former boss from 1997, Jim Doyle, who was now part of the recently formed Cold Case Team.

'Roy,' he said. 'Those missing pages from the Rachael Ryan cold-case file – about the white van seen near her flat on Christmas morning, 1997?'

'Yes?'

'We've found out who last signed that file out. I think you're going to like this rather a lot.'

70

'I'm all ears,' Roy Grace said.

The next words from Jim Doyle stunned him. Totally stunned him. After they had fully sunk in, he said, 'You're not serious, Jim.'

'Absolutely I am.'

In his nineteen years in the police force to date, Roy Grace had found his fellow officers tended to be good, decent people and, for the most part, people whose company he enjoyed both at work and socially. Sure there were a few prats: some, like Norman Potting, who at least had the redeeming feature of being a good detective, and others, very occasionally, who were a total waste of space. But there were only two people he could really genuinely say that he did not like.

The first was his acerbic former ACC, Alison Vosper, who seemed to have made her mind up from the start that she and Grace were not going to get on; the second was a London Metropolitan Police detective who'd had a brief sojourn here last year, and had tried very hard to stick the boot into him. His name was Cassian Pewe.

Grace excused himself and stepped out of the room, closing the door behind him.

'Cassian Pewe? Are you serious, Jim? You're saying

that Cassian Pewe was the last person to sign that file out?'

'*Detective Superintendent* Cassian Pewe. He was working here in the autumn, wasn't he?' Doyle said. 'Hadn't he moved here from the Met, to help you out on cold cases?'

'Not to help me out, Jim, to take over from me – and not just on cold cases, but on everything. That was his plan, courtesy of Alison Vosper! He was out to eat my sodding lunch!'

'I heard there was a bit of friction.'

'You could call it that.'

Grace had first met Pewe a few years ago, when the man was a detective inspector. The Met had sent in reinforcements to help police Brighton during the Labour Party Conference, Pewe being one of them. Grace had had a big run-in with him and found him supremely arrogant. Then, to his utter dismay, last year Pewe had moved down to Sussex CID with the rank of detective superintendent, and Alison Vosper had given him Grace's cold-case workload – plus the clear signal that the former Met officer would be taking over more and more of Grace's duties.

Cassian Pewe fancied himself as a ladies' man. He had golden hair, angelic blue eyes and a permanent tan. He preened and strutted, exuding a natural air of authority, always acting as if he was in charge, even when he wasn't. Working secretly, behind Grace's back, Pewe had taken it upon himself to ruin Grace's career by trying to reopen investigations into Sandy's disappearance – and point suspicion at him. Returning from a trip to New York last October, Grace found, to his utter incredulity, that Pewe had assembled a Police Search Unit team to scan and dig up his garden for Sandy's suspected remains.

Fortunately, that had proved a step too far. Pewe left Sussex CID and returned to the Met not long after, with his tail between his legs.

After a few more questions to Jim Doyle, Grace hung up and then stood thinking for some moments. There was no way, at this stage, he could mention anything openly to his team. Questioning another officer as high-ranking as Pewe as a suspect would have to be done discreetly, regardless of his personal feelings towards the man.

He would do this himself and it would be a pleasure.

71

twitter
jessiesheldonuk

Working late today. Audit review – soooo boring!
But Benedict taking me out after for sushi meal
at Moshi Moshi. Yayyyy!

He read the text which had just Tweeted through on his phone. *Sushi*, he thought disdainfully. He didn't understand that stuff. What was the point of going to a restaurant to eat uncooked fish? Seemed like easy money for the chef. He'd read somewhere that in Japan there were restaurants where you could eat sushi off the naked bodies of women. He could think of much better things to do with naked women.

He was looking forward to doing those things with Jessie Sheldon.

Too bad Jessie was going to be busy tonight. But it didn't matter. Dee Burchmore was making her speech at the Martlets lunch tomorrow. She would be wearing her blue satin Manolo Blahniks with the diamanté buckles. He knew where she was going to park and the place was perfect. He was going to enjoy her.

Meantime, Jessie Sheldon would be keeping in touch. She had 322 followers on Twitter. It was so thoughtful of her to let him know all her movements.

72

Back in his office after the morning briefing, Roy Grace was deep in thought. Was it possible that a serving police officer could be the Shoe Man?

There had been bad apples in the Sussex Police, as in all other forces around the country in the past, at some time or other. Murderers, rapists, thieves, porn merchants, drug dealers and fraudsters hiding behind one of the ultimate façades of respectability and trust. It was rare, but with a team of over 5,000 people in Sussex alone, it could never be ruled out.

And it fitted. The inside information that had been fed to the press on the Shoe Man back in 1997, and now on the current investigation, could have been supplied by anyone with the access codes to the Sussex Police computer network. Cassian Pewe had access to them back in October last year. Who knew what he could have copied or taken then?

He dialled the central internal number for the London Metropolitan Police, his thoughts on what he planned to say crystal clear.

After two minutes of being shunted around various extensions, he heard Detective Superintendent Pewe's voice, as sharp and invasive as a dentist's drill, and as charming as a pipette full of sulphuric acid.

'Roy! How good to hear from you! Need me back, do you?'

Cutting to the chase, he said, 'No, I need some information from you. When you were with us, you logged out a cold-case file from the storeroom. You are the last signature on the form. It's regarding a missing person, Rachael Ryan, who disappeared on Christmas morning, 1997. Ring a bell?'

'I looked at a lot of files in the brief time I was with you, Roy.' His voice sounded pained.

'Well, there are two pages missing from this one, Cassian. Just wondering if by any chance you had given them to anyone else? A researcher perhaps?'

'Let me think. No, absolutely not. No way! I wanted to review everything myself.'

'Did you read that particular file?'

'I honestly can't remember.'

'Try harder.'

Pewe sounded uneasy suddenly. 'What is this, Roy?'

'I'm asking you a question. Did you read that file? It's only a few months ago.'

'It rings a faint bell,' he said defensively.

'Would you have noticed if the last two pages were missing?'

'Well, yes, of course I would.'

'So they weren't missing when you read them?'

'I don't think so.'

'Do you remember what they said?'

'No – no, I don't.'

'I need you to remember what they said, because they may now be crucial to a current investigation.'

'Roy!' He sounded pained. 'Come on. Do you remember stuff you read three months ago?'

'Yes, actually, I do. I have a good memory. Isn't that what detectives are supposed to have?'

'Roy, I'm sorry. I'm really busy at the moment on a report I need to have finished by midday.'

'Would it help to refresh your memory if I had you arrested and brought you back down here?'

Grace heard a sound like the blade of a lawnmower striking a half-buried flint. 'Ha-ha! You are joking, aren't you?'

On an operation last October, Roy Grace had saved Cassian Pewe's life – at considerable risk to himself. Yet Pewe had barely thanked him. It was hard to imagine that he could ever feel more contempt for any human than he felt for this man. Grace hoped it wasn't clouding his judgement, although at this moment he didn't really care that much if it was.

'Cassian, Tony Case, our Senior Support Officer, whom you will remember from when you were with us, has informed me that since Sussex House became operational, back in 1996, all cold-case files have been kept down in a secure storeroom in the basement. Access is strictly controlled, for chain-of-evidence purposes. A digital alarm protects it and anyone entering needs access codes, which are registered. He has a log, signed by you, showing that you returned the Shoe Man's file to one of his assistants last October. No one has looked at that file subsequently, until the Cold Case Team this week. OK?'

He was greeted with silence.

'You were in Brighton during the Labour Party Conference of 1997, weren't you? On secondment from the Met when you were working for Special Branch. You then continued working in Brighton straight after that, on an inquiry into a series of armed jewellery raids in London that were linked with Brighton. You bought a flat, with a view to living here. Correct?'

'Yes. So?'

'The dates you were in this city coincide exactly with the dates that the Shoe Man committed his offences. You spent Christmas Eve, 1997, in Brighton, didn't you?'

'I can't remember without checking my diary.'

'One of my staff can verify that, Cassian. Bella Moy? Remember her?'

'Should I?'

'You tried to shag her in the back of your car at about midnight, after a boozy night out with a bunch of local officers. You drove her home, then tried to stop her getting out of your car. Remember now?'

'No.'

'Probably a good thing. She remembers it well. You're lucky she didn't press charges for sexual harassment.'

'Roy, are you trying to tell me you've never snogged a girl pissed?'

Ignoring him, Grace said, 'I want to know what you did after you left Bella outside her mother's house. Those hours between midnight and Christmas morning? I want to know what you did on Halloween, 1997. I have more dates for you. I want to know where you were a fortnight ago on New Year's Eve. Where were you last Thursday evening, 8 January? Where were you last Saturday evening, 10 January? I hope you are writing all those down, Cassian.'

'You're wasting police time, Roy!' He tried to sound good-humoured. 'Come on. Do you really expect me to be able to tell you where I was at any given moment twelve years ago? Could you tell me where you were?'

'I could, Cassian. I could tell you exactly. So tell me, this past New Year's Eve – where did you spend it?'

There was a long silence. Then Pewe said reluctantly, 'In Brighton, actually.'

'Can someone vouch for you?'

There was another long silence before Pewe said, 'I'm sorry, Roy, I'm not prepared to continue this conversation. I don't like your tone. I don't like your questions.'

'And I don't like your answers,' Grace replied.

73

Yac was tired. At 3 a.m. the city had been quiet. The second Tuesday in January and people were staying home. He'd cruised around because the man who owned the taxi got angry if he stopped too early, but he'd only had two fares since midnight – barely enough to cover the cost of the fuel. He'd been about to head home when a call had come in to take two people up to Luton Airport. He'd only got back to the boat just before 7 a.m. Exhausted, he'd fed the cat and crashed out in his berth.

Footsteps woke him. A steady *clump, clump, clump* on the deck above his head. He sat up and looked at the clock. It showed 2 p.m.

Tea! was his first thought. His second was, *Who the hell is up there?*

He never had visitors. Ever. Apart from the postman and delivery men. But he was not expecting any deliveries.

It sounded like a whole group of people up there. Was it kids? Kids had been on the boat a few times, jeering and shouting at him, before he'd chased them off.

'Go away!' he shouted at the ceiling. 'Piss off! Sod off! Screw off! Fuck off! Take a hike! Get lost, kids!' He liked using words he heard in the taxi.

Then he heard knocking. A sharp, insistent *rap, rap, rap.*

Angrily, he swung his legs out of his bunk and staggered into the saloon, padding across the wooden floor, partially covered with rugs, in his underpants and T-shirt.

Rap, rap, rap.

'Go to hell!' he shouted. 'Who are you? Didn't you hear me? What do you want? Are you deaf? Go away! I'm asleep!'

Rap, rap, rap!

He climbed up the wooden steps, into the sun lounge at the top. It had glass patio doors and a big brown sofa, and windows all around with views out on the grey afternoon across the mudflats. It was low tide.

A man in his fifties, balding, with a comb-over, wearing a shabby tweed jacket, grey flannel trousers and scuffed brown brogues, was standing outside. He held up a small black leather wallet and mouthed something at him that Yac did not understand. Behind him stood a whole group of people wearing blue jackets with POLICE written on them, and helmets with visors. One of them was lugging a big yellow cylinder that looked like a fire extinguisher.

'Go away!' Yac shouted. 'I'm sleeping!'

Then he turned and started walking back down the stairs. As he did so he heard the *rap, rap, rap* again. It was starting to annoy him. *They should not be on his boat. This was private property!*

The sound of splintering glass stopped him in his tracks just as he stepped on to the saloon floor. Anger surged inside him. That idiot. That stupid idiot had knocked too hard! Well, he would go and teach him a lesson!

But as he turned, he heard a cacophony of leather and rubber-soled footsteps.

A voice shouted out, 'POLICE! DON'T MOVE! POLICE!'

The man with the comb-over was clattering down the steps, followed by several police officers in their yellow vests. The man was still holding up the wallet. Inside it was a badge of some kind and writing.

'John Kerridge?' the man asked him.

'I'm Yac,' he replied. 'My name is Yac. I'm a taxi driver.'

'I'm Detective Sergeant Potting, Sussex CID.' The man was now holding up a sheet of paper. 'I have a warrant to search these premises.'

'You'll have to speak to the owners. I'm just looking after it for them. I have to feed the cat. I'm late doing that, because I slept in today.'

'I'd like to have a few words with you, Yac. Perhaps we can sit down somewhere?'

'Actually I have to go back to bed now, because I need my sleep. It's quite important for my night shift, you see.' Yac looked around at the police officers standing in the saloon beside him and behind him. 'I'm sorry,' he said. 'I have to speak to the owners before I allow you on this boat. You will have to wait outside. It might be difficult getting hold of them because they are in Goa.'

'Yac,' Norman Potting said, 'there's an easy way to do this and a hard way. Either you cooperate and help us, or I arrest you. Simple as that.'

Yac cocked his head. 'Simple as what?'

Potting looked at him dubiously, wondering if all the man's lights were fully switched on. 'The choice is yours. Do you want to spend tonight sleeping in your bed, or in a cell at our custody unit?'

'I have to work tonight,' he said. 'The man who owns the taxi will be very angry if I don't.'

'OK, sunshine, then you'd better cooperate.'

Yac looked at him. 'I don't think the sun is always shining.'

Potting frowned, ignoring the comment. 'Bit of a fisherman, are you?'

'I'm a taxi driver.'

Potting jerked a thumb up at the deck. 'You've got fishing lines out.'

Yac nodded.

'What do you catch here? Mostly crabs?'

'Plaice,' Yac replied. 'Flounder. Sometimes Dover soles.'

'Good fishing, is it? I'm a bit of a fisherman myself. Never fished up this far.'

'You broke my patio doors. You'd better fix those. They will be very angry with you. I'm not allowed to break anything.'

'To tell you the truth, Yashmak, I don't give a toss about your patio doors. I don't actually give much of a toss about you either, and I don't like your taste in underpants, but don't let's get personal. Either you're going to cooperate or I'm going to arrest you, then take this floating skip apart, plank by plank.'

'If you do that it will sink,' Yac said. 'You need some of the planks. Unless you're a good swimmer.'

'A comedian, are you?' Potting said.

'No, I'm a taxi driver. I do night shifts.'

Potting held his temper with some difficulty. 'I'm looking for something on this boat, Yashmak. Anything you've got here you'd like to tell me about – and show me?'

'I have my high-flush toilet chains, but they're private. You can't see those – except the ones I have in my berth. I can show you those.' Yac perked up suddenly. 'There's a really good high-flush toilet near Worthing Pier – I could take you over there and show you them if you like?'

'I'll flush you down your own sodding toilet if you don't shut it,' Potting said.

Yac stared back at him, then grinned. 'I wouldn't fit,' he said. 'The diaphragm's too small!'

'Not by the time I finished with you, it wouldn't be.'

'I – I'll bet you!'

'And I'll bet you, sunshine. I'll bet you we find something here, all right? So why don't you save us all lot of time and show us where the ladies' shoes are?'

He saw the flicker in the strange man's face and instantly he knew he had hit the mark.

'I don't have any shoes. Not ladies' shoes.'

'Are you sure?'

Yac eyeballed him for a moment, then looked down. 'I don't have any ladies' shoes.'

'That's good to hear, Yashmak. I'll get my team to verify that and then we'll be off.'

'Yes,' Yac said. 'But they can't touch my toilet chains.'

'I'll let them know that.'

Yac nodded, perspiration running down him. 'I've been collecting them a long time, you see.'

'Toilet chains?' Norman Potting said.

Yac nodded.

The Detective Sergeant stared at him for some moments. 'Tell you what, Yashmak, how about I flush you down the sodding toilet now?'

1998

74

Roy Grace hated coming to this place. He got the heebie-jeebies every time he drove in through the wrought-iron gates. The gold lettering made them seem like the entrance to some grand house, until you took a closer look at the wording: BRIGHTON AND HOVE MORTUARY.

Not even the Rod Stewart cassette playing on his car's stereo, which he'd put on to try to cheer himself up, was having any effect on his gloomy mood. There was a line of cars occupying all the spaces close to the entrance, so he had to drive to the far end and park beside the exit doors to the covered receiving bay. As if to make it even worse, the rain started coming down harder – solid, pelting stair-rods. He switched the engine off and 'Maggie May' died with it. The wipers scratched to a halt across the screen. Then he touched the door handle and hesitated.

He was really not looking forward to this. His stomach felt as though it had curdled.

Because of the heat of the burning van in the field and the difficulty of getting any fire hoses down to it, it had been midday yesterday before the vehicle had cooled enough to allow an inspection, and for it to be identified as stolen. The stench of scorched grass, burnt rubber, paint, fuel, plastic and seared human flesh had made him

437

retch several times. Some smells you never ever got used to, no matter how often you'd experienced them before. And some sights too. The van's unfortunate occupant had not been a pretty one.

Nor had Sandy's expression been when he'd arrived home, at 4 a.m. on Wednesday, to get his head down for a few hours before returning to the scene.

She had said nothing – she was in one of her silent moods. It was what she always did when she was really angry, just went silent on him, sending him to Coventry, shutting him out, sometimes for days. Not even the massive bunch of flowers he'd bought her had thawed her.

He had not been able to sleep, but it wasn't because of Sandy. She'd get over it eventually, she always did, and then it would be forgotten. All night he'd just lain in bed thinking one thought, over and over. Was the body in the van the missing Rachael Ryan?

Charred human corpses were the worst thing of all, so far as he was concerned. As a rookie PC, he'd had to help recover the remains of two children, aged five and seven, from a burnt-out house in Portslade after an arson attack; the horror had been made ten times worse because it was children. It had given him nightmares for months.

He knew what he was about to see in the mortuary would have a similar effect and would be staying with him for a long time. But he had no choice.

Already late because his SIO, Jim Doyle, had called an early briefing which had overrun, he climbed out of the car, locked it, then hurried to the front door of the mortuary, holding the collar of his mackintosh tight around his neck.

The briefing had been attended by a sergeant from

the Accident Investigation Unit, the team which forensi-
cally examined all vehicles involved in serious crashes. It
was early days with the van, the sergeant had told them,
but on first impressions the fire was extremely unlikely to
have been caused by the accident.

He rang the bell and moments later the door was
opened by the Senior Mortician herself, Elsie Sweetman,
wearing a green apron over blue surgical scrubs that were
tucked into long white wellington boots.

In her late forties, with a bob of curly hair, Elsie had
a kind face and a remarkably cheery demeanour, consid-
ering the horrific things she had to deal with on a daily –
and nightly – basis. Roy Grace always remembered she'd
been kind to him when he had nearly keeled over at the
first post-mortem he'd attended. She had led him into her
sitting room and made him a cup of tea, telling him not
to worry, that half the coppers on the force had done the
same thing.

He stepped in through the door, which was like the
front door of any suburban bungalow, into the narrow
entrance hallway, and there the similarities ended, start-
ing with the pervading reek of Jeyes Fluid and Trigene
disinfectant. Today his nostrils detected something else,
and the curdling in his stomach worsened.

In the small changing room he wrestled a green apron
over his head and tied the tapes, then put on a face
mask, tied that securely too, and slipped his feet into
a pair of short white rubber boots that were too big. He
clumped out along the corridor and turned right, pass-
ing the sealed, glassed-in room where corpses that had
died of suspected contagious diseases were examined,
then walked into the main post-mortem room, trying to
breathe in through his mouth only.

There were three stainless-steel tables on wheels, two of which were pushed to one side against a cupboard. The third was in the centre of the room, its occupant, lying on her back, surrounded by people similarly clad to himself.

Grace swallowed. The sight of her made him shiver. She didn't look human, her blackened remains like some terrible monster created by the special effects team on a horror or sci-fi movie.

Is this you, Rachael? What happened? If it is you, how did you come to be in this stolen van?

Leaning over her, with a surgical probe in one gloved hand and tweezers in the other, was the Home Office pathologist, Dr Frazer Theobald, a man Grace always thought was a dead ringer for Groucho Marx.

Theobald was flanked by a fifty-year-old retired police officer, Donald Whitely, now a Coroner's Officer, Elsie Sweetman, her assistant mortician, Arthur Trumble, a drily humorous man in his late forties, with Dickensian mutton chops, and a SOCO photographer, James Gartrell, who was intently focusing his lens on a section of the woman's left leg that had a measuring rule lying across it.

Almost all of the dead woman's hair was gone and her face was like melted black wax. It was difficult to make out her features. Grace's stomach was feeling worse. Despite breathing through his mouth, and the mask over his nose, he could not avoid the smell. The Sunday lunchtime smell of his childhood, of roast pork and burnt crackling.

It was obscene to think that, he knew. But the smell was sending confused signals to his brain and his stomach. It was making him feel increasingly queasy and he was beginning to perspire. He looked at her again, then away, breathing deeply through his mouth. He glanced at the others in the room. They were all smelling the same thing, with the same associations too; he knew that, they'd talked about this before, yet none of them seemed affected by it the way he was. Were they all so used to it?

'Here's something interesting,' the pathologist announced nonchalantly, holding up an oval object, about an inch wide, in his tweezers.

It was translucent, scorched and partially melted.

'See this, Detective Sergeant Grace?' Theobald seemed to be addressing him specifically.

Reluctantly, he moved closer to the corpse. It looked like it might be a contact lens of some kind.

'This is most curious,' the pathologist said. 'Not what I would have expected to find in someone driving a motor vehicle.'

'What is it?' Grace asked.

'An eye shield.'

'Eye shield?'

Theobald nodded. 'They're used in mortuaries. The eyes start to sink quite quickly post-mortem, so morticians pop them in between the eyelids and the globes – makes them look nicer for viewing.' He gave a wry smile. 'As I said, not what I'd expect the driver of a motor vehicle to be wearing.'

Grace frowned. 'Why might this woman have been wearing it?'

'I suppose possibly if she had a false eye, or had had some kind of reconstructive surgery, it could be there for cosmetic purposes. But not in both eyes.'

'Are you suggesting she was blind, Dr Theobald?' Arthur Trumble said, with a mischievous twinkle.

'A bit more than that, I'm afraid,' he replied. 'She

was dead quite a long time before she was put into this vehicle.'

There was a long silence.

'Are you absolutely certain?' the Coroner's Officer asked him.

'There's a small amount of lung tissue that's survived, which I'll need to take and examine in the lab, but from what I can see with my naked eye there is no sign of smoke or flame inhalation – which, to put it bluntly, means she wasn't breathing when the fire started.'

'You're saying she was dead before the accident happened?'

'Yes, I am,' he said. 'I'm certain she was.'

Trying to make sense of this in his mind, Grace asked, 'Are you able to estimate her age, Dr Theobald?'

'I would say she's quite old – late seventies, eighties. I can't be specific without tests, but certainly she's no younger than mid-fifties. I can get you a more accurate estimate in a couple of days.'

'But definitely no younger than mid-fifties?'

Theobald nodded. 'Absolutely not.'

'What about dental records?' Grace asked.

The pathologist pointed his probe at her jaw. 'I'm afraid one of the effects of intense heat is to cause the crowns to explode. There's nothing I can see remaining that would get you anywhere with dental records. I think DNA's going to be your best chance.'

Grace stared back down at the corpse again. His revulsion was fading just a fraction, as he got more accustomed to the sight of her.

If you're not Rachael Ryan, who are you? What were you doing in this van? Who put you there?

And why?

NOW

75

Roy Grace followed Tony Case down the back stone staircase into the basement of the CID headquarters. No one could accuse Sussex Police of squandering money on the decor here, he observed wryly, walking past cracked walls with chunks of plaster missing.

Then the Senior Support Officer led him along the familiar, gloomily lit corridor that felt like it was leading to a dungeon. Case stopped in front of a closed door and pointed at the digi-alarm pad on the wall, then raised his index finger.

'OK, first thing, Roy. Anyone wanting access would need the code for this – only a handful of people, such as your good self, have it – and I've given it to them personally.'

Case was a solidly built man in his mid-fifties, with close-cropped hair and tough good looks, dressed in a fawn suit, shirt and tie. A former police officer himself, he had rejoined the force as a civilian after retirement. With a small team, he ran the CID headquarters and was responsible for all the equipment here, as well as in the three other Major Crime Suites in the county. He could be an invaluable aide to those officers he respected and a total pain in the butt to those he didn't, and his judgement was usually right. Fortunately for Roy Grace, they got on well.

Tony Case then raised a second finger. 'Anyone who comes down here – workmen, cleaners, anyone like that – is escorted all the time.'

'OK, but there must be some occasions when they would be left alone – and could rummage through files.'

Case looked dubious. 'Not in a place as sensitive as this evidence store, no.'

Grace nodded. He used to know his way around here blindfolded, but the new team had rearranged the filing. Case opened the door and they went in. Wall-to-ceiling red-painted cages, all with padlocks, stretched into the distance. On the shelves behind them were red and green crates stacked with files, and sealed evidence bags.

'Anything in particular you want to see?'

'Yes, the files on the Shoe Man.' Although Grace had summary files in his office, all the actual evidence was kept securely in here.

Case walked along several yards, then stopped, selected a key from a bunch dangling from his belt and opened a padlock. Then he pulled open the cage door.

'I know this one,' he said, 'because it's currently being accessed by your team.'

Grace nodded. 'Do you remember Detective Superintendent Cassian Pewe, who was here last autumn?'

Case gave him a bemused look. 'Yeah, don't think I'll forget him in a hurry. Treated me like his personal lackey. Tried to get me hanging pictures in his office for him. Nothing bad happened to him, I hope. Like he didn't fall off another cliff and this time didn't have you around to save him.'

Grace grinned. Saving Pewe's life had turned out to be the least popular thing he'd ever done.

'Unfortunately not.'

'Can't understand why you didn't get a bravery medal for what you did, Roy.'

'I can.' Grace smiled. 'I'd only have got it if I'd let him fall.'

'Don't worry. He's a shit. Know what they say about shit?'

'No.'

'Shit always falls, eventually, from its own weight.'

76

Wednesday 14 January

Thirty minutes later, Grace sat down in front of ACC Peter Rigg's vast desk at Malling House, the Sussex Police headquarters. It was 4 p.m.

'So, Roy, you wanted to see me. Do you have some good news on the Shoe Man?'

'Possibly, sir.' Grace gave him a general update and told him he hoped to have more for him after the evening briefing at 6.30 p.m. Then he went on: 'I have a rather delicate situation that I want to run by you.'

'Go ahead.'

Grace gave him the background on Cassian Pewe and what had happened during the brief time he had been with Sussex CID. Then he went on to outline his current concerns about the man.

Rigg listened intently, making occasional notes. When Grace had finished he said, 'So, let me get this clear. Detective Superintendent Pewe was in the right places to be a potential suspect during the Shoe Man's original attacks back in 1997?'

'It would appear so, sir.'

'And again, during these past two weeks, his movements might fit with the current attacks?'

'I've asked him to account for his whereabouts at the times of these three recent attacks, yes, sir.'

'And you think Detective Superintendent Pewe could be the person who took the pages from the file that could contain crucial evidence?'

'Pewe was one of only a handful of people with access to that file.'

'Could he be responsible for these past and present leaks to the press, in your view?'.

'It's quite possible,' Grace said.

'Why? What's in it for him to do that?'

'To embarrass us? Perhaps me in particular?'

'But why?'

'I can see it quite clearly now, sir. If he could make me look incompetent by undermining me in various ways, he might get me transferred out of CID HQ – and safely away from the cold-case files which could incriminate him.'

'Is that just theory, or do you have anything concrete?'

'At the moment it's just theory. But it fits.' He shrugged. 'I just hope I'm not letting the past history cloud my judgement.'

The ACC looked at him. He had a wise face. Then he gave Roy a kindly smile. 'You mustn't let this get personal, you know.'

'I want to avoid that at all costs, sir.'

'I know your experiences with him were less than satisfactory – and that you put yourself at enormous personal risk in saving him, which has been noted – but he is a very widely respected officer. It's never good to make enemies. Know that old proverb?'

Grace thought he seemed to he hearing rather a lot of expressions this afternoon. 'No?'

'One thousand friends are too few; one enemy is too many.'

Grace smiled. 'So I should let it drop with Pewe, even if I suspect he may be our man?'

'No, not at all. I want to start our working relationship on a footing of mutual trust. If you genuinely think he might be our offender, then you should arrest him and I'll stand by you. But this is a politically sensitive issue and it won't be too clever if we screw up.'

'You mean if *I* screw up?'

Rigg smiled. 'You'll be including myself and the Chief Constable in the screw-up, by association. That's all I'm saying. Make very sure of your facts. There'll be an awful lot of egg on our faces if you're wrong.'

'But even more if I'm right and another woman is attacked and we did nothing.'

'Just make sure your evidence against him is as watertight as your logic.'

77

Roy Grace's rapidly expanding team on *Operation Sword-fish* was now too big to fit comfortably into MIR-1, so he held the 6.30 p.m. briefing in the Conference Room in the Major Incident Suite.

The room could hold twenty-five people seated on the red chairs around the open-centred rectangular table and another thirty standing. One of its uses was for Major Crime briefings for press conferences, and it was to provide a visual backdrop for these that there stood, at the far end opposite the video screen, a concave, two-tone blue board, six feet high and ten feet wide, boldly carrying the Sussex Police website address and the *Crimestoppers* legend and phone number.

The Detective Superintendent sat with his back to this, facing the door, as his team filed in, half of them on their phones. One of the last to enter was Norman Potting, who strutted in, looking very pleased with himself.

At 6.30 sharp, Roy Grace opened the meeting by announcing, 'Team, before I start on the agenda, DS Potting has some news for us.' He gestured to him to begin.

Potting coughed, then said, 'I'm pleased to report I've arrested a suspect.'

'Brilliant!' Michael Foreman said.

PETER JAMES

'He's in custody now while we continue a search of his home, a houseboat moored on the Adur at Shoreham Beach.'

'Who is he, Norman?' Nick Nicholl asked.

'John Kerridge, the man I mentioned at this morning's briefing. A local taxi driver. Calls himself by a nickname, Yac. We conducted a search of his premises and discovered a cache of eighty-seven pairs of ladies' high-heeled shoes concealed in bags in the bilges.'

'Eighty-seven pairs?' Emma-Jane Boutwood said, astonished.

'There may be more. The search is continuing,' he said. 'I suspect we're going to find the ones taken from our first two victims – and past ones.'

'You don't have those yet?' Nick Nicholl asked.

'No, but we'll find 'em. He's got a whole stack of current newspaper cuttings about the Shoe Man that we've seized, as well as a wodge of printouts from the Internet on the Shoe Man back in 1997.'

'He lives alone?' Bella Moy asked.

'Yes.'

'Any wife? Separated? Girlfriend, or boyfriend?'

'Doesn't sound like it.'

'What reason did he give for having these cuttings – and the shoes?' she asked.

'He didn't. When I asked him that question he went into a sulk and refused to speak. We also found a large number of toilet chains concealed, as well as the shoes, which he got extremely agitated about.'

Branson frowned, then made a flushing movement with his arm. 'Toilet chains? You mean as in *bog* chains, right?'

Potting nodded.

'Why?' Branson continued.

Potting looked around, a little hesitantly, and then stared at Roy Grace. 'Dunno if it's politically correct to say it – um – chief.'

'The suspense is killing us,' Grace replied, with good humour.

Potting tapped the side of his head. 'He's not got all his lights on.'

There was a titter of laughter. Potting smiled proudly. Grace watched him, glad for this man to have shown his value to the team. But at the same time, he was thinking hard about Pewe, privately concerned that while this current suspect under arrest ticked a lot of boxes, he left one big unanswered question.

He turned his attention back to DS Potting's prisoner in custody. Great they had an arrest, and here was a story the *Argus* would lead with in the morning. But he was experienced enough to know there was a big gap between arresting a suspect and establishing he was the offender.

'How is he reacting, Norman?' he asked.

'He's angry, chief,' Potting said. 'And we could have a problem. His brief's Ken Acott.'

'Shit,' Nick Nicholl said.

There were a number of Legal Aid solicitors available to suspects, and their abilities and attitudes varied widely. Ken Acott was the smartest of all of them, and the bane of any arresting officer's life.

'What's he saying?' Grace asked.

'He's requesting a medical examination of his client before he speaks any further to us,' the Detective Sergeant replied. 'I'm arranging that. Meantime I'm holding Kerridge in custody overnight. Hopefully the search team will find further evidence.'

'Perhaps we'll get a DNA match,' DC Foreman said.

'So far the Shoe Man has shown himself very forensi-cally aware,' Grace said. 'It's one of the big problems that we've never obtained anything from him. Not one damned hair or fibre.' He looked at his notes. 'OK, excel-lent work, Norman. Let's move on for a moment. Glenn, you have something to report on another possible suspect.'

'Yes, boss. I'm pleased to say we've identified the driver of the Mercedes E Class saloon. The one that was seen driving at speed away from the Pearces' house in Droveway Avenue around the time of the attack on Mrs Roxanna Pearce, and we've now interviewed him. It explains the romantic dinner for two she was preparing, but it's not helpful news, I'm afraid.' Branson shrugged, then went on. 'His name's Iannis Stephanos, a local restaurateur. He owns Timon's down in Preston Street, and Thessalonica.'

'I know that!' DC Foreman said. 'Took my wife there for our anniversary last week!'

'Yeah, well, me and E-J went and spoke to Stephanos this afternoon. He admitted with some embarrassment that he and Mrs Pearce were having an affair. She's subsequently confirmed this. She'd invited him over because her husband was away on a business trip – which we know to be the case. He'd gone to the house but not been able to gain access. He said he'd hung around outside, ringing the doorbell and phoning. He was sure she was in because he'd seen shadows move behind the curtains. In the end, he wasn't sure what she was playing at – then had a sudden fit of panic that perhaps the husband had returned home early, which was why he left at speed.'

'Do you believe him?' Grace looked first at him, then at Emma-Jane Boutwood.

Both of them nodded.

'Doesn't make any sense that he should have raped her if he'd been invited over.'

'Can you be sure she didn't cry *rape* because her husband returned and she felt guilty?' Michael Foreman asked.

'Her husband didn't return until we contacted him the next day,' Branson replied.

'Does he know about the affair?' Grace asked Glenn.

'I've tried to be discreet,' he said. 'I think we'd best keep that to ourselves, for the moment.'

'I've had Mr Pearce on the phone several times, asking about our progress,' Grace said. He looked at the SOLO, Claire Westmore. 'Are you happy for us to try to keep it quiet?'

'I don't see any value in making things worse than they already are for Mrs Pearce, at this stage, sir,' she replied.

*

After the meeting, Grace asked DC Foreman to come to his office, and there he briefed him, in confidence, about his suspicions concerning Detective Superintendent Pewe.

Foreman had not been around during the time Cassian Pewe was with Sussex CID, so no one would be able to accuse him of being biased against the man. He was the perfect choice.

'Michael, I want you to check all Detective Super-intendent Cassian Pewe's alibis back in 1997 and now. I have concerns about him, because so much fits. But if we arrest him, it has to be on watertight evidence. We don't have that yet. See what you can come up with. And remember, you're going to be dealing with a very devious and manipulative person.'

'I'm sure I'm his match, boss.'

Grace smiled. 'That's why I've chosen you.'

1998

78

The lab tests confirmed the age of the woman who had been partially incinerated in the van as being between eighty and eighty-five.

Whoever she was – or rather had been – she was not the missing Rachael Ryan. Which now left Detective Sergeant Roy Grace with a second problem. Who was she, who had put her in the van, and why?

Three big unticked boxes.

So far no undertakers had reported a missing body, but Grace could not get the image of the woman out of his mind. During the past couple of days some of her details had been filled in for him. She was five feet, four inches tall. White. Lab tests carried out by Dr Frazer Theobald on her lung tissue and on the small amount of flesh intact on her back confirmed that she had been dead for some considerable time before the van caught fire – several days before. She had died from cancer secondaries.

But, it seemed, the county of Sussex was knee deep in little old ladies who were terminally ill. Some of its towns, like Worthing, Eastbourne and Bexhill, with their high elderly populations, were jokily known as God's waiting rooms. To contact every undertaker and every mortuary was a massive task. Because of the pathologist's findings, the case was regarded as bizarre rather than as a major crime, so resources allocated to it were limited. It was virtually down to Roy Grace alone.

She had been someone's child, he thought. Someone's daughter. She'd had children herself, so she had been someone's wife or lover. Someone's mother. Probably someone's grandmother. Probably a caring, loving, decent person.

So how come her last journey had been buckled into the driver's seat of a stolen van?

Was it a sick prank by a bunch of youths?

But if so, where had they taken her from? If an undertaker's premises had been broken into and a corpse stolen, surely it would have been reported as a matter of urgency? But there was nothing on the serials. He'd checked them all, for three weeks back.

It just did not make sense.

He expanded his enquiries to undertakers and mortuaries beyond Sussex and into all the bordering counties, without success. The woman must have had family. Perhaps they were all dead, but he hoped not. The thought made him sad. It also saddened him to think that no undertaker had noticed her absence.

The indignity of what had happened to her made matters worse too.

If she wasn't the helpless victim in some sick prank, was there something he was missing?

He replayed the scenario over and over in his mind. For what possible reason would someone steal a van and then put a dead old lady into it?

How stupid would you have to be not to know there were tests that would prove the old woman had not been driving, and that her age would be worked out?

A prank was the most likely. But where had they got the body from? Every day he was broadening his search of undertakers and mortuaries. There had to be one, somewhere in this country, that had a body that was missing. Surely?

It was a mystery that was to remain with him for the next twelve years.

NOW

79

Norman Potting sat on the green chair in the interview room in the Custody Suite adjoining the CID head-quarters. There was a window, high up, a CCTV camera and a microphone. The heavy green door, with its small viewing window, was closed and locked.

Opposite the DS, across a small table the colour of granite, sat John Kerridge, dressed in a regulation-issue, ill-fitting blue paper jump suit and plimsolls. Beside him sat a Legal Aid solicitor who had been allocated to him, Ken Acott.

Unlike many of his duty solicitor colleagues, who tended not to fuss too much about their clothing as they weren't needing to impress their clients, Acott, who was forty-four, was always impeccably dressed. Today he wore a well-cut navy suit, with a freshly laundered white shirt and a sharp tie. With his short, dark hair and genial good looks, he reminded many people of the actor Dustin Hoffman, and he had plenty of the theatrical about him, whether protesting his client's rights in an interview room or addressing the bench in a courtroom. Of all the criminal practice solicitors in the city, Ken Acott was the one that arresting officers disliked coming up against the most.

Kerridge seemed to be having problems sitting still. A

man of about forty, with short hair brushed forward, he was squirming, writhing, as if attempting to free himself from imaginary bonds, and repeatedly looking at his watch.

'They haven't brought my tea,' he said anxiously.

'It's on its way,' Potting assured him.

'Yes, but it's ten past,' Yac said nervously.

On the table sat a tape recorder with slots for three cassettes, one for the police, one for the defence and one file copy. Potting inserted a cassette into each slot. He was about to press the Play button when the solicitor spoke.

'DS Potting, before you waste too much of my client's time, and my own, I think you should take a look at these, which were recovered from my client's home on the *Tom Newbound* houseboat during the night.'

He pushed a large brown envelope across the table to the Detective Sergeant.

Hesitantly, Potting opened it and pulled out the contents.

'Take your time,' Acott said with an assurance that made Potting feel uneasy.

The first item was an A4 printout, which he stared at. It was a receipt from an eBay transaction for a pair of Gucci high-heeled shoes.

During the next twenty minutes, Norman Potting read, with increasing gloom, the receipts from second-hand clothes shops and eBay auctions for eighty-three of the eighty-seven pairs of shoes they had seized from the houseboat.

'Can your client account for the last four pairs?' Potting asked, sensing he was clutching at straws.

'I am told that they were left in his taxi,' Ken Acott

said. 'But as none of these, or any of the others, fit the descriptions of the ones in the recent series of attacks, I would respectfully ask that my client be released from custody immediately, so he does not suffer further loss of earnings.'

Potting insisted on proceeding with the interview. But Acott made his client reply *No comment* to every question. After an hour and a half, Potting left to speak to Roy Grace. Then he returned and conceded defeat.

'I'll accept bailing him 47(3), to come back in two months while our enquiries are continuing,' Potting suggested as a compromise.

'He also wants his property returned to him,' Ken Acott said. 'Any reason why he shouldn't have back the shoes and newspaper cuttings that were seized, his computer and his mobile phone?'

Despite a tantrum from Kerridge, Potting insisted on retaining the shoes and the cuttings. The phone and the laptop were not a problem, as the High-Tech Crime Unit had extracted all they needed from the phone, and they had cloned the hard drive of the computer, which they would continue to analyse.

Acott gave in on the shoes and cuttings, and twenty minutes later Yac was released. The solicitor drove him home with his computer and phone.

80

It was a rush to get here and he had misjudged how heavy the seafront traffic would be. Unless he was imagining it, there seemed to be more police out than usual.

He drove into the car park behind the Grand Hotel shortly after 3 p.m., worried she might have already left. In her new blue satin Manolos. Then, to his relief, he saw her black VW Touareg.

It was in such a good place for his purposes. She could not have picked a better bay. Bless. It was one of the few areas on this level that was out of sight of any of the CCTV cameras in here.

Even better, the space beside her was empty.

And he had her car keys in his pocket. The spare set that he had found where he hoped he would, in a drawer in her hall table.

Reversing the van in, he left enough space behind him to be able to open the rear doors. Then he hurriedly climbed out to check, aware he did not have much time, then looked around carefully. The car park was deserted.

Dee Burchmore would be coming soon from her ladies' luncheon, because she had to get home – she was hosting a meeting of the West Pier Trust there at 4 p.m. Then she was due back into the city centre for drinks in the Mayor's Parlour at Brighton Town Hall at 7 p.m., where she was attending a *Crimestoppers* fund-raising event at the Police Museum. She was a model citizen, supporting lots of different causes in Brighton. And its shops.

And she was such a good girl, posting all her schedules up on Facebook.

He hoped she had not changed her mind and that she was wearing those blue satin Manolo Blahniks with the diamanté buckles. Women had a habit of changing their minds, which was one of the many things he did not like about them. He'd be very angry if she had different shoes on and would have to teach her a lesson about not disappointing people.

Of course, he would punish her even more if she *was* wearing them.

He pressed the door unlock button on the key fob. The indicators flashed and there was a quiet *clunk*. Then the interior light came on.

He pulled the solid-feeling driver's door open and climbed in, noticing the rich smell of the car's leather upholstery and traces of her perfume, Armani Code.

Glancing through the windscreen to ensure that all was clear, he checked the buttons for the interior lights, until he found the one that kept them switched off, and pressed it.

All set.

So much to think about. In particular all those CCTV cameras everywhere. It wasn't enough just to put fake number plates on the van. Many police cars drove around with onboard ANPR. These could read a number plate and in a split second get all the details of the vehicle from the licensing department in Swansea. If the registration did not match the vehicle, they would know instantly. So the registration plates he had on this van were a copy of those on an identical van to this – one he'd seen parked in a street in Shoreham.

Just to make sure that the van in Shoreham didn't go anywhere for a day or two, in case by chance they should both be spotted by the same police patrol, he'd emptied a couple of bags of sugar into its petrol tank. He liked to think he had covered every eventuality. That was how you stayed free. Always cover your tracks. Always have an explanation for everything.

He climbed across on to the back seat, then pulled the black hood over his head, adjusting it until the slits were aligned with his eyes and mouth. Then he squeezed himself down on to the floor, between the front and rear seats, out of sight to anyone peering in the window – not that they would see much through the tinted privacy glass anyway. He took a deep breath and pressed the button on the key fob to lock the doors.

Soon now.

81

Thursday 15 January

Dee Burchmore had a golden rule, never to drink before she gave a talk. But afterwards, boy, did she need one! It didn't matter how many times she had done it before, standing up and speaking in public always made her nervous; and today for some reason, she didn't know why – perhaps because this was a particularly big and prestigious event – she had been even more nervous than usual giving her fund-raising speech for the Martlets hospice.

So afterwards, although she had been anxious to get home in good time to greet her guests for her 4 p.m. meeting, she'd stayed chatting to friends. Before she knew it, she'd drunk three large glasses of Sauvignon Blanc. Not smart, as she'd barely eaten one mouthful of her food.

Now, entering the car park, she felt decidedly unsteady on her legs and was having trouble focusing. She should leave the car, she realized, and take a taxi, or walk – it wasn't that far. But it had just started to rain and she did not want to get her brand-new Manolos sodden.

Even so, it was not a good idea to drive. Quite apart from the danger, she was thinking about the embarrassment it would cause to her husband if she was stopped for it. She stepped up to the pay machine, then fumbled in her bag for the ticket. As she pulled it out, it fell from her fingers.

Cursing, she knelt down, then had problems picking it up.

I'm smashed!

She tried to remember if she had an umbrella in the car. She was sure she did. And of course her flat driving shoes were in there too! Brilliant! She would put them on and walk home – and that would be the best way to sober up.

She put the ticket back in her bag, then staggered on up to Level 2.

82

He heard the echoing *clack-clack-clack* of her heels on the concrete floor. Getting closer. Walking fast.

He liked the sound of heels getting closer. He'd always liked that sound. So much better than the sound of them receding into the distance. Yet, at the same time, they had frightened him as a child. The sound of heels fading meant his mother was going out. The sound getting louder meant she was returning.

Which meant she was probably going to punish him. Or make him do things to her.

His heart thudded. He could feel the adrenalin rush, like the hit of a drug. He held his breath. She was coming nearer.

This had to be her. *Please be wearing the blue satin Manolos.*

CLUNK.

The noise startled him. It was like five simultaneous gunshots all around him, as all five door locks of the car released together. He nearly cried out.

Then another sound.

Clack-clack-clack.

Footsteps walking to the rear of the car. Followed by the hiss of the gas struts of the tailgate rising. What was she putting in there? Shopping? More shoes?

473

Almost silently, with a practised hand, he popped off the lid of the plastic travelling soap dish in his pocket and eased the chloroform pad out with his gloved hand. Then braced himself. In a moment she would get into the car, close the door and put her seat belt on. That was the moment he would strike.

To his total surprise, instead of the driver's door, she pulled the rear door open. He stared up at her startled face. Then she backed away in shock as she saw him.

An instant later, she screamed.

He levered himself up, made a lunge at her face with the pad, but misjudged the height of the car above the ground, stumbled and fell on his face. As he scrambled to his feet, she stepped back, screaming again, then again, then turned, running, screaming, her shoes *clack-clack-clacking*.

Shit, shit, shit, shit, shit.

He watched her, crouched in the space between the Touareg and his van for some moments, debating whether to run after her. She would be in full view of the cameras now. Someone was going to hear her screams.

Shit, shit, shit, shit, shit.

He was trying to think clearly but he couldn't. His brain was a muzz of stuff.

Got to get out, away from here.

He ran around the rear of the van, climbed in through the doors and pulled them shut, then stumbled forward, climbed over the seat-back, eased himself behind the steering wheel and started the engine. Then he shot forward out of the bay and turned left, accelerating hard, following the arrows to the down ramp and the exit.

As he turned left, he saw her halfway down the ramp, stumbling on her heels, waving her arms hysterically. All he needed to do was to accelerate and he'd wipe her out. The idea flashed through his mind. But that would bring more complications than it would solve.

She turned at the sound of his engine and waved her arms even more frantically.

'Help me! Please help me!' she screamed, stepping into his path.

He had to brake sharply to avoid hitting her.

Then, as she peered through the windscreen, her eyes widened in terror.

It was his hood, he realized. He'd forgotten he still had it on.

She backed away almost in slow motion, then turned and ran, as fast as she could again, tripping, stumbling, screaming, her shoes falling off, first the left one, then the right one.

Suddenly a fire exit door to his right opened and a uniformed police officer came running out.

He floored the accelerator, screeching the van around and down the next ramp, then raced towards the twin exit barriers.

And suddenly realized he hadn't paid his ticket.

There was no one in the booth, but in any case he didn't have time. He kept on accelerating, bracing himself for the impact. But there was no impact. The barrier flew off as if it was made of cardboard and he sped on, up into the street, and kept going, dog-legging left, then right around the rear of the hotel, until he reached the traffic lights at the seafront.

Then he remembered his hood. Hastily he tugged it off and shoved it in his pocket. Someone behind him hooted angrily. The light had turned green.

'OK, OK, OK!'

He accelerated and stalled the van. The vehicle behind hooted again.

'Fuck you!'

He started the van, jerked forward, turned right and headed west along the seafront towards Hove. He was breathing in short, sharp gulps. Disaster. This was a disaster. Had to get away from here as quickly as he could. Had to get the van off the road.

The traffic lights ahead were turning red. The drizzle had transformed his windscreen to frosted glass. For an instant he debated whether to run the lights, but a long, articulated lorry had already started moving across. He halted, nervously pounding the steering wheel with the palms of his hand, then flicked on the wipers to clear the screen.

The lorry was taking forever to move across. It was towing a bloody trailer!

Out of the corner of his eye he saw something. Someone to his right was waving at him. He turned his head and his blood froze.

It was a police car.

He was boxed in. That damned lorry towing the trailer belonged to a circus or something and was moving at the speed of a snail. Another great big artic was right behind him.

Should he get out and run?

The officer in the passenger seat continued waving at him, and pointing, with a smile. The officer pointed at his own shoulder, then at him, then back at his own shoulder again.

He frowned. What the hell was his game?

Then he realized.

The officer was telling him to put on his seat belt!

He waved back and pulled it on quickly. *Clunk-click.*

The officer gave him a thumbs-up. He returned it. All smiles.

Finally, the lorry was gone and the lights turned green. He drove on steadily, keeping strictly to the limit, until, to his relief, the police car turned off into a side street. Then he upped his speed, as fast as he dared.

One mile to go. One mile and he would be safe.

But that bitch would not be.

83

Glenn Branson's driving had always reduced Roy Grace to a state of silent terror, but even more so since he had got his green pursuit ticket. He just hoped never to have the misfortune to be in a car when his colleague used it in earnest.

But this Thursday afternoon, as the Detective Sergeant bullied the unmarked silver Ford Focus through the Brighton rush-hour traffic, Grace was silent for a different reason. He was immersed in thought. He didn't even react as he saw the old lady step out from behind the bus and hastily jump back as they drove past well over the speed limit.

'It's OK, old-timer, I saw her!' Glenn said.

Grace did not reply. Norman Potting's suspect had been released at midday, and now this afternoon, in exactly the place the profiler, Dr Julius Proudfoot, had predicted, an attempted attack had taken place.

Of course, it might not be connected to the Shoe Man, but from the limited amount he had heard so far, it had all the hallmarks. Just how good was it going to look if the man they had released was the man who had now done this?

Glenn switched on the blues and twos to help them through the snarled-up traffic at the roundabout in front of the Pier, reaching to the panel and altering the tones of the sirens every few seconds. Half the drivers in the city were either too dim-witted to be behind a steering wheel, or deaf, or blind – and some were all three, Grace thought. They passed the Old Ship Hotel, then staying on King's Road, Glenn took the traffic island at the junction with West Street on the wrong side, swerving almost suicidally across the path of an oncoming lorry.

Probably not a good idea to be driven by someone whose marriage was on the rocks and didn't think he had anything to live for any more, Grace thought suddenly. But fortunately they were approaching their destination. The odds on stepping out of the car intact, rather than being cut out of it by a fire engine rescue crew, were improving.

Moments later they turned up the road beside the Grand Hotel and stopped as they reached what looked like a full-scale siege. There were too many police cars and vans clustered around the entrance to the car park behind it to count, all with their blue-light spinners rotating.

Grace was out of the car almost before the wheels had stopped. A cluster of uniformed officers, some in high-visibility jackets and some in stab vests stood around, in front of a blue-and-white chequered crime scene tape, along with several onlookers.

The only person who seemed to be missing was reporter Kevin Spinella from the *Argus*.

One of the officers, the Duty Inspector, Roy Apps, was waiting for him.

'Second floor, chief. I'll take you up there.'

With Glenn Branson, on his phone, striding behind, they ducked under the tape and hurried into the car park.

It smelt of engine oil and dry dust. Apps updated him as they walked.

'We're lucky,' he said. 'A particularly bright young PC, Alec Davies, who was in the car park's CCTV room with the attendant, thought there might be more to this and got it all sealed off before we arrived.'

'Have you found anything?'

'Yes. Something that may be interesting. I'll show you.'

'What about the van?'

'The CCTV room at Brighton nick picked it up travelling west along Kingsway towards Hove. The last sighting was of it turning right up Queen Victoria Avenue. We dispatched all available patrols and a Road Policing Unit car to try to intercept, but so far no contact.'

'We have the index?'

'Yes. It's registered to a decorator who lives in Moulsecoomb. I've got a unit watching his house. I've also got RPU cars covering all exits from the city in the direction he was travelling, and we've got Hotel 900 up.'

Hotel 900 was the police helicopter.

They reached the second level, which was sealed off by a second crime scene tape. A tall, young uniformed constable stood in front of it with a clipboard.

'This is the lad,' Roy Apps said.

'PC Davies?' Grace said.

'Yes, sir.'

'Good work.'

'Thank you, sir.'

'Can you show me the vehicle?'

The PC looked hesitant. 'SOCO are on their way here, sir.'

'This is Detective Superintendent Grace. He's the SIO on *Operation Swordfish*,' Apps reassured him.

'Ah. OK, right. Sorry, sir. This way.'

They ducked under the tape and Grace followed him across to a row of empty parking bays, at the end of which was a shiny black Volkswagen Touareg with its rear door open.

PC Davies put out a cautionary hand as they approached, then pointed at an object on the ground, just beneath the doorsill. It looked like a wad of cotton wool. Pulling out his torch, the constable directed the beam on to it.

'What is it?' Grace asked.

'It's got a strange smell, sir,' the Constable said. 'Being so close to the scene of the attack, I thought it might have some relevance, so I didn't touch it, in case it's got fingerprints or DNA on it.'

Grace looked at the serious face of the young man and smiled. 'You've got the makings of a good detective, son.'

'That's what I'd like to do, sir, after my two years in uniform.'

'Don't wait until then. If you've done twelve months, I might be able to fast-track you into CID.'

The PC's eyes lit up. 'Thank you, sir. Thank you very much!'

Roy Grace knelt down and put his nose close to the wad. It gave off a smell that was both sweet and astringent at the same time. And almost instantly he became very slightly dizzy. He stood up and felt a little unsteady for some seconds. He was pretty sure he knew that smell, from a course in toxicology he had attended some years back.

The reports from Nicola Taylor and Roxy Pearce were remarkably similar. They tallied with statements from some of the victims of the Shoe Man in 1997. It was the same smell they had described when something had been pressed against each of their faces.

Chloroform.

84

You don't know who I am or where I am, do you, Detective Superintendent Roy Grace? Not a clue! One arrest. Then you had to let him go for lack of evidence. You're panicking.

And I'm not.

Bit of a screw-up this afternoon, I've got to admit that. But I've recovered from far worse. I've been off the radar for twelve years and now I'm back. I might go again, but rest assured, hasta la vista, *baby! I'll be right back! Maybe next week, maybe next month, or next year, or next decade! When I do come back, you'll be very sorry you said that small dick thing about me.*

But I'm not gone just yet. I don't want to leave with unfinished business.

I don't want to leave without giving you something to really panic about. Something that's going to make you look stupid to your new ACC boss. What's that word you used in the Argus *this evening? Hunting! You said that the Shoe Man is hunting.*

Well, you're right, I am! I'm hunting! Stalking!

I didn't get her at the Withdean Sports Stadium, but I'll get her tomorrow night.

I know her movements.

85

Roy Grace was not often in a bad mood, but at this Friday morning briefing he was in a truly vile one, not helped by having had a virtually sleepless night. He'd stayed in MIR-1 with some of his team until past 1 a.m., going through everything they had on the Shoe Man past and present. Then he'd gone to Cleo's house, but she had been called out within minutes of his arrival to recover a body found in a churchyard.

He'd sat up for an hour, drinking whisky and smoking one cigarette after another, thinking, thinking, thinking about what he might be missing, while Humphrey snored loudly beside him. Then he re-read a lengthy report he'd brought home, from the High-Tech Crime Unit. Their Covert Internet Investigator had come up with a whole raft of foot- and shoe-fetish websites, chat-room forums and social-networking presences. There were hundreds of them. In the past six days he'd only managed to cover a small percentage of the total. So far with nothing conclusive.

Grace put down the report with some astonishment, deciding that perhaps he'd led too sheltered a life, but not sure he would want to share any fetish he developed with a bunch of total strangers. Then he'd gone to bed and tried to sleep. But his brain was on warp drive. Cleo had come back at about 4.30 a.m., showered, then climbed into bed and fallen asleep. It always amazed him how she could deal with any kind of corpse, no matter how horrific the condition or the circumstances of the death, then come home and fall asleep in moments. Perhaps it was her ability to switch off that enabled her to cope with the stuff her job entailed.

After lying restlessly for another half-hour, totally wired, he decided to get up and go for a run down to the seafront, to try to clear his head and freshen himself up for the day ahead.

And now, at 8.30 a.m., he had a blinding headache and was shaky from a caffeine overdose; but that did not stop him from cradling yet another mug of strong black instant as he sat in the packed briefing room, his inquiry team now extended to over fifty officers and support staff.

A copy of the morning's *Argus* lay in front of him, next to a pile of documents, on the top of which was one from the Crime Policy and Review Branch. It was their '7-Day Review' of *Operation Swordfish*, which had just come in, somewhat delayed.

The *Argus* featured a photograph of a white Ford Transit on the front page, with the caption: *Similar to the one used by the suspect.*

Inset separately, and with good dramatic effect, the paper reproduced the cloned registration plate, with a request for anyone who saw this vehicle between 2 p.m. and 5 p.m. yesterday to phone the Police Incident Room or *Crimestoppers*, urgently.

The owner of the van whose registration had been cloned was not a happy bunny. He was a decorator who had been unable to leave the site where he was working to buy some materials he urgently needed because the van would not start. But at least he had the perfect alibi. From 2 p.m. to 5 p.m. yesterday, he had been at the roadside, accompanied by an RAC patrolman who had drained his van's petrol tank, and cleaned out the carburettor. In the patrolman's view, someone had very kindly emptied a bag of sugar into the tank.

Was this another of the Shoe Man's touches, Grace wondered?

The only good news so far today was that the '7-Day Review' was at least positive. It agreed with all he had done in the running of this case – at least in its first seven days. But now they were another nine days on. The next review would be at twenty-eight days. Hopefully the Shoe Man would be getting a taste of prison-issue footwear long before then.

He sipped some more coffee, then, because of the large number of people in the room for the briefing, he stood up to address them.

'So,' he said, skipping his normal introduction, 'how sodding great is this? We release our suspect at midday and in the afternoon the next offence happens. I'm not very happy about it. What's going on? Is this John Kerridge – Yac – character having a laugh on us? The bloody *Argus* certainly is!'

He held the paper aloft. The front page splash read:

SHOE MAN FOURTH VICTIM'S LUCKY ESCAPE?

There was little doubt in anyone's mind that the man who had been waiting in Dee Burchmore's car yesterday was the Shoe Man. The location and the confirmation from an emergency analysis by the path lab that the substance on the cotton wool was chloroform both pointed to it. The car was now in the SOCO workshop, where it would remain for several days, being examined for clothing fibres, hairs, skin cells or any other telltale sign the offender might have left behind, however microscopic.

The timeline, established by Norman Potting, cleared John Kerridge from involvement. The taxi driver's solicitor, Ken Acott, had driven him home to his houseboat. A neighbour had confirmed his alibi, that he was on the boat until 5.30 p.m. yesterday, when he had left to start his evening driving shift.

But there was something else, something personal, that was helping to fuel Roy Grace's mood. DC Michael Foreman had reported back that Pewe was being completely unhelpful. So far he had made no progress at all with the Detective Superintendent.

The temptation to arrest Pewe was so strong. But the words of his new ACC were even stronger.

'You mustn't let this get personal, you know.'

He had to admit to himself that to arrest Pewe now, on the flimsy evidence he had to date, would smack of being *personal*. And to arrest and then have to release a second suspect without charge would look like he was clutching at straws. Instead, reluctantly, he told Foreman to keep working on it.

To rub the final salt into the wound, Nick Nicholl had reported that he'd viewed CCTV footage from the Neville pub. The image was poor and he was having it enhanced, but it showed someone who *might* be Darren Spicer drinking there until past 1.30 a.m. on New Year's Day. If it did turn out to be him, that would clear the serial burglar of involvement in the attack on Nicola Taylor. However, the man had no corroboration for his alibi as to where he was at the time of the attack on Roxy

Pearce, other than restating he was at the greyhound stadium – a mere fifteen minutes' walk from her house. Nor did he have any corroboration for his alibi for last Saturday night, at the time when Mandy Thorpe was attacked on the ghost train at Brighton Pier.

That timeline was interesting to Roy Grace. She was attacked at around 7.30 p.m. – one hour before the curfew at St Patrick's night shelter, where Spicer was staying. He *could* have committed the attack and still been back at the shelter in time.

But the evidence at this moment was too circumstantial to warrant arresting the man. A smart brief like Ken Acott would rip them to shreds. They needed a lot more, and at this stage they did not have it.

'Right,' Grace said. 'I want to review all the facts that we have so far. Fact one: our Analysts have established that back in 1997 all five of the Shoe Man's known victims, as well as the sixth possible victim, Rachael Ryan, who disappeared never to be found, were known to have bought a new and expensive pair of designer shoes from shops in Brighton within seven days of being attacked.'

There were several nods of confirmation.

'Fact two: three of our four victims and potential victims, in the past sixteen days – including Mrs Dee Burchmore – have done the same. The exception is Mandy Thorpe. I'm including her for the present moment in our enquiries, although I personally suspect that her attacker was not the Shoe Man. But I won't go there right now.'

He looked at Julius Proudfoot. The forensic psychologist gave him a faintly hostile glare back.

'Fact three: the location of yesterday's attack fits

exactly the prediction made by our forensic psychologist. Julius, perhaps you'd like to come in at this juncture.'

Proudfoot puffed his chest out importantly. 'Yes, well, the thing is, you see, I think there's a lot more than we realize. We have a lot of imponderables, but we know a few important things about the Shoe Man. For a start, he's a very damaged man. I suspect that now he's very angry because he's been rebuffed. If, as I believe, we're dealing with someone damaged by his mother, he could be feeling hurt in a sort of *mummy's rejected me* way. A child would react by sulking, but an adult in quite a different way. It's my guess he's now in a very dangerous and violent frame of mind. He didn't get his way yesterday, but he's damned well going to soon.'

'With the same victim?' Michael Foreman asked.

'No, I think he'll move on to another one. He may return to this victim, Dee Burchmore, at some future point, but not immediately. I think he'll go for a softer target.'

'Do we know how Mrs Burchmore is?' Bella Moy asked.

Claire Westmore, the Sexual Offences Liaison Officer, replied, 'She's very traumatized, as you might expect. There's also an issue on how the offender got into her car – a Volkswagen Touareg with all the latest security bells and whistles. The spare keys are apparently missing.'

'In my experience, women are always losing keys,' Norman Potting said.

'Oh, and never men?' retorted Bella Moy.

'The Burchmores kept them in a drawer in their house,' Claire Westmore went on, ignoring both of them. 'Which raises the question whether the offender might have entered the house and stolen them at some point. They are both extremely distressed about this possibility.'

'*Penetrating* the victim's home!' Proudfoot announced, with a triumphant smile. 'The Shoe Man would enjoy that. It's all part of his gratification.'

'We know he's got breaking and entering skills,' Bella Moy said. 'His attack on Roxy Pearce and his previous attack in the private house in 1997 show that.'

'Darren Spicer's speciality,' Glenn Branson said. 'Right? This fits with him.'

'There's something else which might be significant,' Proudfoot said. 'In 1997 all five of the Shoe Man's attacks occurred late at night. This new spate, apart from New Year's Eve, have taken place mid-afternoon or early evening. This indicates to me the possibility that he might have married, which would explain why he stopped offending. Something is now wrong in the marriage, which is why he has started again.'

DS Bella Moy raised her hand. 'I'm sorry, I don't understand your reasoning – about why he would be attacking earlier just because he's married.'

'Because he needs to be home at night to avoid arousing suspicion,' Proudfoot replied.

'Or be back in time for evening lock-in at St Patrick's night shelter?' Bella responded.

'Possibly so, indeed,' Proudfoot conceded. 'Yes, that too.'

'So how would he have got away with it on New Year's Eve if he was married?' Michael Foreman asked. 'Has anyone checked the meter in this man Kerridge's taxi? Would that not show what he was doing at the time of the Metropole attack on Nicola Taylor?'

'I've spoken to the owner of the taxi he drives and

requested the full log since 31 December,' Potting answered. 'At this stage we just don't have enough evidence to justify impounding the taxi and having the meter analysed.'

'What do we need, in your view, Norman?' Roy Grace asked.

'The shoes of the victims, boss. Or forensic evidence linking Kerridge with them. We don't have it, not yet. Not without rearresting him. He gives the impression of being a harmless nutter who likes shoes. The brief tells me he has mental health issues. He's on the autism spectrum.'

'Does that give him some kind of exemption from prosecution for rape?' Glenn Branson asked.

'It makes the interrogation process a lot harder,' Grace said. 'We'd have to have him assessed, go through all that procedure. DS Potting's right. We don't have enough on him.' He sipped some coffee. 'Were you able to ascertain, Norman, if Kerridge has carried any of the victims in his taxi, as passengers?'

'I showed him all their photos,' he said. 'He claims not to recognize any of them.'

Grace turned to DC Nicholl. 'How soon will you have the enhancement of the CCTV images from the Neville pub?'

'Later today, I hope, sir.'

Proudfoot went on. 'I've been doing some more geographic profiling, which I think we're going to find helpful.'

He turned and pointed at a large map of the central area of the city attached to the whiteboard on the wall behind him. Five red circles were drawn on it.

'I talked you through the offender matrix of the Shoe Man back in 1997 and the current attacks. After his botched attack, the Shoe Man's first reported rape in 1997 was at the Grand Hotel. His first reported attack this year was at the Metropole Hotel – which is almost next door. His second reported attack in 1997 was in a house in Hove Park Road and his second reported attack this year was in a house in Droveway Avenue, one street north. His third attack then was under the pier – then known as the Palace Pier. His third attack now was on the ghost train of this same pier. His fourth attack then was in the Churchill Square car park. Now we have yesterday's attack, in the car park behind the Grand Hotel. A few hundred yards south.'

He paused to let the significance sink in. 'The fifth attack, if Detective Superintendent Grace is correct, occurred in Eastern Terrace, just off Paston Place and St James's Street.' He turned back to the map and pointed at the fifth circle. 'In the absence of anything better to go on, I'm going to predict that the Shoe Man's next attack will take place in a location close to this. He's wounded by his last failure. He's angry. He's likely to default to his comfort zone.' Proudfoot pointed to the street above and the street below St James's. 'Eastern Road and Marine Parade. Now, Marine Parade has only buildings on one side – it has the promenade on the other. Eastern Road is the one that is most similar to St James's. There's a warren of streets running off it and that's where I think he is most likely to strike again, either tonight or tomorrow. My guess is tomorrow is more likely, because the streets will be a bit busier, giving him more cover.'

'Eastern Road is a long road,' DC Foreman said.

'If I had a crystal ball, I'd give you a house number,' Proudfoot said, with a smug grin. 'But if I was running this operation, that's where I would concentrate.'

'Do you think he has selected his next victim already?' Grace asked.

'I may have something interesting on that,' the Analyst, Ellen Zoratti, cut in. 'Something I'd like you to see.'

86

Ellen Zoratti picked up a remote control and pressed a button. A white screen lowered, covering Julius Proudfoot's map.

'We know that the room where the first victim of the Shoe Man was raped, in the Grand Hotel in 1997, was booked in the name of Marsha Morris,' she said. 'We also know that the room where Nicola Taylor was raped in the Metropole on New Year's morning was also booked in this same name. I've now got the CCTV footage from the front desk at the Metropole and I'd like you to see it. Unfortunately they don't have sound.'

Ellen pressed the remote again. A time-delay sequence of grainy black-and-white images appeared. They showed several people with luggage queuing at the front desk of the hotel. She put down the remote, picked up a laser pointer and shone the red dot on the head of a female figure standing in the queue. She had bouffant, shoulder-length blonde hair, huge dark glasses masking much of the top half of her face and a shawl wound around her neck that concealed most of her mouth and chin.

'I believe this is *Marsha Morris*, checking in at the Metropole at 3 p.m. on New Year's Eve, just over two weeks ago. Now, look very closely at her hair, OK?'

She pressed the remote and the scene changed to a time-delay sequence of CCTV images from one of Brighton's premier shopping areas, East Street.

'I came across this in a trawl of CCTV images from all cameras in close proximity to shoe shops in the city. There are several within a couple of hundred yards of this particular camera. They include Last, L. K. Bennett, Russell and Bromley, and Jones. Now take a look at this footage.'

In the next sequence of frames an elegantly dressed woman in her forties, with flyaway blonde hair, wearing a long dark coat and high-heeled boots, strode confidently along towards the camera, then passed it.

'That's Dee Burchmore, who was attacked yesterday,' Ellen Zoratti said. 'This footage was recorded last Saturday, 10 January. Keep watching!'

Moments later a slim woman with light, bouffant hair, wearing a long camel coat, a shawl around her neck, a shoulder bag and shiny wet-look boots, strode into view. She had a determined air, as if on a mission.

An instant later she collided with a man walking in the opposite direction and fell sprawling to the ground. The bouffant hair, which was a wig, rolled on to the pavement. A pedestrian stopped, blocking their view of the man's exposed head.

Within seconds she – or, as looked more likely, he – had grabbed the wig and jammed it, slightly crookedly, back on to her head. Then she scrambled to her feet, checked her handbag and an instant later hurried out of frame, hands up, adjusting the wig.

It was impossible, from the angle of the camera and the poor quality of the image, to make out the person's features. Other than that they were distinctly masculine.

'Marsha Morris?' said Michael Foreman.

'You can always tell them shemale poofs by their Adam's apples,' Potting said. 'That's the giveaway.'

'Actually, Norman,' said Bella Moy, 'I've read that they can have them surgically removed now – or at least reduced. And I'm not quite sure why you're calling them *poofs*?'

'This person was wearing a roll neck,' Nick Nicholl said, ignoring them. 'Whether he – or she – had an Adam's apple or not, it couldn't be seen.'

'Is that the enhanced image, Ellen?' Grace said.

'I'm afraid so, sir,' she replied. 'It's the clearest I could get from the lab. Not great, but it tells us a couple of important things. The first is that the Shoe Man might stalk his victims in drag. The second is that Mrs Burchmore bought an expensive pair of shoes that day. Take a look at this next sequence. I'm afraid the image quality is also poor, it was taken from the shop's own CCTV.'

She pressed the remote control and on the screen appeared the interior of a shoe shop, again in a sequence of frames from a static camera.

'This is one of the Profile shops in Duke's Lane,' Ellen said.

A blonde woman was sitting on a chair, hunched over what looked like her iPhone or BlackBerry, pecking at the keys. Ellen pointed the red laser dot on her face.

'This is Dee Burchmore, five minutes on from the footage you just saw in East Street.'

An assistant jerked into frame, holding a pair of high-heeled shoes.

In the background, the camera showed a woman with bouffant hair, in a long coat, dark glasses and a shawl covering much of the lower part of her face, entering the shop. It was the same person they had just seen fall over.

Ellen pointed the laser dot on her.

'It's good old Marsha Morris again!' DC Foreman said. 'With her wig back on the right way around!'

They watched the transvestite jerk left and right across the frame in the background, while Dee Burchmore purchased her shoes. She then appeared to chat to the assistant at the counter as the young woman entered details on her computer keypad. Marsha Morris stood close by, appearing to examine some shoes, but clearly listening.

Then Dee Burchmore left with her purchase in a carrier bag.

After only a few seconds, Marsha Morris also left. Then Ellen halted the tape.

'Do we know,' asked Norman Potting, 'if the person who attacked Dee Burchmore yesterday was in drag?'

'He was wearing a dark hood with eye slits,' Claire Westmore said. 'It's the only description she's been able to give so far. But historically the only two attacks in which the Shoe Man wore drag were at the Grand Hotel, in 1997, and early on New Year's Day, at the Metropole. None of the subsequent victims has mentioned drag.'

'I think he's wearing it as a disguise,' Proudfoot said. 'Not for sexual gratification. It's gets him into ladies' shoe shops without suspicion and it's a good disguise at the hotels.'

Grace nodded in agreement.

Proudfoot went on: 'Looking at the case file from 1997, the victim who was attacked in the Churchill Square car park was a creature of habit. She always parked in the same car park, on the top floor, because it was the emptiest. There's a parallel with Dee Burchmore, who always parked on Level 2 of the car park behind the Grand Hotel. They both made it very easy for someone stalking them.'

The SOLO added, 'Dee has told me that she regularly posts her movements on the social networking sites Facebook and Twitter. I've had a look at some of her posts over this past week and it wouldn't have taken a rocket scientist to plot her whereabouts on an almost hourly basis. All three previous victims have had a Facebook presence for a while also, and Mandy Thorpe Tweeted regularly as well.'

'So,' Nick Nicholl said, 'we've narrowed the Shoe Man's next victim down to someone who's bought an expensive pair of shoes in the past week and has a presence on either Facebook or Twitter, or both.' He grinned.

'We might be able to be more specific than that,' Ellen Zoratti said. 'The age of the victims could be significant. Nicola Taylor is thirty-eight, Roxy Pearce is thirty-six, Mandy Thorpe is twenty, and Dee Burchmore is forty-two. These four ages correspond closely to the age range of the Shoe Man's victims back in 1997.'

The Crime Analyst paused to let this sink in, then went on: 'If Detective Superintendent Grace is correct that Rachael Ryan was the Shoe Man's fifth victim back in 1997, maybe it can help us narrow down who his next will be now – assuming there will be another one.'

'There will be,' Proudfoot said confidently.

'Rachael Ryan was twenty-two years old,' Ellen said. She turned to the forensic psychologist. 'Dr Proudfoot, you've already told us you think the Shoe Man could be repeating his pattern because that's his comfort zone. Might that comfort zone extend to the age of his next victim? Someone of corresponding age to his fifth victim in 1997? A twenty-two-year-old?'

Proudfoot nodded pensively. 'We can't be sure about Rachael Ryan, of course,' he said pompously, and gave Roy Grace a pointed look. 'But if we assume for the moment that Mandy Thorpe was a victim of the Shoe Man and that Roy is right about Rachael Ryan, then yes, Ellen, your assumption is one we shouldn't rule out. It's very possible he'll go for someone of that age. If he attacked poor Rachael Ryan, and she's never been found, and he's never been caught for whatever he did to her, then it's quite likely, after yesterday's shock, that he'll go for the familiar. Someone more vulnerable than an experienced middle-aged woman. Someone who'll be a soft touch. Yes, I think that's who we should be focusing on. Young women in high heels and with a Facebook presence.'

'Which means just about every young woman in Brighton and Hove. And everywhere else in this country,' E-J said.

'There can't be that many who can afford the prices of the shoes that attract the Shoe Man,' Bella Moy said. 'I would think we could get a list of recent customers in that age bracket from the local shops.'

'Good thinking, Bella, but we haven't got the time,' Grace said.

'It could be narrowed down, sir,' Ellen Zoratti said. 'The connection could be this person in the bouffant wig. If we could find footage of a woman in her early twenties in a shop and footage of this person close to her, we might have something.'

'We've had the Outside Inquiry team viewing all the footage they can from cameras inside shoe shops, but it's a nightmare, because of the January sales,' Bella Moy said. 'I've been in the CCTV room at Brighton nick, looking at footage from cameras close to some of the city's shoe shops. There are hundreds of people of that age out and about shopping. And the problem is there's hundreds and hundreds of hours of CCTV footage.'

Grace nodded.

'Sir,' Claire Westmore said, 'a lot of shoe shops these days take down customer details for their mailing lists. The chances are that the shop that has sold – or has yet to sell – the shoes of the next potential victim will have her name and address on its system.'

Grace considered this. 'Yes, worth a try. We have a list of all the shops in the city that sell expensive designer shoes.' He looked down at his notes. 'Twenty-one of them. The victim is likely to have bought her shoes within the past week – if she has bought them yet. We could try a trawl of all the shops, and get the names and addresses of all the customers who fit this profile who've bought shoes, but with the resources we have this is going to take days. Our problem is we don't have the luxury of that time.'

'How about putting out some decoys, sir?' DC Boutwood said.

'Decoys?'

'Send some of us out shopping.'

'You mean send you out to buy expensive shoes?'

She nodded, beaming. 'I'd volunteer!'

Grace grimaced. 'Women and nice shoes in the January sales. It's like looking for a bloody needle in a haystack! We'd need dozens of decoys to hit the right shops at the right times. Dr Proudfoot thinks the Shoe Man will attack again tonight or tomorrow.' He shook his head. 'It's an interesting idea, E-J, but it's too much of a long shot – and we just don't have the time. We need to get the Eastern Road area under observation by 3 p.m. today.'

He looked at his watch. It was coming up to 9 a.m. He had just six hours.

The CCTV surveillance camera was a clever invention, Roy Grace thought. But there was a big issue with them. There were currently hundreds of cameras running 24/7 in this city. But there simply wasn't the manpower to physically examine all the footage – and half of it was crap quality anyway. He needed some kind of super computer program to check it automatically – and he didn't have one. All he had was a limited number of human beings with limited concentration spans.

'Sir, you were involved yourself with the Rachael Ryan disappearance, weren't you?' Ellen Zoratti said.

Grace smiled. 'I still am. The file's still open. But yes, I was, very involved. I interviewed the two friends she had been out with on that Christmas Eve several times. Rachael was into shoes, big time, which was why I've always suspected the Shoe Man's involvement. She'd bought a very expensive pair of shoes a week before, from Russell and Bromley in East Street, I think.' He shrugged. 'That's another reason I'm not sure we'd gain anything by sending people out shopping today. I think he plans ahead.'

'Unless he's feeling frustrated by yesterday, chief,' Glenn Branson said. 'And just decides to go for someone at random.'

'Our best hope at the moment,' Proudfoot said, 'is that after yesterday afternoon he's feeling rattled, and that maybe he'll rush into something unprepared. Perhaps you succeeded in rattling his cage by insulting his manhood in the *Argus* – which is how he came to make his mistake.'

'Then I think we'd better find a way of rattling his cage again, and this time even harder,' Grace said.

87

The job at the Grand Hotel was not working out the way Darren Spicer had hoped. There were security systems in place to prevent him creating his own room keys on the system, and a supervisor who kept watch on him and his co-workers from the minute he started in the morning to the minute he signed off each evening.

Sure, he was getting paid for his work, renovating the hotel's antiquated electrical system, replacing miles of wiring along its labyrinth of basement corridors, where the laundry, kitchens, boilers, emergency generators and stores were housed. But in taking this particular job, he'd had hopes of being able to do a little more than spend his days unspooling lengths of new electric cables from huge reels and hunt for wires chewed by mice.

He'd imagined he would be getting access to the 201 bedrooms, and the contents left in their safes by their well-off occupants, but so far this first week he had not found a way. He needed to be patient, he knew. He could do patience all right. He was very patient when he fished, or when he waited outside a house he planned to burgle for the occupants to go out.

But there was such temptation here, he was keen to get started.

Because 201 bedrooms meant 201 bedroom safes!

And the hotel was busy, 80 per cent occupancy all year round.

A mate in prison had told him the way to do hotel safes. Not how to break into them – he didn't need that, he had all the kit he needed for the safes in the Grand. No, this was how to steal from safes without getting found out.

It was simple: you stole only a little. You mustn't get greedy. If someone left 200 quid in cash or some foreign currency, you took just a small amount. Always cash, never jewellery; people missed jewellery, but they weren't going to miss twenty quid out of 200. Do that ten times a day and you were on to a nice little earner. A grand a week. Fifty Gs in a year. Yeah. Nice.

He had made his decision that he was going to keep out this time. Stay free. Sure, Lewes Prison had more comforts than St Patrick's night shelter, but soon he'd get his MiPod, then hopefully, a couple of months after he'd have enough cash together for a deposit on his own place. Something modest to start with. Then find himself a woman. Save, maybe get enough cash together to rent a flat. And maybe one day buy one. Ha! That was his dream.

But at this moment, trudging back along Western Road towards St Patrick's, at 6.30 on this freezing, dry Friday night, shoulders stooped, hands in the pockets of his donkey jacket, the dream was a long way off.

He stopped in a pub, the Norfolk Arms by Norfolk Square, and had a pint with a whisky chaser. Both tasted good. This was something he missed when doing bird. The freedom to have a drink in a pub. Simple things like that. Life's little pleasures. He bought a second pint, took it on to the pavement and smoked a cigarette. An old man, who was also holding a pint and was puffing on a pipe, tried to strike up a conversation, but Spicer ignored him. He was thinking. He couldn't just rely on the hotel, he was going to have to do other stuff. Emboldened by his drinks, he was thinking, *Why not start now?*

Between 4 and 5 on winter afternoons was a good time for burgling homes. It was dark but people were still out at work. Now was a bad time, for homes. But there was a place he'd seen on his walk around his neighbour-hood in Hove last Sunday, when he'd been looking for opportunities. A place that, around 6.30 on a Friday evening, was almost certain to be unoccupied. A place that had intrigued him.

A place, he was sure, that had possibilities.

He finished his drink and his cigarette without hurrying. He had plenty of time to go to St Patrick's and get the bag containing all the specialist kit he'd acquired or made himself over the years. He could do this job and still be back at the night shelter by lock-in time. Yeah, for sure.

Lock-in, he thought, the drink definitely getting to him a little. *Lock-in, lock-up.*

That made him grin.

'Want to share the joke?' the old man with the pipe said.

Spicer shook his head. 'Not really,' he said. 'Nah.'

88

Friday 16 January

At 6.45 p.m., Roy Grace, running on adrenalin and caffeine, sat in a small office at the end of the Ops Room, on the third floor of Brighton Central police station. The John Street location of the huge, six-storey building, right on the edge of Kemp Town and just a couple of hundred yards from Edward Street – part of the area where Julius Proudfoot was predicting the Shoe Man's next attack would take place – made it ideal for this current operation.

In the short space of time since this morning's briefing, with the aid of some helpful pressure in the right places from ACC Rigg, the Detective Superintendent had assembled a Covert Team of twenty officers, and was busily working on increasing that to his target of thirty-five for tomorrow.

He currently had a surveillance team of eight out on the streets, on foot and in vehicles, and another twelve, including some members of his own inquiry team, together with several constables, Specials and PCSOs he had commandeered, who were located in buildings at strategic intervals along Edward Street and Eastern Road – as it became – and some of the nearby side streets. Most of them, as was common in surveillance, were in upstairs rooms of private houses or flats, with the consent of their owners.

A bank of CCTV monitors covered most of the wall in

front of his desk. Grace could instantly call up on them views from any of the 350 cameras situated around the city's downtown area, as well as zooming, panning and tilting them. The room was used for the officer in charge, the Gold Commander, at all major public order events, such as party political conferences or for monitoring major demonstrations, and for major operations in the city, as this had now become.

His number two on this, his Silver Commander, was the Crime and Ops Superintendent at John Street, who was currently in the Ops Room, liaising by secure radio with the two Bronze commanders. One, a female detective inspector who ran the Force Surveillance Teams from CID headquarters, was out in an unmarked car, coordinating the street surveillance team. The other, Roy Apps, a senior uniform inspector at John Street, was running the static team, who radioed in anything of potential interest from their observation points.

So far all had been quiet. To Grace's relief it was not raining – many police officers jokingly referred to foul weather as *policeman rain*. Crime levels always dropped during heavy rain. It seemed that villains didn't like getting wet any more than anyone else did. Although the Shoe Man appeared, on past form, to have a penchant for light drizzle.

The rush hour was drawing to an end and Eastern Road was quietening down. Grace flicked through all the screens showing views close to his observation points. He stopped as he saw one unmarked surveillance car slow down and park.

Taking a quick break, he phoned Cleo, telling her he was likely to be late and not to wait up. She was exhausted after last night, she said, and was going to bed early.

'I'll try not to wake you,' he said.

'I *want* you to wake me,' she replied. 'I want to know you're home safe.'

He blew her a kiss and turned back to his task.

Suddenly his internal command phone rang. It was the Silver Commander.

'Boss,' he said. 'Just had an alert from an RPU car – it's picked up the index of the taxi driven by John Kerridge on its ANPR and just clocked it turning left into Old Steine from the seafront.'

Grace tensed, feeling the hollow sensation he often got in the pit of his stomach when things were starting.

'OK, alert the Bronzes.'

'I'm on to it.'

Grace switched his radio to pick up all comms from the Bronzes to any members of their team. He was just in time to hear the excited voice of one of the surveillance team, through a radio crackling with interference, 'Target turning right-right, into Edward Street!'

Moments later there was a response from an observation post just to the east of John Street. 'Target passing, continuing east-east. Hang on – he's stopping. Picking up one male passenger.'

Bugger! Grace thought. *Bugger! Bugger!*

If Kerridge stopped for a passenger, that meant he wasn't hunting. Yet it seemed curious that he had turned into the very area where they suspected the next attack would take place.

Coincidence?

He wasn't so sure. Something about this John Kerridge character bothered him. From his years of experience, offenders like the Shoe Man often turned out to be oddball loners and Kerridge ticked that box. They might have had to let him go because of lack of evidence at this moment, but that did not mean he wasn't their man.

If I was driving a cab, plying for fares, why would I drive along almost deserted Eastern Road at this time on a Friday night? Why not along St James's Street, one street to the south, which was always teeming with people? Or North Street, or London Road, or Western Road?

He phoned Streamline Taxis, stated who he was and asked if John Kerridge had been sent to Eastern Road to do a pick-up. The controller confirmed back to him that he had.

Grace thanked her. So there was an innocent explanation for the taxi driver's presence here.

But he still had a bad feeling about him.

89

Spicer was perspiring, despite the cold. The innocuous-looking Tesco supermarket carrier bag, filled with his tools, weighed a ton, and the walk from St Patrick's to the junction with The Drive and Davigdor Road seemed much further tonight than it had on Sunday. The two pints of beer and the whisky chaser, which an hour ago had fuelled his courage, were now sapping his energy.

The old apartment block loomed on his left. The traffic on the road was light and he had passed few pedestrians on his way here. Half a dozen vehicles on his right, travelling north up The Drive, were waiting for the red light to change. Spicer slowed his pace, also waiting for it to change, not wanting to risk anyone noticing him, just in case. You never knew . . .

Finally the cars moved off. Hurriedly, he turned left, down the steep driveway beside the apartment block, crossed the car park at the front and walked around the side of the building, towards the row of lock-up garages around the corner at the rear that were in almost total darkness, lit only by the glow of lights from some of the apartment windows above.

He walked along to the one at the far left end, the one that had interested him so much on his recce on

Sunday. All of the others had just a single, basic lock inset into their door handles. But this one had four heavy-duty deadlocks, two on each side. You didn't put locks like that on a garage unless you had something of serious value inside.

Of course, it could just be a vintage car, but even then he knew a dealer who would pay good money for instruments from vintage cars; steering wheels, gear levers, badges, bonnet mascots and anything else that could be removed. But, if he was lucky, he might find a stash of valuables of some kind. He knew from his years of experience that burglars like himself favoured anonymous lock-up garages as storage depots. He'd used one himself for many years. They were good places to keep valuables that could be easily identified by their owners until things had quietened down and he could then fence them, maybe a year or so later.

He stood still in the darkness, looking up at the apartment building, checking for shadows at the window that might signal someone looking out. But he could see no one.

Quickly, he delved into his bag and set to work on the first of the locks. It yielded after less than a minute. The others followed suit, equally easily.

He stepped back into the shadows and again checked all around him and above. No sign of anyone.

He pulled open the up-and-over door, then stood still in astonishment, for some moments, absorbing what he was looking at. This was not what he had expected at all.

He stepped inside nervously, yanked the door down behind him, pulled his torch out of his carrier and switched it on.

'Oh shit,' he said, as the beam of light confirmed it for him.

Scared as hell, he backed out, his thoughts in a whirl. With trembling hands he locked it up again, not wanting to leave any tracks. Then he hurried away into the night.

90

Facebook

Jessie Sheldon

View photos of me (128)

Jessie now has 253 friends on Facebook

Benedict's meeting my parents tonight at
charity ball for first time. I'm nervous!!! Got my
early-evening kick-boxing class first, so if there
are any issues and they start being horrible to
him, they'd better watch out. And . . . will be
wearing my new Anya Hindmarch shoes with
five-inch stilettos!!!!

He read Jessie's latest Facebook entry with a thin smile.
*You are so good to me, Jessie. You let me down at the
Withdean Sports Stadium, but you won't let me down
tonight, will you? You will finish your kick-boxing at the
usual time, then walk back the half-mile to your Sudeley
Place flat and change into your beautiful dress and your
new shoes – dressed to kill. Then you will step out into
Benedict's car, which will be waiting outside. That's your
plan, isn't it?*

Sorry to be a party pooper . . .

91

Because of the surveillance operation, Roy Grace had cancelled yesterday's evening briefing. Now, at the 8.30 a.m. Saturday briefing, there was a whole twenty-four hours of activity for the team to catch up on.

Plenty of activity but little progress.

Ellen Zoratti and her colleague analyst still had no results in their nationwide trawl of sexual offences that could be linked to the Shoe Man and the High-Tech Crime Unit still had no potential leads for them.

The Outside Inquiry Team's questioning of the managers and working girls at all thirty-two of the city's known brothels was now complete and had produced nothing tangible so far. Several of their regular punters had shoe or feet fetishes, but as none of the managers kept names and addresses of their clientele, all they could do was promise to phone when any of them next made an appointment.

It was looking more and more as if whatever the Shoe Man might have been up to during these past twelve years, he'd done a damned good job of keeping it quiet.

Last night had also been quiet. The whole city had felt like a graveyard. Having partied hard over the Christmas holidays, it seemed that now its inhabitants, last night at least, were well and truly homebodies in recovery mode and feeling the bite of the recession. And despite his team's long vigil, there had been no further sighting of taxi driver John Kerridge – Yac – since his earlier, brief appearance in the area.

One positive was that Grace now had the full surveillance complement of thirty-five officers he needed to blanket cover the Eastern Road vicinity tonight. If the Shoe Man showed up, his team was going to be ready for him.

Dr Julius Proudfoot remained confident that he would.

As the meeting ended, an internal phone began ringing. Glenn Branson made his way towards the exit of the packed Conference Room to call Ari – he'd blocked one from her during the briefing. He knew why she was calling, which was to ask him to take the kids today. No chance, he thought sadly. Much though he would have given anything to have been able to.

But just as he stepped out through the doorway, Michael Foreman called out to him, 'Glenn! For you!'

He squeezed back through the crowd of people leaving and picked up the receiver, which Foreman had laid on the table.

'DS Branson,' he answered.

'Oh, yeah. Er, hello, Sergeant Branson.'

He frowned as he recognized the rough-sounding voice.

'It's *Detective* Sergeant Branson,' he corrected.

'Darren Spicer here. We met, at the—'

'I know who you are.'

'Look, I have – er – what you might call a delicate situation here.'

'Lucky you.'

Branson was anxious to get him off the line and call Ari. She always hated it when he killed her incoming calls. He'd also found another unwelcome letter from her solicitor awaiting him at Roy Grace's house, when he'd finally got home last night, or rather earlier this morning, and he wanted to talk to her about it.

Spicer gave him a half-hearted, uncertain laugh. 'Yeah, well, I've got a problem. I need to ask you a question.'

'Fine, ask it.'

'Yeah, well, you see – I got this problem.'

'You just told me that. What's your question?'

'Well, it's like – if I said to you that I was, like – like, I saw something, right? Like – someone I know saw something, like, when they were somewhere that they shouldn't ought to be? Yeah? If they, like, gave you information that you really needed, would you still prosecute them because they were somewhere they shouldn't have been?'

'Are you trying to tell me you were somewhere you shouldn't have been and saw something?'

'It wasn't like I breached my licence restrictions or anything. It wasn't like that.'

'Do you want to come to the point?'

Spicer was silent for a moment, then said, 'If I saw something that might help you catch your Shoe Man, would that give me immunity? You know, from prosecution.'

'I haven't got that power. Calling to collect the reward, are you?'

There was a sudden silence at the other end, then Spicer said, '*Reward?*'

'That's what I said.'

'Reward for what?'

'The reward for information leading to the arrest of the man who attacked Mrs Dee Burchmore on Thursday afternoon. It's been put up by her husband. Fifty thousand pounds.'

Another silence, then, 'I didn't know about that.'

'No one does yet, he only informed us this morning. We're about to pass it on to the local media, so you've got a head start. So, anything you'd like to tell me?'

'I don't want to go back inside. I want to stay out, you know, try to make a go of it,' Spicer said.

'If you've got information, you could call *Crimestoppers* anonymously and give it to them. They'll pass it on to us.'

'I wouldn't get the reward then, would I, if it was anonymous?'

'Actually, I believe you might. But you're aware that withholding information's an offence, aren't you?' Branson said.

Instantly he detected the panic rising in the old lag's voice.

'Yeah, but wait a minute. I'm phoning you, to be helpful, like.'

'Very altruistic of you.'

'Very what?'

'I think you'd better tell me what you know.'

'What about if I just give you an address? Would that qualify me for the reward if you find something there?'

'Why don't you stop fucking about and tell me what you have?'

92

Shortly after 2 p.m. Roy Grace drove in through the front entrance of a large, tired-looking apartment block, Mandalay Court, then down an incline at the side, as he had been directed. He was curious to see what Darren Spicer's tip-off revealed.

As he headed around the rear of the building, his wipers clearing away a few tiny spots of drizzle, he saw a long row of shabby lock-up garages that did not look like they had been used for years. At the far end were three vehicles: Glenn Branson's unmarked silver Ford Focus, identical to the one Grace had come in; the little blue van, which he presumed belonged to the locksmith; and the white police van, containing two members of the Local Support Team, who had been requested in case they had to break their way in, and had brought a battering ram with them as backup. Not that there were many doors, in Grace's experience, that could defeat ever-cheery Jack Tunks, whose day job was maintaining the locks at Lewes Prison.

Tunks, in heavy-duty blue overalls, a grimy bag of tools on the ground beside him, was busy inspecting the locks.

Grace climbed out of the car, holding his torch, and greeted his colleague, then nodded towards the last of the garages in the row. 'This the one?'

'Yep. No. 17, not very clearly marked.' Branson double-checked the search warrant that had been signed half an hour ago by a local magistrate. 'Yep.'

'Blimey,' Tunks said. 'What's he got in there? The blooming crown jewels?'

'Does seem a lot of locks,' Grace agreed.

'Whoever's had these put on isn't messing about. I'll guarantee the door's reinforced behind too.'

Grace detected a degree of grudging respect in his voice. The recognition of one professional's work by another.

While Tunks applied himself to his task, Grace stood rubbing his hands against the cold. 'What do we know about the owner of this garage?' he asked Branson.

'I'm on to it. Got two PCSOs going round the apartment block now so see if anyone knows who the owner is, or at least one of the tenants. Otherwise I'll see what we can get from the Land Registry online.'

Grace nodded, dabbed a drip from his nose with his handkerchief, then sniffed. He hoped he didn't have a cold coming – he especially didn't want to give any infection to Cleo while she was pregnant.

'You've checked this is the only way in?'

The Detective Sergeant, who was wearing a long, cream, belted mackintosh, with epaulettes, and shiny brown leather gloves, made a *duh!* motion with his head, rocking it from side to side. 'I know I'm not always the sharpest tack in the box, old-timer, but yeah, I did check.'

Grace grinned, then took a walk around the side to check for himself. It was a long garage, but there was no window or rear door. Returning to Branson, he said, 'So, what news on the Ari front?'

'Ever see that film *War of the Roses*?'

He thought for a moment. 'Michael Douglas?'

'You got it. And Kathleen Turner and Danny DeVito. Everything gets smashed up. We're about there – only worse.'

'Wish I could give you some advice, mate,' Grace said.

'I can give you some,' Glenn replied. 'Don't bother getting married. Just find a woman who hates you and give her your house, your kids and half your income.'

The locksmith announced he was done, and pulled the door back and up a few inches, to show it was now free. 'Would one of you like to do the honours?' he said, and stepped away, a tad warily, as if worried a monster was going to leap out.

Branson took a deep breath and pulled the door up. It was much heavier than he had imagined. Tunks was right, it had been reinforced with steel plating.

As the door clanged home on its rollers, sliding parallel with the roof, all of them stared into the interior.

It was empty.

In the shadows they could make out an uneven dark stain towards the far end, which looked like it had been made by a parked vehicle dripping oil. Roy Grace detected a faint, car-park smell of warm vehicle. On the right-hand side of the far end wall was floor-to-ceiling wooden shelving. An old, bald-looking vehicle tyre was propped against the left-hand side. A couple of spanners and an old claw hammer hung from hooks on the wall to their left. But nothing else.

Glenn stared gloomily into the void. 'Having a laugh on us, is he?'

Grace said nothing as he shone his torch around the walls, then the ceiling.

'I'll tear fucking Spicer's head off!' Glenn said.

Then they both saw it at the same time, as the beam fell on the two plain, flat strips of plastic on the floor. They strode forward. Grace snapped on a pair of latex gloves, then knelt and picked the up first strip.

It was a vehicle front registration plate, black lettering on a reflective white surface.

He recognized the index instantly. It was the cloned registration on the van which had shot away from the Grand Hotel car park on Thursday afternoon, almost certainly driven by the Shoe Man.

The second plastic strip was the rear plate.

Had they found the Shoe Man's lair?

Grace walked across to the end wall. On one shelf was a row of grey duct-tape rolls. The rest of the shelves were bare.

Glenn Branson started walking across to the left wall. Grace stopped him. 'Don't trample everywhere, mate. Let's try to retrace our steps, leave it as clean as we can for SOCO – I want to get them in here right away.'

He looked around carefully, thinking. 'Do you think that's what Spicer saw? These licence plates?'

'I don't think he's smart enough to have put two and two together from just licence plates. I think he saw something else.'

'Such as?'

'He won't talk unless we give him immunity. I have to say, at least he was smart relocking the door.'

'I'll speak to the ACC,' Grace said, stepping as lightly as he could on the way back out. 'We need to know what he saw in here. We need to know what might have been here that isn't here now.'

'You mean he could have nicked something?'

'No,' he replied. 'I don't think Spicer nicked what was

in here. I think what he probably saw in here was a white van. An engine's been running in here within the last few hours. If the van's gone, then where the hell is it? And, more to the point, *why's* it gone? Go and talk to him. Twist his arm. Tell him if he wants a crack at that reward, he has to tell us what he saw, otherwise no deal.'

'He's scared he'll get banged up again for breaking and entering.'

Grace looked at his mate. 'Tell him to lie, to say that the door was open, unlocked. I'm not interested in nicking him for breaking and entering.'

Branson nodded. 'OK, I'll go and talk to him. Just had a thought – if you put SOCO in and the Shoe Man returns and sees them, he'll do a runner. Aren't we smarter having someone covert watching it? Get Tunks to lock it up again so he doesn't know we've been here?'

'Assuming he's not watching us now,' Grace said.

Branson glanced around, then up, warily. 'Yeah, assuming that.'

*

Grace's first action when he arrived at the Ops Control Room at John Street, twenty minutes later, was to inform his Silver and Bronze Commanders that any white Ford Transit van sighted in the vicinity of Eastern Road, for the rest of the day and night, was to be kept under close observation. Then he put out a broader request to all patrols in the city to keep a vigilant eye on all current model white Ford Transit vans.

Twelve years ago, if he was right, the Shoe Man had used a white van in his attack. It would fit Proudfoot's theory on his symmetry if he did the same thing again tonight.

Was that the reason those particular pages had been taken from the file, he wondered? The ones relating to an eyewitness report about a woman abducted in a white van? Did they contain vital clues about his behaviour? His MO? The identity of the van?

Something that had been bothering him about the lock-up garage was bothering him even more now. If the Shoe Man had driven the van out of the garage, why had he bothered to lock all four locks? There was nothing in there to steal except two useless licence plates.

That really did not make sense to him.

93

Saturday 17 January

The only passengers Yac disliked more than drunks were the ones who were high on drugs. This girl on the back seat was almost bouncing off the roof.

She talked and she talked and she talked. She had spewed words non-stop since he had collected her from an address close to the beach in Lancing. Her hair was long and spiky, the colour of tomato ketchup and pea soup. She talked rubbish and she was wearing rubbish shoes. She reeked of cigarettes and Dolce & Gabbana Femme, and she was a mess. She looked like a Barbie doll that had been retrieved from a dustbin.

She was so out of it, he doubted she would notice if he drove her to the moon, except he didn't know how to get to the moon. He hadn't worked that one out yet.

'Thing is, you see,' she went on, 'there's a lot of people going to rip you off in this city. You want quality stuff. You tell them you want brown and they just give you shit, yep, shit. You had that problem?'

Yac wasn't sure whether she was talking into her mobile phone, which she had been for much of the journey, or to him. So he continued driving in silence and looking at the clock and fretting. After he dropped her off in Kemp Town he would park up and ignore any calls on his data unit from the dispatcher, wait for 7 p.m. and then drink his tea.

'Have you?' she asked more loudly. 'Have you?'

He felt a prod in his back. He didn't like that. He did not like passengers touching him. Last week he had a drunk man who kept laughing and thumping him on the shoulder. He had begun to find himself wondering what the man's reaction would be if he hit him in the face with the heavy, four-way steel brace for removing wheel nuts that was stored in the boot.

He was starting to wonder how this girl would react if he did that now. He could easily stop and get it out of the boot. She'd probably still be sitting in the back, talking away, even after he had hit her. He'd seen someone do that in a film on television.

She prodded him again. 'Hey? So? Have you?'

'Have I what?'

'Oh shit, you weren't listening. Like, right, OK. Shit. Haven't you got any music in this thing?'

'Size four?' he asked.

'Size *four*? Size *four* what?'

'Shoes. That's what you are.'

'You a shoemaker when you're not driving or something?'

Her shoes were really horrible. Fake leopard skin, flat and all frayed around the edges. He could kill this woman, he decided. He could. It would be easy. He had lots of passengers he did not like. But this was the first one he actually thought he might like to kill.

But it was probably better not to. You could get into trouble for killing people if you got caught. He watched *CSI* and *Waking the Dead* and other shows about forensic scientists. You could learn a lot from those. You could learn to kill a stupid person like this woman, with her stupid hair and her stupid black nail paint and her breasts almost popping free of their scarlet cups.

As he turned left at the roundabout in front of Brighton Pier and headed up around the Old Steine, she suddenly fell silent.

He wondered if she could read his mind.

94

Saturday 17 January

Roy Grace, seated in the office at the end of the Ops Room, was working his way through a horrible slimy and almost stone-cold mound of chicken and shrimp chow mein that some well-meaning officer had brought him. If he hadn't been ravenous, he would have binned it. But he'd eaten nothing since an early-morning bowl of cereal and needed the fuel.

All had been quiet at the garage behind Mandalay Court. But the number and quality of the locks on the door continued to bother him. ACC Rigg had agreed readily to allowing Darren Spicer to tell them what he saw without incriminating himself, but as yet Glenn had been unable to find him. Grace hoped the serial villain wasn't playing a macabre game with them.

He dug the plastic fork into the foil dish, while staring at the gridded image on the computer screen on the desk in front of him. All the cars and the thirty-five officers on his operation were equipped with transponders which gave him their exact position to within a few feet. He checked the location of each in turn, then the images of the city streets on the CCTV cameras. The images on the screens on the wall showed their night-vision sight as clear as daylight. The city was definitely busier today. People might have stayed home yesterday evening, but

Saturday was starting to look like it might be something of a party night.

Just as he munched on a desiccated shrimp, his radio phone crackled into life and an excited voice said, 'Target One sighted! Turning right-right into Edward Street!'

Target One was the code designated to John Kerridge – Yac. *Target Two*, and further numbers, would be applied to any white van or pedestrian arousing suspicion.

Instantly, Grace put down the foil dish and tapped the command to bring up, on one of the wall-mounted monitors, the CCTV camera trained on the junction of Edward Street and Old Steine. He saw a Peugeot estate taxi, in the turquoise and white Brighton livery, accelerate out of the camera's view along the road.

'One female passenger. He is proceeding east-east!' he heard.

Moments later Grace saw a small Peugeot heading in the same direction. The transponder showed on the grid this was one of his covert cars, no. 4.

He called up the next image in sequence on the CCTV screens and saw the taxi crossing the intersection with Egremont Place, where Edward Street became Eastern Road.

Almost exactly the same pattern as last night, Grace thought. But this time, although he could not have explained why, he sensed there was a difference. At the same time, he was still worried about the amount of faith he had put in Proudfoot's judgement.

He spoke on the internal phone to his Silver. 'Have we found out his destination from the taxi company?'

'No, chief, didn't want to alert them, in case the operator says anything to the driver. We've enough cover to keep him in view if he stays in the area.'

'OK.'

Another excited voice crackled on the radio phone. 'He's turning right – right into – what's that street – Montague, I think. Yes, Montague! He's stopping! Rear door opening! She's out of the car! Oh, my God, she's running!'

95

Saturday 17 January

He had come early in the afternoon, to ensure he got a parking space in one of the pay-and-display bays close to her flat. One that she would have to walk past on her way back from her kick-boxing class.

But every damned one of them was taken when he arrived. So he had waited, at the end of the road, on a yellow line.

This area to the south of Eastern Road was a warren of narrow streets of two- and three-storey Victorian terraced houses, popular with students and singles, and in the heart of the gay community. There were several estate agent's hoardings, advertising properties for sale or to let. Cars, mostly small and grimy, and a few vans were parked along both sides.

He'd had to wait over an hour, to almost 3.30 p.m. before, to his relief, a rusty old Land Cruiser had driven off, leaving behind a space big enough for him. It was just thirty feet from the front door of the pale blue house, with bay windows, where Jessie Sheldon had the upstairs flat. The gods were smiling on him!

It was perfect. He had put sufficient coins in to cover him until 6.30 p.m., when the parking restrictions expired. It was now just past that time.

An hour and ten minutes ago, Jessie had come out of

her front door in her tracksuit and trainers, and walked straight past him on her way to her kick-boxing class – the one she attended every Saturday afternoon, and which she had chattered about on Facebook. He could have taken her then, but it wasn't quite dark enough, and there had been people around.

But now it was dark and, for the moment, the street was deserted.

She would have to hurry home, he knew. She had informed the world that she was going to have to rush in order to get changed into her finery, to take Benedict to meet her parents for the first time.

I am sooooooooooo nervous about that meeting! she had put on Facebook.

What if they don't like him?

She added that she was *sooooooooooo* excited about the Anya Hindmarch shoes she had bought!

He was *sooooooooooo* excited about the pair of Anya Hindmarch shoes he had bought too. They were lying on the floor right behind him, waiting for her! And he was *sooooooooooooo* nervous also. But nervous in a nice, excited, tingly-all-over way.

Where are you tonight, Detective Superintendent Big-Swinging-Dick Detective Superintendent Roy Grace?

Not here, are you? You haven't a clue! Again!

He had parked so that he could watch her approaching through the crack in the rear window curtains, although these were hardly necessary. He'd applied dense black-out privacy film to all the rear and side windows. It was impossible to see in from outside, even in broad daylight. Of course, he knew, aficionados of these classic VW camper vans would frown at such a thing as darkened windows. Fuck them.

He checked his watch, pulled on his latex gloves, then his baseball cap, and raised his night-vision binoculars to his eyes. Any minute now she would appear around the corner, either walking or perhaps running. It was 200 yards from that street corner to her front door. If she was running he would have twenty seconds; if she was walking, a little longer.

All that mattered was that she was alone, and that the street was still deserted.

If not, then he'd have to switch to his alternative plan, to take her inside her house. But that would make it harder for him to then get her outside again and into the camper van undetected. Harder, but not impossible; he had that worked out too.

He was shaking with excitement as he once again went through his checklist. His heart was thudding. He opened the sliding door, grabbed the fake fridge he had made from plywood and moved it closer to the door. Then he took his baseball cap off, pulled his hood on and tugged his baseball cap down again, to disguise the hood as much as possible. Then he looked at the shoes on the floor. Identical to the ones she had bought.

He was ready. After the mess-up on Thursday, he had planned today much more carefully, the way he normally did. He had everything covered, he was quite confident of that.

96

Saturday 17 January

'Hey!' Yac shouted in fury. 'Hey! Hey!'

He couldn't believe it. She was doing a runner on him! He'd driven her all the way from Lancing, a £24 fare, and as he pulled over at the address she'd given him, she opened the rear door and legged it.

Well, he wasn't having it!

He yanked off his seat belt, hurled open the door and stumbled out on to the pavement, shaking with anger. Without even switching off the engine or shutting the door, he began sprinting after the fast-disappearing figure.

She raced along the pavement, downhill, then turned left into the busy thoroughfare of St George's Road, which was more brightly lit, with shops and restaurants on both sides. Dodging past several people, he was gaining on her. She glanced over her shoulder, then suddenly darted into the road, right across the path of a bus, which blared its horn at her. Yac didn't care, he followed her, running between the rear of the bus and a car that was following, hearing the scream of brakes.

He was gaining!

He wished he had the wheel brace to hit her with, that would bring her down!

He was only yards behind her now.

At one of the schools he had attended, they'd made him play rugby, which he hated. But he was good at tackling. He had been so good at tackling they'd stopped him from playing any more rugby, because they said he hurt the other boys and frightened them.

She threw another glance at him, her face lit up in the glare of a street light. He saw fear.

They were heading down another dark, residential street, towards the bright lights of the main seafront road, Marine Parade. He never heard the footsteps closing behind him. Never saw the two men in jeans and anoraks who appeared in front of her at the end of the street. He was utterly focused on his fare.

On his £24.

She was not getting away with it.

Closing the gap!

Closing!

He reached out and clamped a hand on her shoulder. Heard her squeal in fear.

Then, suddenly, arms like steel pincers were around his waist. He smacked, face first, on to the pavement, all the air shot out of him by a crashing weight on his spine.

Then his arms were jerked harshly back. He felt cold sharp steel on his wrists. Heard a snap, then another.

He was hauled, harshly, to his feet. His face was stinging and his body hurt.

Three men in casual clothing stood around him, all panting, breathless. One of them held his arm painfully hard.

'John Kerridge,' he said, 'I'm arresting you on suspicion of sexual assault and rape. You do not have to say anything, but it may harm your defence if you do not mention when questioned something which you later rely on in court. Anything you do say may be given in evidence. Is that clear?'

97

Saturday 17 January

Suddenly, he could see her. She was coming around the corner at a steady jog, a slender green figure against the grey tones of the darkness, through his night vision binocular lenses.

He turned, all panicky now it was happening, shooting a quick glance up and down the street. Apart from Jessie, who was fast closing on him, it was deserted.

He slid open the side door, grabbed the fake fridge with both arms and staggered one step back on to the kerb, then screamed with pain. 'Oh, my back, my back! Oh, God, help me!'

Jessie stopped in her tracks as she saw the back of a clumsy-looking figure in an anorak, jeans and baseball cap holding a fridge half in and half out of the Volkswagen camper van.

'Oh, God!' he screamed again.

'Can I help you?' she asked.

'Oh, please, quick. I can't hold it!'

She hurried over to assist him, but when she touched the fridge it felt strange, not like a fridge at all.

A hand grabbed the back of her neck, hurling her forward into the van. She slithered across the floor, cracking her head against something hard and unyielding. Before she had time to recover her senses, a heavy weight on her back pinned her down, crushing her, then something sickly sweet and damp was pressed over her face, stinging her nose and throat and blinding her with tears.

Terror seized her.

She tried to remember her moves. Still early days, she was just a novice, but she had learned one basic. *Bend before kicking.* You didn't get enough power if you just kicked. You brought your knees towards you, then launched your legs. Coughing, spluttering, trying not to breathe the noxious stinging air, but already feeling muzzy, she clenched her elbows hard into her ribs and rolled sideways, her vision just a blur, trying to break free, bending her knees, then kicking out hard.

She felt them strike something. She heard a grunt of pain. Heard something clattering across the floor, kicked again, shook her head free, twisted, feeling dizzy now and weaker. The sickly sweet wetness pressed against her face again, stinging her eyes. She rolled sideways, breaking free of it, kicking hard with both feet together, feeling even dizzier now.

The weight lifted from her back. She heard sliding, then the slam of the door. She tried to get up. A hooded face was staring down at her, eyes peering through the slits. She attempted to scream, but her brain was working in slow motion now and disconnected from her mouth. No sound came out. She stared at the black hood, which was all blurry. Her brain was trying to make some sense of what was happening, but the inside of her head was swirling. She felt a deep, nauseous giddiness.

Then the sickly, stinging wetness again.

She went limp. Engulfed in a vortex of blackness. Falling deeper into it. Hurtling down a helter-skelter in a void.

98

There was an almost celebratory mood in the Ops Room at Brighton Central. Roy Grace ordered the surveillance team to stand down; they were free to go home. But he was in no mood to share any of their elation and it was going to be a while yet before he got to head home.

This John Kerridge – Yac – character had bugged him all along. They'd released him too damned easily, without thorough enough questioning and investigation. He just thanked his lucky stars that the creep had been caught before harming another victim, which would have made them all look like even bigger idiots.

As it was, difficult questions were going to be asked, to which he was going to have to provide some damned good answers.

He was cursing himself for having allowed Norman Potting to run the initial interview, and for so readily agreeing with Potting's decision that Kerridge should be released. He intended to be fully involved in planning the interview strategy and in the whole interview process of this suspect from now on.

Thinking hard, he left Brighton police station and drove back towards the Custody Centre, behind Sussex House, where Kerridge had been taken. He was fully

538

expecting a phone call at any moment from Kevin Spinella at the *Argus*.

It was shortly after 7 p.m. when he pulled the Ford Focus estate into the bay in the front of the long, two-storey CID HQ building. He phoned Cleo to tell her that, with luck, he might be home earlier than he had thought, before midnight at any rate, then climbed out of the car. As he did so, his phone rang. But it wasn't Spinella.

It was Inspector Rob Leet, the Golf 99 – the Duty Inspector in charge of all critical incidents in the city. Leet was a calm, extremely capable officer.

'Sir, in case this is connected, I've just had a report from East Sector – a unit is attending a van on fire in remote farmland north of Patcham.'

Grace frowned. 'What information do you have on it?'

'It seems to have been on fire for some time – it's pretty well burnt out. The fire brigade's on its way. But this is why I thought it might be of interest. It's a current model Ford Transit – sounds similar to the one you have an alert out on.'

The news made Grace uneasy. 'Any casualties?'

'It appears to be empty.'

'No one seen running away from it?'

'No.'

'Anything from its registration?'

'The licence plates are burned beyond recognition, I'm told, sir.'

'OK, thanks,' he said. 'We have our man in custody. It may not be connected. But keep me updated.'

'I will, sir.'

Grace ended the call and entered the front door of Sussex House, nodding a greeting to the night security man.

'Hi, Duncan. How's the running?'

The tall, athletic forty-year-old smiled at him proudly. 'Completed a half-marathon last weekend. Came fifteenth out of seven hundred.'

'Brilliant!'

'Working up for the London marathon this year. Hope I can touch you for some sponsorship – for St Wilfred's Hospice?'

'Absolutely!'

Grace walked through to the rear of the building and out of the door, crossing the courtyard. He passed the wheelie bins and the SOCO vehicles which were permanently housed there, then went up the steep incline towards the custody block. As he pressed his key card against the security panel to unlock the door, his phone rang again.

It was Inspector Rob Leet once more.

'Roy, I thought I'd better call you right away. I know you have the Shoe Man in custody, but we've got a unit on site in Sudeley Place, Kemp Town, attending a Grade One.'

This was the highest category of emergency call, requiring immediate attendance. Grace knew Sudeley Place. It was just south of Eastern Road. The tone of Leet's voice worried him. What the Duty Inspector had to say fuelled that worry further.

'Apparently a local resident happened to be looking out of her window and saw a woman having a fight with a man over a fridge.'

'A fridge?'

'He was in some sort of van – a camper of some kind – she's not very good on vehicles, couldn't give us the make. She reckons he hit her, then drove off at high speed.'

'With her on board?'

'Yes.'

'When was this?'

'About thirty-five minutes ago – just after 6.30 p.m.'

'He could be anywhere by now. Did she get the registration?'

'No. But I'm treating this as a possible abduction and I've cordoned off that section of pavement. I've asked Road Policing to check all camper vans on the move in the vicinity of the city. We're going to see if we can get anything from CCTV.'

'OK. Look, I'm not quite sure why you're telling me this. We have our Shoe Man suspect in custody. I'm about to go and see him.'

'There's a reason why I think it could be significant for you, sir.' Leet hesitated. 'My officers attending have found a woman's shoe on the pavement.'

'What kind of a shoe?'

'Very new, apparently. Black patent leather, with a high heel. The witness saw it fall out of the camper.'

Grace felt a falling sensation deep in the pit of his stomach. His mind was whirling. They had the Shoe Man. At this very moment they were booking John Kerridge into custody.

But he did not like the sound of the burning van.

And he liked the sound of this new incident even less.

99

In the CCTV room of Sussex Remote Monitoring Services, Dunstan Christmas shifted his twenty-stone bulk on the chair, careful not to lift his weight off altogether and trigger the alarm sensor. It was only 7.30 p.m. Shit. Another hour and a half to wait before he would be relieved for a five-minute comfort break.

He was not due on nights for another two weeks, but he'd agreed to cover for someone who was sick because he needed the overtime pay. Time wasn't even crawling by; it felt like it had stopped altogether. Maybe it was even going backwards, like in a sci-fi movie he'd watched recently on Sky. It was going to be a long night.

But thinking about the money he was making cheered him. Mr Starling might be a strange boss, but he paid well. The money here was good; much better than in his previous job, watching X-rayed luggage at Gatwick Airport.

He reached forward, pulled a handful of Doritos out of the giant-size packet in front of him, munched them and washed them down with a swig of Coca-Cola from the two-litre bottle, then belched. As he routinely ran his eyes over all twenty screens, his hand close to the microphone button in case he should happen to spot any intruder, he noticed that No. 20, which had been dead when he had started his shift, was still not showing any images. It was the old Shoreham cement works, where his dad had been a driver.

He pressed the control toggle to change the image on the screen, in case it was just one of the twenty-six CCTV cameras that was on the blink. But the screen remained blank. He picked up the phone and dialled the night engineer.

'Hi, Ray. It's Dunstan in Monitor Room 2. I've not had any image on screen 17 since I started my shift.'

'Mr Starling's instruction,' the engineer replied. 'The client hasn't paid his bill. Over four months now apparently. Mr Starling's suspended the service. Don't worry about it.'

'Right, thanks,' Dunstan Christmas said. 'I won't.'

He ate some more Doritos.

100

A terrible pain, like a vice crushing her head, woke Jessie. For an instant, utterly disoriented, she had no idea where she was.

In Benedict's room?

She felt all muzzy and queasy. What had happened last night? What had happened at the dinner dance? Had she got drunk?

She felt a crashing jolt. There was a constant whooshing sound beneath her. She could hear the steady blatter of an engine. Was she in a plane?

Her queasiness deepened. She was close to throwing up.

Another jolt, then another. There was a banging sound like a loose door. Fear squirmed through her. Something felt very wrong; something terrible had happened. As she became more conscious, her memory trickled back, reluctantly, as if something was trying to hold it at bay.

She couldn't move her arms or her legs. Her fear deepened. She was lying face down on something hard and constantly jolting. Her nose was bunged up and she was finding it harder and harder to breathe. She tried, desperately, to breathe in though her mouth, but something was clamped over it and no air would come through. She couldn't breathe through her nose now either. She tried to cry out but just heard a dull moan and felt her mouth reverberating.

Panicking, juddering, fighting for breath, she sniffed harder. She could not get enough air in through her nose to fill her lungs. She squirmed, moaned, twisted on to her side, then on to her back, sniffing, sniffing, sniffing, fighting for air, close to blacking out. Then, after a few moments of lying on her back, the blockage freed a little and more air came in. Her panic subsided a little. She took several long, deep breaths, calming a fraction, then tried to call out again. But the sounds stayed trapped in her mouth and gullet.

Bright lights lit up the darkness for an instant and she could see above her the roof of the vehicle. Then darkness again.

Another bright light and she saw a hunched figure in the driver's seat, just shoulders and the back of a baseball cap. The light passed and was instantly replaced by another. Headlights of oncoming cars, she realized.

Suddenly there were bright lights to her right, as a vehicle overtook them. For a fleeting instant she saw part of his face reflected in the interior mirror. She froze in terror. It was still masked by the black hood.

His eyes were on her.

'Just lie back and enjoy the ride!' he said in a bland, small voice.

She tried to speak again, struggling once more to move her arms. They were behind her back, her wrists clamped together. There was no slack, nothing to get a purchase on. She tried to move her legs, but they felt as if they had been welded together at the ankles and knees.

What time was it? How long had she been here? How long since . . .

She should be at the dinner dance. Benedict was going to meet her parents. He was coming round to pick her up. What was he thinking now? Doing now? Was he standing outside her flat ringing the bell? Phoning her? As headlights again brightened the interior, she looked around. Saw what seemed to be a small kitchen unit; one cupboard door was swinging, banging but not closing. Now they were slowing down. She heard him change gear, heard an indicator click-clicking.

Her fear deepened even more. Where were they going?

Then she heard a siren wailing, faintly at first, then louder. It was behind them. Now louder still! And suddenly her spirits soared. Yes! Benedict had come round to collect her and called the police when he realized she wasn't there. They were coming! She was safe. Oh, thank God! Thank God!

Shards of blue light, as if from a shattered chandelier, flooded the interior of the van and the air filled with the scream of the siren. Then, in an instant, the blue lights were gone. Jessie heard the siren recede into the distance.

No, you idiots, no, no no no, no. Please. Come back! Please come back!

She slithered across the floor to her left, as the van made a sharp right. Two hard, jarring jolts and it pulled up. She heard the ratchet of the handbrake. *Please come back!* Then a torch beam flashed into her eyes, momentarily dazzling her.

'Nearly there!' he said.

All she could see when he moved the beam away from her face were his eyes through the slits in the hood.

She tried to speak to him. 'Please, who are you? What do you want? Where have you taken me?' But all that came out was the reverberating moan, like a muffled foghorn.

She heard the driver's door open. The engine ticked over with a steady clatter. Then she heard metal clanking – it sounded like a chain. It was followed by the creaking sound of rusty hinges. A gate being opened?

Then she heard a familiar sound. A soft, rasping buzzing. Hope suddenly sprang up inside her. It was her mobile phone! She'd switched it to silent, vibrate, for her kick-boxing class. It sounded as if it was coming from somewhere up front. Was it on the passenger seat?

Oh, God, who was it? Benedict? Wondering where she was? It stopped after four rings, going automatically to voicemail.

Moments later he jumped back in, drove forward a short distance, then jumped out again, once more leaving the engine ticking over. She heard the same creaking sound, then the same metal clanking of a chain again. Wherever they were, they were now on the far side of locked gates, she realized, her terror deepening even more. Somewhere private. Somewhere that police patrols would not drive by. Her mouth was dry and she felt as if she was going to throw up, bile rising in her throat, sharp and bitter. She swallowed it.

The van lurched, then lurched again – speed humps, she thought – dipped down an incline, sending her sliding forward, her shoulder bashing painfully into something, then rose up, so that she slid back again, helplessly. Then they were driving along a smooth surface, with a steady bump-bump every few moments, like joins in concrete. It was pitch dark in here and he seemed to be driving without lights on.

For an instant her terror turned to anger, then to wild, feral fury. *Let me out! Let me out! Untie me! You have no fucking right to do this!* She struggled against her bonds, pulling her wrists, her arms, with all her strength, shaking, thrashing. But whatever was binding them did not budge.

She lay limp and sniffing air, her eyes filled with tears. She should be at the dinner dance tonight. In her beautiful dress and her new shoes, holding Benedict's arm as he chatted wittily to her parents, winning them over, as she was sure he would. Benedict had been nervous as hell. She had tried to reassure him that they would be charmed by him. Her mother would adore him and her father, well, he seemed a tough guy when you first met him, but underneath he was a big softie. They would adore him, she had promised him.

Yeah, right, until they find out I'm not Jewish.

The van continued its journey. They were turning left now. The headlights came on for a brief second and she saw what looked like the wall of a tall, derelict, slab-like structure with panes of broken glass. The sight sent a vortex of icy air corkscrewing through her. It was like one of the buildings the film *Hostel* was set in. The building where innocent people who had been captured were taken and tortured by wealthy sadists who paid for the privilege.

Her imagination was in freefall. She'd always been a horror movie fan. Now she was thinking about all the deranged killers in movies she had seen, who kidnapped their victims, then tortured and killed them at their leisure. Like in *Silence of the Lambs*, *The Texas Chainsaw Massacre*, *The Hills Have Eyes*.

Her brain was shorting out in terror. She was breathing in short, sharp, panicky bursts, her chest thudding, thudding, thudding, and she was so angry inside.

The van stopped. He got out again. She heard the rumbling of a metal door, then a terrible grinding of metal against some other hard surface. He climbed back in, slammed his door shut and drove forward, putting his lights on again.

Have to talk to him, somehow.

Now she could see through the windscreen that they were inside some vast, disused industrial building, the height of an aircraft hangar, or several aircraft hangars. The headlights briefly showed a railed steel walkway going around the walls high up and a network of what looked like giant, dusty Apollo rocket fuel cylinders stretching into the distance, supported by massive steel and concrete cradles. As they turned, she saw rail tracks disappearing into dust and rubble, and a rusted open goods carriage, covered in graffiti, which did not look like it had moved in decades.

The van halted.

She was shaking so much in terror she could not think straight.

The man got out and switched the engine off. She heard him walking away, then the groaning noise of metal, a loud, echoing clang, following by the clanking of what sounded like a chain. She heard him walking back towards the camper.

Moments later she heard the door slide open and now he was inside the rear with her. He shone the torch down at her, first at her face, then at her body. She stared up at his hooded face, shaking in terror.

She could kick him, she thought wildly. Although her legs were strapped together, she could bend her knees, then lash out at him, but unless she could free her arms, what good would that achieve? Other than to anger him.

She needed to speak to him. She was remembering tips from all she had read in newspapers about hostages who had survived capture. You needed to try to bond with your captors. It was harder for them to harm you if you established a rapport. Somehow she had to get him to free her mouth so she could talk to him. Reason with him. Find out what he wanted.

'You shouldn't have kicked me,' he said suddenly. 'I bought you nice new shoes, the same as the ones you were going to wear tonight to take Benedict to meet your parents. You're all the same, you women. You think your-selves so powerful. You put on all these sexy things to snare your man, then ten years later, you're all fat and horrible, with cellulite and a slack belly. Somebody has to teach you a lesson, even if I have to do it with only one shoe.'

She tried to speak again.

He leaned down and, in a sudden movement that took her by surprise, flipped her over on to her stomach, then sat on her legs, pinioning them to the floor, crushing them painfully with his weight. She felt something being wound around her ankles and knotted tight. He stood up and suddenly her legs were being pulled over to the left. Then, after some moments, she felt them being pulled to the right. She tried to move them, but couldn't.

Then she heard the clank of metal and an instant later felt something cold and hard being wound around her neck and pulled tight. There was a sharp snap that sound liked a lock closing. Suddenly her head was jerked forward, then to the right. She heard another snap, like another lock. Then her head was being pulled to the left. Another snap.

She was stretched out as if she was on some medieval rack. She could not move her head or her legs or her arms. She tried to breathe. Her nose was blocking up again. She shimmied in growing panic.

'I have to go now. I'm expected for dinner,' he said. 'I'll see you tomorrow. *Hasta la vista!*'

She moaned in terror, trying to plead with him. *No, please! No, please don't leave me face down. I can't breathe. Please, I'm claustrophobic. Please—*

She heard the door sliding shut.

Footsteps. A distant rending and echoing bang of metal.

Then the sound of a motorcycle engine starting up, revving and fading into the distance, roaring away, fading rapidly into silence. As she listened, quaking in terror, fighting for air she felt a sudden, unpleasant warm sensation spreading around her groin and along her thighs.

101

Roy Grace sat in the small interview room in the Custody Centre, alongside DC Michael Foreman, who, like himself, was a trained Witness and Suspect Cognitive Interviewer. But at this moment, none of that past training was doing them any good. John Kerridge had gone *no comment* on them. Thanks but no thanks to his smart-alec lawyer, Ken Acott.

The tape recorder with three blank cassettes sat on the table. High up on the walls, two CCTV camera lenses peered down at them like mildly inquisitive birds. There was a tense atmosphere. Grace was feeling murderous. At this moment he could have happily reached across the narrow interview table, grabbed John Kerridge by the neck and strangled the truth out of the little shit, disability or no disability.

His client was on the autism spectrum, Ken Acott had informed them. John Kerridge, who kept insisting he be called Yac, suffered from Asperger's syndrome. His client had informed him that he was in pursuit of a passenger who had run off without paying. It was patently obvious that it was his client's passenger who should have been apprehended, not his client. His client was being discriminated against and victimized because of his disability.

Kerridge would make no comment without a specialist medical expert present.

Grace decided he would like to strangle Ken sodding Acott too at this moment. He stared at the smooth solicitor in his elegantly tailored suit, his shirt and tie, and could even smell his cologne. In contrast his client, also in a suit, shirt and tie, cut a pathetic figure. Kerridge had short dark hair brushed forward, and a strangely haunted face that might have been quite handsome, were his eyes not a little too close together. He was thin, with rounded shoulders, and seemed unable to keep totally still. He fidgeted like a bored schoolboy.

'It's nine o'clock,' Acott said. 'My client needs a cup of tea. He has to have one every hour, on the hour. It's his ritual.'

'I've got news for your client,' Grace said, staring pointedly at Kerridge. 'This is not a Ritz-Carlton hotel. He'll get tea outside of the normal times that tea is provided here if and when I decide he can have it. Now, if your client would care to be more helpful – or perhaps if his solicitor would care to be more helpful – then I'm sure something could be done to improve the quality of our room service.'

'I've told you, my client is not making any comment.'

'I have to have my tea,' Yac said suddenly.

Grace looked at him. 'You'll have it when I decide.'

'I have to have it at nine o'clock.'

Grace stared at him. There was a brief silence, then Yac eyeballed Grace back and said, 'Do you have a high-flush or low-flush toilet in your home?'

There was a vulnerability in the taxi driver's voice, something that touched a chord in Grace. Since the news of the reported abduction in Kemp Town two hours ago, and the discovery of a shoe on the pavement where it had allegedly taken place, there had been a development. A young man had arrived to collect his fiancée for an evening out at a black-tie function, thirty minutes after the time of the abduction and she had not answered the door. There was no response from her mobile phone, which rang unanswered, then went to voicemail.

It had already been established that the last person to have seen her was her kick-boxing instructor, at a local gym. She'd been in high spirits, looking forward to her evening out, although, the instructor had said, she was nervous at the prospect of introducing her fiancé to her parents for the first time.

So she could have funked out, Grace considered. But she didn't sound the type of girl to stand up her boyfriend and let down her family. The more he heard, the less he liked the way the whole scenario was developing. Which made him even angrier here.

Angry at the smugness of Ken Acott.

Angry at this creepy suspect hiding behind *no comment* and behind his condition. Grace knew a child with Asperger's. A police officer colleague and his wife, with whom he and Sandy had been friends, had a teenage son with the condition. He was a strange but very sweet boy who was obsessed with batteries. A boy who was not good at reading people, lacking normal social skills. A boy who had difficulty distinguishing between right and wrong in certain aspects of behaviour. But someone, in his view, who was capable of understanding the line between right and wrong when it came to things as major as rape or murder.

'Why are you interested in toilets?' Grace asked Kerridge.

'Toilet chains! I have a collection. I could show you them some time.'

'Yes, I'd be very interested.'

Acott was glaring daggers at him.

'You didn't tell me,' Kerridge went on. 'Do you have high flush or low flush in your home?'

Grace thought for a moment. 'Low flush.'

'Why?'

'Why do you like ladies' shoes, John?' he replied suddenly.

'I'm sorry,' Acott said, his voice tight with anger. 'I'm not having any questioning.'

Ignoring him, Grace persisted. 'Do you find them sexy?'

'Sexy people are bad,' Yac replied.

102

Roy Grace left the interview room feeling even more uneasy than when he had gone in. John Kerridge was a strange man and he sensed a violent streak in him. Yet he did not feel Kerridge possessed the cunning or sophistication that the Shoe Man would have needed to get away undetected with his crimes of twelve years ago and those in the past few weeks.

Of particular concern to him at the moment was the latest news of the possible abduction of Jessie Sheldon this evening. It was the shoe on the pavement that really worried him. Jessie Sheldon had been in her tracksuit and trainers. So whose was the shoe? A brand-new ladies' shoe with a high heel. The Shoe Man's kind of shoe.

But there was something else gnawing at him even more than John Kerridge and Jessie Sheldon at this moment. He couldn't remember exactly when the thought had first struck him – some time between leaving the garage behind Mandalay Court this afternoon and arriving at the Ops Room at the police station. It was bugging him even more now.

He walked out of Sussex House and over to his car. The drizzle had almost stopped and now the wind was getting up. He climbed in and started the engine. As he did so, his radio crackled. It was an update from one of the officers attending the burning van at the farm north of Patcham. The vehicle was still too hot to enter and search.

A short while later, coming up to 10.15 p.m., he parked the unmarked Ford Focus in the main road, The Drive, some way south of his destination. Then, with his torch jammed out of sight into his mackintosh pocket, he walked a couple of hundred yards up to Mandalay Court, trying to look like a casual evening stroller, not wanting to risk putting off the Shoe Man, or whoever used the garage, should he decide to return.

He'd already spoken to the on-site surveillance officer, to warn him he was coming, and the tall figure of DC Jon Exton, from the Covert Team, stepped out of the shadows to greet Grace as he walked down the ramp.

'All quiet, sir,' Exton reported.

Grace told him to stay on lookout and to radio him if he saw anyone approaching, then walked around the rear of the block of flats and along past the lock-ups to the one at the far end, no. 17.

Using his torch now, he strode along the length of it, counting his paces. The garage was approximately twenty-eight feet long. He double-checked as he retraced his steps, then walked back around to the front and pulled on a pair of latex gloves.

Jack Tunks, the locksmith, had left the garage unlocked for them. Grace lifted the up-and-over door, closed it behind him and shone his torch beam around the inside. Then he counted his paces to the end wall.

Twenty feet.

His pulse quickened.

Eight feet difference.

He rapped on the wall with his knuckles. It sounded

hollow. False. He turned to the floor-to-ceiling wooden shelves on the right-hand side of the wall. The finishing on them was poor and uneven, as if they were home-made. Then he looked at the row of rolls of grey duct tape. The stuff was a favoured tool of kidnappers. Then, in the beam of the torch, he saw something he had not noticed on his visit here earlier today. The shelves had a wooden backing to them, bringing them out a good inch from the wall.

Grace had never been into DIY, but he knew enough to question why the lousy handyman who had made these shelves had put a backing on them. Surely you only put a backing to shelves to hide an ugly wall behind them? Why would someone bother in a crappy old garage?

Holding the torch in his mouth, he gripped one of the shelves and pulled hard, testing it. Nothing happened. He pulled even harder, still nothing. Then he gripped the next shelf up and instantly noticed some play in it. He jiggled it and suddenly it slid free. He pulled it out and saw, recessed into the groove where the shelf should have fitted, a sliding door bolt. He propped the shelf against the wall and unlatched the bolt. Then he tried first pulling, then pushing the shelving unit. It would not budge.

He checked each of the remaining shelves and found that the bottom one was loose too. He slid that out and discovered a second bolt, also recessed into the grove. He slid that open, then stood up, gripped two of the shelves that were still in place and pushed. Nothing happened.

Then he pulled, and nearly fell over backwards as the entire shelving unit swung backwards.

It was a door.

He grabbed the torch and shone the beam into the void behind. And his heart stopped in his chest.

His blood froze.

Icy fingers crawled down his spine as he stared around him.

There was a tea chest on the floor. Almost every inch of the walls was covered in old, yellowing newspaper cuttings. Most of them were from the *Argus*, but some were from national papers. He stepped forward and read the headlines of one. It was dated 14 December 1997:

SHOE MAN'S LATEST VICTIM CONFIRMED BY POLICE

Everywhere that he pointed his torch, more headlines shouted out at him from the walls. More articles, some showing photographs of the victims. There were photographs of Jack Skerritt, the Senior Investigating Officer. And then, prominently displayed, a large photograph of Rachael Ryan stared out from beneath a front-page headline from the *Argus* from January 1998:

IS MISSING RACHAEL SHOE MAN'S VICTIM NO. 6?

Grace stared at the photograph, then at the headline. He could remember when he had first seen this page of the paper. This chilling headline. It had been the shout-line on every news-stand in the city.

He tested the lid of the tea chest. It was loose. He lifted it up and stood, his eyes boggling, at what was inside.

It was crammed with women's high-heeled shoes, each wrapped and sealed in cellophane. He rummaged through them. Some packages contained a single shoe and a pair of panties. Others, a pair of shoes. All of the shoes looked as if they'd barely been worn.

Shaking with excitement, he needed to know how many. Mindful of not wanting to damage any forensic evidence, he counted them out and laid them on the floor in their wrapping. Twenty-two packages.

Also bundled together in one taped-up sheet of cellophane were a woman's dress, tights, panties and bra. The Shoe Man's drag gear, maybe. He wondered. Or were these the clothes taken from Nicola Taylor at the Metropole?

He knelt, staring at the shoes for some moments. Then he returned to the cuttings on the wall, wanting to ensure he did not miss anything significant that might lead him to his quarry.

He looked at each one in turn, focusing on the ones on Rachael Ryan, big and small, which covered a large section of one wall. Then his eyes fell on an A4 sheet of paper that was different. This wasn't a newspaper cutting; it was a printed form, partly filled out in ballpoint pen. It was headed:

J. BUND & SONS, FUNERAL DIRECTORS

He walked across so that he could read the small printing on it. Beneath the name it said:

Registration Form

Ref. D5678

Mrs Molly Winifred Glossop

D. 2 January 1998. Aged 81.

He read every word of the form. It was a detailed list:

- ☑ Church fee
- ☑ Doctor's fee
- ☐ Removal of pacemaker fee

☐ Cremation fee

☑ Gravedigger's fee

☑ Printed service sheets fees

☑ Flowers

☑ Memorial cards

☑ Obituary notices

☑ Coffin

☐ Casket for remains

☐ Organist's fee

☑ Cemetery fee

☐ Churchyard burial fee

☑ Clergy's fee

☑ Church fee

Funeral on: 12 January 1998, 11 a.m.
Lawn Memorial Cemetery, Woodingdean.

He read the sheet again. Then again, transfixed.

His mind was racing back to twelve years ago. To a charred body on a post-mortem table at Brighton and Hove Borough Mortuary. A little old lady, whose remains had been found, incinerated, in the burnt-out shell of a Ford Transit van, and who had never been identified. As was customary, she had been kept for two years and then buried in Woodvale cemetery, her funeral paid for out of public funds.

During his career with the police to date, he'd seen many horrendous sights, but most of them he had been able to put out of his mind. There were just a few, and he could count them on the fingers of one hand, that he knew he would carry to his grave. This old lady, and the mystery accompanying her, he had long thought would be one of them.

But now, standing in the back of this shabby old lock-up garage, something was starting, finally, to make sense.

He had a growing certainty that he now knew who she was.

Molly Winifred Glossop.

But then who had been buried at 11 a.m. on Monday 12 January 1998 in the Lawn Memorial Cemetery in Woodingdean?

He was pretty damned sure he knew the answer.

103

Jessie heard the vibrating sound of her phone, yet again, in the half-darkness. She was parched. Once in a while she drifted into a fitful doze, then woke again in stark panic, unable to breathe through her bunged-up nose and fighting for air.

She had agonizing pains in her shoulders, from her arms being stretched out in front of her. There were noises all around her: clankings, creakings, bangings, grindings. With every new sound, she was terrified that the man was returning, that he might be creeping up behind her at this very moment. Her mind swirled in a constant vortex of fear and confused thoughts. Who was he? Why had he brought her here, wherever it was? What was he planning to do? What did he want?

She couldn't stop thinking about all the horror films that had most scared her. She tried to shut them out, to think of happy times. Like her last holiday with Benedict on the Greek island of Naxos. The wedding they had been discussing, their life ahead.

Where are you now, darling Benedict?

The vibrating sound continued. Four rings, then it stopped once more. Did that mean there was a message? Was it Benedict? Her parents? She tried again and again, desperately, to free herself. Shaking and tossing, struggling to loosen the bonds on her wrists, to work one of her hands free. But all that happened was that she bounced around, painfully, her shoulders almost wrenched out of their sockets, her body crashing down against the hard floor, then up again, until she was exhausted.

Then all she could do was lie here in utter frustration, the damp patch around her groin and thighs no longer warm and starting to itch. She had an itch on her cheek too that she desperately wanted to scratch. And all the time she was fighting constantly to swallow back the bile that kept rising in her throat, which could choke her, she knew, if she allowed herself to vomit with her mouth still clamped shut.

She cried again, her eyes raw with the salt from her tears.

Please help me, somebody, please.

For a moment she wondered whether she should just let herself vomit, choke on it and die. End it all before the man came back to do whatever terrible things he had in mind. To at least deprive him of that satisfaction.

Instead, putting a faltering half-trust in the man she loved, she closed her eyes and prayed for the first time in as long as she could remember. It took her a while before she could properly remember the words.

No sooner had she finished than her phone rang again. The usual four rings, then it stopped. Then she heard a different sound.

A sound she recognized.

A sound that froze her.

The roar of a motorbike engine.

104

The Coroner for the city of Brighton and Hove was a doughty lady. When she was in a bad mood, her demeanour was capable of scaring quite a few of her staff, as well as many hardened police officers. But, Grace knew, she possessed a great deal of common sense and compassion, and he'd never personally had a problem with her, until now.

Perhaps it was because he'd just called her at home after midnight and woken her – from the sleepy sound of her voice. As she became more awake, she grew increasingly imperious. But she was professional enough to listen intently, only interrupting him when she wanted clarification.

'This is a big thing you're asking, Detective Superintendent,' she said, when he had finished, distinctly school-marmy now.

'I know.'

'We've only ever had two of these in Sussex. It's not something that can be granted lightly. You're asking a lot.'

'It's not normally a life or death situation, madam,' Grace said, deciding to address her formally, 'but I really believe it is here.'

'Solely on the evidence of the missing girl's friend?'

'In our search for Jessie Sheldon, we contacted a

number of her friends, from a list given to us by her fiancé. The one who is apparently her best friend received a text from Jessie last Tuesday, with a photograph of a pair of shoes she had bought specifically for this evening. The shoes in that photograph are identical to the one shoe found on the pavement outside her flat, exactly where her reported abduction took place.'

'You're certain her fiancé is not involved in any way?'

'Yes, he's eliminated as a suspect. And all three of our current prime suspects for the Shoe Man are eliminated from being involved.'

Cassian Pewe was confirmed as being at a residential course at the Police Training Centre at Bramshill. Darren Spicer had returned to St Patrick's night shelter at 7.30 p.m., which did not work with the timeline of the abduction, and John Kerridge was already in custody.

After a few moments, the Coroner said, 'These are always carried out early in the morning, usually at dawn, to avoid distress to the public. That would mean Monday morning at the very earliest.'

'That's too long to wait. It would mean a whole thirty hours before we could even begin to start searching for any forensic evidence that might help us. We'd be looking at the middle of this coming week, at the very earliest, on any possible matches. I think every hour could be crucial. We can't leave it that long. This really could be the difference between life and death.'

There was a long silence. Grace knew he was asking for a massive leap of faith. He was taking a huge personal gamble in making this request. It still was not 100 per cent certain that Jessie Sheldon had been abducted. The likelihood was that, after twelve years, there would be no forensic evidence that could help his inquiry anyway. But he'd spoken to Joan Major, the forensic archaeologist that Sussex CID regularly consulted, who told him that it would at least be worth a try.

With the pressures on him at this moment, he was willing to clutch at any straw. But he believed what he was requesting now was much more than that.

Her voice becoming even more imperious, the Coroner said, 'You want to do this in a public cemetery, in broad daylight, on a Sunday, Detective Superintendent? Just how do you think any bereaved people, visiting the graves of their loved ones on the holy day, might feel about this?'

'I'm sure they'd be very distressed,' he replied. 'But not half as distressed as this young woman, Jessie Sheldon, who is missing. I believe the Shoe Man may have taken her. I could be wrong. We could be too late already. But if there's a chance of saving her life, that's more important than temporarily hurting the feelings of a few bereaved people who'll probably leave the cemetery and head off to do their shopping in ASDA or Tesco, or wherever else they shop on the *holy* day,' he said, making his point.

'OK,' she said. 'I'll sign the order. Just be as discreet as you can. I'm sure you will.'

'Of course.'

'I'll meet you at my office in thirty minutes. I take it you've never been involved in one of these before?'

'No, I haven't.'

'You won't believe the bureaucracy that's involved.'

Grace could believe it. But at this moment he was more interested in saving Jessie Sheldon than in worrying about pleasing a bunch of pen-pushers. But he didn't want to risk saying anything inflammatory. He thanked the Coroner and told her that he would be there in thirty minutes.

105

Jessie heard the familiar grating clatter of the side door of the camper van opening. Then the vehicle rocked slightly and she was aware of footsteps right beside her. She was quaking in terror.

An instant later, she was dazzled by the beam of a torch straight in her face.

He sounded furious. 'You stink,' he said. 'You stink of urine. You've wet yourself. You filthy cow.'

The beam moved away from her face. Blinking, she looked up. He was now directing the beam on to his own hooded face deliberately, so she could see him.

'I don't like dirty women,' he said. 'That's your problem, isn't it? You're all dirty. How do you expect to pleasure me when you stink like you do?'

She pleaded with her eyes. *Please untie me. Please free my mouth. I'll do anything. I won't fight. I'll do anything. Please. I'll do what you want, then let me go, OK? Deal? Do we have a deal?*

She was suddenly desperate to pee again, even though she had drunk nothing for what seemed an eternity and her mouth was all furred. What time was it? It was morning, she guessed, from the light that had momentarily filled the interior of the van a few minutes ago.

'I have a Sunday lunch engagement,' he said. 'I don't have time to sort you out and get you cleaned up, I'll have to come back later. Too bad I can't invite you. Are you hungry?'

He shone the torch back on her face.

She pleaded with her eyes for water. Tried to form the word inside her clamped mouth, inside her gullet, but all that came out was an undulating moan.

She was desperate for water. And shaking, trying to keep control of her bladder.

'Can't quite understand what you're saying – are you wishing me bon appétit?'

'Grnnnnmmmmmooooowhhh.'

'That's so sweet of you!' he said.

She pleaded with her eyes again. *Water. Water.*

'You probably want water. I'll bet that's what you're saying. The problem is, if I bring you some, you're just going to wet yourself again, aren't you?'

She shook her head.

'No? Well, we'll see then. If you promise to be a very good girl, then maybe I'll bring you some.'

She continued trying desperately to control her bladder. But even as she heard the sound of the sliding door closing, she felt a steady warm trickle again spreading around her groin.

106

The Lawn Memorial Cemetery at Woodingdean was located high up, on the eastern perimeter of Brighton, with a fine view out across the English Channel. Not that the residents of this cemetery were likely to be able to appreciate it, Roy Grace thought grimly, as he stepped out from the long, blue, caterpillar-shaped tent into the blustery wind, and crossed over to the smaller changing room and refreshments tent, his hooded blue paper suit zipped to the neck.

The Coroner had not been wrong when she had talked about the bureaucracy involved in an exhumation. The granting and signing of the order were the easy parts. Much harder, early on a Sunday morning, was to assemble the team that was required.

There was a commercial firm that specialized in exhumations, its main business being the removal of mass graves to new sites for construction companies, or for churches that had been deconsecrated. But they would not be able to start until tomorrow morning without punitive overtime charges.

Grace was not prepared to wait. He called his ACC and Rigg agreed to sanction the costs.

*

The team assembled for the briefing he'd held at John Street an hour ago was substantial. A Coroner's Officer, two SOCOs, including one forensic photographer, five employees of the specialist exhumation company, a woman from the Department of the Environment, who made it clear she resented giving up her Sunday, a now mandatory Health and Safety Officer and, because it was consecrated ground, a clergyman. He'd also had present Joan Major, the forensic archaeologist, as well as Glenn Branson, whom he had put in charge of crowd control, and Michael Foreman, whom he had made an official observer.

Cleo, Darren Wallace – her number two at the mortuary – and Walter Hordern, who was in charge of the city's cemeteries, and drove the Coroner's discreet dark green van to body recoveries, were also present. He only needed two of them, but because none of the mortuary trio had been to an exhumation before, they were keen to attend. Clearly, Grace thought, none of them could get enough of dead bodies. What did that say, he sometimes wondered, about Cleo's love for him?

It wasn't only the mortuary staff who had been curious. He had received phone calls throughout the morning from other members of the CID as word had spread, asking if there was any chance of attending. For many of them, it would be a once-in-a-career opportunity, but he'd had to say no to all of them on the grounds of lack of space, and, in his tired and increasingly tetchy state, he had nearly added that it wasn't a bloody circus.

It was 4 p.m. and absolutely freezing. He stepped back out of the tent, cradling a mug of tea. The daylight was fading rapidly, and the glare of the mobile lights, situated around the cemetery, illuminating the vehicle path to the tent covering Molly Glossop's grave, and several around it, was getting brighter.

The site was ring-fenced by a double police cordon. All entrances to the cemetery were sealed off by a police guard and so far the public reaction had been more one of curiosity than anger. Then there was a second line of police tape directly around the two tents. No press had been allowed closer than the street.

The team inside the main tent were getting close to the bottom of the grave. Grace hadn't needed anyone to tell him, they all knew from the worsening stench. The smell of death was the worst smell in the world, he always thought, and he was catching whiffs of it now, as he stood out in the open air. It was the reek of a long-blocked drain suddenly being cleared, of the rotten meat in a fridge after a two-week power cut in the summer's heat, a heavy, leaden smell that seemed to suck your own spirits into it as it sank to the ground.

None of the experts had been able to predict what condition the body in this coffin would be in, as there were too many variables. They did not know what body – if any – was in here, or how long it had been dead before being buried. The humidity of any burial ground would be a major factor. But with this one being on chalky soil, on high ground, it was hopefully above the water table and would be relatively dry. Judging by the worsening smell, they would find out in a few minutes now.

He finished his tea and was about to go back inside when his phone rang. It was Kevin Spinella.

'Has the *Argus* hot-shot been having a Sunday lie-in?' Grace said, by way of a greeting.

There was a lot of wind roar, and the rumble of the huge portable generator, close by.

'Sorry!' the reporter shouted. 'Couldn't hear you!'

Grace repeated what he had said.

'Actually I've been doing a tour of local cemeteries, trying to find you, Detective Superintendent. Any chance I could come in?'

'Sure, book a plot here, then go and get hit by a bus.'

'Ha-ha! I mean now.'

'I'm sorry, no.'

'OK. So what do you have for me?'

'Not much more than you can see from the perimeter at the moment. Bell me back in an hour, I might have more then.'

'Excuse me, but I thought you were hunting for a young lady who disappeared last night, Jessie Sheldon? What are you doing here digging up an eighty-year-old lady?'

'You do your work by digging stuff up, sometimes I do mine that way too,' Grace replied, wondering how, yet again, the reporter had such an inside track.

Joan Major suddenly emerged from the entrance to the main tent, waving at him. 'Roy!' she called out.

He hung up.

'They've reached the coffin! Good news. It's intact! And the plaque on it reads *Molly Winifred Glossop*, so we have the right one!'

Grace followed her back in. The stench was horrific now and as the flap closed behind him he tried to breathe in only through his mouth. The crowded interior of the tent felt like a film set, with the battery of intense bright lights on stands all focused around the grave and the mound of earth at the far end, and several fixed video cameras recording all that was happening.

Most of the people in here were having problems

with the stench too, with the exception of the four officers from the Specialist Search Unit. They were wearing white bio-chemical protective suits with breathing apparatus. Two of them were kneeling on the roof of the coffin, screwing heavy-duty hooks into the sides, ready to attach cables to block and tackle lifting gear once the sides of the coffin had been cleared, which the other two were now manoeuvring into position, a good yard above the top of the grave.

Joan Major took over the excavation work, for the next hour painstakingly excavating down the sides, and under the base at each end of the coffin, for lifting straps to be placed there. As she worked she carefully bagged soil samples from above, the side and beneath the coffin for later examination of any possible leaked fluids from the contents of the coffin.

When she was finished, two of the exhumation specialists then clipped ropes to each of the four hooks, and to the underneath of the coffin front and back, and clambered out of the grave.

'OK,' one said, moving clear. 'Ready.'

Everyone moved back.

The police chaplain stepped forward, holding a prayer book. He asked for silence, then, standing over the grave, read out a short, non-denominational prayer, welcoming back to earth whoever it might be that was in the coffin.

Grace found the prayer strangely touching, as if they were greeting some long-lost returning traveller.

The other members of the exhumation team began heaving on a sturdy rope. There was a brief, anxious moment when nothing happened. Then a strange sucking noise that was more like a sigh, as if the earth was only very reluctantly yielding something it had claimed for its own. And suddenly the coffin was steadily rising.

It came up, swinging, scraping against the sides, the pulley creaking, all the way until the bottom of the coffin was several inches clear of the grave. It swayed. Everyone in the tent watched for some moments in silent awe. A few clumps of earth tumbled and fell back into the grave.

Grace stared at the light-coloured wood. It did look remarkably well preserved, as if it had been down there for only a few days, rather than twelve years. *So, what secrets do you contain? Please God, something that will connect us to the Shoe Man.*

The Home Office pathologist, Nadiuska De Sancha, had already been contacted, and would head straight to the mortuary as soon as the body was loaded into the Coroner's van.

Suddenly there was a deafening crack, like a clap of thunder. Everyone in the tent jumped.

Something that was the shape and size of a human body, shrouded in black plastic wrapping and duct tape, plunged through the bottom of the coffin and disappeared into the grave.

107

Jessie was fighting for breath again. Panicking, she thrashed about, frantically trying to turn her head sideways to clear her nose a little. *Benedict, Ben, Ben, please come. Please help me. Please don't let me die here. Please don't.*

It hurt like hell, every muscle in her neck feeling as if it was being torn free from her shoulders. But at least now she could get some air. Still not enough, but her panic momentarily subsided. She was desperate for water. Her eyes were raw from crying. The tears trickled down her cheeks, tantalizing her, but she couldn't taste them with her mouth clamped tightly shut.

She prayed again. *Please God, I've just found such incredible happiness. Ben is such a lovely man. Please don't take me away from him, not now. Please help me.*

Through her living hell, she tried to focus her mind, to think clearly. Some time, she did not know when, but some time, probably soon, her captor was going to return.

If he was going to bring her the water he had talked about, unless he was just taunting her, he would have to untie her – at least enough so she could sit up and drink. If she was going to have a chance, it would be then.

Just one chance.

Even though every muscle in her body hurt, even

though she felt exhausted, she still had her strength. She tried to think of different scenarios. How clever was he? What game could she play to fool him? Play dead? Pretend to have a fit? There must be something, something she had not thought of.

That he had not thought of.

What time was it? In this long, dark void in which she was suspended, she suddenly felt a burning need to measure time. To figure out what time it was, how long she had been here.

Sunday. That was all she knew for sure. The lunch he had talked about must be Sunday lunch. Was it an hour since he had gone? Thirty minutes? Two hours? Four? There had been faint grey light but that had gone now. She was in pitch darkness.

Maybe there was a clue in the sounds she could hear. The endless, mostly faint clangings, clatterings, squeakings and bangings of loose windows, doors, panels of corrugated iron, sheet metal or whatever it was outside the building. There was just one that seemed to have a rhythm to it, she noticed. One of the banging sounds that reverberated. She heard it again now and counted.

One thousand and one, one thousand and two, one thousand and three, one thousand and four. Bang. One thousand and one, one thousand and two, one thousand and three, one thousand and four. Bang.

Her father was a keen photographer. She remembered as a small child, before digital photography had taken over, her father had a darkroom where he developed films himself. She liked to stand in the darkness with him, either the total darkness, or in the glow of the weak red light bulb. When he opened a film roll, they would stand in total darkness and her father would get her to count the seconds, the way he had taught her. If you said, *One thousand and one* slowly, that equalled, quite accurately, one second. It worked the same for all numbers.

So now she was able to calculate that the banging occurred every four seconds. Fifteen times a minute.

She counted out one minute. Then five. Ten. Twenty minutes. Half an hour. Then a surge of anger ripped through her at the futility of what she was doing. *Why me, God, if you bloody exist? Why do you want to destroy the love between Benedict and me? Because he's not Jewish, is that what this is about? Boy, are you one sick God! Benedict's a good man. He's dedicated his life to helping people less well off than himself. That's what I try to do also, in case you hadn't sodding noticed.*

Then she began sobbing again.

And counting automatically, like the banging was a metronome. Four seconds. Bang. Four seconds. Bang. Four seconds. Bang.

Then a loud, sliding clang.

The vehicle rocked.

Footsteps.

108

The Brighton and Hove mortuary had recently undergone substantial building works. The reason for this was that more people were eating themselves to death and then were too fat to fit into the fridges. So now new super-sized fridges had been installed to accommodate them.

Not that it required an extra-wide fridge to accommodate the desiccated remains of the woman who lay on the stainless-steel table, in the centre of the newly refurbished main post-mortem room, at 5.30 p.m. this Sunday afternoon.

Even after half an hour in here, Grace had not got used to the horrendous smell and breathing though his mouth only helped a little. He could understand why almost all pathologists used to smoke and carry out their work on corpses with a cigarette between their lips. Those who didn't put a blob of Vicks just above their upper lips. But that tradition appeared to have stopped along with the smoking ban a few years back. He could have sure done with something now.

Was he the only one in here who was affected?

Present in the room, and all gowned, masked and rubber-booted, were the Coroner's Officer, the forensic archaeologist, Joan Major, the SOCO photographer, James

Gartrell, who was busy alternately videoing and photographing every stage of the examination, Cleo and her assistant, Darren Wallace, and, centre stage, Nadiuska De Sancha. Spanish born and of Russian descent, the Home Office pathologist was a statuesque beauty almost every male police officer in Sussex lusted after – and liked to work with, as she was fast and good-humoured.

Also present was Glenn Branson – not that it was necessary for him to be here, but, Grace had decided, it was better to keep him occupied, rather than leaving him on his own to mope about his calamitous separation.

It was always strange attending a post-mortem when Cleo was at work. She was almost a stranger to him, bustling around, efficient and impersonal. Apart from the occasional smiling glance at him.

Since the start of the post-mortem, Nadiuska had painstakingly taped every inch of the dead woman's skin, bagging each strip of tape separately, in the hope that it might contain an errant skin or semen cell invisible to the naked eye, or a hair or clothing fibre.

Grace stared down at the body, mesmerized. The skin was almost black from desiccation, in a virtual mummified state. Her long brown hair was well preserved. Her breasts, although shrunken, were still clearly visible, as were her pubic hairs and her pelvis.

There was an indent in the rear of her skull, consistent with a heavy blow or fall. Before going into a detailed examination, just from what she could see, Nadiuska said that would be enough, in that part of the skull, to kill a normal person.

Joan said that her teeth indicated the woman was between late teens and mid-twenties.

Rachael Ryan's age.

Is that how Rachael Ryan would look now?
Dead like you? If you are not her.

In an attempt to ascertain her age more accurately, Nadiuska was now removing some of the skin around the corpse's neck to expose her collar bone. As she did so, Joan Major watched intently.

The forensic archaeologist suddenly became increasingly animated.

'Yes, look! Look at the clavicle, see? There's no sign of fusion on the medial clavicle, or even the beginning of it. That normally occurs around the age of thirty. So we can say pretty much for certain she was well below thirty – in her early twenties, I would estimate. I'll be able to get a more accurate age estimate when we've exposed more of the skeleton.'

Grace stared at the dead woman's face, feeling desperately sad for her.

Rachael Ryan, is that who you are?

He was feeling increasingly certain that it was.

He remembered so vividly talking to her distraught parents on those terrible days following her disappearance at Christmas 1997. He could recall her face, every detail of it, despite all that had happened in the intervening years. That smiling, happy, pretty face; such a young face, so full of life.

Have I found you at last, Rachael? Too late, I know. I'm sorry it's much too late. I apologize. I tried my best.

A DNA test would tell him if he was right and there was going to be no problem getting a good sample. Both the pathologist and the forensic archaeologist were profoundly impressed with the condition of the corpse. Nadiuska declared that it was better preserved than some bodies that were only weeks old, and attributed it to the fact that she had been wrapped in the two layers of plastic sheeting, and buried in a dry place.

At this moment, Nadiuska was conducting vaginal scrapings, carefully bagging and tagging each separate sample as she worked her way deeper up inside it.

Grace continued to stare at the body, the twelve years slipping away. And suddenly he wondered if, one day, he'd be in a mortuary, somewhere, looking at a body and nodding his head that it was Sandy.

'It is quite remarkable!' Nadiuska announced. 'The vagina is absolutely intact!'

Grace could not take his eyes from the body. The long brown hair looked in almost obscenely fresh condition, compared to the wizened scalp it sprouted from. There was a myth that hair and nails kept growing long after death. The prosaic truth was that skin contracted – that was all. Everything stopped at death, except for the parasitic cells inside you, which revelled in the fact that your brain no longer launched the antibodies to destroy them. So as your skin slowly shrank, shrivelling, being eaten away from inside, so more of your hair and nails became exposed.

'Oh, my God!' Nadiuska suddenly exclaimed. 'Look what we have here!'

Grace turned towards her, startled. She was holding up, in her gloved hand, a small metal object with a thin handle. Something dangled on the end of it. At first he thought it was a piece of torn flesh.

Then, looking more closely, he realized what it actually was.

A condom.

109

He ripped away the duct tape covering Jessie's mouth, and as he pulled off the last layer, tearing it from her skin and lips and hair, she croaked in pain, then moments later, almost oblivious of the stinging pain, began gulping down air. Momentary relief that she was able to breathe normally flooded through her.

'Nice to meet you properly,' he said through the mouth slit in his hood, in his small voice.

He put the interior light in the van on and for the first time she could get a proper look at him. Sitting on a seat, staring down at her, he didn't appear particularly big or strong, even dressed in his macho head-to-toe motor-cycling leathers. But the hood chilled her. She saw his helmet lying on the floor, with heavy gauntlets folded into it. On his hands now he just wore surgical gloves.

'Thirsty?'

He had moved her on the floor, propped her back against the wall, but leaving her trussed up. She looked in desperation at the open water bottle he held out to her and nodded. 'Please.' It was hard to speak, her mouth was so dry and gummed up. Then her eyes darted to the ser-rated hunting knife he held in the other gloved hand. Not that he needed it; her arms were pinioned behind her back and her legs were still bound at the knees and the ankles.

She could kick him, she knew. She could bend her knees and kick out and really hurt him. But what use would that be? Just enrage him further, and make him do something worse to her than he already had in mind?

It was vital to keep her powder dry. She knew from her nursing days where the vulnerable points were; and from her kick-boxing training, where to land a venomous kick, one that, if she struck the right place, would disable him for a few seconds at the very least, and if she was lucky, longer.

If she got the chance.

She would have only one chance. It was absolutely crucial she didn't blow it.

She swigged down the water greedily, gulping, gulping, until she couldn't swallow fast enough and it overflowed down her chin. She choked, coughing hard. When she had finished coughing, she drank some more, still parched, then thanked him, smiling, looking straight at him pleasantly, as if he was her new best friend, knowing that somehow she had to establish a rapport with him.

'Please don't hurt me,' she croaked. 'I'll do whatever you want.'

'Yes,' he answered. 'I know you will.' He leaned forward and held up the knife in front of her face. 'It's sharp,' he said. 'Do you want to know how sharp?' He pressed the flat of the cold steel blade against her cheek. 'It's so sharp, you could shave with it. You could shave off all your disgusting bodily hairs – especially your pubes, all soaked in urine. Do you know what else I could do with it?'

He kept the flat of the blade to her face as she replied, shaking in terror, almost in a whisper. 'No.'

'I could circumcise you.'

He let the words sink in.

She said nothing. Her brain was kicking off in every direction. *Rapport. Must establish a rapport.*

'Why?' she said, trying to sound calm, but it came out as a gasp. 'I mean – why would you want to do that?'

'Isn't that what happens to all Jewish boys?'

She nodded, feeling the blade starting to bite into her skin, just beneath her right eye.

'Tradition,' she said.

'But not girls?'

'No. Some cultures, but not Jewish.'

'Is that right?'

The blade was pressing so hard she daren't move her head any more. 'Yes.' She only mouthed the word; the sound was trapped, by terror, in her throat.

'Circumcising a woman stops her from getting sexual pleasure. A circumcised woman can't have an orgasm, so after a short while she doesn't bother to try. Which means she doesn't bother being unfaithful to her husband, there's no point. Did you know that?'

Again her reply would not leave her throat. 'No,' she mouthed.

'I know how to do it,' he said. 'I've studied it. You wouldn't like me to circumcise you, would you?'

'No.' This time it came out as a faint whisper. She was quaking, trying to breathe steadily, to calm herself down. To think straight. 'You don't need to do that to me,' she said, her voice a fraction louder now. 'I'll be a good girl to you, I promise.'

'Will you wash yourself for me?'

'Yes.'

'Everywhere?'

'Yes.'

'Will you shave your pubes off for me?'

'Yes.'

Still keeping the knife to her cheek he said, 'I've got water in this van – warm running water. Soap. A sponge. A towel. A razor. I'm going to let you take all your clothes off so you can clean yourself up. Then we're going to play with that shoe.' He pointed at the floor with the water bottle. 'Recognize it? Identical to the pair you bought on Tuesday in Marielle Shoes in Brighton. It's a shame you kicked one out of the van or we could have played with a pair. But we'll have fun with just one, won't we?'

'Yes,' she said. Then, trying to sound bright, she added, 'I like shoes. Do you?'

'Oh, very much. I like the ones with high heels. Ones that women can use like a dildo.'

'Like a dildo? You mean use on themselves?'

'That's what I mean.'

'Is that what you'd like to do?'

'I'll tell you what you're going to do when I'm ready,' he snapped suddenly, anger flaring from nowhere. Then he pulled the knife away from her cheek and began to cut free the duct tape binding her knees together.

'I'm going to give you one word of warning, Jessie,' he said, his tone all friendly again. 'I don't want anything to spoil our fun, yeah? Our little session that we're going to have, OK?'

She pursed her lips and nodded her agreement, giving him all she could manage of a smile.

Then he raised the knife blade so that it was right in front of her nose. 'If you try anything, if you try to hurt me or escape, then what I'm going to do is tie you up again, but without any tracksuit bottoms or panties, yeah? Then I'm going to circumcise you. Just think about that when you're on your honeymoon with Benedict. And every time your husband makes love to you, for the rest of your life. Just think what you'll be missing. Do we understand each other?'

'Yes,' she mouthed.

But she was thinking.

He wasn't big. He was a bully.

She had been bullied at school. Bullied for her hooked nose, bullied for being the rich kid whose parents collected her in flash cars. But she'd learned how to deal with them. Bullies expected to get their own way. They weren't prepared for people to stand up to them. She once whacked her school's biggest bully, Karen Walder-grave, on the knee with a hockey stick during a game. Hit her so hard she'd shattered the bone, and she had to have an artificial kneecap made. Of course, it was an accident. One of those unfortunate things that happen in sport – at least, that was how it seemed to the teachers. No one ever bullied her again.

The instant she had her chance, this man wasn't going to bully her again either.

He cut free the tape securing her ankles. As she gratefully began moving her legs, to get the circulation back, he went to the sink and ran a tap. 'Get it nice and warm for you!' He turned back and looked hard at her. 'I'm going to free your hands now, so you can wash and shave for me. Remember what I've told you?'

She nodded.

'Say it out aloud.'

'I remember what you've told me.'

He cut the bonds joining her wrists, then told her to remove the duct tape.

She shook her hands for some seconds to get them working again, then picked at the strands of tape, getting purchase and ripping them free. He held the knife up, all the time, stroking the flat of the blade with his opaque, gloved finger.

'The floor is fine,' he said, as he noticed her wondering what to do with the curled strips.

Then he reached down, picked up the leather shoe from the floor and handed it to Jessie. 'Smell it!' he said.

She frowned.

'Hold it to your nose. Savour the smell!'

She sniffed the strong smell of fresh leather.

'Good, isn't it?'

His eyes, for an instant, were on the shoe and not her. She saw a glint in them. He was distracted. The shoe was at this moment the focus of his attention, not her. She held it up beneath her nose again, pretending to savour it, and surreptitiously changed her grip on it, so she was holding it by the toe. At the same time, on the pretext of working circulation back into her legs, she began to bend her knees.

'Are you the one they talked about in the papers, with the little winkie?' she asked suddenly.

He jerked towards her at the insult. As he did so, she arched her back and straightened her knees, springing both her legs up as hard as she could, striking him beneath the chin with the toes of her trainers, physically lifting him up, and slamming his head into the ceiling of the camper van. He fell, dazed, to the floor, the knife clattering away from him.

Before he had a chance to recover his wits, she was up on her feet, tearing the hood from his head. He looked almost pathetic without it, like a little startled mole. Then she slammed the shoe, stiletto heel first, as hard as she could into his right eye.

He screamed. A terrible howl of pain and shock and fury. Blood sprayed from his face. Then, grabbing the knife from the floor, she jerked open the sliding door and stumbled out, almost tumbling head first into pitch darkness. Behind her she heard the terrible howl of pain of a maddened, wounded beast.

She ran and crashed into something solid and unyielding. Then streaks of bright light darted around her.

Shit, shit, shit.

How could she have been so stupid? She should have taken the bloody torch!

In the beam, she momentarily saw the disused goods carriage on the dusted-over tracks. A gantry. Part of the steel walkway halfway up the walls. What looked like massive suspended turbines.

Where was the door?

She heard a shuffle. He was screaming out, in pain and fury. 'YOU THINK YOU'RE GOING TO GET AWAY – YOU ARE NOT, YOU BITCH.'

She gripped the knife. The beam shone straight in her face, dazzling her. She turned. Saw huge double doors, over the railway tracks. For the carriages to come in and out through. She sprinted towards them, the beam guiding her all the way there.

All the way to the padlocked chain between them.

110

Jessie turned and stared straight into the beam, her brain racing. He didn't have a gun, she was pretty sure of that, otherwise he'd have pulled that on her, not the knife. He was wounded. He was not big. She had the knife. She knew some self-defence. But he still frightened her.

There must be another exit.

Then the torch went off.

She blinked at the darkness, as if that might make it go away, or somehow lighten it. She was shaking. She could hear herself panting. She struggled to quieten her breathing down.

Now they were equal, but he had an advantage. He presumably knew the layout in here.

Was he creeping up on her now?

In the torch beam, she'd seen to her left a vast space with what looked like some kind of silo at the end of it. She took a few steps and almost instantly stumbled. There was a loud metal *pinggggggg* as something rolled away from under her feet and fell with a swoosh, splashing into water below seconds later.

Shit.

She stood still. Then she remembered her phone!

If she could get back to the van, she could call for help. Then with panic rising, she thought again, *Call who?*

Where was she? Trapped inside some fucking great disused factory building somewhere. How great would that sound if she told the 999 operator?

*

He was already back at the camper van. His face was throbbing in agony and he couldn't see out of his right eye, but he didn't care, not at this moment. He did not care about anything except getting that bitch. She'd seen his face.

He had to find her. Had to stop her getting away.

Had to, because she could bring him down.

And he knew how.

He did not want to reveal his position by switching on the torch, so he moved as slowly as he could, feeling his way around the interior of the van until he found what he was looking for. His night-vision binoculars.

It took him only seconds to spot her. A green figure through the night-vision lens, moving slowly, inching her way left, walking like someone in slow motion.

Think you are so smart, don't you?

He looked around for an implement. Something heavy and solid that would bring her down. He opened the cupboard beneath the sink, but it was too dark to see in, even with his night-vision. So he briefly switched on the torch. The night-vision flared, shooting searing light into his right eye, startling him so much he dropped the torch and stumbled back, falling over.

*

Jessie heard the crash. She looked over in its direction and instantly saw light inside the camper. She hurried further away towards the silo she had seen, fumbling her way, tripping over something, then banging her head into a sharp protruding object. She stifled a groan. Then carried on, feeling with her hands in the darkness until they reached an upright steel stanchion.

One of the pillars supporting the silo?

She crept forward, feeling the downward curve of the base of the silo, and crawled under it, then, still inching her way with her hands, she stood up, breathing in a dry dusty smell. Then she touched something that felt like the rung of a ladder.

*

He carried on searching with the torch, frantically opening each of the drawers. In the last one he found a bunch of tools. Among them was a big, heavy spanner. He picked it up, feeling the pain in his eye worsening with every second, feeling the blood streaming down his face. He retrieved the binoculars and moved to the door, staring out through them.

The bitch had vanished.

He didn't care. He would find her. He knew the whole of this cement works like the back of his hand. He'd supervised the installation of all the surveillance cameras in here. This building housed the giant kilns that heated the combined limestone, clay, sand and bottom ash to 1,500 degrees Celsius, then fed it into twin giant cooling turbines, forward to the grinding mills and, when processed, into a series of storage silos to feed into waiting empty goods trucks. If the bitch wanted to hide, there were plenty of places.

But there was only one exit.

And he had the keys to the padlock in his pocket.

111

Roy Grace delayed the Sunday evening briefing to 7.30 p.m., to give him time to report on the findings from the exhumation.

He left Glenn Branson in the mortuary, to cover any new developments that might occur, as the post-mortem was still not completed and was not likely to be for some while yet. The corpse had a broken jawbone and fractured skull, and it was the blow to the skull that had almost certainly killed her.

His best hopes, both of identifying the dead woman and of achieving his aim in having this exhumation, lay in the hair follicles and skin samples taken from the corpse, along with the condom which contained, in the views of Nadiuska De Sancha and Joan Major, what might be intact traces of semen. The forensic archaeologist thought that although it was twelve years old there was a good chance of DNA being extracted intact from that.

These items had been couriered in an icebox to the DNA laboratory he favoured for fast turnarounds and with whom he had a good working relationship, Orchid Cellmark Forensics. They had promised to start work the moment the items arrived. But there was a slow sequencing process and even if the lab worked around the clock, the earliest they could expect any results would be mid-afternoon tomorrow, Monday. Grace was assured he would be notified instantly by phone.

He took his place and addressed his team, bringing them up to date, then asked for progress reports.

Bella Moy went first, handing out photographs of a young woman with wild hair. 'Sir, this is a photograph up in Brighton nick of one of the wanted persons in the city. Her current name – she's used several aliases – is Donna Aspinall. She's a known user, with a string of previous for fare dodging, both on trains and in taxis. She's got an ASBO and she's currently wanted on three separate counts of violent assault, GBH and actual assault. She's been identified by two covert officers in the operation last night – one of whom she bit on the arm – as the person John Kerridge, the taxi driver, was chasing.'

Grace stared at the photograph, realizing the implication. 'You're saying that Kerridge is telling the truth?'

'This would imply that he might be telling the truth about this passenger, sir.'

He thought for a moment. Kerridge had now been held for twenty-four hours. The maximum period for detaining a suspect without charge and without obtaining a court extension was thirty-six hours. They would have to release the taxi driver at 9.30 tomorrow, unless they had enough reason to convince a magistrate to hold him longer. They didn't yet have evidence that Jessie Sheldon's disappearance was the work of the Shoe Man. But if Kerridge's solicitor, Acott, got hold of this – and he undoubtedly would and probably already had – they'd have a fight on their hands to get an extension. He needed to think about this, and getting an emergency magistrates' court appearance tonight to request a further extension.

'OK, thanks. Good work, Bella.'

Then Norman Potting raised his hand. 'Boss, I've had a lot of help today from the mobile phone company, O_2. I spoke to Jessie Sheldon's fiancé early this morning, who told me that's the supplier her iPhone's registered with. They provided me half an hour ago with the tracking report on her phone. We may have a result here.'

'Go on,' Grace said.

'The last call she made on it was logged at 6.32 p.m. last night, to a number I've identified as belonging to her fiancé, Benedict Greene. He confirms he received a call from her at approximately that time, telling him she was heading home from her kick-boxing lesson. He told her to hurry, because he was picking her up at 7.15 p.m. The phone then remained in standby mode. No further calls were made, but it was plotted, from contact with base stations in the city, moving steadily west from approximately 6.45 p.m. – the time of the abduction. At 7.15 p.m. it stopped moving and has remained static since then.'

'Where?' Grace asked.

'Well,' the DS said, 'let me show you.'

He stood up and pointed to an Ordnance Survey map stuck to a whiteboard on the wall. A squiggly blue line ran the entire length of it. There was a red oval drawn on the map, with two red Xs at the top and bottom.

'The two crosses mark the O2 base stations that Jessie Sheldon's phone is currently communicating with,' Potting said. 'It's a pretty big area and unfortunately there's no third base station within range to give us the triangulation which would enable us to pinpoint her position more accurately.'

He pointed at the squiggly blue line. 'This is the River Adur, which runs up from Shoreham.'

'Shoreham's where John Kerridge lives,' Bella Moy said.

'Yes, but that's not helpful to us, since he's in custody,' Potting replied in a patronizing tone. Then he continued: 'There's open countryside on both sides of the river and Coombes Road, a busy main road which runs between these two base stations. There are a few detached private houses, a row of cottages that used to belong to the old cement works, and the cement works itself. It would seem that Jessie Sheldon, or at least her mobile phone, is somewhere inside this circle. But it's a big area.'

'We can rule out the cement works,' said DC Nick Nicholl. 'I attended there a couple of years ago when I was on Response. It's got extremely high security – round-the-clock monitoring. If a bird shits, it pings an alarm.'

'Excellent, Nick,' Grace said. 'Thank you. OK. Immediate action. We need to get a ground search of the entire area at first light. A POLSA and as many Uniform, Specials and PCSOs as we can muster. I want the river searched – we'll put the Specialist Search Unit in there. And we'll get the helicopter up right away. They can do a floodlight search.'

Grace made some notes, then looked up at his team.

'According to the Land Registry records, the lock-up is owned by a property company, sir,' Emma-Jane Boutwood said. 'I'll go to their offices first thing in the morning.'

He nodded. Despite round-the-clock surveillance, no one had shown up there. He was not hopeful that anyone would now.

He wasn't sure what to think.

He turned to the forensic psychologist. 'Julius, anything?'

Proudfoot nodded. 'The man who has taken Jessie Sheldon, he's your man,' he said emphatically. 'Not the chap you have in custody.'

'You sound very certain.'

'Mark my words. The right location, the right time, the right person,' he said, so smugly that Grace wished desperately, for an instant, that he could prove the man wrong.

*

When he returned to his office after the briefing had ended, Grace found a small FedEx package awaiting him.

Curious, he sat down and tore it open. And his evening just got a whole lot worse.

There was a handwritten note inside, on Police Training College, Bramshill headed paper, and attached to it was a photocopy of an email dated October last year.

The email was addressed to him, from Detective Superintendent Cassian Pewe. It informed him that there were some pages missing from the file on the Shoe Man that Grace had asked him to look through. The same crucial pages on the witness who had seen the van in which Rachael Ryan might have been abducted back in 1997.

The handwritten note said breezily. *Found this in my Sent box, Roy! Hope it's helpful. Perhaps your memory's not what it was – but hey, don't worry – happens to all of us! Cheers. Cassian.*

After ten minutes of searching through his email system, Grace found the original sitting among hundreds of others that were unread. It had been chaos around that time and Pewe seemed to have taken delight in bombarding him with dozens of e-missives daily. If he had read them all, he'd never have got anything done.

Nonetheless, it was going to leave him with a red face, and one less suspect.

112

Jessie had always been petrified of heights and for that reason at least she was grateful for the darkness. She had no idea where she was, but she had just climbed, one rung at a time, what she figured might be an inspection ladder inside the silo chute.

She had climbed for so long it felt like the ladder reached up to the skies, and she was glad she could not see down. She looked, every few rungs, scared he might already be climbing up after her, but there was no sign – or sound – of him.

Finally at the top she'd felt a railing and a gridded metal floor, and had hauled herself up on to this. Then she had gone head first into a stack of what felt and smelt like old cement bags, and had crawled on top of them. It was where she crouched now, peering into the blackness all around her and listening, trying to keep still to stop the bags rustling.

But she could hear nothing beyond the regular sounds of her prison. The regular clangings, clatterings, squeakings and bangings that were all much louder up here than they'd been when she was in the van, as the wind battered broken metal sheeting all around her.

She was thinking hard. What was his plan? Why wasn't he using the torch?

Was there another way up here?

The only thing that she could see was the luminous dial of her watch. It was just coming up to 9.30 p.m. Sunday night, she figured, it had to be. Over twenty-four hours since she'd been kidnapped. What was happening at home and with Benedict? He'd be isolated from her parents, she thought, wishing desperately now she had introduced them sooner, so they could all be doing something together.

Were the police involved? They must be. She knew her father. He would get every emergency service in the country involved.

How were they? What was her mother thinking? Her father? Benedict?

She heard the distant clatter of a helicopter. That was the second time in the past half-hour she had heard one.

Maybe it was looking for her.

*

He heard the sound of the helicopter again too. A powerful machine, not one of the smaller training ones from the school at nearby Shoreham Airport. And not many helicopters flew at night either. Mainly military, rescue services, air ambulances – and police.

The Sussex Police helicopter was based at Shoreham. If it was theirs that he was hearing, there was no reason to panic. It could be up for all kinds of reasons. The clatter was fading now; it was heading away to the east.

Then he heard a new sound that worried him much more.

A sharp, insistent buzzing. It was coming from the front of the camper. He lowered the binoculars and saw a weak, pulsing light that was also coming from the same place.

'Oh, shit. No, no, no!'

It was the bitch's mobile phone, which he had taken from her pocket. He thought he had switched the fucking thing off.

He stumbled up to the front, able to see the light from the phone's flashing display, seized it, then threw it on the floor in fury and stamped on it, crushing it like a massive beetle.

He stamped on it again. Then again. Then again.

Maddened with pain from his eye, anger at the bitch and anger at himself, he stood shaking. *Christ! Oh, Christ! Oh, Christ!* How could he have been so stupid?

Mobile phones gave away your location, even when they were only on standby. It would be one of the first things any intelligent police officer would be looking for.

Perhaps the phone companies were not able to access detailed stuff like that on Sundays?

But he knew he could not take the risk. He had to move Jessie Sheldon away from here as quickly as possible. Tonight. During darkness.

Which made it even more imperative to find her and quickly.

She'd made no sound for over an hour. Playing some clever hiding game. She might think she was clever that she had the knife. But he had two far more valuable tools at this moment. The torch and the binoculars.

He'd never had much truck with literature and shit. But there was one line he remembered from somewhere, through his pain: *In the land of the blind, the one-eyed man is king.*

That's what he was now.

He stepped down out of the van on to the concrete floor and raised his binoculars to his face. Hunting.

113

The evening was passing slowly for Roy Grace. He sat in his office, looking at Jessie Sheldon's family tree, which had been assembled by one of his team members. Her computer and mobile phone records were currently being examined by two members of the overloaded and under-manned High-Tech Crime Unit, who had given up their Sundays for the task.

The only report he'd received so far was that Jessie was very active on social networking sites – something she had in common with the woman who had nearly become a victim of the Shoe Man on Thursday afternoon, Dee Burchmore.

Was that how he followed his victims?

Mandy Thorpe had been active on Facebook and on two other sites as well. But neither Nicola Taylor, who had been raped in the Metropole Hotel, early on New Year's Day, nor Roxy Pearce, who had been raped in her home in Droveway Avenue, had presences on any social networking sites, nor did they Tweet.

It came back to the same thing linking each of these women. They had all recently bought expensive shoes from shops in Brighton. All except Mandy Thorpe.

Despite Dr Proudfoot's insistence to the contrary, the Detective Superintendent continued to believe that

Mandy Thorpe had not been raped by the Shoe Man but by someone else. Perhaps by a copycat. Or possibly the timing was coincidental.

His phone rang. It was DC Michael Foreman from MIR-1.

'Just had a report in from Hotel 900, who are going down to refuel, sir. So far they have nothing to report, except for two possible anomalies in the old cement works.'

'*Anomalies*?' Grace queried, wondering what the police helicopter crew meant by that.

He knew they had thermal-imaging equipment on board, which could detect humans in pitch darkness or dense fog just from the body heat they gave off. Unfortunately, while good for following villains who were fleeing from a stolen car and trying to hide in woods, or in alleys, it was easily fooled by animals or by anything that retained warmth.

'Yes, sir. They can't be sure they're human – could be foxes or badgers or stray cats or dogs.'

'OK, get a response unit down there to check it out. Keep me posted.'

*

Half an hour later, DC Foreman rang Grace back. A patrol car had attended the entrance to the old cement works and reported that the place was secure. There were ten-foot-high locked gates, topped with razor wire, and extensive surveillance.

'What kind of surveillance?' Grace asked.

'Remote monitoring. A Brighton firm with a good reputation, Sussex Remote Monitoring Services. If there was anything going on in there it would have been picked up by now by them, sir.'

'I know the name,' Grace said.

'The police use them. I think the Sussex House door pads were all installed by them.'

'Right. OK.' Like everyone in the city, he knew the cement works. It was one of the big landmarks, heading west, and there were rumours that at some point it was going to be reactivated after nearly two decades in mothballs. It was a vast place, situated in a chalk quarry hewn out of the Downs, comprising a group of buildings, each of them bigger than a football pitch. He wasn't even sure who the current owners were, but no doubt there would be a sign on the front.

To do a search he'd either have to get their consent or obtain a search warrant. And for an effective search, he'd have to put a big team in there. It would need to be done in daylight.

He made a note on his pad for the morning.

114

'Jessie!' he shouted. 'Phone call for you.'

He sounded so plausible, she almost believed him.

'Jessie! It's Benedict! He wants to do a deal with me to let you go! But first he needs to know you are OK. He wants to speak to you!'

She remained silent, trying to think this through. Had Benedict rung, which was highly probable, and the creep answered?

Was this about a ransom?

Benedict didn't have any money. What kind of deal could he do? And anyhow, this creep was a pervert, the Shoe Man, or whoever he was. He wanted her to masturbate with her shoe. What deal was he talking about? It didn't make sense.

And she knew, if she shouted, she would give her location away.

Lying on the old cement sacks, aching with cramp and craving water, she realized, for the moment anyway, that despite everything she was safe up here. She'd heard him creeping around the place for nearly two hours, downstairs first, then up on the floor above her, then clambering on to another level that did not sound far below her. At one point he had been so close she could hear him breathing. But mostly he had been silent, just every now and then giving away his position by kicking something, or crunching something underfoot, or with a ping of metal on metal. But he had not switched on his torch.

For a while she'd wondered if he had broken it, or if the battery had run out. But then she'd seen something that chilled her.

A very faint red glow.

It was not an area of technology on which she was clued up, but she remembered a movie in which a character had used night-vision equipment and that had given off a barely detectable red glow. Was that what he was using in here, she wondered?

Something through which he would watch her, without being seen?

So why hadn't he already sneaked up on her? There had to be only one reason: he had not been able to find her.

That's what this pretend call from Benedict was all about.

*

He knew one thing for certain. He'd searched every inch of this floor and she wasn't down here. She had to have climbed up, but where? There were two vast upstairs areas housing the long cooling pipes and the kilns that blasted the hot cement clinker into them. Any number of hiding places, but he thought he had searched them all.

She was clever, this bitch. Maybe she kept moving. He was getting more anxious and desperate with every passing minute. He had to get her away from here and somehow secure her in another place. And he had to be at work tomorrow. It was a very important day. A major new client and a key meeting with the bank about his expansion plans. He was going to have to get some sleep before then.

And his eye needed to be looked at. The pain was worsening all the time.

'Jessie!' he called out again, all friendly. 'It's for yooooooooouuuuu!'

Then, after a few moments silence, he said, 'I know where you are, Jessie! I can see you up there! If Mohammed won't come to the mountain, then the mountain's coming to Mohammed!'

Silence greeting him. Then the bang of a metal flap. Four seconds later, it banged again.

'You're only making this worse for yourself, Jessie. I'm not going to be happy when I find you. I'm really not!'

*

Jessie did not make a sound. She realized one thing. All the time it was dark, this creep had the advantage. But the moment dawn broke and some light started seeping in here, however little, all that changed. He frightened her and she did not know what he was capable of. But she was sure she had hurt his eye badly. And she still had the knife, on the floor, right by her hand.

It was midnight. Dawn would be some time around seven o'clock. Somehow she had to find the strength to forget her raging thirst and her tiredness. Sleep was not an option.

Tomorrow maybe there'd be a chink of light coming through a wall. This place was derelict. In semi ruins. There had to be a hole somewhere that she could crawl through. Even if it was on to the roof.

115

Despite the vigorous protests of the taxi driver's solicitor, Ken Acott, Grace had refused to allow John Kerridge – Yac – to be freed, and insisted on applying to the magistrates' court for a further thirty-six-hour extension. It had been granted readily, since, after the solicitor's insistence on having a specialist medic present, they had not yet been able to start interviewing Kerridge.

Grace was still not happy with this suspect, although he had to admit the evidence against Kerridge did not look strong, so far. The man's mobile phone had yielded nothing. He only had five numbers stored on it. One belonged to the owner of his taxi, one was for the taxi company, two were for the owners of the boat he lived on, who were in Goa – a mobile and a landline – and one for a therapist he had not seen in over a year.

The taxi driver's computer had not revealed anything of interest. Just endless visits to sites involving ladies' shoes – mostly on the fashion rather than fetish side – visits to eBay, as well as countless visits to perfume sites, sites concerned with Victorian period toilets and mapping sites.

A medical expert, a psychologist of some sort who was trained in Asperger's syndrome patients was on her way down. When she arrived, if she assessed Kerridge favourably, Acott said he would allow his client to be interviewed. Hopefully they'd find out more then.

Just as he returned to his office from the morning briefing, his mobile phone rang.

'Roy Grace,' he answered.

It was a technician he knew at the forensic laboratories and she was sounding very pleased with herself. 'Roy, I've got DNA results for you!'

'On what we sent you last night?' he replied, astonished.

'It's a new bit of kit – it's still undergoing trials and it's not reliable enough for court work. But we had such good DNA from both of those samples, we took some to experiment with, knowing the urgency.'

'So, tell me?'

'We have two hits – one for each sample. One is complete, a 100 per cent match, the other is partial, a familial match. The complete match is on DNA from a hair follicle from the corpse. Her name is Rachael Ryan. She disappeared in 1997. Any help?'

'You're certain?'

'The *machine* is certain. We're still running conventionally with the rest of her DNA, so we'll have that result later today. But I'm pretty sure.'

He allowed himself only a couple of seconds for this to sink in. It was what he was expecting, but even so it was a shock. A confirmation of his failure to save this young woman's life. He made a mental note to contact her parents, hoping they were both still alive and still together. At least now they would have closure, if nothing else.

'And the familial match?' he asked.

Familial, Grace knew, meant a near match, but not an exact match. It was normally a match between siblings or a parent and child.

'That's from the semen inside the condom that was found inside the corpse – Rachael Ryan as we now know. It's a woman called Mrs Elizabeth Wyman-Bentham.'

Grace wrote the name down, checking the spelling with her, so excited his hand was shaking. Then the technician gave him her address.

'Do we know why she's on the database?'

'Drink-driving.'

He thanked her, and as soon as he had terminated the call, he dialled Directory Enquiries, gave the name of Elizabeth Wyman-Bentham and her address.

Moments later, he had the number and dialled it.

It went straight to voicemail. He left a message with his name and rank, asking her to call him back urgently on his mobile number. Then he sat down and Googled her name to see if he could find out anything about her, in particular where she worked. It was 9.15 a.m. If she worked she was likely to be there already, or on her way there.

Moments later on his screen appeared the words, *About Lizzie Wyman-Bentham, CEO of WB Public Relations.*

He clicked on them and almost immediately a photograph of a smiling woman, with a mass of frizzed hair, came up, together with a row of details to click on for information about the firm. Just as he clicked on *Contact*, his phone rang.

He answered and heard a rather breathless, effusive female voice. 'I'm so sorry, I missed your call – heard it ringing just as I stepped out of the house! How can I help you?'

'This may sound a strange question,' Roy Grace asked. 'Do you have a brother or a son?'

'A brother.' Then her voice changed to panic. 'Is he

all right? Has something happened? Has he been in an accident?'

'No, he's fine, so far as we know. I need to speak to him in connection with a police inquiry.'

'Gosh, I was worried for a moment!'

'Can you tell me where I can reach him?'

'An inquiry, did you say? Ah yes, of course, probably something to do with work. Silly of me! I think he does a bit of work with you guys. He's Garry Starling and his company – well, he has two – Sussex Security Systems and Sussex Remote Monitoring Services – they're both in the same building in Lewes.'

Grace wrote the information down, and took Starling's office phone number.

'I'm not quite sure why – why exactly have you contacted me?'

'It's a little bit complicated,' Grace replied.

Her voice darkened. 'Garry's not in trouble, is he? I mean, he's a very respectable businessman – he's very well known in this city.'

Not wanting to give anything further away, he assured her that no, her brother was not in trouble. He ended the call, then immediately dialled Starling's office. The phone was answered by a pleasant woman. He did not reveal his identity, but merely asked to speak to Garry Starling.

'He's not in yet,' she said, 'but I'm sure he will be shortly. He's normally in by this time. I'm his secretary. Can I take a message?'

'I'll call back,' Grace said. He had to struggle to keep his voice sounding calm.

The instant he hung up, he hurried along to MIR-1, formulating his plan as he strode down the corridor.

116

There was less light than Jessie had imagined there'd be, which in some ways she thought was good. If she was very, very careful, keeping totally silent, she was able to tiptoe a short distance along the gridded walkway and look down at the camper van.

It sat there, cream and grimy, with its side door open. It was the kind of camper van that used to be one of the symbols of the hippy era – flower power, ban-the-bomb, all that stuff she recalled from what she had read about the 1960s and 1970s.

This creep didn't seem much like a hippy.

He was inside the van at the moment. Had he slept? She doubted it. Once or twice during the darkness she'd nearly dozed off, and on one occasion had almost cried out when an animal of some kind brushed her arm. Then a while later, as dawn brought with it a weak, grey haze of light, a rat came and took a look at her.

She hated rats and after that incident her tiredness was banished.

What was his plan now? What was going on in the outside world? She'd not heard the helicopter again, so maybe it hadn't been looking for her after all. How long would this go on for?

Perhaps he had supplies in the van. She knew he had

water and maybe he had food. He could sit this out indefinitely, if he didn't have a job or a life that was missing him. Whereas, she knew, she could not go on much longer without water and something to eat. She was feeling weak. On edge, but definitely weaker than yesterday. And dog tired. Running on adrenalin.

And determination.

She was going to marry Benedict. This creep was not going to stop her. Nothing was.

I am going to get out of here.

The wind was strong today and seemed to be getting stronger. The cacophony of sounds all around was worsening. Good, because that would help cover any noise she might make moving around.

Suddenly she heard a howl of rage. 'ALL RIGHT, YOU BITCH, I'VE HAD ENOUGH OF YOUR DAMNED GAMES. I'M COMING AFTER YOU. HEAR ME? I'VE WORKED OUT WHERE YOU ARE AND I'M COMING AFTER YOU!'

She tiptoed back to her vantage point and looked down. To her shock she could see him, still with his hood off, with what looked like a big red weal around his right eye. He was running across the ground floor, holding a big spanner in one hand and a carving knife in the other.

He was running straight for the entrance of the silo beneath her.

Then she heard him shouting again, his voice an echoing boom, as if he was shouting through a funnel. 'OH, VERY CLEVER, BITCH. A LADDER UP INSIDE THE SILO! HOW DID YOU FIND THAT?'

Moments later she heard the clanging of the rungs.

117

Glenn Branson was already waiting for Roy Grace in an unmarked car at the entrance to the industrial estate. He had the signed search warrants in his pocket.

The map they had studied earlier, in their hasty plan for this operation, showed there were only two possible routes in or out for vehicles visiting Garry Starling's head-quarters here for his two companies, Sussex Security Systems and Sussex Remote Monitoring Services. Tucked discreetly out of sight, at this moment, were the vehicles of the team he had organized to carry out the arrest – when and if Starling turned up.

He already had four covert officers in place on the estate, in casual clothes. Parked up a side street, and ready to move in the moment Starling returned, were two dog-handler units to cover the exits to his office building. He had one of the Local Support Team vans, with six officers in body armour waiting inside it, plus four plain cars cover-ing access to the network of roads linking into the indus-trial estate should Starling try to make a run for it.

Grace left his unmarked car parked in the next street along and climbed into Glenn Branson's. He felt tense. Relieved, yet hurting from the confirmation of Rachael Ryan's death. Thinking through the plan now. Plenty worried him.

'Rock 'n' roll?'

Grace nodded distractedly. The Shoe Man had never left DNA traces. His victims reported he had been unable to maintain an erection. Did this mean Garry Starling was not the Shoe Man? Or that killing Rachael Ryan – assuming he was the killer – had turned him on enough to ejaculate?

Why was he not in his office this morning?

If he had sex with a woman twelve years ago who was then found dead, how were they going to prove Starling was the killer? If indeed he was. What view would the Crown Prosecution Service take?

A million unanswered questions.

Just a growing certainty in his mind that the man who had murdered Rachael Ryan was the man who had abducted Jessie Sheldon. He desperately hoped he could do a better job of finding her alive – if there was still a chance – than he had done of finding Rachael Ryan. And that he would not be disinterring her from a grave in another twelve years' time.

As they drove up to the smart front entrance of Sussex Security Systems and Sussex Remote Monitoring Services, he noticed the cars parked in allotted bays, and the empty one marked CEO. But what he was looking at more was the row of white vans bearing the companies' joint logo.

It had been a white van that had driven off at speed from the car park on Thursday after the failed attack on Dee Burchmore. And a white van in which Rachael Ryan had been abducted twelve years ago.

They climbed out of the car and walked in through the front door. A middle-aged receptionist sat behind a curved desk with the two logos emblazoned on the front. To their right was a small seating area, with copies of

Sussex Life and several of today's papers, including the *Argus*, laid out.

Grace thought grimly that they probably wouldn't be laying out tomorrow's *Argus*, with the kind of headline it was likely to contain.

'Can I help you, gentlemen?'

Grace showed his warrant card. 'Has Mr Starling come in yet?'

'No – er, no, not yet,' she said, looking flustered.

'Would you say that's unusual?'

'Well, normally, on a normal Monday morning, he's the first one in.'

Grace held the search warrant up and gave her a few seconds to read it. 'We have a warrant to search these premises. I'd be grateful if you could find someone to show us around.'

'I'll – I'll get the manager, sir.'

'Fine. We'll start. Tell him to find us.'

'Yes – right – yes, I will. When Mr Starling turns up, shall I let you know?'

'It's OK,' Grace replied. 'We'll know.'

She looked lost for an answer.

'Where do we find your CCTV monitoring section?' Grace asked.

'That's on the first floor. I'll page Mr Addenberry and he can take you along.'

Glenn pointed at the door to the stairs. 'First floor.'

'Yes, you turn right. Keep going down the corridor, into the accounts department and then the call-handling and you'll come to it.'

Both detectives loped up the stairs. Just as they reached the end of a corridor, with offices on either side, a short, nervous-looking and balding man in his early forties, in a grey suit with a row of pens in the top pocket, scuttled up to them.

'Hello, gentlemen. How can I help you? I'm John Addenberry, the General Manager.' He had a slightly smarmy voice.

When Grace explained who they were and about the search warrant, Addenberry started to look as if he was standing on a live electrical wire.

'Right,' he said. 'Right. Of course. We do a lot of work for Sussex Police. CID HQ are important customers. Very.'

He led the way through into the CCTV control room. Seated at a chair in front of a bank of twenty television monitors was a enormously overweight character, dressed in an ill-fitting uniform and greasy hair, and looking far too old to be sporting bum-fluff on his lip, Grace thought. A large Coca-Cola and a giant-size packet of Doritos sat on a table in front of him, next to a microphone and a small control panel, and a computer keyboard.

'This is Dunstan Christmas,' Addenberry said. 'He's the duty controller.'

But Grace had turned his attention away to the bank of monitors. And he frowned as he stared at one in particular. The front of a smart, ultra-modern house. Then he pointed. 'No. 7 – is that 76 Droveway Avenue, the home of Mr and Mrs Pearce?'

'Yep,' Christmas said. 'She was raped, wasn't she?'

'I didn't see any cameras when I was there.'

Christmas chewed a nail as he spoke. 'No, you wouldn't. I think in that house they're all hidden.'

'Why's no one told me? There might be evidence on this from her attack,' Grace said angrily.

Christmas shook his head. 'No, wasn't working that

night. It was down from mid-afternoon. Didn't go back up until the next morning.'

Grace stared at him hard and saw Branson doing the same thing. Was he hiding something? Or guileless? Then he stared back at the screen. The image had changed to the rear garden.

Down on the night she was attacked. The company was owned by their new prime suspect.

The coincidence was too much.

'Do these often go down?'

Christmas shook his head and chewed on his nail again. 'No. Very rarely. It's a good system and there's normally backup.'

'But the backup wasn't working on the night Mrs Pearce was attacked?'

'That's what I was told.'

'What about that one there?' Glenn Branson said, pointing at the blank screen numbered 20.

Grace nodded his head. 'Yes, I was going to ask the same.'

'Yep, that's down at the moment.'

'What's the property that's being covered?'

'The old cement works at Shoreham,' Christmas replied.

118

Jessie knew what she had to do, but as the moment approached her body went into panic mode and froze on her.

He was getting closer. Each clang of the rung slow, steady, determined. She could hear his breathing now. Getting closer. Closer. Nearing the top.

Above her she could hear a sound, like the clatter of that helicopter again. But she ignored it, not daring to be distracted. She turned, holding the knife in her hand, then finally dared to look down. And nearly dropped the knife in terror. He was only a few feet below her.

His right eyeball was at a grotesque angle, almost as if it was peering back into its own socket, half sunken in a gunge of coagulated blood and grey fluid, the whole socket encircled inside a livid purple bruise. The massive spanner protruded from the top pocket of his anorak and he was holding the rung with one hand, the carving knife with the other, staring up at her with an expression of utter hatred.

It was a long way down. Her brain was spinning. Trying to think clearly, to remember her instructions, but she'd never been taught how to kick in a situation like this. If she could plant both feet hard on his face she could dislodge him, she knew. It was her one chance.

In a swift moment, she squatted, fighting off the vertigo as she stared down, trying to concentrate on him and not the long drop below. She took all her weight on her hands, braced herself, bent her knees, then kicked as hard as she could, clinging to the slats of the grid with her fingers.

Instantly she felt a searing pain in the ball of her right foot.

Then, crying out in pain, she felt a vice-like clamp around her left ankle. He was pulling her. Pulling her. Trying to dislodge her. And she realized in this instant she had made a terrible mistake. He had jammed his knife into her right foot, let go of the rung and was now holding both her ankles. He was much stronger than he had looked. He was pulling her. Trying to dislodge her. He was being suicidal, she suddenly understood. Taking a gamble. Either he dislodged her and they both plunged together, or she was going to have to pull him up.

Then she felt another searing pain in the ball of her right foot, followed by an agonizing one in her right shin. And another. He was holding on with his left hand and slashing at her foot with the knife. Suddenly there was a terrible, terrible pain in the back of her right ankle and her foot felt powerless.

He had sawn through her Achilles tendon, she realized.

In desperation she jerked sharply backwards. And fell on to her back. He had let go.

She scrambled to her feet and promptly fell over again. She heard a clatter as her knife skidded away from her and then, to her horror, it plunged through the railings. Moments later she heard a *ping* a long way below her. Her right foot, in terrible agony, would no longer support her.

Oh, Jesus. Please help me.

He was hauling himself up over the edge, on to the grid, the carving knife still in his hand.

Trying desperately to think clearly despite her agony, she struggled to remember her training. This was a better position. Her left leg was still working.

He was on the gridded platform now, only feet away from her, on his knees and getting to his feet.

She lay still, watching him.

Watching the leer on his face. He was smiling again. Back in control. Coming after her.

Upright now, he towered over her, holding the knife, with blood on the blade, in his right hand and taking out the spanner from his top pocket with his left. He took a lurching step towards her, then raised the spanner.

In less than a second, she calculated, he would bring that spanner down on her head.

She bent her left knee, then kicked forward with every ounce of strength that remained in her body, visualizing a point a yard behind his right kneecap, heard the snap as she connected, driving her foot into the kneecap, just as she had driven that hockey stick all those years before into the knee of the school bully.

Saw the momentary shock in his face. Heard his hideous howl of pain as he fell over backwards, with an echoing clang, on to the grid. Then, hauling herself up with the help of the railings and holding on, began to hop, dragging her right foot, away from him.

'Owwww! My knee! Owwwwww, you fucking, fucking, fucking bitch.'

There was a vertical ladder she'd seen earlier at the far end of this walkway. She lunged at it, not looking down, ignoring the height. Gripping the edge with both hands she half-hopped, half-slipped, down, down, down, down.

He still had not appeared above her.

Then, as she reached the bottom, a pair of hands gripped her waist.

She screamed in terror.

A calm, gentle, unfamiliar voice said, 'Jessie Sheldon?'

She turned, quaking. And found herself staring at a tall man with silver wisps of hair either side of a black baseball cap. On the front of the cap was written the word POLICE.

She fell into his arms, sobbing.

119

'You're unbelievable! You know that? You are un-fucking-believable! You know how much evidence there is against you? It's un-fucking-believable! You filthy pervert! You – you monster!'

'Keep your voice down,' he replied, in a subdued tone.

Denise Starling stared at her husband, in his shapeless blue prison tracksuit, with the black patch over his right eye, sitting opposite her in the large, garishly furnished, open-plan visiting room. A camera watched them from the ceiling and a microphone was silently recording them. A blue plastic table separated them.

Either side of them, other prisoners talked with their loved ones and their relatives.

'Have you read the papers?' she demanded. 'They're linking you with the Shoe Man rapes back in 1997. You did those too, didn't you?'

'Keep your bloody voice down.'

'Why? Are you afraid of what they might do to you in the remand wing? They don't like perverts, do they? Do they bugger you with ladies' shoes in the showers? You'd probably enjoy that.'

'Be quiet, woman. We've got things to discuss.'

'I've got nothing to discuss with you, Garry Starling.

You've destroyed us. I always knew you were a sodding pervert. But I didn't know you were a rapist and a murderer. Had a good time on the ghost train with her, did you? You took me on the ghost train on one of our first dates and jammed your finger up my fanny. Remember? Get your rocks off on the ghost train, do you?'

'I didn't go on any ghost train. It wasn't me. Believe me!'

'Yeah, right, believe you. Ha! Ha fucking ha!'

'It wasn't me. I didn't do that.'

'Sure, right, and it wasn't you at the cement works, was it? Just someone who looked like you.'

He said nothing.

'All that tying me up shit. Making me do things with shoes while you watched and played with yourself.'

'Denise!'

'I don't care. Let them all hear! You've ruined my life. Taken my best years. All that not wanting to have children because you had such an unhappy childhood shit. You're a monster and you're where you deserve to be. I hope you rot in hell. And you'd better get yourself a good solicitor, because I'm not standing by you. I'm going to take you for every penny I can.'

Then she began to sob.

He sat in silence. He had nothing to say. If it had been possible, he would have liked to lean over the table and strangle this bitch with his bare hands.

'I thought you loved me,' she sobbed. 'I thought we could make a life together. I knew you were damaged, but I thought that if I loved you enough maybe I could change you. That I could offer you something that you never had.'

'Give over!'

'It's true. You were honest with me once. Twelve

years ago, when we married, you told me I was the only person who had given you peace in your life. Who understood you. You told me your mother made you screw her, because your father was impotent. That after that you were disgusted by women's private parts, even my own. We went through all that psychology shit together.'

'Denise, shut it!'

'No, I won't shut it. When we got to together I understood that shoes were the only things that turned you on. I accepted that because I loved you.'

'Denise! Bitch! Shut it!'

'We had so many good years. I didn't realize I was marrying a monster.'

'We had good times,' he said suddenly. 'Good times until recently. Then you changed.'

'Changed? What do you mean changed? You mean I got fed up fucking myself with shoes? Is that what you mean by *changed*?'

He was silent again.

'What's my future?' she said. 'I'm now Mrs Shoe Man. Are you proud of that? That you've destroyed my life? You know our good friends, Maurice and Ulla? The ones we have dinner with every Saturday night at the China Garden? They're not returning my calls.'

'Maybe they never liked you,' he replied. 'Maybe it was me they liked and they just put up with you as my whingeing hag wife.'

Sobbing again, she said, 'Do you know what I'm going to do? I'm going to go home and kill myself. Will you care?'

'Just do it properly,' he said.

120

Denise Starling drove home recklessly in her black Mercedes convertible coupé. She stared at the wet road ahead through her mist of tears. The wipers clop-clopped on the windscreen. A chirrupy woman was wittering away on BBC Sussex Radio about disastrous holidays people had experienced, inviting listeners to call in.

Yeah, every sodding holiday with Garry Starling had been a disaster. Life with Garry Starling had been a disaster. And now it was getting even worse.

Shit, you bastard.

Three years into their marriage she'd fallen pregnant. He'd made her abort. He didn't want to bring children into the world. He'd quoted some poem at her, some poet whose name she could not remember, about your parents screwing you up.

What had happened in Garry's childhood had twisted him, that was for sure. Damaged him in ways that she could never understand.

She drove, way over the limit, along the London Road, past Preston Park, and shouted, 'Fuck you!' when the speed camera there she had totally forgotten about flashed her. Then she turned into Edward Street, drove along past the law courts, and Brighton College and the Royal Sussex County Hospital.

A few minutes later she made a right turn, opposite the East Brighton Golf Club, where Garry was a member – not for much longer, she thought, with some strange, grim satisfaction – let him be a sodding pariah too! Then she crested the hill, swung into Roedean Crescent and finally turned right, into the driveway of their large mock-Tudor house, passing the double garage doors, and pulled up in front of Garry's grey Volvo.

Then, her eyes still misted with tears, she unlocked the front door of her house. She had trouble, for some moments, unsetting the alarm. *Typical! The one time we have trouble with the alarm, Garry's not around to get it sorted!*

She slammed shut the front door, then slid the safety chain across. *Sod you, world. You want to ignore me? Fine by me! I'm going to ignore you too. I'm going to open a bottle of Garry's most expensive claret and get rip-roaring sodding pissed!*

Then a quiet voice right behind her said, 'Shalimar! I like Shalimar! I smelt it the first time I met you!'

An arm clamped around her neck. Something damp and sickly-sweet-smelling was pressed across her nose. She struggled, for a few seconds, as her brain began to go muzzy.

As she lapsed into unconsciousness, the last words she heard were, 'You're like my mother. You do bad things to men. Bad things that make men do bad things. You're disgusting. You are evil, like my mother. You were rude to me in my taxi. You destroyed your husband, you know that? Someone has to stop you before you destroy anyone else.'

Her eyes were closed, so he whispered into her ear, 'I'm going to do something to you that I once did to my mother. I left it a little late with her, so I had to do it a different way. But it felt good afterwards. I know I'm going to feel good after this too. Maybe even better. Uh-huh.'

Yac pulled her limp body up the stairs, listening to the bump-bump, bump-bump of her black Christian Louboutins on each tread as he struggled with her weight.

He stopped, perspiring, when he reached the landing. Then he bent down and picked up the blue tow rope he'd found in the garage, in his gloved hands, and knotted one end firmly around one of the mock-Tudor ceiling beams that was in easy reach of the stairs. He'd already prepared the other end into a hangman's noose. And measured the distance.

He placed the noose around the limp woman's neck and heaved her, with some difficulty, over the banister rail.

He watched her fall, then jerk, then spinning around and around.

It was some minutes before she was completely still.

He stared at her shoes. He remembered her shoes the first time she had entered his taxi. Feeling a need to take them from her.

Hanging limply, looking pretty dead so far as he could tell, she reminded him of his mother again now.

No longer able to hurt anyone.

Just like his mother hadn't been.

'I used a pillow on her,' he called out to Denise. But she did not reply. He wasn't really expecting her to.

He decided to leave the shoes, although they were so tempting. After all, taking them was the Shoe Man's style. Not his.

121

Sunday 25 January

It was a good Sunday morning. The tide was in and the baby on the boat next door was not crying. Maybe it had died, Yac thought. He'd heard about cot death syndrome. Perhaps the baby had died from that. Perhaps not. But he hoped so.

He had copies of all this week's *Argus* newspapers laid out on the table in the saloon. Bosun, the cat, had walked over them. That was OK. They'd reached an understanding. Bosun did not walk over his lavatory chains any more. But if he wanted to walk over his newspapers, that was fine.

He was happy with what he read.

The Shoe Man's wife had committed suicide. That was understandable. Her husband's arrest was a big trauma for her. Garry Starling had been a major player in this city. A big socialite. The disgrace of his arrest would have been hard for any wife to bear. She'd been telling people she felt suicidal and then she had hanged herself.

Perfectly reasonable.

Uh-huh.

He liked it best when the tide was in and the *Tom Newbound* was floating.

Then he could pull his fishing lines up.

He had two fishing lines out, each with weights on them so that they sank well into the mud at low tide. Of course he had been worried each time that the police had searched the boat. But he needn't have been. They pulled every plank up from the floor of the bilges. Searched in every cavity there was. But none of them had ever thought to raise one of the fishing lines, like he was doing now.

Just as well.

The second line was tied, at the end, to a weighted waterproof bag. Inside were the shoes of Mandy Thorpe. Fake Jimmy Choos. He didn't like those fake shoes. They deserved to be buried in mud.

And she deserved the punishment he had given her for wearing them.

But, he had to concede, it had been good punishing her. She'd reminded him so much of his mother. Fat like his mother. The smell of his mother. He'd waited a long time to do that to his mother, to see what it felt like. But he'd left it too late and she was too sick by the time he'd gathered the courage. But it had been good with Mandy Thorpe. It had felt like he was punishing his mother. Very good indeed.

But not as good as punishing Denise Starling.

He liked the way she had spun around and around, like a top.

But he hadn't liked being in custody. Hadn't liked the way the police had removed so many of his things from the boat. Going through everything and messing up his collections. That was bad.

At least he had everything back now. It felt like he had his life back.

Best news of all, he'd had a call from the people who owned this boat, to say that they would be staying on at least two more years in Goa now. That made him very pleased.

Life suddenly felt very good. Very peaceful.

And it was a rising tide. Nothing like it.

Uh-huh.

122

Darren Spicer was feeling in a good mood. He stopped off at the pub, which had become his regular staging post on his way back home from work, for his now customary two pints with whisky chasers. He was becoming a creature of habit! You didn't have to be in prison to have a routine; you could have one outside too.

He was enjoying his new routine. Commuting to the Grand from the night shelter – always by foot, to save the pennies and to keep fit. There was a young lady who worked as a chambermaid at the hotel called Tia whom he was getting sweet on – and he reckoned she was getting sweet on him too. She was Filipina, pretty, in her early thirties, with a boyfriend she'd left because he beat her up. They were getting to know each other pretty well, although they hadn't actually yet *done it*, so to speak. But that was just a matter of time now.

They had a date tomorrow. It was difficult in the evenings, because of having to be back for lock-in, but tomorrow they would be spending all day together. She shared a room in a little flat up off the Lewes Road and, giggling, had told him her room-mate was going to be away for the weekend. Tomorrow, with luck, he reckoned, they'd be shagging all day.

He had another whisky to celebrate, a quality one

this time, a single malt, Glenlivet. Mustn't drink too much, he knew, because arriving back at St Patrick's drunk was a sure way to get thrown out. And now he was getting close to his coveted MiPod. So just the one Glenlivet. Not that money was no object – but the old cash situation was improving all the time.

He'd managed to get himself on to room maintenance at the hotel, because they were short of staff. He had a plastic pass key to get him into every guest room in the building. And he had today's takings from the room safes he'd opened up tucked in his pocket. He'd been cautious. He was going to keep his promise to himself to stay out of prison this time for good. All he took was a tiny fraction of any cash he found in the safes. Of course he had been tempted by some of the fancy watches and jewellery, but he'd stuck to his guns, and was proud of his self-discipline.

In these past four and a half weeks, he'd stashed away nearly four grand in his chained suitcase in the locker at St Patrick's. Property prices had come down, thanks to the recession. With what Tia earned, and with what he could put down as a cash deposit in, say, a year's time, he should be able to buy a little flat somewhere in the Brighton area. Or even move right away to somewhere a lot cheaper. Perhaps warmer.

Perhaps Spain.

Maybe Tia would like to be in a warm country.

Of course it was all a pipe dream. He hadn't talked about any future with her yet. The thought of hopefully shagging her tomorrow was about as far as he had got. But he felt good about her. She gave off a warmth that made him feel happy every time he stood near her or talked to her. Sometimes you needed to go with your instincts.

And his instincts, ten minutes later, as he turned right off Western Road into Cambridge Road told him that something was not good.

It was the shiny silver Ford Focus estate double-parked almost outside the front door of the St Patrick's night shelter, with someone sitting in the driving seat.

When you spent your life trying not to get nicked, you developed a kind of second sense, your antennae always up for spotting plain-clothes police and their vehicles. His eyes locked on the four short antennae on the roof of the Ford.

Shit.

Fear crashed through him. For an instant, he debated whether to turn and run, then empty his pockets. But he'd left it too late. The burly, bald, black detective who was standing in the doorway had already clocked him. Spicer decided he'd have to try to bluff it out.

Shit, he thought again, his dream fading away. And tomorrow's shag with sweet Tia. The grim, green walls of Lewes Prison closing around his mind.

'Hello, Darren,' Detective Sergeant Branson greeted him, with a big cheery grin. 'How's it going?'

Spicer looked at him warily. 'All right,' he said. 'Yeah.'

'Wonder if I could have a word with you.' He pointed at the door. 'They're letting us use that interview room – OK with you?'

'Yeah.' Spicer shrugged. 'What's this about?'

'Just a little chat. Got a bit of news I thought you might like to hear.'

Spicer sat down, shaking, very uneasy. He couldn't

think of any news that Detective Sergeant Branson could bring him that he would like to hear.

Branson closed the door, then seated himself across the table, facing him. 'Dunno if you remember when we spoke – you were giving me the nod about the lock-up behind Mandalay Court? About the white van inside it?'

Spicer looked at him warily.

'I mentioned to you there was a reward, right? Fifty thousand pounds? For information leading to the arrest and conviction of the man who attempted to attack Mrs Dee Burchmore? Put up by her husband.'

'Yeah?'

'Well, I've got good news for you. It looks like you're in line for it.'

Spicer broke into a grin, relief flooding through him. Incredible relief.

'You're shitting me?'

Branson shook his head. 'Nope. Actually, Detective Superintendent Grace, the SIO, has put your name forward himself. It's down to you that we've potted our suspect. He's been arrested and charged.'

'When do I get the money?' Spicer asked incredulously.

'When he's convicted. I think a trial date's been set for this autumn – I can let you know when I have the details. But there's not much doubt we've got the right man.' Branson smiled. 'So, sunshine, what are you going to do with all that loot? Shove it up your nose, right, as usual?'

'Nah.' Spicer said. 'I'm going to buy a little flat, you know, as an investment for the future. I'll use the money towards the deposit. Magic!'

Branson shook his head. 'In your dreams. You'll spend it on drugs.'

'I won't. Not this time! I'm not going back inside. I'm going to buy a place of my own and go straight. Yeah.'

'Tell you what, invite us to your house-warming. Just to prove you've changed, all right?'

Spicer grinned. 'Yeah, well, that could be difficult. If it's a party, you know – like – there might be stuff here. You know, like – party stuff. Could be embarrassing for you to be there – you being a cop and all.'

'I don't embarrass easily.'

Spicer shrugged. 'Fifty grand. Incredible! Fucking incredible!'

The DS fixed his eyes on the old lag. 'You know what? I heard they didn't bother changing the sheets in your cell. They know you're going to be back.'

'Not this time.'

'I'll look forward to the invitation. The Governor of Lewes Prison will know where to send it.'

Spicer grinned. 'That's very witty.'

'Just the truth, sunshine.'

Glenn left the room and went outside, to where Roy Grace was waiting in the car. He was looking forward to an end-of-week drink with his mate.

123

I've started talking. Just for one reason, to get even with you, Detective Smug Superintendent Roy Grace.

It's not great in here on the remand wing. People don't like guys like me in this place. Nonces, they call us. I cut my tongue open on a piece of razor blade that was in my Irish stew. I hear rumours that people piss in my soup. One guy's threatened to put my other eye out.

I'm told it will be better after my trial. Then if I'm lucky (ha) I'll be put into the nonces' wing, as it's known. All of us sexual deviants together. How great will that be! Party-party-party!

Some nights I don't sleep at all. I have all this anger everywhere – all around me in this place and deep inside me. I'm angry at whoever it was who did that rape on the ghost train. It meant that the pier was swarming with police afterwards, completely messing up my plans. It was all going so nicely until then. It just didn't go nicely after that.

I'm angry that the bitch escaped the humiliation that she would have faced, being known as my wife. Something's not right about that. Although I don't really care and I don't suppose anyone else does.

But I have even bigger anger inside me that is directed at you, Detective Superintendent Grace. You thought you were clever, telling the world about the size of my dick. You can't be allowed to get away with something like that.

That's why I'm talking now. I'm fessing-up to all the other times I raped and took the shoes. In particular the ghost train. You won't be able to get me on any trick questions – word seems to have got around about all the crimes the Shoe Man perpetrated – the recent ones – every detail of what he did to the women. Including every detail of what happened in the ghost train.

So I'm briefed!

You didn't understand why I changed my MO, from taking one shoe and panties to taking both shoes. You weren't meant to understand, see? I wasn't going to make your job easy for you by just repeating exactly the same stuff over again. Variety's the spice of life, right?

I'm your man, all right! I'm just going to hope that the creep who raped that woman on the ghost train strikes again.

You'll have egg all over your face, Detective Superintendent Grace.

And I'll have a big grin on mine.

And who will have the smaller dick then?

124

'It's good to see you relaxed, my darling,' Cleo said.

It was the evening now. They'd spent the afternoon together, working on the wedding list. Roy Grace had his feet up, a glass of red wine in his hand, and was watching *The Antiques Road Show*, one of his favourite programmes. Most of all he enjoyed watching people as they were given the valuation of their treasured – or otherwise – heirloom. The look of astonishment when some tatty bowl they'd been using to feed the dog was valued at thousands. The look of dismay when some splendid painting, which had been in the family for generations, was pronounced a fake worth only a few quid.

'Yep!' He smiled and just wished he felt relaxed. But he didn't. Doubt was still gnawing away at him, despite the Shoe Man having been caught. And there were still ripples from Starling's wife's suicide. He'd listened to the prison tape, where she'd talked about going home and topping herself. It had sounded like an idle threat. But then she had gone and done it. No note, nothing.

'I mean,' she said, gently lifting Humphrey out of the way and curling up next to him on the sofa, 'as relaxed as you're ever going to be.'

He shrugged, then nodded. 'At least the Shoe Man's

had some comeuppance. He's permanently blinded in one eye.'

'How sad is that? Shame that young woman didn't castrate him while she was at it,' Cleo retorted. 'All of his victims are maimed in some way and one's dead.'

'I just wish we knew who all of them are,' he said. 'He's coughed, but I somehow don't think he's telling us everything. He's one of the nastiest creeps I've ever come across. His home and office computers are full of weird shit. All kinds of foot- and shoe-fetish sites and chatlines – a lot of it sadistic. And he's got a whole cocktail of sleeping and date-rape drugs in his office fridge.'

'Is he going to plead guilty and spare his victims the ordeal of giving evidence?'

'I don't know. Depends on his brief – good old Ken Acott again. We've a ton of evidence against him. The lock-up's in his name. We've found missing pages from the Shoe Man's 1997 files in a safe in his office. There are links to Facebook and Twitter sites of some of his recent victims on his computer and iPhone. DNA evidence from Rachael Ryan's body.'

He drank some wine.

'But we're going to have to wait for psychiatric evaluations as to whether he is fit to stand trial. Great! Garry Starling's able to run one of the biggest companies in the city, to be vice-captain of his golf club and treasurer of his Rotary Club – but he might not be fit to stand trial! Our legal processes suck.'

Cleo smiled sympathetically. She understood some of his frustrations at the criminal justice system.

'Jessie Sheldon should get a medal. How is she? Has she survived her ordeal OK?'

'Remarkably well. I went to see her at home this

afternoon. She's had surgery on her ankle and hopefully it will be fine in time. In fact she seemed in very good spirits, considering. She's looking forward to her wedding this summer.'

'She was engaged?'

'Apparently. She told me it was her determination to get married that kept her going.'

'So don't feel bad about his injury.'

'I don't. Not about his injury, no. I just don't feel we've nailed it. Not completely.'

'Because of those other shoes?'

'I'm not so concerned about those. If we can get him to talk more, eventually, maybe we'll clear those up.'

He sipped some more wine and glanced at the television.

'Is it the one on the ghost train who's bothering you? What's her name?'

'Mandy Thorpe. Yes. I still don't believe it was the Shoe Man who raped her. Even though he says he did. The forensic psychologist is wrong, I'm still convinced.'

'Meaning the perpetrator is still out there?'

'Yes, that's exactly the problem. If Proudfoot's wrong, then he's still out there. And might attack again.'

'If he is out there, you'll get him. One day.'

'I want to get him before he attacks again.'

Cleo pouted her lips playfully. 'You're my hero, Detective Superintendent Grace. You'll always get them eventually.'

'In your dreams.'

'No, not in my dreams. I'm a realist.' She patted her tummy. 'In about four months' time, our little *Bump* is going to be born. I'm depending on you to make it a safe world for him – or her.'

He kissed her. 'There are always going to be bad guys out there.'

'And bad girls!'

'Them too. The world is a dangerous place. We're never going to lock them all up. There'll always be evil people who get away with their crimes.'

'And good people who get locked away?' she said.

'There will always be blurred boundaries. There are plenty of *good* bad guys and *bad* good guys. Life's not clear and it's seldom fair,' he said. 'I don't want our child growing up under the illusion that it is. Shit happens.'

Cleo smiled at him. 'Shit *used* to happen. It stopped happening the day I met you. You rock!'

He grinned. 'You're full of it. Sometimes I wonder why you love me.'

'Do you, Detective Superintendent Grace? I don't. Not for one moment. And I don't think I ever will. You make me feel safe. You have from the day I met you and you always will.'

He smiled. 'You're so easily pleased.'

'Yeah, and I'm a cheap date. I don't even have one pair of designer shoes.'

'Want me to buy you some?'

She stared at him quizzically.

He looked back at her and grinned. 'For the right reasons!'

AUTHOR'S AFTERWORD

'Stranger rape' is actually extremely uncommon. In Sussex, the county in which *Dead Like You* is based, attacks such as those described are, thankfully, rare. It is in fact the very sad truth that virtually all rapes are committed by men known to the victim. The vast majority of rape survivors describe being attacked by a friend or someone they are in a long-term relationship with. The betrayal of trust caused as a result can undermine their ability to form a new relationship subsequently.

It is impossible to generalize about the way victims will respond to being raped, because there is no 'normal' reaction to such an abnormal act. The trauma can manifest itself in many different ways and there are specialist organizations, such as Rape Crisis, that exist to support victims. One local to Sussex is The Lifecentre, which aims to 'rebuild' survivors of rape. I have chosen to support them because I feel they provide a critical service which, incredibly, is not government-funded. Donations are always welcome. Go online and visit their website at www.lifecentre.uk.com if you wish to help. Thank you.

ACKNOWLEDGEMENTS

As ever, there are many people I have to thank for helping me in my research for this novel.

My first thank-you is to Martin Richards, QPM, Chief Constable of Sussex, who allows me such invaluable access to the world of his police force.

My good friend former Detective Chief Superintendent David Gaylor has, as ever, been a brick, a pillar of wisdom, and at times has wielded a bigger stick than my publishers in keeping me to my deadlines!

As always, so many officers of Sussex Police have given me their time and wisdom, and tolerated me hanging out with them and answered my endless questions, that it is almost impossible to list them all, but I'm trying here, and please forgive any omissions. Detective Chief Superintendent Kevin Moore; Chief Superintendent Graham Bartlett; Chief Superintendent Chris Ambler; DCI Trevor Bowles, who has been an absolute star and a brick; Chief Inspector Stephen Curry; DCI Paul Furnell; Brian Cook, Scientific Support Branch Manager; Stuart Leonard; Tony Case; DI William Warner; DCI Nick Sloan; DI Jason Tingley; Chief Inspector Steve Brookman; Inspector Andrew Kundert; Inspector Roy Apps; Sgt Phil Taylor; Ray Packham and Dave Reed of the High-Tech Crime Unit; Lex Westwood; Sgt James Bowes; PC Georgie Edge; Inspector Rob Leet; Inspector Phil Clarke; Sgt Mel Doyle; PC Tony Omotoso; PC Ian Upperton; PC Andrew King; Sgt Sean McDonald; PC Steve Cheesman; Sgt Andy McMahon; Sgt Justin Hambloch; Chris Heaver; Martin Bloomfield; Ron King; Robin Wood; Sue Heard, Press and PR Officer; Louise Leonard; James Gartrell.

DS Tracy Edwards has been incredible in helping me to

understand the reality of the suffering of rape victims, as have Maggie Ellis of The Lifecentre and PCs Julie Murphy and Jonathan Jackson of the Metropolitan Police, London.

Eoin McLennan-Murray, former Governor of Lewes Prison, and Deputy Governor, Alan Setterington, helped me greatly with the psychology of my suspects, as did Jeanie Civil and Tara Lester, who helped me so much with the psychology of the perpetrators, and barrister Richard Cherrill. I had huge help also with the psychology of the perpetrators from Dr Dennis Friedman.

A special thank-you to Caroline Mayhew, and to the team at the St Patrick's Night Shelter, in particular Emma Harrington, Theo Abbs and Amanda Lane.

And, as always, I owe an extremely special and massive thanks to the terrific team at the Brighton and Hove City Mortuary, Sean Didcott and Victor Sindon. And also to Dr Nigel Kirkham; forensic archaeologist Lucy Sibun; Dr Jonathan Pash; Coroner Dr Peter Dean; forensic pathologist Dr Benjamin Swift; Dr Ben Sharp; Marian Down.

Thank you to my terrific consultants on autism, Vicky Warren, who gave me so much of the inspiration for Yac; Gareth Ransome; Tony Balazs; and to wonderful Sue Stopa, manager of Hollyrood – the Disabilities Trust's flagship autism-specific residential home – and its staff and residential clients.

Thanks also to Peter Wingate Saul; Juliet Smith, Chief Magistrate of Brighton and Hove; Paul Grzegorzek; Abigail Bradley and Matt Greenhalgh, Director of Forensics at Orchid Cellmark Forensics; Tim Moore; Anne Busbridge, General Manager of the Brighton Hilton Metropole Hotel, Michael Knox-Johnston, General Manager of the Grand Hotel. And to Graham Lewis, my lock-up garage specialist! Special thanks to Josephine and Howard Belm, owners of the *Tom Newbound* houseboat. A very special thanks to Steve Dudman, owner of the Old Cement Works, whose kind offer to show me round sparked the idea for the location of the climax. Thanks also to Andy Lang, of Languard Alarms. And to Phil Mills. And also to Anne Martin, General Manager, and Peter Burgess, Chief Engineer, of Brighton Pier.

As ever, thank you to Chris Webb of MacService for keeping my Mac alive despite all the abuse I give it! Very big and special thanks to Anna-Lisa Lindeblad, who has again been my tireless and wonderful 'unofficial' editor and commentator throughout the Roy Grace series, and to Sue Ansell, whose sharp eye for detail has saved me many an embarrassment, and my wonderful PA, Linda Buckley.

Professionally I again have a total dream team: the tireless Carole Blake representing me; my awesome publicists, Tony Mulliken, Sophie Ransom and Claire Barnett of Midas PR; and there is simply not enough space to say a proper thank-you to everyone at Macmillan, but I must mention my brilliant former editor, Publishing Director Maria Rejt, my editor, Susan Opie, and copy-editor, Lesley Levene, and a massive welcome to my new editor, the wonderful Wayne Brookes.

As ever, Helen has been my rock, keeping me nourished with saintly patience and constant wisdom.

My canine friends continue to keep me sane. The ever-cheerful Coco has now joined Oscar and Phoebe under my desk, waiting to pounce on any discarded pages of manuscript that should fall to the floor and dutifully shred them.

Lastly, thank you, my readers, for all the incredible support you give me. Keep those emails, tweets and blog posts coming!

Peter James
Sussex, England
www.peterjames.com
Find and follow me on
http://twitter.com/peterjamesuk